A Text Book Of

NETWORK ANALYSIS

For
SEMESTER – II
SECOND YEAR DEGREE COURSE IN ELECTRICAL ENGINEERING

Strictly As Per New Revised Syllabus of University of Pune,
July 2013

WITH MULTIPLE CHOICE QUESTIONS (MCQs)

Dr. SACHIN D. RUIKAR

Associate Professor, E&TC Department
Sinhgad Academy of Engineering
Kondhwa (Bk.) Pune

Network Analysis (P.U.) (S.E. Electrical)

First Edition : January, 2014

© : Authors

ISBN 978-93-83971-29-9

The text of this publication, or any part thereof, should not be reproduced or transmitted in any form or stored in any computer storage system or device for distribution including photocopy, recording, taping or information retrieval system or reproduced on any disc, tape, perforated media or other information storage device etc., without the written permission of Authors with whom the rights are reserved. Breach of this condition is liable for legal action.

Every effort has been made to avoid errors or omissions in this publication. In spite of this, errors may have crept in. Any mistake, error or discrepancy so noted and shall be brought to our notice shall be taken care of in the next edition. It is notified that neither the publisher nor the authors or seller shall be responsible for any damage or loss of action to any one, of any kind, in any manner, therefrom.

Published By :
NIRALI PRAKASHAN
Abhyudaya Pragati, 1312, Shivaji Nagar,
Off J.M. Road, PUNE – 411005
Tel - (020) 25512336/37/39, Fax - (020) 25511379
Email : niralipune@pragationline.com

Printed By :
REPRO INDIA LTD.
50/2 T.T.C. MIDC,
Industrial Area, Mahape, Navi Mumbai
Tel - (022) 2778 2011

DISTRIBUTION CENTRES

PUNE

Nirali Prakashan
119, Budhwar Peth, Jogeshwari Mandir Lane
Pune 411002, Maharashtra
Tel : (020) 2445 2044, 66022708, Fax : (020) 2445 1538
Email : bookorder@pragationline.com

Nirali Prakashan
S. No. 28/27, Dhyari,
Near Pari Company, Pune 411041
Tel : (020) 24690204 Fax : (020) 24690316
Email : dhyari@pragationline.com
bookorder@pragationline.com

MUMBAI
Nirali Prakashan
385, S.V.P. Road, Rasdhara Co-op. Hsg. Society Ltd.,
Girgaum, Mumbai 400004, Maharashtra
Tel : (022) 2385 6339 / 2386 9976, Fax : (022) 2386 9976
Email : niralimumbai@pragationline.com

DISTRIBUTION BRANCHES

NAGPUR
Pratibha Book Distributors
Above Maratha Mandir, Shop No. 3, First Floor,
Rani Jhanshi Square, Sitabuldi, Nagpur 440012,
Maharashtra, Tel : (0712) 254 7129

BENGALURU
Pragati Book House
House No. 1, Sanjeevappa Lane, Avenue Road Cross,
Opp. Rice Church, Bengaluru – 560002.
Tel : (080) 64513344, 64513355,
Mob : 9880582331, 9845021552
Email:bharatsavla@yahoo.com

JALGAON
Nirali Prakashan
34, V. V. Golani Market, Navi Peth, Jalgaon 425001,
Maharashtra, Tel : (0257) 222 0395
Mob : 94234 91860

KOLHAPUR
Nirali Prakashan
New Mahadvar Road,
Kedar Plaza, 1st Floor Opp. IDBI Bank
Kolhapur 416 012, Maharashtra. Mob : 9855046155

CHENNAI
Pragati Books
9/1, Montieth Road, Behind Taas Mahal, Egmore,
Chennai 600008 Tamil Nadu, Tel : (044) 6518 3535,
Mob : 94440 01782 / 98450 21552 / 98805 82331, Email : bharatsavla@yahoo.com

RETAIL OUTLETS
PUNE

Pragati Book Centre
157, Budhwar Peth, Opp. Ratan Talkies,
Pune 411002, Maharashtra
Tel : (020) 2445 8887 / 6602 2707, Fax : (020) 2445 8887
Pragati Book Centre
Amber Chamber, 28/A, Budhwar Peth,
Appa Balwant Chowk, Pune : 411002, Maharashtra,
Tel : (020) 20240335 / 66281669
Email : pbcpune@pragationline.com

Pragati Book Centre
676/B, Budhwar Peth, Opp. Jogeshwari Mandir,
Pune 411002, Maharashtra
Tel : (020) 6601 7784 / 6602 0855
PBC Book Sellers & Stationers
152, Budhwar Peth, Pune 411002, Maharashtra
Tel : (020) 2445 2254 / 6609 2463

MUMBAI
Pragati Book Corner
Indira Niwas, 111 - A, Bhavani Shankar Road, Dadar (W), Mumbai 400028, Maharashtra
Tel : (022) 2422 3526 / 6662 5254, Email : pbcmumbai@pragationline.com

Preface ...

It gives me great pleasure to bring out this text book of **Network Analysis** for the benefit of student community. This text book is designed keeping in need of S.E. (Electrical) students of Pune University.

As per the policy of the University, Engineering Syllabus is revised every five years. Last revision was in the year 2009. **New revision is coming little earlier, as university has introduced online system of examination from year 2012.**

As per the new system, the **online examinations** (Combined Phase-I and Phase-II) will be conducted based on first, second, third and fourth units. The online examinations will have objective types of questions with multiple choices. End semester examination will be based on all the six units and that will be conducted in traditional way.

New text book is written, taking in to account all the new features that have been introduced. All the entrants to the engineering field will definitely find this book, complete in all respect. Students will find the subject matter presentation quite lucid. There are large number of illustrative examples and well graded exercises. **Addition of Multiple Choice Questions will be very useful to the students**, especially for online examinations.

I take this opportunity to express our sincere thanks to Shri. Dineshbhai Furia of Nirali Prakashan, pioneer in all fields of education. Thanks are also due to Shri. Jignesh Furia, whose dynamic leadership is helpful to all the authors of Nirali Prakashan.

I specially appreciate the efforts of Shri. M. P. Munde and entire staff of Nirali Prakashan for making the publication of this book possible, well in time.

I also thankful to Mr. Akbar Shaikh for DTP and Mrs. Prajakta, Mrs. Sonal for Proof Reading.

I have no doubt, that like our earlier texts, student's community will respond favourably to this new venture.

Salient features of this book are :
- **Written strictly according to revised syllabus of Pune University.**
- **Adequate emphasis on both Theory and Problems.**
- **More Multiple Choice Questions.**
- **Unnecessary Theory is avoided.**

Suggestions and Feedback shall be well appreciated and acknowledged.

Authors

14th January, 2014
Makarsankranti
Pune

Syllabus ...

Unit 1 : Introduction to Network Analysis (7 L)

Types of Networks: Lumped and Distributed, Linear and Nonlinear, Bilateral and Unilateral, Time-variant and Time-invariant. Independent and Dependent (Controlled) Voltage and Current Sources. Concept of Voltage and Current Divider, Source Transformation and Shifting.

Network equations: Network equations on Loop basis and Node basis, Choice between Loop Analysis and Nodal Analysis. Concept of Super Node and Super Mesh, Mutual Inductance, Dot Convention for Coupled Circuits, Concept of Duality and Dual Networks.

Unit 2 : Network Theorems (7 L)

Superposition, Thevenin, Norton, Maximum Power Transfer Theorem, Reciprocity, Millman Theorems applied to Electrical Networks with all types of sources.

Unit 3 : Transient Analysis (8 L)

Solutions of differential equations and Network equations using classical method for R-L, R-C and R-L-C circuits, Initial and Final Condition (Series and Parallel).

Unit 4 : Laplace Transform Application to Network (9 L)

Basic Properties of Laplace Transform, Laplace Transform of Basic R, L and C components, Solutions of Differential equations and Network equations using Laplace transform method for R-L, R-C and R-L-C Circuits (Series and Parallel), Inverse Laplace transforms, Transformed Networks with initial conditions. Analysis of Electrical Circuits with applications of step, Pulse, Impulse and Ramp functions, Shifted and Singular functions the Convolution Integral. Laplace transforms various Periodic and Non-periodic Waveforms application of Laplace transforms.

Unit 5 : Two Port Network and Filters (8 L)

Two Port Network: Z, Y, H and Transmission parameters, Interrelations between Parameters. Input power, Power transfer and Insertion loss: Energy and Power, Effective or Root-Mean Square values, Average Power and Complex Power, Problems in Optimizing Power Transfer, Insertion Loss. Introduction to Passive Filters, Low Pass Filters, High Pass Filters and m-Derived LPF and HPF, Filters and Design.

Unit 6 : Network Functions (6 L)

Network functions: Poles and Zeros: Terminal Pairs or Ports, Network functions for the One port and Two ports, The calculation of Network functions, General networks. Poles and Zeros of Network functions, Restrictions on Poles and Zeros locations for transfer functions and driving point function, Time-domain behaviour from the Pole and Zero plot. Stability of active networks. Parallel Resonance, Resonance frequency, Quality factor, Current and resonance.

Contents ...

1. INTRODUCTION TO NETWORK ANALYSIS   1.1 – 1.124
- **Multiple Choice Questions**   1.90

2. NETWORK THEOREMS   2.1 – 2.104
- **Multiple Choice Questions**   2.76

3. TRANSIENT ANALYSIS   3.1 – 3.90
- **Multiple Choice Questions**   2.76

4. LAPLACE TRANSFORM APPLICATION TO NETWORK   4.1 – 4.76
- **Multiple Choice Questions**   4.57

5. TWO PORT NETWORK AND FILTERS   5.1 – 5.130

6. NETWORK FUNCTIONS   6.1 – 6.92

Unit 1

INTRODUCTION TO NETWORK ANALYSIS

Contents ...

1.1 Introduction
1.2 Definitions of Network Variables
    1.2.1 Charge
    1.2.2 Current
    1.2.3 Voltage
    1.2.4 Power
    1.2.5 Energy
1.3 Some Circuit Definitions
    1.3.1 Circuit Element
    1.3.2 Electric Circuit or Network
    1.3.3 Branch
    1.3.4 Mesh or loop
    1.3.5 Node or Junction
1.4 Basic Circuit Elements
    1.4.1 Resistor
    1.4.2 Capacitor
    1.4.3 Inductor
1.5 Network Classification
    1.5.1 Linear and Non-linear Networks
    1.5.2 Unilateral and Bilateral Networks
    1.5.3 Lamped and Distributed Networks
    1.5.4 Time Variant and Invariant Networks
1.6 Energy Sources
    1.6.1 Voltage Source
    1.6.2 Current Source
1.7 Independent and Controlled (Dependent) Sources
1.8 Power
1.9 Open and Short Circuit
    1.9.1 Open Circuit
    1.9.2 Short Circuit (SC)

1.10 Voltage Divider and Current Divider Circuits
    1.10.1 The Voltage Divider Circuit
    1.10.2 The Current Divider Circuit
1.11 Kirchoff's Voltage Law (KVL)
    1.11.1 Ground (Datum) Node and Node-Node Voltages
1.12 Kirchoff's Current Law (KCL)
1.13 Problems Based on KCL and KVL only
1.14 Circuit Elements in Series and Parallel
    1.14.1 Impedances in Series
    1.14.2 Impedances in Parallel
1.15 Energy sources in Series and Parallels
    1.15.1 Series Connection of Voltage Source
    1.15.2 Parallel Connection of Voltage Sources
    1.15.3 Current Sources in Series
    1.15.4 Current Sources in Parallel
1.16 Source Transformation
    1.16.1 Source Transformation Equation
1.17 Source Shifting
    1.17.1 Voltage Source Shifting
    1.17.2 Current Source Shifting
1.18 Mesh (Or loop) or KVL Analysis
1.19 Super Mesh Analysis
1.20 Nodal (KVL) Analysis
1.21 Super Node Analysis
1.22 Analysis of Circuits with Mixed Sources
1.23 Mutual Inductance
    1.23.1 Self Inductance
    1.23.2 Transformers
1.24 Dot Conventions for Coupled Circuits
    1.24.1 Introduction to Coupling Circuits
    1.24.2 Energy Stored into Coupling Circuits
    1.24.3 Ideal Transformers
1.25 Dot Conventions
1.26 Concept of Duality and Dual Networks
Multiple Choice Questions (MCQs)
Exercise

1.1 INTRODUCTION

Given an electrical network, the network analysis involves various methods. The process of finding the network variables namely the voltage and currents in various parts of the circuit is known as network analysis. Before we carry out actual analysis it is very much essential to thoroughly understand the various terms associated with the network. In this Unit, we shall begin with the definition and understanding in detail some of the commonly used terms. Those terms includes a current source, voltage source, independent and controlled source, lumped and distributed network, active and passive networks, linear and non-linear circuits, open and short circuits.

Analysis becomes easier, if we can simplify the given network. We will be discussing various simplifications techniques. These techniques involves combing series and parallel connections of R, L and C elements, series and parallel connection of every sources. Then source transformation and source shifting techniques are discussed. Star-Delta conversion of simplification is also briefly discussed.

KVL and KCL are the two basic electrical laws that can be used to analyse the given network when a network is complex containing many loops and nodes then loop analysis and nodal analysis techniques can be used for analysis. Various theorems are there which can be used to simplify and then analyse the network. Some of the theorem discussed in this chapter includes superposition theorem, Maximum Power Transfer (MPT) theorem, Thevenin's theorem, Norton's theorem, Millman's theorem.

1.2 DEFINITIONS OF NETWORK VARIABLES

Charge, current, follow voltage, power and energy are network variables which can be defined as given below.

1.2.1 Charge

This electrical quantity is the basic property of an atom. There are two types of charges positive and negative. Each atom consist of nucleus with a positive charge and is surrounded by negatively charged particles called electrons. Charge can be neither created nor destroyed. It can be only transferred. This is known as law of conservation of charges.

Basic SI unit of charge is Coulomb and is represented by symbol C. The quantity symbol is Q for constant charge and q for charge that varies with time.

1.2.2 Current

Electric current is produced because of movement of charge. SI unit for current is Ampere with unit symbol A. Quantity symbol is I for constant current and i for variable current.

If a steady flow of 1 C of charge passes a given point in a conductor in 1 second then the resultants current is 1 A.

Time rate of change of transfer of charge is called as current. Thus, we have

$$i(t) = \frac{dq(t)}{dt} \quad \text{...(1.1 a)}$$

$$q(t) = \int_{-\infty}^{t} i(t)\, dt \quad \text{...(1.1 b)}$$

1.2.3 Voltage

"Voltage difference also called potential difference between two points is the work in joules required to move IC of charge from one point to other. The SI unit for voltage is Volt with unit symbol V. The quantity symbol is V or v although E or e is also used. Thus, we have

$$V(\text{volts}) = \frac{W\text{ (jowles)}}{Q\text{ (coloumbs)}} \text{ or } v(t) = \frac{dw}{dq} \quad \text{...(1.2)}$$

1.2.4 Power

Power is defined as the time rate at which energy is transferred. Thus, we have

$$p = \frac{dw}{dt} \quad \text{...(1.3 a)}$$

$$p(t) = v(t)\, i(t) \quad \text{...(1.3 b)}$$

Also $\quad P(\text{watts}) = V(\text{volts}) \times I(\text{amps})$

If P is positive then component absorbs power i.e. it is a consumer of power (or load). If P is negative then the component produces power i.e. it is a source of energy. Positive and negative powers are explained in the Fig. 1.1.

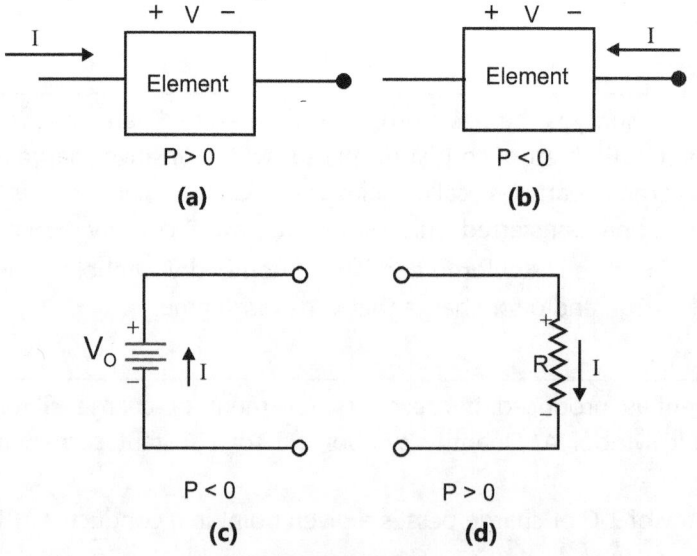

Fig. 1.1: Positive and negative power

1.2.5 Energy

"**Electrical energy used or produced is the product of electric power input or output and the time over which this input or output occurs.**"

Thus, (N/Joules) = P (watts) × t (seconds)

A.C. energy is given by the relation,

$$w = w(t) = \int_0^t P(t)\, d(t) = \int_0^t v(t)\, i(t)\, dt \qquad \ldots (1.4)$$

Joule is a small energy unit. Hence, commercially much large unit called kilowatt hour (kWh). is used.

W (kilowatt hours) = P (kilowatts) × t (Hours)

1.3 SOME CIRCUIT DEFINITIONS

In this section, we shall study some of the commonly used terms associated with the circuit.

1.3.1 Circuit Element

Any individual circuit element (such as inductor, capacitor, resistor, generator) with two terminals by which it may be connected to other circuit elements.

1.3.2 Electric Circuit or Network

An electric network or circuit is an interconnection of circuit elements or branches. It may be two terminals, three terminals or multiterminal network containing active and passive elements.

1.3.3 Branch

A group of elements connected in series or parallel and having two terminals is called a branch.

1.3.4 Mesh or Loop

Mesh or loop is a set of branches forming a closed path in a network such that if one of the branches is removed then the remaining branches do not form a closed path.

Consider Fig .1.2 which is a electric circuit the closed paths forming loops are a-b-d-a, b-c-d-b and a-b-c-d-a.

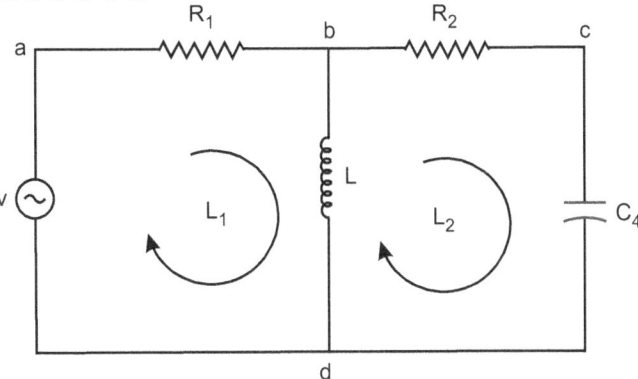

Fig. 1.2: An electric circuit

An **Independent loop** is a loop that contains at least on new element in its path which is not there in other loop.

An **Non - independent** loop is one which do not contains at least one element which is not in the other loop.

In the Fig.1.1, the loops a-b-d-a and b-c-d-b are independent loops. Then loop a-b-c-d-a becomes non - independent loop.

If we choose L_1 (a-b-d-a) and L_3 (a-b-c-d-a) as independent then L_2 (b-c-d-b) becomes non -independent loop.

Note: Selection of independent loops is very important while analyzing network using loop analysis which will be discussed later on.

1.3.5 Node or Junction

It is the common terminal in a network at which one or more branches meets. In the circuit of Fig. 1.2 the nodes are a, b, c and d.

1.4 BASIC CIRCUIT ELEMENTS

There are only three basic circuit elements used. In this section we shall study basic voltage-current relationships of these basic elements.

1.4.1 Resistor

Resistor has the basic property of opposing flow of current. This property is known as resistance. The resistance is denoted by symbol R. It has the unit of ohms Ω. The symbol of resistor is shown in Fig. (1.3).

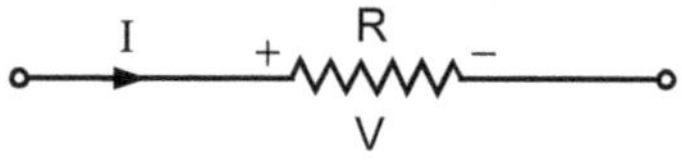

Fig. 1.3: A resistor of 'R' ohms

The voltage and current relationship is given by

$$V = RI \qquad \text{... (1.5 a)}$$

$$I = \frac{V}{R} \qquad \text{... (1.5 b)}$$

Resistor dissipates energy in the form of heat. The power consumed (absorbed) by a resistor is

$$P = VI = I^2R = \frac{V}{R} \qquad \text{... (1.5 c)}$$

Using relationship (1.3 a) amount of energy dissipated into loop is given by

$$W = \int Pdt = I^2 \, R.t. = V.I.t. \text{ (joules)} \qquad \text{... (1.5 d)}$$

The resistance of a material is proportional to length and is inversely proportional to cross section area and is given by:

$$R = \frac{\rho}{A}$$

Where ρ is called resistivity which is constant for a given material.

1.4.2 Capacitor

Capacitor is the element that stores electrical energy in the form of electrostatic field. The capacitance of a capacitor is denoted by symbol 'c'. It has basic unit of Farads (F). Farad being bigger unit, smaller unit of micro farads (µF) or milli farads (mF) are used. The symbol of a capacitor is shown in Fig. 1.4.

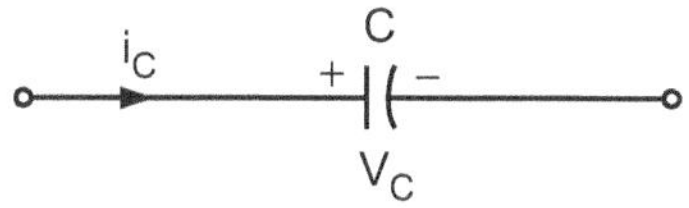

Fig. 1.4: A capacitor of 'C' Farads

The basic voltage and current relationship is given by

$$V_c = \frac{1}{C}\int_{-\infty}^{t} i\, dt \qquad \ldots (1.6\ a)$$

$$i_c = \frac{C\, dv_c}{dt} \qquad \ldots (1.6\ b)$$

The capacitor if already stored by a charge q_0 then voltage on capacitor is given by relation

$$V_c = V_0 + \frac{1}{C}\int_{-\infty}^{t} i_c\, dt \qquad \ldots (1.6\ c)$$

Where V_0 is called Initial voltage.

The electric energy stored in a capacitor is given by,

$$W_c = \frac{1}{2} C V_c^2 \qquad \ldots (1.6\ d)$$

1.4.3 Inductor

Inductor is the element that stores magnetic energy in the form of electromagnetic field. The inductance of an inductor is denoted by symbol 'L'. It has basic unit of Henry (H). Henry being bigger unit, smaller unit of milli Henry (mH)) or micro Henry (µH) are used. The symbol of a inductor is shown in Fig. 1.5.

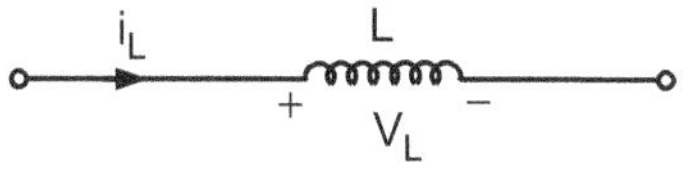

Fig. 1.5: An inductor of 'L' Henry

The basic voltage and current relationship is given by

$$i_L = \frac{1}{L}\int_{-\infty}^{t} V_L\, dt \qquad \ldots (1.7\ a)$$

$$V_L = L\frac{di_L}{dt} \qquad \ldots (1.7\ b)$$

The inductor if already energized, then the current is given by

$$i_L = I_0 + \frac{1}{L} \int_0^t V_L \, dt \qquad \ldots (1.7\ c)$$

Where I_0 is the initial current due to initial energy stored.

The magnetic energy stored in the inductor is given by

$$W_m = \frac{1}{2} L i_L^2 \qquad \ldots (1.7\ d)$$

Note: In addition to basic elements of inductor, capacitor, and resistor, the network can contain other elements such as energy sources and transformer. Energy sources will be discussed later on while transformer is not used at all in this book.

1.5 NETWORK CLASSIFICATION

Based on the characteristics of elements used, some of the types of networks are discussed below.

1.5.1 Linear and Non-linear Networks

A linear element is one in which current and voltage relation is a Linear Differential Equation (LDE) with constant coefficients.

A resistor (R) is a linear element as it is governed by linear equation $V = RI$. Similarity uncharged capacitor with current $(i_c) = C \frac{dv_c}{dt}$ and unenergised inductor with voltage $v_L = \frac{di_L}{dt}$ are also linear elements.

"A circuit containing only linear elements is called as linear circuit."

"If the circuit contain at least one non-linear element then it is called as non-linear circuit".

Examples of non-linear circuit are one containing non-linear elements such as charged capacitor, energized inductor, diode, transistor etc.

Reciprocity and Superposition theorems are valid for only linear circuit. Thus, alternatively. "A linear circuit is defined as the circuit for which Superposition theorem and Reciprocity theorem is valid."

1.5.2 Unilateral and Bilateral Networks

An bilateral element is one in which the voltage current relationship do not alters if we interchange the two terminals. The bilateral elements are resistor, capacitor and inductor.

An unilateral element is one in which the voltage - current relationship changes if we interchange the two terminals. The best example of two terminal bilateral element is diode.

"A circuit whose characteristic and behaviour do not change irrespective of direction of current flow through various elements is called "Bilateral Network."

"A circuit whose characteristic and behaviour does change with the direction of current flow through various elements is called unilateral network."

Thus, network containing at least one element as diode is definitely a unilateral network. But if it contains only R-L-C elements and energy sources then it may be unilateral or bilateral.

1.5.3 Lamped and Distributed Networks

"**An Lumped network is one in which all the circuit elements are physically identifiable and separable.**" If a network is formed by interconnecting energy sources, resistors, inductor, and capacitors then it is a lumped circuit. Most of the electronic circuits are lumped circuits.

"**An distributed network is one in which circuit elements such as resistor, capacitor, inductor can not be isolated and physically separable.**"

Best example for distributed network is transmission lines. In the later Unit, we shall understand that in a transmission line such as telephone lines, power cables or coaxial cables/TV cable, the circuit elements (resistor, capacitor, inductor) can not be identified and physically separated. But they exists through the wire length.

Note: All the network theorems, basic laws such as KCL, KVL or even Ohm's law are valid only for the distributed networks. They are not valid for the transmission line which is a lumped network.

1.5.4 Time-Invariant and Time-Variant Networks

A system is called time-invariant or fixed, if a time-shaft (delay or advance) in the input signal causes the same time shift in the output signal. That is its input-output relationship does not change with time, i.e. if $H[x(t)] = y(t)$, then $H[x(t - \tau)] = y(t - \tau)$ for any value of τ.

For example, the system described by $y(t) = x(t) + Ax(t - T)$ is time-invariant if A and T are constants.

For a discrete-time system, the system is time-variant if $H[x(n - k)] = y(n - k)$ for any value of k.

In the time-invariant systems the shape of the response $y(t)$ depends only on the shape of the input $x(t)$ and not on the time when it is applied. When one more coefficients are function of time, the system is called time-varying system.

1.6 ENERGY SOURCES

Voltage source and current source are said to be energy sources because they supply energy to the linear circuit. Let us study these sources in detail.

1.6.1 Voltage Source

An voltage source provides potential to the circuit. "**An ideal voltage source is an energy unit that gives constant voltage across its terminal irrespective of the current drawn through its terminals.**"

Symbol for an ideal voltage source and its V-I characteristic is shown in Fig. 1.6.

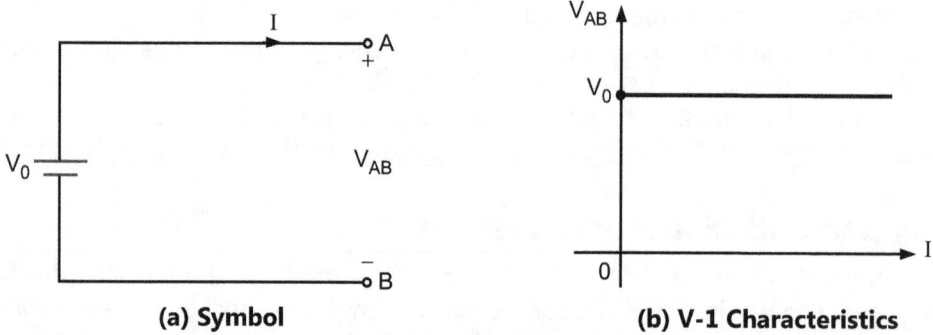

(a) Symbol   (b) V-1 Characteristics

Fig. 1.6: Ideal voltage source

Practical Voltage Source: Every voltage source has some series resistance across its terminals known as "source resistance" and is represented as Rs. For ideal voltage source Rs = 0. But in a practical [Non-Ideal] voltage source value of Rs is not zero but may have small value. Because of this Rs voltage across terminal decreases with increase in current. This is shown in Fig. 1.7.

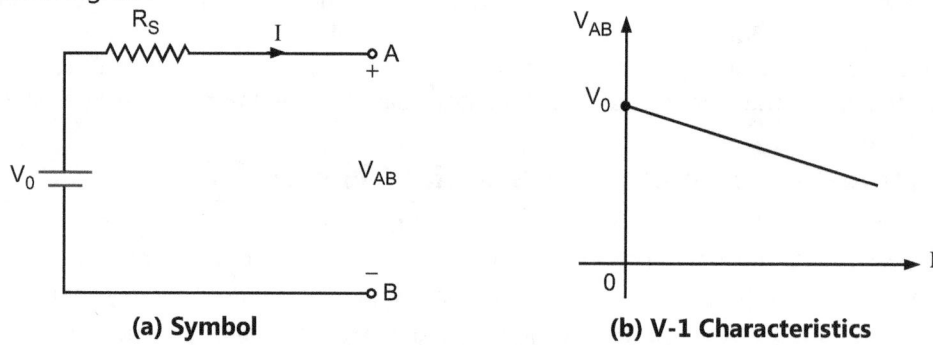

(a) Symbol   (b) V-1 Characteristics

Fig. 1.7: Practical (Non-Ideal) voltage source

Terminal voltage of an practical voltage source is given by

$$V_{AB} = V_0 - R_s I \quad \text{... (a)}$$

By above equation it is obvious that as the terminal current increases terminal voltage will be decreasing slightly. It is practically impossible to obtain ideal voltage source. Some of the practical voltage sources are battery cells. Battery eliminators and regulated power supply.

Note: Unless otherwise specified all the voltage sources in a given network are assumed to be ideal sources ($R_s = 0$).

1.6.2 Current Source

An current source provides current through terminal in a network. **"Ideal current source is an energy unit that will give constant current through its terminals irrespective of the voltage appearing across its terminals."**

Symbol for ideal current source and its V-I characteristic is shown in Fig. 1.8.

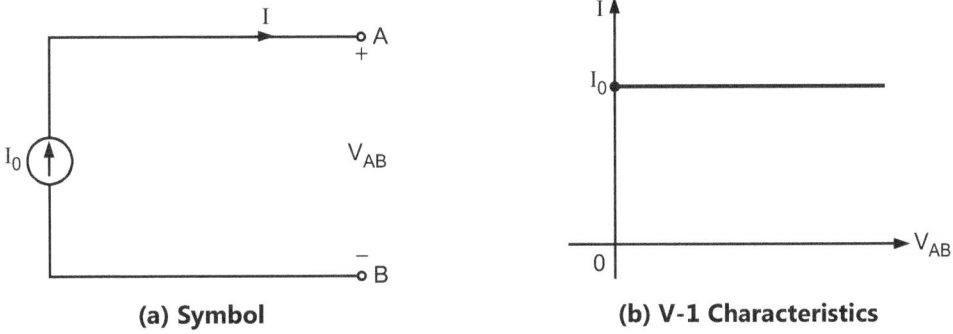

(a) Symbol   (b) V-1 Characteristics

Fig. 1.8: Ideal current source

Practical Current Source: Every current source have some resistance in parallel across its terminals known as source resistance and is represented as R_p. For ideal current source value of R_p is infinity (∞). But in practical (Non-ideal) Current source R_a is not infinity but may have a large value. Thus, because of this large R_p current through its terminals slightly decreases as voltage across terminals increases. This is shown in Fig. 1.9.

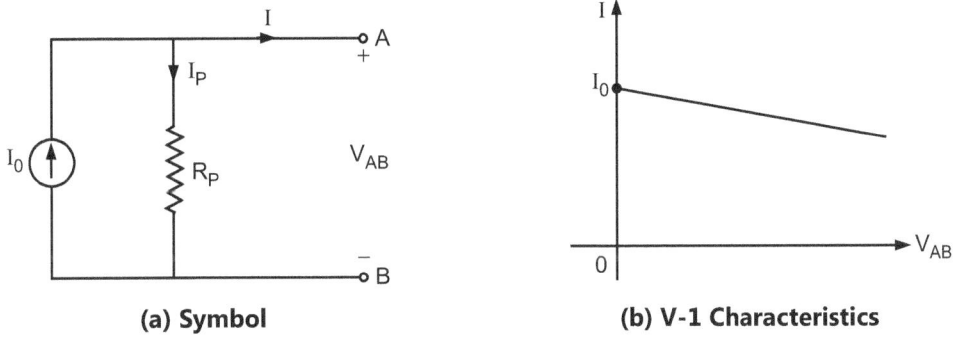

(a) Symbol   (b) V-1 Characteristics

Fig. 1.9

Terminal current of a practical current source is given by

$$I = I_0 - I_p = I_0 = \frac{V_{AB}}{R_P} \qquad \ldots (b)$$

From equation (b) it is obvious that as V_{AB} increased from zero current (I) goes on decreasing.

Current sources are formed using complex electronic circuits that uses OP - AMP or transistor as active elements. These are non-ideal current sources. It is practically impossible to obtain an ideal current source.

Note: Unless or otherwise specified all the current sources given in the circuit are assumed to be ideal sources ($R_p = \infty$).

1.7 INDEPENDENT AND CONTROLLED (DEPENDENT) SOURCES

In general in a electric circuit we use capital letters to designate quantities which are time invariant (Do not vary with time). Thus V or V_0 designate time invariant (or constant) or D.C. voltage; Similarly, I or I_0 represent D.C. (or constant) current. The symbol for them are shown in Fig. 1.10. (a).

If a quantity does vary with time then it will be represented by lower case letters such as v or v(t) and i or i(t) for current source. Symbol for such time variant sources is shown in

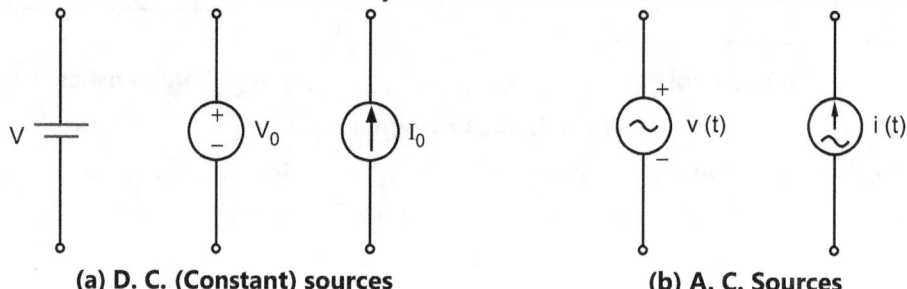

(a) D. C. (Constant) sources   (b) A. C. Sources

Fig. 1.10: Independent energy sources

(a) Independent Energy Sources:

"Independent energy source is a voltage or current source whose value does not depend upon other voltages or currents or the circuit to which these sources are connected."

Independent sources are represented by circle with internal polarity marked. All the sources represented in Fig. 1.10 are independent energy sources. These sources can be time invariant (D.C.) or time variant (A.C.)

(b) Dependent (controlled) Energy Source

"Dependent energy source is a voltage or current source whose value depends upon some other voltage or current in the circuit. These sources are also called as controlled energy sources."

Such sources are common in electronic circuits and are indicated by diamond shaped symbols as in Fig. 1.11 controlled sources are always associated with some equations such as $v = ki_1$, $i_1 = k_iv_2$, $i_2 = k_2i_2$ etc. where i_1, i_2, v_2 are currents or voltage in some other parts of circuit. KVL, KCL and other circuit laws are valid for circuit containing both independent and controlled energy sources.

Dependent (or controlled) Energy sources are of the following four types

1. Voltage controlled voltage sources (VCVS)
2. Current controlled voltage source (CCVS or ICVS)
3. Voltage controlled current source (VCIS or VCCS)
4. Current controlled current source (ICIS or CCCS)

All these sources are shown in Fig. 1.11.

In Fig. 1.11 (a) and Fig. 1.11 (b) terminal voltage is specified as a function of some variable x which is a current or voltage i.e. i = f(x).

In Fig. 1.11 (c) and Fig. 1.11 (d) the terminal currents is specified as a function of some variable x which again is a voltage or current i.e. I = f(x).

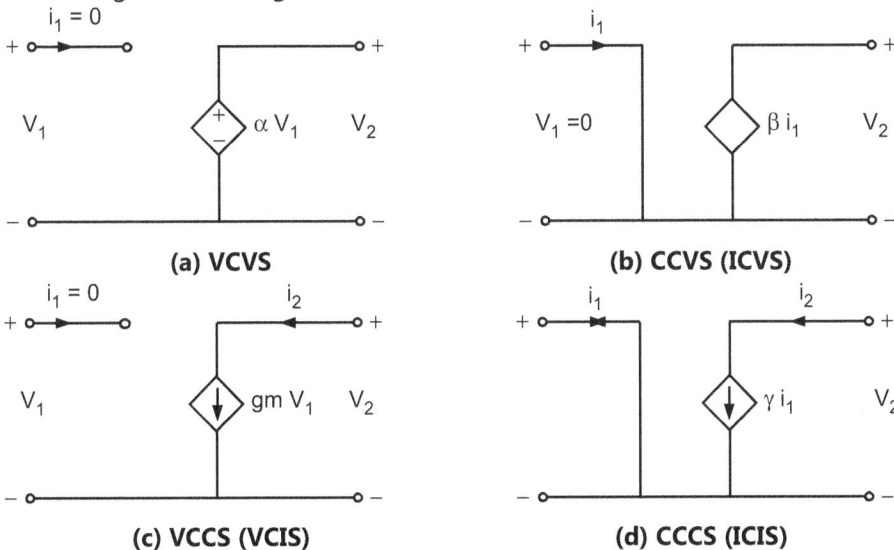

Fig. 1.11: Dependent (Controlled) sources

1.8 POWER

The total work done in a time (t) in an electric circuit is called as energy

$$P = \frac{Work\ (E)}{Time\ (t)} = \frac{W}{t}$$

The power can be written as

$$Power\ (P) = Voltage\ (V) \times Current\ (I)$$
$$P = V \times I \quad watts\ (W)$$

From Ohm's law

$$V = I \cdot R$$
$$I = \frac{V}{R}$$
$$\therefore P = I^2 R$$
$$= \frac{V^2}{R}$$

1.9 OPEN AND SHORT CIRCUIT

Open and short circuits are two circuit connections that have special importance in the network analysis.

1.9.1 Open Circuit

Two points in a circuit are open circuited if there is no circuit element or a direct connection between them as shown in Fig. 1.12 (b).

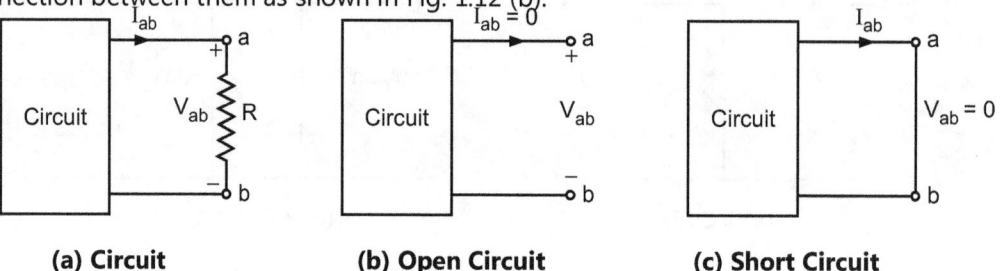

(a) Circuit   (b) Open Circuit   (c) Short Circuit

Fig. 1.12: Open and short circuit

In open circuit since there is no connection between a and b current $I_{ab} = 0$ while voltage (V_{ab}) is determined by rest of the circuit. Consider circuit shown in Fig. 1.13. The current $I_{ab} = 0$. But voltage (V_{ab}) = $10 \times \dfrac{5}{10}$ = + 5V.

Thus, **"two points with arbitrary voltage between them and zero current between them represents an open circuit (OC)"**.

Since, $I_{ab} = \dfrac{V_{ab}}{R}$, If $V_{ab} \neq 0$ but $I_{ab} = 0$ then $R = \infty$

Thus, in a open circuit resistance between two points is infinity.

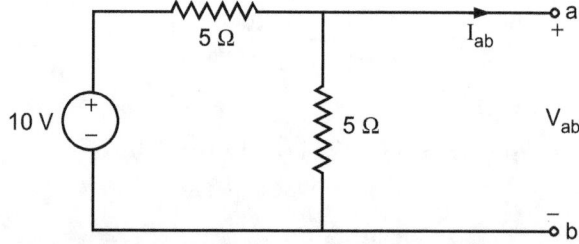

Fig. 1.13: Circuit to explain open circuit (OC)

1.9.2 Short Circuit (SC)

Two points in a circuit are said to be short circuited when two points are connected by a good conducting wire as shown in Fig. 1.12 (c).

In a short circuit (SC) voltage between two points is zero (V_{ab}) = 0 but current between two points is determined by rest of the circuit.

Consider circuit shown in Fig. (1.14).

The voltage V_{ab} is zero while current $(i_{ab}) = 2 \times \dfrac{5}{10} = +1A$

Thus, "two points with arbitrary current through its terminals but zero voltage between is called as short circuit (SC)".

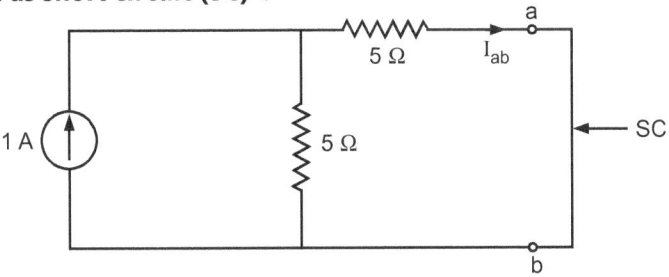

Fig. 1.14: Circuit to explain short circuit (SC)

Since $V_{ab} = RI_{ab}$ if $I_{ab} = 0$ but $V_{ab} = 0$ this means $R = 0$. "Thus in a short circuit the resistance two points is zero."

Thus, the terms **"Zero resistance"** and **"Short circuit"** can be used interchangeably. Similarly the terms **"Infinite resistance"** and **"Open circuit"** are interchangeably used.

1.10 VOLTAGE DIVIDER AND CURRENT DIVIDER CIRCUITS

Voltage and current divider circuits are most commonly used in the analysis. Let us study two circuits in detail.

1.10.1 The Voltage Divider Circuit

Consider an voltage divider circuit shown in Fig. 1.15.
Here two series resistors R_1 and R_2 are driven by a voltage source V_0.

The current(I) is given by $\quad I = \dfrac{V_0}{R_1 + R_2}$

Hence, voltage V_1 is $\quad V_1 = IR_2 = \dfrac{V_0 R_2}{R_1 + R_2} \quad \ldots (1.8)$

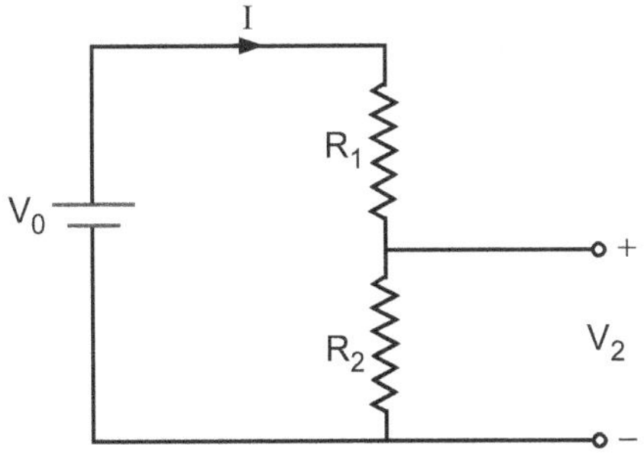

Fig. 1.15: Voltage divider circuit

Equation 1.8 gives output voltage in terms of input voltage (V_0) and two resistors (R_1, R_2) and is called voltage divider equation. This principle can be extended to many number of voltage divider points as explained in Example (1.1) below.

Ex. 1.1: Design the resistors in Fig. 1.16 to provide the following voltage on the taps. $V_2 = 2V$, $V_3 = 6V$ and $V_4 = 10V$. Assume that taps are unloaded. All voltages are measured with respect to ground. Assume that $R_4 = 4$ ohms.

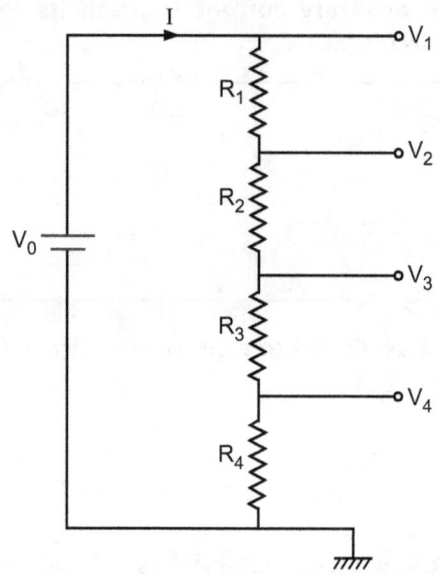

Fig. 1.16: Figure for Ex. (1.1)

Sol.: Since, taps are unloaded no current flows through the tap terminal. Hence, all resistors are in series. The current in the circuit is given by

$$I = \frac{V_0}{R_1 + R_2 + R_3 + R_4}$$

$$= \frac{12}{R_1 + R_2 + R_3 + R_4}$$

Now $V_2 = R_4$, $V_2 = 2V$ (given), $R_4 = 4\Omega$

Hence, circuit current $I = 0.5A$

$$V_3 = (R_4 + R_3)\, I$$
$$= (4 + R_3) \times 0.5$$
$$= 6$$

Hence, $R_3 = 8\Omega$

Finally, $V_4 = 12V$
$$= (R_1 + R_2 + R_3 + R_4) \times 0.5$$
$$= (R1 + 20) \times 0.5$$

Solving this given $R_1 = 4\Omega$

Thus, designed values are $R_2 = 8\Omega$, $R_3 = 8\Omega$, $R_1 = 4\Omega$

1.10.2 The Current Divider Circuit

Consider circuit shown in Fig. 1.17 in which two resistors R_1, R_2 are in parallel across Vo. The total current (I) through battery is $I = I_1 + I_2$.

$$I_1 = \frac{V_0}{R_1} \text{ and } I_2 = \frac{V_0}{R_2}$$

Hence,
$$I_1 = \frac{V_0}{R_1} + \frac{V_0}{R_2}$$

$$= V_0 \left[\frac{R_1 + R_2}{R_1 R_2} \right]$$

$$\text{Current } (I_1) = \frac{V_0}{R_1} = \frac{1}{R_1} \left[\frac{R_1 R_2}{R_1 + R_2} \right] I = \frac{R_2 I}{R_1 + R_2} \quad \ldots (1.9 \text{ a})$$

$$\text{Current } (I_2) = \frac{V_0}{R_2} = \frac{1}{R_2} \left[\frac{R_1 R_2}{R_1 + R_2} \right] I = \frac{R_1 I}{R_1 + R_2} \quad \ldots (1.9 \text{ b})$$

If $R_1 = R_2$ then $I_1 = I_2 = \frac{I}{2}$.

From equations 1.8 and 1.9 it is obvious that the voltage division is directly related to the resistor across which voltage is measured. While for current divider the division is related to other resistor also. The current division principles are explained in the Example (1.2) given below.

Ex. 1.2: A battery of 10 V carries a current of 10 mA. Design a current divider circuit such that the current in one of the resister is 1/3 of other resister current.

Sol.: The current divider circuit is shown in Fig. 1.17.

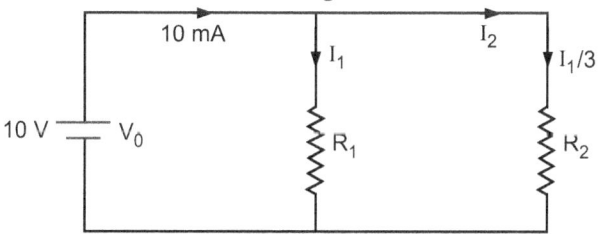

Fig. 1.17: Circuit for Ex. (1.2)

We have,
$$10 = I_1 + \frac{I_1}{3} = \frac{4}{3} I_1$$

Hence we have, $I_1 = 7.5$ mA

Also,
$$I_1 = \frac{10}{R_1} = 7.5 \text{ mA gives } \boxed{R_1 = \frac{4}{3} \text{ k}\Omega}$$

Also
$$\frac{I_1}{3} = 2.5 \text{ mA} = \frac{10}{R_2} \text{ gives } \boxed{R_2 = 4 \text{ k}\Omega}$$

1.11 KIRCHOFF'S VOLTAGE LAW (KVL)

This is one of the fundamental laws used in network analysis.

Statement: "The algebraic sum of the voltage around a closed loop in a circuit must be equal to zero"

OR
$$\sum_{\text{Loop}} \text{Voltage across elements} = 0 \qquad \ldots (1.10\ a)$$

The term algebraic is used since there are both positive and negative voltage around the loop. The positive (+ve) voltages are termed as "voltage rise" while negative (-ve) voltages are termed as "voltage fall" or 'voltage drop'.

Sign conventions for KVL: The positive and negative voltages while using KVL is shown in Fig. (1.18).

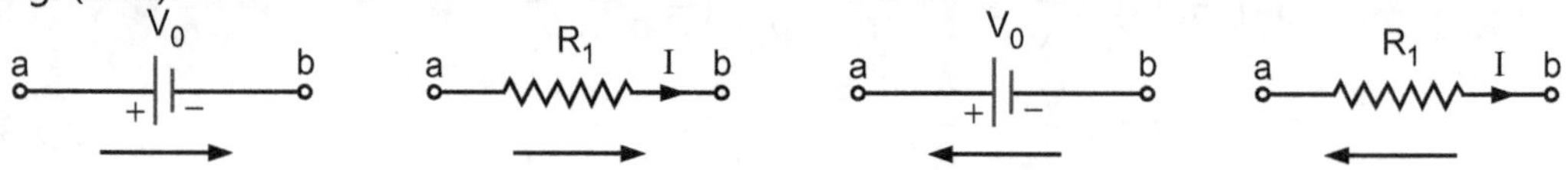

(a) Drop ($-V_0$)   (b) Drop ($-R_1 I$)   (c) Rise ($+V_0$)   (d) Rise ($+R_1 I$)

Fig. 1.18: Sign conventions for KVL

Arrow indicates the direction in which we are moving. In Fig. 1.18 (a), we are moving from higher potential to lower potential [i.e. +ve to –ve of battery] hence take this as Voltage drop i.e. $V_{ab} = V_0$. In Fig. 1.18 (b) we are moving in the direction of current hence take the voltage $V_{ab} = -IR$, which is again a voltage drop.

In Fig. 1.18 (c) we are moving from lower potential to higher potential in the battery. Hence take voltage between a and b as $V_{ab} = +V$. which is a voltage rise. In Fig. 1.18 (d), we are moving against the current hence take $V_{ab} = +R, I$ which is again a voltage rise.

Note: Some books take exactly opposite conventions for voltages. But to avoid confusion stick to above conventions only which is used in this text book.

Now consider equation (1.10 a) in which all the voltages appears either as a voltage rise with positive sign OR they appear as voltage drop with negative sign. Hence equation (1.10 a) can be written as

$$\sum_{\text{Loop}} \text{Voltage drops} - \sum_{\text{Loop}} \text{Voltage rises} = 0$$

OR
$$\sum_{\text{Loop}} \text{Voltage drops} = \sum_{\text{Loop}} \text{Voltage rises} \qquad \ldots (1.10\ b)$$

The alternatively KVL can be defined as **"sum of all the voltage rises is equal to the sum of all the voltage drops around a closed loop in a circuit"**

Now let us study how we can use the KVL in analyzing single loop circuit. The steps involved in a single loop analysis are:

1. Identify and assign loop current with direction and voltage polarities across all elements in the loop.
2. Apply Kirchoff's Voltage Law (KVL) across the loop, use Ohm's law for the resistors.
3. Solve the equation obtained above to get the loop current (I). If the current is negative then the assumed current direction is wrong.

Ex. 1.3: For the single loop circuit of Fig. 1.19 use KVL to find the current (I).

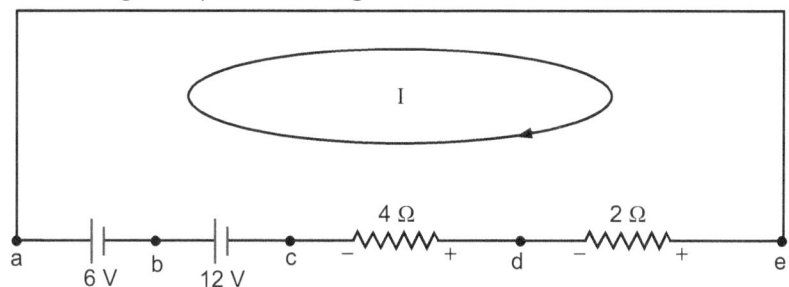

Fig. 1.19: Circuit for Ex. (1.3)

Sol.: Loop current (I) with direction is already given. Also the polarities across resistor is given.

Using KVL across loop (a-e-d-c-b-a), we get,

$V_{ae} + V_{ed} + V_{dc} + V_{cb} + V_{ba} = 0$

$0 - 2I - 4I + 12 + 6 = 0$

$6I = 18$ OR $I = + 3A$

Since, current is positive the assumed direction of current is correct. If we assume opposite direction then only sign of current (I) would be negative. But the magnitude remains 3Amp.

1.11.1 Ground (Datum) Node and Node-Node Voltages

Ground or Reference or Datum node in a circuit is a node whose voltage we assume to be 0V (zero) and the voltages of all other nodes are expressed with respect to this node. **Please note that no current sinks into ground.**

Consider the circuit of Fig. 1.20. Even though any node can be taken as ground generally the bottom most node is considered as a ground for our convenience. Here node d is considered as datum node i.e. we assume voltage $V_d = 0V$

Node voltage V_a, V_b and V_c are known as node-datum voltages.

For example, $\quad V_{ad} = V_a - V_d = V_a - 0 = V_a$

If $V_a = + 8V$ this means that voltage of node 'a' is at higher potential than ground by 8V. If $V_b = - 5V$ or $V_c = - 2V$ this means voltages of nodes b and c are at lower potentials than ground voltage.

Now V_{ab}, V_{bc}, V_{ac} are known as Node–Node voltages. With the above assumed values for V_a, V_b, V_c, we have

$V_{ab} = V_a - V_b = 8 - (- 5) = + 13V$

$V_{bc} = V_b - V_c = -5 - (-2) = - 3V$

$V_{ac} = V_a - V_c = + 8 - (- 2) = + 10V$

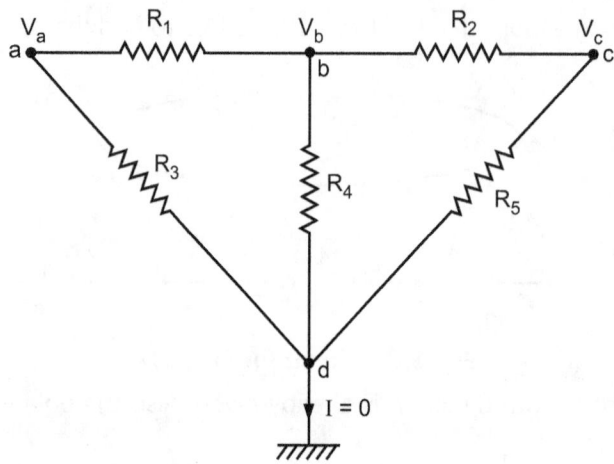

Fig. 1.20: Ground (Reference) node

Note: When voltage is expressed with respect to the reference (or ground) erode then single suffix is used as in V_a, V_b and V_c. If voltages between two nodes neither of which is ground node, then two suffixes are used. For example V_{ab}, V_{bc}, V_{ac} etc.

1.12 KIRCHOFF'S CURRENT LAW (KCL)

This is also most fundamental law along with KVL used in the network analysis.

Statement: "The algebraic sum of currents at a node (or Junction) in a circuit is zero". Alternatively "The sum of currents directed into any node in a circuit is equal to the sum of the currents coming out of same node in a circuit".

$$\sum_{\text{node 'n'}} \text{Current in} = \sum_{\text{node 'n'}} \text{Current out} \qquad \ldots (1.11\ a)$$

OR

$$\sum_{\text{node}} \text{Algebraic current} = 0 \qquad \ldots (1.11\ b)$$

Sign Convention for KCL: Generally, current leaving an node is taken as having positive sign. The currents entering an node is taken as having negative sign. We can assume other way also without any error being committed. But always stick to the convention given which we use in this text.

Consider a portion of circuit given as in Fig. 1.21. The dotted line indicates remaining part of the circuit.

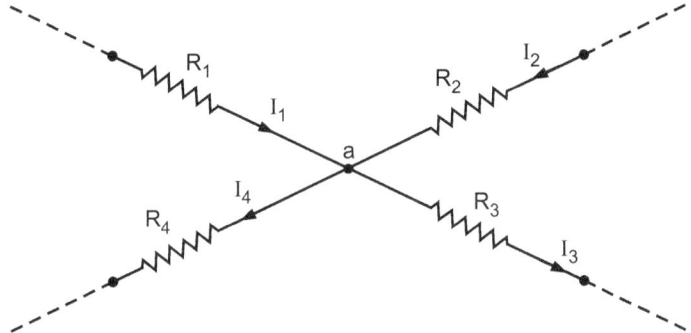

Fig. 1.21: A node of a circuit used to explain KCL

Using the above sign convention given, the KCL at node 'a' as given by equation (1.11 b) is

$$-I_1 - I_2 + I_3 + I_4 = 0$$

OR
$$I_1 + I_2 = I_3 + I_4$$

This also verify the equation (1.11 a).

While analyzing a given circuit KCL at a node enables us to determine node voltage. The following example explain this.

Ex. 1.4: Using Kirchoff's current law find the currents in the resistors of 5Ω, 10Ω and 2Ω.

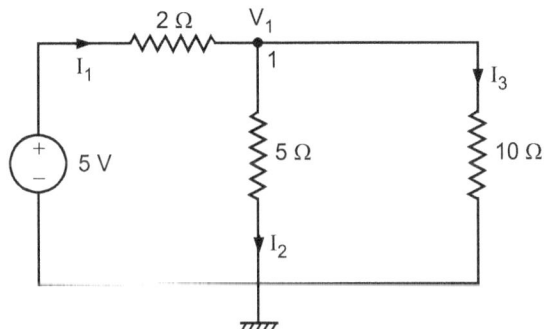

Fig. 1.22: Circuit for Ex. (1.4)

Sol.: All the branch currents are given, along with ground (reference) node. Now applying KCL at node '1' we get,

$$+ I_3 - I_1 + I_2 = 0$$

$$+ \frac{V_1}{10} - \left(\frac{5 - V_1}{2}\right) + \frac{V_1}{5} \text{ OR } \frac{V_1}{10} + \frac{V_1}{5} = \left(\frac{5 - V_1}{2}\right)$$

Given
$$5(5 - V_1) = 2V_1 + V_1$$

OR
$$V_1 = +\frac{25}{8} \text{ Volts}$$

Current in 5Ω resistor = $I_2 = \dfrac{V_1}{5} = \dfrac{+5}{8}$ Amp.

Current in 10Ω resistor = $I_3 = \dfrac{V_1}{10} = \dfrac{5}{10}$ Amp.

Current in 2Ω resistor = $I_1 = \left(\dfrac{5-V_1}{2}\right) = +\dfrac{15}{16}$ Amp.

Thus, $I_1 = \dfrac{15}{16} = I_2 + I_3 = \dfrac{5}{8} + \dfrac{5}{16} + \dfrac{15}{16}$ Amp.

1.13 PROBLEMS BASED ON KCL AND KVL ONLY

Two fundamental laws of KVL and KCL together forms an powerful tool in a circuit analysis. Following examples explain how they can be used effectively.

Ex. 1.5: Determine variables I_1, I_2 and V_A in the circuit using KVL and KCL.

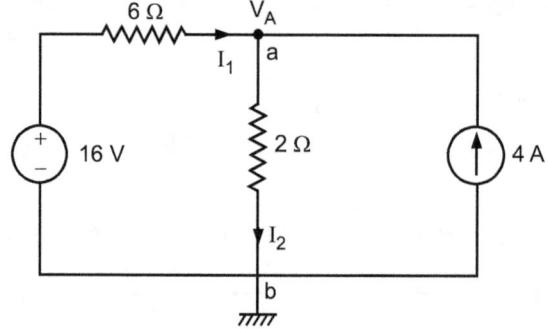

Fig. 1.23: Circuit for Ex. (1.5)

Sol.: KCL at node a gives $\quad I_2 = 4 + I_1$ ... (a)

KVL across loop (a – b – c – a) gives $V_{ab} + V_{bc} + V_{ca} = 0$

$\quad -2I_2 + 16 - 6I_1 = 0v \quad$ OR $\quad 3I_1 + I_2 = 8$ ... (b)

Solving equation (a) and (b) gives

$\quad I_1 + 4 = 8 - 3I \quad$ OR $\quad I_1 = +1A$

Hence $\quad I_2 = 4 + 1 = 5A \quad$ i.e. $\quad I_2 = +5A$

Thus, $\quad V_A = 2I_2 + 10\,V \quad$ i.e. $\quad V_A = +10V$

Ex. 1.6 Using Kirchoff's laws, determine current I_1 in the circuit shown.

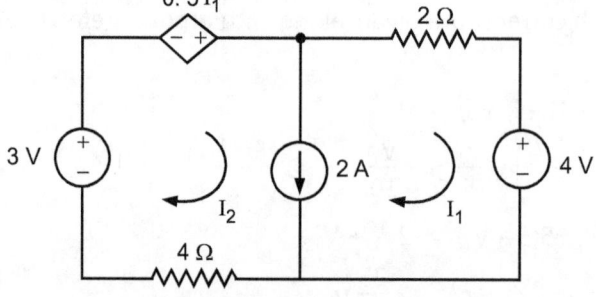

Fig. 1.24: Circuit for Ex. (1.6)

Sol.: The circuit can be redrawn as in Fig. (1.25) where nodes are taken as a, b, c. d and e.

Now KCL at b gives $\quad I_2 = I_1 + 2$ ... (a)

There are two unknown variables I_1 and I_2 for this we need two equations. The other equation can be obtained by applying KVL across outer loop (a - b - c - d - e - a).

$$+0.5I_1 - 2I_1 - 4 - 4I_2 + 3 = 0$$

OR $\quad\quad 1.5 I_1 + 4 I_2 = -1$ ... (b)

Solving (a) and (b) we get,

$$1.5 I_1 + 4 (I_2 + 2) = -1$$

OR $\quad\quad I_1 = \dfrac{-9}{5.5} = 1.636$ Amp.

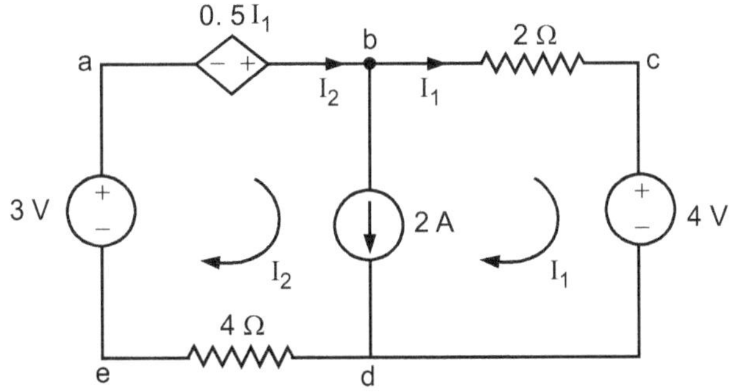

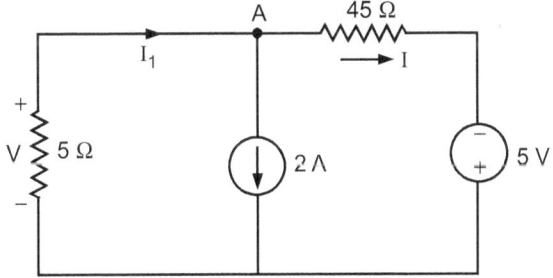

Fig. 1.25: Redrawn circuit for Ex. (1.6)

Ex. 1.7: For the circuit shown determine I and V, use KCL and KVL.

Fig. 1.26: Circuit of Ex. (1.7)

Sol.: KCL at A gives $\quad I_1 = I + 2$ ... (a)

We have $\quad\quad V = -5I_1 = -5 (I + 2)$ ... (b)

Applying KVL across outer loop gives

$$-5I_1 - 45I + 5 = 0$$

$-5 (I + 2) - 45I = -5 \quad$ OR $\quad I = -0.1$ A ... from (a)

Hence by (b) $\quad\quad V = -5 (-0.1 + 2) = -9.5$ volts.

1.14 CIRCUIT ELEMENTS IN SERIES AND PARALLEL

The basic circuit elements are R, L, C and energy sources. Many times in a complex circuits these elements themselves are connected in series or parallel. By combining them we can simplify the circuits. In this section, we shall study how to combine the series or parallel connected network elements. This is one of the basic simplification technique used.

1.14.1 Impedances In Series

Consider three impedances Z_1, Z_2 and Z_3 in series as shown in Fig. 1.6 (a) with a voltage source V.

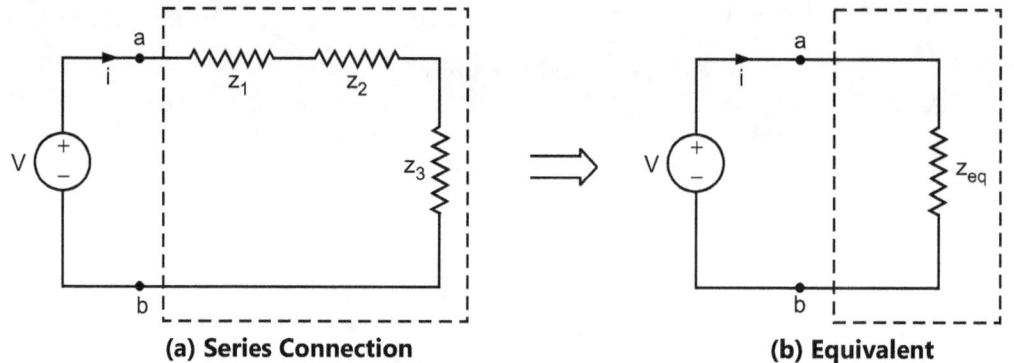

(a) Series Connection   (b) Equivalent

Fig. 1.27: Impedances in series

Since, same current (i) flows through all impedances we have

$$V = I[Z_1 + Z_2 + Z_3] = i \cdot Z_{eq}$$

Hence $\quad Z_{eq} = Z_1 + Z_2 + Z_3$ ... (1.12)

(a) Resistors in series $[R_{eq} = R_1 + R_2 + R_3 + ...]$

(b) Inductors in series $[L_{eq} = L_1 + L_2 + L_3 + ...]$

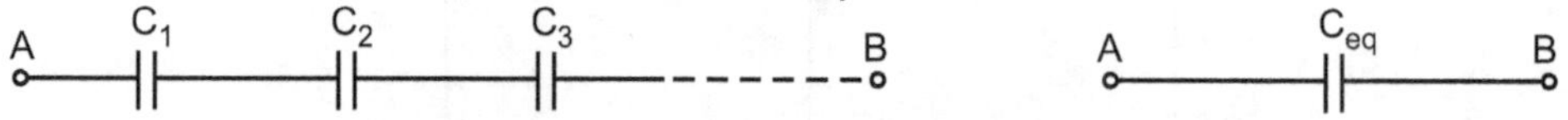

(c) Capacitors in series $\left[\dfrac{1}{C_{eq}} = \dfrac{1}{C_1} + \dfrac{1}{C_2} + \dfrac{1}{C_3} + ...\right]$

Fig. 1.28: R, L, C elements in series

The equivalent circuit will have same voltage and current across terminals a-b as shown in Fig. 1.27 (b).

"Thus in series connection of the impedances the equivalent impedance is addition of all the impedances.

The impedances can be resistors or inductors or capacitors The elements and their equivalent values is shown in Fig. 1.28.

1.14.2 Impedances in Parallel

Consider three impedances Z_1, Z_2, Z_3 in parallel as shown in Fig. 1.29 (a). An common voltage source V is connected across them.

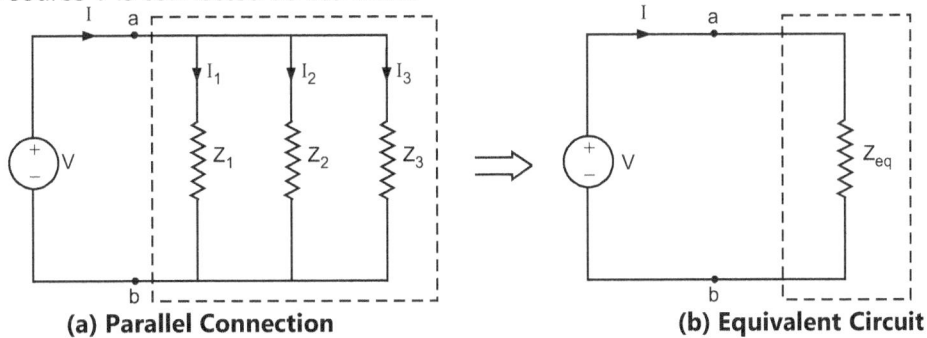

(a) Parallel Connection (b) Equivalent Circuit

Fig. 1.29: Impedances in parallel

Since, all impedances have same voltage across them by KCL at a we get:

$$I = I_1 + I_2 + I_3 = 0 \quad \ldots (a)$$

In the equivalent circuit of Fig. 1.32 (b)

$$I = \frac{V}{Z_{eq}} \quad \ldots (b)$$

Hence,

$$\frac{1}{Z_{eq}} = \frac{1}{Z_1} + \frac{1}{Z_2} + \frac{1}{Z_3} \quad \ldots (1.13)$$

If 'N' impedances are connected in parallel then

$$\frac{1}{Z_{eq}} = \frac{1}{Z_1} + \frac{1}{Z_2} + \frac{1}{Z_3} + \ldots\ldots\ldots + \frac{1}{Z_n}$$

If two impedances (Z_1, Z_2) are connected in parallel which is most commonly found in many circuit the equivalent resistance is

$$Z_{eq} = \frac{Z_1 Z_2}{Z_1 + Z_2}$$

The impedances can be resistor, inductor or capacitor. The elements and their equivalent values are shown in Fig. 1.29. As far as equivalent value is concerned resistors in series is equivalent to the inductors in series and capacitors in parallel. The resistors in parallel is equivalent to inductor in parallel and capacitor in series.

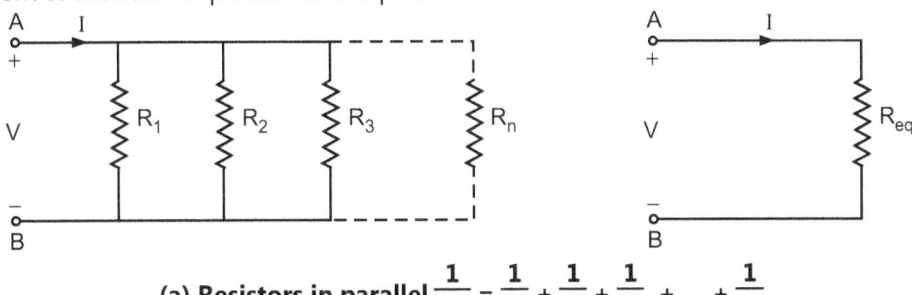

(a) Resistors in parallel $\frac{1}{R_{eq}} = \frac{1}{R_1} + \frac{1}{R_2} + \frac{1}{R_3} + \ldots + \frac{1}{R_n}$

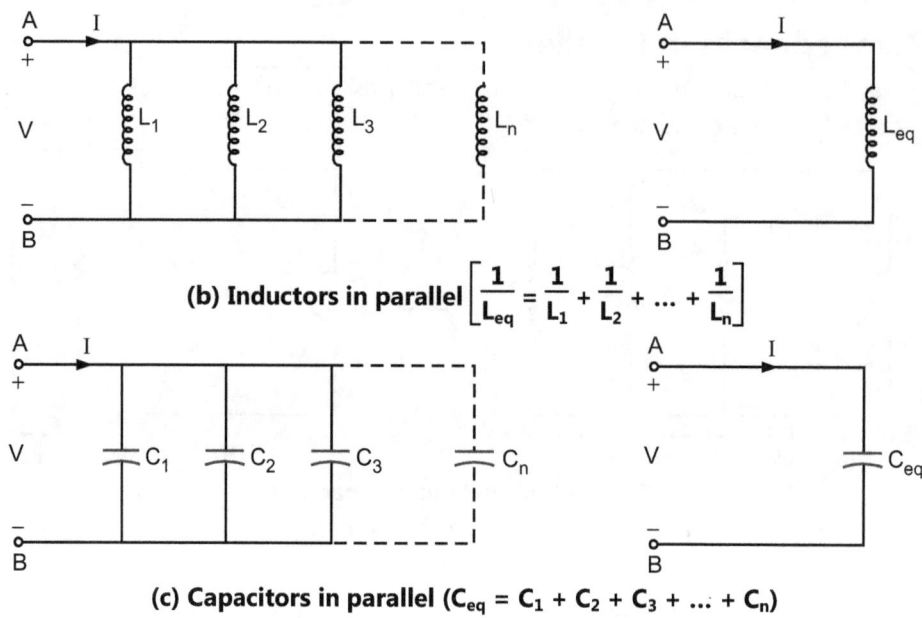

(b) Inductors in parallel $\left[\dfrac{1}{L_{eq}} = \dfrac{1}{L_1} + \dfrac{1}{L_2} + \ldots + \dfrac{1}{L_n}\right]$

(c) Capacitors in parallel ($C_{eq} = C_1 + C_2 + C_3 + \ldots + C_n$)

Fig. 1.30: R, L, C elements in parallel

1.15 ENERGY SOURCES IN SERIES AND PARALLEL

Last section we have seen how to combine R, L, C element when they are in series or parallel. In this section, we will consider equivalent value when two or move voltages or currents in series and parallel.

1.15.1 Series Connection of Voltage Sources

Various types of series connections and their equivalents are shown in Fig. (1.31).

From the Fig. 1.31 it is obvious that if positive terminal of a voltage source is connected to the negative (−ve) terminal of other voltage source [Fig. 1.31 (a) and (b)] then two voltages are added to get equivalent voltage sources.

If the positive (+ve) terminal of one voltage source is connected to negative (−ve) terminal of other voltage source [Fig. 1.31 (c) and (d)] then equivalent voltage source is the difference between individual voltages.

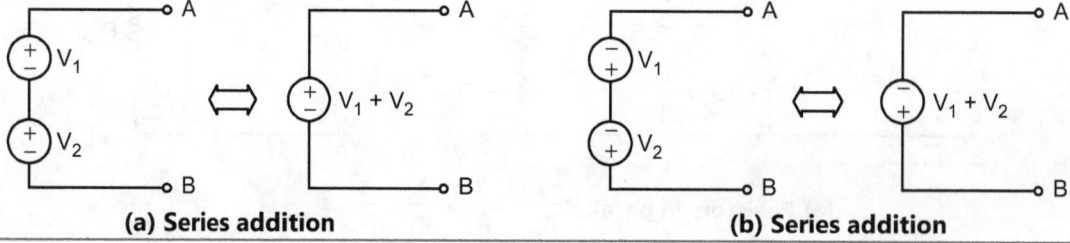

(a) Series addition (b) Series addition

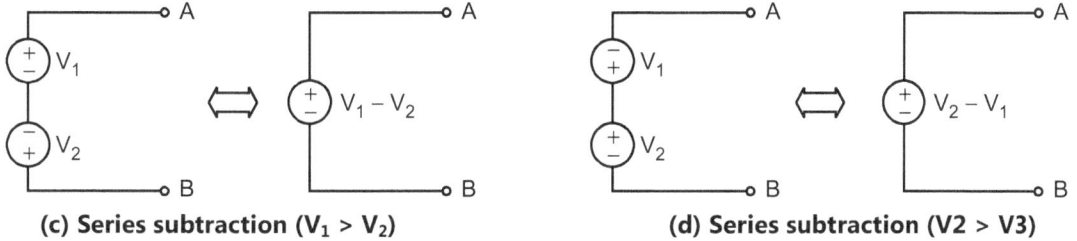

(c) Series subtraction ($V_1 > V_2$)   (d) Series subtraction ($V2 > V3$)

Fig. 1.31: Voltage Sources in Series

To explain why voltage sources are connected in series we shall consider a practical situation. Suppose that we have many batteries with 1.5 V and 0.1 A ratings. Now we have a circuit that needs 12V and a current of 0.1 A maximum. Then 8 of such batteries can be connected in series.

"**Thus, to get the higher voltage with same current rating we are connecting voltage sources in series**".

Note: To connect voltage sources in series all the sources must have same current ratings, but they may have same or different current ratings.

1.15.2 Parallel Connection of Voltage Sources

Two voltage sources connected in parallel is shown in Fig. (1.32) unlike series connection there are not many ways in which sources can be connected in parallel.

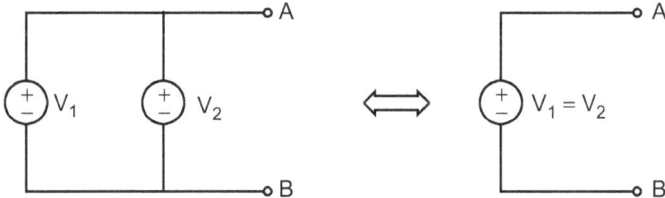

Fig. 1.32: Voltage sources in parallel

To explain why voltage sources are connected parallel, let us consider an practical situation. As before suppose we have a lot of batteries with 1.5 V and 0.1 A ratings. Now suppose we have a circuit that needs an supply of 1.5V and 1A rating. Then we can well connect 10 such batteries in parallel. "**Thus, to get the higher current rating with same voltage rating the voltage sources are connected in parallel**".

Note: While connecting two or more voltage sources in parallel all the voltage sources must be having same voltage rating but can have different current ratings. If two voltage sources of unequal voltage ratings are connected in parallel then heavy current will flow through both the sources and can damage them.

1.15.3 Current Sources In Series

Series connection of two current sources is shown in Fig. (1.33).

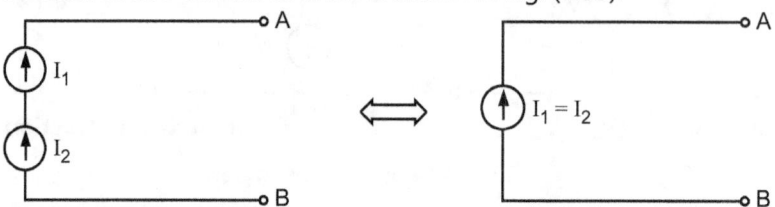

Fig. 1.33: Current sources in series

To explain why current sources are connected in series consider a practical situation. Suppose we have many current sources with 2A and 10V ratings. Now if a circuit needs a current source with 2A and 30V rating then three such sources can be connected in series. **"Thus, to get higher voltage rating with same current rating two or more current sources are connected in series."**

Note: While connecting the current sources in series all the current sources must have same current ratings but their voltage ratings can be different.

1.15.4 Current Sources In Parallel

Various ways in which current sources can be parallel connected is shown in Fig. 1.34.

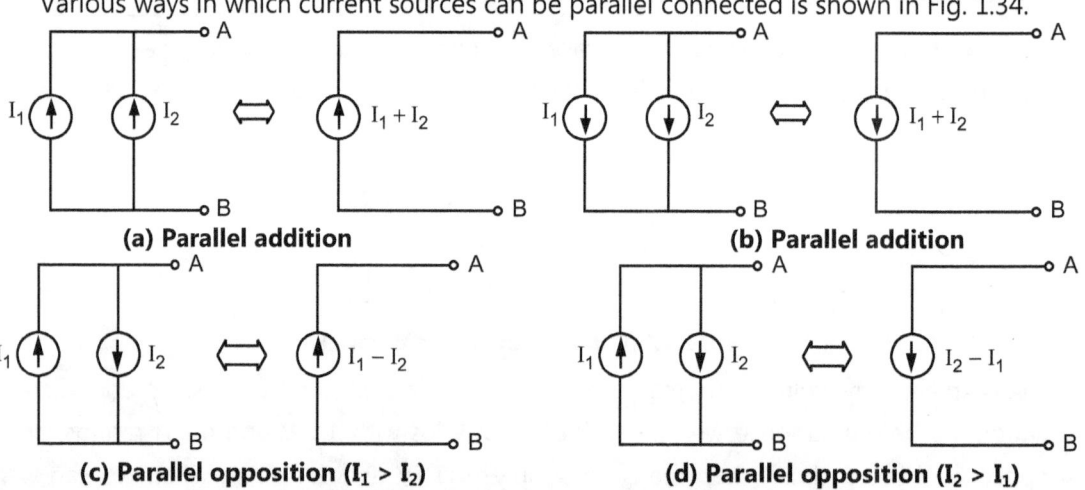

(a) Parallel addition (b) Parallel addition

(c) Parallel opposition ($I_1 > I_2$) (d) Parallel opposition ($I_2 > I_1$)

Fig. 1.34: Current sources in parallel

To explain why current sources are parallel connected again consider a practical situation. As before we had many current sources of 2A and 10V rating each. Now if a circuit needs an current source of 6A and 10V rating then three such current "sources can be connected in parallel. Thus, to get higher current rating with same voltage rating two or more current sources are connected in parallel.

Note: While current sources are connected in parallel, all the sources must have same voltage rating but they can have same or different current ratings.

Now let us consider a peculiar situation in which voltage and current sources together are connected in series and parallel as shown in Fig. (1.35).

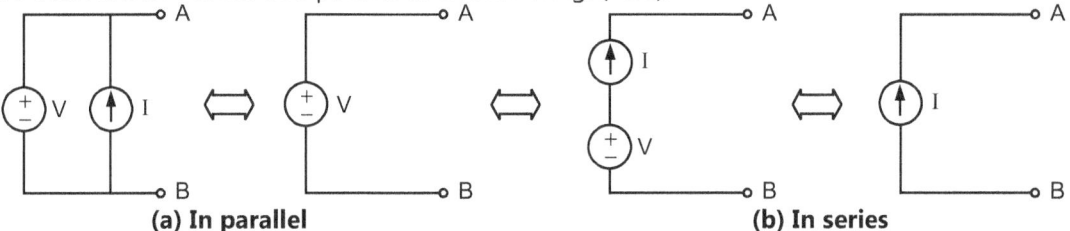

(a) In parallel   (b) In series

Fig. 1.35: Voltage and current sources

In Fig. 1.35 (a), since internal resistance of the voltage source is zero, the output current from the current source flows through voltage source without any effects on its output voltage. Hence, the configuration has exactly the same properties as that of a voltage source alone.

In Fig 1.35 (b), since voltage rating of the current source is undefined addition of voltage of voltage source still leaves the quantity undefined. Thus, the combination will have same properties as that of current source alone.

1.16 SOURCE TRANSFORMATION

Some times while analyzing an network we want all the sources to be same type either current sources or voltage sources. For example in "Loop analysis" all the sources preferably must be voltage sources while in "Nodal analysis" all the sources preferably must be current sources. Thus, conversion of one type of source into other type is very much essential in many network analysis. This conversion can be accomplished by source transformation equation which is discussed below.

1.16.1 Source Transformation Equation

If an voltage source has a series resistor then it can be converted into an current source. Similarly if an current source has a resistor in parallel with it then it can be converted into a equivalent voltage source. The conversion should not a effect the terminal property. Source transformation equation can be used for this purpose. Let us now derive this equation.

Consider the circuit shown in Fig. 1.36 (a) (a) across terminal a-b there is a voltage source (V_0) in series with resistor (R). The equivalent circuit which converts the voltage source into a current source (I_0) is shown in Fig. 1.36 (b). The two circuits must have same terminal voltage (V_x) and terminal current (I_x).

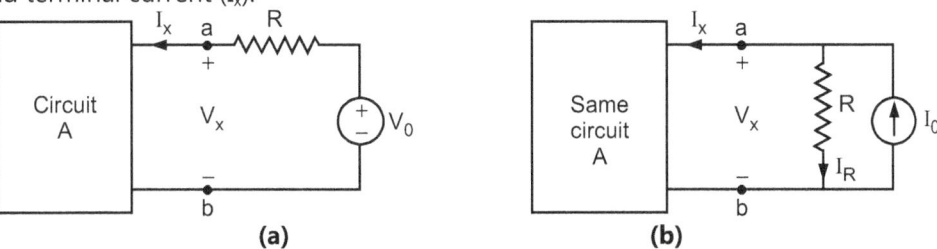

(a)   (b)

Fig. 1.36: Source transformation

In Fig. 1.39 (a) KVL across a-b-a gives,

$$+ RI_x - V_0 + V_x = 0 \quad \text{or} \quad V_0 = V_x + RI_x \quad \ldots \text{(a)}$$

In Fig. 1.39 (b) KCL at node a gives

$$I_R + I_x = I_0 \quad \text{or} \quad \frac{V_x}{R} + I_x = I_0$$

Hence, we have $\quad V_x + RI_x = RI_0 \quad \ldots \text{(b)}$

For the two circuits to be equivalent (that is one can be replaced by the other) the two equations must be same.

Thus, we have $\quad \boxed{V_0 = RI_0} \quad \ldots \text{(1.14 a)}$

or $\quad \boxed{I_0 = \frac{V_0}{R}} \quad \ldots \text{(1.14 b)}$

Equation (1.14) is known as **"Source transformation equation."**

Thus, we conclude that **"A voltage source V_0 in series with an resistor (R) can be converted into a current source (I_0) of value $\frac{V_0}{R}$ which is in parallel with resistor (R)".**

Conversely **"A current source (I_0) in parallel with the resistor (R) can be converted into a voltage source (V_0) of value (V_0) = RI_0 in series with resistor (R).**

Note: In equation (1.14) (a) and (b) if R = 0 then I_0 will be infinite and if R = ∞ then V_0 = ∞. Thus source transformation has no meaning if R= 0 or R = ∞.

Following examples explains how source transformation is useful in circuit analysis.

Ex. 1.8: Using source transformation find voltage (V) in the circuit shown below.

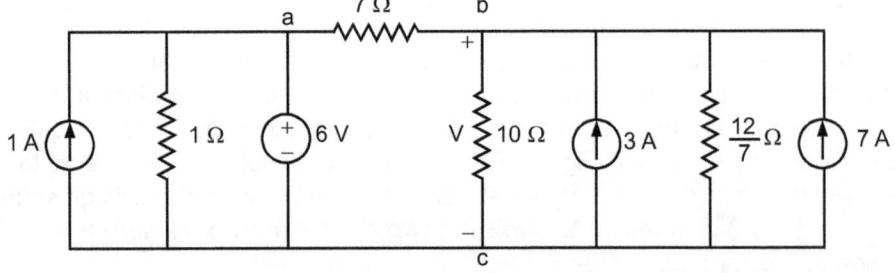

Fig. 1.37 (a): Circuit for Ex. (1.18)

Sol.: Now $3\Omega \parallel 4\Omega = \frac{12}{7}\Omega$. This is in series with 12 V source. This can be converted into a current source of $12 \times \frac{7}{12} = 7A$ in parallel with $\frac{12}{7} \Omega$. The circuit can be redrawn as shown in Fig. 1.37 (a).

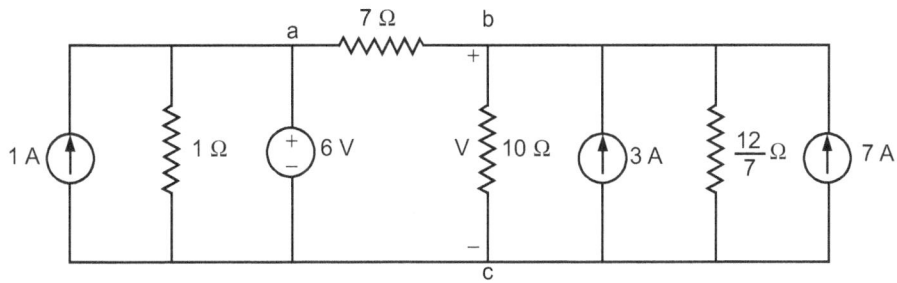

(i) Equivalent circuit of Fig. 1.37 (a)

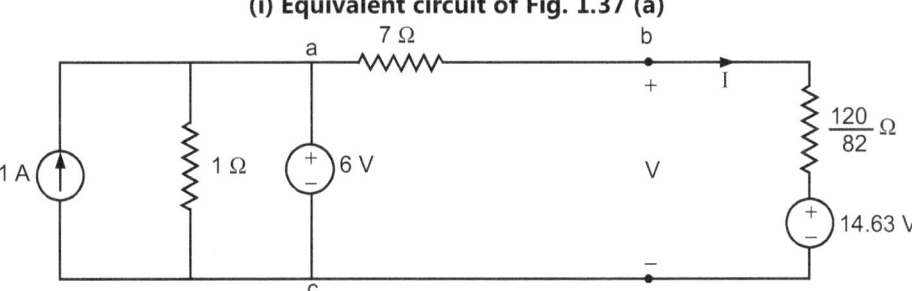

(ii) Simplified equivalent circuit of Fig. 1.37 (a)

Fig. 1.37 (b): Equivalent circuits for Ex. (1.8)

Now 7A and 3A are in parallel addition that gives 10A current source. 10Ω and $\frac{12}{7}$ Ω resistors are in parallel to give equivalent resistance (R_{eq}) of

$$R_{eq} = \frac{\frac{12}{7} \times 10}{\frac{12}{7} + 10} = \frac{120}{82} \, \Omega$$

With this simplification and after source transformation the circuit can be redrawn as in Fig. 1.37 (b).

KVL across right loop (a-b-c-a) given

$$-7I - \frac{120}{82} I - 14.63 + 6 = 0$$

Or $\qquad$ I [7 + 1.463] = 6 − 14.63

$\qquad\qquad\qquad\quad = -8.63$

Hence, $\qquad$ I = − 1.02 Amp.

Thus, $\qquad$ V = + $\frac{120}{8}$ I + 14.63

$\qquad\qquad\qquad = -1.492 + 14.63$

Thus, $\qquad$ V = +13.137 volts.

Ex. 1.9: Using source transformation, find I_1 that gives V_2 = 6.5V in the circuit shown.

(Dec. 2004) (8 marks)

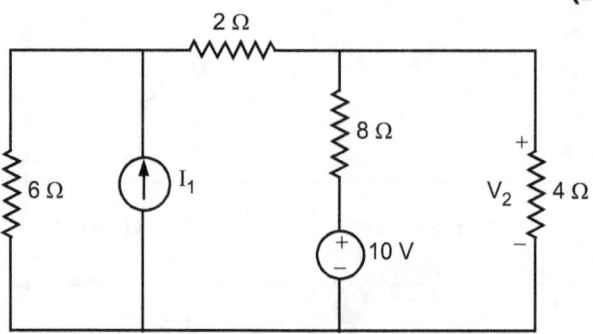

Fig. 1.38: Circuit for Ex. (1.9)

Sol.: 10V in series with 8Ω can be converted into a current source of $\frac{5}{4}$ in parallel with 8Ω as in Fig. 1.39 (a).

Now 8Ω and 4Ω in parallel gives equivalent resistance of $\frac{8 \times 4}{8 + 4} = \frac{24}{12} = \frac{8}{3}$ Ω as shown in Fig. 1.39 (b).

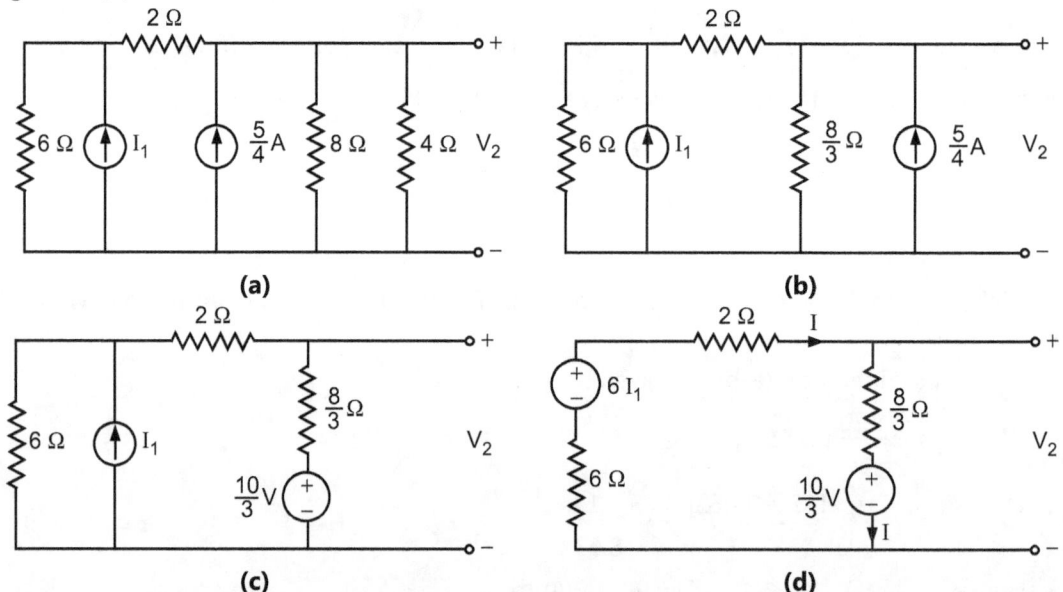

Fig. 1.39: Various steps involved in simplification of Fig. 1.38

Thus, $\frac{5}{4}$ A current source and $\frac{8}{3}$ Ω resistor in parallel can be converted into voltage source of $\frac{10}{3}$ V in series with $\frac{8}{3}$ Ω as shown in Fig. 1.39 (c).

The final circuit after current source transformation is shown in Fig. 1.39 (d). Assume loop current (1) and using Ohm's across outer branch gives,

$$V_2 = 6.5$$
$$= \frac{8}{3}I + \frac{10}{3}$$

Solving this gives, $I = \frac{19}{16} A$

Now KVL across the whole loop gives,
$$-6I + 6I_1 - 2I - V_2 = 0$$
i.e. $\quad -8I + 6I - 6.5 = -0$
or $\quad 6I_1 = 6.5 + 8I$
$$= 6.5 + 9.5 = 16$$

Hence $\quad I_1 = \frac{16}{6} = \frac{8}{3} A$

Thus, a current source of $\frac{8}{3}$ A in the circuit of Fig. 1.43 gives a voltage of V_2 6.5 V.

Ex. 1.10: Using source transformation, find current I in the circuit shown.

(Dec.2005) (6 marks)

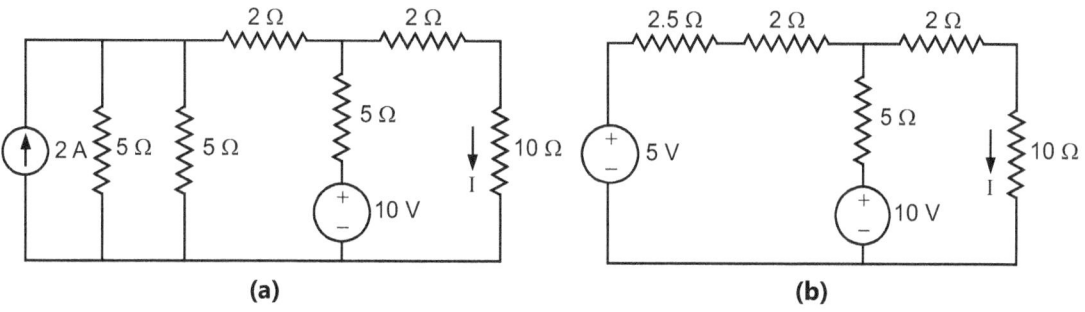

Fig. 1.40: Circuit for Ex. (1.10)

Sol.: Various steps involved in the simplification of the circuit given are shown in Fig. (1.41).

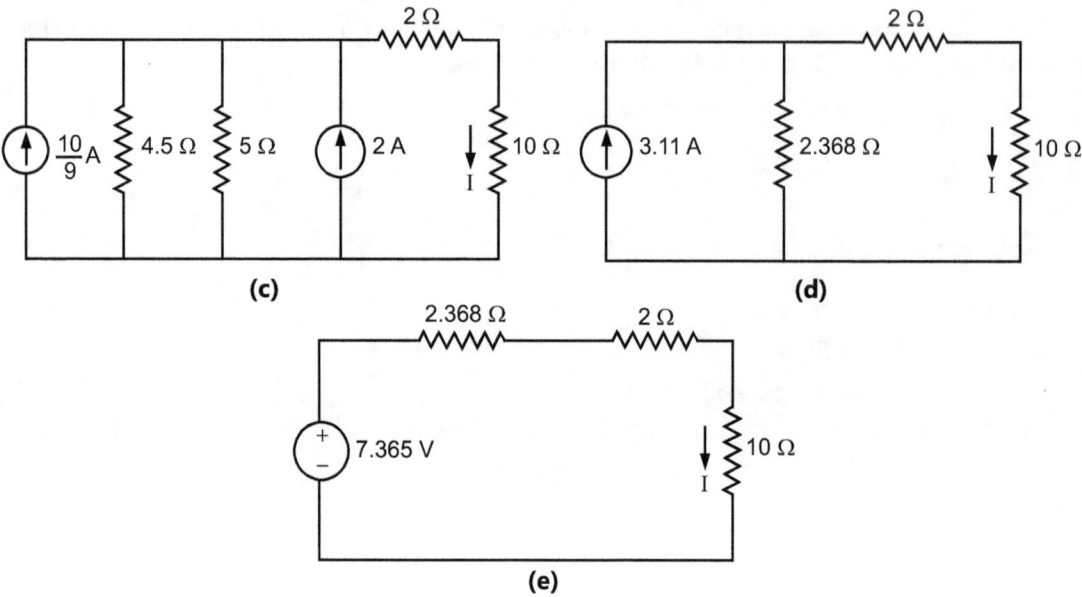

Fig. 1.41: Various step involved in simplification of Fig. 1.40

Convert 10V in series with 5Ω into a current source of 2A parallel with 5Ω as in Fig. (1.41 a).

5Ω || 5Ω gives 2.5Ω resistor. This resistor is parallel with 2A current source. This combination is converted into an voltage source of 5V in series with 2.5Ω as shown in Fig. 1.41 (b).

Convert the two voltage sources in series with resistors into current sources in parallel as in Fig. 1.41 (c).

Two current sources of two parallel resistors are combined to get circuit of Fig. 1.41 (d), where 4.5Ω || 5Ω gives 2.368 Ω resistor.

Finally, converting 3.11 A in parallel with 2.368Ω into voltage source of 3.11 × 2.368 = 7.365V in series with resistor 2.368Ω as shown in Fig. 1.41 (e).

Using KVL gives   7.365 = (2 + 10 + 2.368)

Or   I = 0.512 Amp.

Ex. 1.11: Make use of source transformations to determine values of V and I in the circuit shown.

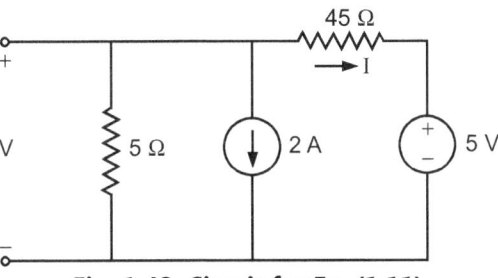

Fig. 1.42: Circuit for Ex. (1.11)

Sol.: In the given circuit 2A is in parallel with 5Ω. This can be converted into a voltage source of 2 × 5 = 10V in series with 5Ω. This conversion makes the circuit into a single loop as shown in Fig. 1.43.

KVL across the loop gives + 5 + 45I + 5I + 10 = 0

$$50I = -15 \quad \text{or } I = -0.3A$$

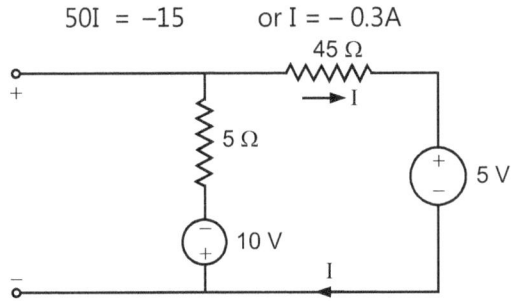

Fig. 1.43: Equivalent circuit of Fig. (1.42)

Now, $\quad V = -10 - 5I = -10 - 5(-0.3) = -8.5$ V

Also, $\quad V = +45I + 5 = 45 \times -0.3 + 5 = -8.5$ V

1.17 SOURCE SHIFTING

In source transformation it is required that there must be a resistor in series with a voltage source or a resistor in parallel with the current source. If this is not the case then source transformation cannot be achieved. But we can go for source shifting if it is possible to do.

1.17.1 Voltage Source Shifting

Consider a circuit where there is no resistor in series with voltage source as in Fig. 1.44 (a). Here voltage (V_1) do not have a resistor in series. Now voltage source shifting can be achieved by pushing it into the arms containing resistors R_1 and R_2 as shown Fig. 1.44 (b). Nodes a and b are maintained at same potential (V_1) with respect to ground in both the circuits. Also the KVL applied to both the loops yields same equations in both the circuits. Hence, two circuits are equivalent to each other.

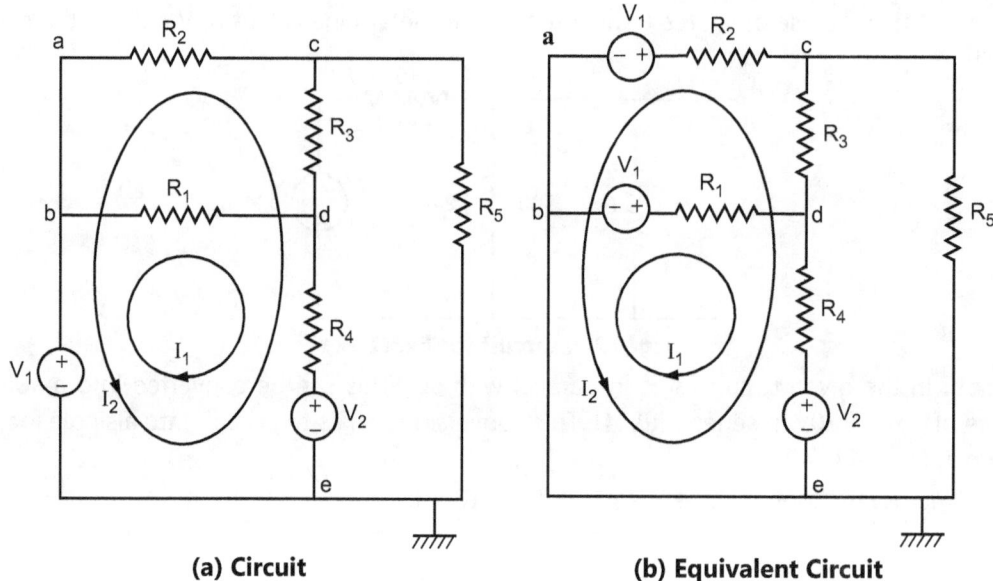

(a) Circuit (b) Equivalent Circuit
Fig. 1.44: Voltage source shifting

Thus "Voltage source shifting is nothing but pushing a voltage source through a node." This is explained in the Fig. 1.45.

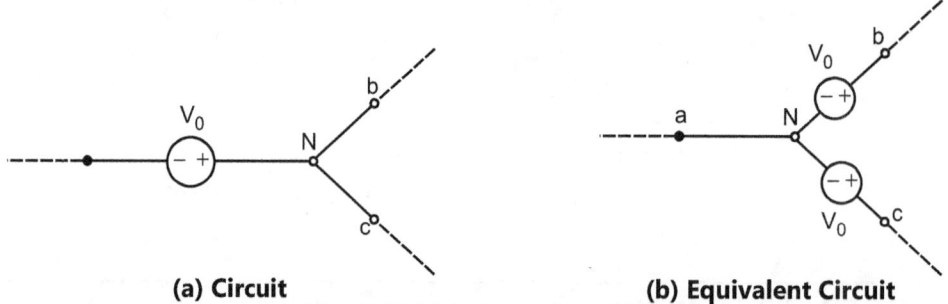

(a) Circuit (b) Equivalent Circuit
Fig. 1.45: Voltage source shifting

Voltage between a-b and a-c in both the circuit is V_0 While $V_{bc} = 0$ in both the circuit.

If there are three connected branches then voltage, source would be shifted to all the branches as shown in Fig. 1.46.

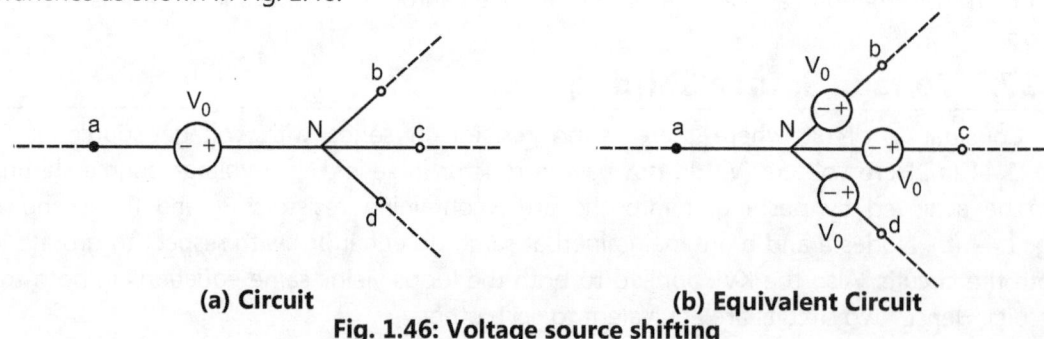

(a) Circuit (b) Equivalent Circuit
Fig. 1.46: Voltage source shifting

1.17.2 Current Source Shifting

When there is no single resistor in parallel with current source then current source shifting can be used. Consider the circuit of Fig. 1.47 (a). Here current source (I_0) is connected between a and b terminals but source transformation is not possible since there is no single resistor in parallel with current source. Hence we can shift the current source and convert it into two sources as shown in Fig. 1.47 (b). By doing so the current at three nodes a, b and c are same in both the circuits. In Fig. 1.47 (b) Current at node c is zero as current (I_0) entering and leaving the node. Hence, net current at node c is zero in both the circuits. Thus, even after source shifting the two circuits are equivalent.

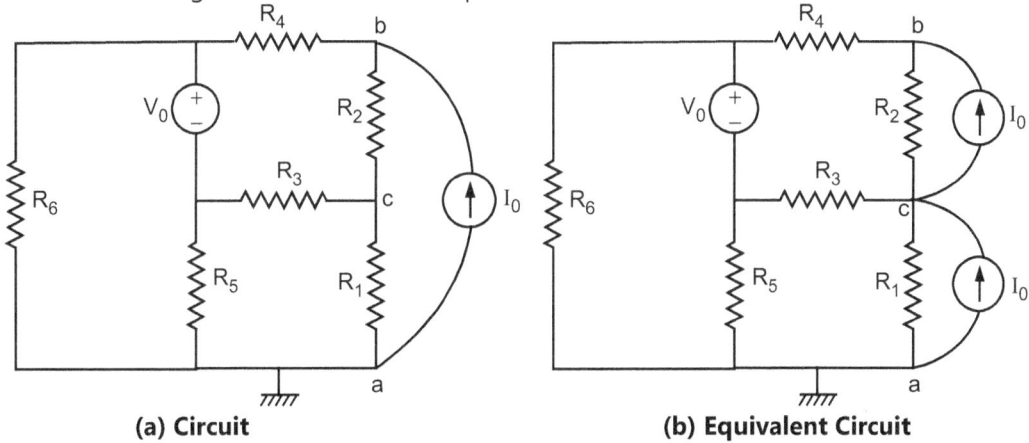

(a) Circuit   (b) Equivalent Circuit

Fig. 1.47: Current source shifting

Voltage source and current source shiftings are two important network simplification techniques that can be used to analyze given network. Following few examples explain how there are useful in the simplification and then analysis of the network. They can be used in any part of the network as and when required.

Ex. 1.12: Using source transformation and source shifting simplify the circuit of Fig. 1.48 and then determine the potential of node 'a'.

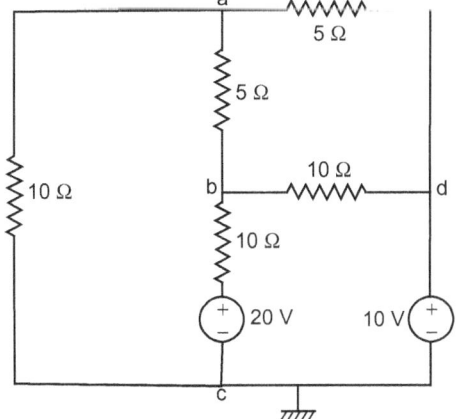

Fig. 1.48: Circuit for Ex. (1.12)

Sol.: 10V voltage source is shifted to adjacent branches as shown in Fig. 1.49 (a) as a first step. Various other steps involved in simplification are shown in Fig. 1.49.

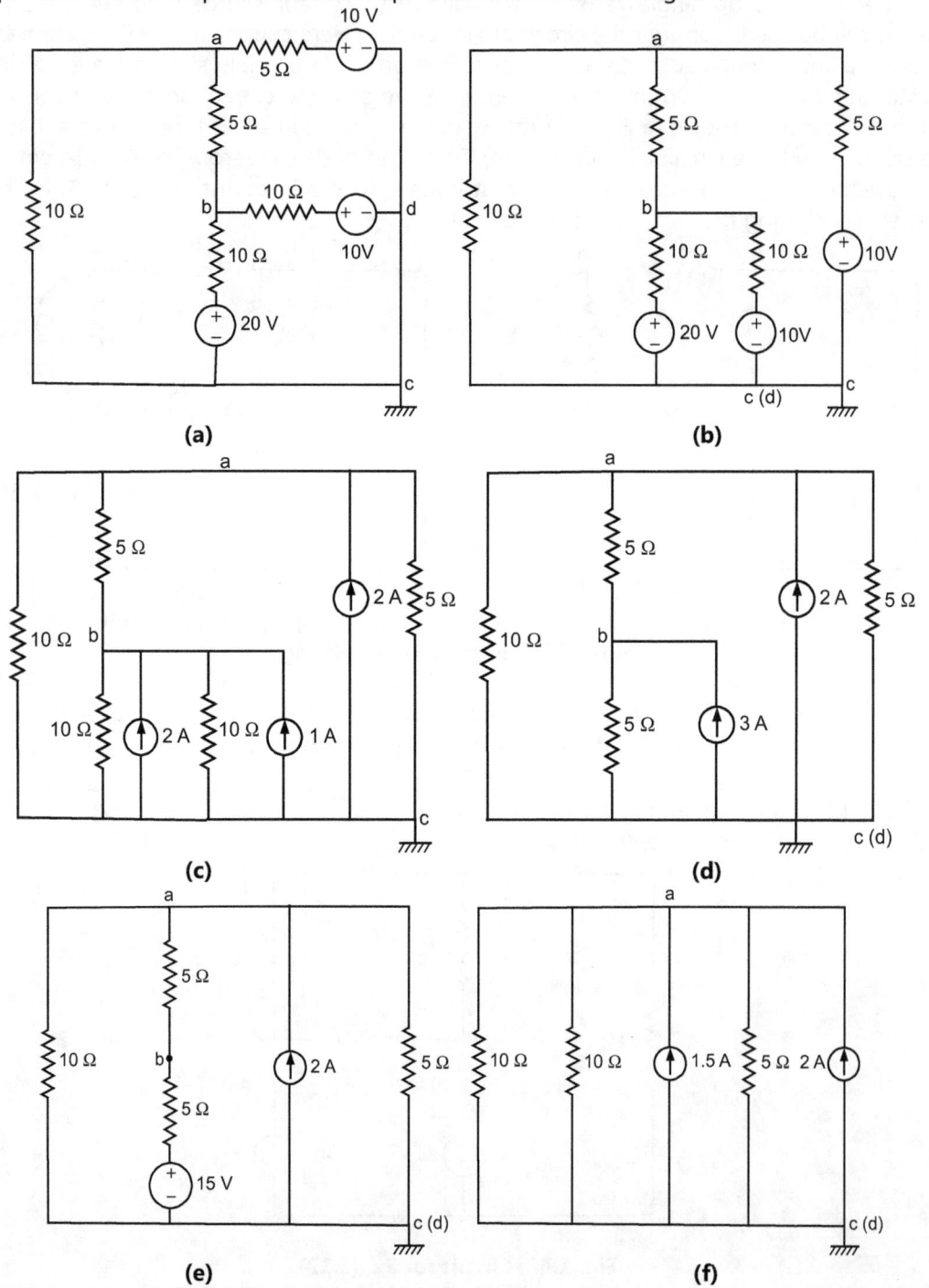

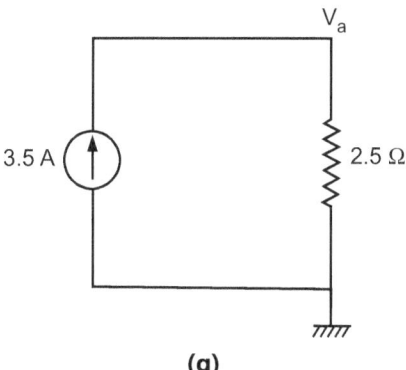

(g)

Fig. 1.49: Various steps involved in simplification of Fig. 1.48

In Fig. 1.49 (f) 10Ω || 10Ω || 5Ω gives an equivalents resistance (R_{eq}) = 5Ω || 5Ω = 2.5Ω. Hence, by Fig. (1.49 g) we have

$$Va + 3.5 \times 2.5 = + 8.75 \text{ V}$$

Ex. 1.13: Using source shifting and source transformation procedure simplify the circuit of Fig. 1.50 in such a way that the voltage V_x is determined. Also find value of V_x.

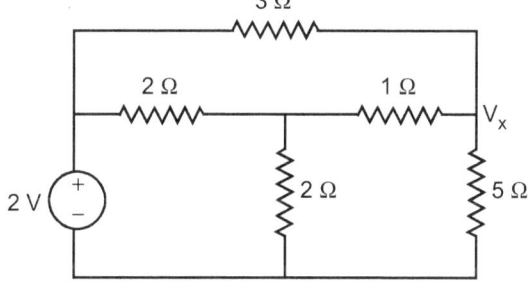

Fig. 1.50: Circuit for Ex. (1.13)

Sol.: First of all shift 3V source into adjacent resistor branch of 2Ω and 3Ω as in Fig. 1.51 (a). Various other steps in simplification are given in Fig. 1.51

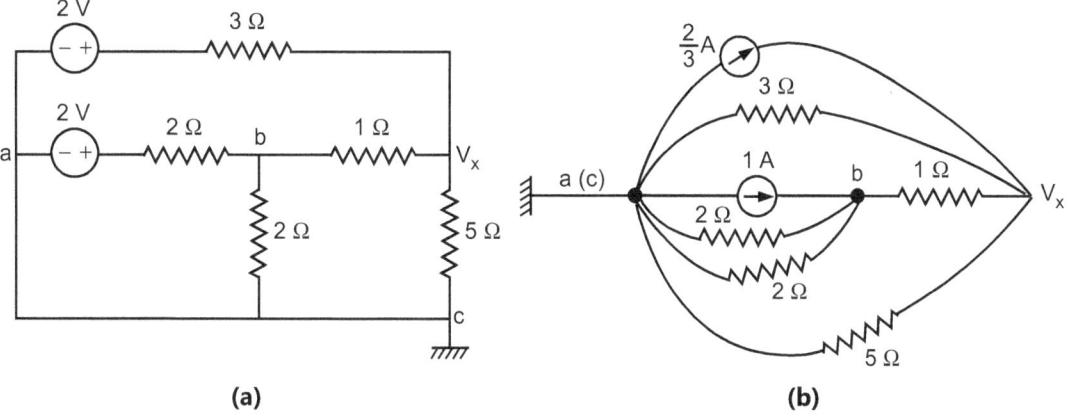

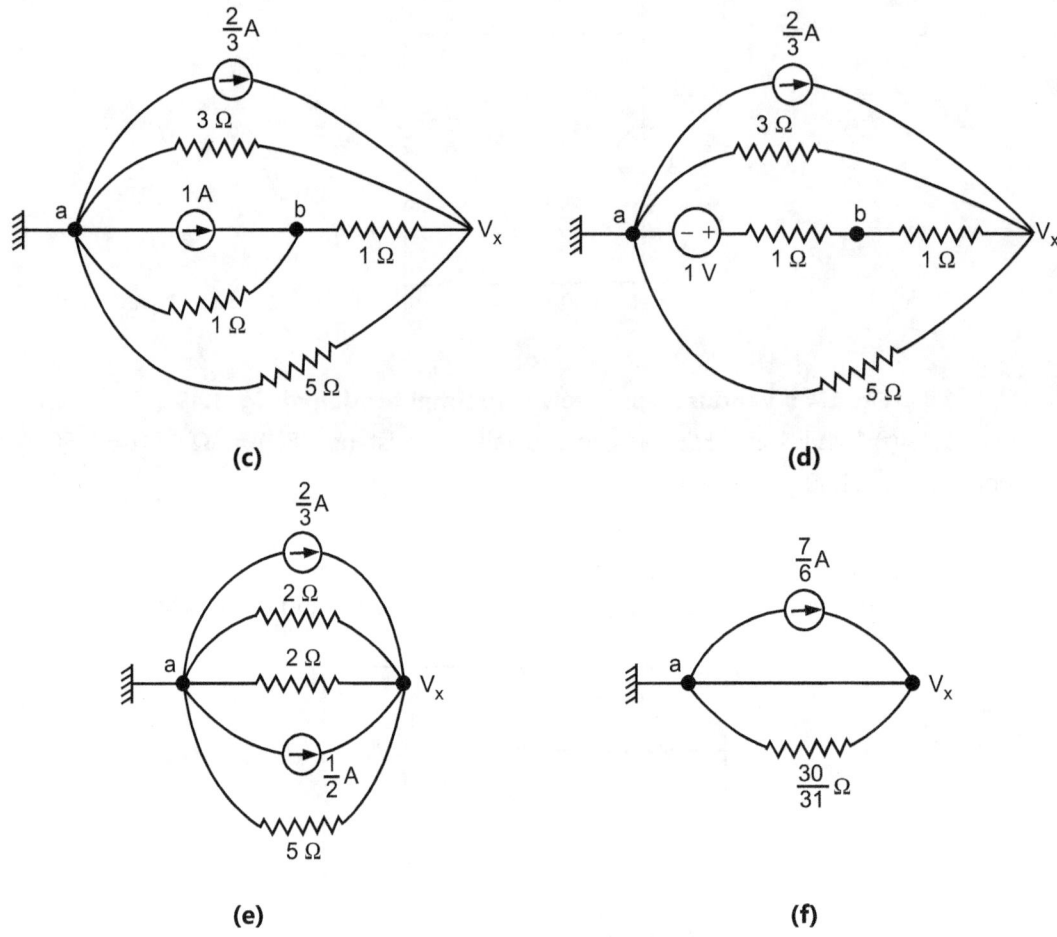

Fig. 1.51: various steps involved in simplification of Fig 1.50

In Fig. 1.51 (e) three resistors of 2Ω, 3Ω and 5Ω are in parallel. The equivalent resistance is given by,

$$\frac{1}{R_{eq}} = \frac{1}{3} + \frac{1}{5} + \frac{1}{2} = \frac{10 + 6 + 15}{30} = \frac{31}{30} \, \mho$$

or

$$R_{eq} = \frac{30}{31} \, \Omega$$

Finally the simplified circuit of Fig. 1.51 (f) gives the node voltage (V_x) as,

$$V_x = \frac{30}{31} \times \frac{7}{6} = +\frac{35}{31} = +1.13 \text{ volts}$$

Ex. 1.14: Using source transformation show that following two circuits of Fig. 1.52 are equivalent.

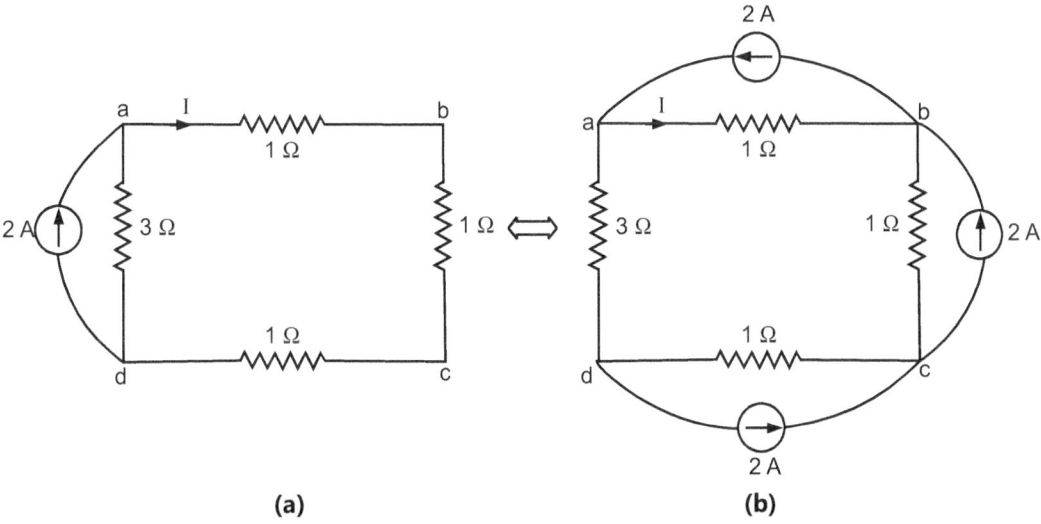

(a)   (b)

Fig. 1.52: Circuits for Ex. (1.14) that explains current source shifting

Sol.: Above circuit is an excellent example of current source shifting technique. We can say that the two circuits are equivalent if voltages between various branches of both circuits is same.

In circuit of Fig. 1.53 (a) all three 1Ω resistors are in series. Hence, 2A current from source divides equally between 3Ω resistor and three 1Ω resistors as 1 Amp. each

Hence, for circuit of Fig. 1.63 (a) we have,

$$\left. \begin{array}{l} V_{ab} = V_{bc} = V_{cd} = +1\text{ V} \\ V_{ad} = 3 \times 1 = +3\text{V} \end{array} \right\} \quad \ldots \text{(a)}$$

Now using source transformation the circuit of Fig. 1.52 (b) can be redrawn as equivalent circuit of Fig. 1.53.

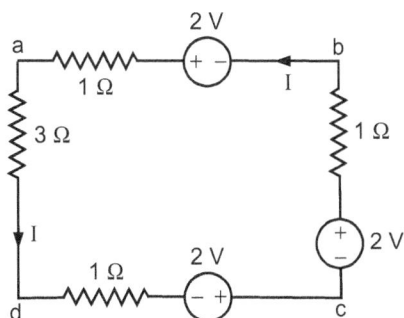

Fig. 1.53: Equivalent circuit of Fig. 1.52 (b) after source transformation

Now there is a single loop and let I be loop current. The KVL across d-a-b-c-d gives
+ 3I + I − 2 + I − 2 − 2 + I = 0
6I = 6 or I = 1A

Hence, voltages across various branches are

$$V_{ab} = V_{bc} = V_{cd} = 2 - I = 2 - 1 = +1V$$
$$V_{ad} = 3I = 3 \times 1 = +3V$$ ... (b)

From (a) and (b) since branch voltages are equal in both the circuits; two circuits of Fig. 1.52 are equivalent.

1.18 MESH (OR LOOP) OR KVL ANALYSIS

When a network is complex containing many energy sources and impedances than KVL and KCL are not enough to analyze the circuit. In such cases we can use loop analysis or nodal analysis. In this section, we shall study how Mesh analysis can be used for analyze a complex circuit. **Since, this analysis makes use of KVL this is also called KVL analysis.**

Consider the circuit of Fig. (1.54). The circuit has two independent loops. These loops are L_1 (a-b-d-a) with loop current I_1 and L_2 (b-c-d-b) with loop current I_2. There is also a loop L_3 (a-b-c-d-a) but it is not an-independent loop (It does not contain any new element which are not in loop L_1 and Loop L_2). The assumption of loop current for this non-independent loop does not yield any new equations of variables.

There are two unknown currents (I_1, I_2) hence, we need two equations to obtain their values. These two equations can be obtained by applying KVL across two independent loops.

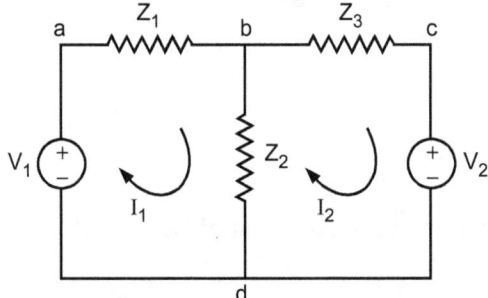

Fig. 1.54: Circuit to explain loop (or Mesh) analysis

KVL across loop L_1 (a-b-d-a) gives,

$$- Z_1 I_1 + Z_2 (I_2 - I_1) + V_1 = 0$$ ... (a)

Or
$$I_1 (Z_1 + Z_2) - I_1 I_2 = V_1$$

KVL across loop L_2 (b-c-d-b) gives

$$- Z_3 I_2 - V_2 - Z_2 (I_2 - I_1) = 0$$

Or
$$- Z_2 I_1 + (Z_1 + Z_3) I_2 = - V_2$$ ... (b)

Above equations can be written in matrix form as

$$\begin{bmatrix} (Z_1 + Z_2) & -Z_2 \\ -Z_2 & (Z_2 + Z_3) \end{bmatrix} \begin{bmatrix} I_1 \\ I_2 \end{bmatrix} = \begin{bmatrix} V_1 \\ -V_2 \end{bmatrix} \qquad \ldots \text{(c)}$$

These equations can be solved to obtain loop currents I_1 and I_2. Once these currents are obtained then the branch currents can be calculated.

It is not absolutely necessary that the loop currents (I_1, I_2 ...) should be clockwise always. These can be both clockwise and anticlockwise currents. But, for our convenience, the loop currents are always assumed in clockwise direction. These current directions are as shown in Fig. 1.55 below.

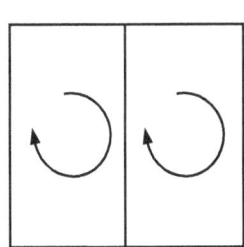 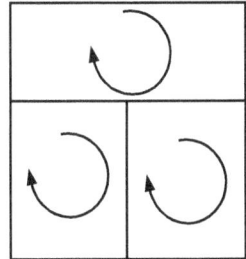 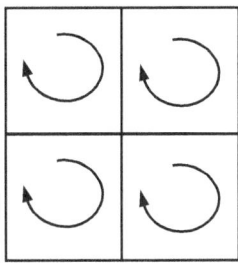

Fig. 1.55: General loop current directions

If all loop currents are clockwise and V_1, V_2, V_3 etc. are sum of the voltage drop (– ve) in the current direction, then for 3 loop circuit the equation will be in the form of.

$$\begin{bmatrix} V_1 \\ V_2 \\ V_3 \end{bmatrix} = \begin{bmatrix} Z_{11} & -Z_{12} & -Z_{13} \\ -Z_{21} & Z_{22} & -Z_{23} \\ -Z_{31} & -Z_{32} & Z_{33} \end{bmatrix} \begin{bmatrix} I_1 \\ I_2 \\ I_3 \end{bmatrix} \qquad \ldots \text{(1.15)}$$

Where, Z_{11} = sum of all impedances in loop L_1 i.e. self impedance of Loop L_1.

Z_{12} = sum of impedances common to L_1 and L_2 i.e. mutual impedance of loop L_1 or L_2.

Cramer's rule can be used to solve variable I_1, I_2 and I_3 in equations (1.15).

Analysis procedure for Mesh (or loop) Analysis:

In general following steps can be used to carry out Mesh analysis.

Step I : First of all chose the independent loops (L_1, L_2, L_3 etc.) in the given circuit.

Step II : Assume all loop currents (I_1, I_2, I_3 etc.) in clockwise direction for convenience (even though currents can be anticlockwise).

Step III : Apply KVL across each loop in the circuit. Write equations in standard form interms of loop currents. Make use of Ohm's law.

Step IV : Solve simultaneous algebraic equations obtained in step III to obtain loop currents (I_1, I_2, I_3 etc. etc.).

Step V : Once loop currents are obtained then branch currents and node voltages can be obtained.

Things to be remembered for Loop (Mesh) Analysis:

1. Always choose independent loops, which gives minimum but sufficient number of loops for analysis.
2. Convert all current sources into voltage source if possible. This is because mesh analysis makes use of KVL.
3. When current in a particular branch is required then choose loop current in such a way that only one loop current links with the branch.

Following examples explain the mesh analysis method.

Ex. 1.15: Use loop analysis for the circuit of Fig. 1.56 to obtain branch currents and node voltage at node A.

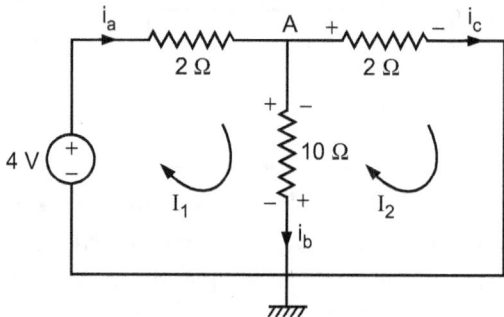

Fig. 1.56: Circuit for Ex. (1.15)

Sol.: Here two independent loops and their loop currents are already given. Hence, we can start with step III. KVL across loop I_1 gives,

$$-1(I_1 - I_2) + 4 - 2I_1 = 0 \quad \text{or} \quad 3I_1 - I_2 = 4 \quad \ldots \text{(a)}$$

KVL across loop I_2 gives

$$-2I_2 + 1(I_1 - I_2) = 0 \quad \text{or} \quad 3I_2 - I_1 = 0 \quad \ldots \text{(b)}$$

Solving equation (a) and (b) gives I_1 and I_2 as

$$I_2 = \frac{1}{2} A \quad \text{and} \quad I_1 = \frac{3}{2} A$$

Thus,
$$i_a = I_1 = 1.5 \text{ Amp.}$$
$$i_c = I_2 = 0.5 \text{ Amp.}$$
$$i_b = (I_1 - I_2) = (1.5 - 0.5) = +1 \text{ Amp.}$$
$$V_A = 1[I_1 - I_2] = 1 \times 1 = +1 \text{ Volts}$$

Also,
$$V_A = +2I_2 = 2 \times 1 = +1 \text{ Volts}$$

Ex. 1.16: Make use of loop analysis to find current i_1 and i_2 and from this information determine voltages V_x in the circuit shown in Fig. 1.57.

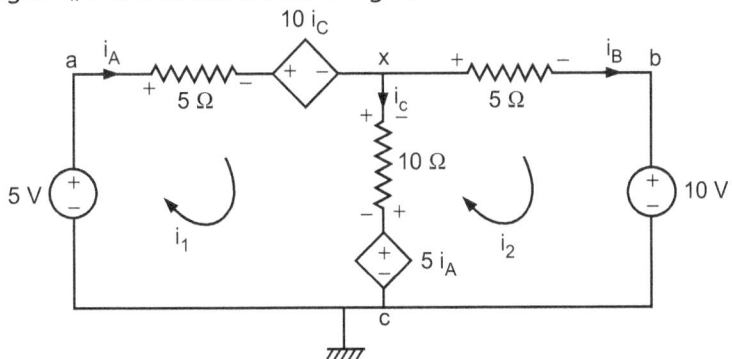

Fig. 1.57: Circuit for Ex. (1.16)

Sol.: Here two independent loops and their loop currents are already given. Hence, we can start with step III.

KVL across loop i_1 (c – x – a – c) gives,

$$+ 5i_A + 10(i_1 - i_2) + 10i_c + 5iA = 5$$

But $i_A = i_1$, $i_c = i_1 - i_2$ and $i_B = i_2$

Hence, we have $+ 5i_1 + 10(i_1 - i_2) + 10(i_1 - i_2) 5i_1 = 5$

Or, $30i_1 - 20i_2 = 5$

i.e. $6i_1 - 4i_2 = 1$ ... (a)

KVL across loop i_2 (c – b – x – c) gives

$$+ 10 + 5i_B + 10(i_2 - i_1) - 5i_A = 0$$
$$10 + 5i_2 + 10(i_2 - i_1) - 5i_1 = 0$$

Or $15i_1 - 15i_2 = 10$

i.e. $3i_1 - 3i_2 = 2$ ... (b)

From (a) and (b) solve for current i_1 and i_2

By (b) $3i_1 = 2 + 3i_2$, putting this in equation (a) gives,

$2 \times [2 + 3i_2] - 4i_2 = 1$ or $i_2 = -1.5$ Amp.

Hence, by (a) $6i_1 = 1 + 4i_2 = 1 - 4 \times 1.5 = -5$

Thus, we have $i_1 = -\dfrac{5}{6}$ Amp.

The branch currents are:

$$i_A = i_1 = \dfrac{-5}{6} \text{ A}, \; i_B = i_2 = -1.5 \text{ A}, \; i_c = (i_1 - i_2) = +\dfrac{2}{3} \text{ Amp.}$$

$$V_x = 10 + 5i_B = 10 - 5 \times 1.5 = +2.5 \text{ V}$$

Also $V_x = 10i_c + 5i_A = 10 \times \dfrac{2}{3} - 5 \times \dfrac{5}{6} = +2.5$ V

Ex. 1.17: Set up the mesh equations for the circuit and use them to find voltage drop from point a to point b in the circuit shown below.

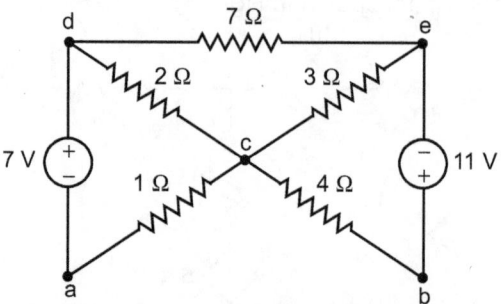

Fig. 1.58: Circuit for Ex. (1.17)

Sol.: There are three independent loops. These loops with loop currents I_1, I_2 and I_3 are shown below.

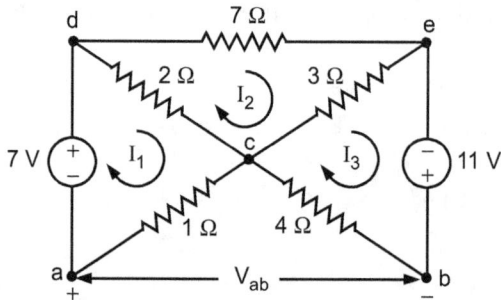

Fig. 1.59: Redrawn circuit with loop current

KVL across loop with current I_1 (d - c - a - d) gives,

$$-2(I_1 - I_2) - I_1 + 7 = 0$$

Or $\qquad 3I_1 - 2I_2 + 0I_3 = 7$ ... (a)

KVL across loop with loop current I_2 (a – e – c – d) gives

$$-7I_2 - 3(I_2 - I_3) + 2(I_1 - I_2) = 0$$

Or $\qquad -2I_1 + 12I_2 - 3I_3 = 0$ ... (b)

KVL across loop with loop current I_3 (e – b – c – e) gives

$$+ 11 - 4I_3 + 3(I_2 - I_3) = 0$$

Or $\qquad 0I_1 - 3I_2 + 7I_3 = 11$ ... (c)

Above three equation can put into a standard form as given by equation. (1.15).

$$\begin{bmatrix} 3 & -2 & 0 \\ -2 & 12 & -3 \\ 0 & -3 & +7 \end{bmatrix} \begin{bmatrix} I_1 \\ I_2 \\ I_3 \end{bmatrix} = \begin{bmatrix} 7 \\ 0 \\ 11 \end{bmatrix} \qquad \text{... (d)}$$

Now voltage between a – b is given by applying KVL across outer loop.
$$-11 + 7I_2 - 7 - V_{ab} = 0$$
Or
$$V_{ab} = 7I_2 - 18 \qquad \ldots (e)$$

From (e) it is obvious that only I_2 need to be found to calculate V_{ab}. Hence, solve for I_2 from equation (d) using Cramer's law,

$$I_2 = \frac{\Delta_2}{\Delta} \frac{\begin{bmatrix} 3 & 7 & 0 \\ -2 & 0 & -3 \\ 0 & 11 & 7 \end{bmatrix}}{\begin{bmatrix} 3 & -2 & 0 \\ -2 & 12 & -3 \\ 0 & -3 & 7 \end{bmatrix}} = \frac{3(0+33) - 7(-14)}{3(84-9) + 2(-14-0)}$$

$$= \frac{197}{197} + 1 \text{ Amp.}$$

Hence, by (e) $\quad V_{ab} = 7 \times 1 - 18 = -11$ Volts.

Thus, voltage between a – b is – 11 V which means 'b' is at higher potential than a by 11 V.

1.19 SUPER MESH ANALYSIS

While using mesh analysis preferably we requires all the voltage sources in the circuit. If there is a current source in the loop we choose, We can not use KVL since the voltage across the current source is not known directly. Consider the circuit shown in Fig. 1.60.

Here there are two loops which contains a current source (I_0) within loop. We cannot use KVL across loops since voltage between the current source is not known. There are two unknowns and hence two equations are needed in terms of currents I_1 and I_2.

The first equation can be obtained by the current source itself. Since, current in the branch is equal to source current (I_0), the first equation is given by,
$$I_1 - I_2 = I_0 \qquad \ldots (a)$$

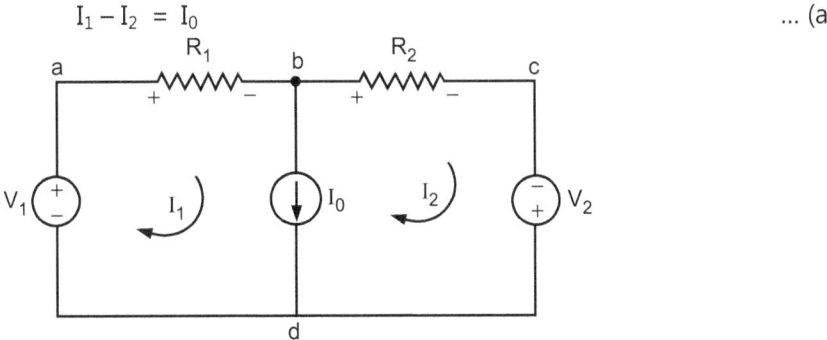

Fig. 1.60: Circuit to explain super mesh

If we assume that current source (I_0) **is removed** temporarily then mesh (a - b - c - d - a) is formed that contains R_1, R, and two voltage sources. This mesh is known as **super mesh. Thus, as super mesh is mesh formed when current source is assumed to be temporarily removed.**

Now KVL across super mesh (a - b - c - d - a) gives the second equation, which is as shown below.

$$-R_1 I_1 - R_2 I_2 + V_2 + V_1 = 0$$

Or
$$R_1 I_1 + R_2 I_2 = V_1 + V_2 \quad \text{(b)}$$

Thus, these two equations can be solved to get the two unknown currents (I_1, I_2).

Ex. 1.18: Find mesh currents in the circuit given. Use loop analysis method.

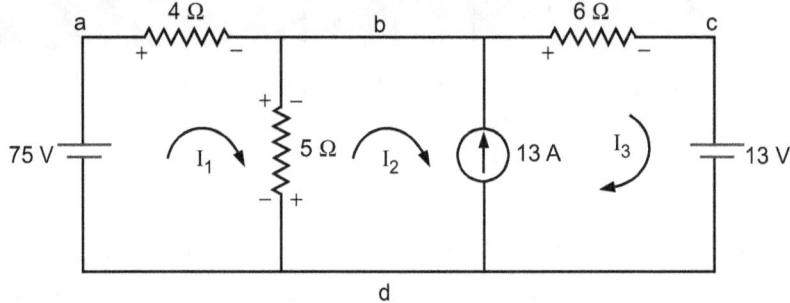

Fig. 1.61: Circuit for Ex. (1.18)

Sol.: One method to analyze this circuit is to convert current source of 13A parallel with 5Ω into an voltage source with a 5Ω series resistor across b – d. This will convert the circuit into two loops and make the loop current (I_2) zero. Therefore we cannot use this method.

Hence, we can make use of super mesh analysis. Super mesh (b - c - d - b) is formed if current source assumed to be temporarily removed. KVL across this super mesh (b - c- d - b) gives.

$$-6I_3 - 13 + 5(I_1 - I_2) = 0$$
$$5I_1 - 5I_2 - 6I_3 = 13 \quad \text{... (a)}$$

KVL across loop I_1 (a - b - d - a) gives,
$$-4I_1 - 5(I_1 - I_2) + 75 = 0$$
$$9I_1 - 5I_2 + 0I_3 = 75 \quad \text{... (b)}$$

The third equation can be obtained by current source of 13A it self and is given as,
$$I_3 - I_2 = 13 \quad \text{or} \quad 0I_1 - I_2 + I_3 = 13 \quad \text{... (c)}$$

These three equations can be put into standard form of equation (1.15) as below.

$$\begin{bmatrix} 5 & -5 & -6 \\ 9 & -5 & 0 \\ 0 & -1 & 1 \end{bmatrix} \begin{bmatrix} I_1 \\ I_2 \\ I_3 \end{bmatrix} = \begin{bmatrix} 13 \\ 75 \\ 13 \end{bmatrix}$$

I_1, I_2 and I_3 can be solved using Cramer's law, gives,
$$I_1 = +5A, I_2 = -6A \text{ and } I_3 = +7A$$

Ex. 1.19: Use mesh analysis to find voltage V_0 in the circuit shown below.

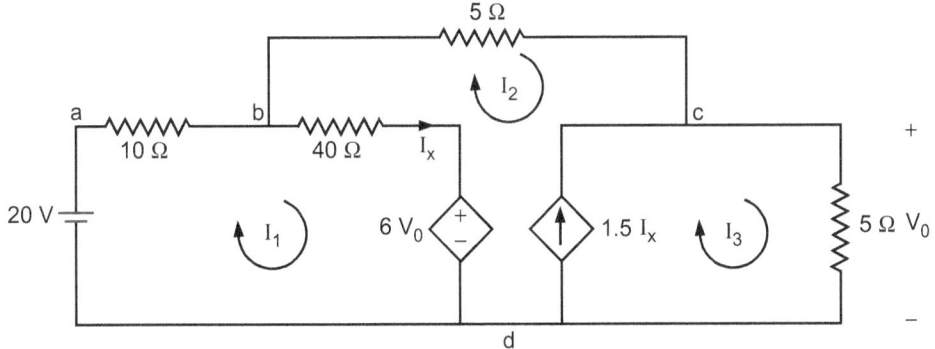

Fig. 1.62: Circuit for Ex. (1.19)

Sol.: We have $\quad I_x = I_1 - I_2$ ... (a)

And $\quad V_0 = 5I_3$ ... (b)

We need three equations in terms of I_1, I_2, I_3 to solve for these currents.

We cannot use KVL for loop 2 and loop 3 since they contains current source in between. When current source is temporarily removed a super mesh is formed (b – c – d – b) containing 5Ω, 5Ω, 40Ω and $6V_0$ source. KVL across this super mesh (b – c – d – b) gives.

$$-5I_2 - 5I_3 + 6V_0 + 40(I_1 - I_2) = 0$$

Or $\quad -5I_2 - 5I_3 + 6 \times 5I_3 + 40(I_1 - I_2) = 0$

$$-40 I_1 + 45 I_2 - 25 I_3 = 0 \quad \text{... (c)}$$

KVL across loop with current I_1 (a – b – d – a) gives,

$$-10I_1 - 40(I_1 - I_2) - 6V_0 + 20 = 0$$

$$-10I_1 - 40I_1 + 40I_2 - 6 \times 5I_3 + 20 = 0$$

$$50I_1 - 40I_2 + 30I_3 = 20 \quad \text{... (d)}$$

The third equation can be obtained by applying KCL at node V which is $1.5 I_x = I_3 - I_2$. Using equation (a) for I_x we get $1.5 \times (I_1 - I_2) = I_3 - I_2$.

Hence, $\quad 1.5I_1 - 0.5I_2 - I_3 = 0$ ... (e)

These three equations can be put into standard form as,

$$\begin{bmatrix} -40 & 45 & -25 \\ 50 & -40 & 30 \\ 1.5 & -0.5 & -1 \end{bmatrix} \begin{bmatrix} I_1 \\ I_2 \\ I_3 \end{bmatrix} = \begin{bmatrix} 0 \\ 20 \\ 0 \end{bmatrix} \quad \text{... (f)}$$

Solving for current I_3 using Cramer's law, we get

$$I_3 = \frac{\begin{bmatrix} -40 & 45 & 0 \\ 50 & -40 & 20 \\ 1.5 & -0.5 & 0 \end{bmatrix}}{\begin{bmatrix} -40 & 45 & -25 \\ 50 & -40 & 30 \\ 1.5 & -0.5 & -1 \end{bmatrix}} = 0.792 \text{ Amp.}$$

Hence, by (b) $\quad V_0 = 5I_3 = 5 \times 0.792 = +3.96$ V.

1.20 NODAL (KVL) ANALYSIS

This is another technique to analysis a complicated electrical circuit. Nodal analysis make use of KCL. Hence, it is also known as KCL analysis.

To explain this analysis consider the circuit shown in Fig. (1.63). Node '0' is taken as reference (ground) node and voltages of node 1 and 2 is taken as V_1 and V_2 respectively with respect to ground. Choose unknown branch currents as i_1, i_2 and i_3 arbitrarily.

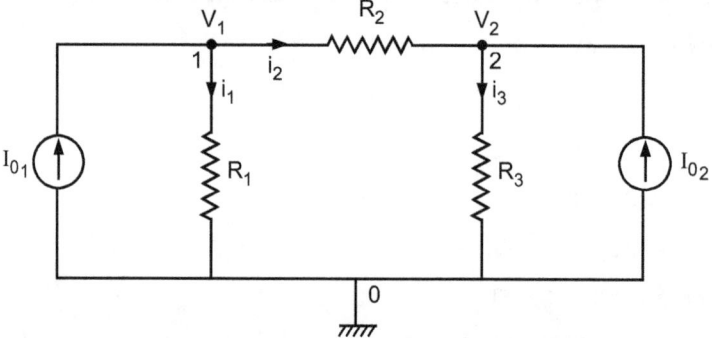

Fig. 1.63: Circuit to explain nodal analysis

Our aim is to find voltages V_1 and V_2. Once these are known, then branch currents can be found out.

KCL at node 1 gives,

$$I_1 + I_2 = I_{01}$$

Or $\quad \dfrac{V_1}{R_1} + \left[\dfrac{V_1 - V_2}{R_2}\right] = I_{01}$

Hence $\quad V_1 + \left[\dfrac{1}{R_1} + \dfrac{1}{R_2}\right] - \dfrac{V_2}{R_2} = I_{01}$ ... (a)

KCL at node 2 gives $I_3 - I_2 = I_{02}$

Or $$\frac{V_2}{R_3} - \left[\frac{V_1 - V_2}{R_2}\right] = I_{02}$$

$$-\frac{V_1}{R_2} + \left[\frac{1}{R_2} + \frac{1}{R_3}\right] V_2 = I_{02}$$

If R_1, R_2, R_3 and I_{01}, I_{02} are known then voltages V_1, V_2 can be found out. For example, if $R_1 = 5\Omega$, $R_2 = 10\Omega$, $R_3 = 10\Omega$ and $I_{01} = 5A$, $I_{02} = 10$ A then.

By (a) $$\frac{V_1}{5} + \left[\frac{V_1 - V_2}{10}\right] = 5$$

Or $\qquad 3V_1 - V_2 = 50 \qquad\qquad\qquad …\text{(c)}$

By (b) $$\frac{-V_1}{10} + \left[\frac{1}{10} + \frac{1}{10}\right] V_2 = 10$$

Or $\qquad 2V_2 - V_1 = 100 \qquad\qquad\qquad …\text{(d)}$

Solving (c) and (d) gives $V_1 = 40V$ and $V_2 = 70V$

Hence, $$I_1 = \frac{40}{5} + 8A$$

$$I_2 = \frac{40 - 70}{10} = \frac{-30}{10} = -3A$$

and $$I_3 = \frac{70}{10} = +7A$$

Thus, nodal analysis enables to find us currents in various branches of a circuit by finding various node voltages.

Analysis Procedure for Nodal analysis

In general following steps can be used to carry out nodal analysis.

Step I : Simplify the circuit by combining impedances in parallel or series and combining current sources in parallel.

Step II : Choose a reference (or ground) node. Any node can be choosen as ground but preferably for convenience, we choose bottom node as reference. Assign unknown node voltages as V_1, V_2, V_3 etc. With respect to the ground (0V).

Step III : Assign arbitrarily currents in various branches of the circuit where current is not known.

Step IV : Apply KCL at each node except at ground Node. Make use of ohm's law to obtain branch currents.

Step V : Simplify the equations algebraically to put them in standard form in terms of V_1, V_2, V_3.

Step VI : Solve the above simultaneous equations for the unknown node voltages V_1, V_2, V_3 etc.

Step VII : Using these node voltages, current in all or any required branch can be determined.

In general the standard form of nodal equations will be as below.

$$\begin{bmatrix} I_{01} \\ I_{02} \\ I_{03} \end{bmatrix} = \begin{bmatrix} Y_{11} & -Y_{12} & -Y_{13} \\ -Y_{21} & Y_{22} & -Y_{23} \\ -Y_{31} & -Y_{32} & -Y_{33} \end{bmatrix} \begin{bmatrix} V_1 \\ V_2 \\ V_3 \end{bmatrix} \quad \ldots (1.16)$$

Where, V_1, V_2, V_3 are unknown node voltages.
I_{01}, I_{02}, I_{03} are known current sources.
Y_{11} = Sum of admittances connected to node V_1 = Self admittance.
Y_{12} = Admittance connected between nodes 1 and 2 = mutual admittance.

Things to be remembered for Nodal (KCL) analysis:
1. Nodal analysis prefers all sources to be current sources. If there are any voltage sources convert them into current sources.
2. Do not apply KCL at ground (or reference) node.
3. Currents in unknown branches can be choosen arbitrarily with arbitrary direction. Following examples explains node analysis in detail.

Ex. 1.20: Determine Node to Datum voltages for the circuit shown, use nodal analysis method.

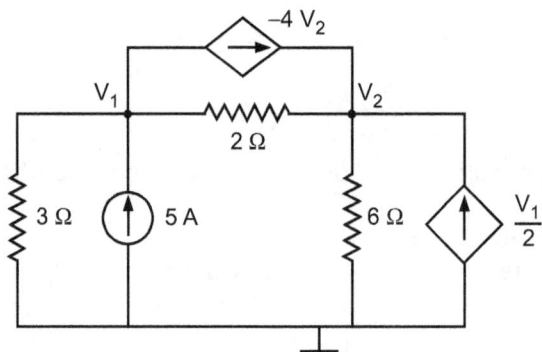

Fig. 1.64: Circuit for Ex. (1.20)

Sol.: Assume currents in various branches arbitrarily as shown in redrawn circuit of Fig. (1.83).

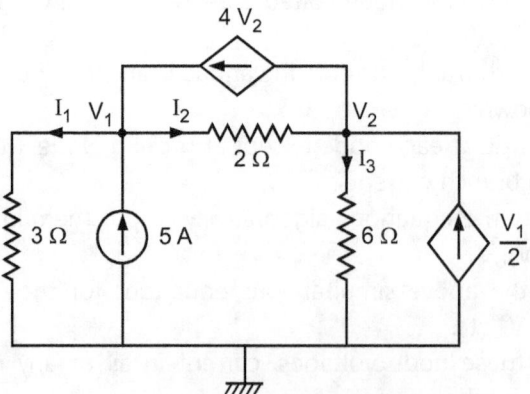

Fig. 1.65: Redrawn circuit

KCL at V_1 gives $I_1 + I_2 = 5 + 4V_2$.

Or $\quad \dfrac{V_1}{3} + \left(\dfrac{V_1 - V_2}{2}\right) - 4V_2 = 5$

Hence, $\quad 5V_1 - 27 V_2 = 30$ ... (a)

KCL at V_2 gives, $I_3 + 4V_2 = I_2 + \dfrac{V_1}{2}$

Or $\quad I_3 - I_2 + 4V_2 \dfrac{-V_1}{2} = 0$

$\dfrac{V_2}{6}\left(\dfrac{V_1 - V_2}{2}\right) + 4V_2 - \dfrac{V_1}{2} = 0$

Hence, $6V_1 = 28V_2$, OR $V_2 = \dfrac{3}{14} V_1$ ... (b)

By (a), $5V_1 - 27 \times \dfrac{3}{14} V_1 = 30$. Solving this gives $V_1 - 38.12$ V.

Hence, by (b) $\quad V_2 = \dfrac{3}{14} \times (-38.12) = -8.18$ V

Thus both nodes are at less potential than ground node.

Ex. 1.21: Using nodal analysis find node voltage V_b in the circuit.

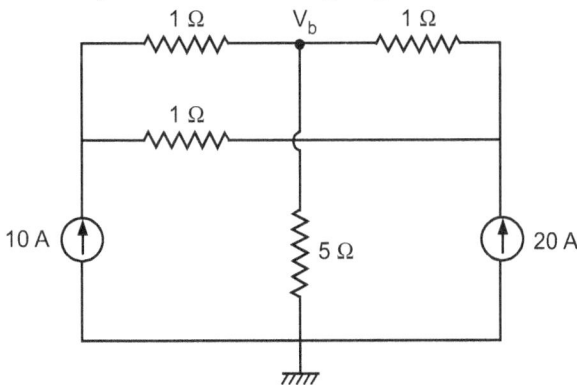

Fig. 1.66: Circuit for Ex. (1.21)

Sol.: Let other two unknown node voltages be V_a and V_c. Assume arbitrarily currents in various branches. The redrawn circuit is shown in Fig. (1.67).

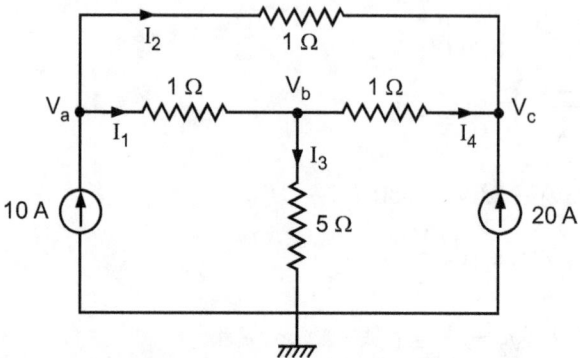

Fig. 1.67 Redrawn circuit

KCL at node 'a' with voltage V_a gives $I_1 + I_2 = 10$

$$\left(\frac{V_a - V_b}{1}\right) + \left(\frac{V_a - V_c}{1}\right) = 10$$

Or $\qquad 2V_a - V_b - V_c = 10 \qquad$ ... (a)

KCL at node 'b' with voltage V_b gives $I_3 + I_4 = I_1$

$$\frac{V_b}{5} + \left(\frac{V_b - V_c}{1}\right) = \left(\frac{V_a - V_b}{1}\right)$$

Or $\qquad V_a - 2.2\,V_a + V_c = 0 \qquad$ ... (b)

KCL at node 'c' with voltage V_c gives $I_4 + I_2 + 20 = 0$

$$\left(\frac{V_b - V_c}{1}\right) + \left(\frac{V_a - V_c}{1}\right) + 20 = 0$$

$$V_b + V_a - 2V_c = -20 \qquad \text{... (c)}$$

In matrix form these can be written as:

$$\begin{bmatrix} 2 & -1 & -1 \\ 1 & -2.2 & 1 \\ 1 & 1 & -2 \end{bmatrix} \begin{bmatrix} V_a \\ V_b \\ V_c \end{bmatrix} = \begin{bmatrix} 10 \\ 0 \\ -20 \end{bmatrix} \qquad \text{... (d)}$$

Solve for V_b using Cramer's law

$$V_b = \frac{\begin{vmatrix} 2 & 10 & -1 \\ 1 & 0 & 1 \\ 1 & -20 & -2 \end{vmatrix}}{\begin{vmatrix} 2 & -1 & -1 \\ 1 & -2.2 & 1 \\ 1 & 1 & -2 \end{vmatrix}} = \frac{2(20) - 10(-3) - 1(-20)}{2(-5.4) + 1(-3) - 1(3.2)} = \frac{90}{-17} = -5.3 \text{ Volts}$$

Ex. 1.22: Using nodal analysis to find voltage V_y in the circuit shown.

(May 2005, 6 Marks)

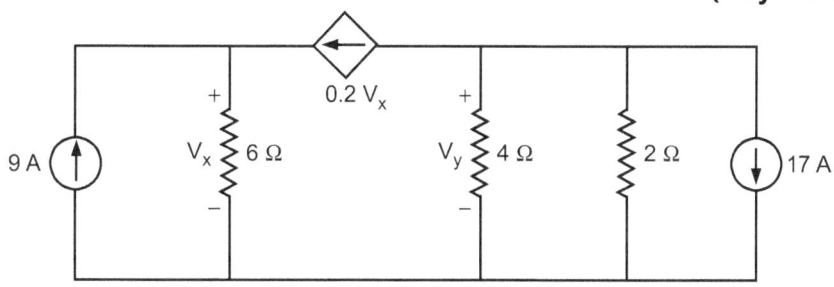

Fig. 1.68: Circuit for Ex. (1.22)

Sol.: Let bottom node be at ground (0V). Then two unknown node voltages will be V_x and V_y. Combine $2\Omega \parallel 4\Omega$ into a single resistor of $\frac{4}{3}$ ohms. The redrawn circuit is shown in Fig. (1.69).

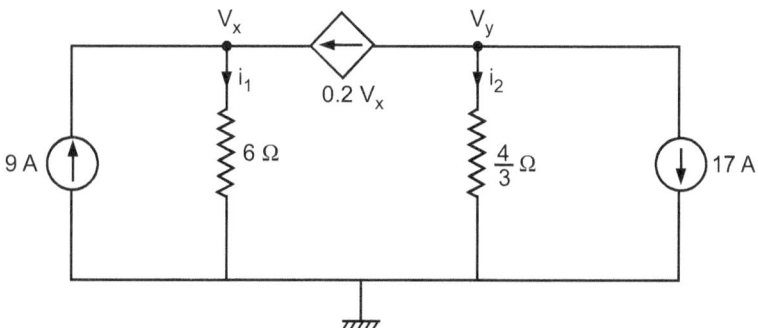

Fig. 1.69: Redrawn equivalent circuit

KCL at node 'x' with voltage V_x gives $i_1 = 9 + 0.2\,V_x$.

Or $\quad \dfrac{V_x}{6} - 0.2\,V_x = 9$

Hence, $\quad V_x[1 - 1.2] = 54$

Thus, $\quad$ Voltage $V_x = \dfrac{54}{-0.2}$

$\quad\quad\quad\quad\quad\quad = -270$ V

KCL at node 'y' with voltage V_y gives $i_2 + 0.2\,V_x + 17 = 0$.

Or $\quad \dfrac{V_y}{4/3} + 0.2 \times [-270] + 17 = 0$

Hence, $\quad V_y = \dfrac{4}{3}[54 - 17] = +49.33$ V

Thus, voltage of node y is $V_y = +49.33$ V.

1.21 SUPER NODE ANALYSIS

Consider the circuit shown in Fig. 1.70 in which there is a voltage source between two unknown nodes V_1 and V_2 with many other circuit elements. The region (shown by dotted line) connecting two nodes by a voltage source directly are known as **super node**. Thus, V_1, V_2 along with voltage source V_x form a **super node**.

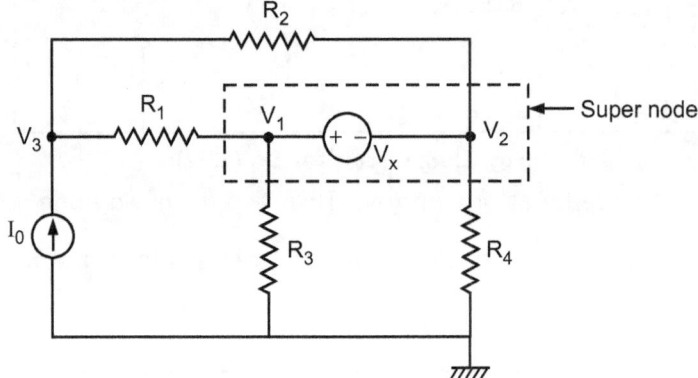

Fig. 1.70: Circuit to explain super node

One of the equation can be obtained by the super node itself where $V_1 - V_2 = V_x$ ... (a)

Since, we do not know what is current flowing in voltage sources, we cannot apply KCL at nodes V_1 and V_2 directly. The current through voltage source connecting super nodes must be expressed in terms of the branch currents and hence node voltage of other nodes.

Following few examples explains how super node circuit analysis can be achieved.

Ex. 1.23: In the circuit shown find node voltage V, using nodal analysis.

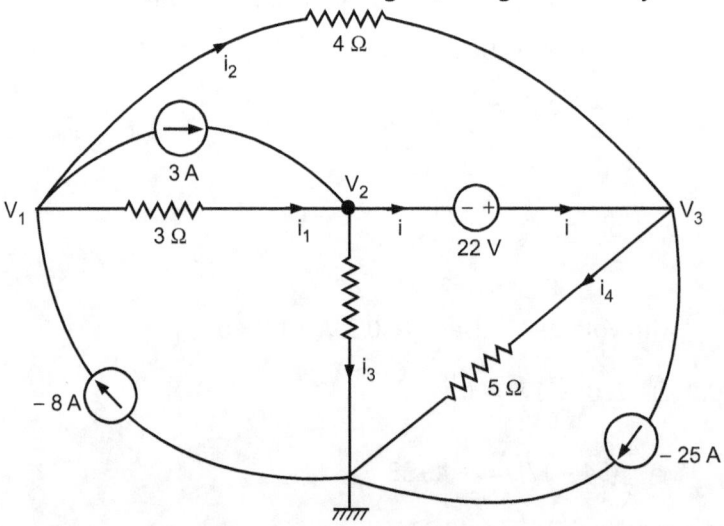

Fig. 1.71: Circuit for Ex. 1.23

Sol.: In the circuit V_2, V_3 and 22V source together forms a super node. There are three unknown voltages and hence we need three equations in terms of V_1, V_2 and V_3. One of the equations is given by super node itself.

Thus, $V_3 - V_2 = 22$ or $0V_1 - V_2 + V_3 = 22$ ... (a)

Current i leaving node V_2 must be equal to current entering the node V_3. This current can be expressed in terms of other branch current. Thus,

$$i = 3 + i_1 - i_3 = i_4 - 25 - i_2$$

Or $\qquad 3 + 3(V_1 - V_2) - V_2 = 5V_3 - 25 - 4(V_1 - V_3)$

Hence, we get second equation as

$$-7V_1 + 4V_2 + 9V_3 = 28 \qquad \text{... (b)}$$

The third equation can be obtained by applying the KCL at node V_1 as $i_1 + i_2 + 3 + 8 = 0$

$\qquad 3(V_1 - V_2) + 4(V_1 - V_3) + 11 = 0$

Or $\qquad +7V_1 - 3V_2 - 4V_3 = -11$ ... (c)

These equations can be put into matrix form as below.

$$\begin{bmatrix} 0 & -1 & 1 \\ -7 & +4 & 9 \\ 7 & -3 & -4 \end{bmatrix} \begin{bmatrix} V_1 \\ V_2 \\ V_2 \end{bmatrix} = \begin{bmatrix} 22 \\ 28 \\ -11 \end{bmatrix} \qquad \text{... (d)}$$

Solve for V_1 using Cramer's rule as

$$V_1 = \frac{\Delta_1}{\Delta} = \frac{\begin{vmatrix} 22 & -1 & 1 \\ 28 & 4 & 9 \\ -11 & -3 & -4 \end{vmatrix}}{\begin{vmatrix} 0 & -1 & 1 \\ -7 & 4 & 9 \\ 7 & -3 & -4 \end{vmatrix}}$$

$$= \frac{22(-16 + 27) + 1(-112 + 99) + 1(-84 + 44)}{0 + 1(28 - 63) + 1(21 - 28)}$$

$$= \frac{242 - 13 - 40}{-35 - 7}$$

$$= \frac{189}{-42}$$

$$= -4.5 \text{ volts}$$

Ex. 1.24: Find node voltages in the circuit shown using nodal analysis.

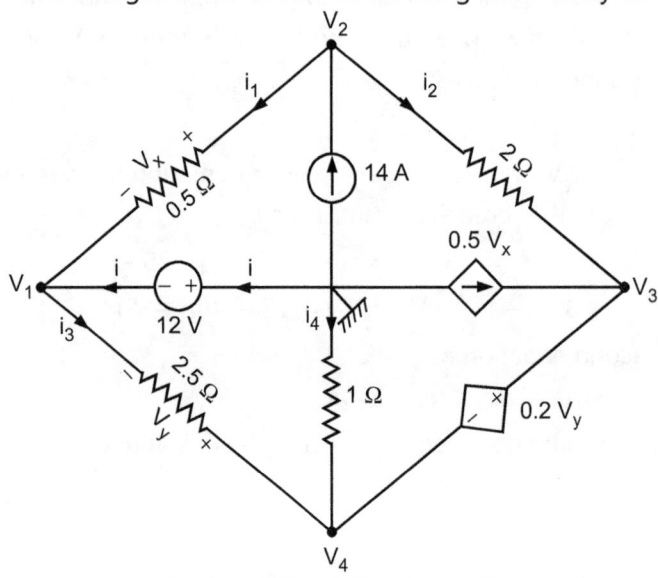

Fig. 1.72: Circuit for Ex. (1.24)

Sol.: In this circuit central node is grounded (0V) instead of bottom most node (V_4). Node V_1 and the reference (0V), along with 12V battery source represents a super node. Hence, we get voltage of node (V_1) as

$$V_1 = -12 \text{ V} \quad \ldots \text{(a)}$$

KCL at node (V_2) gives
$$\frac{V_2 - V_1}{0.5} + \frac{V_2 - V_3}{2} = 14$$

Or
$$2.5 V_2 - 2V_1 - 0.5 V_3 = 14 \quad \ldots \text{(b)}$$

Since current i is flowing through 12V source we have,

$$i = i_1 + i_3 = -14 - 0.5 V_x - i_4$$

$$i = \left(\frac{V_1 - V_4}{2.5}\right) - \left(\frac{V_2 - V_1}{0.5}\right)$$

$$= -14 - \frac{(0 - V_4)}{1} - 0.5 (V_2 - V_1)$$

Solving this gives

$$1.9 V_1 - 1.5 V_2 + 0 V_3 - 1.4 V_4 = -14 \quad \ldots \text{(c)}$$

The fourth equation required can be obtained as below, from another super node consisting of V_3, V_4 and $0.2 V_y$.

We have, $\quad 0.2 V_y = V_3 - V_4 = 0.2 (V_4 - V_1)$

Hence, $0.2 V_1 + 0 V_2 + V_3 - 1.2 V_4 = 0 \quad \ldots \text{(d)}$

Solving these equations gives $\quad V_2 = 4V, V_3 = 0V, V_4 = -2V$ and $V_1 - 12V$

Ex. 1.25: Using nodal analysis solve for voltages of all the nodes with reference to node 'e' in the circuit shown. **(Dec. 2004) (8 marks)**

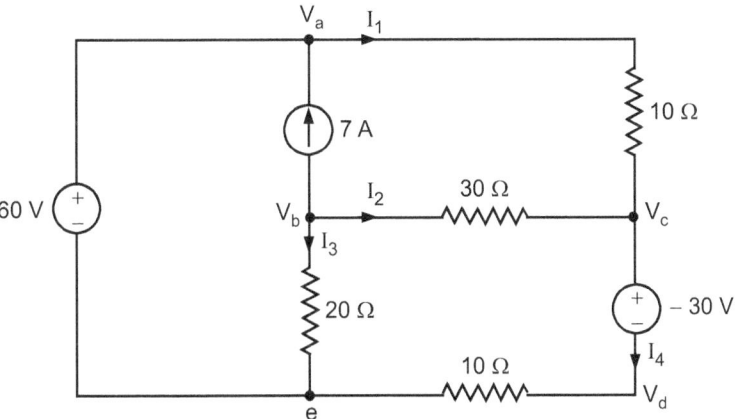

Fig. 1.73: Circuit for Ex. (1.25)

Sol.: Choose 'e' node as references. Let V_a, V_b, V_c and V_d be the other node voltages with reference to ground. Assume arbitrarily currents in various branches. The redrawn circuit is shown below in Fig. 1.74.

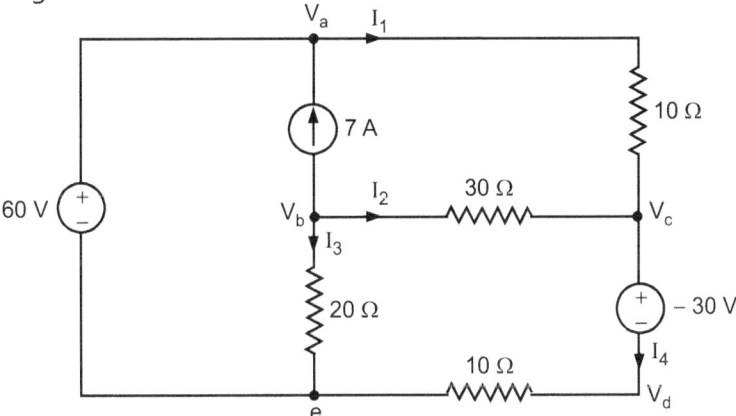

Fig. 1.74: Redrawn circuit

There are four nodes. Hence we need four equations. Now V_a, reference node and 60V source together form a super node.

This gives first equation as $V_a = +60V$ ... (a)

The voltage source of 30V, V_c and V_d nodes together forms another super node. This gives second equation as $V_a - V_c = 30$ ... (b)

KCL at node 'b' with voltage V_b gives third equation and is given by equation,

$$I_3 + I_2 + 7 = 0$$

$$\frac{V_b}{20} + \left(\frac{V_b - V_c}{30}\right) + 7 = 0$$

Or $\quad 2V_c - 5V_b = 420$ ... (c)

The fourth equation can be obtained by applying the KCL at node c and is given by equation,

$$I_1 + I_2 - I_4 = 0$$

$$\left(\frac{60 - V_c}{10}\right) + \left(\frac{V_b - V_c}{30}\right) - \left(\frac{V_c + 30}{10}\right) = 0$$

Or $3(60 - V_c) + (V_b - V_c) - 3(V_c + 30) = 0$

Or $\quad 7V_c - V_b = 90 \quad \ldots$ (d)

[Current I_4 is given by equation $V_c = 10 \times I_4 - 30$]

Source equations (a), (b), (c) and (d) to get required node voltages. Putting equations (d) into equation (c) gives

$$2V_c - 5[7V_c - 90] = 420$$

Hence $\quad V_c = +0.91$ V

By (d) $\quad V_b = 7V_c - 90 = -83.64$ V

By (d) $\quad V_d = 30 + V_c = +30.91$ V

1.22 ANALYSIS OF CIRCUITS WITH MIXED SOURCES

In section (1.17) we have studied mesh analysis where all energy sources uses voltage sources. Thus, mesh (KVL) analysis preferably requires all energy sources as voltage sources. Similarly in section (1.19) we have studied nodal (KCL) analysis in which all the energy sources were current source.

But generally networks consists of both the voltage as well as current sources. Such circuits are called as the circuits with mixed sources. Analysis of such circuits can not be carried out directly. If the circuit is to be analysed on loop basis then all the current sources must be converted into voltage sources. Similarly if the circuit is to be analysed on nodal basis then all the voltage sources are to be converted into current sources. Following few examples explains the analysis of circuits with mixed sources.

Ex. 1.26: Using nodal analysis find the node voltages V_1 and V_2 in the circuit of Fig. 1.75.

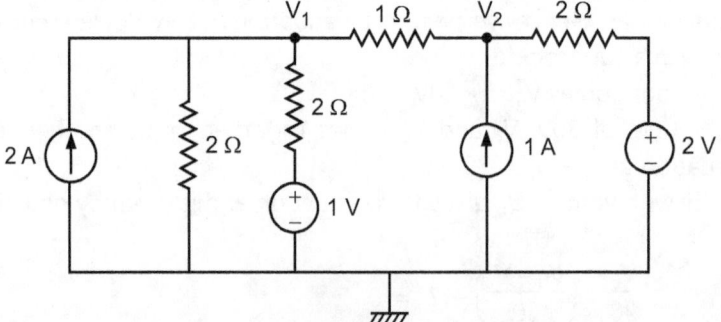

Fig. 1.75: Circuit for Ex. (1.26)

Sol.: Since, the circuit is to be analysis in nodal basis all the voltage sources need to be inverted into the current sources. The circuit after conversion is shown in Fig. 1.76 (a). The resistors are combined and so also are current sources. The simplified final equivalent circuit with all the assumed branch currents is shown in Fig. 1.76 (b).

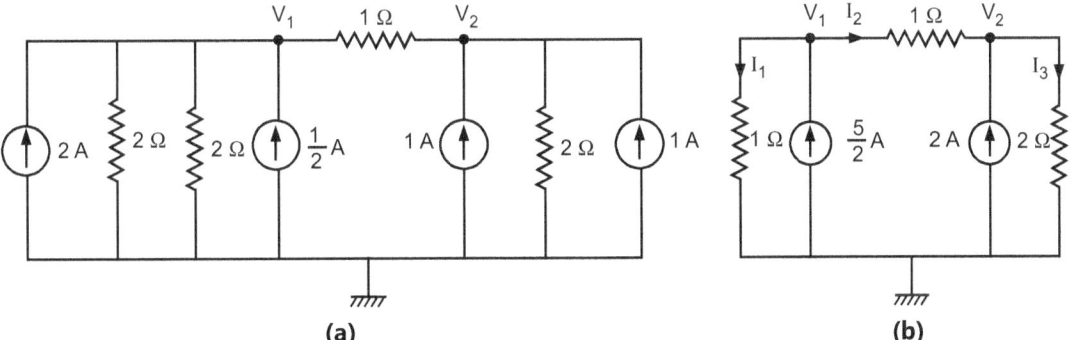

(a) (b)

Fig. 1.76: Equivalent circuits

Now KCL at node with voltage V_1 gives $I_1 + I_2 = \dfrac{5}{2}$

$$\dfrac{V_1}{1} + \left(\dfrac{V_1 - V_2}{1}\right) = 2.5 \text{ or } 2V_1 - V_2 = 2.5 \quad \ldots \text{(a)}$$

KCL at node with voltage V_2 gives $I_3 - I_2 = 2$

$$\dfrac{V_2}{2} - \left[\dfrac{V_1 - V_2}{1}\right] = 2 \text{ or } -2V_1 - 3V_2 = 4 \quad \ldots \text{(b)}$$

Solve (a) and (b) to get voltages V_1 and V_2
Adding (a) and (b) gives $2V_2 = 6.5$ hence $V_2 = +\, 3.25$V
By (a) $2V_1 = 2.5 + V_2 = 5.75$ hence $V_1 = 2.875$V

Ex. 1.27: The circuit contains both the voltage and current sources. Analyse the circuit on loop basis to find the value of current I_a.

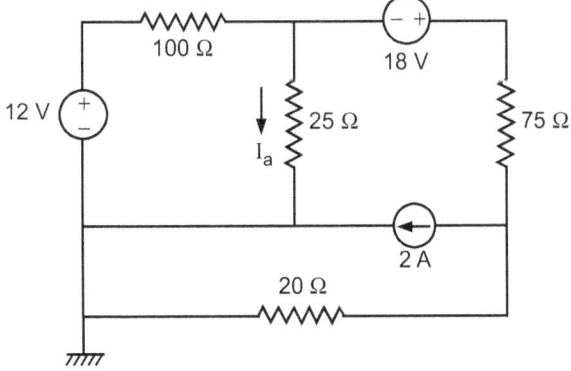

Fig. 1.77: Circuit for Ex. (1.27)

Sol.: Since, the circuit is to be analysed on loop basis convert the current source (2A) parallel with 20Ω into the voltage source of 40V in series with 20Ω. The modified equivalent circuit with loop currents I_1 and I_2 is shown in Fig. (1.78). Source conversion converts the three loops circuits into a two loops circuit.

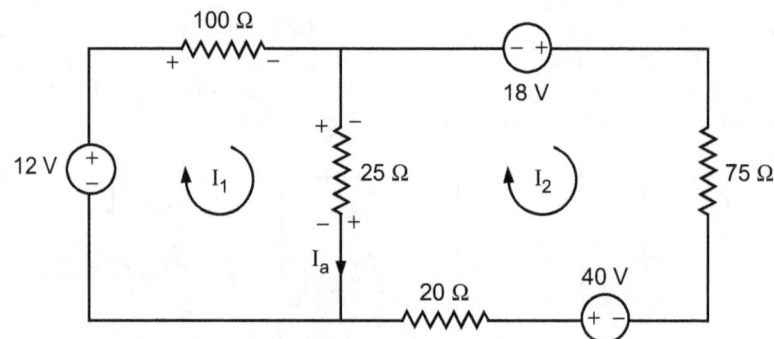

Fig. 1.78: Modified equivalent circuits

KVL across loop I_1 gives
$$-100 I_1 - 25(I_1 - I_2) + 12 = 0$$
Or
$$125 I_1 - 25 I_2 = 12 \quad \ldots \text{(a)}$$
KVL across loop I_2 gives $+18 - 75I_2 + 40 - 20I_2 + 25(I_1 - I_2) = 0$
$$-25 I_1 + 120 I_2 = 58 \quad \ldots \text{(b)}$$
From (a) and (b) solve for I_1 and $_2$

Thus, $I_1 = \dfrac{\Delta_1}{\Delta} = \dfrac{\begin{vmatrix} 12 & -25 \\ 58 & 120 \end{vmatrix}}{\begin{vmatrix} 125 & -25 \\ -25 & 120 \end{vmatrix}} = \dfrac{1440 + 1450}{15000 - 625} = 0.2$ Amp.

By (a)
$$25 I_2 = 125 I_1 - 12 = 13.13$$
$$I_2 = +0.5252 \text{ Amp}$$
Hence,
$$I_a = I_1 - I_2 = 0.2 - 0.5252 = -0.325 \text{ Amp}.$$

Ex. 1.28: For the circuit of Fig. 1.79 find the current (I) flowing through 2Ω resistance.

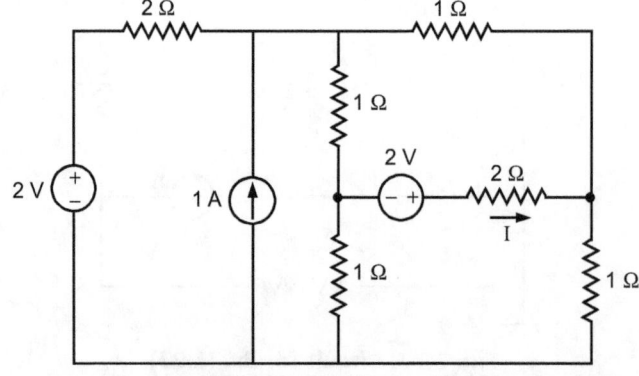

Fig. 1.79: Circuit for Ex. (1.28)

Sol.: We have to use loop analysis which is more easier for this problem than using nodal analysis. Convert 2V in series with 2Ω into a current source of 1A parallel with 2Ω. And two parallel current sources of 1A each into 2A current source. Again convert 2A in parallel with 2Ω into a voltage source of 4V in series with 2Ω. The final simplified circuit with assumed loop currents is shown in Fig. 1.80.

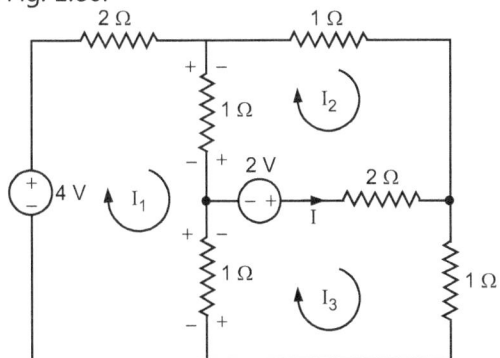

Fig. 1.80: Modified equivalent circuit

KVL across loop with loop current I_1 gives:
$$-2I_1 - (I_1 - I_2) - (I_1 - I_3) + 4 = 0$$
Or
$$4I_1 - I_2 - I_3 = 4 \quad \ldots \text{(a)}$$
KVL across loop with loop current I_2 gives.
$$-2 - I_2 + 2(I_3 - I_2) - (I_2 - I_1) = 0$$
Or
$$-I_1 - 4I_2 - 2I_3 = -2 \quad \ldots \text{(b)}$$
KVL across loop with loop current I_3 gives:
$$+2 - 2(I_3 - I_2) - I_3 - (I_3 - I_1) = 0$$
Or
$$-I_1 - 2I_2 + 4I_3 = 2 \quad \ldots \text{(c)}$$
Since, current in 2Ω resistor $= I = I_3 - I_2$, solve for I_2 and I_3

Thus, $$I_2 = \frac{\Delta_2}{\Delta} = \frac{\begin{vmatrix} 4 & 4 & -1 \\ -1 & -2 & -2 \\ -1 & 2 & 4 \end{vmatrix}}{\begin{vmatrix} 4 & -1 & -1 \\ -1 & 4 & -2 \\ -1 & -2 & 4 \end{vmatrix}} = \frac{12}{36} = +\frac{1}{3} \text{ Amp.}$$

Thus, $$I_3 = \frac{\Delta_3}{\Delta} = \frac{\begin{vmatrix} 4 & -1 & 4 \\ -1 & 4 & -2 \\ -1 & -2 & 2 \end{vmatrix}}{36} = \frac{36}{36} = +\frac{1}{3} \text{ Amp.}$$

Hence, $I = I_3 - I_2 = 1 - \frac{1}{3} = +\frac{2}{3}$ Amp.

1.23 MUTUAL INDUCTANCE

Suppose we hook up an AC generator to a solenoid so that the wire in the solenoid carries AC. Call this solenoid the primary coil. Next place a second solenoid connected to an AC voltmeter near the primary coil so that it is coaxial with the primary coil. Call this second solenoid the secondary coil. See the Fig. 1.81 at the right.

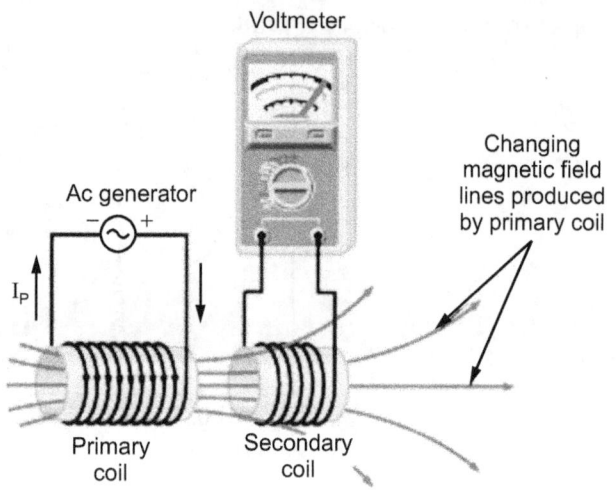

Fig. 1.81

The alternating current in the primary coil produces an alternating magnetic field whose lines of flux link the secondary coil (like thread passing through the eye of a needle). Hence the secondary coil encloses a changing magnetic field. By Faraday's law of induction this changing magnetic flux induces an emf in the secondary coil. This effect in which changing current in one circuit induces an emf in another circuit is called **mutual induction**.

Let the primary coil have N_1 turns and the secondary coil have N_2 turns. Assume that the same amount of magnetic flux Φ_2 from the primary coil links each turn of the secondary coil. The net flux linking the secondary coil is then $N_2\Phi_2$. This net flux is proportional to the magnetic field, which, in turn, is proportional to the current I_1 in the primary coil. Thus we can write $N_2\Phi_2 \propto I_1$. This proportionality can be turned into an equation by introducing a constant. Call this constant M, the **mutual inductance** of the two coils:

$$N_2\Phi_2 = MI_1 \text{ or } M = \frac{N_2\Phi_1}{I_1}$$

the unit of inductance is $\frac{wb}{A}$ = henry (H) named after Joseph Henry.

The emf induced in the secondary coil may now be calculated using Faraday's law:

$$E_2 = -N_2 \frac{\Delta\Phi_2}{\Delta t} = -\frac{\Delta(N_2\Phi_2)}{\Delta t} = -\frac{(MI_1)}{\Delta t} = -M\frac{\Delta I_1}{\Delta t}$$

$$\boxed{E_2 = -M\frac{\Delta I_1}{\Delta t}}$$

The above formula is the **emf due to mutual induction**.

Ex. 1.29: The apparatus used in Experiment EM-11B consists of two coaxial solenoids. A solenoid is essentially just a coil of wire. For a long, tightly-wound solenoid of n turns per unit length carrying current I the magnetic field over its cross-section is nearly constant and given by B = μ_0nI. Assume that the two solenoids have the same cross-sectional area A. Find a formula for the mutual inductance of the solenoids.

The magnetic flux is the primary coil is

$$\Phi_1 = \mu_0 \frac{N_1 I_1}{l_1} A \text{ where } l_1 \text{ is the length of the primary coil}$$

$$M = \frac{N_2 \Phi_2}{I_1}$$

But $\Phi_2 = \Phi_1$

$\therefore$
$$M = \frac{N_2 \Phi_2}{I_1} = \frac{N_2}{I_1} \mu_0 \frac{N_1 I_1}{l_1} A;$$

$$\boxed{M = \mu_0 \frac{N_1 N_2}{l_1} A} \qquad \ldots (1.18)$$

(Note how M is independent of the current I_1).

1.23.1 Self-Inductance

A current-carrying coil produces a magnetic field that links its own turns. If the current in the coil changes the amount of magnetic flux linking the coil changes and, by Faraday's law, an emf is produced in the coil. This emf is called a self-induced emf.

Let the coil have N turns. Assume that the same amount of magnetic flux Φ links each turn of the coil. The net flux linking the coil is then NΦ. This net flux is proportional to the magnetic field, which, in turn, is proportional to the current I in the coil. Thus we can write N$\Phi \propto$ I. This proportionality can be turned into an equation by introducing a constant. Call this constant L, the **self-inductance** (or simply **inductance**) of the coil:

$$N\Phi = LI \text{ or } L = \frac{L\Phi}{I} \qquad \ldots (1.19)$$

As with mutual inductance, the unit of self-inductance is the henry.

The self-induced emf can now be calculated using Faraday's law:

$$E = -N\frac{\Delta \Phi}{\Delta t} = -\frac{\Delta(N\Phi)}{\Delta t} = -\frac{\Delta(LI)}{\Delta t} = -L\frac{\Delta I}{\Delta t}$$

$$\boxed{E = -L\frac{\Delta I}{\Delta t}} \qquad \ldots (1.20)$$

The above formula is the **emf due to self-induction**.

The formula for the self-inductance of a solenoid of N turns, length l, and cross-sectional area A. Assume that the solenoid carries a current I. Then the magnetic flux in the solenoid is

$$\Phi = \mu_0 \frac{NI}{l} A \cdot L = \frac{N\Phi}{I} = \frac{N}{I} \mu_0 \frac{NI}{l} = A$$

$$L = \mu_0 \frac{N^2}{l} \text{ or } \boxed{L = \mu_0 n^2 Al} \quad \ldots (1.21)$$

where $n = \frac{N}{l}$

Note how L is independent of the current I).

1.23.2 Transformers

A **transformer** is a device for increasing or decreasing an AC voltage. It consists of an iron core with two coil wrappings: a primary coil with N_p turns and a secondary coil with N_s turns. See the figure at the right.

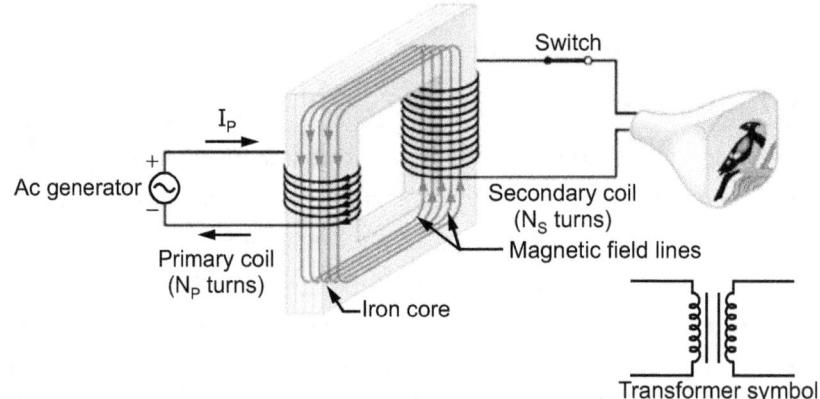

Fig. 1.82

Assume an AC source, such as an AC generator, produces an alternating current I_p in the primary coil. The primary coil creates a changing magnetic flux Φ in the core which links the turns of both the primary and secondary coils. In the secondary coil the induced emf arises from mutual induction and is given by Faraday's law as

$$E_s = -N_s \frac{\Delta\Phi}{\Delta t} \quad \ldots (a)$$

In the primary coil the induced emf is due to self-induction and is given by Faraday's law as

$$E_p = -N_p \frac{\Delta\Phi}{\Delta t} \quad \ldots (b)$$

The term ΔΦ/Δt is the same in both equations since the same amount of magnetic flux Φ passes through both coils. Dividing the equations gives

$$\frac{E_s}{E_p} = \frac{N_s}{N_p} \quad \ldots (c)$$

If the resistances of the coils are negligible the terminal voltages V_s and V_p of the coils are nearly equal to the magnitudes of the emfs E_s and E_p. Hence we can write

$$\boxed{\frac{V_s}{V_p} = \frac{N_s}{N_p}} \quad \ldots (1.22)$$

This is called the **transformer equation**.

The power delivered to an ideal transformer on its primary circuit will match the power output on its secondary circuit and we can write $I_p V_p = I_s V_s$ or

$$\frac{I_s}{I_p} = \frac{V_p}{V_s} = \frac{N_p}{N_s} \quad \ldots (1.23)$$

1.24 DOT CONVENTIONAL FOR COUPLED CIRCUITS

1.24.1 Introduction to Coupling Circuits

A constant current produces a constant magnetic field that forms a closed loops of magnetic flux lines in the vicinity of the inductor.

A changing current causes these closed loops to expand or contract, thereby cutting the turns in the windings that makes up the indicator.

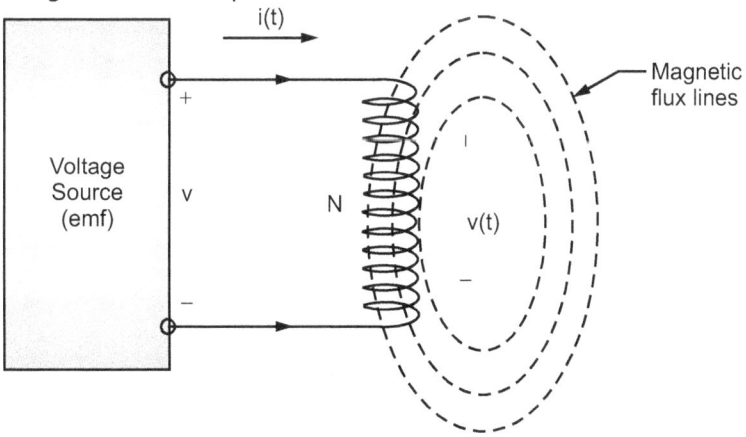

Fig. 1.83

As the current change with time, the magnetic flux due to this current will change with time. This changing flux creates an induced emf in the circuit.

Faraday's law states that the voltage across the indicator (emf) is equal to the time rate of change of the total flux linkage.

The direction of the induced emf in the circuit opposite the direction of the source emf; this results in a gradual (rather than instantaneous) increase in the source current to its final value.

This phenomenon is said resulted from the self inductance of the coil.

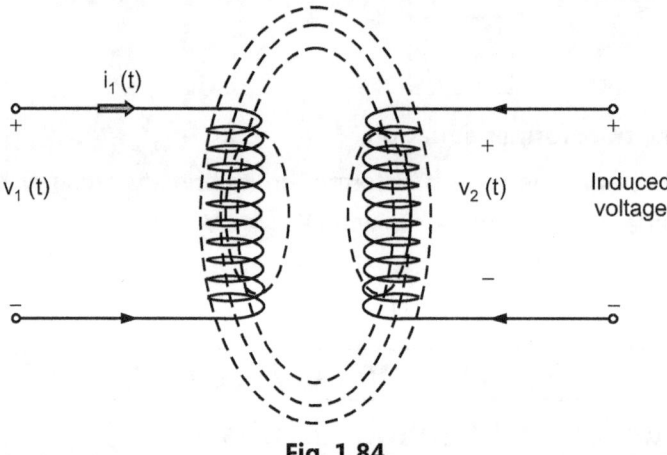

Fig. 1.84

Suppose a second inductor is brought closed to the first so that the flux from the first indicator links with the turns of the second indicator. If the current in the first inductor is changing, then the flux linkage will generate a voltage in the second inductor.

The magnetic coupling between the changing current in the first inductor and the voltage generate in the second indicator produces mutual inductance.

Assuming that the two inductors are part as shown in the Fig. 1.85. Each inductor prouces a flux, $\phi(t)$:

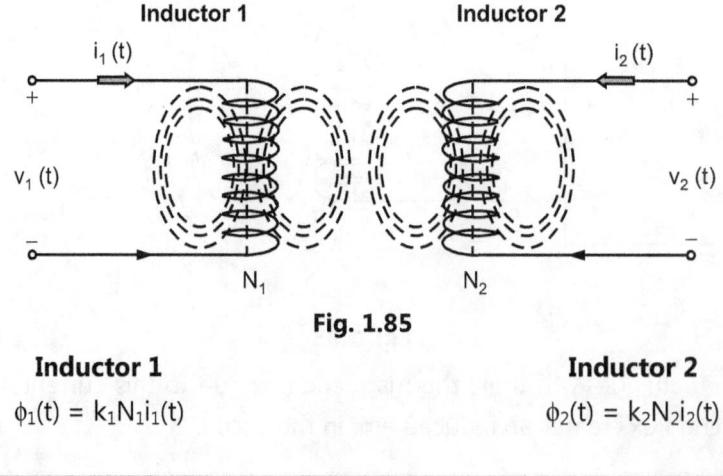

Fig. 1.85

Inductor 1   **Inductor 2**

$\phi_1(t) = k_1 N_1 i_1(t)$ $\phi_2(t) = k_2 N_2 i_2(t)$

k_1 and k_2.

The flux linkage in each inductor is proportional to the number of turns:

Inductor 1
$\lambda_{11}(t) = N_1\phi_1(t)$

Inductor 2
$\lambda_{22}(t) = N_2\phi_2(t)$

By Faraday's law, the voltage across the indicator is equal to the time rate of change of the total flux linkage.

Inductor 1: $\quad v_{11}(t) = \dfrac{d\lambda_{11}(t)}{dt} = N_1\dfrac{d\phi_1(t)}{dt} = [k_1N_1^2]\dfrac{di_1(t)}{dt}$

Inductor 2: $\quad v_{22}(t) = \dfrac{d\lambda_{22}(t)}{dt} = N_2\dfrac{d\phi_2(t)}{dt} = [k_2N_2^2]\dfrac{di_2(t)}{dt}$

These equations provide the i-v relationships for the indicators when there is no mutual coupling.

Suppose that the two indicators are brought close together so that part of the flux (not necessary all) produced by each inductor intercepts the other as shown in Fig. 1.86. The inductors a fluxes: $\phi_{12}(t)$ and $\phi_{21}(t)$.

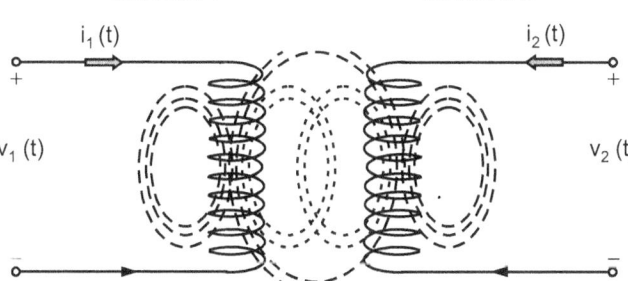

Fig. 1.86

$\phi_{12}(t)$: flux intercepting inductor 1 due to the current in inductor 2
$\phi_{22}(t)$: flux intercepting inductor 2 due to the current in inductor 1

Inductor 1
$\phi_{12}(t) = k_{12}N_2i_2(t)$

Inductor 2
$\phi_{21}(t) = k_{21}N_1i_1(t)$

k_{12} and k_{21} are proportionality constants.

The total flux linkage in each inductor is proportional to the number of turns:

Inductor 1
$\lambda_{12}(t) = N_1\phi_{12}(t)$

Inductor 2
$\phi_{21}(t) = N_2\phi_{21}(t)$

By Faraday's law, the voltage across the indictor is equal to the time rate of change of the total flux linkage.

Inductor 1: $\quad v_{12}(t) = \dfrac{d\lambda_{12}(t)}{dt} = N_1\dfrac{d\phi_{12}(t)}{dt} = [k_{12}N_1N_2]\dfrac{di_2(t)}{dt} \quad \ldots 1.25\ (a)$

Inductor 2: $\quad v_{21}(t) = \dfrac{d\lambda_{21}(t)}{dt} = N_2\dfrac{d\phi_{21}(t)}{dt} = [k_{12}N_1N_2]\dfrac{di_1(t)}{dt} \quad \ldots 1.25\ (b)$

These equations provide the i-v relationships describing the cross coupling between the inductors when there is a mutual coupling.

When the magnetic medium supporting the fluxes is linear, the superposition principle applies and the total voltage across the inductors is the sum of the voltages with and without mutual coupling.

The total voltages are:

Inductor 1
$$v_1(t) = v_{11}(t) + v_{12}(t)$$
$$= [k_1 N_1^2]\frac{di_1(t)}{dt} + [k_{12} N_1 N_2]\frac{di_2(t)}{dt} \qquad \ldots 1.26\,(a)$$

Inductor 2
$$v_2(t) = v_{21}(t) + v_{22}(t)$$
$$= [k_{21} N_1 N_2]\frac{di_1(t)}{dt} + [k_2 N_2^2]\frac{di_2(t)}{dt} \qquad \ldots 1.26\,(b)$$

Identifying the following four inductance parameters then:

The self-inductances of the inductors are:
$$L_1 = k_1 N_1^2 \quad \text{and} \quad L_2 = k_2 N_2^2 \qquad \ldots 1.27\,(a)$$

The mutual inductances are:
$$M_{12} = K_{12} N_1 N_2 \quad \text{and} \quad M_{21} = k_{21} N_1 N_2 \qquad \ldots 1.27\,(b)$$

In a linear magnetic medium,
$$k_{12} = k_{21} = k_M \quad \text{and} \quad M_{12} = M_{21} = k_M N_1 N_2 = M$$

Inductor 1
$$v_1(t) = v_{11}(t) + v_{12}(t)$$
$$v_1(t) = L_1 \frac{di_1}{dt} + M \frac{di_2}{dt} \qquad \ldots 1.28\,(a)$$

Inductor 2
$$v_2(t) = v_{21}(t) + v_{22}(t)$$
$$v_2(t) = M \frac{di_1}{dt} + L_2 \frac{di_2}{dt} \qquad \ldots 1.28\,(b)$$

Note:
1. Coupling inductors involve three inductance parameters, the two self-inductances L_1 and L_2 and the mutual inductance M.
2. The preceding development assumes that the cross-coupling is additive. The general from for both additive and subtractive coupling is:
$$v_1(t) = L_1 \frac{di_1}{dt} \pm M \frac{di_2}{dt} \qquad \ldots 1.29\,(a)$$
and
$$v_2(t) = \pm M \frac{di_1}{dt} + L_2 \frac{di_2}{dt} \qquad \ldots 1.29\,(b)$$

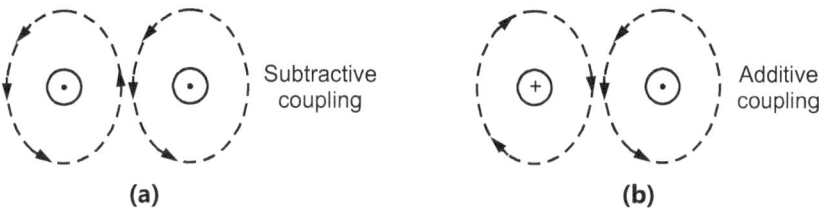

Fig. 1.87

It is very important to know when to use the positive sign or the negative one.

3. Assuming the coupled circuit is excited with a sinusoidal source. Then, the voltages and the currents can be presented in phasor form as:

$$V_1 = j\omega L_1 I_1 + j\omega M I_2 \quad \ldots 1.30\ (a)$$
$$V_2 = j\omega L_2 I_2 + j\omega M I_1 \quad \ldots 1.30\ (b)$$

1.24.2 Energy Stored into Coupling Circuits

We would like to determine the total energy stored in a coupled network. The general form of the voltages in a mutual coupling circuit is

$$v_1(t) = L_1 \frac{di_1}{dt} \pm M \frac{di_2}{dt}$$

$$v_2(t) = \pm M \frac{di_1}{dt} + L_2 \frac{di_2}{dt}$$

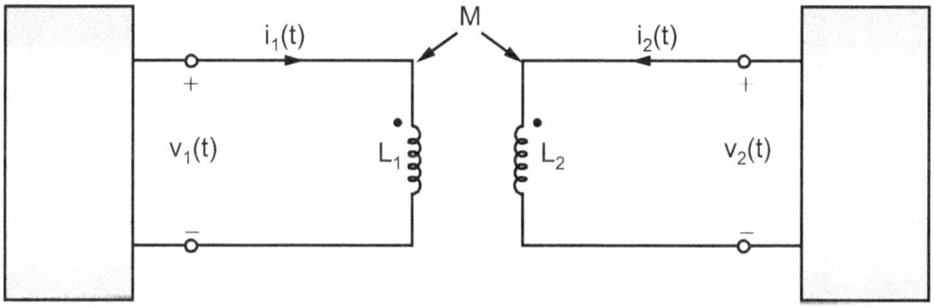

Fig. 1.88

Multiplying the voltage by the currents in each inductor, the power absorbed in each indictor is:

$$p_1(t) = i_1(t)\, v_1(t) = L_1 i_1(t) \frac{di_1(t)}{dt} \pm M i_1(t) \frac{di_2(t)}{dt} \quad \ldots (a)$$

$$p_2(t) = i_2(t)\, v_2(t) = \pm M i_2(t) \frac{di_1(t)}{dt} + L_2 i_2(t) \frac{di_2(t)}{dt} \quad \ldots (b)$$

The total power absorbed with inductors 1 and 2 is:

$$p(t) = p_1(t) + p_1(t)$$

$$p(t) = L_1 \left[i_1(t) \frac{di_1(t)}{dt} \right] \pm M \left[i_1(t) \frac{di_2(t)}{dt} + i_2(t) \frac{di_1(t)}{dt} \right] + L_2 \left[i_1(t) \frac{di_2(t)}{dt} \right] \quad \ldots (1.31)$$

Each of the bracketed terms is a perfect derivative. Therefore,

$$i_1(t)\frac{di_1(t)}{dt} = \frac{1}{2}\frac{d}{dt}i_1^2(t)$$

$$i_2(t)\frac{di_2(t)}{dt} = \frac{1}{2}\frac{d}{dt}i_2^2(t)$$

$$i_1(t)\frac{di_2(t)}{dt} + i_2(t)\frac{di_1(t)}{dt} = \frac{d}{dt}i_1(t)\,i_2(t)$$

Therefore,
$$p(t) = L_1\left[\frac{1}{2}\frac{di_1^2(t)}{dt}\right] + M\frac{di_1(t)\,i_2(t)}{dt} + L_2\left[\frac{1}{2}\frac{di_1^2(t)}{dt}\right]$$

or
$$p(t) = \frac{d}{dt}\left[\frac{1}{2}L_1\,i_i^2(t) \pm Mi_1(t)\,i_2(t) + \frac{1}{2}L_2\,i_2^2(t)\right]$$

Power is defined as the time rate of change of energy, therefore the energy is:

$$w(t) = \frac{1}{2}L_1 i_1^2(t) \pm Mi_1(t)\,i_2(tr) + \frac{1}{2}L_2\,i_2^2(t)) \qquad \dots (1.32)$$

Note:
1. The self-inductance terms are always positive. However, the mutual-inductance term can either positive or negative.
2. The total energy must be positive. This energy consideration dictate that for any pair of coupled inductors the product of the self-inductances must exceed the square of the mutual-inductance.

   or $\qquad L_1 L_2 \geq M^2$

   Let $\qquad k = \dfrac{M}{\sqrt{L_1 L_2}} \leq 1$

   Note: $L_{eq} > 0$, $L_1 L_2 - M^2 \geq 0$.

   where, k is the coefficients of coupling and ranges between 0 and 1.

   $$0 \leq k \leq 1$$

   k = 0 $\qquad$ M = 0 $\qquad$ No flux linking in the coil
   k = 1 $\qquad$ M = $\sqrt{L_1 L_2}$ $\qquad$ Perfect coupling

   Perfect coupling means all flux in each coil is linking the other coil. Practical design can produce coupling coefficients of 0.99 and lower.
3. For energy calculation, the positive sign for the mutual term is selected if both currents enter or leave the dotted terminals of the coils. The negative sign is selected others.

Ex. 1.30: Compute the energy stored in the perfected coupled inductors at t = 5 ms.

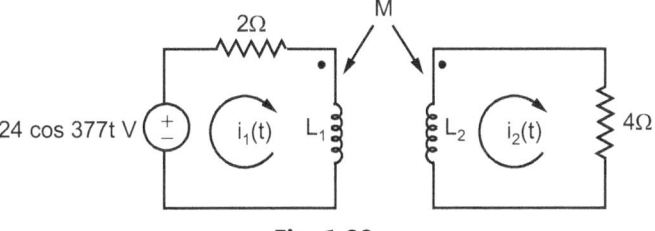

Fig. 1.89

Sol.: Perfect coupling, then k = 1.

$$k = \frac{M}{\sqrt{L_1 L_2}} \text{ or } M = 5.31 \text{ mH and } j\omega M = j2$$

$$\omega L_1 = 377 \times 2.653 \times 10^{-3} = 1\Omega \text{ and } \omega L_2 = 4\Omega$$

Assuming passive sign convention, the circuit is drawn in the frequency domain.

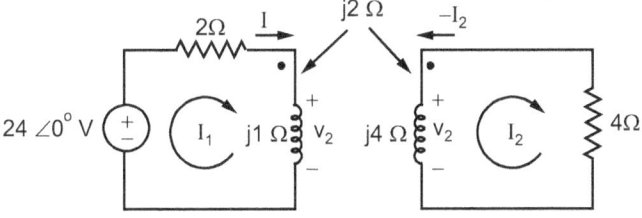

Fig. 1.89 (a)

$$V_1 = j1I_1 - j2I_2 \text{ and } V_2 = j2I_1 - j4I_2$$
$$2I_1 + V_1 = 24 \angle 0°$$
$$4I_2 - V_2 = 0$$

Merge the writing of the loop and coupled inductor equations in one step

$$2I_1 + (j1I_1 - j2I_2) = 24 \angle 0°$$
$$4I_2 - (j2I_1 - j4I_2) = 0$$

Solving the equations

$$I_1 = 9.41 \angle -11.31° \text{ (A)}$$
$$I_2 = 3.33 \angle 33.69° \text{ (A)}$$

The currents in the time domain are:

$$i_1(t) = 9.41 \cos(377t - 11.31°) \text{ (A)}$$
$$i_2(t) = 3.33 \cos(377t - 33.69°) \text{ (A)}$$

Note that the term 377 t is in radians.

At $\quad$ t = 0.005 s

$$377t = 1.885 \text{ (rad)} \Leftrightarrow 108°$$

Ex. 1.31: Determine the energy stored at t = 10 ms.

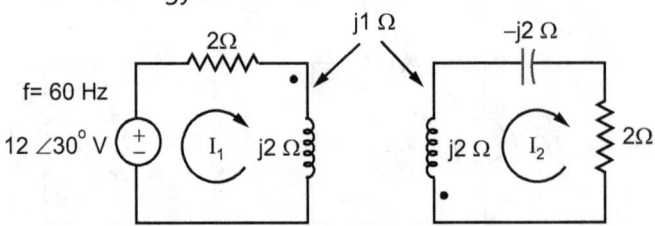

Fig. 1.90

Sol.: f = 50 Hz, L_1 = 0.0053 (H) and L_2 = 0.0053 (H) and M = 0.00265 (H)

Assuming passive sing convention, the circuit is drawn in the frequency domain.

$$V_1 = j2I_1 + j1I_2 \quad \text{and} \quad V_2 = j1I_1 + j2I_2$$

The loop equations are:

$$2I_1 + V_1 = 12 \angle 30°$$
$$(2 - j2) I_2 + V_2 = 0$$

Fig. 1.90 (a)

Merge the writing of the loop and coupled inductors equations in one step

	$2I_1 + (j2I_1 + j1I_2) = 12\angle 30°$	... (a)
	$(j1I_1 + j2I_2) + (2 - j2)I_2 = 0$	... (b)
or	$(2 + j2) I_1 + jI_2 = 12\angle 30°$	... (c)
	$jI_1 + 2I_2 = 0$	... (d)
and	$I_2 = -0.5\, jI_1$	... (e)

Substituting (e) into (c)

$$(2 + j2 - j\,0.5) I_2 = 12 \angle 30°$$

$$I_1 = \frac{12\angle 30°}{2.0 + j1.5} = \frac{12\angle 30°}{2.5\angle 36.87°} = 4.8 \angle -6.87°$$

$$I_2 = -0.5\, jI_1$$
$$= 0.5 \angle -90° \times 4.8 \angle -6.87°$$
$$= 2.4 \angle -96.87°$$

The currents in the time domain are:

$$i_1(t) = 4.8 \cos(377t - 6.87°) \text{ (A)}$$
$$i_2(t) = 2.4 \cos(377t - 96.87°) \text{ (A)}$$

Note that the term 377 t is in radians

At t = 0.01s

$$377t = 3.77 \text{ (rad)} \Leftrightarrow = 216°$$
$$i_1(0.01) = 4.8 \cos(216 - 6.87°) = -4.19 \text{ A}$$
$$i_2(0.01) = 2.4 \cos(216 - 96.87°) = -1.17 \text{ A}$$

For energy calculation, the positive sign for the mutual term is selected because both currents enter the dotted terminals of the coils.

$$w(t) = \frac{1}{2} L_1 i_1^2(t) \pm M i_1(t) i_2(t) + \frac{1}{2} L_2 i_2^2(t)$$

$$w(0.100) = 0.5 \times 0.0053 \times (-4.19)^2 + 0.00265 \times (-4.19)(-1.17)$$
$$+ 0.5 \times 0.0053 \times (-1.17)^2 \text{ (J)}$$

$$w(0.010) = 63 \text{ mJ}$$

1.24.3 Ideal Transformers

Transformer is a device utilize magnetic coupling between two inductors. It is used by power utilities to step-up or step-down a.c. voltages and currents. Transformers are commonly used in electronic and communication circuits to raise or reduce the voltages and to isolate one circuit from another.

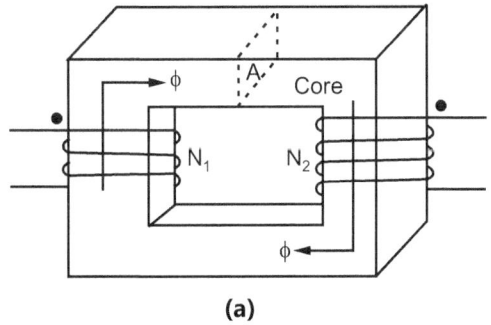
(a)

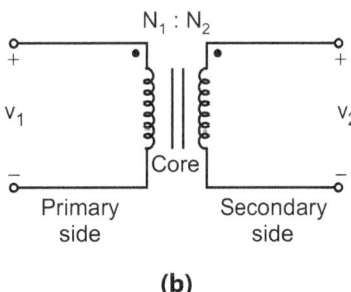
(b)

Fig. 1.91

The ideal transformer is a circuit element in which coupled inductors are assumed to have perfect coupling and zero power loss.

Therefore, for an ideal transformer.

Coupling coefficient   k = 1
Winding Resistance $R_{primary} = 0 = R_{secondary}$

From section 1.24.1 "Introduction to Coupling Circuits", for a linear magnetic medium, the proportionality constants are:
$$k_{12} = k_{21} = k_M$$
And perfect coupling requires, the proportionality constants:
$$k_1 = k_{21} \quad \text{and} \quad k_2 = k_{12}$$

Primary voltage:

$$v_1(t) = [k_1 N_1^2]\frac{di_1(t)}{dt} \pm [k_1 N_1 N_2]\frac{di_2(t)}{dt}$$

$$v_1(t) = [k_M N_1^2]\frac{di_1(t)}{dt} \pm [k_M N_1 N_2]\frac{di_2(t)}{dt} \qquad \ldots (1.33)$$

Secondary voltage:

$$v_2(t) = \pm [k_{21} N_1 N_2]\frac{di_1(t)}{dt} + [k_2 N_2^2]\frac{di_2(t)}{dt}$$

$$v_2(t) = \pm [k_M N_1 N_2]\frac{di_1(t)}{dt} + [k_M N_2^2]\frac{di_2(t)}{dt} \qquad \ldots (1.34)$$

Taking N_1 common from (1.33) and $\pm N_2$ common from (1.34).

$$v_1(t) = N_1\left[k_M \frac{di_1(t)}{dt} \pm k_M N_2 \frac{di_2(t)}{dt}\right] \qquad \ldots (1.35)$$

$$v_2(t) = \pm N_2\left[k_M N_1 \frac{di_1(t)}{dt} \pm k_M N_2 \frac{di_2(t)}{dt}\right] \qquad \ldots (1.36)$$

Dividing (1.36) by (1.35) then, the **First ideal transformer equation is:**

$$\frac{v_2(t)}{v_1(t)} = \pm \frac{N_2}{N_1} = \pm n \qquad \ldots (1.37)$$

For zero power loss transformer,
$$v_1(t)\, i_1(t) - v_2(t)\, i_2(t) = 0$$
$$\frac{i_2(t)}{i_1(t)} = \frac{v_1(t)}{v_2(t)}$$

Using (1.37) then the **Second equation for the ideal transformer is:**

$$\frac{i_2(t)}{i_1(t)} = \frac{v_1(t)}{v_2(t)} = \pm \frac{N_1}{N_2} = \pm \frac{1}{n} \qquad \ldots (1.38)$$

Using ohm's law,
$$V_2 = Z_L I_2$$

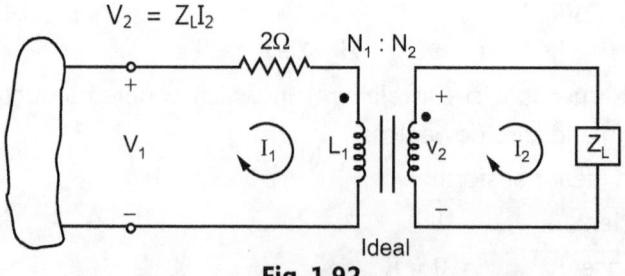

Fig. 1.92

Using (1.37) and (1.38)

$$V_1 \frac{N_2}{N_1} = Z_L I_1 \frac{N_1}{N_2} \quad \text{or} \quad V_1 = \left(\frac{N_1}{N_2}\right)^2 Z_L I_1$$

$$\frac{V_1}{I_1} = Z_1 = \left(\frac{N_1}{N_2}\right)^2 Z_L$$

Transferring Z_L from the secondary side to the primary side helps in circuit analysis.

Z_1 = The secondary impedance (Z_L) as reflected into the primary side

The complex power at primary side is:

$$S_1 = V_1 I_1^* = \left(V_2 \frac{N_1}{N_2}\right)\left(I_2 \frac{N_2}{N_1}\right)^*$$

$$= V_2 I_1^* = S_2 \text{ The complex power at secondary side is}$$

Note:
1. The turns ratio is defined as:
$$n = \frac{N_2}{N_1}$$

2. Phasor equations for an ideal transformer are:
$$V_1 = \pm \frac{V_2}{n} \quad \text{and} \quad I_1 = \pm n I_2$$

$$Z_1 = \frac{Z_L}{n^2} \quad \text{and} \quad S_1 = S_2$$

Rules for Voltage and Current sign Relations

Rule 1: If V_1 and V_2 are both positive or both negative at the dotted terminals, use positive (+n). Otherwise, use – n.

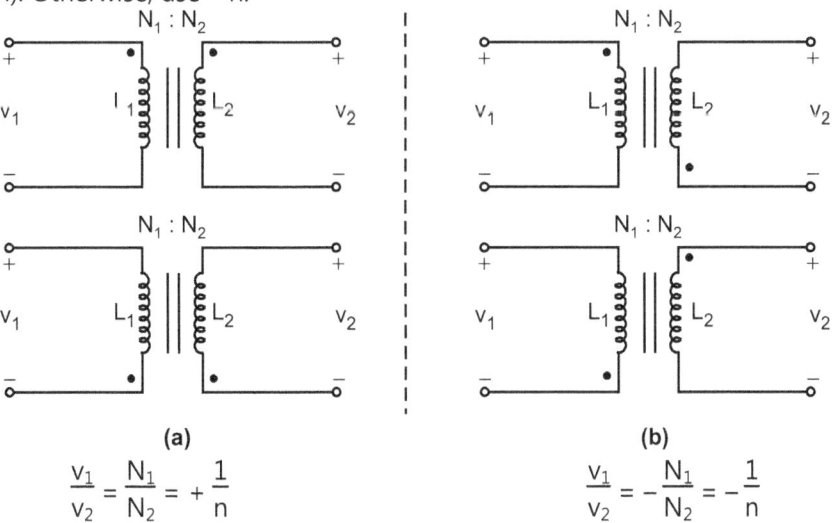

(a)   (b)

$$\frac{V_1}{V_2} = \frac{N_1}{N_2} = +\frac{1}{n} \qquad \frac{V_1}{V_2} = -\frac{N_1}{N_2} = -\frac{1}{n}$$

Fig. 1.93

Rule 2: If I_1 and I_2 are both enter or both leave at the dotted terminals, use negative ($-n$). Otherwise, use $+n$.

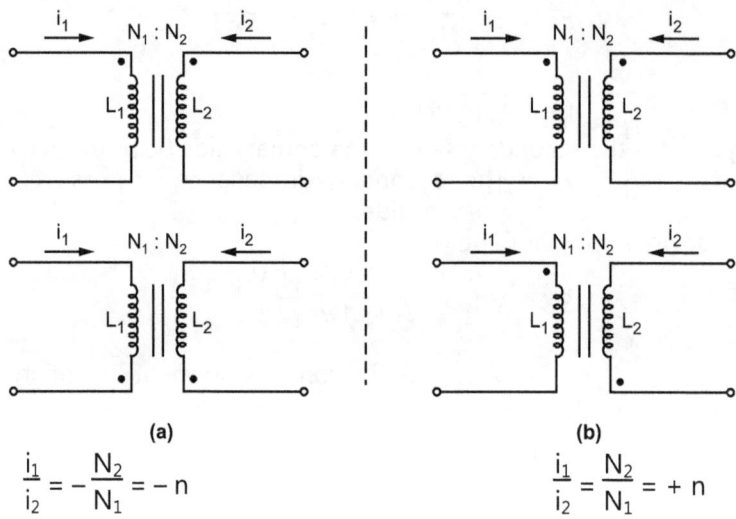

Fig. 1.94

Ex. 1.32:
Rule 1: If V_1 and V_2 are both positive or both negative at the dotted terminals, use positive ($+n$). Otherwise, use $-n$.

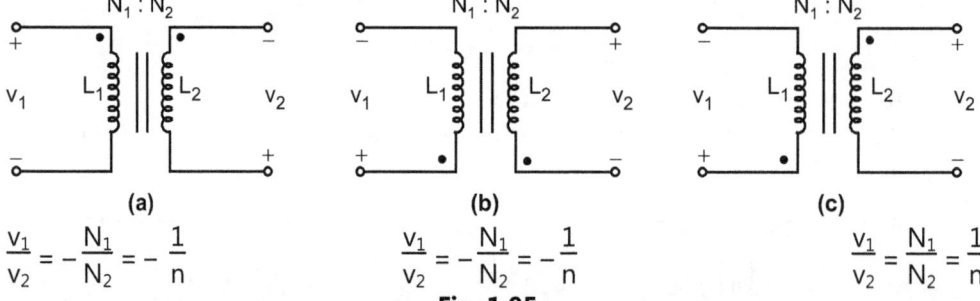

Fig. 1.95

Rule 2: If I_1 and I_2 are both enter or both leave at the dotted terminals, use negative ($-n$). Otherwise, use $+n$.

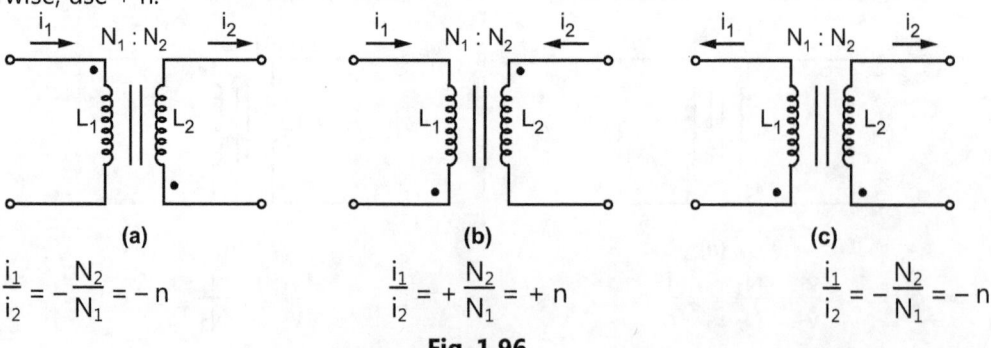

Fig. 1.96

Ex. 1.33: Determine all indicated voltages and currents.

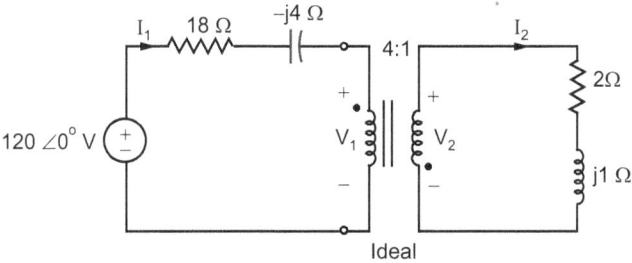

Fig. 1.97

Sol.: The turns ratio is: $n = \dfrac{N_2}{N_1}$

$$n = \dfrac{1}{4} = 0.25$$

Reflect secondary impedance into the primary side, then

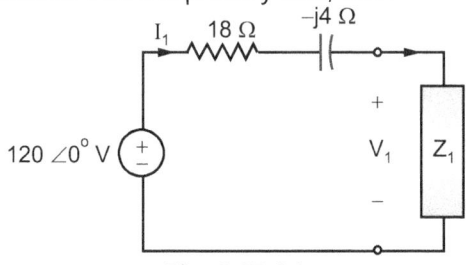

Fig. 1.97 (a)

$$Z_1 = \dfrac{Z_L}{n^2} = \dfrac{2 + j1}{(1/4)^2} = 32 + j15 \; \Omega$$

$$I_1 = \dfrac{V_s}{Z_T} = \dfrac{120 \angle 0°}{50 + j12} = \dfrac{120 \angle 0°}{51.42 \angle 13.5°} = 2.33 \angle -13.5°$$

$$V_1 = Z_1 I_1 = (32 + j16)(2.33 \angle -13.5°) = 83.5 \angle 13.07°$$

Considering voltage properties and current direction:

Rule 1: $\quad V_2 = -nV_1 = -0.25\, V_1 = 20.87 \angle 193.07$

Rule 2: $\quad I_2 = -\dfrac{I_1}{n} = -4I_1 = 9.33 \angle 166.50$

Ex. 1.34: Find the current I_1 and V_0.

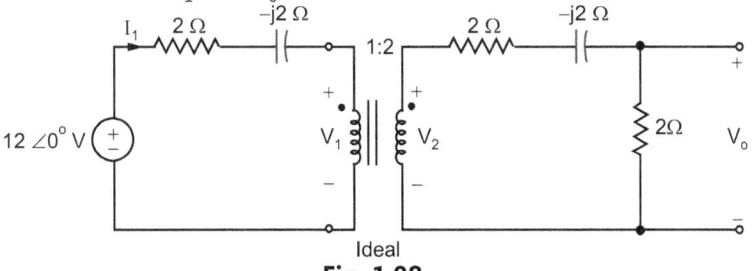

Ideal
Fig. 1.98

Sol.: The turns ratio is: $n = \dfrac{N_2}{N_1} = 2$

Reflect secondary impedance into the primary side, then

$$Z_1 = \dfrac{4-j2}{4} = 1 - j\,0.5\ \Omega$$

$$I_1 = \dfrac{V_s}{Z_T} = \dfrac{120\angle 0°}{3+j2.5} = \dfrac{120\angle 0°}{3.91\angle 39.81°} = 3.07\angle 39.81°\ (A)$$

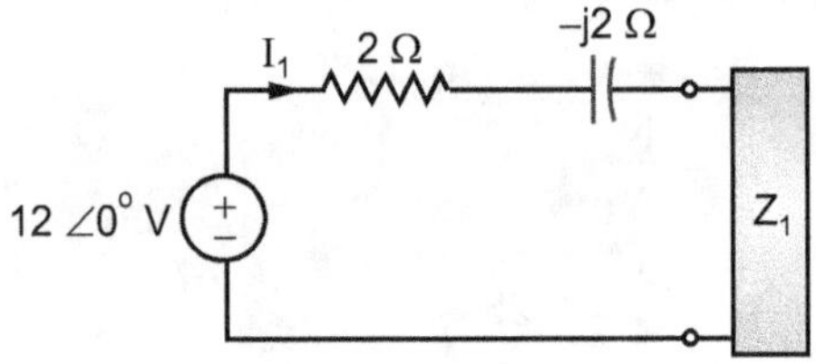

Fig. 1.98 (a)

The current in secondary

Current leaving dot $\quad \dfrac{I_1}{I_2} = \dfrac{N_2}{N_1} = +n \quad \text{or} \quad I_2 = \dfrac{I_1}{2}$

Therefore, $\quad V_0 = 2\Omega \times \dfrac{I_1}{2} = 3.07\angle 39.81°\ (V)$

1.25 DOT CONVENTION

The general from of the voltages in a mutual coupling circuit is:

$$v_1(t) = L_1 \dfrac{di_1}{dt} \pm M \dfrac{di_2}{dt}$$

and $\quad v_2(t) = \pm M \dfrac{di_1}{dt} + L_2 \dfrac{di_2}{dt}$

The correct sign depends on two things:
1. The spatial orientation of the two windings.
2. The reference marks given to the currents and voltages.

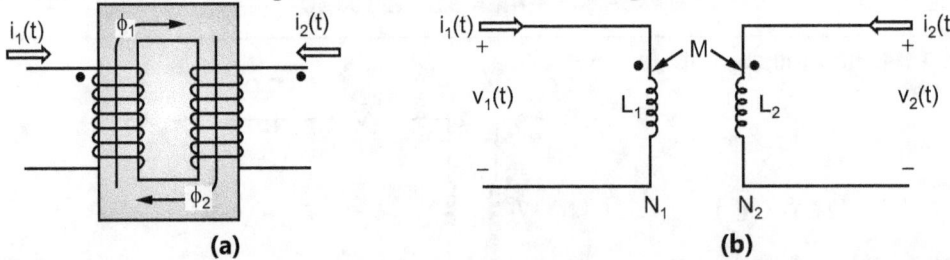

Fig. 1.99

Fig. 1.99 shows the additive coupling. The direction of the flux produced by the current is found using the right-hand rule.

Both currents produce clockwise flux.

$$v_1(t) = L_1 \frac{di_1}{dt} \pm M \frac{di_2}{dt} \qquad \ldots (1.39\,(a))$$

and
$$v_2(t) = M \frac{di_1}{dt} + L_2 \frac{di_2}{dt} \qquad \ldots (1.39\,(b))$$

Fig. 1.100 shows the subtractive coupling. The direction of the flux produced by the current is found using the right-hand rule.

(a) $I_1(t)$ produces clockwise flux and
$I_2(t)$ produces clockwise flux

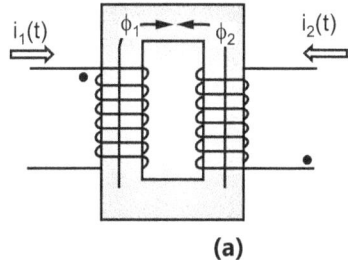
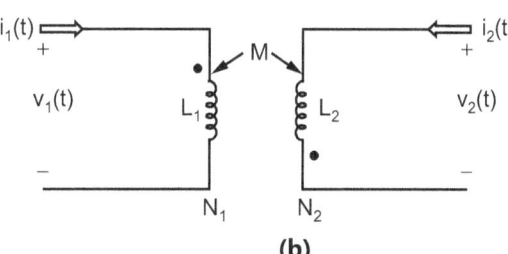

(a) (b)

Fig. 1.100

The four possible current and voltage reference assignments:

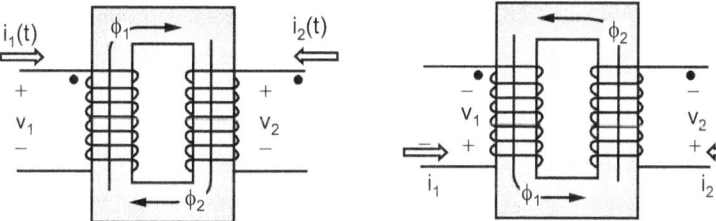

(c) Additive coupling
Fig. 1.100

$$v_1(t) = L_1 \frac{di_1}{dt} + M \frac{di_2}{dt} \qquad \ldots (1.39\,(c))$$

and
$$v_2(t) = M \frac{di_1}{dt} + L_2 \frac{di_2}{dt} \qquad \ldots (1.39\,(d))$$

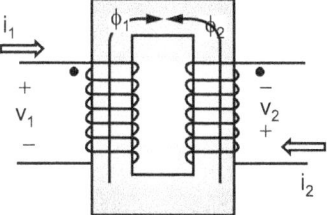
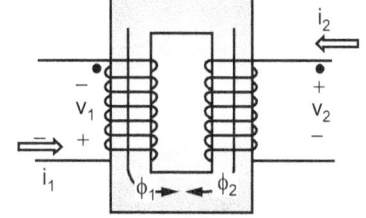

(d) Subtractive coupling
Fig. 1.100

$$v_1(t) = L_1 \frac{di_1}{dt} - M \frac{di_2}{dt} \quad \ldots (1.39\ (e))$$

and
$$v_2(t) = -M \frac{di_1}{dt} + L_2 \frac{di_2}{dt} \quad \ldots (1.39\ (f))$$

From these four possible cases we derive the following rule (using passive sign convention):

Rule 1: Mutual inductance is additive when both current reference directions point toward or both point away from the dotted terminals, otherwise, it is subtractive.

Rule 2: Mutual inductance is additive when the voltage reference marks are both positive or both negative at the dotted terminals, otherwise, it is subtractive.

Note: The polarity of the induced voltage in the second coil depends on the direction of the current in the first coil.

1. If a current enters the dotted terminals of one coil, the reference polarity of the mutual voltage in the second coil is positive at the dotted terminal of the second coil.
2. If a current leaves the dotted terminals of one coil, the reference polarity of the mutual voltage in the second coil is negative at the dotted terminal of the second coil.

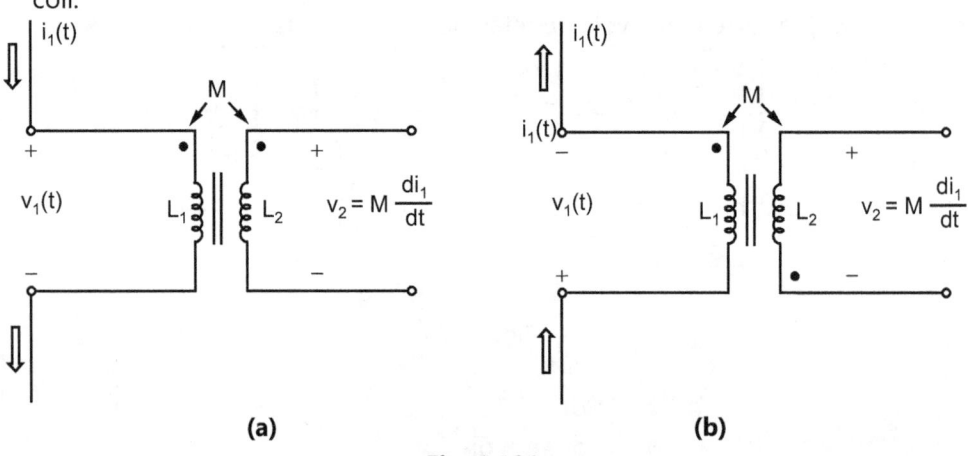

Fig. 1.101

Ex. 1.35: Find the output voltage V_o.

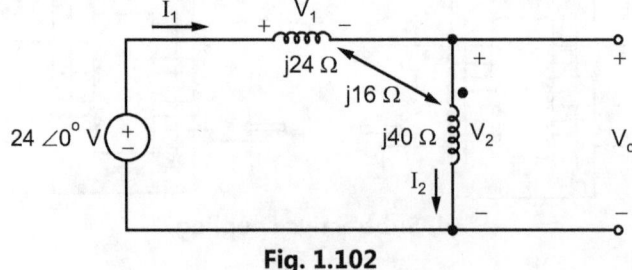

Fig. 1.102

Sol.: Using Rule 1: Mutual inductance is additive when both current reference directions point toward or both point away from the dotted terminals, otherwise, it is subtractive.

$$V_1 = j\omega L_1 I_1 + j\omega M I_2 \quad \text{and} \quad V_2 = j\omega L_2 I_2 + j\omega M I_1$$
$$V_1 = j24 I_1 + j16 I_2 \quad \text{and} \quad V_2 = j40 I_2 + j16 I_1$$
$$I_1 = I_2 = I$$

Using KVL:
$$V_s = V_1 + V_2 = (j24I + j16I) + (j40I + j16I)$$
$$24 = j96I \quad \text{or} \quad I = \frac{24}{j96}$$
$$V_o = V_2 = j56I = j56 \frac{24}{j96} = 14V$$

Ex. 1.36: Find the current I_o.

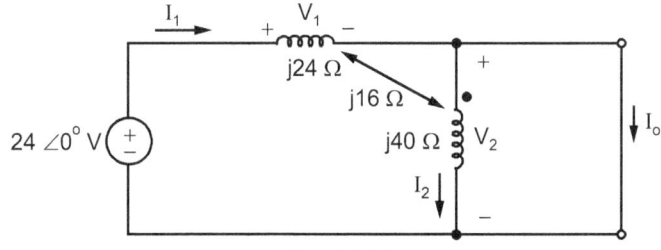

Fig. 1.103

Sol.: Using Rule 1: Mutual inductance is additive

$$V_2 = j40 I_2 + j16 I_1 = 0 \quad \text{or} \quad I_1 = -\frac{40}{16} I_2 = -2.5 I_2$$
$$V_1 = j24 I_1 + j16 I_2 \quad \text{or} \quad V_1 = (j24(-2.5) + j16)I_2 = -j44 I_2$$
$$V_s = V_1 = 24 \quad \text{or} \quad I_2 = \frac{24}{-j44} = j\frac{6}{11}$$

Using KCL:
$$I_o = I_1 - I_2 = (-2.5 I_2 - I_2) = -3.5 I_2$$
$$I_o = -3.5 \frac{j6}{11} = j1.909$$

Ex. 1.37: The coupled inductors can be connected in four different ways. Find he total inductance for each case

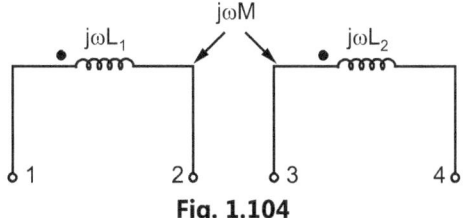

Fig. 1.104

Sol.: Case 1: Mutual inductance is additive when both current reference directions point toward or both point away from the dotted terminals, (same as rule 2). Note that the polarity are selected assuming passive sing convention.

$$V = V_1 + V_2 \quad \text{or} \quad I_1 = I_2 = I$$
$$V_1 = j\omega L_1 I_1 + j\omega M I_2 \quad \text{or} \quad V_2 = j\omega M I_1 + j\omega L_2 I_2$$

Substituting $\quad V = j\omega(L_1 + L_2 + 2M) I = j\omega L_{eq} I$

$$L_{eq} = L_1 + L_2 + 2M$$

Fig. 1.105 (a)

Case 2:

Rule 2: Mutual inductance is additive when the voltage reference marks are both positive or both negative at the dotted terminals, (same as rule 1).

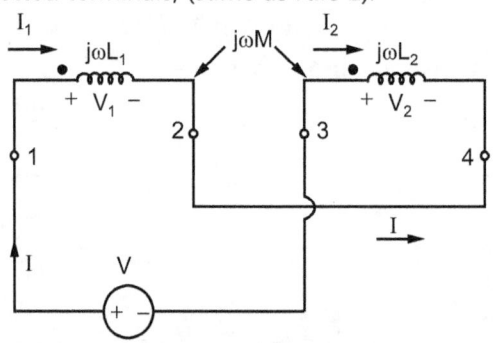

Fig. 1.105 (b)

$$V_1 = j\omega L_1 I_1 + j\omega M I_2$$
$$V_2 = j\omega M I_1 + j\omega L_2 I_2$$
$$I_1 = I \text{ and } I_2 = 1 \quad \text{or} \quad V_1 = j\omega L_1 I - j\omega M$$
$$V_2 = j\omega M I - j\omega L_2 I$$

Using KVL: $\quad V = V_1 - V_2$

Substituting: $\quad V = j\omega(L_1 - 2M + L_2) I$

$$L_{eq} = L_1 - 2M + L_2$$

$L_{eq} \geq 0$ imposes a physical constraint on the value of M

Case 3:

Rule 1 or Rule 2: Mutual inductance is additive

$$V = V_1 = V_2$$
$$V_1 = V = j\omega L_1 I_1 + j\omega M I_2$$
$$V_2 = V = j\omega M I_1 + j\omega L_2 I_2$$

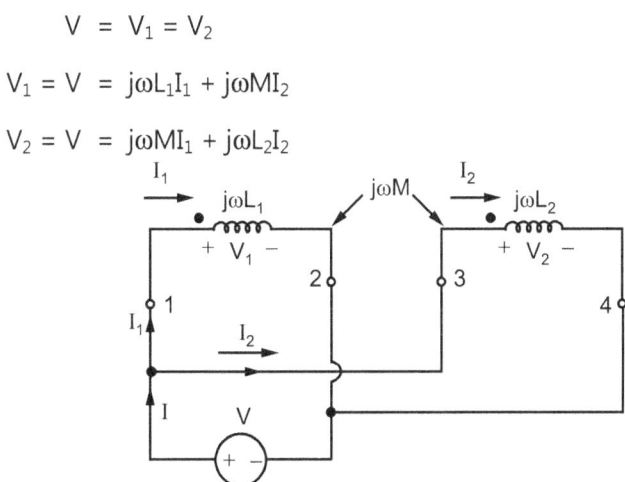

Fig. 1.105 (c)

Solving the two equations:

$$I_1 = \frac{V(L_2 - M)}{j\omega(L_1 L_2 - M^2)} \quad \text{and} \quad I_2 = \frac{V(L_1 - M)}{j\omega(L_1 L_2 - M^2)}$$

or $\quad I = I_1 + I_2 \quad$ or $\quad I_2 = I - I_2$

Subtracting $\quad V = j\omega L_1 I_1 + j\omega M(I - I_1)$

$$V = j\omega M I_1 + j\omega L_2 (I - I_1)$$
$$V = -j\omega(L_1 - M) I_1 + j\omega M I$$
$$V = -j\omega(L_2 - M) I_1 + j\omega L_2 I$$

or $\quad V = j\omega(L_1 - M) I_1 + j\omega M I \quad\quad *(L_2 - M)$
$\quad V = -j\omega(L_2 - M) I_1 + j\omega L_2 I \quad\quad *(L_1 - M)$

Solving for I and using KCL:

$$I = I_1 + I_2$$
$$I = \frac{V(L_1 + L_2 - 2M)}{j\omega(L_1 L_2 - M^2)} = \frac{V}{j\omega L_{eq}}$$

Note: $L_{eq} \geq 0$
$L_1 L_2 - M^2 \geq 0$

or $\quad L_{eq} = \dfrac{L_1 L_2 - M^2}{L_1 + L_2 - 2M}$

Case 4:
Rule 1 or 2: Mutual inductance is additive

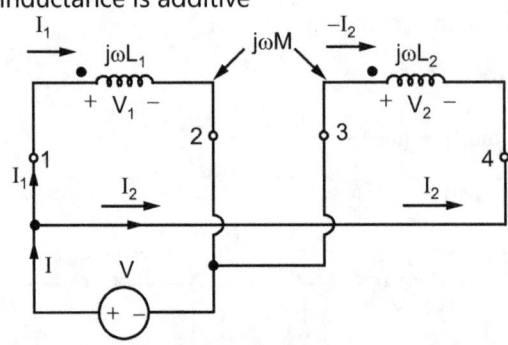

Fig. 1.105 (d)

We have $I = I_1 + I_2$ or $I_2 = I - I_1$
$V = V_1$ and $V = -V_2$

Substituting

$V_1 = V = j\omega L_1 I_1 + j\omega M(-I_2)$
$V_2 = -V = j\omega M I_1 + j\omega L_2(-I_2)$

or $V = j\omega L_1 I_1 - j\omega M I_2$
$-V = j\omega M I_2 - j\omega L_2 I_2$

Solving the two equations:

$$V = j\omega \frac{L_1 L_2 - M^2}{L_1 + L_2 + 2M} I$$

and $$L_{eq} = \frac{L_1 L_2 - M^2}{L_1 + L_2 + 2M}$$

Note: $L_{eq} \geq 0$
$L_1 L_2 - M^2 \geq 0$

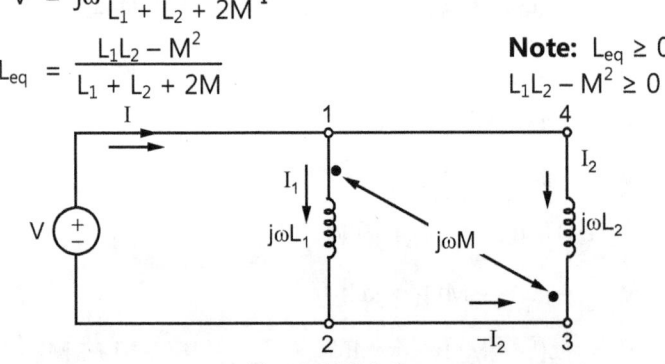

Fig. 1.105 (e)

Ex. 1.38: Find the output voltage V_o.

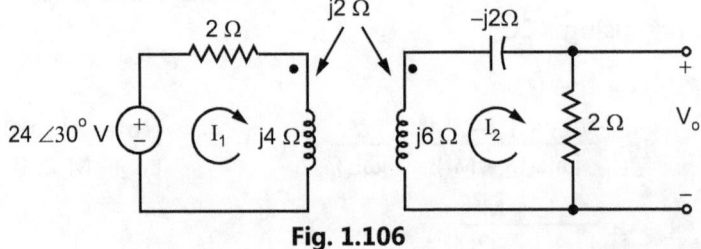

Fig. 1.106

Sol.: Assume passive sign convention and defined the direction of the currents and polarity of the voltages.

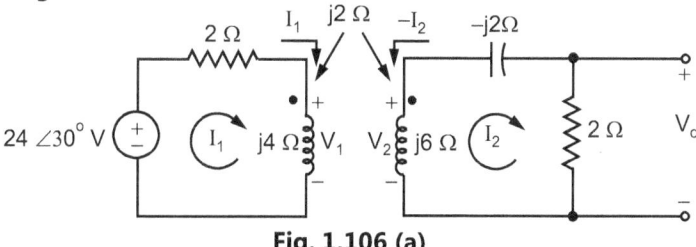

Fig. 1.106 (a)

Use rule 1 or rule 2 to defined the voltage equations:

$$V_1 = j\omega L_1 I_1 + j\omega M I_2 \quad \text{and} \quad V_2 = j\omega L_2 I_2 + j\omega M I_1$$
$$V_1 = j4I_1 + j2(-I_2) \quad \text{and} \quad V_2 = j2I_1 + j6(-I_2)$$

Using KVL, write loop equations in terms of coupled inductor voltages

$$24\angle 30° = 2I_1 + V_1 \quad \text{and} \quad -V_2 - j2I_2 + 2I_2 = 0$$

Substituting $\quad 24\angle 30° = 2I_1 + j4I_1 + j2(-I_2)$

$$0 = -(j2I_1 - j6I_2) - j2I_2 + 2I_2$$

or $\quad 24\angle 30° = (2 + j4)I_1 - j2I_2$

$$0 = -j2I_1 + (2 - j2 + j6) I_2$$

Solving the two equations:

$$I_2 = \frac{j2(24\angle 30°)}{-8 + j16} = 2.68 \angle 3.345°$$

$$V_0 = 2I_2 = 5.37 \angle 3.42°$$

Ex. 1.39: Find I_1, I_2, V_0

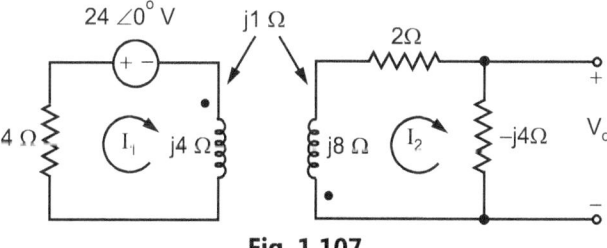

Fig. 1.107

Sol.: Assume passive sign convention and defined the direction of the currents and polarity of the voltages.

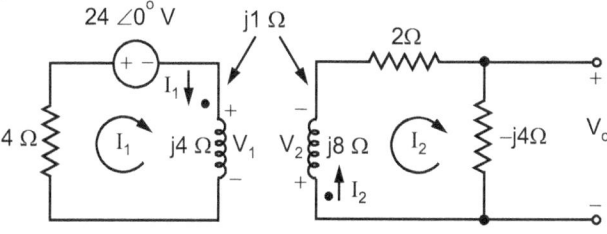

Fig. 1.108

Unit 1 | 1.87

Use rule 1 and rule 2 to defined the voltages equations:

$$V_1 = j\omega L_1 I_1 + j\omega M I_2 \quad \text{and} \quad V_2 = j\omega L_2 I_2 + j\omega M I_1$$
$$V_1 = j4I_1 + jI_2 \quad \text{and} \quad V_2 = jI_1 + j8I_2$$

Using KVL, write loop equations in terms of coupled inductor voltages

$$V_s + V_1 + 4I_1 = 0 \quad \text{and} \quad V_2 + (2-j4)I_2 = 0$$

Substituting
$$(4 + j4) I_1 + jI_2 = -V_s \quad \quad \ldots (a)$$
$$jI_2 + (2 + j4) I_2 = 0 \quad \quad \ldots (b)$$

Solving the two equations:

$$(4 + j4) I_1 + jI_2 = -V_s \quad \times /-j$$
$$\underline{jI_2 + (2 + j4) I_2 = 0}$$
$$(1 + 8(1-j)(1+2j)) I_2 = jV_s$$

$$I_2 = \frac{jV_s}{-6 + 24j} \times \frac{-j}{-j}$$

$$= \frac{24 \angle 0°}{24 + 7j}$$

$$= \frac{24 \angle 0°}{25 \angle 16.26°}$$

$$= 0.96 \angle -16.26° \text{ (A)}$$

Using equation (b) $\quad jI_1 + (2 + j4) I_2 = 0 \quad /\times j$

$$I_1 = j(2 + j4) I_2$$
$$I_1 = 1 \angle 90° \times 4.47 \angle 63.43° \times 0.96 \angle -16.26°$$
$$= 4.29 \angle 137.17° \text{ (A)}$$

$$V_0 = -j4I_2$$
$$= 1 \angle -90° \times 4 \times 0.96 \angle -16.26°$$
$$V_0 = 3.84 \angle -106.26° \text{ (V)}$$

1.26 CONCEPT OF DUALITY AND DUAL NETWORKS

Two networks are said to be the dual network when the mesh equation of one network are the same as the nodal equation of other network. The kirchhoff's voltage low (KVL) and kirchhoff's current law (KCL) are same, word for word, with voltage substituted for current, independent loop for independent node pair, etc. Similarly, two graphs G_1 and G_2 are said to be the dual of each other, if the incidence matrix A of any one of the network is equal to the circuit matrix Q of the other. These duality principle is applicable to plannar network only without matual impedance. Some of the dual relation are given below:

Voltage (V) ↔ Current (I)
Resistance (R) ↔ Conductance (G)
Inductance (L) ↔ Capacitance (C)
Impedance (z) ↔ Admittance (Y)
Voltage source (V_s) ↔ Current source (I_s)
KVL ↔ KCL
Mesh ↔ Node
Mesh current ↔ Node voltage
Mesh Equations ↔ Nodal equations
Tree ↔ Co-tree
Twig ↔ Link
Cut set ↔ Loop
Short circuit ↔ Open circuit
Parallel path ↔ Series path

The steps to be followed for constructing the dual of network

(i) Place a node within each mesh of the given network. These nodes are called as independent nodes which correspond to the independent nodes in the dual network.

(ii) The datum node is placed outside the given network.

(iii) All internal nodes to be connected in the adjacent mesh by dashed lines crossing the common branches. It is convenient to consider the sources as separates branches for the purpose of constructing the dual.

(iv) All internal nodes to be connected to the external node by dashed line corresponding to all external branches. These external branches dual will form the branches connecting independent nodes and the datum node.

(v) The KVL equation of one node is the KCL equation of another node.

(vi) A current equation in clockwised direction in a mesh corresponds to a positive polarity at the dual independent node.

(vii) A rise in voltage in the clockwise direction of mesh current corresponds to a current flowing towards the dual independent node.

Ex. 1.40: Draw the dual of the network as shown in Fig. 1.109 below.

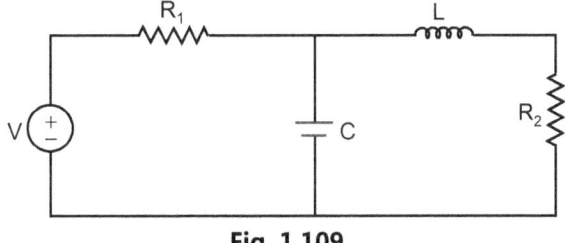

Fig. 1.109

Sol.:
(a) Place a node within each mesh

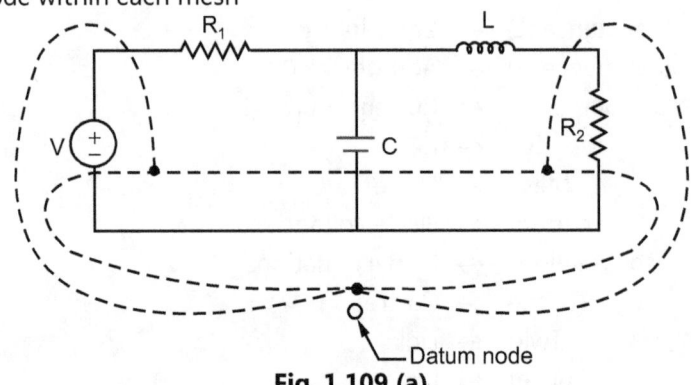

Fig. 1.109 (a)

(b) Place a node outside the node which is called as datum node.
(c) All the internal nodes are connected through dotted line. The element which is dual o+ the common branch which is the inductor here, which will form the branch connecting the corresponding independent node in the dual network.
(d) All the internal nodes are connected to the external node by dashed line crossing all the branches. The dual of these branches will form the branches connecting the independent node and datum node.

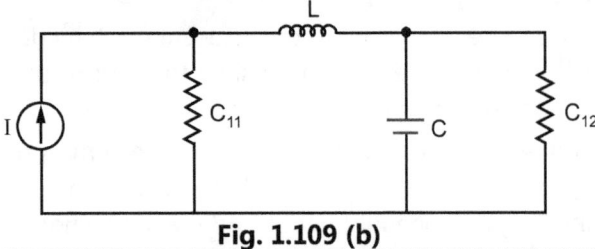

Fig. 1.109 (b)

MULTIPLE CHOICE QUESTIONS (MCQs)

1. The drop across 6 kΩ resistor as shown in figure is equal to

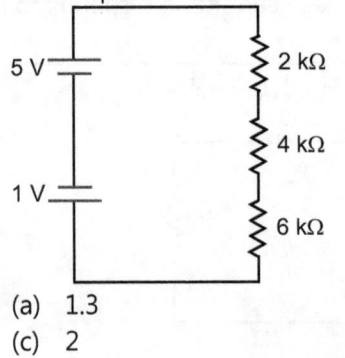

(a) 1.3 (b) 0.67
(c) 2 (d) 4

2. The drop across 4 kΩ resistor as shown in figure is equal to

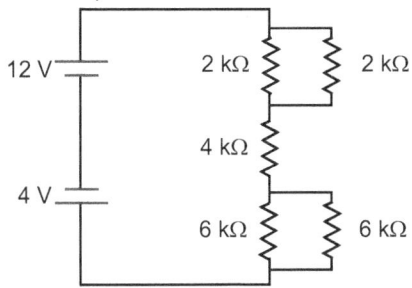

(a) 4
(b) 1.6
(c) 2.67
(d) none of these

3. A voltage divider circuit is shown in figure. The value of R_1 is equal to

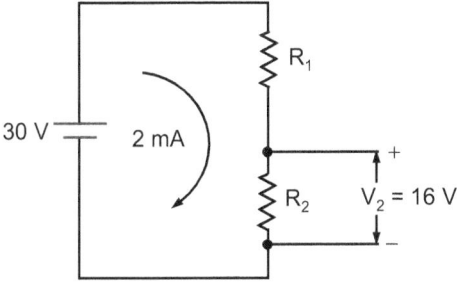

(a) 14 kΩ
(b) 7 kΩ
(c) 28 kΩ
(d) none of these

4. A voltage divider circuit is shown in figure. The voltage drop across R_2 is equal to

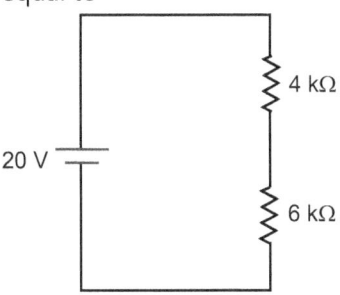

(a) 6 V
(b) 8 V
(c) 12 V
(d) 10 V

5. The power dissipated in R_1 resistor for the circuit shown in figure is equal to

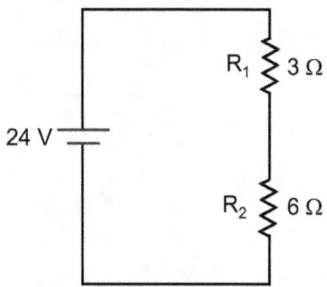

(a) 10.67 W (b) 42.67 W
(c) 85.33 W (d) 21.33 W

6. The power dissipated in R_3 resistor for the circuit shown in figure is equal to

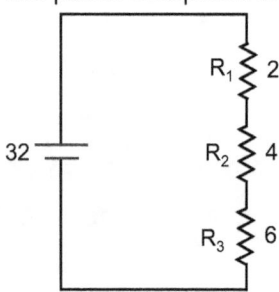

(a) 42.67 W (b) 64 W
(c) 128 W   (d) none of these

7. The total power dissipated in circuit shown in figure is equal to

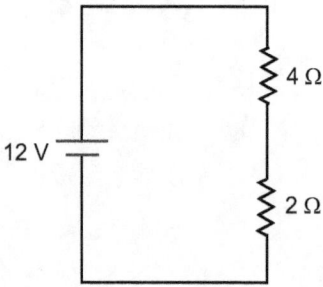

(a) 9 W   (b) 24 W
(c) 17 W (d) none of these

8. The total power dissipated in circuit shown in figure is equal to

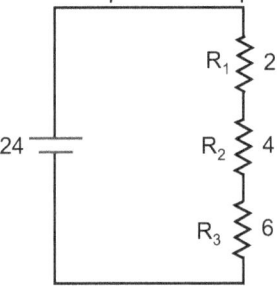

(a) 41.5 W (b) 24 W
(c) 40 W (d) none of these

9. A circuit shown in figure, the voltage V_2 is equal to

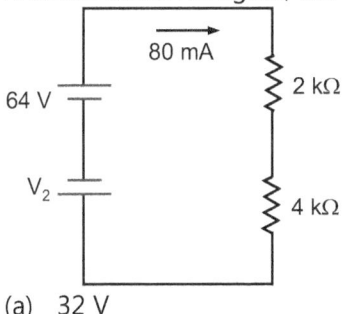

(a) 32 V (b) 6 V
(c) 16 V (d) 48 V

10. A circuit shown in figure. The voltage V_2 is equal to

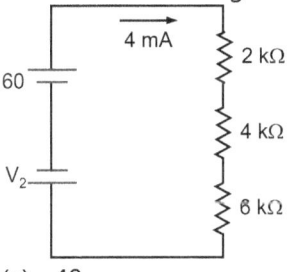

(a) 48 (b) 12
(c) 36 (d) none of these

11. A circuit shown in figure. The current flowing through the R_2 resistor is equal to

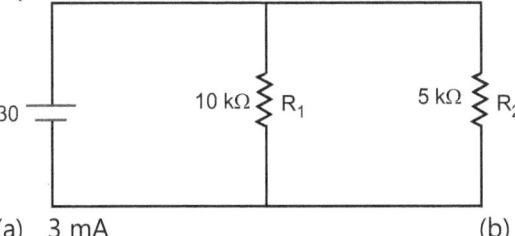

(a) 3 mA (b) 6 mA
(c) 2 mA (d) 30 mA

12. A circuit shown in figure. The current flowing through the R_2 resistor is equal to

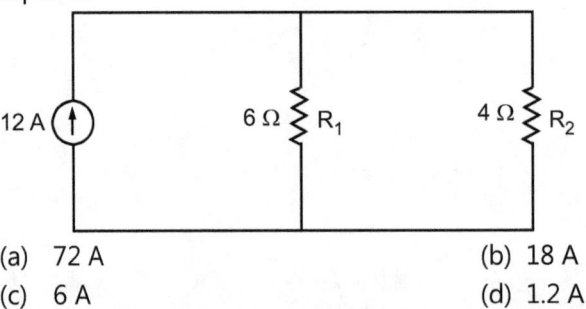

(a) 72 A
(b) 18 A
(c) 6 A
(d) 1.2 A

13. The current flowing through the 10Ω resistor for the circuit shown in figure is equal to

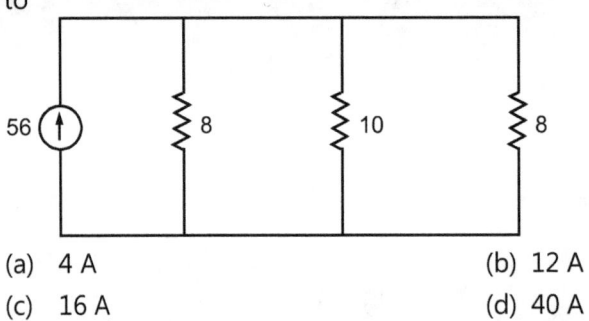

(a) 4 A
(b) 12 A
(c) 16 A
(d) 40 A

14. The current drawn from the supply in the circuit shown in figure is equal to

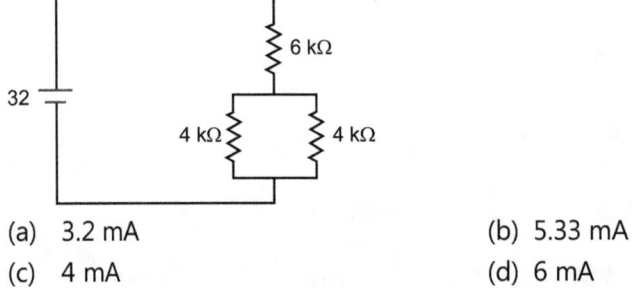

(a) 3.2 mA
(b) 5.33 mA
(c) 4 mA
(d) 6 mA

15. In a circuit shown in figure, the current flowing through the 8Ω resistor is equal to

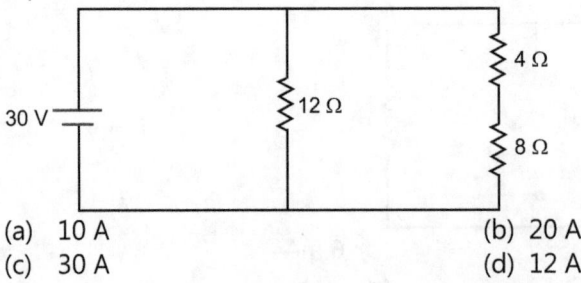

(a) 10 A
(b) 20 A
(c) 30 A
(d) 12 A

16. In a circuit shown in figure, the current flowing through the 6Ω resistor is equal to

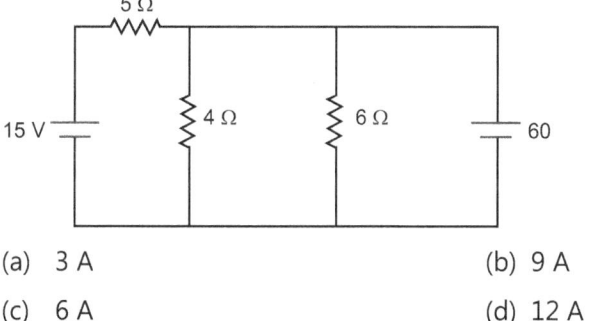

   (a) 3 A (b) 9 A
   (c) 6 A (d) 12 A

17. Alternating current flow in an inductor depends on the
   (a) applied voltage and current
   (b) applied voltage and inductive reactance of the inductor
   (c) applied current and inductive reactance of the inductor
   (d) none of these

18. Alternating current flow in a capacitor depends on the
   (a) supply voltage and supply current
   (b) supply current and capacitive reactance
   (c) supply voltage and capacitive reactance
   (d) none of these

19. When an alternating voltage is applied to a pure inductance, the current flows through the inductance
   (a) leads the terminal voltage by 45°
   (b) leads the terminal voltage by 90°
   (c) lags the terminal voltage by 45°
   (d) lags the terminal voltage by 90°

20. When an alternating voltage is applied to a pure capacitor, the alternating current through a capacitor
   (a) lags the capacitor terminal voltage by 45°
   (b) lags the capacitor terminal voltage by 90°
   (c) leads the capacitor terminal voltage by 45°
   (d) leads the capacitor terminal voltage by 90°

21. The current in a purely inductive circuit
    (a) leads the voltage by $\frac{\pi}{4}$ radians
    (b) leads the voltage by $\frac{\pi}{2}$ radians
    (c) lags the voltage by $\frac{\pi}{4}$ radians
    (b) lags the voltage by $\frac{\pi}{2}$ radians

22. The current in a purely capacitive circuit
    (a) leads the voltage by $\frac{\pi}{4}$ radians
    (b) leads the voltage by $\frac{\pi}{2}$ radians
    (c) lags the voltage by $\frac{\pi}{4}$ radians
    (b) lags the voltage by $\frac{\pi}{2}$ radians

23. A series RL circuit shown in figure, the voltage across the inductor is equal to

    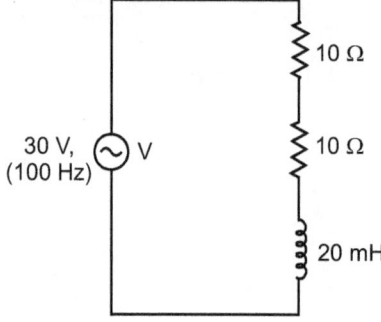

    (a) 15.95 V
    (b) 17.2 V
    (c) 18.3 V
    (d) 19.6 V

24. A series RL circuit shown in figure. An inductor having an internal resistance of 20 Ω, the value of voltage across an inductor is equal to

    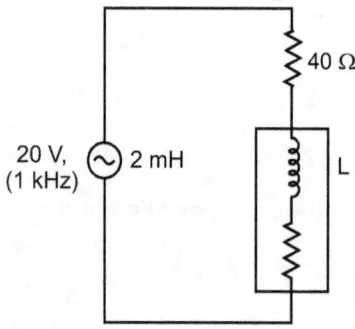

    (a) 41.84 mV
    (b) 62.83 mV
    (c) 62.83 V
    (d) 41.84 V

25. A series RC circuit shown in figure, the voltage across capacitor is equal to

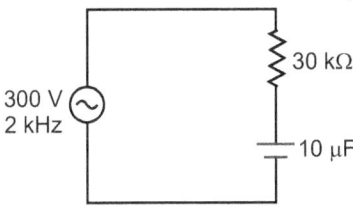

(a) 50.23 (b) 75.37
(c) 79.57 mV (d) none of these

26. The current drawn in a circuit is shown in figure is equal to

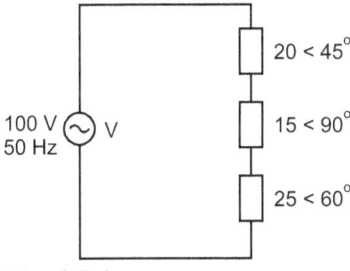

(a) 1.5 A (b) 2.5 A
(c) 2.67 A (d) 1.67 A

27. The current flowing in the circuit shown in figure is equal to

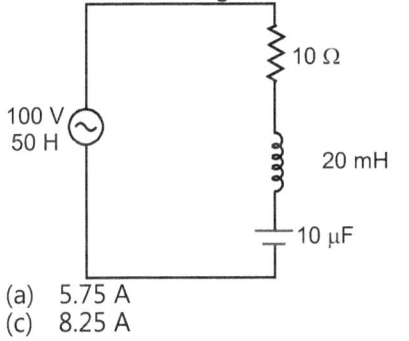

(a) 5.75 A (b) 6.75 A
(c) 8.25 A (d) 10 A

28. The current flowing in the circuit shown in figure is equal to

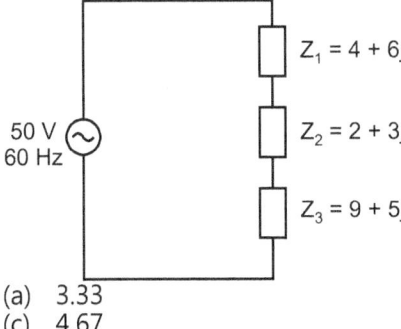

(a) 3.33 (b) 3.44
(c) 4.67 (d) 5.67

29. A circuit shown in figure, the current flowing through the Z_2 impedance is equal to

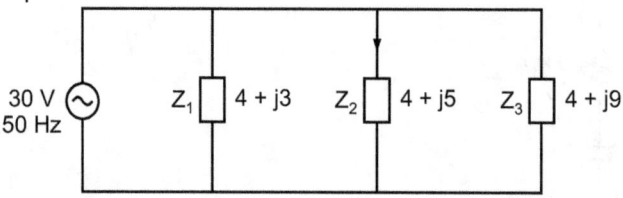

(a) 2.17 A
(b) 3.43 A
(c) 4.65 A
(d) 5.3 A

30. A circuit shown in figure, the current flowing through the Z_2 impedance is equal to

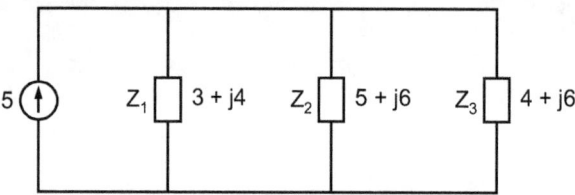

(a) 2.67 A
(b) 1.25 A
(c) 1.37 A
(d) 4.5 A

31. The circuit shown in figure, the current I flowing through the circuit is equal to

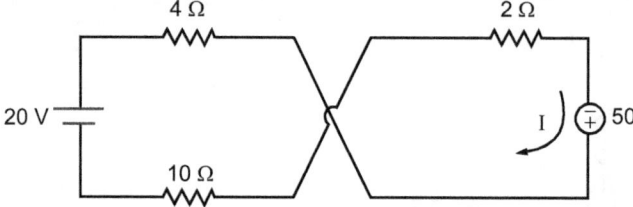

(a) – 1.875 A
(b) – 4.375 A
(c) 1.875 A
(d) 4.375 A

32. A circuit shown in figure. The current flowing through the resistor R_1 is equal to

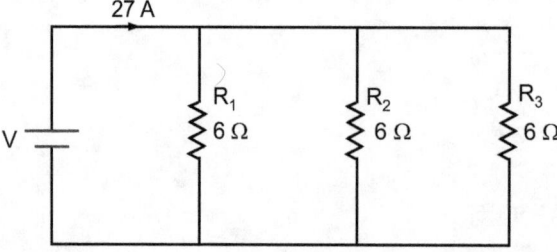

(a) 6 A
(b) 3 A
(c) 9 A
(d) none of these

33. For the given network, the current flowing through the 20Ω resistor is equal to

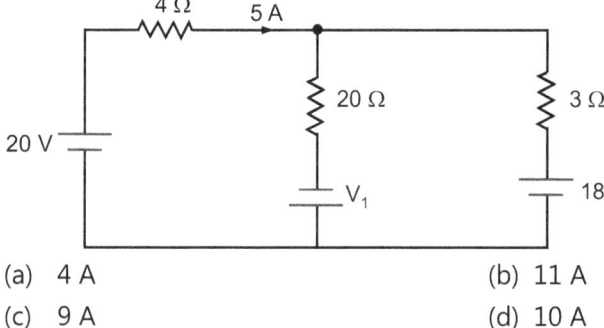

(a) 4 A (b) 11 A
(c) 9 A (d) 10 A

34. For the given network, shown in figure, the voltage across 5Ω resistor is equal to

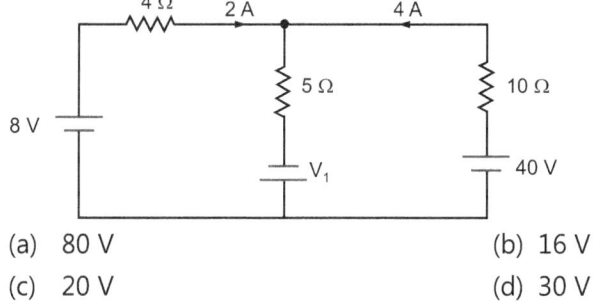

(a) 80 V (b) 16 V
(c) 20 V (d) 30 V

35. For the circuit shown in figure, the voltage across terminal A and B is equal to

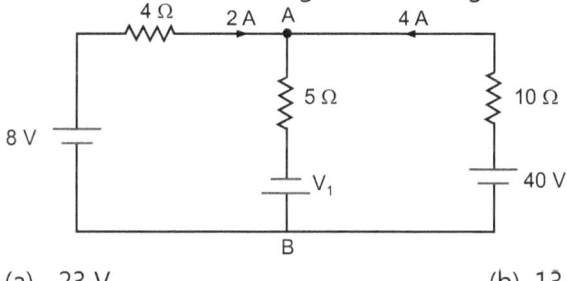

(a) 23 V (b) 13 V
(c) 11 V (d) 1 V

36. The voltage drop across of 4 Ω resistor for the circuit shown in figure is equal to

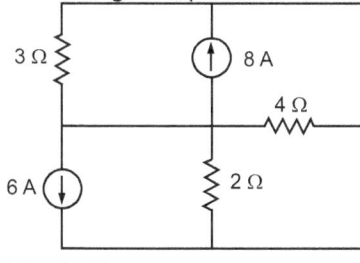

(a) 1.56 (b) 1.85
(c) 12.93 (d) none of these

37. In the circuit shown in figure, the voltage drop across the point A and B is equal to

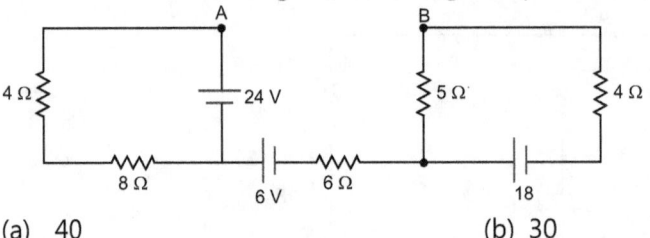

(a) 40 (b) 30
(c) 20 (d) none of these

38. In the circuit shown in figure, the voltage drop across the point A and B is equal to

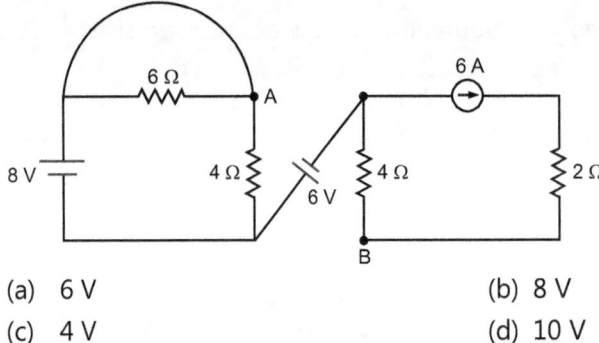

(a) 6 V (b) 8 V
(c) 4 V (d) 10 V

39. For the circuit shown in figure, the voltage across the terminal AB is equal to

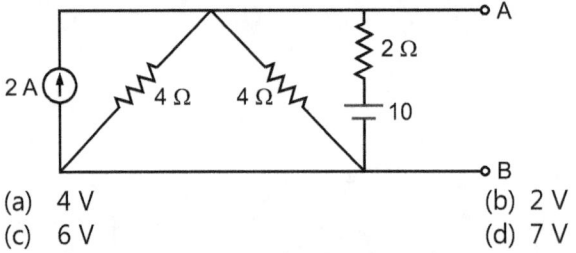

(a) 4 V (b) 2 V
(c) 6 V (d) 7 V

40. For the circuit shown in figure, the voltage across the terminal AB is equal to

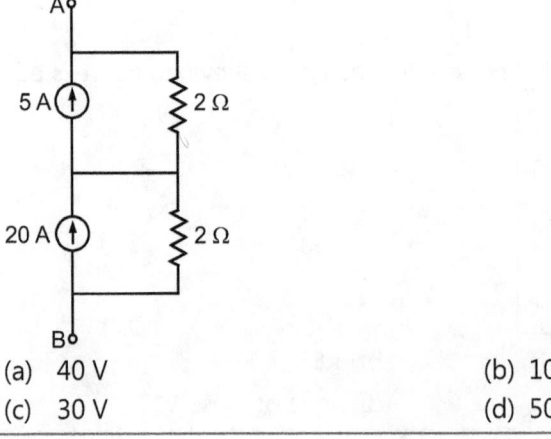

(a) 40 V (b) 10 V
(c) 30 V (d) 50 V

41. A network shown in figure, the voltage across terminal AB is equal to

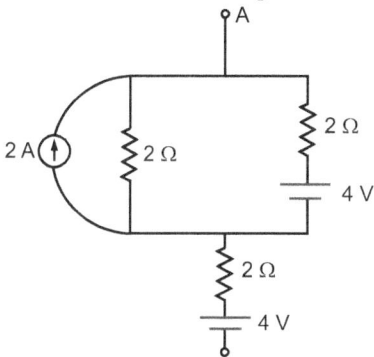

(a) 8 V
(b) 4 V
(c) 9 V
(d) 1 V

42. A network shown in figure, the voltage across terminal AB is equal to

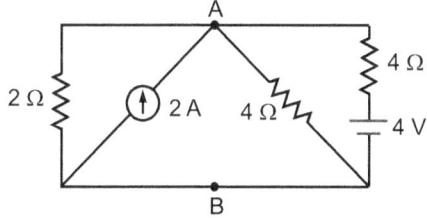

(a) 1 V
(b) 0 V
(c) 4 V
(d) 8 V

43. A network is shown in figure, the current flowing through the 4Ω resistor is equal to

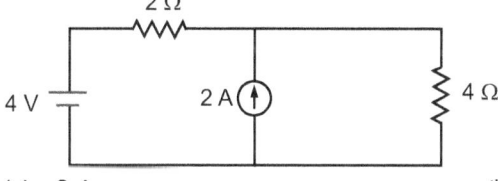

(a) 2 A
(b) 4 A
(c) 8 A
(d) 1.33 A

44. A network shown in figure the voltage V across resistor 5Ω is equal to

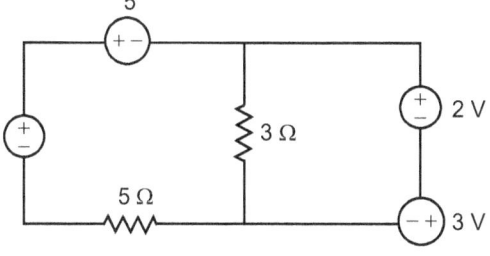

(a) 10 V
(b) 6 V
(c) 1 V
(d) 4 V

45. A network shown in figure, the voltage across the terminal AB is equal to

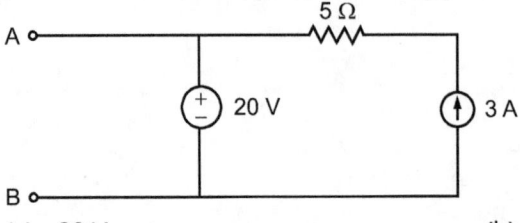

(a) 20 V
(b) 5 V
(c) 15 V
(d) none of the above

46. A network is shown in figure the value of the unknown voltage source V_A is equal to

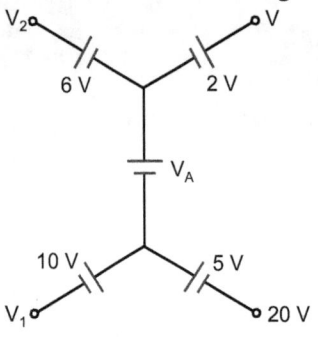

(a) 16 V
(b) 27 V
(c) 9 V
(d) none of the above

47. A network shown in figure, an equivalent resistance of the network is equal to

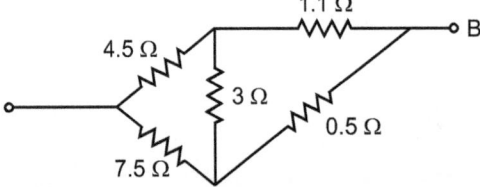

(a) 2.25 Ω
(b) 5.6 Ω
(b) 3.25 Ω
(d) 4.25 Ω

48. A network shown in figure. The total resistance across terminal AB is equal to

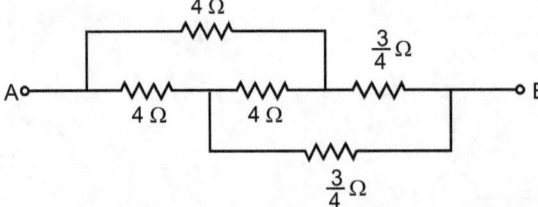

(a) 2.083 Ω
(b) 1.4 Ω
(c) 0.75 Ω
(d) 2.37 Ω

49. A network shown in figure, an equivalent resistance across terminal AB is equal to

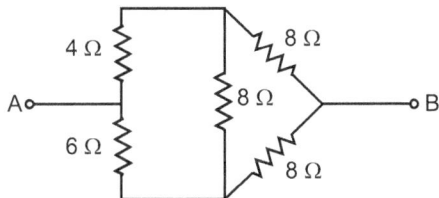

(a) 17.34 Ω (b) 11.64 Ω
(c) 12.48 Ω (d) 15.67 Ω

50. The current equation for supermesh for a given network shown in figure is equal to

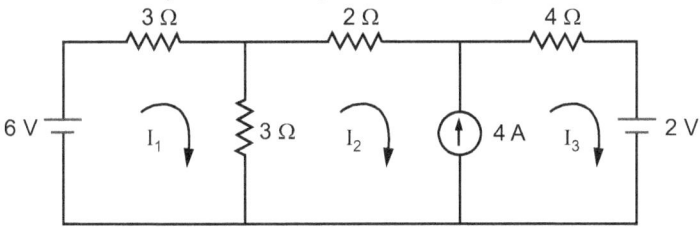

(a) $I_2 - I_3 = 4$ (b) $I_3 - I_2 = 4$
(c) $I_2 + I_3 = 4$ (d) none of these

51. A network is shown in figure. The supermesh equation for a given network is equal to

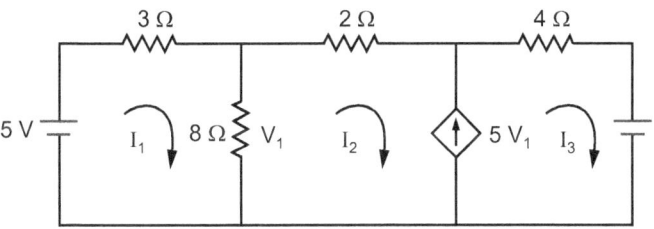

(a) $I_3 - I_2 = 5V_1$ (b) $I_2 - I_3 - 5V_1$
(c) $I_3 + I_2 = 5V_1$ (d) none of these

52. For the network shown in figure, the current flowing through the 10 Ω resistor is equal to

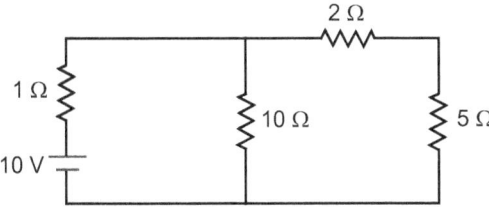

(a) 0.4 A (b) 0.6 A
(c) 0.8 A (d) 1 A

53. For the network shown in figure, the current flowing through the 10Ω resistor is equal to

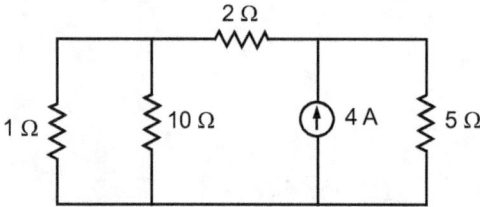

(a) 0.23 A (b) 0.37 A
(c) 0.67 A (d) none of these

54. A network shown in figure, the current flowing the 6Ω resistor is equal to

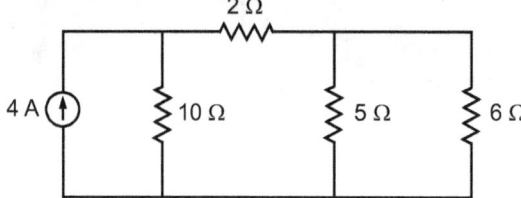

(a) 0.5 A (b) 0.67 A
(c) 1.23 A (d) 2.5 A

55. A network shown in figure, the current passing through 6Ω resistor is equal to

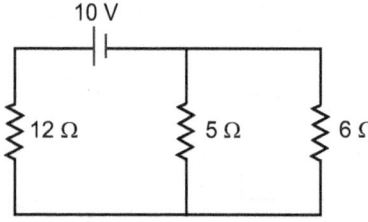

(a) − 0.61 A (b) − 0.31 A
(c) 0.5 A (d) 0.87 A

56. A network shown in figure, the current passing through the 6Ω resistor is equal to

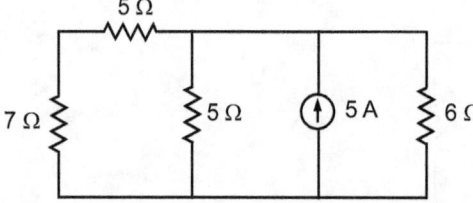

(a) 1.5 A (b) 1.85 A
(c) 2 A (d) 2.35 A

57. A network is shown in figure, the voltage across the terminal AB is equal to

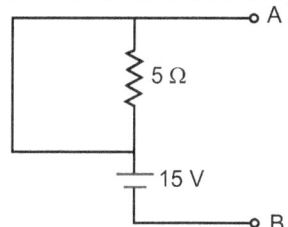

(a) 3 V (b) 10 V
(c) 15 V (d) none of these

58. The network shown in figure, the current I flowing through the 6Ω resistor is equal to

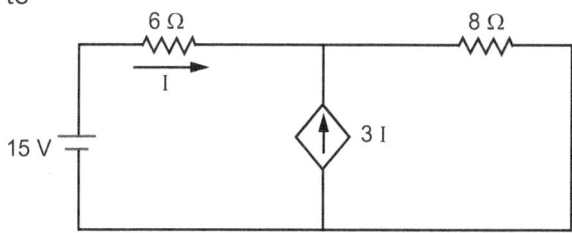

(a) 0.2 A (b) 0.3 A
(c) 0.4 A (d) none of these

59. A network shown in figure, the current I flowing through the 5Ω resistor is equal to

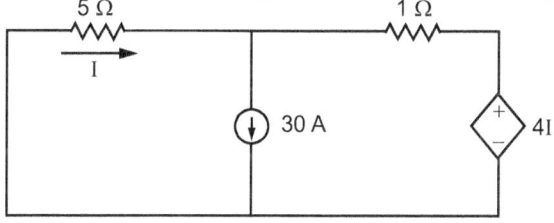

(a) 6 A (b) 30 A
(c) 3 A (d) none of these

60. A network is shown in figure, the current I flowing through the 10Ω resistor is equal to

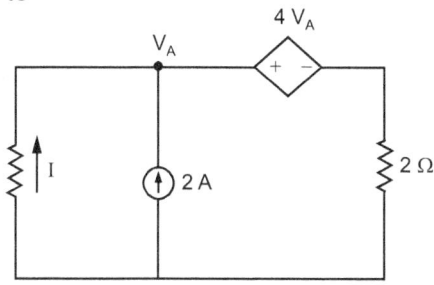

(a) 0.14 (b) 0.52
(c) 0.38 (d) none of these

61. A network shown in figure, he current I passing through the 3Ω resistor is equal to

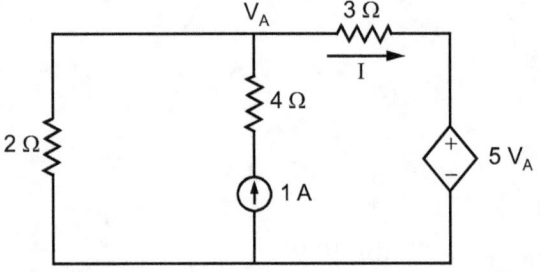

(a) 3.4
(b) 1.6
(c) 1 A
(d) none of these

62. For a network shown in figure, the voltage across terminal AB is equal to

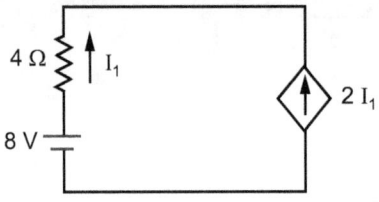

(a) 2 V
(b) 4 V
(c) 6 V
(d) 8 V

63. A network shown in figure, the current I passing through the 6Ω resistor is equal to

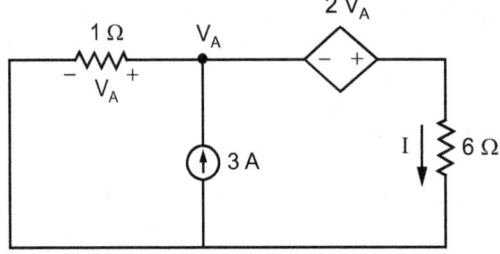

(a) 3 A
(b) 1.5 A
(c) 1 A
(d) none of these

64. A network is shown in figure, the value of current I_2 in the network is equal to

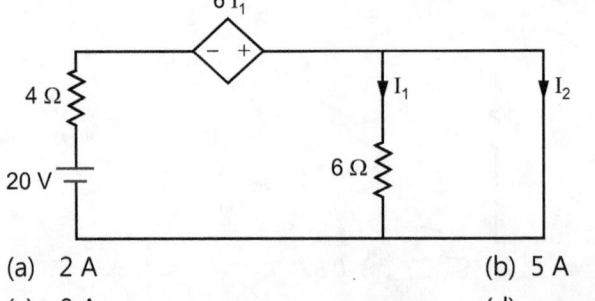

(a) 2 A
(b) 5 A
(c) 0 A
(d) none of these

65. For a network shown in figure, the current I_1 flowing through the branch is equal to

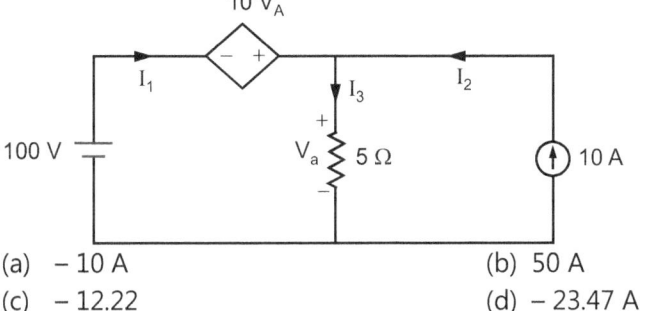

(a) −10 A
(b) 50 A
(c) −12.22
(d) −23.47 A

66. For a network shown in figure, the value of the current I_2 flowing through the network is equal to

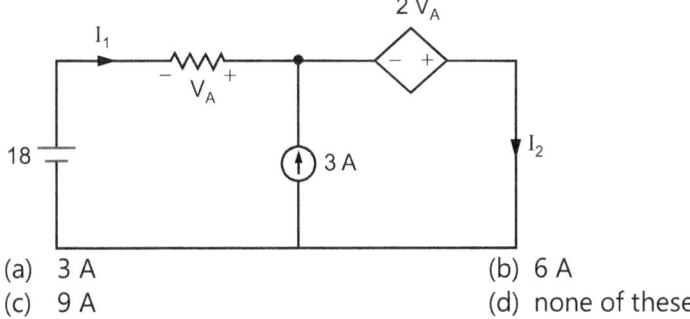

(a) 3 A
(b) 6 A
(c) 9 A
(d) none of these

67. A network is shown in figure, the value of current I_2 in the network is equal to

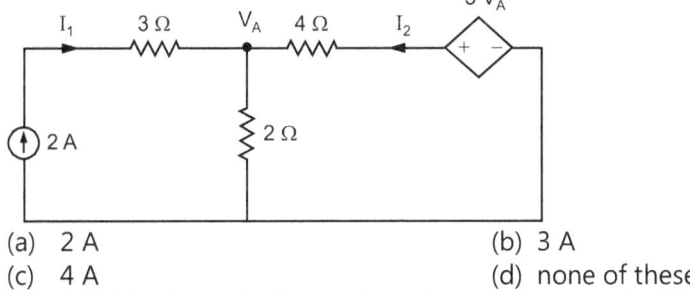

(a) 2 A
(b) 3 A
(c) 4 A
(d) none of these

68. A network is shown in figure, the voltage across terminal AB is equal to

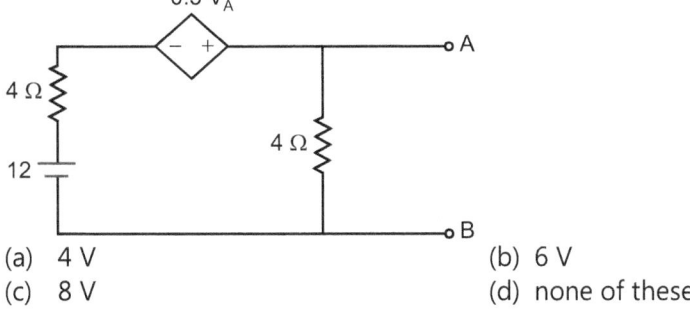

(a) 4 V
(b) 6 V
(c) 8 V
(d) none of these

69. A network is shown in figure, the voltage across terminals AB is equal to

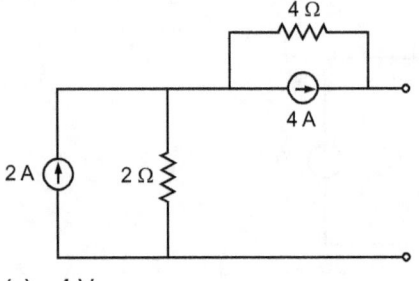

(a) 4 V (b) 16 V
(c) 20 V (d) 12 V

70. A network is shown in figure, the voltage across the terminals AB is equal to

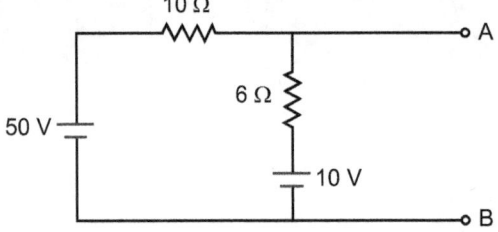

(a) 10 V (b) 50 V
(c) 25 V (d) none of these

71. A network is shown in figure, the current I flowing through the network is equal to

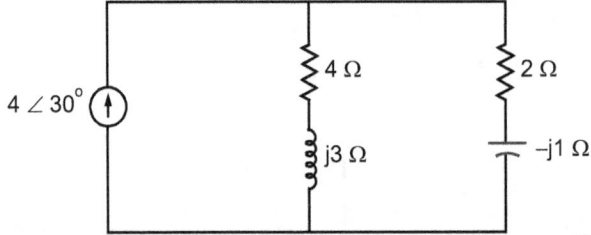

(a) 1.414 < 30° (b) 1.414 < −30°
(c) 1.414 < 15° (d) 1.414 < 15°

72. A circuit is shown in figure, the source voltage V_s is equal to

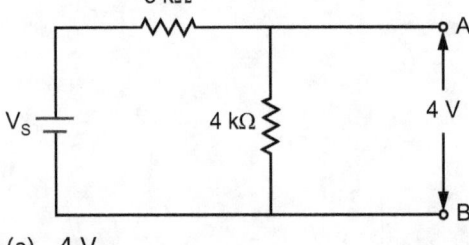

(a) 4 V (b) 6 V
(c) 8 V (d) none of these

73. A circuit is shown in figure, the source current I_s is equal to

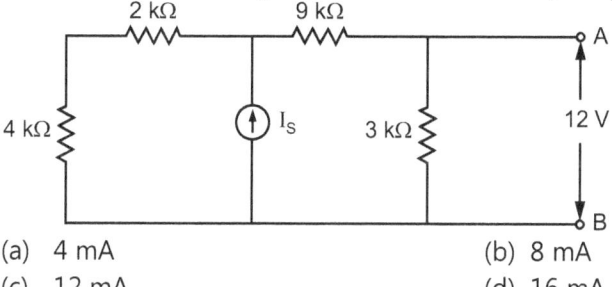

(a) 4 mA (b) 8 mA
(c) 12 mA (d) 16 mA

74. A circuit is shown in figure, the voltage across terminal AB is equal to

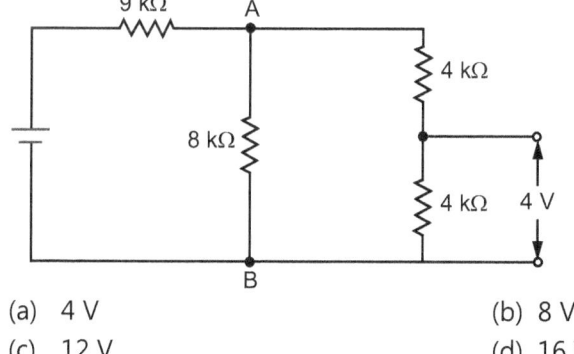

(a) 4 V (b) 8 V
(c) 12 V (d) 16 V

75. A circuit is shown in figure, the current I_A passing through 10 kΩ is equal to

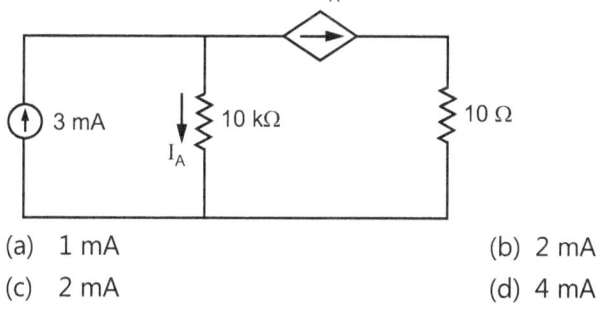

(a) 1 mA (b) 2 mA
(c) 2 mA (d) 4 mA

76. A network is shown in figure, the current I passing through the 3 kΩ is equal to

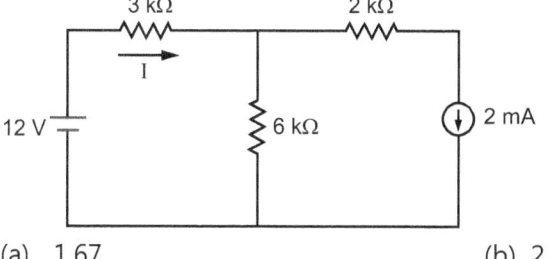

(a) 1.67 (b) 2.67
(c) 3.67 (d) none of these

77. A circuit is shown in figure, the current I passing through the resistor is equal to

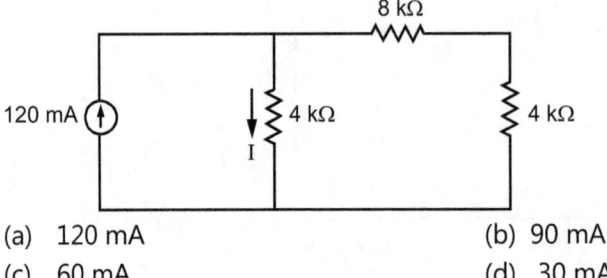

(a) 120 mA
(b) 90 mA
(c) 60 mA
(d) 30 mA

78. A circuit is shown in figure, the current I passing through the 4 kΩ resistive is equal to

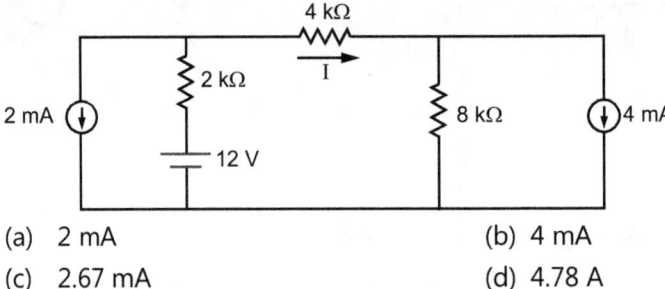

(a) 2 mA
(b) 4 mA
(c) 2.67 mA
(d) 4.78 A

79. A circuit is shown in figure, the current I flowing through the circuit is equal to

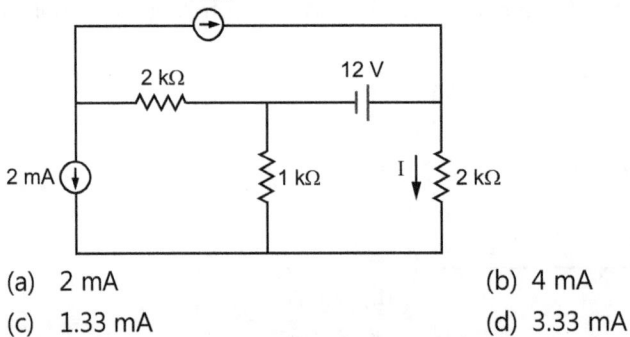

(a) 2 mA
(b) 4 mA
(c) 1.33 mA
(d) 3.33 mA

80. A circuit is shown in figure, the voltage across AB terminal is equal to

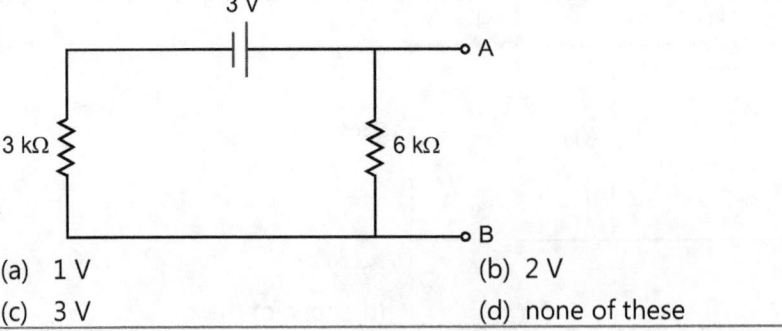

(a) 1 V
(b) 2 V
(c) 3 V
(d) none of these

81. A circuit is shown in figure, the voltage across AB terminal is equal to

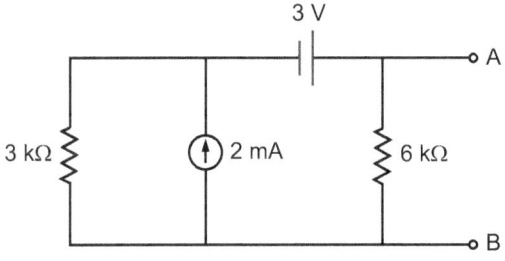

(a) 1 V (b) 3 V
(c) 6 V (d) none of these

82. A circuit is shown in figure, the voltage across AB terminal is equal to

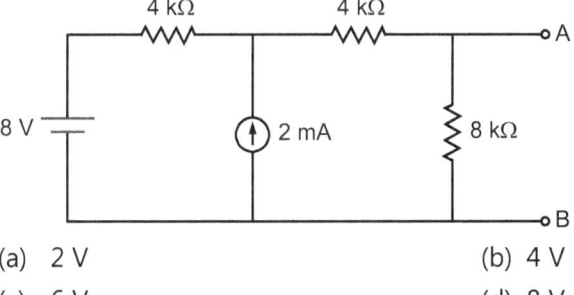

(a) 2 V (b) 4 V
(c) 6 V (d) 8 V

83. A circuit is shown in figure, the voltage across AB terminal is equal to

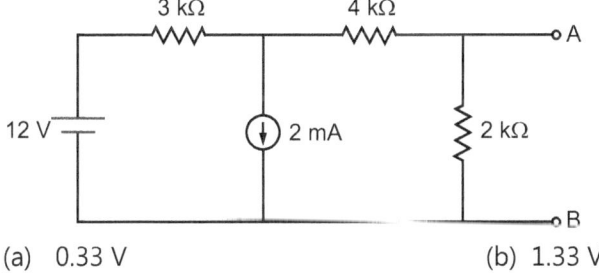

(a) 0.33 V (b) 1.33 V
(c) 2.33 V (d) None of these

84. A circuit is shown in figure, the current I passing through the circuit is equal to

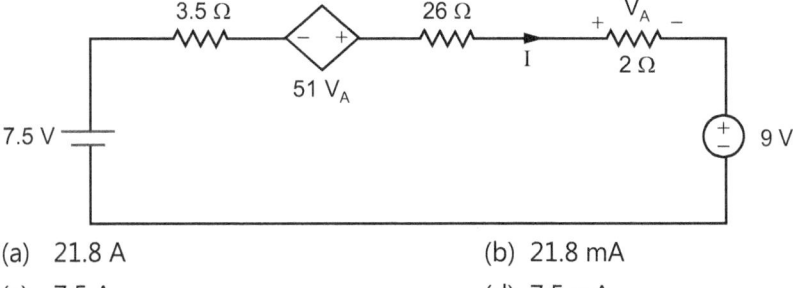

(a) 21.8 A (b) 21.8 mA
(c) 7.5 A   (d) 7.5 mA

85. A circuit is shown in figure, the current I passing through 4 Ω resistor is equal to

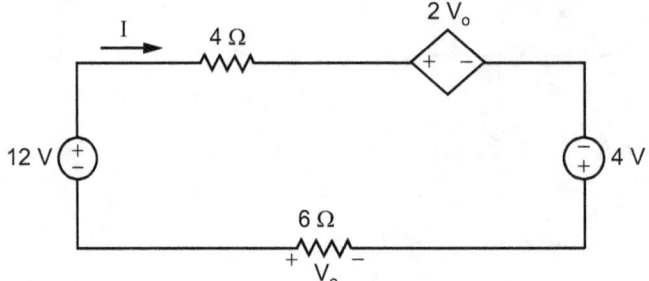

   (a) 8 A
   (b) – 8 A
   (c) 16 A
   (d) none of these

86. The total energy supplied to the inductor
   (a) When the current is decreased from 0 to I
   (b) When the current is increased from 0 to I
   (c) When the voltage is increased from 0 to V
   (d) When the voltage is decreased from 0 to V.

87. The total energy supplied to the capacitor
   (a) When the potential difference is decreased from 0 to V
   (b) When the potential difference is decreased from 0 to V
   (c) When the current is increased from 0 to I.
   (d) When the current is decreased from 0 to I.

88. The value of the voltage across independent voltage source is
   (a) independent of the value or direction of the current flows through it.
   (b) dependent of the value or direction of the current flow.
   (c) dependent on the value
   (d) independent on the direction of current flow.

89. The value of direction of the independent current source is
   (a) independent of the value or direction of the voltage across the terminals of the source.
   (b) dependent of the value of the voltage across the terminals of the source.
   (c) independent of the value of the voltage across the terminals of the source.
   (d) independent on the value across the terminals of the source.

90. In a voltage controlled voltage source, the voltage depends on
   (a) the voltage of the current gain.
   (b) the current and the voltage gain.
   (c) the voltage and the voltage gain
   (d) the current and the current gain

91. In a voltage controlled current source, the current depends on
    (a) control current and the transconductance
    (b) control voltage and the transconductance.
    (c) control voltage and the transresistance
    (d) control current and the transresistance
92. In a current controlled voltage source, the voltage depends on the
    (a) control current and the transconductance
    (b) control voltage and the transconductance
    (c) control current and the transresistance
    (d) control voltage and the transresistance.
93. In a current controlled current source, the current source, the current depends on
    (a) the control current and voltage gain
    (b) the control voltage and voltage gain
    (c) the control voltage and current gain
    (d) the control current and current gain
94. The kirchoff's current law states that
    (a) the algebraic sum of currents meeting at a junction is not zero
    (b) the algebraic sum of currents meeting at a junction is not equal
    (c) the algebraic sum of current meeting at a junction is zero.
    (d) the algebraic sum of current meeting at a junction is equal.
95. Kirchoff's voltage law states that
    (a) the algebraic sum of all the voltages in any closed loop is equal.
    (b) the algebraic sum of all the voltages in any closed loop is not equal.
    (c) the algebraic sum of all the voltages in any closed loop is zero.
    (d) The algebraic sum of all the voltages in any closed loop is not zero.
96. A rise in potential can be assumed to ...... while fall in potential can be considered ......
    (a) negative, positive   (b) negative, negative
    (c) positive, positive   (d) positive negative
97. Source shifting technique is used when there is no resistor in ...... with a voltage source or a resistor in ...... with a current source
    (a) series, series   (b) parallel, series
    (c) series, parallel   (d) parallel, parallel
98. Mesh analysis is defined as a loop which
    (a) does not contain loops within it   (b) contain loop with it
    (c) plane surface with crossover   (d) none of above

99. Mesh analysis is applicable to
    (a) planar network
    (b) non planar network
    (c) both
    (d) none of these
100. Meshesh that share a current source with other meshes form
    (a) super node
    (b) super mesh
    (c) super current
    (d) super voltage
101. Nodal analysis is based on
    (a) kirchoff's voltage law
    (b) kirchoff's current law
    (c) ohm's law
    (d) voltage divider law
102. Nodes that are connected to each other by voltage source form
    (a) super mesh
    (b) super node
    (c) super current
    (d) super voltage
103. Find the current in 4Ω resistor in figure.

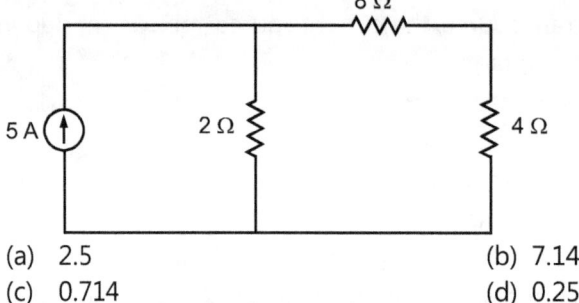

    (a) 2.5
    (b) 7.14
    (c) 0.714
    (d) 0.25
104. Find the voltage v across 4Ω resistor in figure.

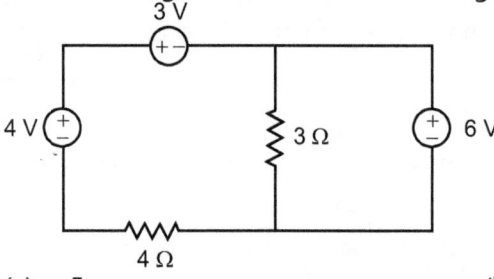

    (a) −5
    (b) 5
    (c) −3
    (d) 3
105. Find the voltage V across ab terminal in figure, if the current in the circuit is 1A.

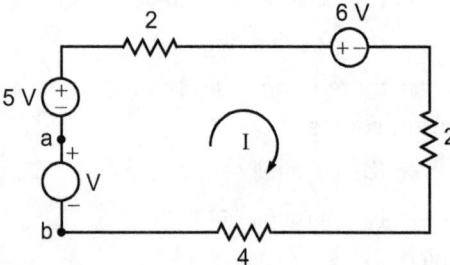

    (a) 11
    (b) −11
    (c) 9
    (d) −9

106. Determine the voltage across 6Ω resistor in figure.

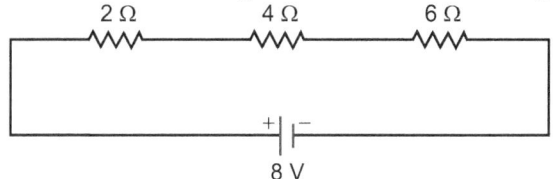

(a) 6.4 (b) 5.16
(c) 4   (d) 2.67

107. Calculate the current I flowing through the circuit shown in figure.

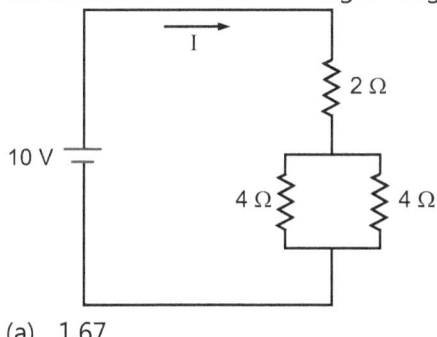

(a) 1.67 (b) 2.5
(c) 1   (d) None of these

108. Find the voltage V across the ab terminal shown in figure.

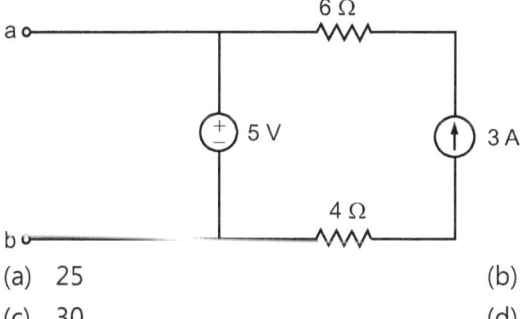

(a) 25 (b) 6
(c) 30 (d) 5

109. Find the current I flowing through the circuit shown in figure.

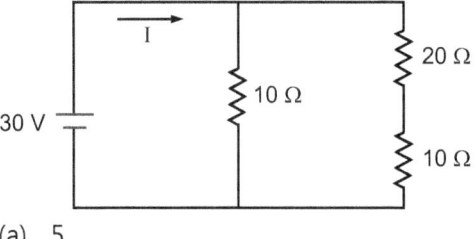

(a) 5 (b) 3
(c) 4 (d) 2

110. Calculate the equivalent resistance of the circuit shown in figure.

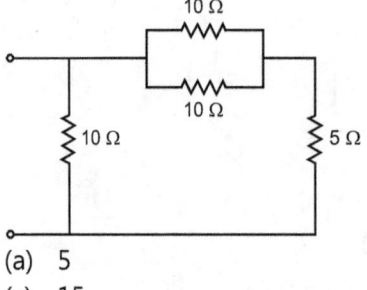

(a) 5 (b) 10
(c) 15 (d) 20

111. Find the voltage V across the ab terminal in circuit as shown in figure.

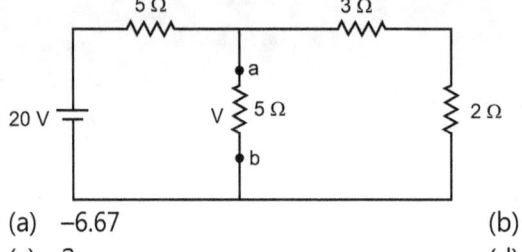

(a) −6.67 (b) 6.67
(c) 2 (d) −2

112. Find an equivalent resistance of the circuit shown in figure.

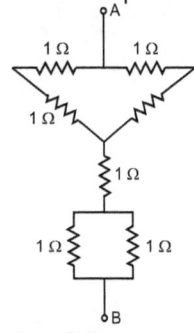

(a) 3.5 (b) 2.5
(c) 1.5 (d) None of the above

113. A star connected network is shown in figure. Find the elements of the delta connected circuit shown in figure.

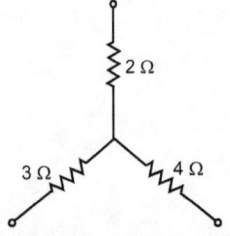

(a) $R_A = 6\Omega$, $R_B = 8\Omega$, $R_C = 12\Omega$
(b) $R_A = 4\Omega$, $R_B = 0.2\Omega$, $R_C = 8.3\Omega$
(c) $R_A = 6.3\,\Omega$, $R_B = 8\Omega$, $R_C = 8\Omega$
(d) $R_A = 6.5\,\Omega$, $R_B = 8.67\,\Omega$, $R_C = 13\Omega$

114. A delta connected network is shown in figure. Find the elements R_1, R_2 and R_3 of star connected network

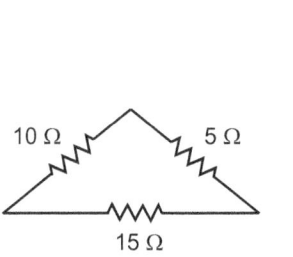 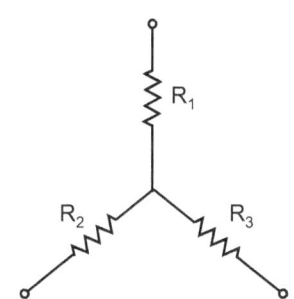

  (a) 1.67 Ω, 5Ω, 2.5Ω   (b) 5Ω, 3Ω, 7.5 Ω
  (c) 1.67Ω, 3Ω, 2.5Ω   (d) 2.5Ω, 5, 3.5 Ω

115. An air gap provided in the iron core of an inductor prevents
  (a) flux leakage   (b) core saturation
  (c) heat generation   (d) hysteresis loss

116. A coil with 100 turns carrying a current of 8A produces a flux of 6×10^{-6} Wb. The inductance of the coil will be
  (a) 0.000075 H   (b) 0.075 H
  (c) 0.0075 H   (d) 0.75 H

117. The inductance of a circuit is 16 henrys and a current of 6 amperes flows through it. The energy stored will be
  (a) 288 joules   (b) 1536 joules
  (c) 144 joules   (d) 556 joules

118. An inductor stores energy in
  (a) core   (b) electrostatic field
  (c) electromagnetic field   (d) magnetic field

119. The current through an inductance follows
  (a) a linear graph   (b) an exponential decay
  (c) an exponential growth   (d) a linear decay

120. Power factor for a pure inductor is
  (a) unity   (b) 0.707
  (c) zero   (d) infinite

121. Which statement about the inductance is incorrect?
  (a) an inductance does not oppose direct currents
  (b) inductive reactance can be measured by an ohm-meter
  (c) the inductive reactance varies directly as the frequency of the applied voltage
  (d) the inductance of coil can be increased by adding few more turns to the coil

122. The inductance of a coil can be increased by
    (a) increasing core length
    (b) using core material of high relative permeability
    (c) reducing number of turns
    (d) any of the above

123. The inductive reactance of an ac circuit having 0.08 henry inductance at 60 Hz frequency will be
    (a) 20 Ω
    (b) 10 Ω
    (c) 25 Ω
    (d) 30 Ω

124. The emf in the volts induced in a coil of 200 turns when the magnetic flux changes from 0.001 Wb to 0.0025 Wb in 0.1 sec., will be
    (a) 7.5 V
    (b) 4.5 V
    (c) 3.0 V
    (d) 1.5 V

125. A network which contain one or more than one source of emf is known as
    (a) passive network
    (b) active network
    (c) electric network
    (d) non-linear network

126. A coil with 1000 turns carrying a current of 8 amperes produces a flux of 6×10^{-6} Wb. The inductance of the coil will be
    (a) 0.0075 H
    (b) 0.075 H
    (c) 0.00075 H
    (d) 0.75 H

127. A coil having an inductance of 75 H is carrying a current of 1A. If the current is reduced to zero in 0.2. second, the self-inductance emf will be
    (a) 375 V
    (b) 125 V
    (c) 750 V
    (d) 500 V

128. An ideal voltage source
    (a) has zero internal resistance
    (b) has terminal voltage in proportion to current
    (c) has terminal voltage in proportion to load
    (d) has open circuit voltage nearly equal to the voltage on full load

129. Which of the following is bilateral element?
    (a) capacitance
    (b) constant current source
    (c) constant voltage source

130. The relationship between voltage and current in same for two opposite directions of current in case of
    (a) passive network
    (b) active network
    (c) unilateral network
    (d) bilateral network

131. A circuit having neither any energy source nor emf source is termed the
    (a) bilateral circuit
    (b) passive circuit
    (c) active circuit
    (d) unilateral circuit

132. A coil with large distributed capacitance has
    (a) low quality factor
    (b) low resonant frequency
    (c) low resistance
    (d) high resonant frequency

133. An ideal current source has zero
    (a) voltage on no load
    (b) internal resistance
    (b) internal conductance
    (d) ripple

134. The rating given on the name plate of a transformer indicates the
    (a) true power which it draws from the supply mains
    (b) true power which it can supply
    (c) apparent power which it draws from the supply mains
    (d) apparent power which it can supply

135. An a.c. circuit has an inductance of $(5 + j6)\ \Omega$ for the fundamental frequency. For the third harmonic the impedance will be
    (a) $5 + j2$
    (b) $15 + j18$
    (c) $5 + j18$
    (d) $15 + j2$

136. The transient currents are due to
    (a) changes in stored energy in inductors and capacitors
    (b) circuit impedance
    (c) voltage applied to the circuit
    (d) circuit resistance

137. The condition $AD - BC = 1$ for a 2 part network implies that the network is
    (a) reciprocal
    (b) loss less
    (c) unilateral element network
    (d) lumped element network

138. The dual of a capacitor is
    (a) capacitor
    (b) conductor
    (c) inductor
    (d) resistor

139. The power factor of a practical inductor is
   (a) leading
   (b) lagging
   (c) unity
   (d) zero

140. The network which contain one or more than one source of emf is known as
   (a) electric network
   (b) non-linear network
   (c) active network
   (d) passive network

141. A coil with 1000 turns carrying a current of 8A produces flux of 6×10^{-8} Wb. The inductance of the coil will be
   (a) 0.0075 H
   (b) 0.00075 H
   (c) 0.75 H
   (d) 0.075 H

142. A coil having an inductance of 75 H is carrying a current of 1 A. If the current is reduced to zero in 0.2. Second, the self-inductance emf will be
   (a) 125 V
   (b) 500 V
   (c) 750 V
   (d) 375 V

143. Two resistance are connected in parallel and each dissipates 40 watts. The total and each dissipates 40 watts. The total power supplied by the source equals
   (a) 80 watts
   (b) 40 watts
   (c) 20 watts
   (d) 160 watts

144. Voltage v = 100 sin 1000 t is applied to a resistor of 10 Ω. The reading of a.c. ammeter connected in series will be
   (a) 70.7 amp
   (b) 10 amp
   (c) 7.07 amp
   (d) 100 amp

145. AC 50 Hz voltage across a fixed resistor is gradually varied. Which of the following figure correctly represents the expected relationship between power consumed W and the voltage V?

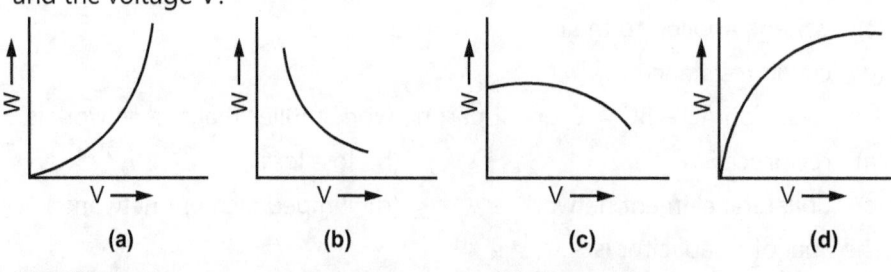

   (a) Figure A
   (b) Figure B
   (c) Figure C
   (d) Figure D

146. Power consumed in the given circuits is

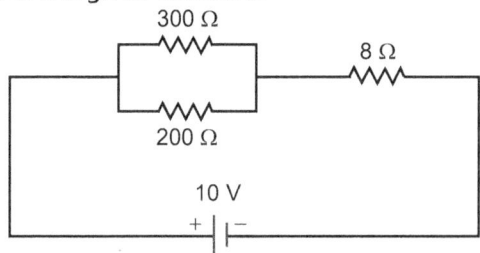

(a) 5 watts (b) 100 watts
(c) 40 watts (d) 20 watts

147. The power dissipated in the given circuit is

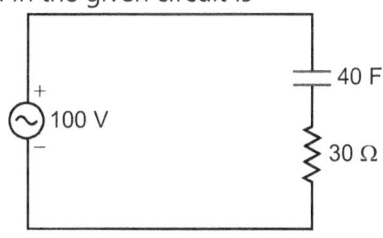

(a) zero (b) 33.3 watts
(c) 300 watts (d) 120 watts

148. Power is drawn from a source at power factor 0.8, P_{av} = 200 watts. The reactive power is given by
(a) 100 VARS (b) 200 VARS
(c) 150 VARS (d) 300 VARS

149. The average power loss in the 10 ohm resistor across which a voltage of $v(t) = 4 + 4 \sin \omega t + 2 \sin 2\omega t + 2 \cos 2\omega t + 2 \sin 3\omega t$ is applied is
(a) 1 watt (b) 2 watt
(c) 3 watt (d) 4 watt

150. The average value of the waveform is

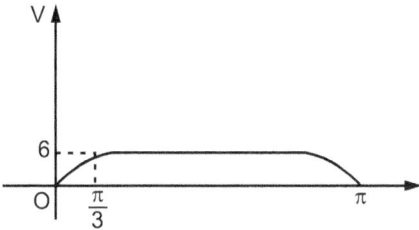

(a) $\dfrac{6}{\pi}$ (b) 4 V

(c) $\dfrac{6}{\pi/2}$ (d) $\int_0^{\pi} 6\theta \, d\theta$

ANSWERS

1. (c)	2. (a)	3. (b)	4. (c)	5. (d)	6. (a)	7. (c)	8. (a)	9. (c)	10. (b)
11. (b)	12. (b)	13. (d)	14. (c)	15. (b)	16. (b)	17. (b)	18. (c)	19. (d)	20. (d)
21. (d)	22. (b)	23. (a)	24. (d)	25. (c)	26. (d)	27. (d)	28. (b)	29. (b)	30. (c)
31. (c)	32. (c)	33. (b)	34. (d)	35. (a)	36. (c)	37. (a)	38. (c)	39. (d)	40. (d)
41. (c)	42. (c)	43. (d)	44. (b)	45. (a)	46. (b)	47. (c)	48. (a)	49. (c)	50. (b)
51. (a)	52. (c)	53. (a)	54. (c)	55. (b)	56. (b)	57. (c)	58. (c)	59. (c)	60. (a)
61. (b)	62. (d)	63. (c)	64. (b)	65. (c)	66. (c)	67. (c)	68. (c)	69. (c)	70. (c)
71. (d)	72. (b)	73. (c)	74. (c)	75. (a)	76. (b)	77. (b)	78. (c)	79. (d)	80. (b)
81. (b)	82. (a)	83. (b)	84. (b)	85. (b)	86. (b)	87. (a)	88. (a)	89. (d)	90. (c)
91. (b)	92. (c)	93. (d)	94. (c)	95. (c)	96. (d)	97. (c)	98. (a)	99. (a)	100. (b)
101. (b)	102. (b)	103. (c)	104. (b)	105. (c)	106. (d)	107. (b)	108. (d)	109. (c)	110. (a)
111. (b)	112. (b)	113. (d)	114. (a)	115. (c)	116. (a)	117. (a)	118. (d)	119. (c)	120. (c)
121. (b)	122. (b)	123. (d)	124. (b)	125. (b)	126. (c)	127. (a)	128. (a)	129. (a)	130. (d)
131. (b)	132. (d)	133. (c)	134. (d)	135. (c)	136. (a)	137. (a)	138. (c)	139. (b)	140. (c)
141. (b)	142. (d)	143. (a)	144. (c)	145. (d)	146. (a)	147. (d)	148. (c)	149. (c)	150. (b)

EXERCISE

1. Distinguish between independent and dependent energy sources.
2. Define following terms:
    (a) Capacitor (b) Current (c) Voltage (d) Power (e) Energy
3. Explain voltage-current (V-I) relationship between following circuit elements:
    (a) Capacitor (b) Resistor (c) Inductor
4. Explain the difference between short circuit (SC) and open circuit (OC) with an example.
5. What you mean by a lumped network and a distributed network?
6. Explain why voltage sources are connected in series and parallel. Give the requirement of voltage sources when they are to be connected in series or parallel.
7. Explain why current sources are connected in series and parallel. Give the requirements of current sources when they are to be connected in parallel or series.
8. What is source transformation? State and prove state transformation equation.

9. State and explain KVL and KCL.
10. With an example explain the general procedure to analyse a network using mesh (loop) analysis.
11. With an example explain the general procedure to the analysis of the given network using nodal (KCL) analysis.
12. Write short note on:
    (a) Mutual inductance
    (b) Dual networks
    (c) Coupling circuits
13. Determine current I_2. Use source shifting and the KVL analysis.

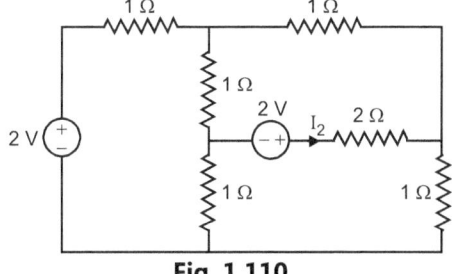

Fig. 1.110

14. Using KCL and KVL, find voltage V_1 in the circuit.

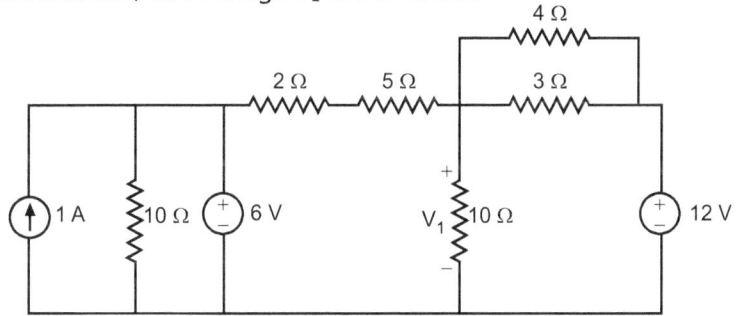

Fig. 1.111

15. Find I_1, I_2, V_1, V_2 and V_3 in the circuit shown. Make use of loop analysis.

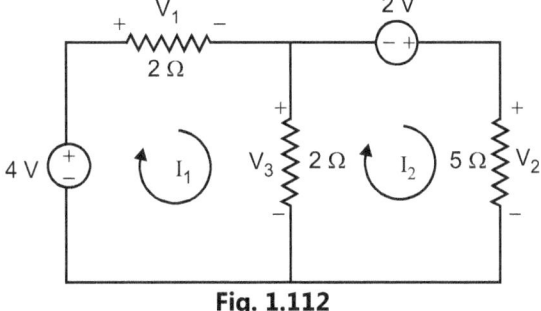

Fig. 1.112

16. Write Node equation for the circuit shown, solve for the voltage V_2 and V_3.

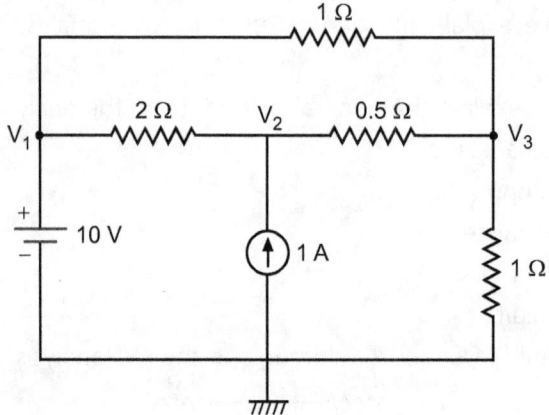

Fig. 1.113

17. Use nodal analysis to find V_1, V_2 and V_x in the circuit shown.

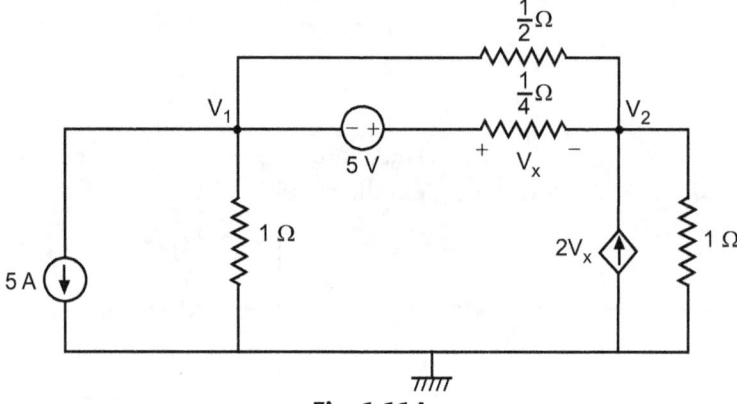

Fig. 1.114

Unit 2

NETWORK THEOREMS

Contents ...

2.1 Superposition Theorem
2.2 Thevenin's Theorem
2.3 Norton's Theorem
2.4 Maximum Power Transfer (MPT) Theorem
    2.4.1 MPT Theorem for DC Circuits
    2.4.2 MPT Theorem for AC circuits
    2.4.3 Corollary of Maximum Power Transfer (MPT)
2.5 Millman's Theorem
2.6 Additional Solved Problems on AC Circuits
Multiple Choice Questions (MCQs)
Exercise

2.1 SUPERPOSITION THEOREM

In the last sections, we have studied two powerful technique of mesh and nodal analysis to find the network variables. Network variable can also be out by using network theorems. In this section, we shall discuss one of the most basic theorem called Superposition theorem. Remaining theorems are discussed in the subsequent sections.

Utility of Theorem: Superposition theorem is used to find voltage across any (or all) branches and current through any (or all) branches in a circuit containing impedances and more than one independent energy source.

Statement: "In a linear circuit containing linear and bilateral elements and energy sources. voltage across any branch or current in any branch is given by algebraic sum of voltage or current due to each energy sources considered separately (with other sources turned off)".

While turning off energy sources they are replaced by their internal impedances. The voltage source is replaced by short circuit and current source is replaced by open circuit across the two terminals where they are connected.

Proof: To prove this theorem, we can consider a simple two loops circuit with voltage and current sources as shown in Fig. 2.1.

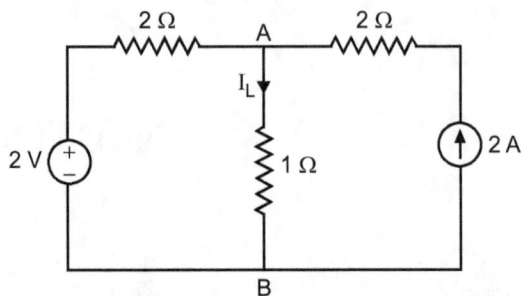

Fig. 2.1: Circuit to prove Superposition theorem

Let us find current (I_L) in 1 Ω across A-B by KVL and KCL and then verify the current by using Superposition theorem.

Current (I_L) by use of KCL and KVL: Using KCL current in 2Ω resistor is ($I_L - 2$) Amp. as shown in Fig. 2.2.

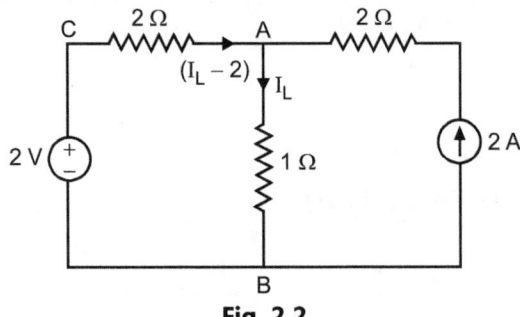

Fig. 2.2

Now KVL across loop (B-A-C-B) gives

$$I_L + 2(I_L - 2) - 2 = 0 \text{ or } 3I_L = 6 \text{ or } I_L = 3A$$

Current (I_L) by using Superposition theorem: Current (I_L) can be found out by considering one source at a time.

Step I: Consider 2V source alone. Make current source zero (Open the terminal since current source has infinite resistance between terminals). The circuit will be as shown in Fig. 2.3 (a).

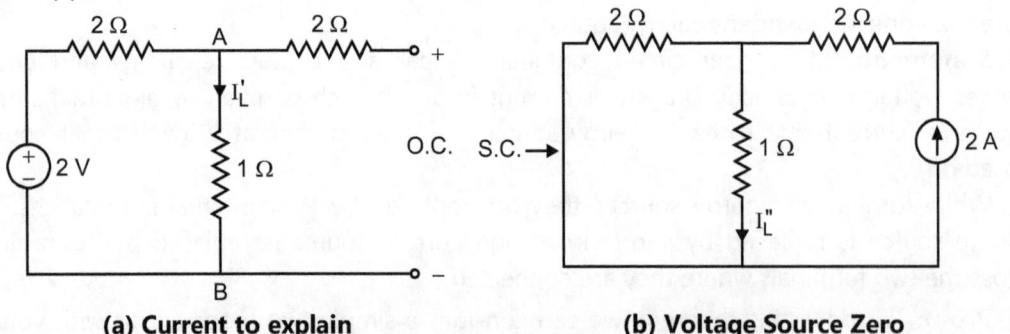

(a) Current to explain (b) Voltage Source Zero

Fig. 2.3: Circuits to explain Superposition theorem

Now current in $2\Omega = I_L' = \dfrac{2}{2+1} = \dfrac{2}{3}$ Amp.

Step II: Consider 2A source alone. Make voltage source zero (short the terminals since ideal voltage source has zero resistance between terminals). The circuit will be as shown in Fig. 2.3 (b).

Now by current divider equation

$$I_L'' = \dfrac{2 \times 2}{3} = \dfrac{4}{3} \text{ A}$$

Step III: By Superposition theorem

$$I_L = I_L' + I_L'' = \dfrac{2}{3} + \dfrac{4}{3} = 3\text{A}$$

Conclusion: Since, current (I_L) found out by using Superposition theorem is same as that by using KCL and KVL, the Superposition theorem is proved.

Note: Superposition theorem is valid for circuit with linear impedances. It is not applicable to circuit containing at least one or more nonlinear elements such as charged capacitor, energized inductor, diodes, transistors, incandescent lamp, vacuum tube or gas tubes.

Superposition theorem can also be used in a network supplied by generators with several different frequencies to compute currents as a sum of individual currents due to each frequency. Change in reactances to different frequencies should be considered while computing the currents.

Following examples explains principles of Superposition theorem.

Ex. 2.1: Using Superposition theorem determine node voltages V_1 and V_2 in the circuit shown.

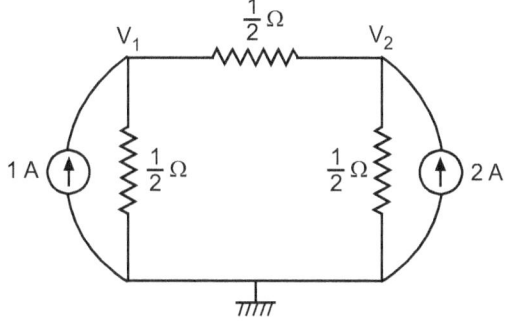

Fig. 2.4

Proof: Step I: Consider 1A current source alone 2A source is made by opening terminals as in Fig. 2.5 (a).

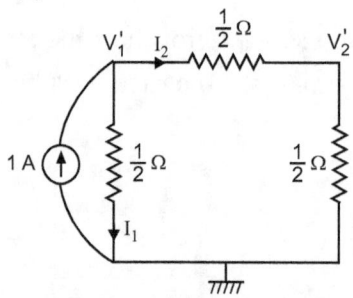 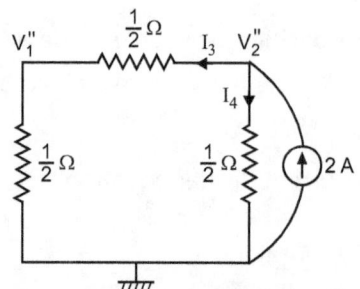

(a) Circuit for Step I   (b) Circuit for Step II

Fig. 2.5: Circuit to find required at variables

Current $\quad I_1 = \dfrac{1 \times 1}{1 + \dfrac{1}{2}} = \dfrac{2}{3}$ and current $I_2 = \dfrac{1}{3}$ A

Hence $\quad V_1' = \dfrac{1}{2} \times \dfrac{2}{3} = \dfrac{1}{3}$ V and $V_2' = \dfrac{1}{2} \times \dfrac{1}{3} = \dfrac{1}{6}$ V

Step II: Consider 2A current source alone. A current source is made zero by opening its terminals as shown as in Fig. 2.5 (b).

Current $\quad I_3 = \dfrac{2 \times 1/2}{1 + 1/2} = \dfrac{2}{3}$ A current $I_4 = \left(2 - \dfrac{2}{3}\right) = \dfrac{4}{3}$ A

Hence $\quad V_2'' = \dfrac{1}{2} \times I_4 = \dfrac{2}{3}$ V

$\quad V_1'' = \dfrac{1}{2} \times I_3 = \dfrac{1}{2} \times \dfrac{2}{3} = \dfrac{1}{3}$ V

Step III: By applying Superposition theorem, we have

$$V_1 = V_1' + V_1'' = \dfrac{1}{3} + \dfrac{1}{3} = \dfrac{2}{3} \text{ V}$$

$$V_2 = V_2' + V_2'' = \dfrac{1}{6} + \dfrac{2}{3} = \dfrac{5}{6} \text{ V}$$

Ex. 2.2: Make use of Superposition theorem to determine the voltage V in the circuit shown.

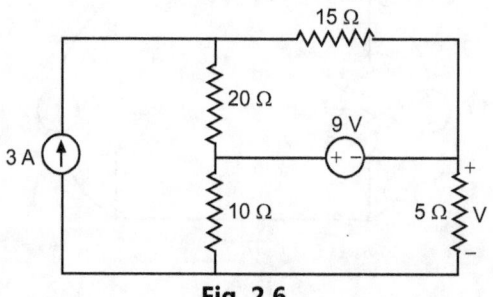

Fig. 2.6

Sol.: Step I: Consider 3A current source alone. Make the 9V source zero as in Fig. 2.7 (a).

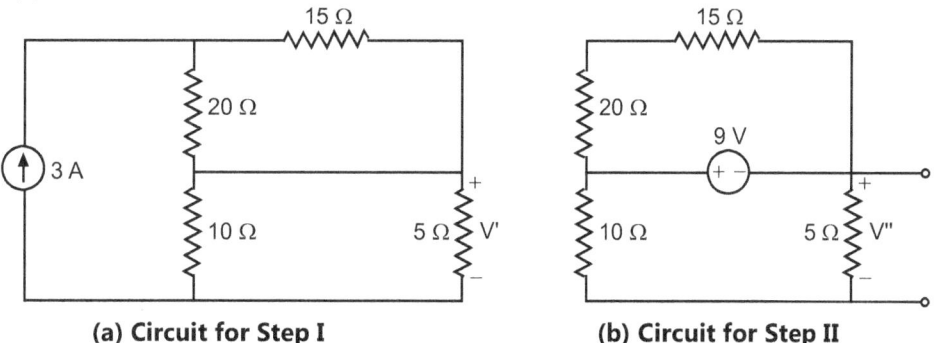

(a) Circuit for Step I   (b) Circuit for Step II
Fig. 2.7: Circuit to find required variables

We have 10Ω and 5Ω resistors in parallel to give equivalent resistance of $\frac{10}{3}$ Ω. Current of 3A flows through it.

Hence, we have
$$V' = \frac{10}{3} \times 3 = 10V$$

Step II: Consider 9V source alone. Make the 3A current source zero as shown in Fig. 2.8 (b).

Now 10Ω and 5Ω are in series and this series combination is in parallel with the 9V source. Hence, by voltage divider, we have
$$V'' = -5 \times \frac{9}{15} = -3V$$

Step III: By Superposition theorem, we have
$$V = V' + V'' = 10 - 3 = 7 \text{ Volts.}$$

Ex. 2.3: In the circuit shown find the open circuit voltage (V_{Th}) across a-b using Superposition theorem.

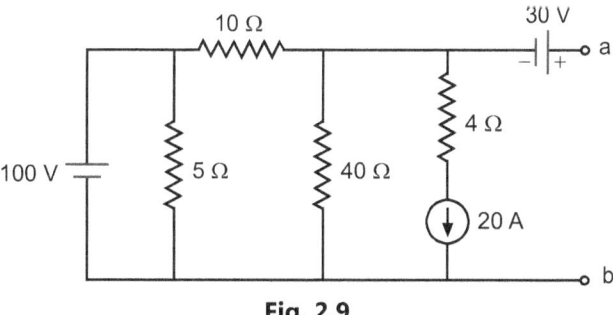

Fig. 2.9

Sol.: Step I: Consider 30V source alone. Make other sources zero i.e. short 100V source and open 20A source. As no current flows through circuit the open circuit voltage (V_{Th}) will be V_{Th} = 30 V.

Step II: Consider 100 V source only make other sources zero. The circuit will be as shown in Fig. 2.10 (a)

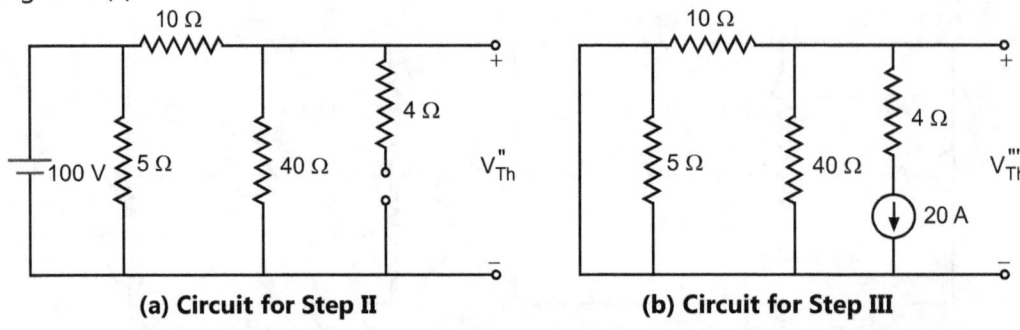

(a) Circuit for Step II   (b) Circuit for Step III

Fig. 2.10

Voltage across 40Ω resistor is the output voltage (V_{Th}). By voltage divider circuit, we have,

$$V_{Th}'' = \frac{40 \times 100}{40 + 10} = 80V$$

Step III: Consider 20Ω current source alone make other sources zero as shown in Fig. 2.10 (b). 40Ω and 10 Ω are in parallel to give equivalent resistance of 8Ω. 20A current will flow through this combination to give output voltage (V_{Th}) of

$$V_{Th}'' = -8 \times 20$$
$$= -160V$$

Step IV: Hence by Superposition theorem, we have

$$V_{Th}' + V_{Th}'' + V_{Th}''' = 30 + 80 - 160$$
$$= -50 \text{ Volts}$$

Ex. 2.4: Using Superposition theorem determine voltage V_{AB} in the circuit, shown

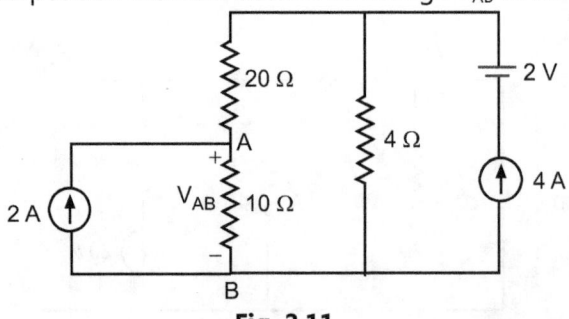

Fig. 2.11

Sol.: Step I: Consider only 2V source. Open the two current sources. Then voltage source is open circuited. Hence, no current flows through the circuit resistors. Thus, we have $V_{AB}' = 0V$.

Step II: Consider 2A source only. Make the other two sources zero. The circuit will be as shown in Fig. 2.12 (a).

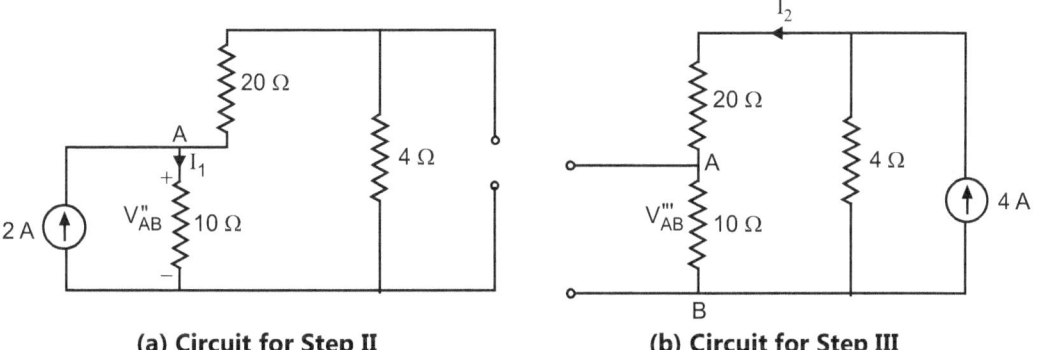

(a) Circuit for Step II   (b) Circuit for Step III

Fig. 2.12: Circuit to find required variable

Now,   Current $I_1 = 2 \times \dfrac{24}{24 + 10}$

$= 1.41$ Amp.

Thus we have, $V''_{AB} = I_1 \times 10$

$= 14.12$ V

Step III: Consider 4A source only. Make other two sources as shown in Fig. 2.12 (b). By current divider action the current,

$$I_2 = 4 \times \dfrac{4}{4 + 30} = \dfrac{16}{34} = \dfrac{8}{17} \text{ Amp}$$

Hence, $V'''_{AB} = 10\, I_2 = +\dfrac{80}{17}$

$= 4.7$ Volts

Step IV: Hence by Superposition theorem we have

$$V_{AB} = V'_{AB} + V''_{AB} + V'''_{AB} = 0 + 14.12 + 4.7 = 18.82 \text{ V}$$

Ex. 2.5: Using Superposition theorem find I_1 that gives voltage $V_2 = 6.5$ V in the circuit shown.

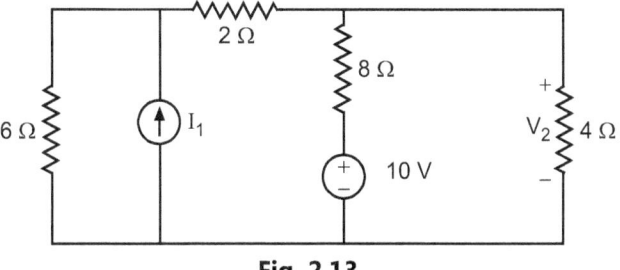

Fig. 2.13

Sol.: Step I: Consider current source I_1 alone. Make the voltage source of 10V zero as shown in Fig. 2.14 (a).

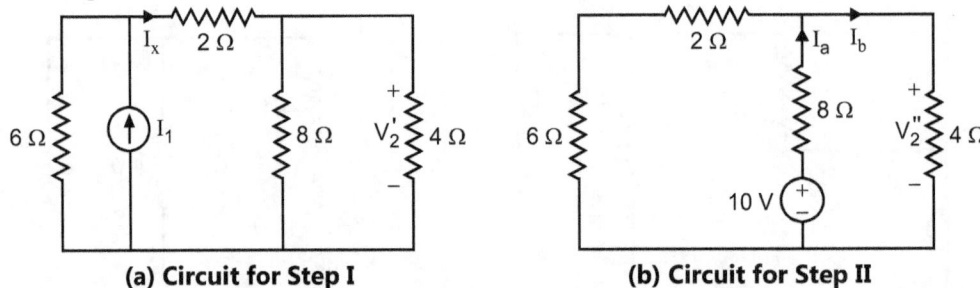

(a) Circuit for Step I   (b) Circuit for Step II

Fig. 2.14: Circuits to find required variables

$8\Omega \parallel 4\Omega$ gives 2.67Ω resistor. This is in series with 2Ω resistor. Now by current divider circuit, we have the current.

$$I_x = \frac{I_1 \times 6}{6 + 2 + 2.67} = \frac{6I_1}{10.67}$$

$$= 0.562\, I_1$$

This current flows through equivalent 2.67Ω resistor. Hence, we get V_2' as

$$V_2' = 2.67 \times I_x$$

$$= 1.5\, I_1 \text{ volts}$$

Step II: Consider 10V source alone. Make the current source zero as shown in Fig. 2.14 (b).

Now $(6 + 2) = 8\Omega$ resistor is in parallel with 4Ω resistor.

The Total current $= I_a = \dfrac{10}{8 + 8 \parallel 4} = \dfrac{10}{8 + 2.67}$

$$= 0.937 \text{ Amp.}$$

Now by current divider action, we have,

$$I_b = I_a \times \frac{8}{8 + 4} = \frac{2}{3} \times I_a = 0.625 \text{ A}$$

Hence   Output voltage $= V_2'' = 4I_b = 2.5$ V

Step III: By Superposition theorem, we have,

$$V_2 = 6.5 = V_2' + V_2'' = 1.5 I_1 + 2.5$$

Hence, $1.5 I_1 = 4$ or $I_1 = \dfrac{8}{3}$ Amp.

Thus, an current of $I_1 = \dfrac{8}{3}$ A produces $V_2 = 6.5$ Volts

Ex. 2.6: Use Superposition theorem to find current I in the circuit shown.

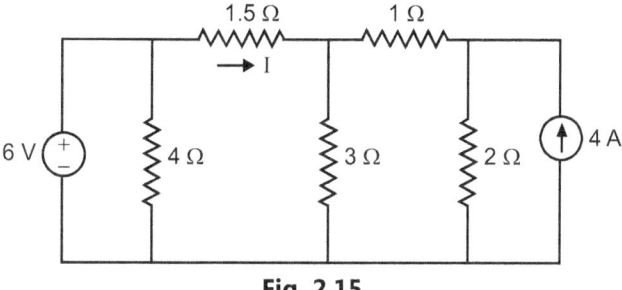

Fig. 2.15

Sol.: Consider one source at a time to find the total current as a summation of two currents.

Step I: Consider 6V source alone. Make the 4A current source zero as shown in Fig. 2.16 (a). Now 1Ω and 2Ω are in series. This 3Ω is in parallel with 3Ω resistor to give 1.5Ω across a-b. This is in series with 1.5 Ω resistor. This total resistance of 3Ω is in parallel with 6V source.

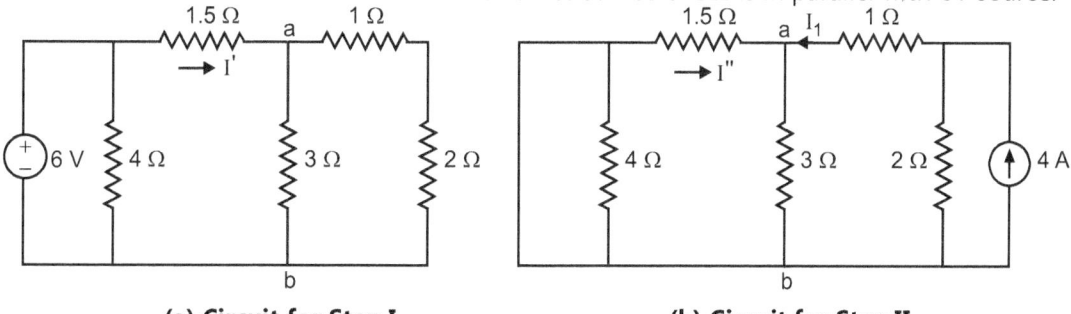

(a) Circuit for Step I (b) Circuit for Step II

Fig. 2.16: Circuits to find required variables

Thus, Current $(I') = \dfrac{6}{(1.5 + 1.5)} = \dfrac{6}{3} = 2A$

Step II: Now consider 4A current source alone. Make the 6V voltage source zero as shown in Fig. 2.16 (b). Because of short 4Ω resistance becomes zero. Now 1.5 Ω and 3Ω are in parallel to give an equivalent of 1Ω. Now by current divider action

$$I_1 = \dfrac{4 \times 2}{2 + 1 + 1} = 2A$$

Now again using divider action, we have,

$$I'' = -I_1 \times \dfrac{3}{3 + 1.5} = -I_1 \times \dfrac{3}{4.5} = -2 \times \dfrac{2}{3} = \dfrac{-4}{3} \text{ A}$$

Step III: By Superposition theorem we have I = I' + I"

$$I = 2 - \dfrac{4}{3} = \dfrac{2}{3} \text{ Amp.}$$

Ex. 2.7: Determine the voltage V_1 in the circuit by using Superposition Theorem.

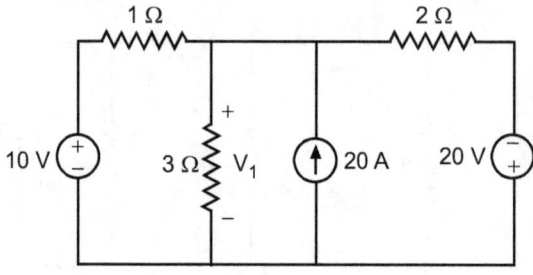

Fig. 2.17

Sol.: Step I: Consider 10V source alone. Make other two sources zero as in Fig. 2.18 (a).

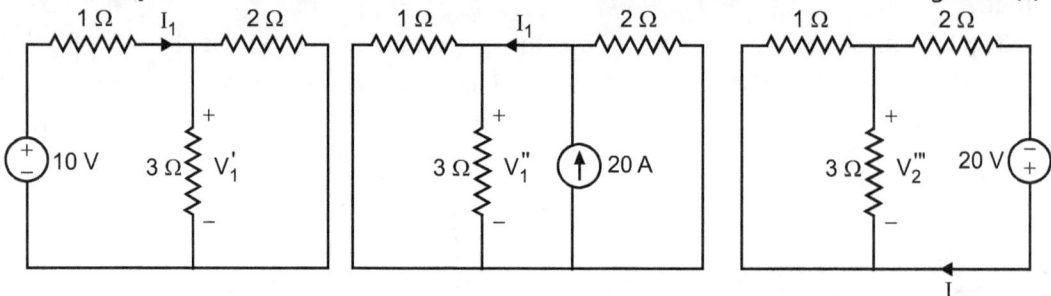

(a) Circuit for Step I   (b) Circuit for Step II   (c) Circuit for Step III

Fig. 2.18: Circuit to find required variables

Now 3Ω and 2Ω in parallel gives $\frac{6}{5}$ Ω resistor. The voltage V_1' is across this resistor.

Hence, by voltage divider action.

$$V_1' = \frac{10 \times \frac{6}{5}}{1 + \frac{6}{5}} = 10 \times \frac{6}{11} = 5.45 \text{ V}$$

Step II: Consider 20A current source alone. Make other two sources zero as shown in Fig. 2.18 (b). Now 1Ω || 3Ω gives an equivalent resistance of 0.75Ω. By current divider action, we have,

$$I_2 = 20 \times \frac{2}{2 + 0.75} = 14.545 \text{ Amp.}$$

Hence,
$$V_1'' = 0.75 \times I_1$$
$$= 10.9 \text{ V}$$

Step III: Consider 20V source alone. The other two sources are zero as shown in Fig. 2.18 (c). 1Ω || 3Ω gives an equivalent of 0.75Ω. Now by voltage divider action.

We have $V_1''' = -20 \times \dfrac{0.75}{0.75 + 2} = -5.45$ V

Step IV: By Superposition theorem we have

$$V_1 = V_1' + V_1'' + V_1''' = 5.45 + 10.9 - 5.45 = 10.9 \text{ V}$$

Ex. 2.8: Find current I using Superposition Theorem.

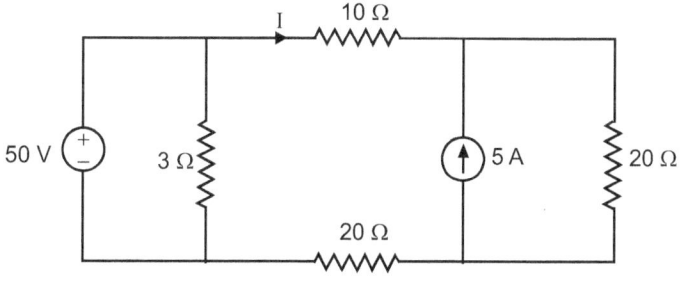

Fig. 2.19

Sol.: Step I: Consider 50V source alone. Make current source zero as shown in Fig. 2.20 (a).

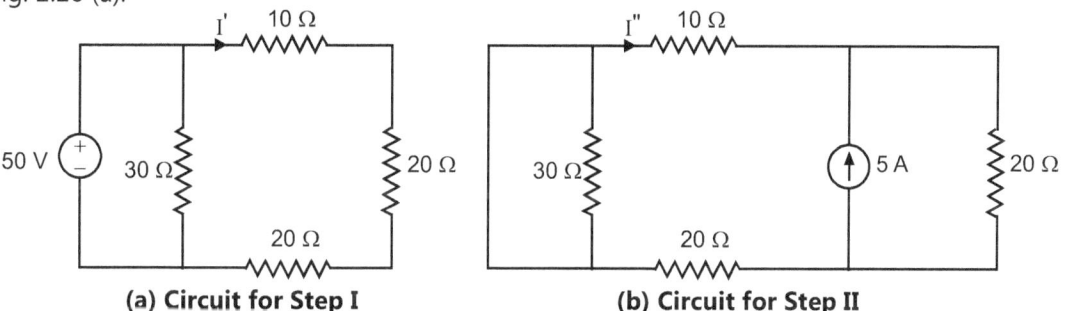

(a) Circuit for Step I (b) Circuit for Step II
Fig. 2.20: Circuits to find required variables

Now 10Ω, 20Ω and 20Ω all in series to give a total resistance of 50Ω. This 50Ω resistor is in parallel with 50V source.

Hence, $I' = \dfrac{50}{50} = 1$ Amp.

Step II: Consider 5A current source alone. Make the voltage source zero as shown in Fig. 2.20 (b). Now 30Ω resistor becomes zero. 10Ω and 20Ω resistors are in series. By current divider action we have,

$$I'' = -5 \times \dfrac{20}{20 + 30} = -5 \times \dfrac{2}{5} = -2 \text{ Amp.}$$

Step III: By Superposition theorem $I = I' + I'' = 1 - 2 = 1$ Amp.

Ex. 2.9: Find current through capacitor branch in the circuit by Superposition theorem.

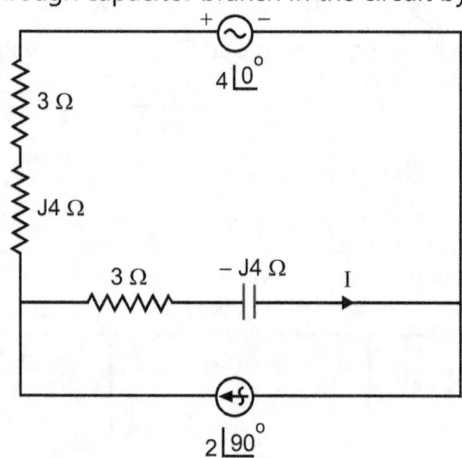

Fig. 2.21

Sol.: Superposition theorem can also be applied to AC circuits. This example explain how A.C. circuits are analysed using Superposition theorem.

Step I: Consider voltage source alone. Make current source zero as shown in Fig. 2.22 (a).

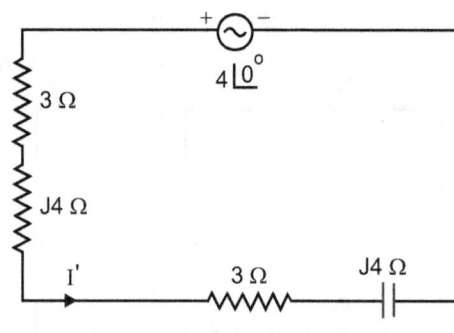
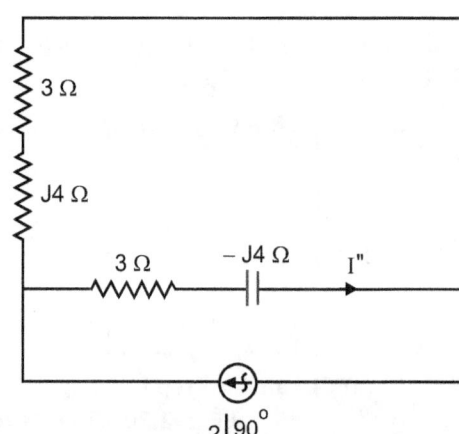

(a) Circuit for Step I   (b) Circuit for Step II

Fig. 2.22: Circuits to find required variables

Current $\qquad I' = \dfrac{4\angle 0°}{(3+J4)+(3-J4)} = \dfrac{4\angle 0°}{6} = \dfrac{2}{3}\angle 0°$ Amp.

Step II: Consider current source alone. Make voltage source zero as shown in Fig. 2.22 (b). Now by current divider action.

We have $\qquad I'' = 2\angle 90° \times \dfrac{(3+J4)}{(3+J4)+(3-J4)} = \dfrac{2\angle 90° \times (3+J4)}{6}$

$$= \dfrac{1}{3}\angle 90° \times 5\angle 53.13° = 1.65 \angle 143.3°$$

$$= (-1.33 + J1) \text{ Amp.}$$

Step III: By Superposition theorem I = I' + I"

$$I = (0.67 + J0) + (-1.33 + J1)$$
$$= (-0.66 + J1) \text{ Amp.}$$
$$= 1.20 \angle 124.4° \text{ Amp.}$$

Note: Many times controlled sources are also present in the circuit along with independent energy sources. While applying steps to Superposition Theorem the **controlled sources are not to be considered as a separate source. Only independent energy source need to be considered.**

Following examples explain this.

Ex. 2.10: Use Superposition theorem to find current (I) in the circuit shown.

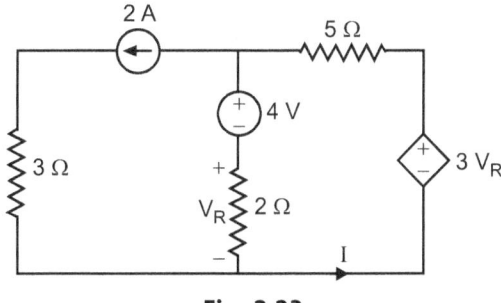

Fig. 2.23

Sol.: There are two independent source. Hence, only two step to find current I. The controlled source of $3V_R$ is not separately considered.

Step I: Consider 2A current source alone. Make 4V sources zero as shown in Fig. 2.24 (a).

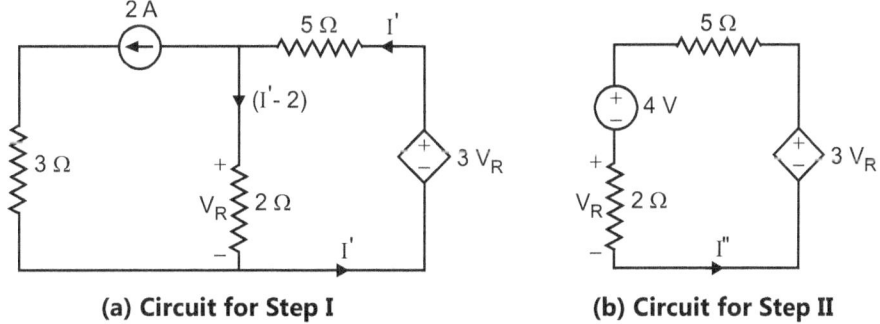

(a) Circuit for Step I   (b) Circuit for Step II

Fig. 2.24: Circuits to find required variables

By KCL current in 2Ω branch is (I' − 2). Hence, $V_R = 2(I' - 2)$

KVL across right side loop gives

$$3V_R - 5I' - 2(I' - 2) = 0$$

OR $3 \times 2(I' - 2) - 5I' - 2I' + 4 = 0$

Solving this gives   I' = − 8 Amp.

Step II: Consider 4V source alone. Make current source zero as shown in Fig. 2.25 (b). Now there is a single loop with loop current I". We have $V_R = 2I"$. KVL across the loop gives

$$3V_R - 5I" - 4 - V_R = 0$$

i.e.
$$2V_R - 5I" - 4 = 0$$
$$2 \times 2I" - 5I" - 4 = 0$$

Hence $I" - RA$

Step III: By Superposition theorem $I = I' + I" = -8 - 4 = -12$ Amp.

Ex. 2.11: By Superposition theorem find current I in the circuit.

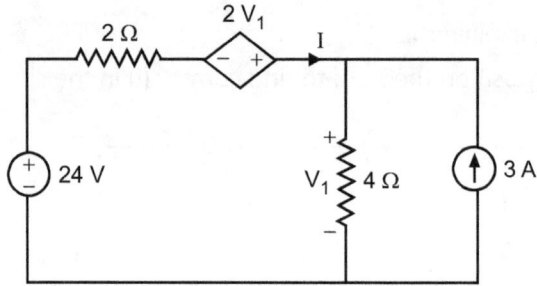

Fig. 2.26

Sol.: Consider 24V and 3A only. Do not consider controlled source of $2V_1$ separately.

Step I: Consider 24V alone. Make 3A source zero as shown in Fig. 2.27 (a). Now there will be a single loop with loop current I'. Now $V_1 = 4I'$ and hence KVL across whole loop gives,

$$+ V_1 - 2V_1 + 2I' - 24 = 0 \quad \text{or} \quad -V_1 + 2I' - 24 = 0$$
$$-4I' + 2I' - 24 = 0 \quad \text{gives}, I" = -12 A$$

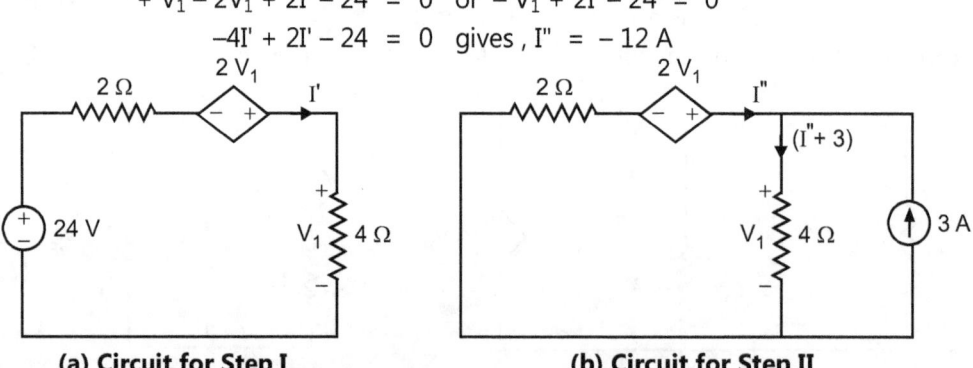

(a) Circuit for Step I   (b) Circuit for Step II

Fig. 2.27: Circuit to find required variables

Step II: Consider 3A source alone. Make voltage source zero as shown in Fig. 2.27 (b). KCL gives current in 4Ω resistor as (I" + 3) Amps. Hence, voltage $V_1 = 4$ (I" + 3), and KVL across the left side the loop gives

$$+ V_1 + 2I" - 2V_1 = 0$$

or
$$2I" - V_1 = 0 \quad \text{i.e. } 2I" - 4 (I" + 3) = 0$$

Solving this gives $I" = -6A$

Step III: By Superposition theorem
$$I = I' + I'' = -12 - 6 = -18A$$

Current (I) from KVL and KCL:

To verify the Superposition theorem for this circuit let us find current I directly for circuit of Fig. 2.135. By KCL current in 4Ω resistor is (I + 4) Amp. The voltage $V_1 = 4(I + 4)$, and KVL across left loop as before gives

$$V_1 - 2V_1 + 2I - 24 = 0 \text{ or } -V_1 + 2I - 24 = 0$$

i.e. $\quad -4(I + 4) + 2I - 24 = 0 \text{ or } -2I = -36$

Hence, $\quad I = -18$

This is the same current we found out using Superposition theorem. Thus Superposition theorem is verified for this circuit.

Ex. 2.12: Find current in 6Ω resistor (I_L) by using the Superposition theorem.

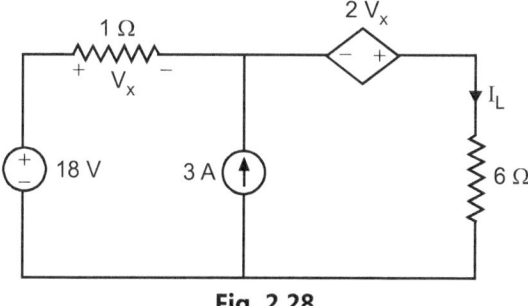

Fig. 2.28

Sol.: Step I: Consider 18V only. Make current source zero as shown in Fig. 2.29 (a). The circuit is converted into a single loop with loop current I_L'. Now $V_x = I_L'$ and KVL across whole loop gives

$$+6I_L' - 2V_x + V_x - 18 = 0 \text{ or } 6I_L' - V_x = 18$$

i.e. $\quad 6I_L' - I_L' = 18 \text{ or } I_L' = +\dfrac{18}{5} = 3.6 \text{ Amp.}$

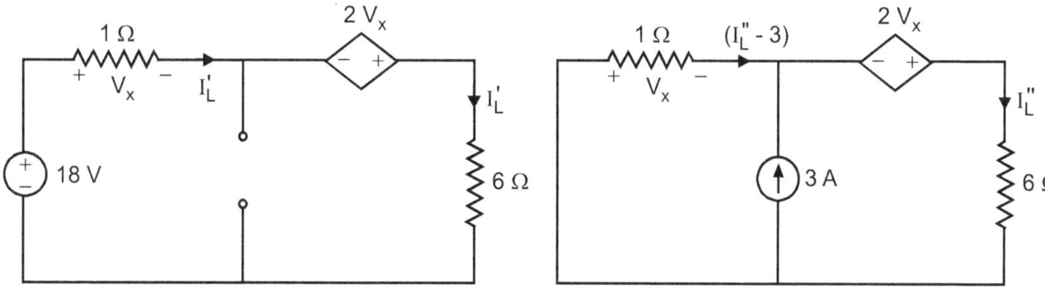

(a) Circuit for Step I (b) Circuit for Step II

Fig. 2.29: Circuits to find required variables

Step II: Consider 3A current source alone. Make the voltage source zero as shown in Fig. 2.29 (b). Now KCL gives current in 1Ω resistor branch as $(I_L'' - 3)$. Now applying KVL to outer loop (loop without 3A source in between) gives,

$$6I_L'' - 2V_x + V_x = 0 \text{ or } V_x = 6I_L'' = I(I_L'' - 3) \quad \text{where } V_x = (I_L'' - 3)$$

Solving this gives $\quad I_L'' = \dfrac{-3}{5} = -0.6$ Amp.

Step III: By Superposition theorem $I_L = I_L' + I_L'' = (3.6 - 0.6)$

i.e. $\quad I_L = 3.0$ Amp.

Ex. 2.13: Find current in 3Ω resistor (I) by using the Superposition theorem.

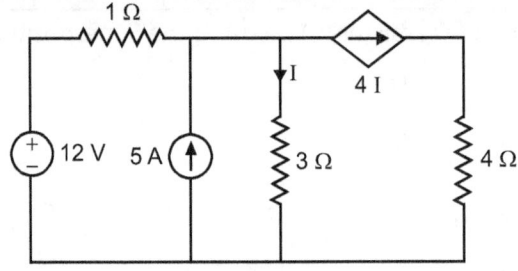

Fig. 2.30

Sol.: Step I: Consider 12V source alone. Make 5A current source zero as shown in Fig. 2.31 (a). By KCL the current in 1Ω branch is $+ 5I'$. KVL across the input loop gives

$$3I' + 5I' - 12 = 0 \text{ or } I' = +1.5A$$

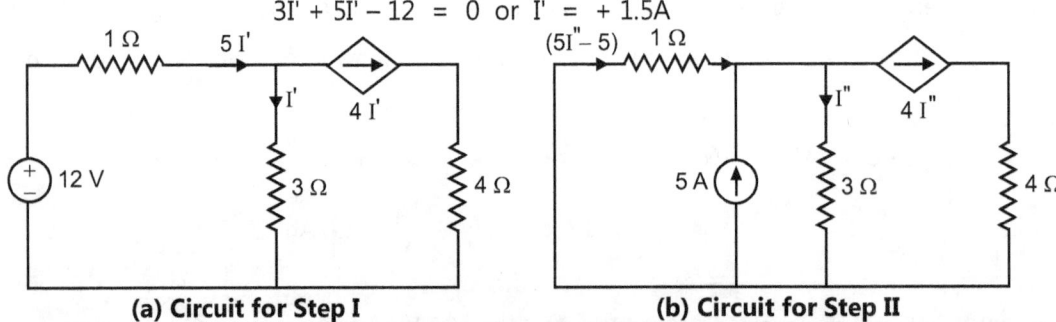

(a) Circuit for Step I   (b) Circuit for Step II

Fig. 2.31: Circuits to find required variables

Step II: Now consider 5A source make voltage source zero as shown in Fig. 2.31 (b). KCL at node gives current in 1Ω resistor as $(5I'' - 5)$. KVL across loop formed by the 3Ω and 1Ω resistor is

$$+3I'' + 1(5I'' - 5) = 0 \text{ or } I'' = \dfrac{5}{8} \text{ Amp.}$$

Step III: By Superposition theorem $I = I' + I'' = \dfrac{3}{2} + \dfrac{5}{8} = \dfrac{17}{8}$

Thus, $\quad$ current (I) $= 2.125$ Amp.

Ex. 2.14: By using Superposition theorem find current (I) in the circuit shown.

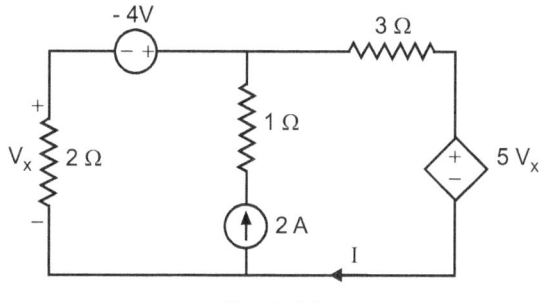

Fig. 2.32

Sol.: There are only two independent energy sources. Consider 4V source alone. Make current source zero as shown in Fig. 2.33 (a). The circuit is converted into a single loop with loop current (I'). We have $V_x = -2I'$ and KVL across loop is gives $5V_x + 3I' + 4 - V_x = 0$.

i.e. $\qquad 4V_x + 3I' + 4 = 0$

i.e. $\qquad 4(-2I') + 3I' + 4 = 0$ or $I' = 0.8$ Amp.

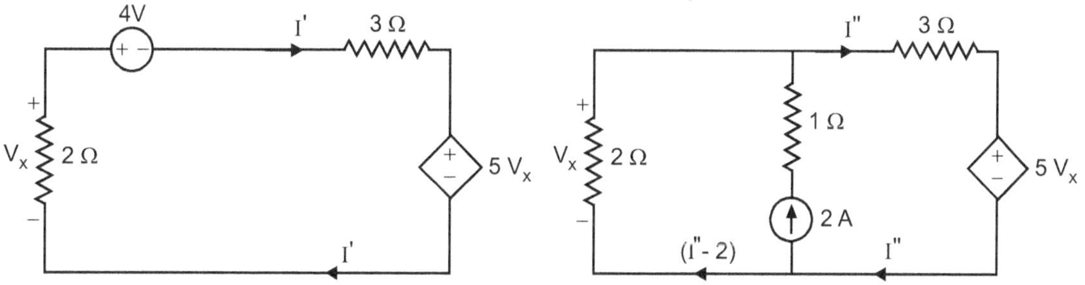

(a) Circuit for Step I　　　　　　　**(b) Circuit for Step II**

Fig. 2.33: Circuit to find required variables

Step II: Now consider current source only. Make voltage source zero as shown in Fig. 2.33 (b). KCL gives the current in 2Ω resistor as $(I'' - 2)$. Now $V_x = -2(I'' - 2)$ and KVL across outer loop gives

$$+ 5V_x + 3I'' - V_x = 0$$

OR $\qquad 4V_x + 3I'' = 0$

i.e. $\qquad 4 \times -2(I'' - 2) + 3I'' = 0$

gives, $\qquad I'' = \dfrac{16}{5} = 3.2$ A

Step III: By Superposition theorem $I = I' + I'' = 0.8 + 3.2 = 4A$

Hence, $\qquad$ current (I) = 4A

Ex. 2.15: Using Superposition theorem find current I in the circuit shown.

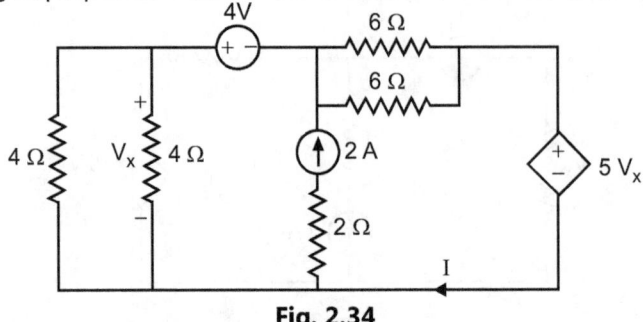

Fig. 2.34

Sol.: Two 4Ω resistors are in parallel. Effective resistance is 4Ω || 4Ω = 2Ω. Also 6Ω in parallel with 6Ω gives equivalent of 3Ω. This will reduce the circuit which is same as that is given in Fig. 2.34 for Ex. (2.15) except that this has 2Ω resistor in series with 2A source of 1Ω.

Since, any resistor in series with current source do not change current through that branch and hence is of no meaning (Similarly resistor in parallel directly across the voltage source). The analysis will be exactly same as given for Ex. (2.15).

Thus,   current (I) = (0.8 + 3.2) = 4.0 Amp.

2.2 THEVENIN'S THEOREM

Thevenin's theorem and Norton's theorem are two important network theorems used for the analysis of the electrical networks.

Utility of Thevenin's Theorem: Thevenin's theorem is used when we want to find current (or voltage) across a particular branch of the given complicated circuit consisting of many energy sources and impedances. It cannot be used to find current (or voltage) across all the branches in the circuit.

Thevenin (voltage source) Equivalent Circuit: Before we study Thevenin's theorem let us consider Thevenin Equivalent circuit by considering following problem. Suppose that we had a complicated network (N) containing many impedance (R, L, C) and energy sources (Independent or dependent or both). Let Z_L be the load Impedance across any two terminals a-b as shown in Fig. 2.35 (a).

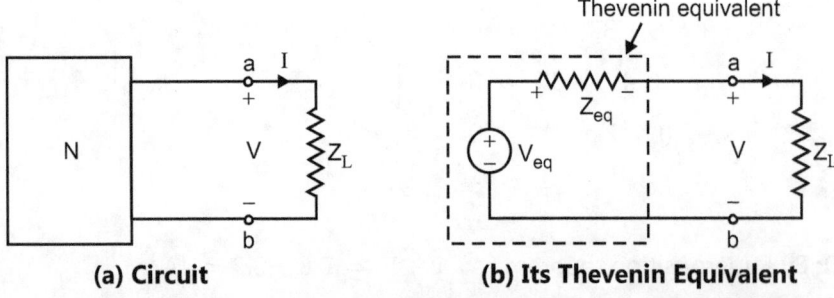

(a) Circuit   (b) Its Thevenin Equivalent

Fig. 2.35: Circuit to explain Thevenin (Voltage source) Equivalent

Our aim is to replace whole the circuit across a-b by equivalent circuit consisting of a voltage source (V_{eq}) in series with a impedance (Z_{eq}). This is known as Thevenin Equivalent Circuit. The two circuits are equivalent regardless of whatever load (Z_L) connected. This means voltage across terminal a-b (V) and current through terminal (I) must be same in both the circuits.

For Fig. 2.35 (b) $\qquad V_{eq} = Z_{eq} I + V \qquad$ ...(a)

Value of V_{eq} and Z_{eq} can be found out by considering two simple loads.

(a) To find the voltage V_{eq}: Consider Z_L being temporarily removed by open circuiting as shown in Fig. 2.36.

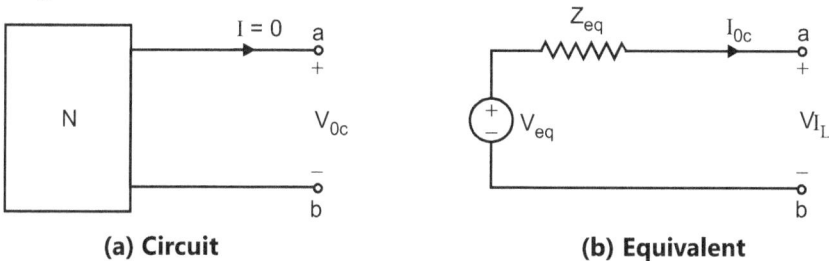

(a) Circuit (b) Equivalent

Fig. 2.36: Circuit used to find V_{eq}

As a-b are open ($Z_L = \infty$) we have $I = I_{oc} = 0$
and $\qquad V = V_{oc} = V_{eq} \qquad$ ... (2.1)

"Thus, V_{eq} is the open circuit voltage (V_{oc}) between the two terminals"

(b) To find value of equivalent Impedance (Z_{eq}): There are two methods by which Z_{eq} can be determined.

Method I: Consider Load (Z_L) is replaced by a short circuit (SC) as shown in Fig. 2.37.

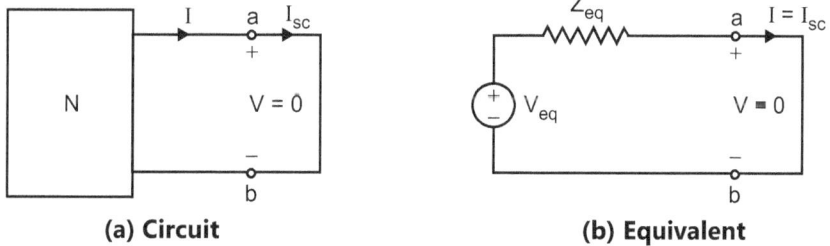

(a) Circuit (b) Equivalent

Fig. 2.37: Circuits to find Z_{eq}

As a-b is short $V = 0$ and $Z_L = 0$

By equation (a) $\qquad V_{eq} = Z_{eq} I_{sc} + 0 = Z_{eq} I_{sc}$

Hence $\qquad Z_{eq} = \dfrac{V_{eq}}{I_{sc}} = \dfrac{V_{oc}}{I_{sc}}$

"Thus the Z_{eq} is obtained by taking ratio of open circuit voltage (V_{oc}) and short circuit current (I_{sc})".

Method II: If the network (N) contains only independent energy (voltage or current) sources then Z_{eq} is the impedance seen between terminals a-b of the network with all sources made zero (replace voltage source by short circuit and current source by open circuit).

This is explained in Fig. 2.38.

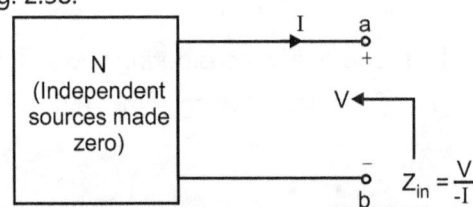

Fig. 2.38: Alternate method to find Z_{eq}

Thus, $$Z_{eq} = Z_{in} = \frac{V}{-I} \quad \ldots (2.2)$$

Z_{eq} is called as "Thevenin equivalent impedance".

Note: (1) To find Z_{eq} by method II [equation (2.2)] the network (N) should not contain any controlled (dependent) energy sources, and must contain only independent energy sources.

(2) If the network (N) contains controlled energy sources then to find Z_{eq} method – I must be used. Infact method I is general that can be used to find Z_{eq} when network contains both independent and controlled energy sources.

Summary: Thevenin Equivalent circuit can be obtained by using the following steps:

Step I: Remove load (Z_L) leaving network (N) with terminals a-b open. Find open circuit voltage (V_{oc}).

Step II: Short terminals a-b ($Z_L = 0$). Find short circuit current (I_{sc})

Then $$Z_{eq} = \frac{V_{oc}}{I_{sc}}$$

Step III: Thevenin equivalent circuit of N is obtained by a voltage source (V_{oc}) in series with impedance (Z_{eq}).

With the study of Thevenin Equivalent circuit now we can define the Thevenin's Theorem and prove it.

Statement of Thevenin's Theorem: "In a linear circuit containing energy sources and linear, bilateral elements, across any two terminals in the circuit the whole circuit can be replaced by a equivalent voltage source (V_{eq}) in series with equivalent impedance (Z_{eq}) where V_{eq} is the open circuit voltage between the terminals and Z_{eq} is the input impedance seen between the terminals with all the energy sources are replaced by their internal impedances".

Proof: To prove the above Theorem let us consider a simple circuit shown in Fig. 2.39 (a).

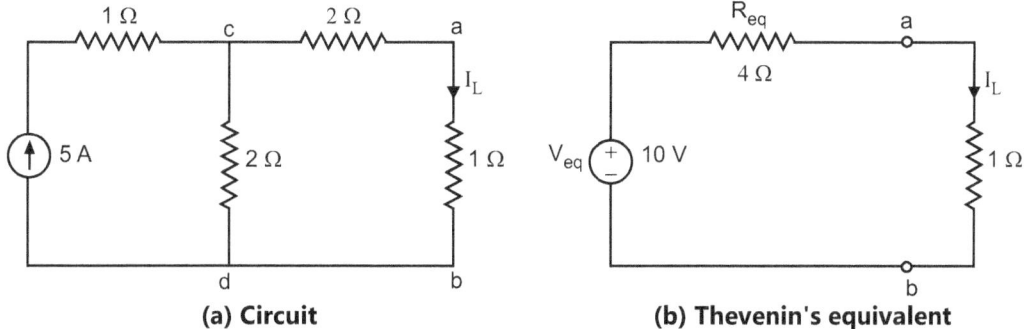

(a) Circuit (b) Thevenin's equivalent
Fig. 2.39: Circuits used to prove Thevenin's theorem

To prove the theorem let us find out load current (I_L). By current divider action this current is given by

$$I_L = 5 \times \frac{2}{2+2+1} = 5 \times \frac{2}{5} = 2A$$

Now we have to prove that current I_L as found from using Thevenin Theorem is also equal to 2A. The equivalent circuit is as shown in Fig. 2.39 (b).

With terminal a-b opened the open circuit voltage is the voltage across 2Ω resistor connected between c-d. This voltage is $V_{eq} = V_{oc} = 2 \times 5 = 10V$.

Now to find R_{eq} between a-b make the current source zero (open the two terminals). Then two 2Ω resistors will be in series across a-b. Hence we have $R_{eq} = 2Ω + 2Ω = 4$ ohms. Hence the load current (I_L) from Fig. 2.39 (b) is given by

$$I_L = \frac{10}{4+1} = \frac{10}{5} = 2A$$

Since, this current is same as the current obtained from current divider action the Thevenins theorem is proved.

Following few examples explains how the Thevenin's theorem can be used effectively in network analysis.

Ex. 2.16: Determine load current (I_L) in 4Ω resistor connected across a-b in the circuit using Thevenin's theorem.

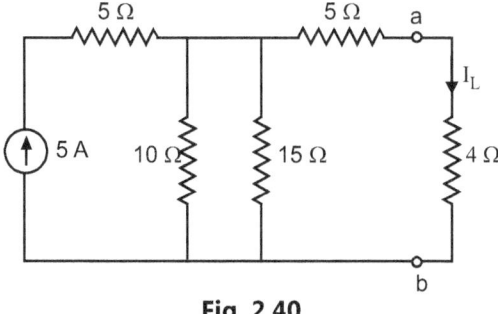

Fig. 2.40

Sol.: Let us find Thevenin equivalent across a-b.

Step I: To find open circuit voltage (V_{oc}): With a-b opened the circuit is shown in Fig. 2.41 (a). Then open circuit voltage = $V_{oc} = V_{eq} = 5 \times [6\Omega] = 30V$ where 6Ω resistor is parallel equivalent of 10Ω and 15Ω.

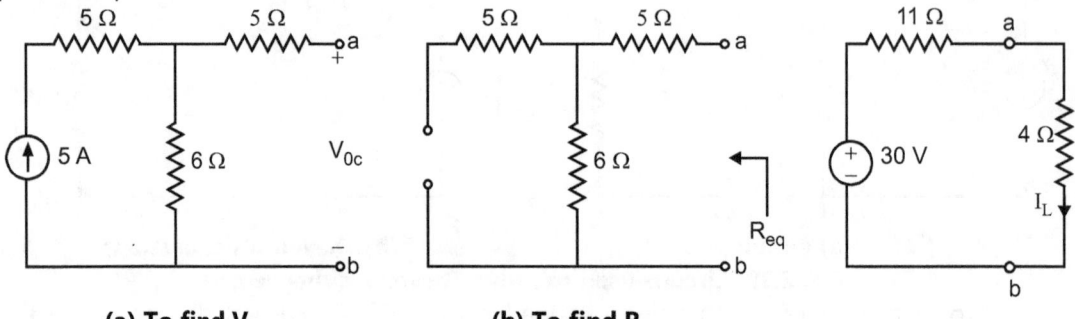

(a) To find V_{CC} (b) To find R_{eq}

Fig. 2.41: Steps to find Thevenin equivalent circuits

Step II: To find Thevenin equivalent Impedance (R_{eq}): Open the current source as in Fig. 2.41 (b). Then resistance between

$$a - b = R_{eg} = (5 + 6) = 11 \, \Omega$$

Step III: Thevenin equivalent circuit: This is shown in the Fig. 2.41 (c). The load current (I_L) is given by

$$(I_L) = \frac{30}{11 + 4} = \frac{30}{15} = 2A$$

Ex. 2.17: Find Thevenin equivalent across terminal a-b in the circuit shown below and find current (I_L).

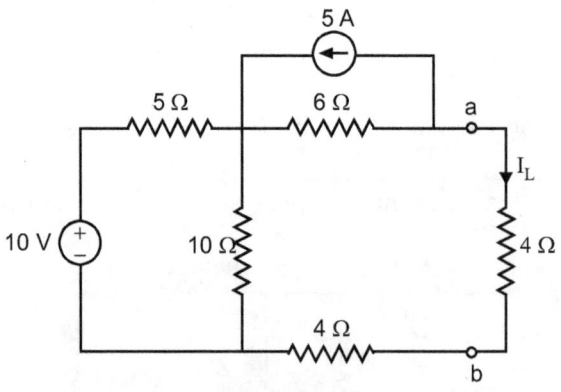

Fig. 2.42

Sol.: Let us find Thevenin's equivalent across a-b.

Step I: To find V_{oc}: Open terminal a-b. Make source transformation of 3A current source the resultant circuit is shown in Fig. 2.43 (a). Current (I) = $\frac{10}{5 + 10} = \frac{2}{3}$ Amp.

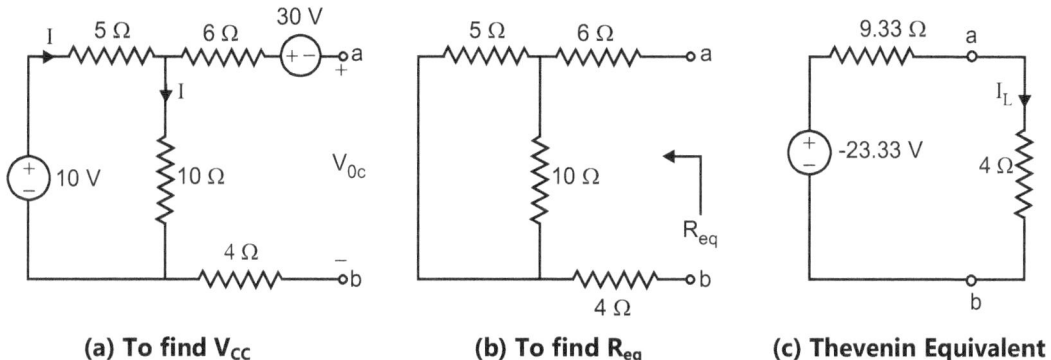

(a) To find V_{cc}   **(b) To find R_{eq}**   **(c) Thevenin Equivalent**

Fig. 2.43: Steps to find Thevenin equivalent circuits

Open circuit (OC) voltave = $V_{oc} = -30 + 10I = -30 + 6.67 = -23.33$ V

Step II: To find R_{eq}: Open the current source and short the voltage source the equivalent circuit to find R_{eq} is shown in Fig. 2.43 (b).

$$R_{eq} = 6 + 5 \| 10 = 6 + \frac{10}{3} = 9.33 \Omega$$

Step III: Thevenin equivalent circuit: This is shown in Fig. 2.43 (b).

$$\text{The load current } (I_L) = \frac{-23.33}{9.33 + 4} = -1.75 \text{ Amps.}$$

Ex. 2.18: Find current (I_L) in 10 Ω resistance across a-b. Make use of Thevenin's theorem.

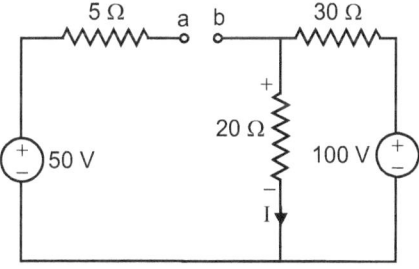

Fig. 2.44

Sol.: Let us find the Thevenin equivalent across a-b.

Step I: To find V_{oc}: As it is terminals a-b are open in the given circuit.

The current $\quad I = \dfrac{100}{20 + 30} = \dfrac{100}{50} = 2.0$ Amp.

Hence voltage between $\quad a - b = V_{ab} = V_{oc} = 50 - 20I = 10$ Volts

Step II: To find R_{eq}: Short the two voltage sources. The equivalent circuit is shown in Fig. 2.45 (a). The two resistors of 30Ω ∥ 20 Ω gives equivalent of 12Ω. Thus, equivalent resistance between a − b = R_{eq} = 5 + 12 = 17 Ω.

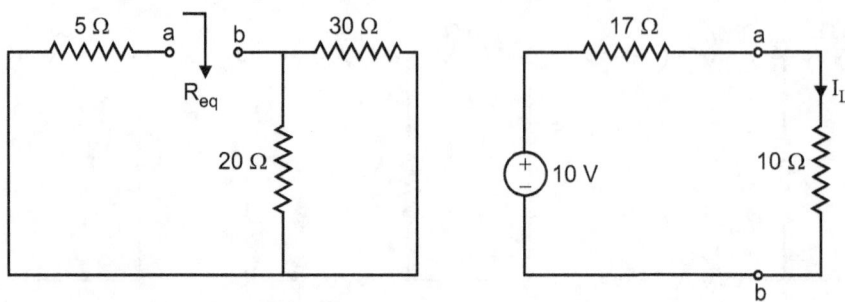

(a) To find R_eq (Method II)   (b) Thevenin's equivalent

Fig. 2.45: Steps to find Thevenin equivalent circuits

Step III: The Thevenin equivalent circuit is shown in Fig. 2.45 (b).

$$\text{The load current } (I_L) = \frac{10}{17 + 10} = \frac{10}{27}$$

$$= 0.37 \text{ Amp.}$$

Ex. 2.19: Find current in 20Ω resistor across a-b in the circuit. Make use of Thevenin's theorem.

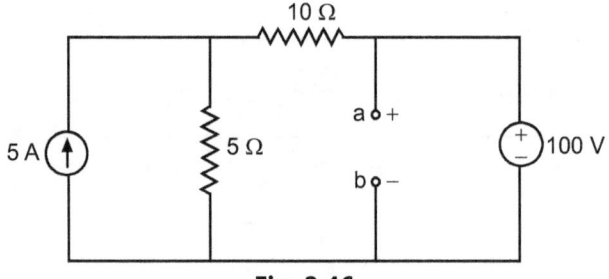

Fig. 2.46

Sol.: Let us find Thevenin equivalent across a-b.

Step I: To find V_{oc}: As it is terminals a-b opened. Since 100V is directly across terminals a-b. The voltage across a-b = V_{ab} = V_{oc} = 100V (Fixed)

Step II: To find R_{eq}: Open the current source and short the voltage source as in Fig. 2.47 (a). As terminals a-b are directly shorted R_{ab} = 0. Thus, R_{eq} = 0 ohms.

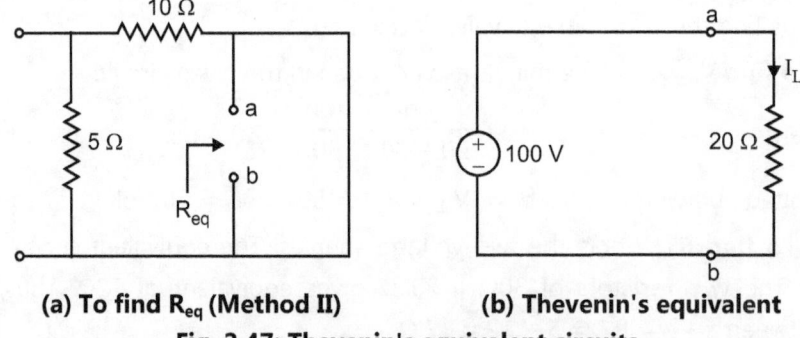

(a) To find R_eq (Method II)   (b) Thevenin's equivalent

Fig. 2.47: Thevenin's equivalent circuits

Step III: Thevenin's equivalent circuit: This is shown in Fig. 2.47 (b). The current in 20Ω is given as

$$(I_L) = \frac{100}{20} = 5A$$

Ex. 2.20: Find Thevenin's equivalent circuit across a-b and then find current in 10Ω resistor connected between a-b.

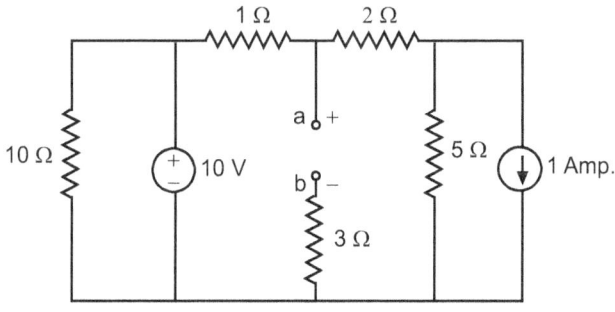

Fig. 2.48

Sol.: Let us find Thevenin equivalent circuit across a-b.

Step I: To find open circuit voltage: Convert current source of 1A into voltage source as shown in Fig. 2.49 (a). The loop current I is given by applying KVL across the loop.

i.e. $+ 10 - I - 2I - 5I + 5 = 0$ or $I = \frac{15}{8}$ Amp.

With terminals a-b open no current flows in 3Ω resistor.

Hence, $V_{ab} = V_{oc} + 7I - 5 = 8.125$ V

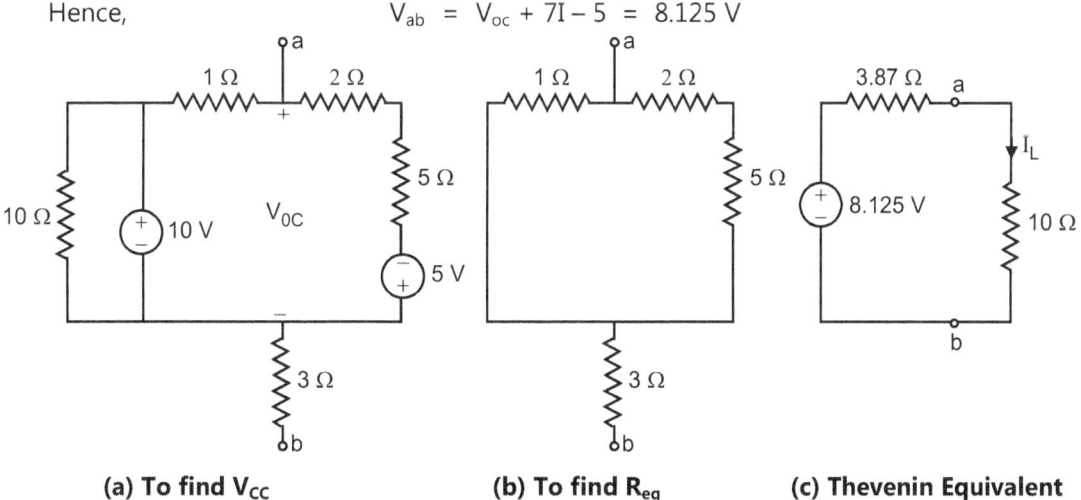

(a) To find V_{CC} (b) To find R_{eq} (c) Thevenin Equivalent

Fig. 2.49: Thevenin's equivalent circuits

Step II: To find R_{eq}: Open the current sources. Short the voltage sources. The resultant circuit is shown in Fig. 2.49 (b). 1Ω is in parallel with (2 + 5) = 7Ω resistor. Hence the equivalent resistance between a-b is

$$R_{eq} = 3 + 1 \| 7 = 3 + \frac{7}{8} = 3.87 \, \Omega$$

Step III: The Thevenin equivalent circuit is shown in Fig. 2.49 (c).

The current between resistor of 10Ω $= I_L = \dfrac{8.125}{10 + 3.87} = 0.585$ A

Ex. 2.21: In the circuit shown find I_L when R_L = 5Ω, 10Ω, 20 Ω.

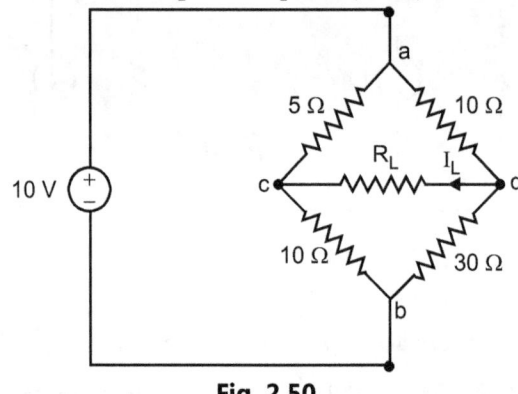

Fig. 2.50

Sol.: Since, we have to find load current (I_L) for three different R_L, it is very laborious to calculate the currents by repeating calculations for different values of R_L. Hence, this problem can be solved by using the Thevenin equivalent across load (R_L). For the time being assume R_L is removed.

Step I: To find Thevenin's voltage (V_{oc}): With R_L removed circuit is shown in Fig. 2.51 (a). The currents I_1 and I_2 are $I_1 = \dfrac{10}{10 + 5} = \dfrac{2}{3}$ A and $I_2 = \dfrac{10}{10 + 30} = 0.25$ A

V_{oc} = Voltage between d and c = $V_{dc} = 30 \, I_2 - 10 \, I_1$
= 30 × 0.25 − 10 × 0.667 = 0.83 V

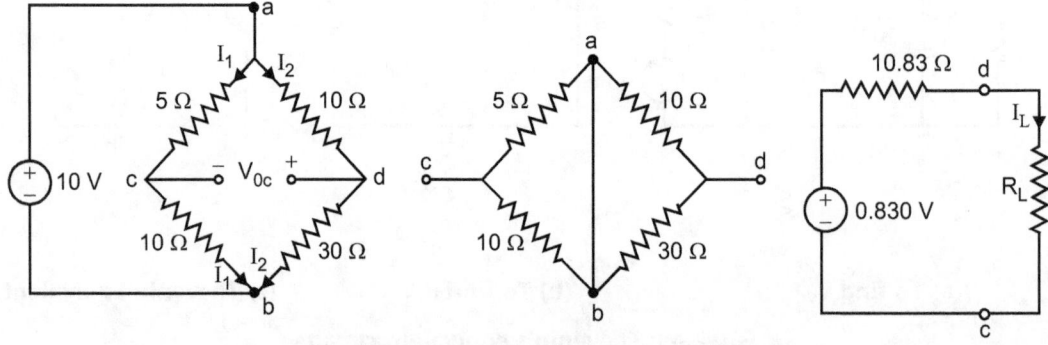

Fig. 2.51: Thevenin's equivalent circuits

Step II: To find R_{eq}: Short the voltage source with R_L being removed the circuit is shown in Fig. 2.51 (b). Now a-b being shorted 10Ω is paralle with 5Ω and 10Ω is parallel with 30Ω. This parallel combination is in series across terminals c and d. Thus, we have,

$$R_{eq} = [5 \| 10] + [10 \| 30] = \frac{10}{3} + 7.5 = 10.83 \; \Omega$$

Step III: Thevenin equivalent circuit is shown in Fig. 2.51 (c).

$$\text{Load current } (I_L) = \frac{0.83}{10.83 + R_L}$$

For $R_L = 5\Omega$ we have $I_{L1} = 52.43$ mA
For $R_L = 10 \; \Omega$ we have $I_{L2} = 39.85$ mA
For $R_L = 20 \; \Omega$ we have $I_{L3} = 26.92$ mA

Note: In last few examples we have seen that the Thevenin equivalent circuit is very convenient and easy to find current (or voltage) across a particular branch of the circuit. It is more convenient especially when load is variable like the one in Ex. (2.21). Thus, the Thevenin's theorem simplify the network analysis to a greater extent. In fact the Thevenin Theorem is considered to be major break through in the circuit analysis.

Ex. 2.22: For the circuit shown find Thevenin's equivalent circuit across terminal a-b.

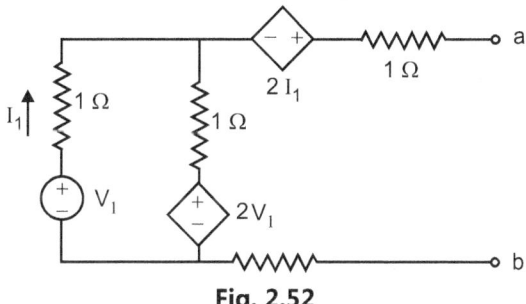

Fig. 2.52

Sol.: Step I: To find V_{oc}: As its terminals are opened current I_1 is given by

$$I_1 = \frac{V_1 - 2V_1}{1 + 1} = \frac{-V_1}{2} \text{ Amp.}$$

$$V_{ab} = V_{co} = 2I_1 + I_1 + 2V_1 = 3I_1 + 2V_1$$

$$= \frac{-3V_1}{2} + 2V_1 = \frac{V_1}{2} \text{ Amp.}$$

Step II: To find R_{eq}: Since, circuit contains controlled sources the impedance is to be determined by using the equation given below.

i.e. $$R_{eq} = \frac{V_{oc}}{I_{sc}}$$

To find I_{sc} use circuit of Fig. 2.53 (a)

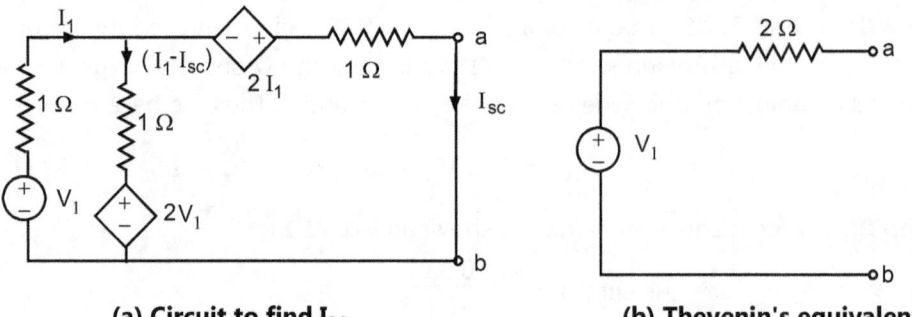

(a) Circuit to find I_{sc} (b) Thevenin's equivalent

Fig. 2.53: Steps to find Thevenin equivalent

KVL across first (Input) loop gives $2V_1 + (I_1 - I_{sc}) + I_1 - V_1 = 0$

$$2I_1 - I_{sc} + V_1 = 0 \text{ or } I_{sc} - 2I_1 = V_1 \qquad \ldots(a)$$

KVL across second (output) loop[gives

$$I_{sc} - 2I_1(I_1 - I_{sc}) - 2V_1 = 0$$

OR $\qquad\qquad -3I_1 + 2I_{sc} = 2V_1 \qquad \ldots(b)$

From (a) and (b) solve for I_{sc}

$$I_{sc} = \frac{\begin{vmatrix} -2 & V_1 \\ -3 & 2V_1 \end{vmatrix}}{\begin{vmatrix} -2 & 1 \\ -3 & 2 \end{vmatrix}} = \frac{-4V_1 + 3V_1}{-4 + 3} = \frac{-V_1}{-1} = V_1$$

$$R_{eq} = \frac{V_1}{V_1/2} = 2\Omega$$

Step III: Thus, Thevenin equivalent across a-b is shown in Fig. 2.53 (b).

Ex. 2.23: Replace the portion within dotted line by Thevenin's equivalent circuit and then find voltage V_1.

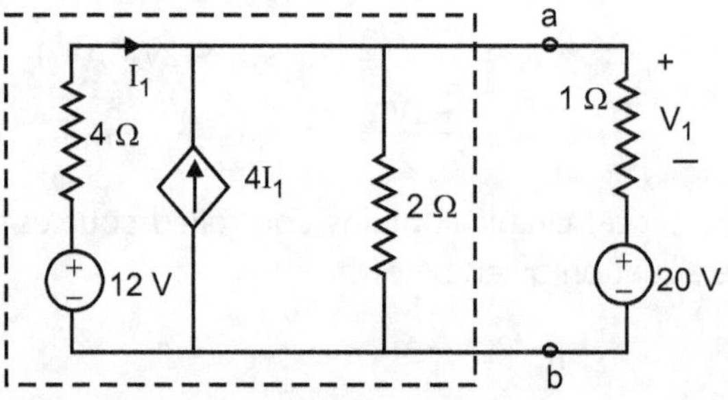

Fig. 2.54

Sol.: We have to find Thevenin equivalent across a-b. For the time being assume that a-b is open circuited.

Step I: To find V_{OC}: The circuit is shown in Fig. 2.55 (a).

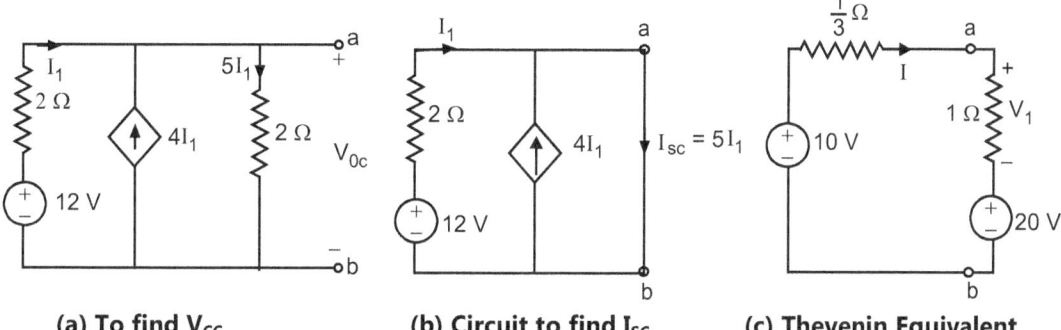

(a) To find V_{CC} (b) Circuit to find I_{SC} (c) Thevenin Equivalent

Fig. 2.55: Steps to obtain Thevenin equivalent circuits

KVL across outer loop gives $2 \times 5I_1 + 2I_1 - 12 = 0$ or $I_1 = 1$ Amp.

Hence $\quad V_{eq} = V_{OC} = 2 \times 5I_1 = 10V$

Step II: To find R_{eq}: Since, circuit contains controlled sources we have to use equation $R_{eq} = \dfrac{V_{OC}}{I_{SC}}$. To find I_{SC} consider the circuit shown in Fig. 2.55 (b).

KVL, across outer loop gives $0 + 2I_1 - 12 = 0$ OR $I_1 = 6A$. Thus I_1 is different from one found in Step I because here I_1 is found by short circuiting a-b while it was found by open circuiting in step I.

Thus, $\quad I_{SC} = 5I_1 = 5 \times 6 = 30A$

Therefore $\quad R_{eq} = \dfrac{V_{OC}}{I_{SC}} = \dfrac{10}{30} = \dfrac{1}{3} \Omega$

Step III: Thevenin equivalent is shown in Fig. 2.55 (c). KVL across whole loop gives current (I). Thus $20 + I + \dfrac{I}{3} - 10 = 0$. Solving this gives current (I) $= \dfrac{30}{4}$ Amp. -7.5 A.

Hence $\quad V_1 = 1 \times I = I = -75$ Volts

Ex. 2.24: Find current in 9Ω resistor by using Thevenin's Theorem.

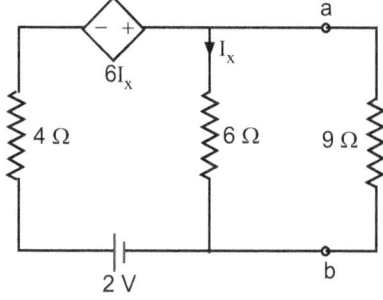

Fig. 2.56

Sol.: Let us first find Thevenin equivalent across a-b.

Step I: To find V_{OC}: Open the terminal a-b by removing the 9Ω resistor as shown in Fig. 2.57 (a). There will be a single loop with loop current I_x.

KVL gives $\quad 6I_x - 6I_x + 4I_x - 2 = 0$ or $I_x = 0.5$ A

Hence $\quad V_{OC} = V_{ab} = V_{eq} = 6I_x = 3V$

Step II: To find R_{eq}: Use $R_{eq} = \dfrac{V_{OC}}{I_{SC}}$ to find the R_{eq}. Now short a-b find I_{SC} as shown in Fig. 2.57 (b).

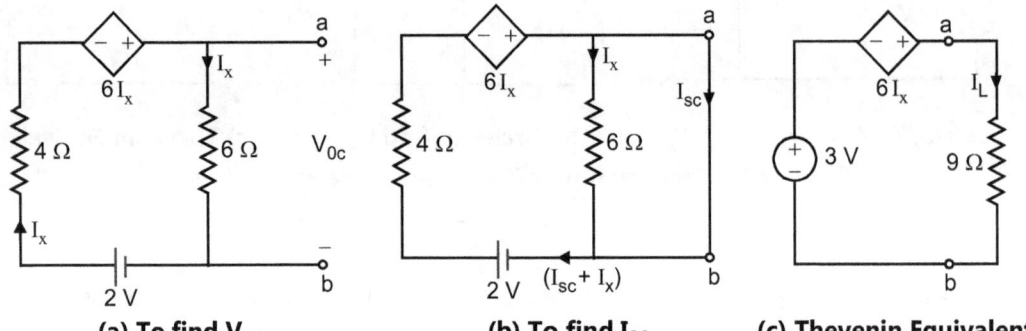

(a) To find V_{CC} (b) To find I_{SC} (c) Thevenin Equivalent

Fig. 2.57: Step to find Thevenin's equivalent

KVL across input loop gives $\quad 6I_x - 6I_x + 4(I_{SC} + I_x) - 2 = 0 \quad$ ...(a)

OR $\quad (I_{SC} + I_x) = 0.5$

KVL across output loop gives $6I_x = 0$ or $I_x = 0$

Hence, we have $\quad I_{SC} = 0.5$ A

Thus, $\quad R_{eq} = \dfrac{V_{OC}}{I_{SC}} = \dfrac{3}{0.5} = 6\,\Omega$

Step III: Thevenin equivalent circuit is shown in Fig. 2.57 (c).

The current through 9Ω resistor $= I_L = \dfrac{3}{6+9} = \dfrac{3}{15} = 0.2$ A

Ex. 2.25: Find current in 10Ω resistor across a-b in the circuit shown. Make use of voltage source equivalent across terminals a-b.

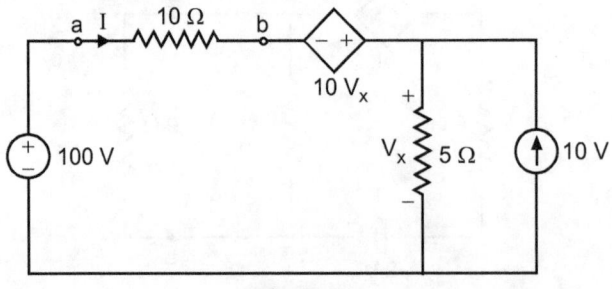

Fig. 2.58

Sol.: We have to find voltage source (Thevenin's) equivalent circuit across terminals a-b.

Step I: To find V_{OC}: Open the terminals a-b as shown in Fig. 2.59 (a). 10 A current flows through 5Ω resistor. Hence V_x = 50 V.

Now, $\qquad V_{OC} = V_{ab} = 100 - V_x + 10V_x = 100 + 9V_x = 550V$

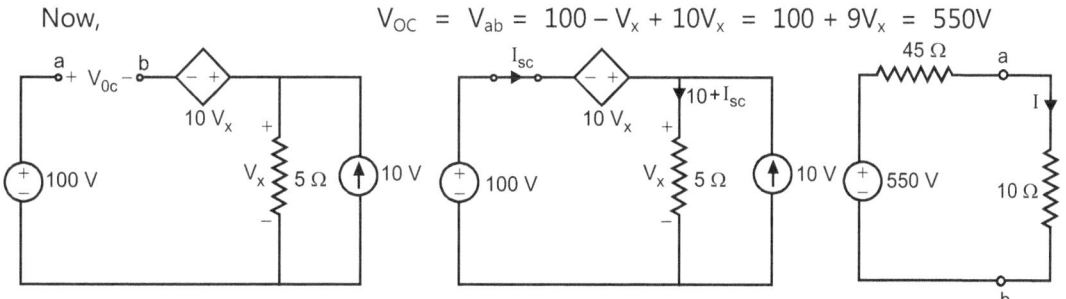

(a) Circuit to find V_{CC} (b) Circuit to find V_{OC} (c) Thevenin Equivalent

Fig. 2.59: Steps to find voltage source equivalent

Step II: To find R_{eq}: Use the formula $R_{eq} = \dfrac{V_{OC}}{I_{SC}}$. To get I_{SC} short terminals a-b as shown in Fig. 2.59 (b). We have $V_x = 5(10 + I_{SC})$. Where $(10 + I_{SC})$ is the current in 5Ω resistor. KVL across input loop gives $V_x - 10 V_x - 100 = 0$ OR $-9V_x = 100$

i.,e. $\qquad\qquad -9[10 + I_{SC}] \times 5 = 100$

Solving this gives $\qquad I_{SC} = \dfrac{500}{45}$ A

Hence, $\qquad\qquad R_{eq} = \dfrac{V_{OC}}{I_{SC}} = 45\ \Omega$

Step III: Thevenin's (Voltage source) equivalent is shown in Fig. 2.59 (c).

2.3 NORTON'S THEOREM

Like Thevenin Theorem, Norton's Theorem is also used to analyse the given network.

Utility of Theorem: It is used when current (or voltage) across a particular branch in a circuit consisting of many sources and impedance is to be found out. However it cannot be used when more than one branch currents (or voltages) are to be found out.

Norton's (Current source) Equivalent circuit: Consider a network (N) consisting of impedances and energy sources is shown in Fig. 2.36 (a). Some time the whole network (N) is to be replaced across a-b by equivalent circuit shown in Fig. (2.60). This is an current source equivalent and is called Norton's equivalent circuit.

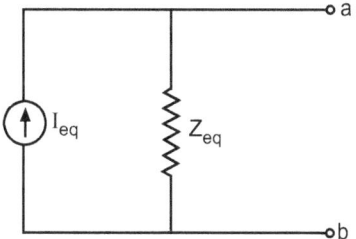

Fig. 2.60: Norton's (Current source) Equivalent circuit

This equivalent can be obtained by source transformation of Thevenin's equivalent circuit of Fig. 2.36 (b) where

$$I_{eq} = I_N = \frac{V_{OC}}{Z_{eq}} \qquad \ldots(2.3)$$

This is the value of equivalent current source. Since.

$$Z_{eq} = \frac{V_{OC}}{I_{SC}}$$

We have, $\qquad I_{eq} = I_N = \frac{V_{OC}}{V_{OC}/I_{SC}} = I_{SC} \qquad \ldots(2.4)$

Thus, Norton's equivalent current source is the short circuit current across terminals in the circuit.

Thus, **"Norton's equivalent circuit is obtained by the source Transformation of Thevenin equivalent circuit or vice versa"**.

Statement of Norton's Theorem: "In a linear circuit containing energy sources and linear and bilateral element across any two terminals in the circuit the whole circuit can be replaced by equivalent current source (I_{eq}) in parallel with equivalent impedance (Z_{eq}) where, I_{eq} is the short circuit current (I_{SC}) between the terminals and Z_{eq} is the input impedance the terminals with all the energy sources replaced by their internal impedances."

Proof: To prove above theorem let us consider again the same circuit as shown in Fig. 2.39 (a) and is reproduced in Fig. 2.61 (a) below.

Let us find the load current (I_L) to prove this theorem. As before current divider action I_L:

$$= \frac{5 \times 2}{2 + 2 + 1} = 2A \text{ for the circuit of Fig. 2.61 (a)}$$

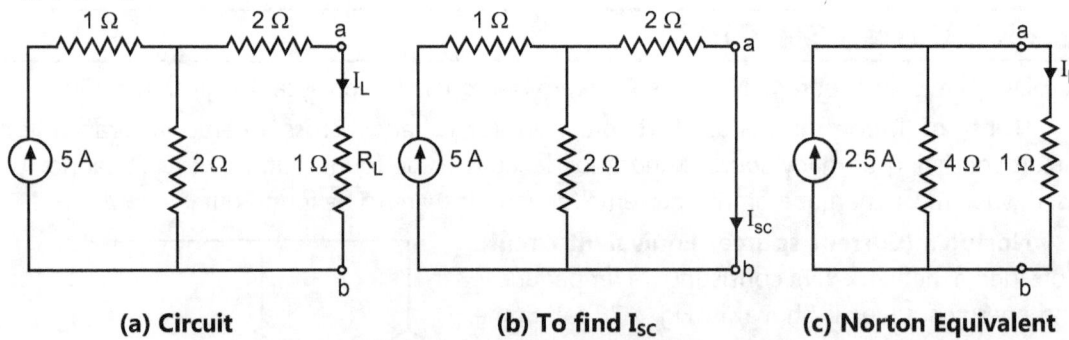

(a) Circuit (b) To find I_{SC} (c) Norton Equivalent

Fig. 2.61: Circuits to prove Norton's Theorem

Now we shall prove that $I_L = 2A$ by Norton's theorem. Now short terminals a-b as shown in Fig. 2.61 (b). Then short circuit current (I_{SC}) which is equivalent current (I_{eq}) is given by

$$I_{eq} = I_{SC} = 5 \times \frac{2}{2 \times 2} = 2.5 \text{ A}$$

As before Z_{eq} is the impedance between a-b with current source made zero (open the terminals). Thus, we have $Z_{eq} = 4\Omega$.

Hence, the Norton's equivalent is shown in Fig. 2.61 (c). For this circuit the current in load (I_L) is given by current divider action as,

$$I_L = 2.5 \times \frac{4}{1+4} = 2A$$

Since, this current is same as that obtained by the current divider action the Norton's theorem is proved.

[Note: Norton's equivalent circuits is also called as the current source equivalent circuit.] Following examples explains the use of the Norton's theorem in circuit analysis.

Ex. 2.26: Find current in 2Ω resistor across a-b by using Norton's theorem.

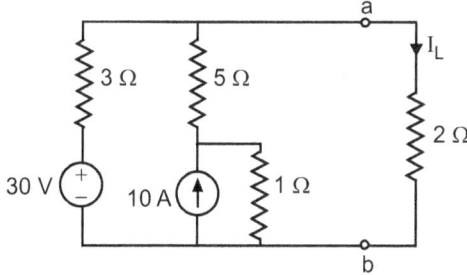

Fig. 2.62

Sol.: Let us find Norton equivalent circuit across a-b.

Step 1: To find I_{eq} (or I_N): To find I_{eq} short a-b as shown in Fig. 2.63 (a). Convert the current source into voltage source. Current I_1 and I_2 together added to get I_{SC}. We have $I_1 = \frac{30}{3} = 10$ A, $I_2 = \frac{10}{6} = \frac{5}{6}$ A. Hence $I_{SC} = I_1 + I_2 = 10 + \frac{5}{3} = 11.67$ Amp.

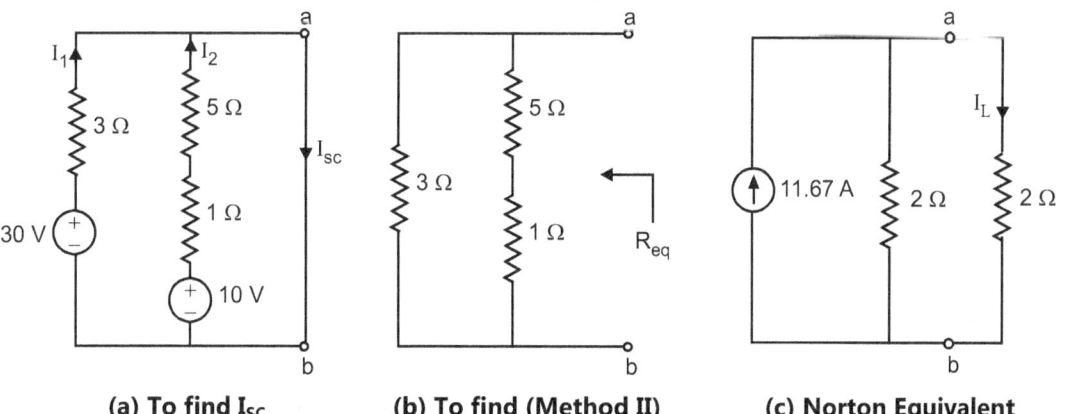

(a) To find I_{SC} (b) To find (Method II)   (c) Norton Equivalent

Fig. 2.63: Steps to obtain Norton's equivalent

Step II: To find R_{eq}: Remove load of 2Ω resistor. Short the voltage source V. Open the current source. The resultant circuit is shown in Fig. 2.63 (b). Hence, we have

$$R_{eq} = 3\,\Omega \parallel 6\,\Omega = \frac{3 \times 6}{3 + 6} = \frac{18}{9} = 2\,\Omega$$

Step III: The Norton equivalent circuit is shown in Fig. 2.63 (c). By current divider action the load current (I_L) is given by

$$I_L = 11.67 \times \frac{2}{2 + 2} = 5.835\ A$$

Ex. 2.27: Find current in 1 ohm resistor by Norton equivalent circuit.

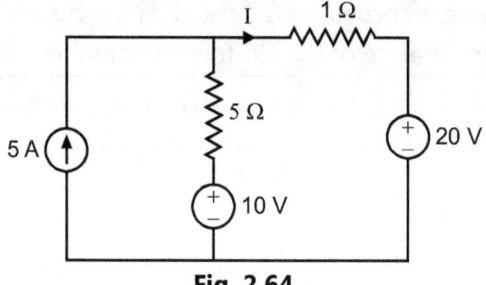

Fig. 2.64

Sol.: Let a-b be the terminals where 1Ω resistor is connected. Let us find Nortons' equivalent circuit across terminals a-b.

Step I: To find I_{eq} (Or I_N): Short the terminals a-b as shown in Fig. 2.65 (a). Let I_{SC} be the short circuit current.

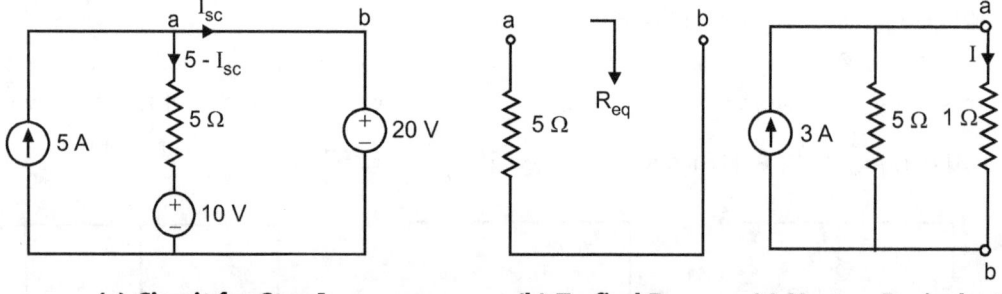

(a) Circuit for Step I (b) To find R_{eq} (c) Norton Equivalent

Fig. 2.65: Steps to obtain Norton's equivalent

By KCL current in 5Ω resistor is $(5 - I_{SC})$. Using KVL across output loop given

$$10 + 5(5 - I_{SC}) - 20 = 0$$

OR

$$I_{SC} = 3A$$

Thus, $I_{eq} = I_N = 3A$

Step II: To find R_{eq}: Open the current source short the voltage sources. Remove the 1Ω resistor. The circuit is shown in Fig. 2.65 (b). The equivalent resistance between a-b is given by $R_{eq} = 5\,\Omega$.

Step III: The Norton's Equivalent circuit is shown in Fig. 2.65 (c). By current divider action, the current in 1Ω reisistor is I = $3 \times \dfrac{5}{5+1}$ = 2.5A

Note: Many times we need to find both Thevenin's and Norton equivalent for the given circuit. Then we can first find any one of them and then the other equivalent can be obtained by using source transformation. Following few examples explains this.

Ex. 2.28: Find Thevenin's and Norton's equivalent across a-b in the circuit shown.

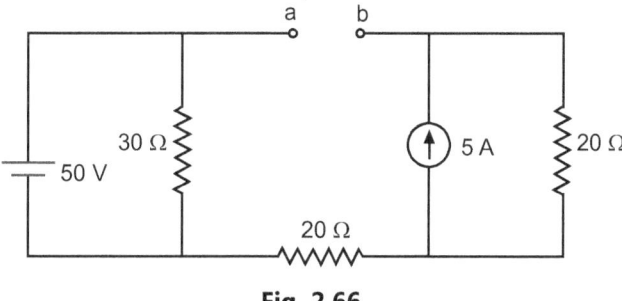

Fig. 2.66

Sol.: Let us find Thevenin's equivalent circuit.

Step I: To find V_{oc}: The circuit is shown n Fig. 2.67 (a). Convert 5A current source into a voltage source. The voltage between a – b = V_{OC} = 50 –100 = –50V

Step II: To find R_{eq}: Open the current source and short the voltage source. Then resistance between a – b = R_{eq} = 20 + 20 = 40 Ω.

Step III: Thevenin equivalent circuit is shown in Fig. 2.67 (b).

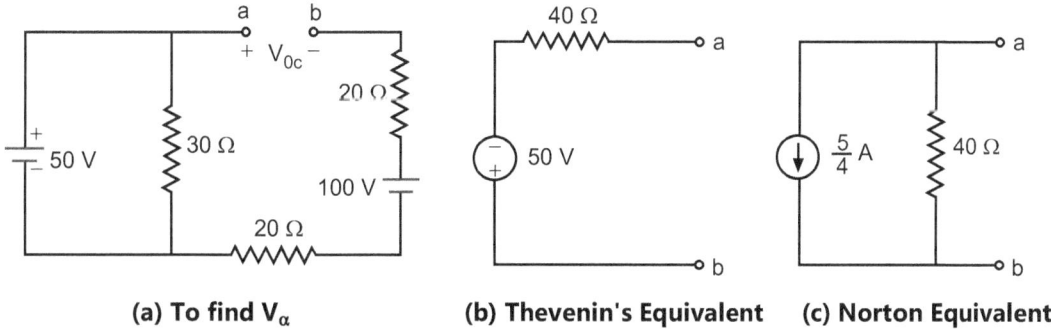

(a) To find V_α (b) Thevenin's Equivalent (c) Norton Equivalent

Fig. 2.67: Steps to find equivalent

Since V_{OC} is – V_e (Negative), the polarity of 50V source is shown reversed.

The Norton's equivalent is obtained by source transformation of Thevenin's equivalent and is shown in Fig. 2.67 (c).

Ex. 2.29: Find Thevenin's and Norton's equivalent circuits across terminal pair a-b in the circuit shown below.

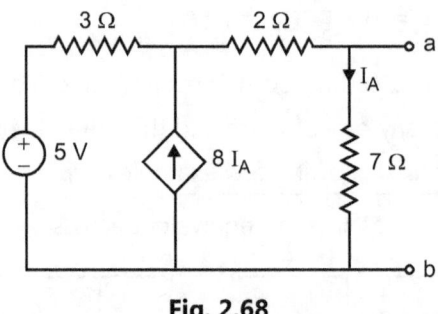

Fig. 2.68

Sol.: Let us first find Thevenine equivalent circuit and then use source transformation to get Norton's equivalent.

Step I: To find V_{OC}: The circuit can be written as shown in Fig. 2.69 (a) KCL gives current in 3Ω resistor as $7I_A$.

KVL across loop b-a-c-d-b gives

$$7I_a + 2I_A - 7I_A \times 3 = 5$$

Solving this gives $\quad I_A = \dfrac{-5}{12}$ Amp.

Hence, $\quad V_{OC} = V_{ab} = 7I_A = \dfrac{-35}{12} = -2.917$ Volts

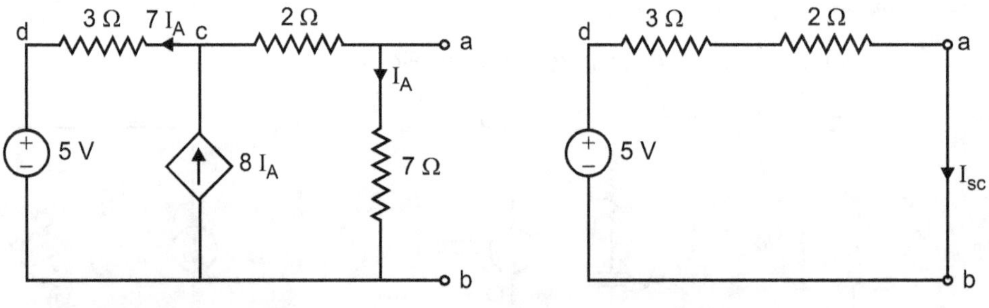

(a) Circuit to find V_α **(b)** To find I_{SC}

Fig. 2.69: Steps to find equivalent

Step II: To find R_{eq}: Use method I and equation to find R_{eq}. Since the circuit contains controlled sources. When a-b are shorted current I_A will be zero. The current source $8I_A$ KVL across loop gives $(2 + 3) I_{SC} = 5$ or $I_{SC} = 1$ Amp.

Thus, $\quad R_{eq} = \left|\dfrac{V_{OC}}{I_{SC}}\right| = \dfrac{35}{12} = 2.917\ \Omega$

Step III: The resultant Thevenin equivalent circuit is shown in Fig. 2.70 (a). By making use of source transformation Norton equivalent of Fig. 2.70 (b) is obtained.

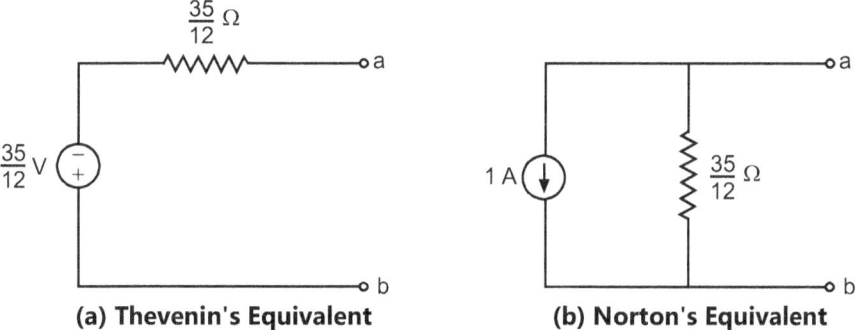

(a) Thevenin's Equivalent (b) Norton's Equivalent
Fig. 2.70: The equivalent circuits

Note: Since V_{OC} is negative the polarity of V_{OC} in the equivalent circuit is reversed.

Ex. 2.30: Find Thevenin's and Norton's equivalent circuits across terminals a-b in the circuit shown.

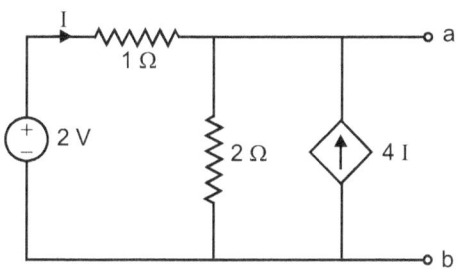

Fig. 2.71

Sol.: Let us first find Thevenin's equivalent circuit.

Step I: To find V_{OC}: With terminal a-b opened as given, KCL gives current in 2Ω resistor as 5I. The circuit is as shown in Fig. 2.72 (a).

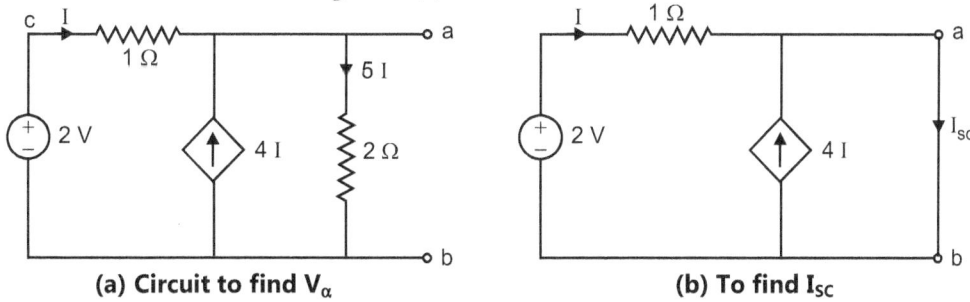

(a) Circuit to find V_α (b) To find I_{SC}
Fig. 2.72: Steps to find equivalent

KVL across loop gives (b-a-c-b)

$$2 \times 5I + I - 2 = 0 \text{ OR } I = \frac{2}{1} \text{ Amp.}$$

Hence, $V_{OC} = V_{ab} = 2 \times 5I = 10I = \frac{20}{11}$ Volts

Step II: To find R_{eq}: Here method I is to be used where $R_{eq} = \dfrac{V_{OC}}{I_{SC}}$, Now short terminals a-b, then the resultant circuit is as shown in Fig. 2.73 (b). The current $(I_{SC}) = 5I$

Now KVL gives $I \times 1 = 2$ OR $I = 2$ Amp.

Hence, short circuit current $(I_{SC}) = I_{eq} = 10A$.

Therefore, $\qquad R_{eq} = \dfrac{20/11}{10} = \dfrac{20}{11} \times \dfrac{1}{10} = \dfrac{2}{11} \, \Omega$

Step III: Thevenin equivalent circuit is shown in Fig. 2.74 (a). The Norton's equivalent is shown in Fig. 2.74 (b).

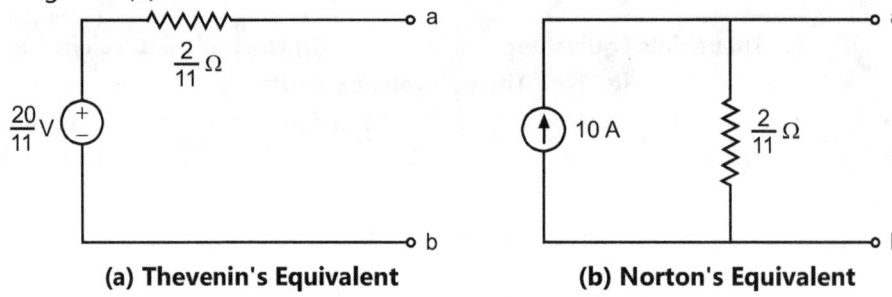

(a) Thevenin's Equivalent   (b) Norton's Equivalent

Fig. 2.73: Equivalent circuits

Ex. 2.31: Find Thevenin's and Norton's equivalent circuits across AB in the circuit shown.

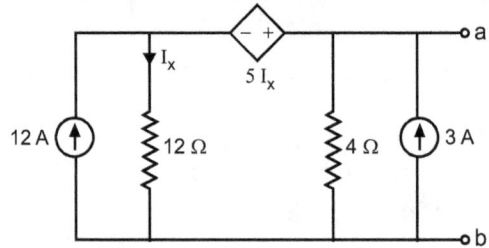

Fig. 2.74

Sol.: Let us first find Thevein equivalent circuit.

Step I: To find V_{OC}: With terminal a-b open the currents in various branches are shown in Fig. 2.75 (a).

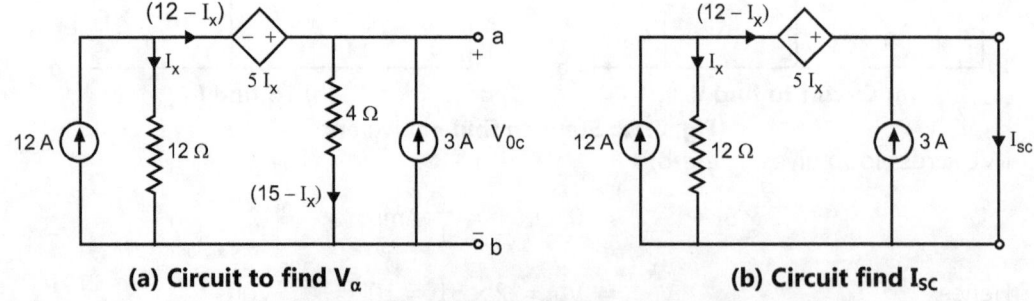

(a) Circuit to find V_α (b) Circuit find I_{SC}

Fig. 2.75: Steps to find equivalents

There is only one unknown (I_x). KVL across the loop gives,.

$$4(15 - I_x) - 5I_x - 12(I_x) = 0 \text{ i.e. } I_x = \frac{60}{21} = \frac{20}{7} \text{ Amp.}$$

Hence,
$$V_{OC} = V_{ab} = 4(15 - I_x)$$
$$= 4\left[15 - \frac{20}{7}\right] = 48.57 \text{ Volts}$$

Step II: To find R_{eq} ; Use method I where $R_{eq} = \frac{V_{OC}}{I_{SC}}$. I_{SC} can be found out by shorting a-b as shown in Fig. 2.75 (b).

where
$$I_{SC} = (3 + 12 - I_x) = 15 - I_x$$

Now KVL gives $- 5I_x - 17I_x = 0$. Since, this equation cannot be satisfied the current $I_x = 0$.

Thus
$$I_{SC} = 15 - 0 = 15 \text{ Amp.}$$

Thus,
$$R_{eq} = \frac{V_{OC}}{I_{SC}} = \frac{48.57}{15} = 3.23 \text{ }\Omega$$

Step III: Thevenin equivalent circuit is shown in Fig. 2.76 (a) while the Norton equivalent is shown in Fig. 2.76 (b).

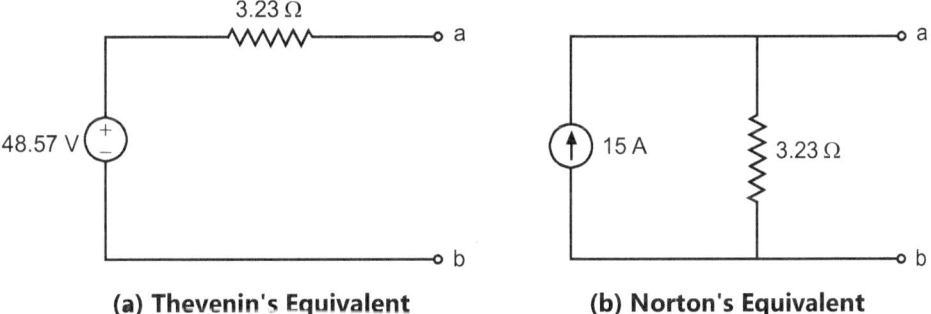

(a) Thevenin's Equivalent　　(b) Norton's Equivalent

Fig. 2.76: The equivalent circuits

Ex. 2.32: Obtain current I_x for the circuit using the Thevenin's Theorem.

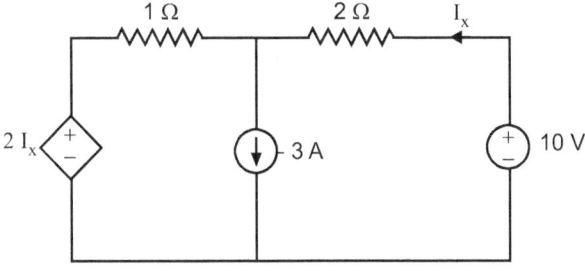

Fig. 2.77

Sol.: Assume for the time being 2Ω removed. Then $I_x = 0$ and we shall find Thevenin equivalent across terminals a-b where 2Ω is connected.

Step I: To find V_{OC}: The circuit is as shown in Fig. 2.78 (a). The controlled source become inactive (0V).

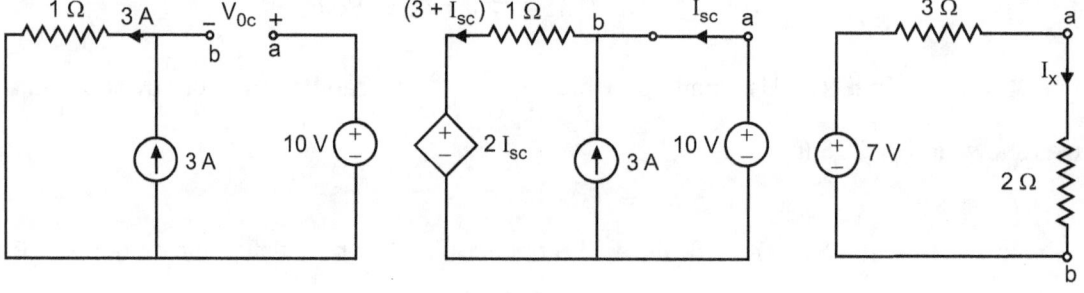

(a) Circuit for V_{CC} (b) Circuit to find I_{SC} (c) Thevenin Equivalent

Fig. 2.78: Steps to find Thevenin equivalent

Step II: To find R_{eq}: We use $R_{eq} = \dfrac{V_{OC}}{I_{SC}}$. To find equivalent resistor short terminal a-b. Let I_{SC} be the current flowing through the shorted terminals. By KCL current in 1Ω resistor is $(3 + I_{SC})$. The resultant circuit is shown in Fig. 2.78 (b). The KVL across loop gives $10 - (3 + I_{SC}) - 2I_{SC} = 0$. Hence $I_{SC} = \dfrac{7}{3}$ Amp.

Thus, $$R_{eq} = \dfrac{V_{OC}}{I_{SC}} = \dfrac{7}{7/3} = 3\,\Omega$$

Step III: The Thevenin equivalent circuit is shown in Fig. 2.78 (c).

Thus, $$I_x = \dfrac{7}{3+2} = \dfrac{7}{5} = 1.4\,A$$

Ex. 2.33: Find Thevenin and Norton equivalent circuit across A-B in the circuit shown.

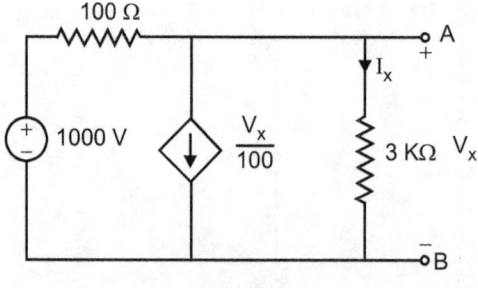

Fig. 2.79

Sol.: Let us first find Thevenin equivalent circuit across A-B.

Step I: To find V_{OC}: As it is terminals are open

We have
$$I_x = \frac{V_x}{3000} = \left(\frac{V_x}{3}\right) \text{ mA}$$

$$\text{Current (I)} = \left(\frac{V_x}{100} + I_x\right)$$

The KVL gives $V_x + 100I - 1000 = 0$

OR $\quad V_x + 100\left(I_x + \dfrac{V_x}{100}\right) = 1000$

Solving this given $\quad V_x = \dfrac{1000}{2.033} = 491.8 \text{ V} = V_{OC}$

The circuit is shown in Fig. 2.80 (a).

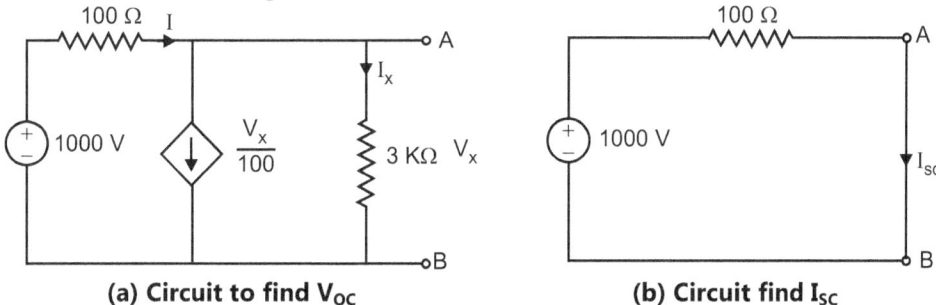

(a) Circuit to find V_{OC} (b) Circuit find I_{SC}

Fig. 2.80: Steps to find equivalent

Step II: To find I_{SC}: Short the terminal A-B. Then $I_x = 0$ an controlled current source becomes zero. The resultant circuit will be as shown in Fig. 2.80 (b).

Now, $\quad I_{SC} = \dfrac{1000}{100} = 10\text{A}$

Hence, $\quad R_{eq} = \dfrac{V_{OC}}{I_{SC}} = 41.18 \text{ ohms}$

Step III: The resultant Thevenin equivalent circuit is shown in Fig. 2.81 (a). The Norton equivalent circuit with $I_{eq} = I_{SC} = 10\text{A}$ is shown in Fig. 2.81 (b).

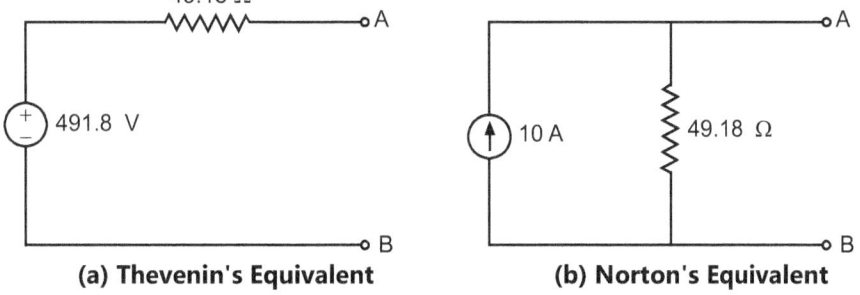

(a) Thevenin's Equivalent   (b) Norton's Equivalent

Fig. 2.81: Equivalent circuits

Ex. 2.34: Find Thevenin and Norton's equivalent circuit across A-B in the circuit shown.

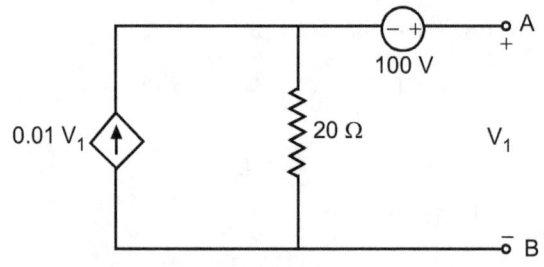

Fig. 2.82

Sol.: Let us first find Thevenin equivalent circuit.

Step I: To find V_{OC}: As it is terminals are opened. The voltage (V_1) is the V_{OC} between terminals. With A-B opened current of 0.01 V_1 flows through 20Ω resistor. KVL across the output loop gives

$$V_1 - 100 - 20 \times 0.02\, V_1 = 0 \quad \text{i.e.} \quad V_1 - 0.2\, V_s = 100$$

OR $\quad V_1 = 125V$ is the open circuit voltage

Step II: To find R_{eq}: Use $R_{eq} = \dfrac{V_{OC}}{I_{SC}}$. To obtain Thevenin resistance short terminal A-B. Since $V_1 = 0$ the current source becomes zero. The resultant circuit is shown in Fig. 2.83 (a).

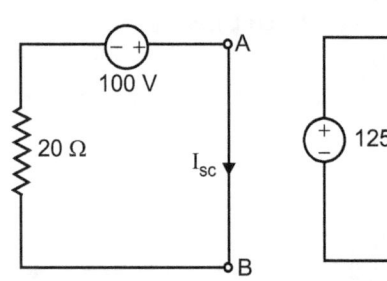 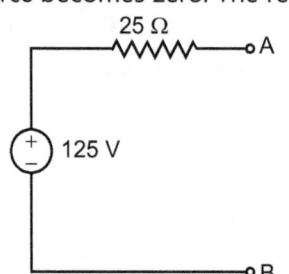 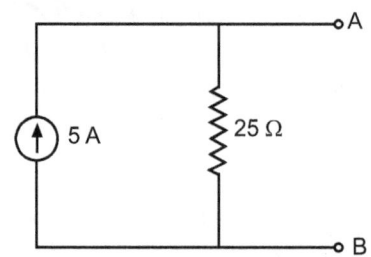

(a) Circuit to find I_{SC} (b) Thevenin's Equivalent   (c) Norton's Equivalent

Fig. 2.83: Equivalent circuits

Now, $\quad I_{SC} = \dfrac{100}{20} = 5A$

Hence, $\quad R_{eq} = \dfrac{V_{OC}}{I_{SC}} = \dfrac{125}{5}$

$= 25\Omega$

Step III: The resultant Thevenin equivalent circuit is shown in Fig. 2.83 (b).

As $\quad I_{SC} = I_{eq} = 5A$

the Norton equivalent is shown in Fig. 2.83 (c).

Ex. 2.35: Find Thevenin and Norton's equivalent circuits across AB in the circuits.

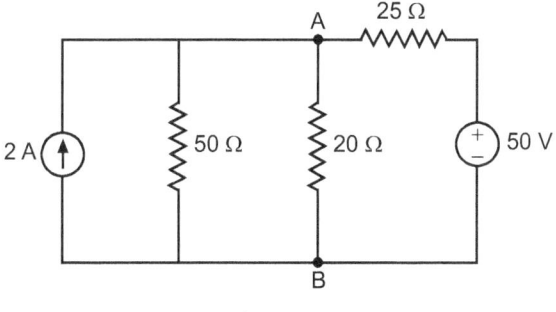

Fig. 2.84

Sol.: Let us first find out Thevenin equivalent circuit.

Step I: To find V_{OC}: Open terminals A-B by removing 20Ω resistor temporarily. Convert 20A current source into a voltage source. The resultant circuit is shown in Fig. 2.85. Let V_{OC} be voltage between A-B. Since, here is a single loop let I be loop current. Now KVL across loop gives.

$$50 + 25I + 50I - 100 = 0 \text{ OR } I = +\frac{2}{3} \text{ Amp.}$$

Voltage between $\quad A - B = V_{AB} = 25I + 50 = 66.67 \text{ V}$

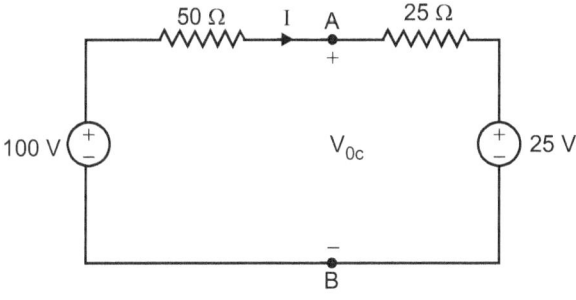   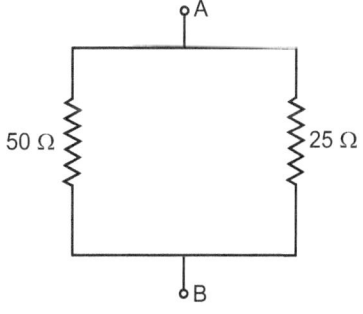

Fig. 2.85: Circuit to find V_{CC}   **Fig. 2.86: Circuit to find R_{eq}**

Step II: Since circuit contains only independent source, use method – II to find R_{eq}, Open current source and short the voltage source the resultant circuit is shown in Fig. 2.86.

Resistance between A-B $= R_{eq} = 50 \parallel 25 = \dfrac{50 \times 25}{75} = 16.67 \, \Omega$

Step III: The resultant Thevenin equivalent circuit in shown in Fig. 2.87 (a). By source transformation the resultant Norton equivalent circuit is shown in Fig. 2.87 (b).

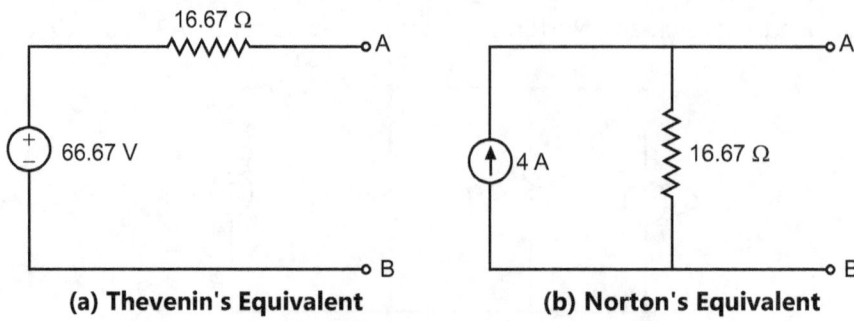

(a) Thevenin's Equivalent (b) Norton's Equivalent

Fig. 2.87: Equivalent circuits

2.4 MAXIMUM POWER TRANSFER (MPT) THEOREM

Sometimes it is necessary to determine the load impedance (Z_L) to be connected across two terminals of the circuit so that maximum power is transferred to load.

For example, consider a circuit (N) consisting of impedances and energy sources as shown n Fig. (2.88), where variable load (Z_L) is connected across A-B. We have to determine load (Z_L) so that maximum power is transferred (dissipated) in the load (Z_L).

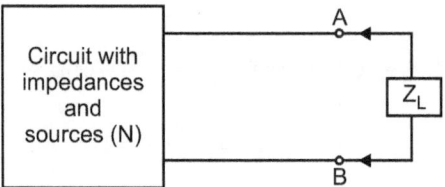

Fig. 2.88: Circuit (N) with variable load

This is given by Maximum Power Transfer (MPT) theorem. There are three different cases depending upon type of network (N) and load (Z_L).

2.4.1 MPT Theorem for DC Circuits

Consider the network contain in only "**DC source and resistance**". No reactive element (L or C) is present in the circuit. Now load Z_L will be purely resistive (R_L) as shown below in Fig. 2.89 (a).

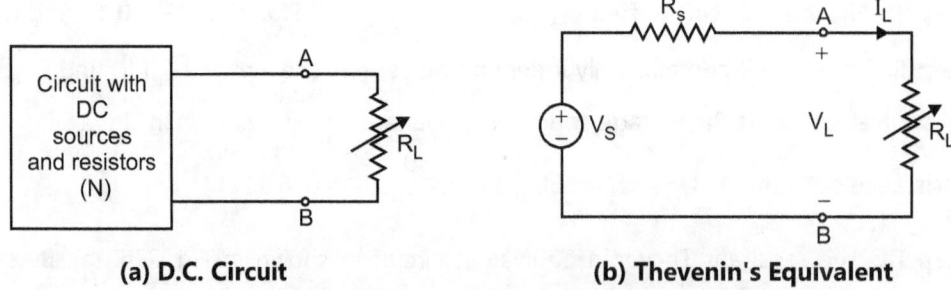

(a) D.C. Circuit (b) Thevenin's Equivalent

Fig. 2.89: Circuit to explain MPT of DC circuits

Now according to Thevenin theorem the whole circuit (N) across A-B can be replaced by an open circuit voltage (V_S) in series with Thevenin resistor (R_S) as shown in Fig. 2.89 (b).

Load R_L is variable while source resistance (R_S) is fixed by the network. Our aim is to find value of R_L that will dissipate maximum power in R_L.

Applying KVL gives
$$I_L = \frac{V_S}{(R_S + R_L)} \quad \ldots(a)$$

Hence, Power in $R_L = P_L = I_L^2 \cdot R_L = \frac{V_S^2}{(R_S + R_L)^2} \times R_L \quad \ldots(2.5)$

To find R_L for which P_L is maximum differentiate P_L with respect to R_L and equate it to zero (according to maxima minima theory). Thus we have,

$$\frac{dP_L}{dR_L} = V_S^2 \left[\frac{(R_S + R_L)^2 \cdot 1 - 2(R_S + R_L) \cdot R_L}{(R_S + R_L)^4} \right] = 0$$

Since, $V_S \neq 0$ and denominator is zero, the numerator must be zero. Equating numerator to zero we have

$$(R_S + R_L)^2 - (R_S + R_L) \cdot R_L = 0$$

OR $\qquad (R_S + R_L) - 2R_L = 0$

OR $\qquad R_S = R_L \quad \ldots(2.6)$

"**Thus, for maximum power transfer across load (R_L), the load resistance must be equal to resistance (R_S)**" with above condition of equation (2.6) which is known as matched condition, the maximum power (P_{Lmux}) is given by equation (2.7) as

$$P_{L\,max} = \frac{V_S^2 \cdot R_L}{(2R_L)^2} = \frac{V_S^2}{4R_L} = \frac{V_S^2}{4R_S} \quad \ldots(2.7)$$

Since, $R_S = R_L$, same amount of power is dissipated in the internal resistances (i.e. R_S in this case). Hence maximum power efficiency is 50%.

Note: If R_L is fixed [fixed load] and internal resistance (R_S) is variable then by equation (2.7) maximum power will be in the load when $R_S = 0$. This maximum power is given by $P_{L\,max} = \frac{V_S^2}{R_L}$ and the power efficiency in this case is 100%.

Thus, it is always advantageous to make source resistance (R_S) as small as possible in order to make the power efficiency larger. But if R_S is not zero, then maximum power efficiency is limited to 50% only.

With the above proof the Maximum Power Transfer Theorem (MPT) for DC circuit can be stated as follows.

Statement of MPT for DC circuit: "In a linear circuit containing linear, bilateral resistance and DC energy sources the maximum power will be transferred in variable load resistance (R_L) connected between any two terminals when value of load resistance (R_L) is equal to source resistance (R_S) or Thevenin equivalent resistance".

The variation of load power (P_L) with variable load (R_L) and fixed source resistance (R_S) as given by equation (2.7) and circuit of Fig. 2.89 (b) is shown in Fig. 2.90. Note that P_L is maximum when $R_L = R_S$.

Fig. 2.90: Variation of power (P_L) with load (R_L)

Following examples explain use of MPT for DC circuits.

Ex. 2.36: For the ladder circuit shown find R_L that will give maximum power to R_L and determine value of P_{Lmax}.

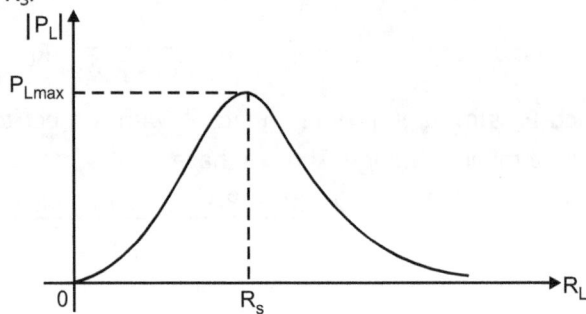

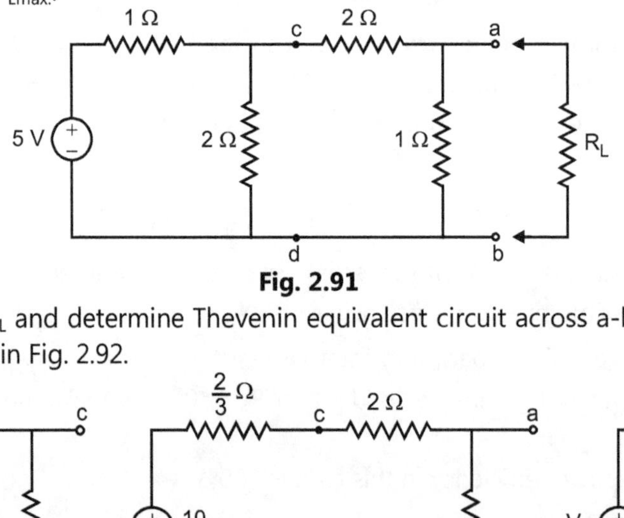

Fig. 2.91

Sol.: Remove R_L and determine Thevenin equivalent circuit across a-b. The various steps involved are shown in Fig. 2.92.

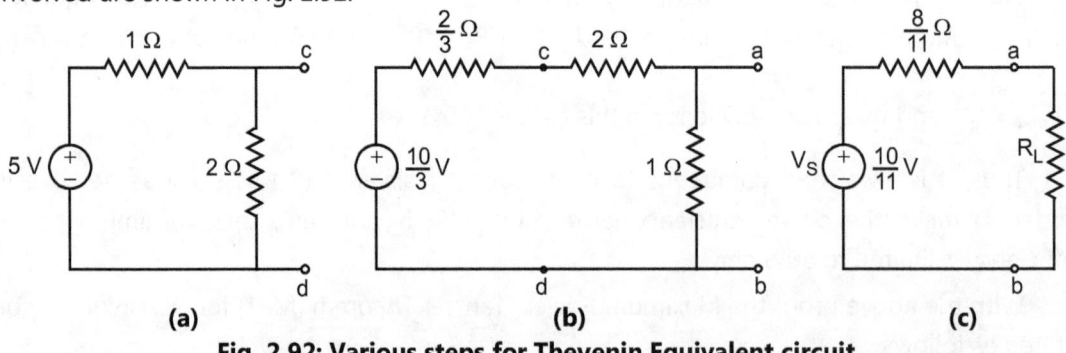

Fig. 2.92: Various steps for Thevenin Equivalent circuit

Assume the network is broken at c-d as shown in Fig. 2.92 (a). First find Thevenin equivalent across c-d which is shown in Fig. 2.92 (b) where

$$V_{OC} = V_{Cd} = \frac{2 \times 5}{2 + 1} = \frac{10}{3} \text{ volts and } R_{eq} = 2\Omega \parallel 1\Omega = \frac{2}{3}\Omega$$

Now add remaining part of network at c-d and then find Thevenin equivalent across R_L or a –b where $V_{OC} = V_{ab} = \dfrac{10/3 \times 1}{1 + 2 + 2/3} = \dfrac{10}{11}$ Volts

and $$R_{eq} = 1\Omega \parallel \left(2 + \frac{2}{3}\right) = 1 \parallel \frac{8}{3} = \frac{1 \times 8/3}{1 + 8/3} = \frac{8}{11}\Omega$$

The final equivalent is shown in Fig. 2.92 (c). By the MPT theorem we have by equation (2.6),

For maximum pwer transfer $R_L = R_S = \dfrac{8}{11}\Omega$

Using equation (2.7), we have

$$P_{Lmax} = \frac{V_S^2}{4R_L} = \frac{(10/11)^2}{4 \times 8/11} = \frac{100}{11 \times 8 \times 4} = 0.284 \text{ watts}$$

Ex. 2.37: For the circuit shown in Fig. 2.93 (1) find R_L that will maximum the power delivered to R_L and find power in R_L for load under matched condition. (2) how much is power dissipated by 1kΩ resistor R_L is selected as matched load?

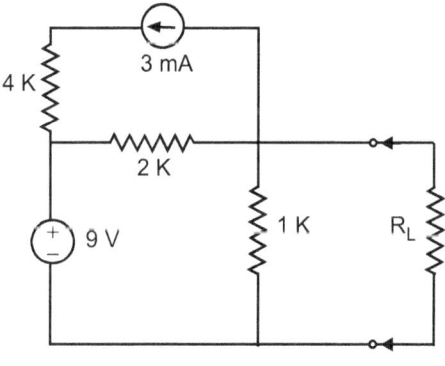

Fig. 2.93

Sol.: Let us first find Thevenin equivalent circuit across R_L. Assume being removed from circuit for the time being. The redrawn circuit is shown in Fig. 2.94 (a).

Step I: To find V_{OC}: By KCL current in 1kΩ resistor is $(I_1 - 3)$ mA where I_1 is the current assumed in 2kΩ resistor. KVL across lower loop gives $(I_1 - 3) \times 1 + 2I_1 - 9 = 0$ solving this gives $3I_1 = 12$ or $I_1 = 4$mA.

Thus, V_{OC} = Open circuit voltage = $1 \times (4 - 3) = 1$ volts

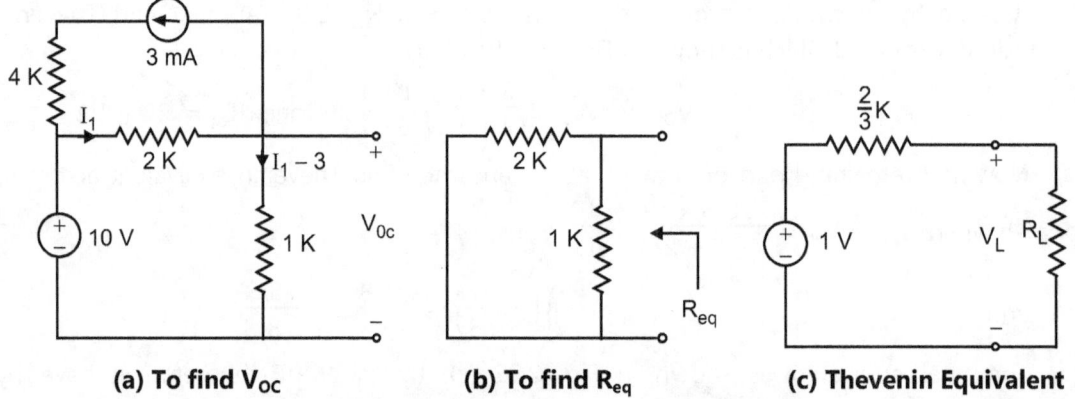

(a) To find V_{OC} (b) To find R_{eq} (c) Thevenin Equivalent

Fig. 2.94: Steps to find Thevenin equivalents

Step II: To find R_{eq}: Use method II where all sources are made zero as shown in Fig. 2.94 (b). We have 2k in parallel with 1k.

Hence the equivalent resistance = R_{eq} = 1k || 2k = $\frac{2}{3}$ kΩ

Step III: The final equivalent circuit is shown n Fig. 2.201 (c).

(1) For maximum power transfer $R_L = \frac{2}{3}$ kΩ

$$P_{Lmax} = \frac{V_S^2}{4R_L} = \frac{(1)^2}{4 \times \frac{2}{3} k} = \frac{3}{8} \text{ mW}$$

(2) When $R_L = \frac{2}{3}$ k is connected then voltage across R_L = 0.5 V. Since 1kΩ is directly in parallel with R_L the voltage across kΩ is also 0.5 V.

Hence, power in 1 kΩ = $\frac{(0.5)^2}{1k\Omega}$ = 0.25 mW = $\frac{1}{4}$ mW

Ex. 2.38: In the circuit shown variable load absorbs power. Find current I [Magnitude and direction] so that it receives maximum power. Also find amount of power absorbed by R_L

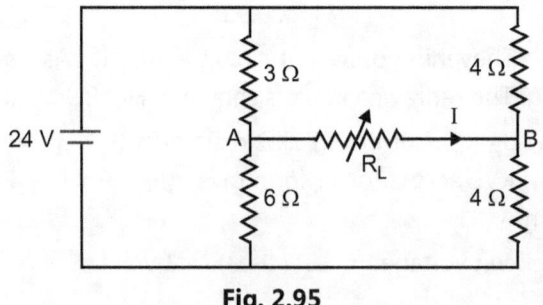

Fig. 2.95

Sol.: Let us determine Thevenin equivalent across R_L assumes for the time being R_L is removed.

Step I: To find V_{OC}: With R_L removed circuit is as shown in the Fig. 2.96 (a). The currents I_1 and I_2 are given by $I_1 = \dfrac{24}{3+6} = \dfrac{8}{6}$ A and $I_2 = \dfrac{24}{4+4} = 3A$

$$V_{OC} = V_{AB} = 6I_1 - 4I_2 = 6 \times \dfrac{8}{3} - 12 = 4V$$

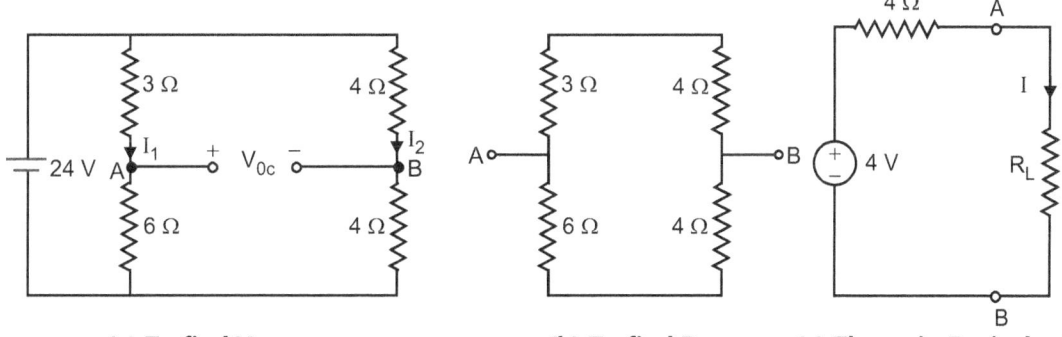

(a) To find V_{OC} (b) To find R_{eq} (c) Thevenin Equivalent

Fig. 2.96: Steps to find Thevenin equivalent

2.4.2 MPT Theorem for AC Circuits

If a network is AC containing AC sources and impedances (R, L and C) then load (Z_L) should also be reactive then MPT Theorem for such circuit is stated as below.

Statement: "The maximum power will be delivered by a network to a load impedance (Z_L) if the impedance (Z_L) is the complex conjugate of impedance (Z_S) of the network measured looking back into terminals of the network".

Proof: To prove the Theorem consider a complex network (N) containing AC energy sources and impedances with a complex load (Z_L) as shown in Fig. 2.97 (a). The Thevenin equivalent across load is shown in Fig. 2.97 (b), where V_S is a phasor containing both magnitude and phase and $Z_S = R_S + jX_S$ is a complex Thevenin equivalent impedance. For maximum power transfer $Z_L = (R_L + jX_L)$ should also be complex in which R_L and X_L are both adjustable.

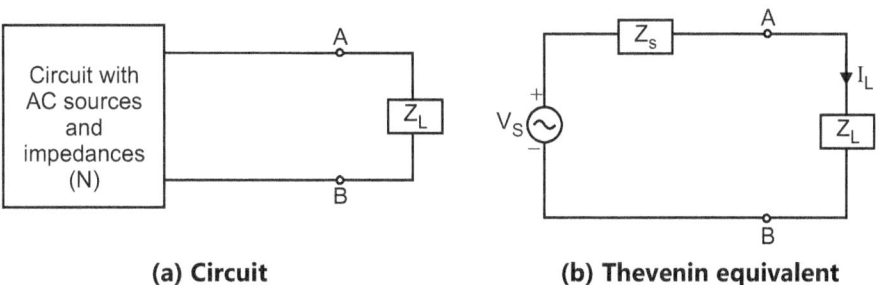

(a) Circuit (b) Thevenin equivalent

Fig. 2.97: Circuit to explain MPT for AC circuits

Thus, we have $Z_S = R_S + jX_S$ = source (Internal) impedance
$$Z_L = R_L + jX_L = \text{Load impedance}$$
Then
$$I_L = \frac{V_S}{Z_S + Z_L} = \frac{V_S}{(R_S + R_L) + j(X_L + X_S)} \quad \ldots \text{(a)}$$

Power delivered in the load (P_L) is given by -

$$P_L = [I_L]^2 R_L = \frac{V_S^2 \cdot R_L}{(R_S + R_L)^2 + (X_S + X_L)^2} \quad \ldots \text{(b)}$$

In above power (P_L) expression R_L and X_L are variable while all other quantities (V_S, R_S, X_S) are fixed for a given circuit.

Case I: Keep R_L fixed and X_L as a variable. Then for maximum power $\frac{dP_L}{dX_L}$ must be zero.

$$\frac{dP_L}{dX_L} = \frac{-2V_S^2 R_L (X_L + X_S)}{[(R_L + R_S)^2 + (X_S + X_L)^2]^2} = 0$$

Hence, $\quad (X_L + X_S) = 0$ **Or** $(X_L = -X_S)$ $\quad \ldots$ (2.7 (a))

Thus, *"Condition for maximum power when only reactance is varied is given by $X_L = -X_S$".*
"Reactance of load must be equal to the reactance of source impedance but of opposite nature (sign)".

Now substituting equation (1.24) into equation (b) we have,

$$P_L = \frac{V_S^2 R_L}{(R_S + R_L)^2} \quad \ldots \text{(c)}$$

Case II: Now vary R_L also. To get maximum power output we have $\frac{dP_L}{dR_L} = 0$.

Differentiating (c) with respect to R_L, we get,

$$\frac{dP_L}{dR_L} = \frac{V_S^2 (R_L + R_S)^2 - V_S^2 \cdot R_L (R_S + R_L)}{(R_L + R_S)^4} = 0$$

Hence, $\quad (R_S + R_L)^2 - R_L(R_S + R_L) = 0$ Or $R_S = R_L \quad \ldots$ (2.8)

'With $X_S = -X_L$ the condition for maximum power transfer is that load resistance must be equal to source resistance'.

Thus, a network of internal impedance of $Z_S = R_S + jX_S$ will delivers maximum power to load impedance (Z_L) when $Z_L = R_S - jX_S$".

Hence, **"Load impedance (Z_L) must be complex conjugate of source impedance (Z_S) for maximum power transfer in load".**

Hence the Theorem is proved.

Power efficiency: When matched load is used i.e. $Z_L = Z_S^*$ then maximum power transfer in load (P_{Lmax}) is given by the equation (b) as

$$P_L(max) = \frac{V_S^2 R_L}{4R_L^2} = \frac{V_S^2}{4R_L} \qquad ...(2.8\,(a))$$

This is same expression as equation (2.7). As equal amount of power is wasted in R_s the maximum power efficiency is 50% only.

Following examples explains this Theorem in detail.

Ex. 2.39: In the network shown w = 200r/s. Determine load (Z_L) for maximum power transfer. Also determine energy delivered to load in 1 hour.

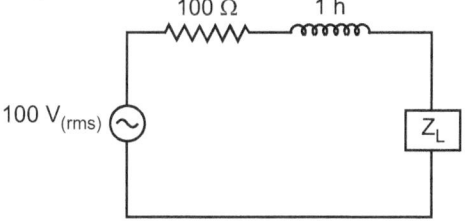

Fig. 2.98

Sol. We have $Z_S = 100 + JwL = (100 + J200)\,\Omega$

Now for maximum power transfer $Z_L = Z_S^* = (100 - J200)\,\Omega$

Where $R_L = 100\,\Omega$ and $X_L = X_C = 200 = \dfrac{1}{wC}$

Hence, $\quad C = \dfrac{1}{w \times 200} = \dfrac{1}{200 \times 200} = 25\,\mu F$

Thus load consists of 100Ω resistor in series with 25µF capacitor.

Power delivered to load $= \dfrac{V_{rms}^2}{4R_L} = \dfrac{(110)^2}{4 \times 100} = 25$ watts

Energy delivered in 1 hour $= \dfrac{25}{1000} \times 1 = 0.025$ kWh

Ex. 2.40: In the circuit w = 400 r/s. Find load impedance (Z_L) that maximizes power transfer and find power transferred when load is matched.

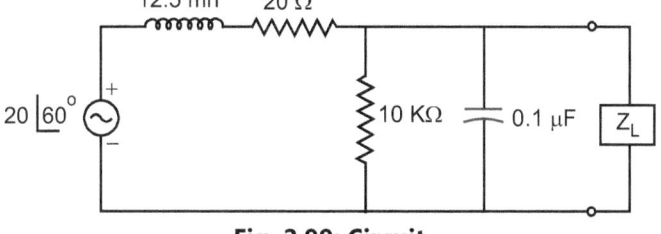

Fig. 2.99: Circuit

Sol.: Assume Z_L being removed for time being.

Let
$$Z_1 = 20 + JwL = (20 + J \times 400 \times 12.5 \times 10^{-3}) = (20 + J5) \, \Omega$$

$$Z_2 = 10k\Omega \parallel \frac{-J}{wC} = 10 \, k\Omega \parallel -25 \, k\Omega$$

$$= \frac{-J250 M\Omega}{(10 - J25) \, K\Omega}$$

$$= \frac{250 \angle -90°}{26.9 \angle -68.2°} \, k\Omega = 9.285 \angle -21.8° \, k\Omega$$

Thus,
$$Z_2 = (8.62 - J3.44) \, k\Omega$$

$$V_{Th} = V_{OC} = \frac{20\angle 60° \times Z_2}{Z_2 + Z_1} = 20\angle 60°$$

And
$$Z_{Th} = Z_2 \parallel Z_1 = Z_1 \approx Z_1$$

Thus,
$$Z_{Th} = (20 + J5) \, \Omega$$

The Thevenin equivalent circuit is shown in Fig. 2.100.

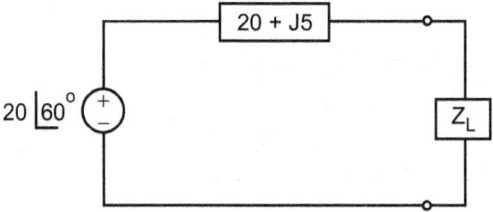

Fig. 2.100: Thevenin equivalent circuit

For maximum power transfer $Z_L = (20 - J5) \, \Omega$

Thus load must consist of 20Ω resistor and a capacitor (C) of $\frac{1}{400 \times 5} = 500 \, \mu F$

when matched load is used then maximum power is transferred and is given by.

$$P_{Lmax} = \frac{V_{rms}^2}{4R_L} = \frac{(20)^2}{4 \times 20} = 5 \text{ watts}$$

Ex. 2.41: In the circuit shown $V_1 = 2\sqrt{2} \sin 2t$. For the element values given find value of 'C' that will cause maximum power in 1 ohm load.

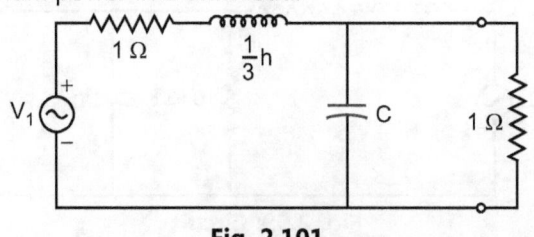

Fig. 2.101

Sol.: With 1Ω load removed, Let us find Z_{Th} across load, w = 2

$$Z_{Th} = (1 + JwL) \parallel \frac{-J}{wC}$$

$$= \left(1 + J\frac{2}{3}\right) \parallel \frac{-J}{2C}$$

$$= \frac{\left(1 + J\frac{2}{3}\right)(-J/2C)}{1 + J\left(\frac{2}{3} - \frac{1}{2C}\right)} = \frac{\left(\frac{1}{3C} - \frac{J}{2C}\right)}{1 + J\left[\frac{2}{3} - \frac{1}{2C}\right]} \quad \ldots \text{(a)}$$

$$= \frac{\left(\frac{1}{3C} - \frac{J}{2C}\right)\left[1 - J\left(\frac{2}{3} - \frac{1}{2C}\right)\right]}{1 + \left[\frac{2}{3} - \frac{1}{2C}\right]^2}$$

For maximum power transfer in load $R_L = 1\Omega$ we must have $Z_{Th} = 1\Omega$. This means real part of Z_{Th} must be 1Ω and imaginary part must be zero.

Thus,
$$\frac{\frac{1}{3C} - \frac{1}{2C}\left[\frac{2}{3} - \frac{1}{2C}\right]}{1 + \left(\frac{2}{3} - \frac{1}{2C}\right)^2} = 1 \quad \ldots \text{(b)}$$

And
$$\frac{1}{2C} + \frac{1}{3C}\left(\frac{2}{3} - \frac{1}{2C}\right) = 0 \quad \ldots \text{(c)}$$

condition (c) gives, $\frac{-1}{3}\left(\frac{2}{3} - \frac{1}{2C}\right) = \frac{1}{2}$ Or $\frac{-2}{3} + \frac{1}{2C} = 1.5$

This gives C = 0.23F

Thus value of capacitor (C) must be 0.23F. Similarly, condition (b) gives another value of 'C' for which maximum power transfer occurs.

Ex. 2.42: In the circuit shown current source has a frequency of 1000 Hz. Find value of load for maximum power transfer also calculate power in load for matched condition and also calculate power efficiency.

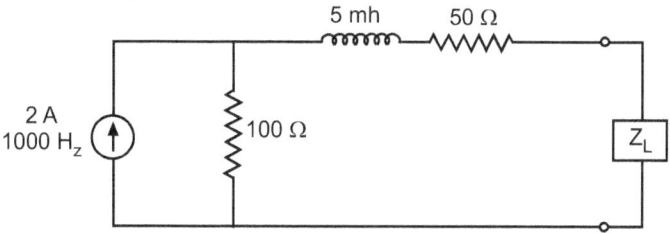

Fig. 2.102: Circuit for Ex. (2.41)

Sol.: Given f = 1000 Hz, X_L = JwL = $J2\pi \times 1000 \times 5 \times 10^{-3}$ = - J31.4Ω
Source transformation gives circuit shown in Fig. 2.103.

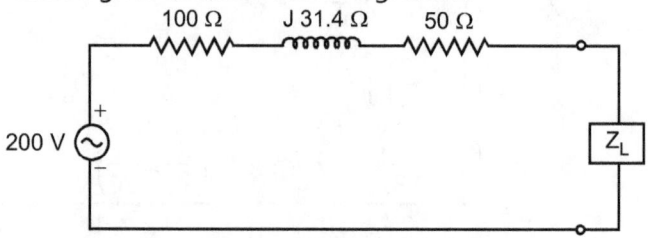

Fig. 2.103: Equivalent circuit

Source impedance = Z_S = (100 + 50 + J31.4) = (150 + J31.4)
Hence, load must be Z_L = (150 – J31.4) for MPT.
With this load connected maximum power delivered is

$$P_{Lmax} = \frac{V_S^2}{4R_L} = \frac{(200)^2}{4 \times 150}$$

= 66.66 watts

Maximum power efficiency = 50%

Note: Load should consists of a resistor of 150Ω in series is with a Capacitor (C) = $\frac{1}{31.4w}$

= $\frac{1}{3.14 \times 2 \pi \times 1000}$ = 5μF

Ex. 2.43: For the circuit shown find load impedance (Z_L) such that maximum power is transferred in load. Also find the power transferred to load under this condition.

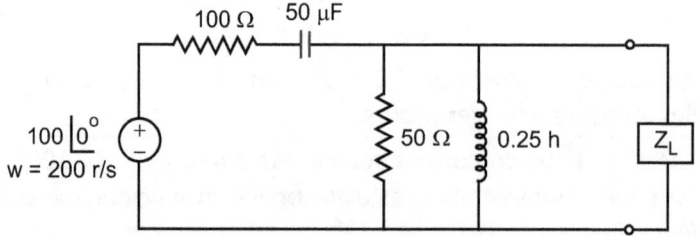

Fig. 2.104: Circuit for Ex (2.42)

Sol.: Let $Z_S = 100 - JX_C = \left(100 - \frac{J}{wC}\right) = \left(100 - \frac{J}{50 \times 10^{-6} \times 200}\right)$

i.e Z_1 = (100 – J100) = 141.42 ∠ – 45°Ω

Z_2 = 50Ω || JwL = 50||J50 = $\frac{2500\angle 90°}{(50 + J50)}$

i.e Z_2 = (25 + J25) = 35.35∠45°

We have, $V_{OC} = 100\angle 0° \times \dfrac{Z_2}{Z_1 + Z_2} = 100 \times \dfrac{35.35\angle 45°}{(125 - J75)}$

$= \dfrac{3535\angle 45°}{145.77\angle -31°} = 24.25\angle 76°$ Volts

$Z_{Th} = Z_1 \| Z_2 = \dfrac{141.42\angle -45° \times 35.35\angle 45°}{(125 - J75)}$

$= \dfrac{5000}{145.7\angle -31} = 34.3\angle 31 = (29.4 + J17.67)\ \Omega$

Thus, for maximum power transfer $Z_L = Z_{Th}^*$.

The load impedance must be $Z_L = (29.4 - J17.67)\ \Omega$

The circuit under matched condition is shown in Fig. 2.105.

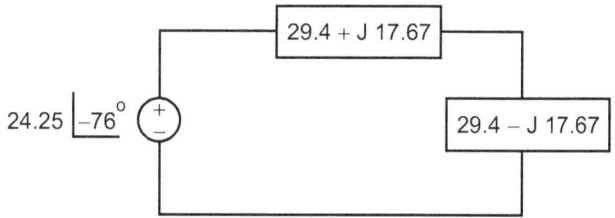

Fig. 2.105: Matched load

Maximum power transferred to load $= \dfrac{(24.25)^2}{4 \times 29.4} = 5$ Watts.

Ex. 2.44: Find Z_L such that maximum power is transferred in Z_L. Also find maximum power transferred.

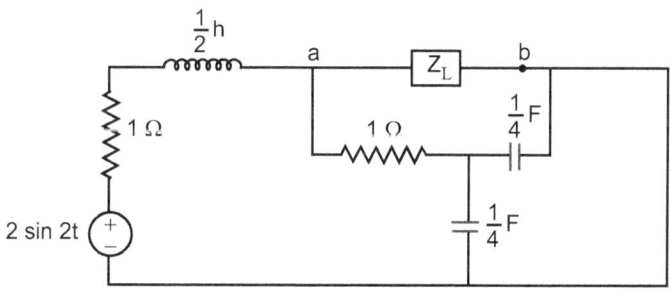

Fig. 2.106

Sol.: Two capacitors are in parallel to given equivalent capacitance of $\dfrac{1}{2}$ F = 0.5 F. The reactance of this capacitor is X_C where, $X_C = \dfrac{1}{wC} = \dfrac{1}{2 \times 0.5} = 1\Omega$, reactance of inductor = $X_L = wL = 2 \times \dfrac{1}{2} = 1\Omega$. The resultant circuit is shown in Fig. 2.107 (a).

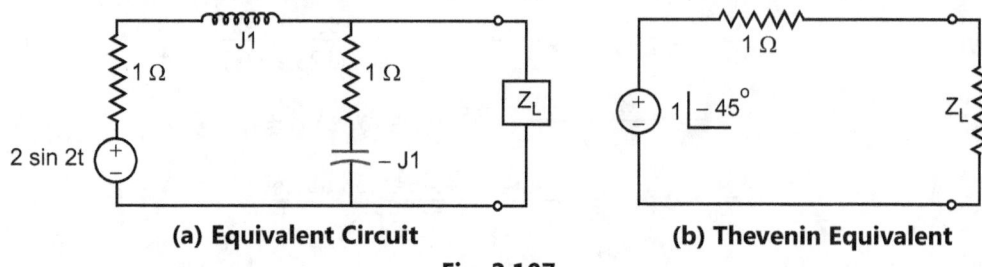

(a) Equivalent Circuit   (b) Thevenin Equivalent

Fig. 2.107

With Z_L removed for the time being we shall find the Thevenin equivalent circuit across load.

$$(1 + J1) \| (1 - J1) = \frac{(1 + J1)(1 - J1)}{(1 + J1) + (1 - J1)}$$

We have $Z_{Th} = \dfrac{1+1}{1+1} = 1\Omega$

The r.m.s value of input voltage $= V_{rms} = \sqrt{2}$ Volts.

Hence, $V_{Th} = \dfrac{\sqrt{2} \times (1 - J1)}{(1 + J1) + (1 - J1)} = \dfrac{\sqrt{2}(1 - J1)}{2} = 1\angle -45°$

$= (1 - J1)$ Volts

The Thevenin equivalent circuit is shown in Fig. 2.107 (b).

For maximum power transfer Z_L should be 1 ohm. With matched load the maximum power transferred is given by $P_{L(max)} = \dfrac{V_{rms}^2}{4R_L} = \dfrac{(1)^2}{4 \times 1} = 0.25$ watts.

2.4.3 Corollary of Maximum Power Transfer (MPT)

If a network is AC containing AC sources and impedances (R, L, C elements) and load is resistive (not reactive) in which only magnitude of load and not the angle can be varied then corollary of maximum power transfer can be used to obtain the condition for maximum power transfer.

Statement: If only the absolute magnitude and not the angle of the load impedance (Z_L) can be varied, then the greatest power is delivered from the network to load if the absolute magnitude of Z_L (i.e. $|Z_L|$ is made equal to absolute magnitude of source Impedance Z_S (i.e. $|Z_S|$)".

Proof: We have $Z_L = (R_L + JX_L) = |Z_L| \angle\theta = Z_L [\cos\theta + I\sin\theta]$

Hence, $R_L = |Z_L| \cos\theta$, $X_L = |Z_L| \sin\theta$

Hence, for the given AC circuit power delivered to load is given by expression (b) of section (2.3.2) as,

$$P_L = \frac{V_S^2 |Z_L| \cos\theta}{[R_S + |Z_L|\cos\theta]^2 + [X_S + |Z_L|\sin\theta]^2} \quad \ldots \text{(a)}$$

As magnitude of impedance (Z_L) can be varied and not the angle, therefore we have $\dfrac{dP_L}{d|Z_L|} = 0$ for maximum power transfer, is given by equation,

$$R_S^2 + (X_S)^2 - |Z_L|^2 [\sin^2 \theta + \cos^2 \theta] = 0$$

Or $\quad R_S^2 + (X_S)^2 = |Z_L|^2$ ... (2.9)

Hence, $\quad |Z_L| = \sqrt{R_S^2 - X_S^2} = |Z_S|$

Thus, if load angle cannot be varied but magnitude can be varied then load impedance ($|Z_L|$) should be made equal to the magnitude of source impedance ($|Z_S|$) for the greatest amount of power transfer. Hence, proved.

Following examples explains the principles of this theorem.

Ex. 2.45: A resistance variable between 0 to 500Ω is available as a load for the circuit shown in Fig. 2.108.

1. What should be the value of resistor (R_L) so as to develop maximum power in the resistor?
2. How much power is developed?
3. Draw the curve of power output versus resistance load (R_L) showing that selected value of resistance does develop maximum power.

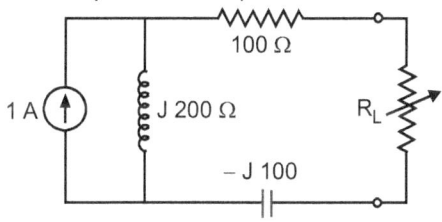

Fig. 2.108

Sol.: Open circuit voltage = V_{OC} = J200 − × 1 = 200 ∠90° volts. Open the current source to find Z_{Th}. thus, we have Z_{Th} = 100 + J200 − J100 = 100 = 141.42∠45°

The Thevenins's equivalent circuit is shown in Fig. 2.109.

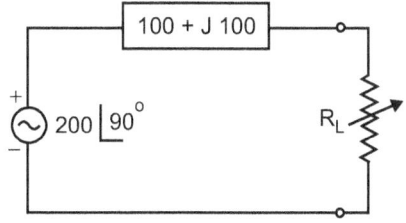

Fig. 2.109: Thevenin equivalent circuit

1. By corollary of MPT and hence by equation (1.26) the value of $|R_L|$ that transfers maximum power in it is given by,

$$R_L = \sqrt{(R_S)^2 + (X_S)^2} = \sqrt{(100)^2 + (100)^2} = 141.4 \text{ ohms}$$

2. Maximum power developed $= P_{RL(max)} = \dfrac{V_S^2}{4R_L} = \dfrac{(200)^2}{4 \times 141.4} = 70.7$ watts.

3. Power developed by load $= P_L = \dfrac{V_S^2 |Z_L|}{[|Z_S| + |Z_L|]^2}$ ... (1)

Now, $|Z_S| = \sqrt{(100)^2 + (100)^2} = 141.4$ ohms

Hence, $P_L = \dfrac{V_S^2 \times |Z_L|}{[141.4 + |Z_L|]^2}$ ... (2)

Since, $|Z_L|$ is resistive (R_L), P_L versus R_L can be plotted by taking different values of R_L and using equation (2).

When
$R_L = 50\,\Omega$ then $P_L = 54.6$ watts.
$R_L = 200\,\Omega$ then $P_L = 68.64$ watts.
$R_L = 500\,\Omega$ then $P_L = 48.6$ watts.
$R_L = 141.4\,\Omega$ then $P_L = 70.7$ watts.
$R_L = 100\,\Omega$ then $P_L = 68.64$ watts.

From above values of P_L and R_L it is obvious that for $R_L = 141.4\,\Omega$ the power delivered to load is maximum and it reduces if $R_L > 141.4\,\Omega$ or $R_L < 141.4\,\Omega$.

The graph of P_L (watts) versus R_L is shown below in Fig. 1.110.

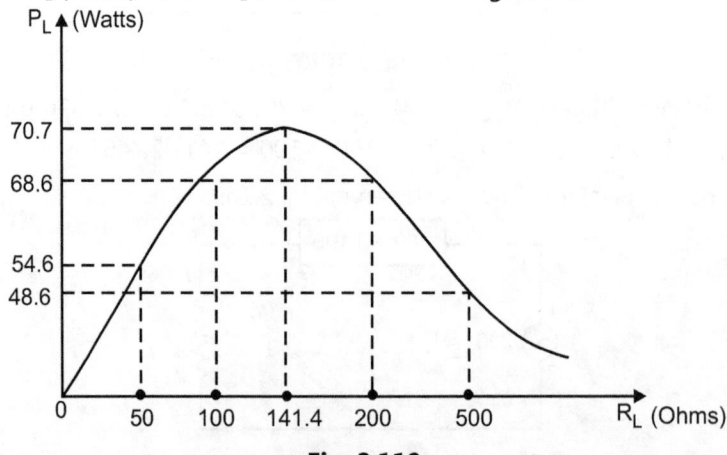

Fig. 2.110

Ex. 2.46: (1) In the circuit shown what is the load needed to obtain maximum power output at the terminals a-b?

(2) What is the generator current, load current, power generated and power delivered to load and matched load condition?

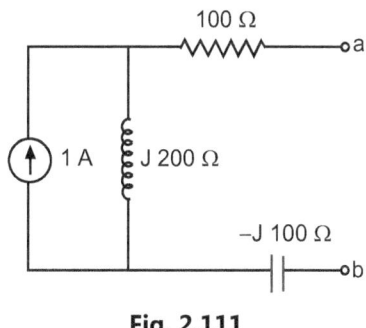

Fig. 2.111

Sol.: Assume load (Z_L) being temporarily removed.

(1) Find Thevenin equivalent resistance between a-b. With current source made zero [open circuited]

We have, $\quad Z_{Th} = Z_S = 100 + J200 - J100 = (100 + J100)$ ohms

For maximum power transfer $Z_L = Z_S = (100 - J100)$ ohms

(2) Circuit with matched load (Z_L) connected is as shown in Fig. 2.112.

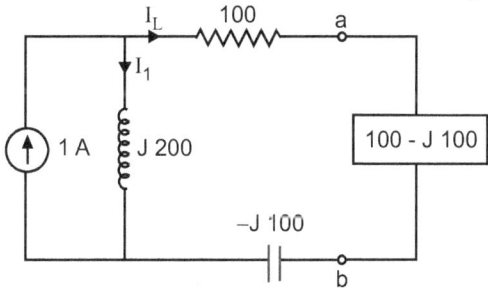

Fig. 2.112: Circuit with matched load

Now current source $1 \angle 0°$ is divided into two currents I_1 and I_L. By current divider action.

$$I_L = I \times \frac{J200}{Z_L + Z_S} = \frac{1 \angle 0° \times 200 \angle 90°}{(100 + J100) + (100 - J100)}$$

$$= \frac{200 \angle 90°}{200}$$

Thus, $\quad I_L = 1 \angle 90°$ Amp.

Power delivered in load $= |I_L|^2 \times R_L = 1 \times 100 = 100$ watts

Power generated = VI cos θ where I is the generator current and V is the generator voltage. θ is angle between two. We have I = $1 \angle 0°$ and V can be calculated by knowing. I_1 which is

$$I_1 = I - I_L = 1 \angle 0° - 1 \angle 90° = (1 - J1)$$

Thus, $\quad I_1 = (1 - J1) = \sqrt{2} \angle -45°$ Amps.

Thus, voltage across generator (V) = J200 J1 = $282.83 \angle +45°$

Thus, $\quad$ power generated = VI cos θ
$\quad\quad\quad\quad\quad\quad\quad\quad\quad\quad$ = 282.84 × 1 × cos (45°) = 200 watts

Since, power efficiency for matched load is 50%, out of total power of 200 watts generated, 100 watts is supplied to load and remaining power of 100 watts is consumed by circuits itself.

2.5 MILLMAN'S THEOREM AND ITS DUAL

Generally voltage source should be in series if we want to add them voltage sources in parallel cannot be added directly. If many voltage sources each with source impedance are in parallel then Millman's theorem gives us formula by which we can add them to get equivalent source in series with an equivalent source impedance. Thus, this theorem enable a number of voltage sources to be combined into a single voltage source.

Statement of Millman's Theorem

If a voltage sources $V_1, V_2 \dots V_n$ having internal impedance [or series impedances] $Z_1, Z_2 \dots Z_n$ respectively are connected in parallel as shown in Fig. 2.113 (a), then these sources may be replaced by a single voltage source (V_m) having internal series impedance (Z_m) as shown in Fig. 2.113 (b). Where V_m and Z_m are given by following formulae.

$$V_m = \frac{V_1Y_1 + V_2Y_2 + V_3Y_3}{Y_1 + Y_2 + Y_3} \quad \dots (2.10)$$

$$Z_m = \frac{1}{Y_1 + Y_2 + Y_3 + \dots} \quad \dots (2.11)$$

where $Y_1, Y_2, Y_3, \dots, Y_n$ are admittances corresponding to $Z_1, Z_2, Z_3, \dots, Z_n$ respectively.

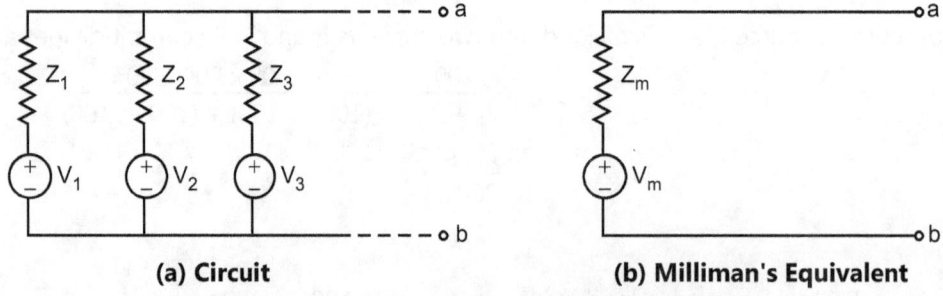

(a) Circuit $\quad\quad\quad\quad\quad\quad\quad\quad\quad\quad$ (b) Milliman's Equivalent

Fig. 2.113: Circuits to explain Millman's theorem

Proof: We know that a voltage source V in series with the series impedance Z can be converted into a current source. I = VY in parallel with the admittance $Y = \frac{1}{Z}$.

Thus, converting all voltage sources into current sources we get the equivalent circuit as shown in Fig. 2.114 (a).

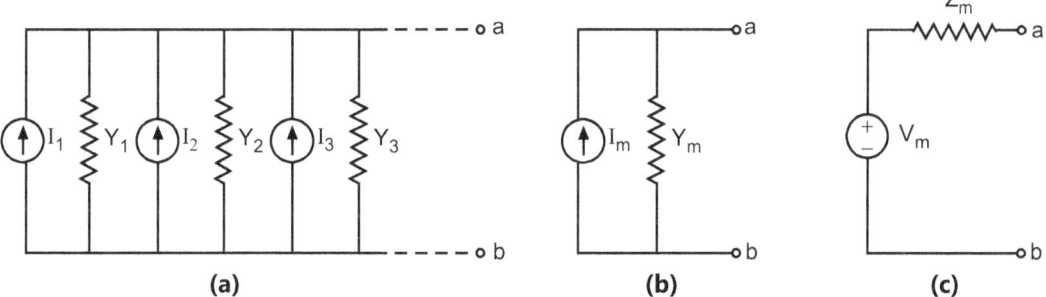

(a)　　　　　　　(b)　　　　　　　(c)

Fig. 2.114: Equivalent circuits

Now current sources in parallel are added

i.e. $\qquad I_m = I_1 + I_2 + I_3 ...$

Admittances in parallel are also added

i.e. $\qquad Y_m = Y_1 + Y_2 + Y_3 ...$

The resultant equivalent circuit is shown in Fig. 1.114 (b). Reconverting current source into voltage source we get the final Millman's equivalent of Fig. 2.114 (c).

where, $\qquad V_m = \dfrac{I_m}{Y_m} = \dfrac{I_1 + I_2 + I_3 ...}{Y_1 + Y_2 + Y_3 ...} = \dfrac{V_1 Y_1 + V_2 Y_2 + V_3 Y_3 ...}{Y_1 + Y_2 + Y_3 ...}$

and $\qquad Z_m = \dfrac{1}{Y_m} = \dfrac{1}{Y_1 + Y_2 + Y_3 ...}$ Hence, proved.

Following examples explains use of Millman's Theorem in simplification and analysis of circuits.

Ex. 2.47: In the circuit shown find voltage between A and B use Millman's theorem.

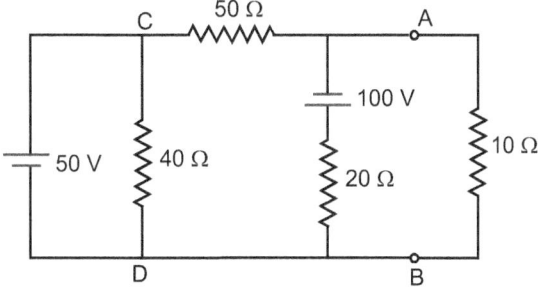

Fig. 2.115: Circuit of Ex. 2.46

Sol.: We have V_{CD} = 50V and the 40Ω resistor is directly in parallel with 50V. Hence, this resistance becomes redundant and can be removed. The resultant equivalent circuit is shown in Fig. 2.116 (a).

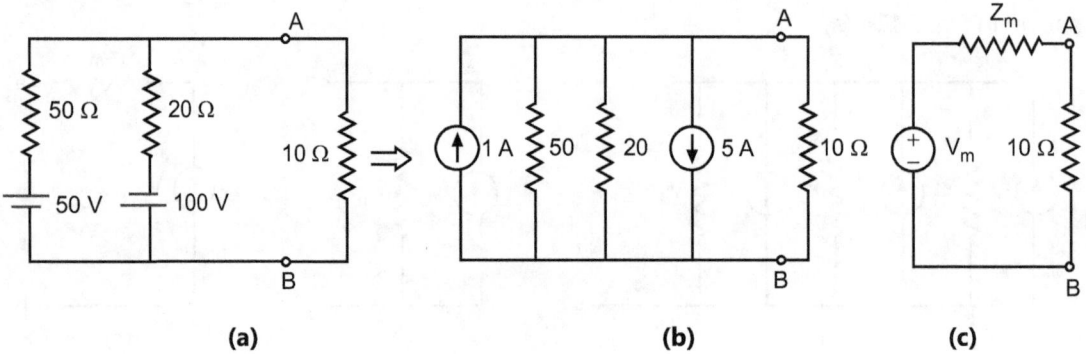

Fig. 2.116: Equivalent circuits

Using Millman's theorem the equivalent circuit is as shown in Fig. 2.116 (c) where V_m and Z_m are given by equations (2.10) and (2.11).

$$V_m = \frac{+50 \times \frac{1}{50} - 100 \times \frac{1}{20}}{\frac{1}{50} + \frac{1}{20}} = \frac{(1-5)}{7/100} = \frac{-400}{7} \text{ volts}$$

$$Z_m = \frac{1}{\frac{1}{50} + \frac{1}{20}} = \frac{100}{7} \Omega = 14.3 \Omega$$

Thus, by voltage divider action V_{AB} is given by

$$V_{AB} = -\frac{400}{7} \times \frac{10}{10 + 14.3} = -23.52 \text{ volts.}$$

Ex. 2.48: Find current in resistor R_3 by using Milliman's theorem.

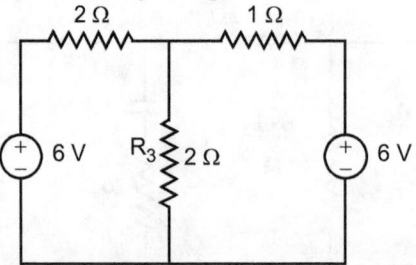

Fig. 2.117: Circuit for Ex. 2.47

Sol.: The circuit can be redrawn as shown in Fig. 2.118 (a). The Millman's equivalent circuit is shown in Fig. 2.118 (b).

Where, $V_m = \dfrac{6 \times \dfrac{1}{2} + 6 \times \dfrac{1}{1}}{\dfrac{1}{2} + \dfrac{1}{1}} = \dfrac{3+6}{3/2} = +6V$, $Z_m = \dfrac{1}{\dfrac{1}{2}+1} = \dfrac{2}{3}\Omega$

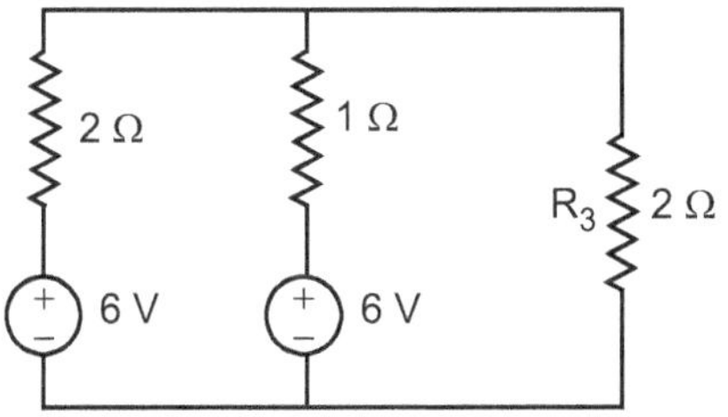

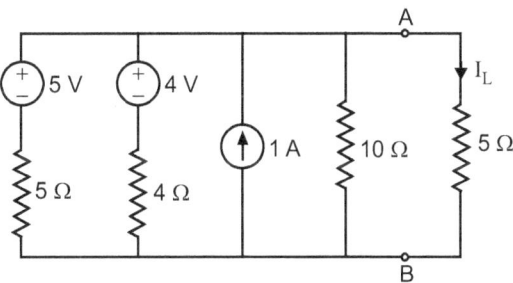

(a) Redrawn circuit 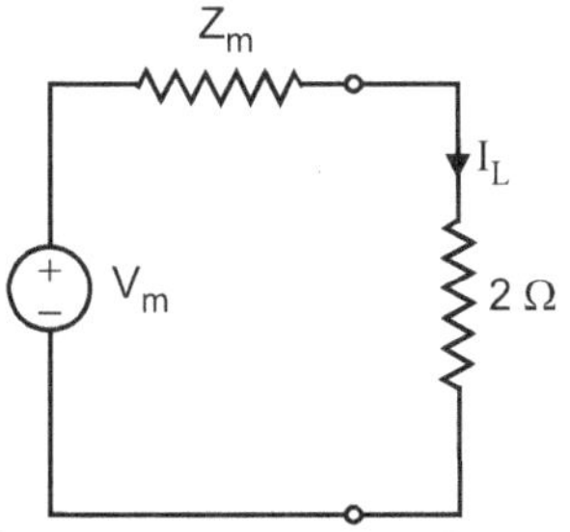   (b) Millman's Equivalent

Fig. 2.118: Equivalent circuits

Thus, current in 2Ω resistor = $I_L = \dfrac{V_m}{Z_m + 2} = \dfrac{6}{\dfrac{2}{3}+2} = \dfrac{18}{8} = 2.25$ Amp.

Ex. 2.49: Using Millman's theorem find the current and voltage in resistor of 5Ω across A-B.

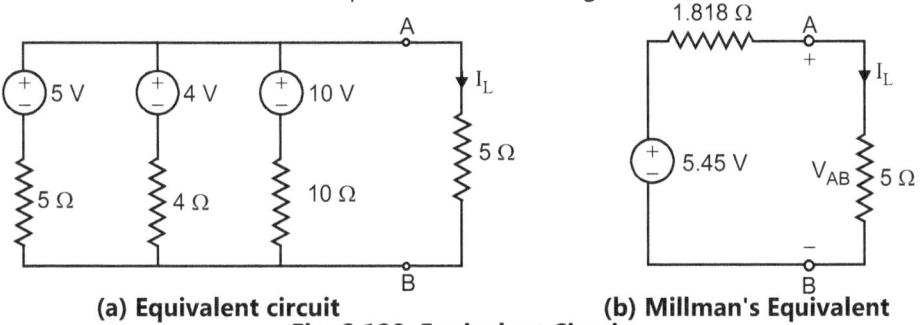

Fig. 2.119: Circuit for Ex. 2.48

Sol.: Current source of 1A parallel with 10Ω can be converted into a voltage source of 10V in series with 10Ω as shown in equivalent circuit of Fig. 2.120 (a).

(a) Equivalent circuit   (b) Millman's Equivalent

Fig. 2.120: Equivalent Circuit

By using equations (2.10) and (2.11) we have,

$$V_m = \frac{+5 \times \frac{1}{5} + 4 \times \frac{1}{4} + 10 \times \frac{1}{10}}{\frac{1}{5} + \frac{1}{4} + \frac{1}{10}} = \frac{1+1+1}{11/20} = \frac{60}{11} = 5.45 \text{ V}$$

$$Z_m = \frac{1}{\frac{1}{5} + \frac{1}{4} + \frac{1}{10}} = \frac{1}{\frac{11}{10}} = \frac{20}{11} \Omega = 1.818 \text{ }\Omega$$

Thus, we have

$$I_L = \frac{5.45}{1.818 + 5} = 0.8 \text{ Amp}$$

And

$$V_{AB} = 5 \times \frac{5.45}{5 + 1.818} = 4 \text{ volts.}$$

Ex. 2.50: Use Millman's Theorem to determine the current drawn by a resistor of 5Ω from 4 batteries that are connected in parallel. The open circuit voltages and internal resistances of the batteries are 18V and 1Ω, 20V and 2Ω, 22V and 5Ω and 24V and 4Ω.

Sol.: The circuit arrangement for the given problem is as shown in Fig. 2.121 (a). The Millman equivalent circuit is as shown in Fig. 2.121 (b).

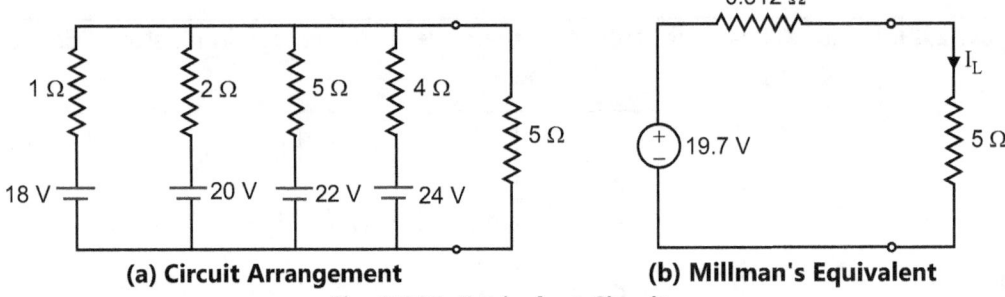

(a) Circuit Arrangement (b) Millman's Equivalent

Fig. 2.121: Equivalent Circuits

By using (2.10) and (2.11) we have,

$$V = \frac{+18 \times \frac{1}{1} + 20 \times \frac{1}{2} + 22 \times \frac{1}{5} + 24 \times \frac{1}{4}}{\frac{1}{1} + \frac{1}{2} + \frac{1}{5} + \frac{1}{4}}$$

$$= \frac{18 + 10 + 4.4 + 6}{39/20} = \frac{38.4 \times 20}{39}$$

$$= 19.7 \text{ volts}$$

$$Z_m = \frac{1}{\frac{1}{1} + \frac{1}{2} + \frac{1}{5} + \frac{1}{4}} = \frac{1}{39/20} = \frac{20}{39} = 0.512 \text{ }\Omega$$

Hence, Current (I) = $\frac{19.7}{5 + 0.512}$ = 3.57 Amp.

Ex. 2.51: Using Millmans theorem find current I in the circuit shown.

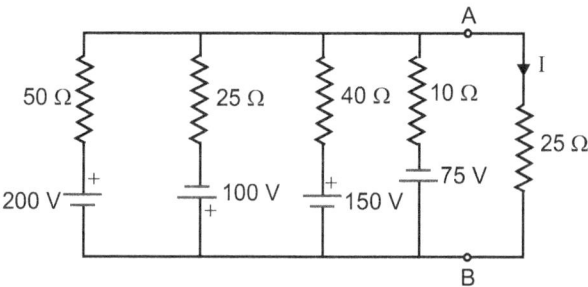

Fig. 2.122: Circuit of Ex. 2.50

Sol.: We can replace whole the circuit on left side of A-B by Millman's equivalent circuit as shown in Fig. 2.123.

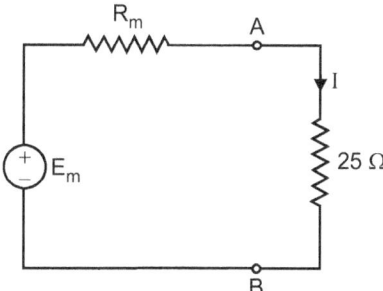

Fig. 2.123: Millman's Equivalent circuit

Using equation (2.10) and (2.11) we get,

$$V_m = \frac{+200 \times \frac{1}{50} - 100 \times \frac{1}{25} + 150 \times \frac{1}{40} - 75 \times \frac{1}{10}}{\frac{1}{50} + \frac{1}{25} + \frac{1}{40} + \frac{1}{10}}$$

$$= \frac{+4 - 4 + 3.75 - 7.5}{\frac{4 + 8 + 5 + 20}{200}}$$

$$= \frac{-3.75}{37/200}$$

$$= -20.27 \text{ V}$$

$$Z_m = \frac{1}{\frac{1}{50} + \frac{1}{25} + \frac{1}{40} + \frac{1}{10}} = \frac{1}{\frac{37}{200}}$$

$$= \frac{299}{37} = 5.4 \, \Omega$$

Hence, Current (I) $= \dfrac{-20.27}{3725 + 5.4} = -0.667$ Amp.

2.6 ADDITIONAL SOLVED PROBLEMS ON AC CIRCUITS

So far all the simplification Techniques and analysis Techniques along with network Theorems are explained considering DC circuits as examples. For the AC circuits containing R, L, C elements and AC sources these can be extended. In the AC circuits we are dealing with impedances where both magnitude and phase are considered. Following few examples explains ac analysis and simplifications.

Ex. 2.52: Determine the voltage V_{23} in the circuit using node analysis method.

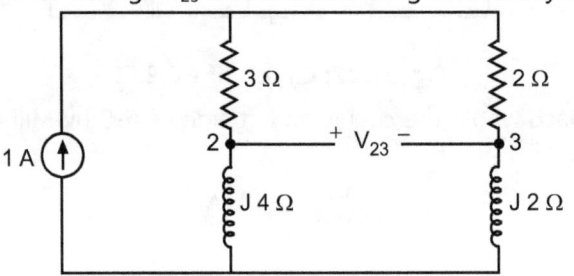

Fig. 2.124: Circuit for Ex. 2.51

Sol.: There are two nodes out of which one is Ground. Let voltage of unknown node may be V_1 as shown below

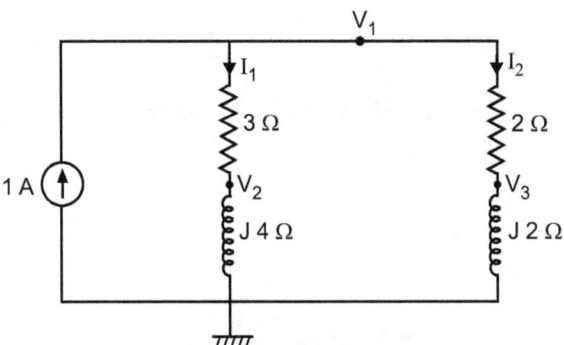

Fig. 2.125: Redrawn Circuit

KCL at node V_1 gives $\qquad I_1 + I_2 = 1$

$$\frac{V_1}{(3 + J4)} + \frac{V_1}{(2 + J2)} = 1$$

$$V_1 \left[\frac{(2 + J2)(3 + J4)}{(3 + J4)(2 + J2)} \right] = 1$$

$$\Rightarrow \qquad V_1 \left[\frac{5 + 16}{6 + 16 + J8 - 8} \right] = 1$$

$$\Rightarrow \qquad V_1 \left[\frac{5 + 16}{-2 + J14} \right] = 1$$

Thus
$$V_1 = \left[\frac{-2 + j14}{5 + j6}\right]$$

$$I_1 = \frac{V_1}{(3 + j4)} = \frac{(2 + j2)}{(5 + j6)}$$

Thus
$$V_2 = j4 \times I_1 = \frac{-8 + j8}{(5 + j6)} = \frac{8(j - 1)}{5 + j6} \text{ Volts}$$

$$I_2 = \frac{V_1}{2 + j2} = \frac{3 + j4}{(5 + j6)}$$

Thus
$$V_3 = j2 \times I_2 = \frac{-8 + j6}{(5 + j6)} \text{ Volts}$$

$$V_{23} = V_2 - V_3 = \frac{8(j - 1)}{(5 + j6)} - \frac{-8 + j6}{(5 + j6)} = \frac{j2}{(5 + j6)}$$

$$= \frac{2\angle 90°}{7.81\angle 50.2°} = 0.256\angle 39.8° \text{ volts}$$

Ex. 2.53: For the network shown determine node voltages using nodal analysis.

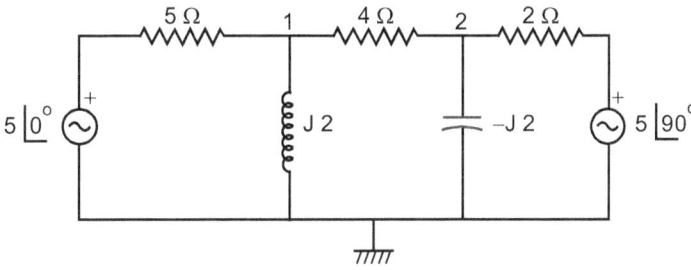

Fig. 2.126: Circuit for Ex. 2.52

Sol.: There are three nodes. The reference node is already given. Let V_1 and V_2 be the voltage of nodes 1 and 2 with respect to ground. Assume the currents in branches arbitrarily as i_1, i_2, i_3, i_4 and i_5 as shown in Fig. 2.127.

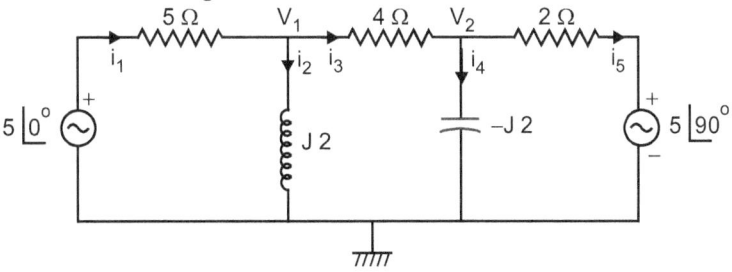

Fig. 2.127: Redrawn circuit

KCL at V_1 gives $i_1 - i_2 - i_3 = 0$

$$\left(\frac{5\angle 0° - V_1}{5}\right) - \frac{V_1}{J2} - \left[\frac{V_1 - V_2}{4}\right] = 0$$

Hence, $\quad V_1[10 + J9] - J5\, V_2 = J20 \quad\quad \ldots(a)$

Similarly KCL at V_2 gives $i_3 - i_4 - i_5 = 0$

$$\left(\frac{V_1 - V_2}{4}\right) + \frac{V_2}{J2} - \left(\frac{V_2 - 5\angle 90°}{2}\right) = 0$$

$$J1\,(V_1 - V_2) + 2V_2 - J2\,(V_2 - J5) = 0$$

$$JV_1 + V_2\,(2 - J3) = 01 \quad\quad \ldots(b)$$

From (a) and (b) solve for V_1 and V_2

$$V_1 = \frac{\begin{vmatrix} J20 & -J5 \\ 10 & (2 - J3) \end{vmatrix}}{\begin{vmatrix} (10 + J9) & -J5 \\ J1 & (2 - J3) \end{vmatrix}}$$

$$= \frac{J40 + 60 + J50}{(20 - J30 + J18 + 27) - 5}$$

$$= \frac{60 + J90}{(42 - J12)} = \frac{108.16\angle 56°}{43.7\angle -16°}$$

$$= 2.47\angle 72° \text{ Volts}$$

$$= (0.76 + J\,2.35) \text{ Volts}$$

Now from (b), we have

$$V_2 = \frac{(10 - JV_1)}{(2 - J3)}$$

i.e. $\quad V_2 = \dfrac{10 - J\,(0.76 + J2.35)}{2 - J3} = \dfrac{10 - J0.76 + 2.35}{(2 - J3)}$

$$= \frac{12.35 - J0.76}{(2 - J3)} = \frac{12.37\angle -3.52°}{3.6\angle -56.3°}$$

$$= 3.436\angle 52.8°$$

Ex. 2.54: Use mesh analysis method to determine the voltage source $V\angle 0°$ volts in the circuit if it delivers a power of 100 watts to the circuit.

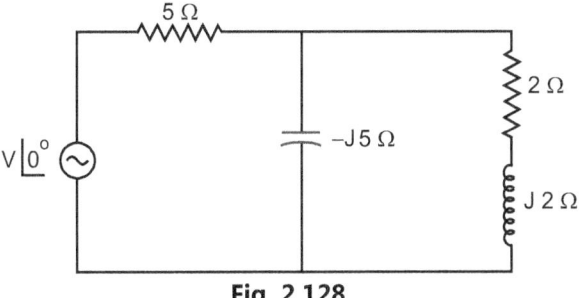

Fig. 2.128

Sol.: Let I_1 and I_2 be loop currents as shown

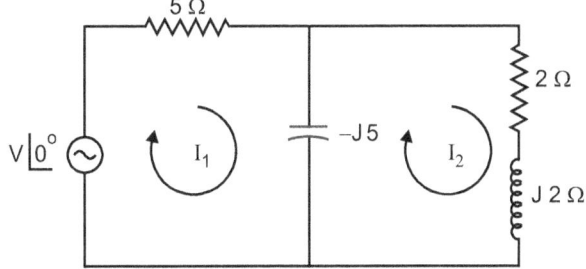

Fig. 2.129: Redrawn circuit

KVL across loop I_1 gives

$$-J5(I_1 - I_2) + 5I_1 = V$$
$$I_1(5 - J5) + J5\,I_2 = V \qquad \ldots(a)$$

KVL across loop I_2 gives

$$(2 + J2)I_2 + J5(I_1 - I_2) = 0$$
$$I_2(2 - J3) = -J5\,I_1 \qquad \ldots(b)$$

From (a) and (b) solve for currents I_1 and I_2. Thus

$$I_1(5 - J5) + J5 \times \left(\frac{-J5\,I_1}{2 - J3}\right) = V$$

$$I_1\left[\frac{10 - J15 - J10 - 15 + 25}{(2 - J3)}\right] = V$$

$$I_1\left[\frac{20 - J25}{2 - J3}\right] = V$$

Thus
$$I_1 = \frac{V(2 - J3)}{(20 - J3)}$$

$$I_1 = V \times \frac{3.6\angle -56.3°}{32\angle -51.3°} = V \times 0.1125\angle -5°\ \text{Amp.}$$

This is the current that flows through the voltage source. Thus power delivered by the source is P = 100 W = $VI_1 \cos\theta$ = V^2 [0.1125] cos (5°)

$$100 = V^2 (0.1125)$$

Thus V^2 = 893 volts

Thus, Voltage source = V = 29.9 $\angle 0°$ volts

Ex. 2.55: Find mesh currents in the circuit shown

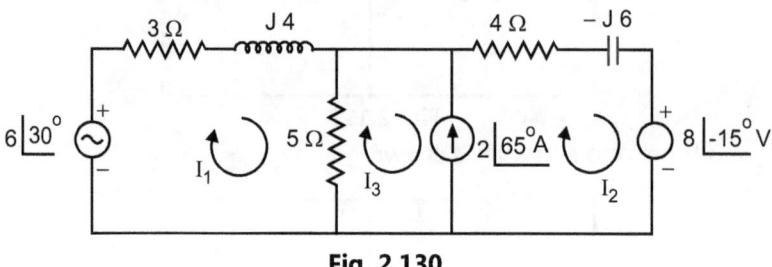

Fig. 2.130

Sol.: Transform $2\angle 65°$ a current source in parallel with 5 Ω into a voltage source of $10\angle 65°$ V in series with 5Ω as shown in Fig. 2.130. This transformation eliminates loop 3 and hence current I_3.

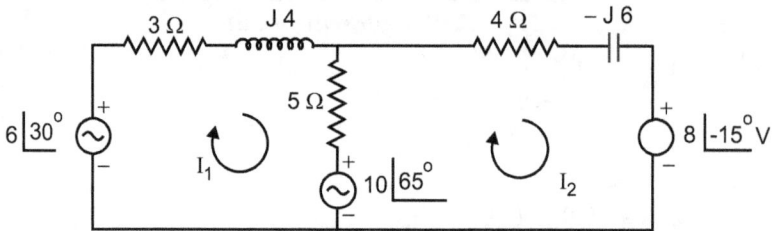

Fig. 2.131: Redrawn circuit

KVL across loop I_1 gives

$$(3 + J4) I_1 + 5 (I_1 - I_2) + 10 \angle 65° - 6 \angle 30° = 0$$

or
$$(8 + J4) I_1 - J5 I_2 = 6 \angle 30° - 10 \angle 65°$$

$$(8 + J4) I_1 - J5 I_2 = 6.14 \angle -81° \quad \ldots(a)$$

KVL across loop I_2 gives

$$J2 (4 - J6) - 5 ((I_1 - I_2) + 8 \angle -15° - 10 \angle 65° = 0$$

$$-5I_1 + (9 - J6) I_2 = 10 \angle 65° - 8 \angle -15°$$

$$-5I_1 + (9 - J6) I_2 = 11.7 \angle 107° \quad \ldots(b)$$

In matrix form these equations are

$$\begin{bmatrix} (8+J4) & -J5 \\ -5 & (9-J6) \end{bmatrix} \begin{bmatrix} I_1 \\ I_2 \end{bmatrix} = \begin{bmatrix} 6.14\angle -81° \\ 11.7\angle 107° \end{bmatrix}$$

Solving these two equations gives

$$I_1 = 0.631\angle -164.4°$$

and $\quad I_2 = -1.13\angle -23.9°$ Amp

Now, from original circuit we have

$$I_2 - I_3 = 2\angle 65°$$

Thus $\quad I_3 = -1.13\angle -23.9° - 2\angle 65°$

$$= -2.31\angle 35.9° \text{ Amp.}$$

Ex. 2.56: Find the voltage source equivalent circuit of the Fig. 2.132 across terminals a-b.

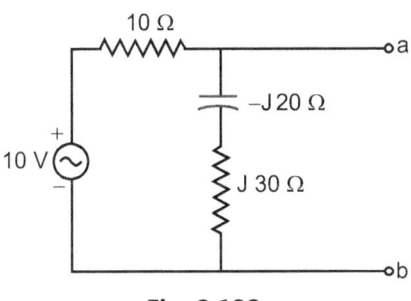

Fig. 2.132

Sol.: The voltage source equivalent is also known as Thevenin's equivalent circuit. As it is the terminals a-b are open. Hence we have

$$V_{oc} = V_{th} = 10 \times \frac{(J30 - J20)}{(10 + J30 - J20)}$$

$$= \frac{10 \times J10}{(10 + J10)}$$

$$= 7.07\angle 45° \text{ volts}$$

$$Z_{eq} = Z_{Th} = 10 \,\|\, J10$$

$$= \frac{10 \times J10}{10 + J10}$$

$$= (5 + J5) \text{ ohms}$$

Thus, voltage source equivalent circuit is as shown below in Fig. 2.133.

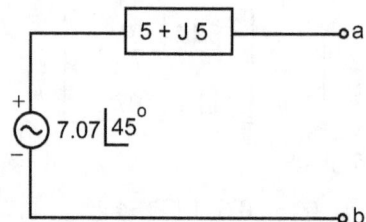

Fig. 2.133: Voltage source equivalent circuit

Ex. 2.57: Calculate the current through Z_L using (1) Thevenin's theorem (2) Nortons Theorem. Verify the result by direct calculations.

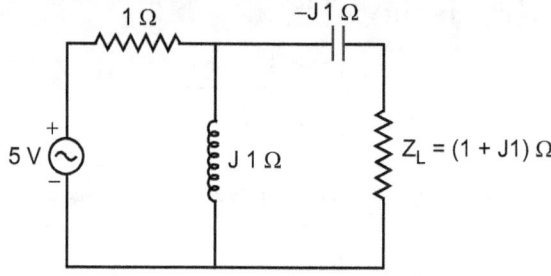

Fig. 2.134

Sol.: Let us first obtain Thevenin's equivalent circuit.

(a) To find open circuit voltage: Remove Z_L the circuit will be as shown in the Fig. 2.135 (a).

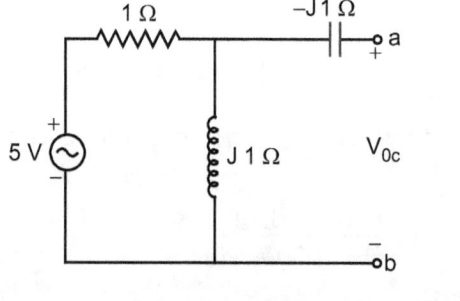

(a) To Find V_{OC}

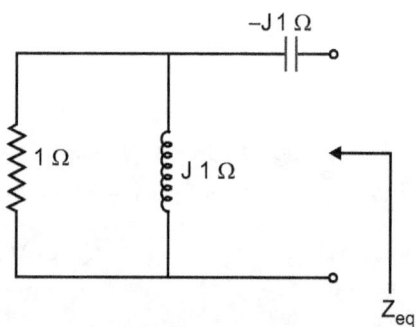

(b) To find Z_{eq}

Fig. 2.135: Circuits to find V_{oc} and V_{eq}

$$V_{oc} = \frac{5 \times J1}{1 + J1} = \frac{5 \angle 90°}{\sqrt{2} \angle 45°}$$

$$= 3.53 \angle 45° \text{ Volts}$$

(b) To find Z_{eq}: Short the voltage source. The circuit will be as shown in Fig. 2.135 (b).

$$Z_{eq} = -J1 + 1 \| J1 = -J1 + \frac{J1}{(1+J1)}$$

$$= -J1 + 0.5 + J0.5 = (0.5 - J0.5)\,\Omega$$

The resultant Thevenin's equivalent circuit is as shown in the Fig. 2.136 (a).

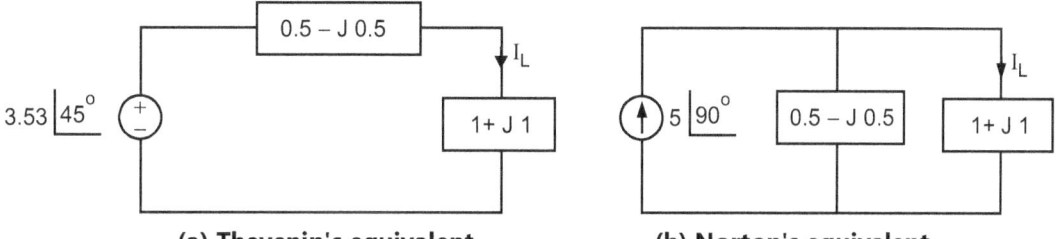

(a) Thevenin's equivalent   (b) Norton's equivalent

Fig. 2.136: Equivalent circuits

$$I_L = \frac{3.53\,\lfloor 45°}{(0.5 - J0.5) + (1 + J1)} = \frac{3.53\,\lfloor 45°}{(1.5 + J0.5)}$$

$$I_L = \frac{3.53\,\lfloor 45°}{1.58\,\lfloor 18.4°} = 2.23\,\lfloor 26.6°\ \text{Amp.}$$

Norton's equivalent circuit is obtained by source transformation of Thevenin's equivalent circuits and is shown in Fig. 2.136 (b).

$$I_{SC} = I_N = \frac{V_{oc}}{Z_{eq}} = \frac{3.53\,\lfloor 45°}{1.5 + J0.5} = 5\,\lfloor 90°\ \text{Amp.}$$

Using current divider option we have,

$$I_{l\Omega} = I_{SC} \times \frac{Z_{eq}}{Z_{eq} + Z_L}$$

$$= 5\,\lfloor 90°\ \times \frac{(0.5 - J0.5)}{(0.5 - J0.5) + (1 + J1)}$$

$$= \frac{3.53\,\lfloor 45°}{1.5 + J0.5} = 2.23\,\lfloor 25.6°\ \text{Amp.}$$

This current is same as obtained from the Thevenin's equivalent circuit.

Direct calculation of load current (I_L): Consider again the original circuit of Fig. 2.134.

$$\text{Source current } (I_S) = \frac{5}{1 + J1 \| (-J1 + 1 + J1)]} = \frac{5}{1 + (1 \| J1)}$$

$$= \frac{5}{1 + 0.5 + J0.5} = \frac{5}{1.5 + J0.5} = 3.16\,\lfloor -18.5°$$

Now by using current divider equation we have

$$\text{Load current } (I_L) = I_s \times \frac{J1}{(1+J1)} = \frac{3.16\angle-18.4° \times 1\angle 90°}{\sqrt{2}\angle 45°}$$

$$= 2.23\angle 26.6°$$

Ex. 2.58: Use Thevenin Theorem to calculate the steady state current through the Inductor of J8Ω in the circuit shown.

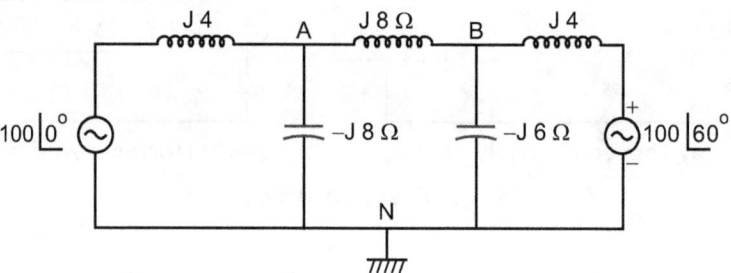

Fig. 2.137: Circuit for Ex. 2.57

Sol.: Remove J8Ω inductor branch temporarily. Let us obtain Thevenin equivalent circuit to the left of AN and to the right of BN.

$$\text{Voltage } V_{oc} \text{ (across AN)} = \frac{100 \times J8}{J4 - J8} = 200\angle 0° = 200 \text{ V}$$

$$\text{Equivalent Impedance } (Z_{AN}) = -J8 \parallel J4 = J8\Omega$$

$$\text{Voltage } V_{oc} \text{ (across BN)} = \frac{100\angle 60° \times -J6}{(J4 - J6)} = 300\angle 60° \text{ volts}$$

$$\text{Equivalent Impedance } (Z_{BN}) = -J6 \parallel J4 = J12 \ \Omega$$

The reduced equivalent circuit is shown below in the Fig. 2.138 below.

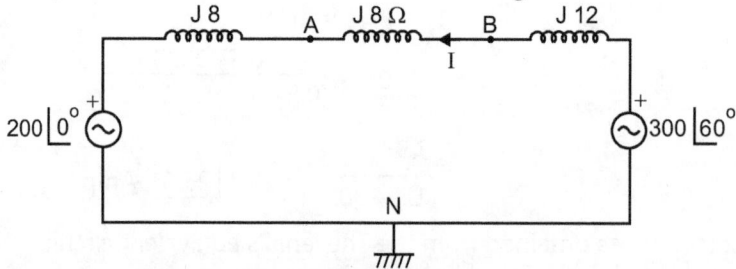

Fig. 2.138: Reduced Equivalent circuit

Let I be the steady state current in J8Ω inductor

$$I = \frac{300\angle 60° - 200\angle 0°}{J8 + J8 + J12} = 9.45\angle 10.9° \text{ Amp.}$$

Ex. 2.59: Use Superposition Theorem to find current (I) in the circuit shown.

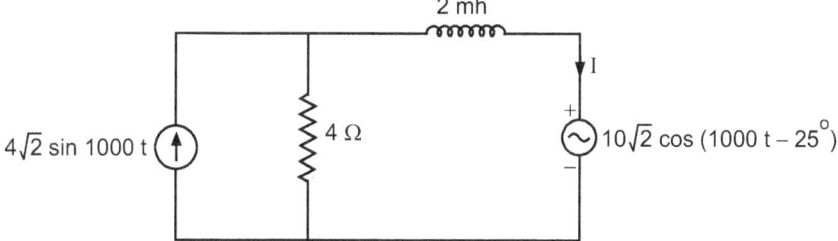

Fig. 2.139: Circuit for Ex. 2.58

Sol.: Here $\omega = 1000$ r/s, $X_L = \omega L = 2 \times 10^{-3} \times 10^3 = 2\,\Omega$
Let us use phasor to determine current (I)
Let phasor of $10\sqrt{2} \sin 1000t$ be $4\sqrt{2}\angle 0°$

Then phasor of $10\sqrt{2} \cos(1000\,t - 25°)$ is $10\sqrt{2}\angle 65°$.
This is because $10\sqrt{2}\cos(1000t - 25°) = 10\sqrt{2}\sin[90° + (1000\,t - 25°)]$

Step I: Consider currents source $4\sqrt{2}\angle 0°$ alone. Make the voltage source zero as in Fig. 2.140 (a).

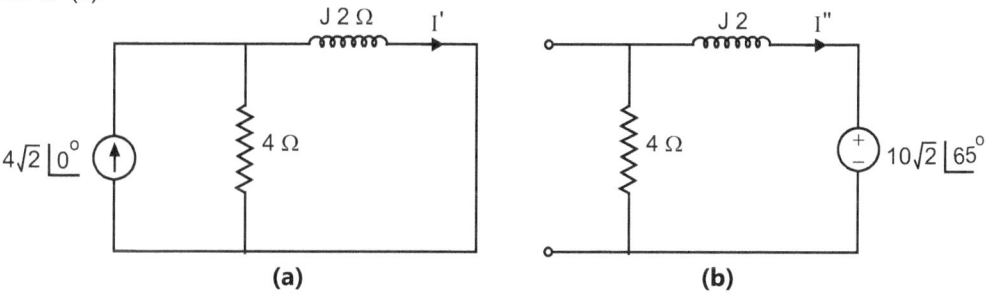

(a)   **(b)**
Fig. 2.140: Steps in Superposition Theorem

$$I' = 4\sqrt{2}\angle 0° \times \frac{4}{(4 + J2)} = 3.58\sqrt{2}\angle -26.6°\ \text{Amp.}$$

Step II: Consider voltage source of $10\sqrt{2}\angle 65°$ V alone. Make current source zero as in Fig. 2.140 (b).

$$I'' = \frac{-10\sqrt{2}\angle 45°}{(4 + J2)} = -2.24\sqrt{2}\angle 38.4°\ \text{Amp.}$$

Step III: By Superposition Theorem phasor of total current (I)

$$I = I' + I'' = \sqrt{2}\left[3.58\angle -26.6° - 2.24\angle 38.4°\right]$$

$$= 3.32\sqrt{2}\angle -64.2°$$

The corresponding sinusoidal current is given by

$$I(t) = 3.32\sqrt{2}\sin[1000\,t - 64.2°]\ \text{Amp.}$$

MULTIPLE CHOICE QUESTIONS (MCQs)

1. A circuit shown in figure, the Thevenin voltage across load terminal AB is equal to

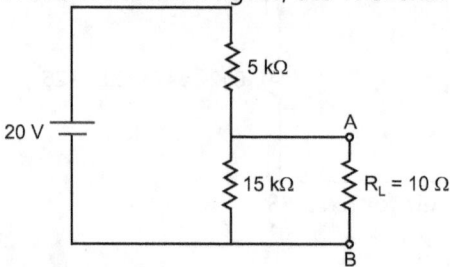

   (a) 5 V (b) 15 V
   (c) 20 V (d) 10 V

2. For the circuit shown in figure the Thevenin equivalent resistance across terminal AB is equal to

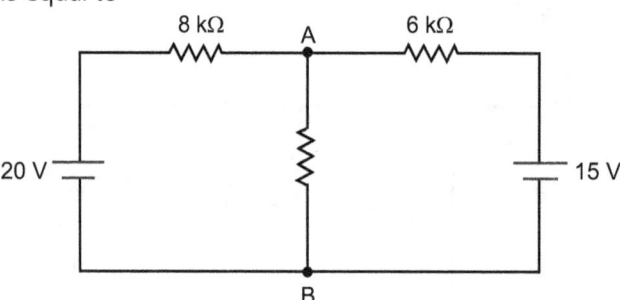

   (a) 8 kΩ (b) 6 kΩ
   (c) 3.43 kΩ (d) 14 kΩ

3. For the circuit shown in figure, the value of Norton equivalent resistance is equal to

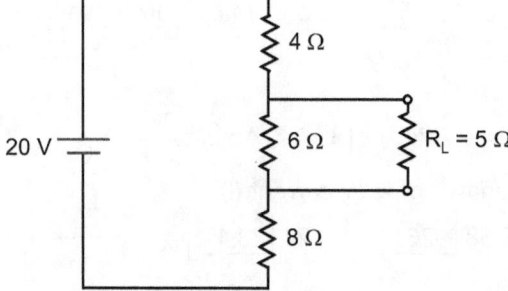

   (a) 12 Ω (b) 18 Ω
   (c) 4 Ω (d) 6 Ω

4. For the circuit shown in figure, the value of Norton current across 8Ω resistor is equal to

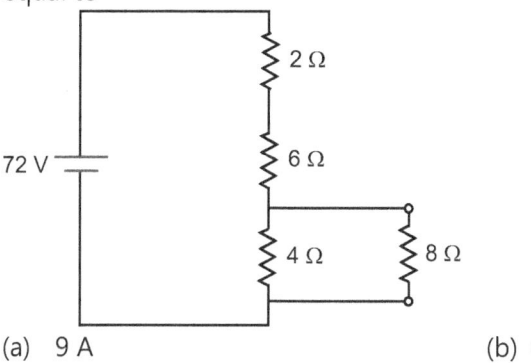

(a) 9 A
(b) 6 A
(c) 4.5 A
(d) 6.6 A

5. Using Thevenin theorem, the thevenin equivalent resistance across AB of the circuit shown in figure is equal to

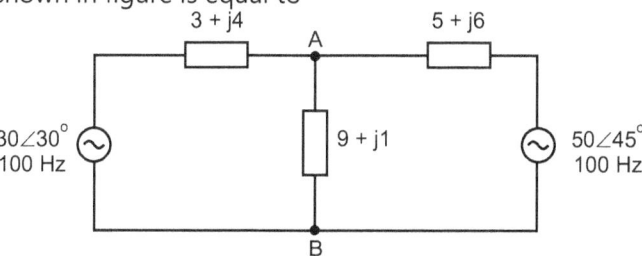

(a) 1.87 + j 2.4
(b) 2.3 + j 1.67
(c) 1.56 + j 3.4
(d) 1.67 + j 3.8

6. The nodal voltage V at node A for the circuit shown in figure is equal to

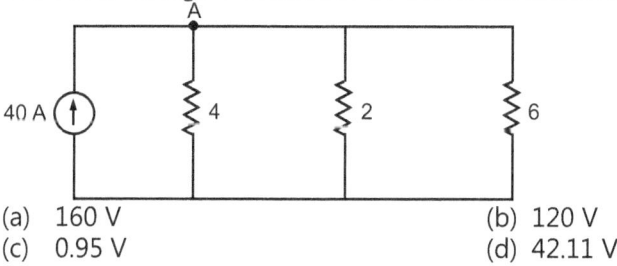

(a) 160 V
(b) 120 V
(c) 0.95 V
(d) 42.11 V

7. For the given circuit shown in figure the nodal voltage V at node A is equal to

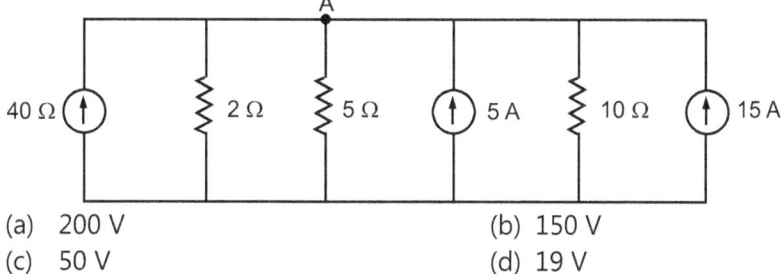

(a) 200 V
(b) 150 V
(c) 50 V
(d) 19 V

8. For the circuit shown in figure, the current I_3 flowing in resistor R_3 is equal to

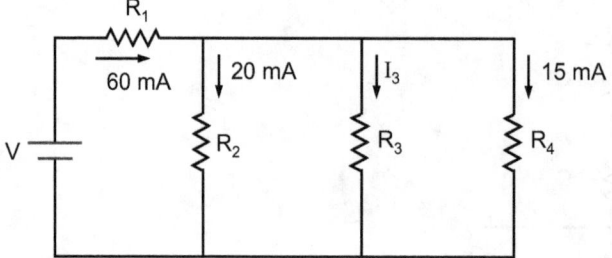

(a) 40 mA (b) 45 mA
(c) 25 mA (d) none of these

9. A network shown in figure, the voltage at node A is equal to

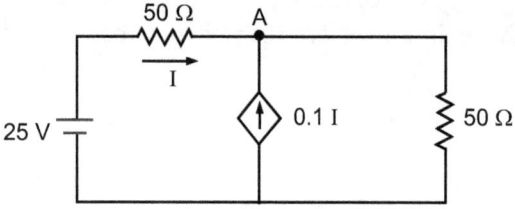

(a) 36.905 V (b) 2.27 V
(c) 13.1 V (d) 47.725 V

10. A network shown in figure, the voltage across node A is equal to

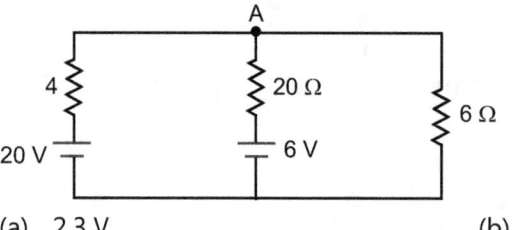

(a) 2.3 V (b) 2.4 V
(c) 2.5 V (d) 2.6 V

11. A network shown in figure, the total current flowing through terminal AB is equal to

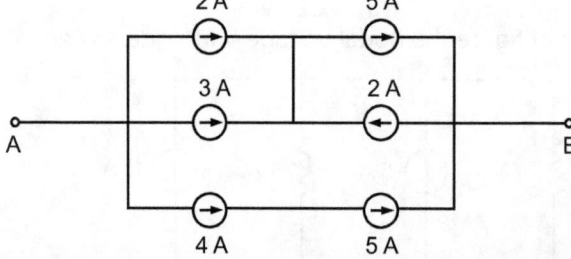

(a) 10 A (b) 17 A
(c) 5 A (d) 8 A

12. A network shown in figure, the voltage at node A is equal to

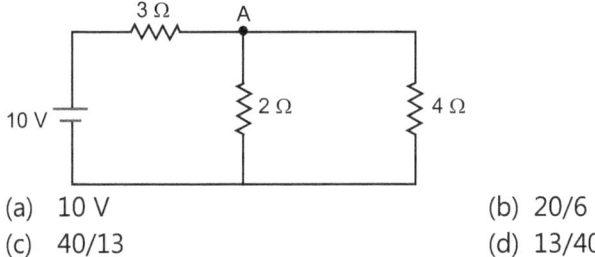

(a) 10 V (b) 20/6
(c) 40/13 (d) 13/40

13. For a given network shown in figure, the current I_1 flowing through the network is equal to

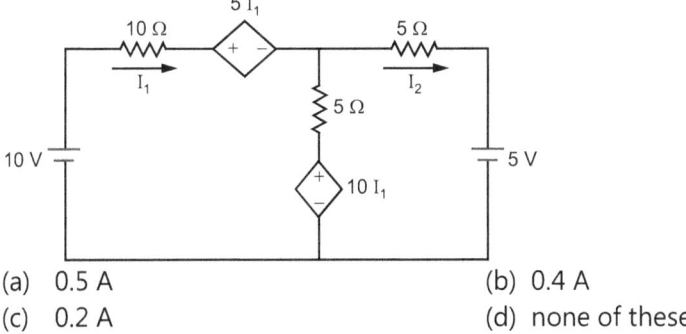

(a) 0.5 A (b) 0.4 A
(c) 0.2 A (d) none of these

14. For a given network shown in figure, the current I_2 flowing through the network is equal to

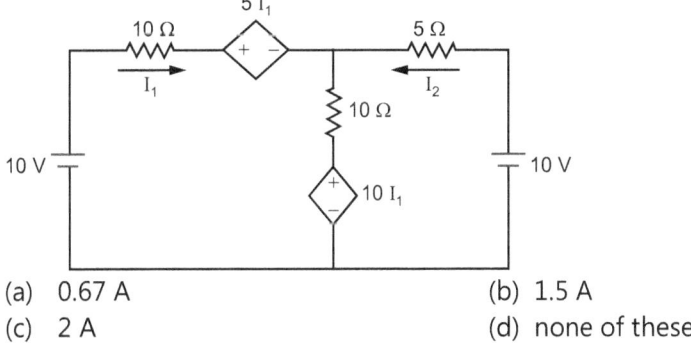

(a) 0.67 A (b) 1.5 A
(c) 2 A (d) none of these

15. A network shown in figure. The voltage across terminals A and B is equal to

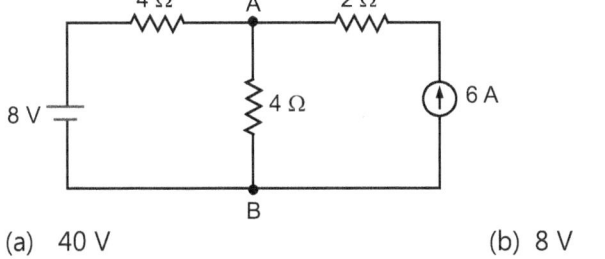

(a) 40 V (b) 8 V
(c) 18 V (d) none of these

16. For the network shown in figure, the voltage across 8Ω resistor is equal to

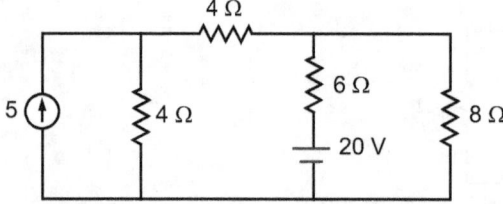

(a) 20 V (b) 16 V
(c) 14 V (d) none of these

17. A network shown in figure, the voltage V_A at node A is equal to

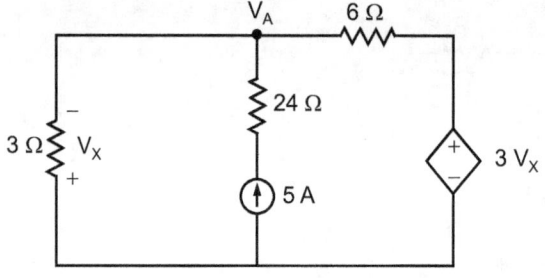

(a) 120 V (b) 5 V
(c) 3 V (d) 6 V

18. The network is shown in figure, the voltage at node A is equal to

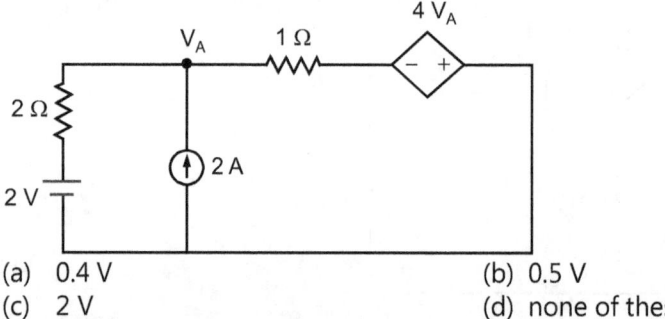

(a) 0.4 V (b) 0.5 V
(c) 2 V (d) none of these

19. A network is shown in figure, the voltage at node V_A is equal to

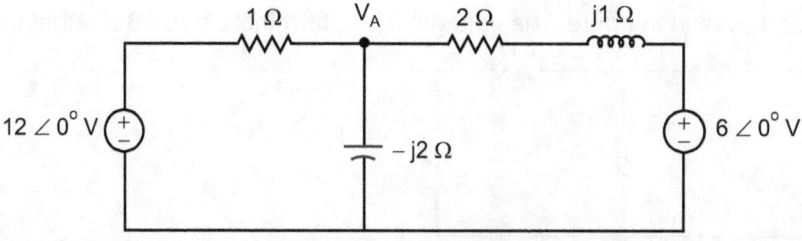

(a) $10 < 0°$ (b) $10 < -16.85$
(c) $10 < 53.76$ (d) none of these

20. A network is shown in figure, the voltage at node V_A is equal to

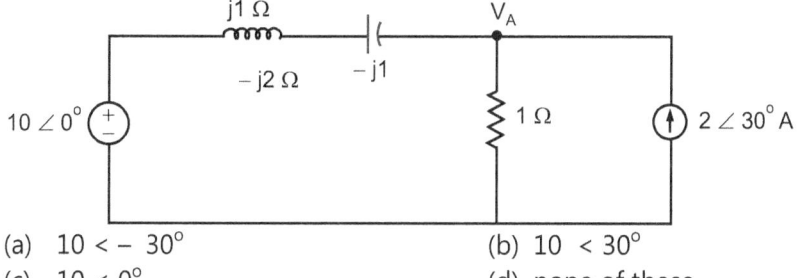

(a) $10 \angle -30°$
(b) $10 \angle 30°$
(c) $10 \angle 0°$
(d) none of these

21. A network is shown in figure, the voltage across the terminal AB is equal to

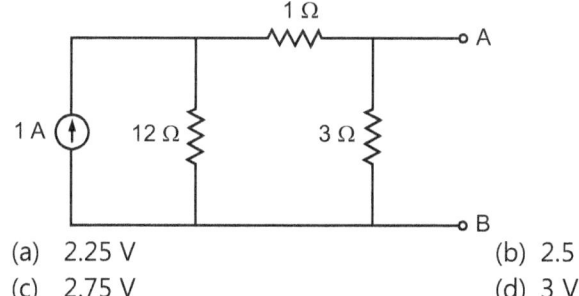

(a) 2.25 V
(b) 2.5 V
(c) 2.75 V
(d) 3 V

22. A circuit is shown in figure, the voltage at the node V_A is equal to

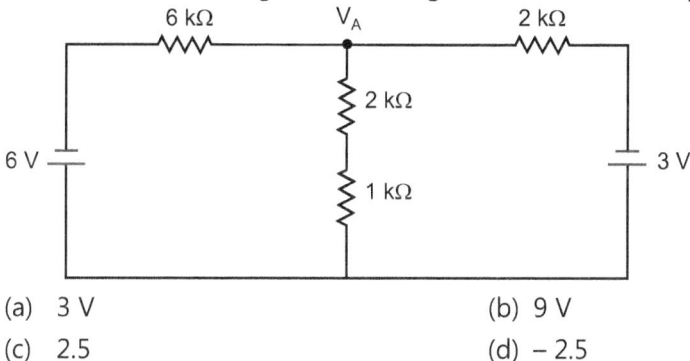

(a) 3 V
(b) 9 V
(c) 2.5
(d) – 2.5

23. A circuit is shown in figure, the voltage at node V_A is equal to

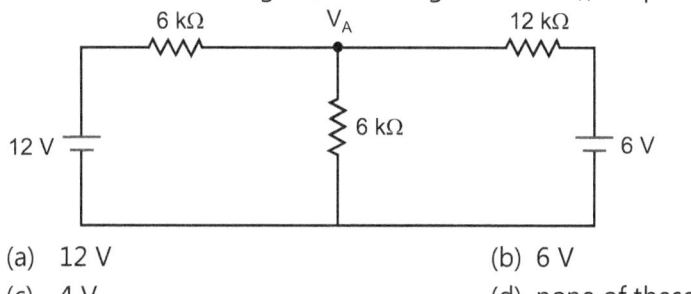

(a) 12 V
(b) 6 V
(c) 4 V
(d) none of these

24. A circuit is shown in figure, the voltage at node V_A is equal to

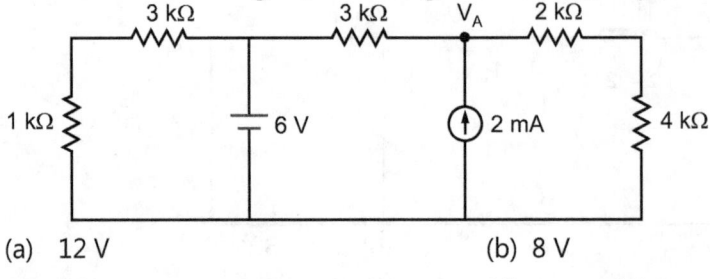

(a) 12 V
(b) 8 V
(c) 4 V
(d) none of these

25. A circuit is shown in figure, the voltage at node V_A is equal to

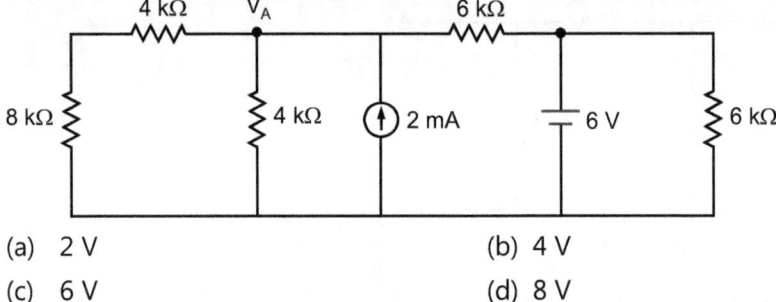

(a) 2 V
(b) 4 V
(c) 6 V
(d) 8 V

26. A circuit is shown in figure, the voltage across terminal AB is equal to

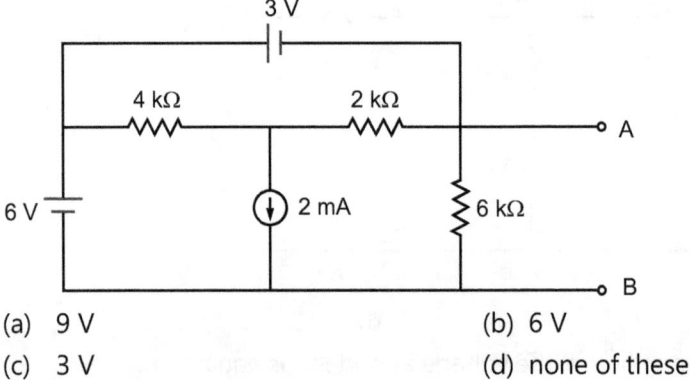

(a) 9 V
(b) 6 V
(c) 3 V
(d) none of these

27. A circuit is shown in figure, the voltage at node V_A is equal to

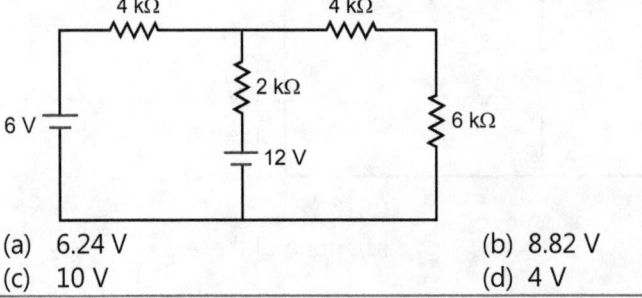

(a) 6.24 V
(b) 8.82 V
(c) 10 V
(d) 4 V

28. A circuit is shown in figure, the voltage across AB terminal is equal to

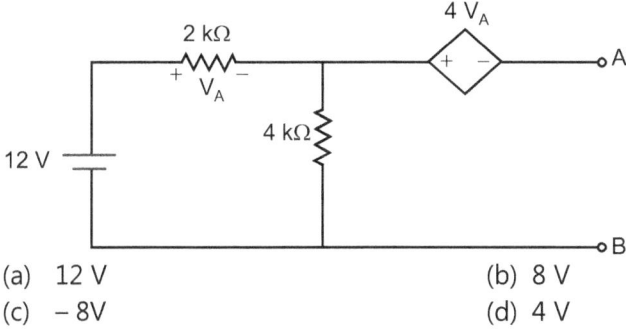

(a) 12 V (b) 8 V
(c) −8V (d) 4 V

29. A circuit is shown in figure, the voltage across AB terminal is equal to

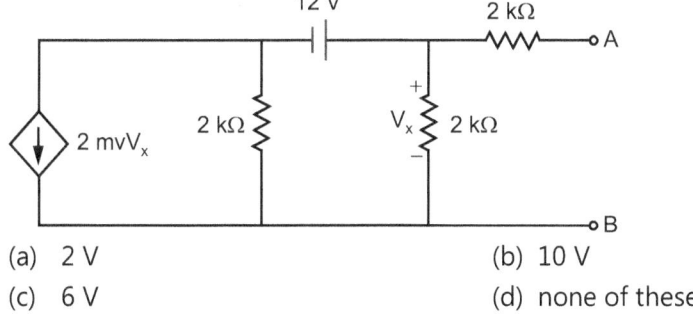

(a) 2 V (b) 10 V
(c) 6 V (d) none of these

30. A circuit is shown in figure, the voltage at node V_A is equal to

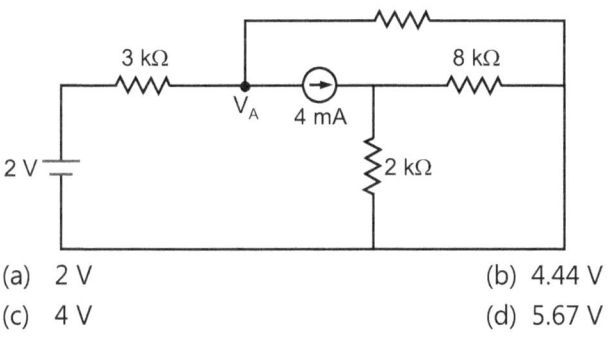

(a) 2 V (b) 4.44 V
(c) 4 V (d) 5.67 V

31. A circuit is shown in figure, the voltage across AB terminal is equal to

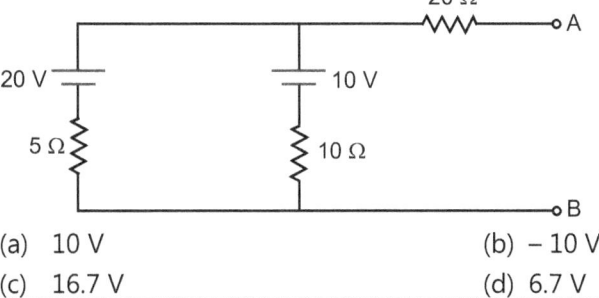

(a) 10 V (b) −10 V
(c) 16.7 V (d) 6.7 V

32. A circuit is shown in figure, the current I passing through the circuit is equal

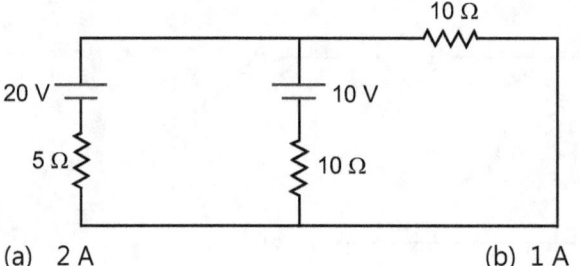

(a) 2 A
(b) 1 A
(c) 4 A
(d) none of these

33. A circuit is shown in figure, the voltage across 6Ω resistor is equal to

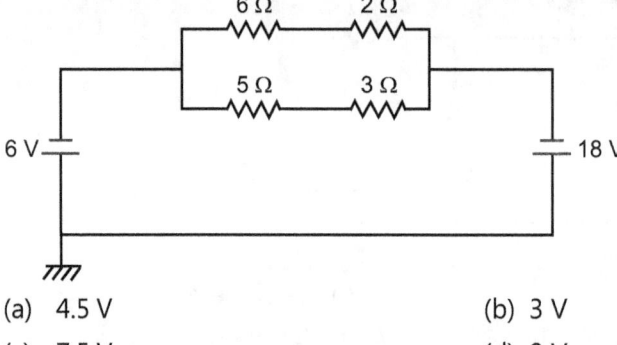

(a) 4.5 V
(b) 3 V
(c) 7.5 V
(d) 9 V

34. A circuit is shown in figure, the current I passing through 2 kΩ resistor is equal to

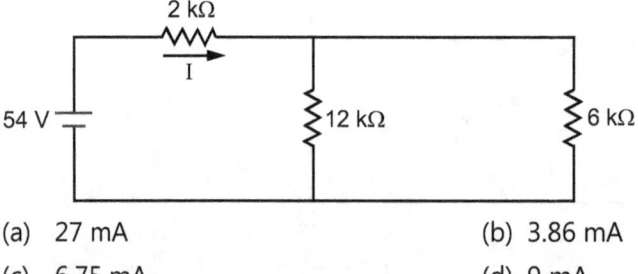

(a) 27 mA
(b) 3.86 mA
(c) 6.75 mA
(d) 9 mA

35. A circuit is shown in figure, the voltage V_A in the circuit across resistor is equal to

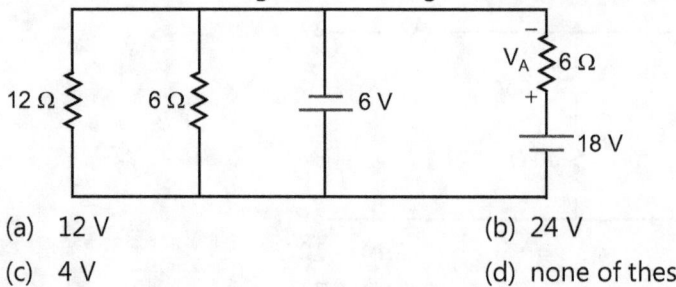

(a) 12 V
(b) 24 V
(c) 4 V
(d) none of these

36. A circuit is shown in figure, the current I passing through 14 Ω resistor is equal to

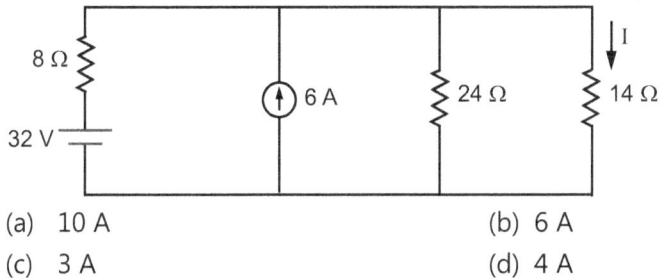

(a) 10 A (b) 6 A
(c) 3 A (d) 4 A

37. A circuit is shown is figure, the nodal voltage at node A is equal to

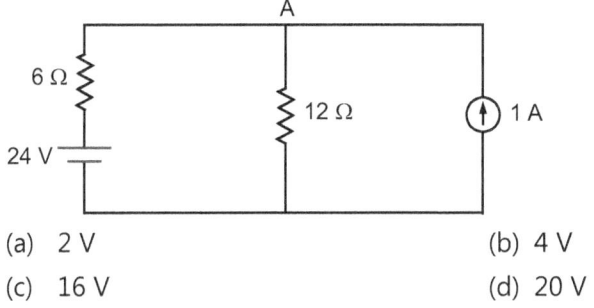

(a) 2 V (b) 4 V
(c) 16 V (d) 20 V

38. A circuit is shown in figure, the voltage across AB terminal is equal to

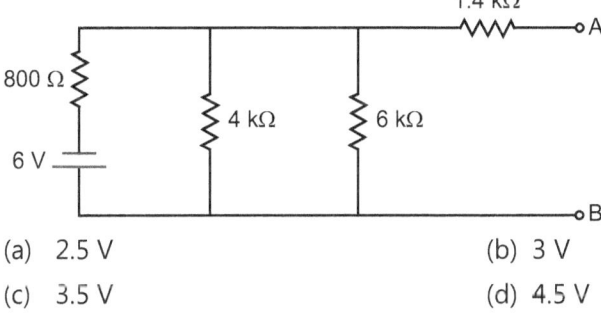

(a) 2.5 V (b) 3 V
(c) 3.5 V (d) 4.5 V

39. A circuit is shown in figure, the value of load resistance form maximum power is equal to

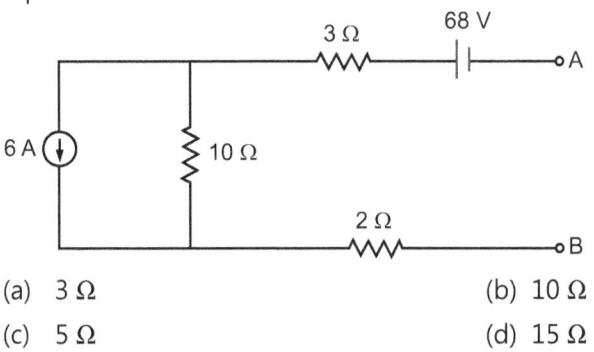

(a) 3 Ω (b) 10 Ω
(c) 5 Ω (d) 15 Ω

40. A circuit is shown in figure, the voltage at node A is equal to

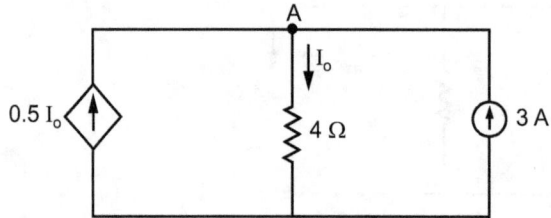

(a) 12 V
(b) 14 V
(c) 24 V
(d) none of these

41. A circuit is shown in figure, the voltage at node A is equal to

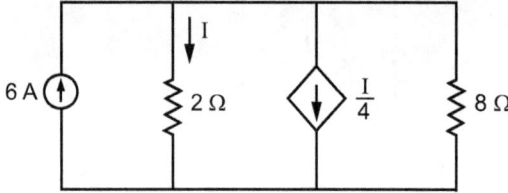

(a) 2 V
(b) 4 V
(c) 6 V
(d) 8 V

42. A circuit is shown in figure, the nodal voltage at node A is equal to

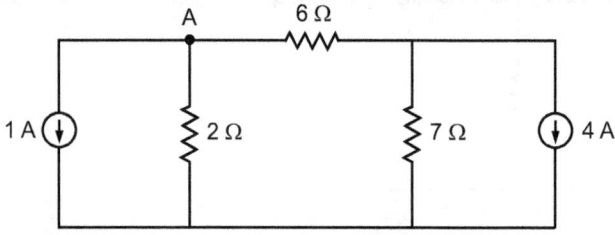

(a) 2 V
(b) – 2 V
(c) 12
(d) – 12 V

43. A circuit is shown in figure, the current passing through 8 Ω resistor is equal to

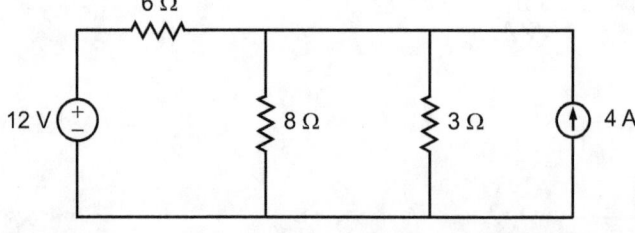

(a) 4 A
(b) 2 A
(c) 0.4 A
(d) 0.2 A

44. A circuit is shown in figure, the voltage across terminal AB is equal to

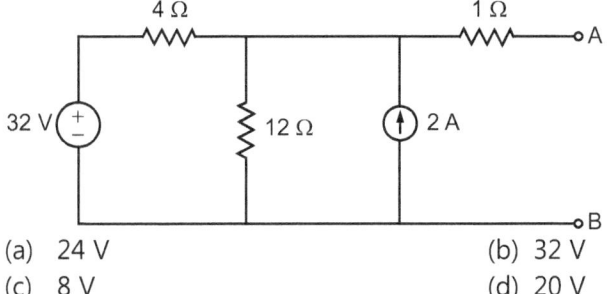

(a) 24 V (b) 32 V
(c) 8 V   (d) 20 V

45. A circuit s shown in figure, the voltage across terminal AB is equal to

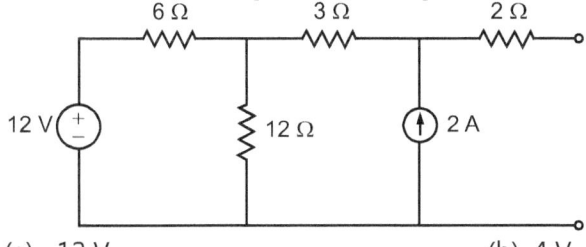

(a) 12 V (b) 4 V
(c) 22 V (d) none of these

46. "Any two terminal of a network can be replaced by an equivalent voltage source and an equivalent series resistance" which is the theorem statement
(a) Superposition theorem   (b) Theveinins theorem
(c) Theveinins theorem   (d) Maximum power transfer theorem

47. Any two terminal of a network can be replaced by an equivalent current source and an equivalent parallel resistance is the statement of
(a) Superposition theorem   (b) Maximum power transfer theorem
(c) Norton theorem   (d) Theveinins theorem

48. The maximum power is delivered from a source to a load when
(a) the load resistance resistance is equal to the source resistance
(b) the load resistance is not equal to the source resistance
(c) both of these
(d) None of these

49. The Thevenin equivalent circuit to the left of AB has R_{eq} given by

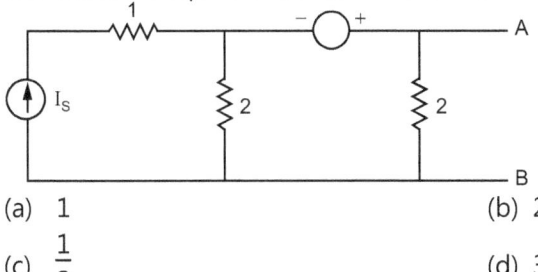

(a) 1   (b) 2
(c) $\frac{1}{2}$ (d) 3

50. In the figure the transformer is ideal with adjustable turns ratio $\frac{n_2}{n_1}$. The turns ratio $\frac{n_2}{n_1}$ for maximum power transfer to the load is

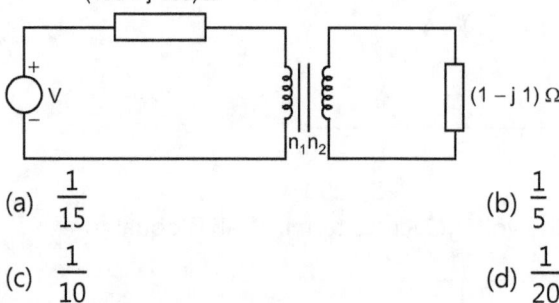

(a) $\frac{1}{15}$ (b) $\frac{1}{5}$

(c) $\frac{1}{10}$ (d) $\frac{1}{20}$

51. The Thevenin equivalent resistance of the two-terminal network as shown in the above figure is

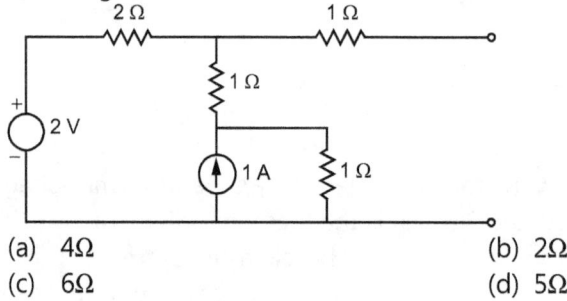

(a) 4 Ω (b) 2 Ω
(c) 6 Ω (d) 5 Ω

52. Thevenin's equivalent impedance of the given circuit is

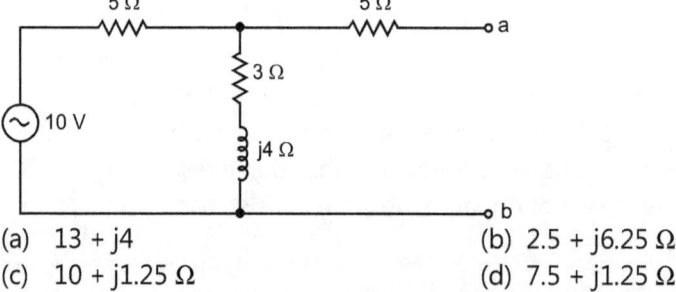

(a) 13 + j4 (b) 2.5 + j6.25 Ω
(c) 10 + j1.25 Ω (d) 7.5 + j1.25 Ω

53. Thevenin's equivalent impedance between terminals a and b in the given circuit is

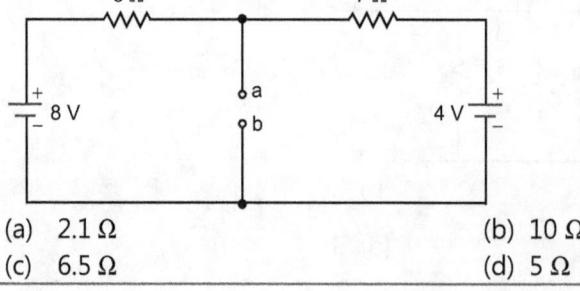

(a) 2.1 Ω (b) 10 Ω
(c) 6.5 Ω (d) 5 Ω

54. Norton's theorem results in
    (a) a current source alone
    (b) a voltage source alone
    (c) a current source with an impedance in parallel
    (d) a voltage source with an impedance in series

55. In an ac circuit having terminal impedance of (R + jx) for maximum transfer of power the load impedance should be
    (a) x
    (b) R − jx
    (c) R
    (d) R + jx

56. For the given circuit Norton's equivalent current source is

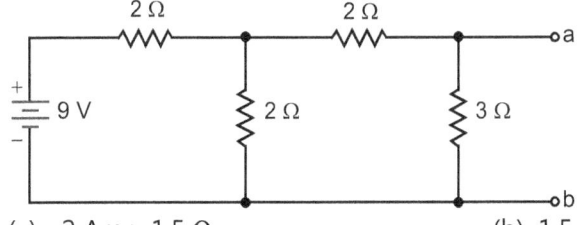

    (a) 2 Amp, 1.5 Ω
    (b) 1.5 Amp, 1.5 Ω
    (c) 1.5 Amp, 2 Ω
    (d) 2 Amp, 2 Ω

57. In the given circuit, maximum transfer to load Z_L takes place when Z_L equals

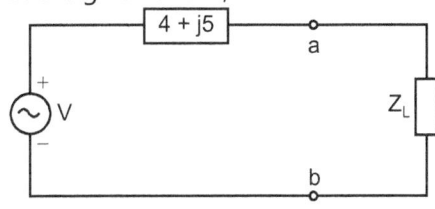

    (a) (4 − j5) Ω
    (b) (4 + j5) Ω
    (c) (5 + j4) Ω
    (d) (5 − j4) Ω

58. In the given circuit load Z_L is adjusted for maximum transfer of power. The power so delivered to the load is

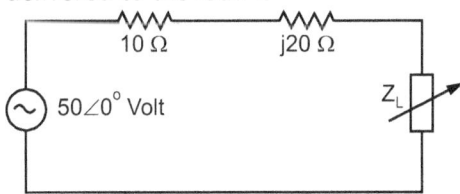

    (a) 62.5 W
    (b) 25 W
    (c) 38.5 W
    (d) 10 W

59. Maximum point transfer is given by
    (a) $\dfrac{V_{th}^2}{R_{th}}$
    (b) $\dfrac{4V_{th}^2}{R_{th}}$
    (c) $\dfrac{V_{th}^2}{2R_{th}}$
    (d) $\dfrac{V_{th}^2}{4R_{th}}$

60. The Superposition theorem with essentially based on the concept of
    (a) duality
    (b) reciprocity
    (c) linearity
    (d) non-linearity

61. Which of the following theorems is applicable for both linear and non-linear circuits?
    (a) Superposition
    (b) Norton's
    (c) Thevenin's
    (d) None of these

62. Millman's theorem yields equivalent
    (a) voltage source
    (b) current source
    (c) voltage or current source
    (d) impedance or resistance

63. Application of Norton's theorem to a network results in equivalent
    (a) current source
    (b) current source and impedance in parallel
    (c) current source and impedance in series
    (d) impedance

64. A non-linear network does not satisfy
    (a) Super-position condition
    (b) homogeneity condition
    (c) both homogeneity as well as Super-position condition
    (d) homogeneity Super-position and associative condition

65. The Super-position theorem is applicable to
    (a) linear, non-linear and time variant
    (b) linear and non-linear responses only
    (c) linear responses only

66. In a pure inductive circuit
    (a) the current lags behind the voltage by 90°
    (b) the current leads the voltage by 90°
    (c) the current can lead or lag by 90°
    (d) the current is in phase with the voltage

67. Time constant of a circuit is the time in seconds taken after the application of voltage to reach
    (a) 90% of maximum value
    (b) 63% of maximum value
    (c) 50% of maximum value
    (d) 25% of maximum value

68. Times constant of an inductive circuit
    (a) increases with decrease of inductance and increase of resistance
    (b) increases with the decrease of inductance and decrease of resistance
    (c) increases with the increase of inductance and the increase of resistance
    (d) increases with increase of inductance and decrease of resistance

69. The Superposition theorem is applicable to
    (a) current only
    (b) voltage only
    (c) current, voltage and power
    (d) both current and voltage
70. The double energy transient occur in the
    (a) R-L circuit
    (b) R-C circuit
    (c) R-L-C circuit
    (d) Purely inductive circuit
71. The transient currents are associated with the
    (a) changes in the stored energy in the inductors and capacitors
    (b) applied voltage to the circuit
    (c) impedance of the circuit
    (d) resistance of the circuit
72. In a pure resistive circuit
    (a) current lags behind the voltage by 90°
    (b) current is in phase with the voltage
    (c) current can lead or lag the voltage by 90°
    (d) current leads the voltage by 90°
73. The Superposition theorem is applicable to
    (a) linear and non-linear resistors only
    (b) linear responses only
    (c) linear, non-linear and time variant responses
    (d) none of the above
74. Application of Norton's theorem to a circuit yields
    (a) equivalent current source
    (b) equivalent impedance
    (c) equivalent current source and impedance in parallel
    (d) equivalent current source and impedance in series
75. Millman's theorem yields
    (a) equivalent voltage or current source
    (b) equivalent voltage source
    (c) equivalent impedance
    (d) equivalent resistance
76. For maximum transfer of power, internal resistance of the source should be
    (a) greater than the load resistance
    (b) less than the load resistance
    (c) equal to load resistance
    (d) none of the above

77. The common voltage across parallel branches with different voltage sources can be determined by the relation

$$V = \frac{V_1}{R_1} + \frac{V_2}{R_2} + \frac{V_3}{R_3} \cdots$$

The above statement is associated with

(a) Milliman's theorem
(b) Norton's theorem
(c) Thevenin's theorem
(d) Superposition theorem

78. A non-linear network does not satisfy

(a) homogeneity condition
(b) Superposition condition
(c) both homogeneity as well as Superposition condition
(d) homogeneity, Superposition and associative conditions

79. Using Thevenin's theorem, the circuit in branch NS of the network system shown in Fig. will be

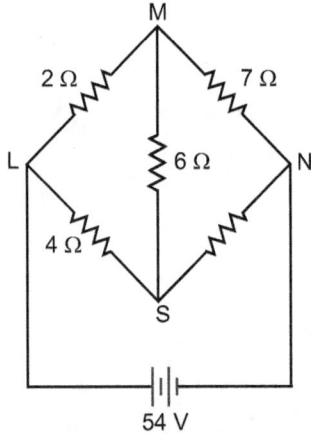

(a) 0.6 A
(b) 2.7 A
(c) 1.6 A
(d) 3.7 A

80. "In any network containing more than one source of e.m.f. the current in any branch is the algebraic sum of a number of individual fictitious currents (the number being equal to the number of sources of e.m.f.), each of which is due to separate action of each source of e.m.f. taken in order, when the remaining sources of e.m.f. are replaced by conductors the resistances of which are equal to the internal resistances of the respective sources". The above statement is associated with

(a) Norton's theorem
(b) Superposition theorem
(c) Thevenin's theorem
(d) none of the above

81. Thevenin's equivalent (E_{th}, R_{th}) for the circuit shown in Fig. will be

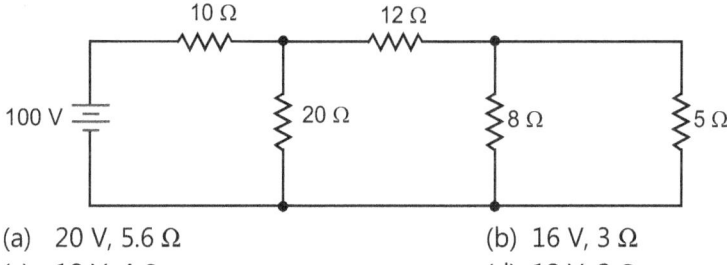

   (a) 20 V, 5.6 Ω
   (b) 16 V, 3 Ω
   (c) 18 V, 4 Ω
   (d) 12 V, 2 Ω

82. The current down from 4V battery in the network shown in the Fig. will be

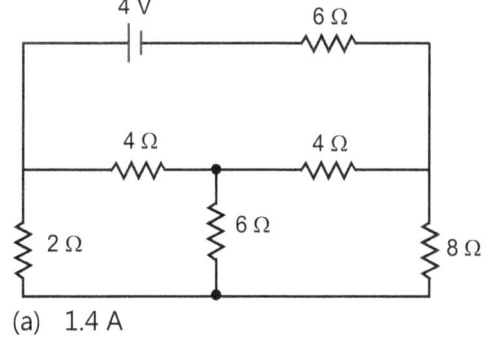

   (a) 1.4 A
   (b) 0.6 A
   (c) 0.9 A
   (d) 0.39 A

83. Efficiency of power transfer when maximum transfer of power occurs is
   (a) 50%
   (b) 75%
   (c) 80%
   (d) 100%

84. "In any linear bilateral network, if a source e.m.f. E in any branch produces a current I in any other branch then same e.m.f. acting in the second branch would produce the same current I in the first branch".
   The above statement is associated with
   (a) Compensation theorem
   (b) Reciprocity theorem
   (c) Superposition theorem
   (d) none of the above

85. In the circuit shown in the Fig. R_{th} equals

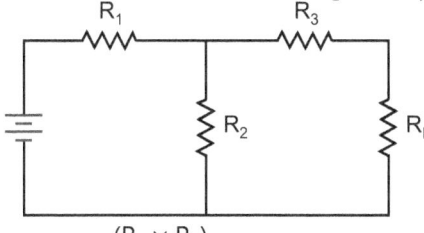

   (a) $R_1 + \dfrac{(R_2 \times R_3)}{R_2 + R_3}$
   (b) $R_2 + \dfrac{(R_3 \times R_1)}{R_3 + R_1}$
   (c) $R_3 + \dfrac{(R_1 \times R_2)}{R_1 + R_2}$
   (d) none of the above

86. Time constant of a capacitive circuit
    (a) increase with increase of capacitance and increase of resistance
    (b) increases with decrease of capacitance and decrease of resistance
    (c) increases with decrease of capacitance and increase of resistance
    (d) increases with increase of capacitance and decrease of resistance

87. A capacitor with no initial charge at t = ∞ acts
    (a) current source   (b) voltage source
    (c) open-circuit   (d) short-circuit

88. Which of the following theorems enables a number of voltages (or current) sources to be combined directly into a single voltage (or current) source?
    (a) Thevenin's theorem   (b) Millman's theorem
    (c) Superposition theorem   (d) Compensation theorem

89. "Maximum power output is obtained from a network when the load resistance is equal to the output resistance of the network as seen form the terminals of the load". The above statements is associated with
    (a) Superposition theorem   (b) Maximum power transfer theorem
    (c) Thevenin's theorem   (d) Millman's theorem

90. "Any number of current sources in parallel may be replaced by a single current source whose current is the algebraic sum of individual source currents and source resistance is the parallel combination of individual source resistances".
    The above statement is associated with
    (a) Millman's theorem   (b) Thevenin's theorem
    (c) Maximum power transfer theorem (d) none of the above

91. Thevenin's equivalent (E_{th}, R_{th}) for the circuit shown in Fig. will be

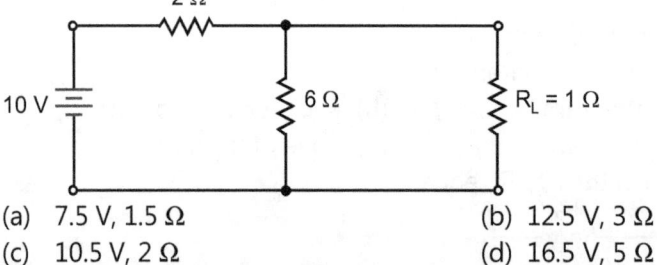

    (a) 7.5 V, 1.5 Ω   (b) 12.5 V, 3 Ω
    (c) 10.5 V, 2 Ω   (d) 16.5 V, 5 Ω

92. The concept of which Superposition theorem is based on
    (a) duality   (b) linearity
    (c) non-linearity   (d) reciprocity

93. Thevenin resistance R_{th} is found
    (a) by short-circuiting the given two terminals
    (b) between any two 'open' terminals
    (c) between same open terminals as for E_{th}
    (d) by removing voltage sources along with their internal resistances

94. The Thevenin's equivalent between points L and M for the network shown in Fig. is given by

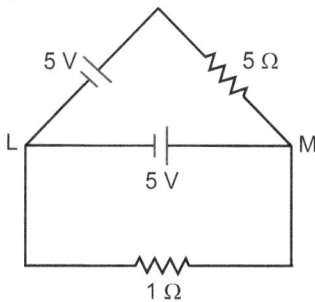

   (a) 5 V, 0 ohm (b) 5 V, 10 ohm
   (c) 5 V, 5 ohm (d) none of the above

95. In a linear circuit, the Superposition principle can be applied to calculate the
   (a) voltage and current (b) voltage and power
   (c) current and power (d) voltage, current and power

96. In any network of linear impedances the current flowing at any point is equal to the algebraic sum of the currents caused to flow at that point by each of the sources of emf taken separately with all other emf's reduced to zero.
   This statements represents
   (a) Norton's theorem (b) Superposition theorem
   (c) Thevenin's theorem (d) Kirchoff's law

97. Superposition theorem can be applied only to circuits having
   (a) resistive elements (b) non-linear elements
   (c) linear bilateral elements (d) passive elements

98. The value of the resistance R in the circuit shown in the given figure is varied in such a manner that the power dissipated in the 3 ohm resistor is maximum. Under this condition, the value of R will be

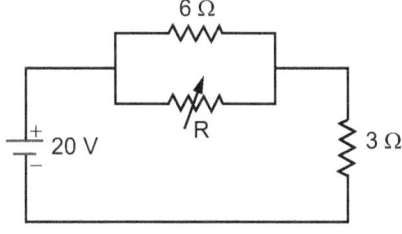

   (a) 6 Ω (b) 12 Ω
   (c) 9 Ω (d) 3 Ω

99. In the circuit shown in the given figure R_L will absord maximum power when its value is

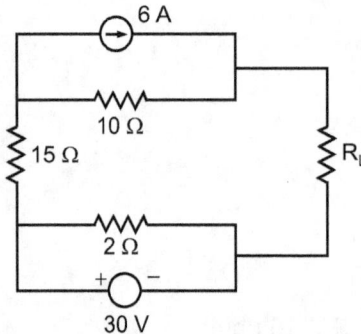

(a) 7.5 Ω
(b) 25 Ω
(c) 2.75 Ω
(d) none of these

100. A loud speaker is connected across terminals A and B of the network shown below. What should its impedance to be obtain maximum power dissipation in it?

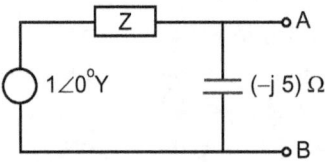

(a) $3 - j1$
(b) $7.5 + j2.5$
(c) $3 + j9$
(c) $7.5 - j2.5$

101. The Norton's equivalent of the circuit given below will be

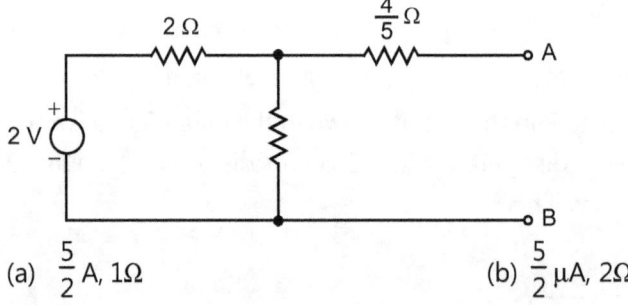

(a) $\frac{5}{2}$ A, 1Ω
(b) $\frac{5}{2}$ μA, 2Ω
(c) $\frac{2}{5}$ A, 1Ω
(d) $\frac{2}{5}$ A, 2Ω

102. Substitution theorem applies to
   (a) non-linear networks
   (b) linear networks
   (c) linear time invariant network
   (d) any network

103. For the circuit shown in figure four equivalent (A), (B), (C) and (D) are shown. Which circuit represents Thevenin equivalent circuit?

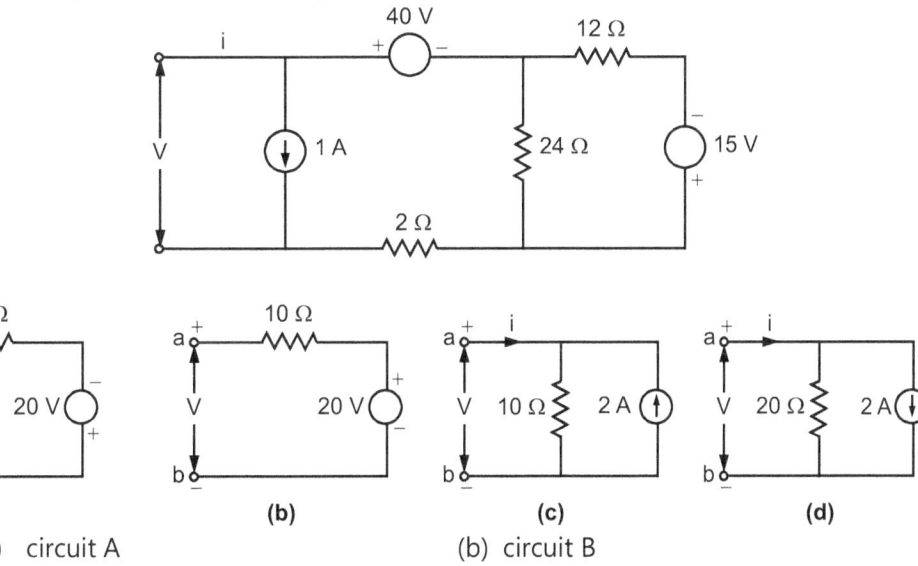

(a) circuit A
(b) circuit B
(c) circuit C
(d) circuit D

104. In the forgoing figure which circuit represents the Norton equivalent circuit?
 (a) Circuit A
 (b) Circuit B
 (c) Circuit C
 (d) Circuit D

105. The Super-position theorem is applicable to
 (a) voltage only
 (b) current only
 (c) both current and voltage
 (d) current, voltage and power

106. In order to find Z in Thevenin's theorem
 (a) all independent voltage sources are open circuited and all independent current sources are short circuited
 (b) all independent current sources are short circuited and independent voltage sources are open circuited
 (c) all independent voltage sources are short circuited and all independent current sources are open circuited
 (d) all independent voltage are current sources are short circuited

107. In Thevenin's theorem to find Z
 (a) all independent voltage and current sources are short-circuited
 (b) all independent voltage sources are short circuited and all independent current sources are open-circuited
 (c) all independent voltage sources are open-circuited and all independent current sources are short-circuited
 (d) all independent current sources are short-circuited and independent voltage sources are open-circuited

108. The Superposition theorem requires as many circuit to be solved as there are
    (a) sources
    (b) nodes
    (c) sources and nodes
    (d) sources, nodes and meshes
109. Millman's theorem is best to find
    (a) equivalent voltage or current source
    (b) equivalent voltage and resistance of a circuit
    (c) equivalent voltage source
    (d) none of the above
110. Norton's theorem reduces a two terminal network to
    (a) a constant current source and an impedance in parallel
    (b) a constant voltage source and an impedance in parallel
    (c) a constant voltage source and an impedance in series
    (d) a constant current source and an impedance in series
111. Steady state conditions are considered to be achieved in R-L circuits at the end of .... time constant
    (a) two
    (b) one
    (c) five
    (d) four
112. While calculating R_{th} in Thevenin's theorem and Norton equivalent
    (a) all independent sources are made dead
    (b) only voltage sources are made dead
    (c) only current sources are made dead
    (d) all voltage and current sources are made dead
113. The Superposition theorem requires as many circuits to be solved as there are
    (a) sources
    (b) nodes
    (c) meshes
    (d) none of the above
114. In a circuit containing a complex impedance maximum power transfer takes palce when
    (a) load is equal to the complex impedance
    (b) load is pure resistance
    (c) load is conjugate complex of the circuit impedance
    (c) none of the above
115. Norton theorem results in
    (a) a current source only
    (b) a current source in parallel with an impedance
    (c) a current source and an impedance in series
    (d) a voltage source only

116. The Superposition theorem requires as many circuit to be solved as there are
   (a) nodes
   (b) meshes
   (c) sources
   (d) all of the above are valid

117. In the circuit shown in figure maximum power will be transferred when

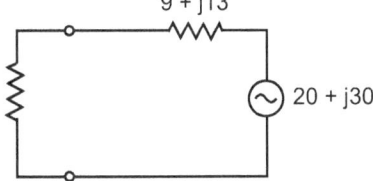

   (a) $Z_L = 9 - j13$
   (b) $Z_L = 9 + j13$
   (c) $Z_L = 13 + j9$
   (d) $Z_L = 13 - j9$

118. Millman's theorem is best to find
   (a) equivalent voltage source
   (b) equivalent voltage and resistance of a circuit
   (c) equivalent voltage or current source
   (d) none of the above

119. In Thevenin's theorem to find Z
   (a) all voltages and current sources are short-circuited
   (b) all independent voltage sources and dependent current sources are open-circuited
   (c) all independent voltage sources are open-circuited and all independent current sources are short-circuited
   (d) all independent voltage sources are short-circuited and all independent current sources are open-circuited

120. A loud-speaker is connected across terminals A and B of the network illustrated. What should its impedance be to obtain maximum power dissipation in it?

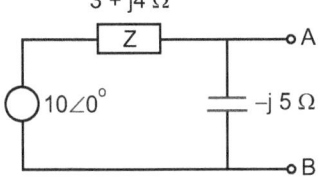

   (a) $3 - j1$
   (b) $3 + j9$
   (c) $7.5 - j2.5$
   (d) $7.5 + j2.5$

121. Find the Norton's equivalent of the circuit given below:

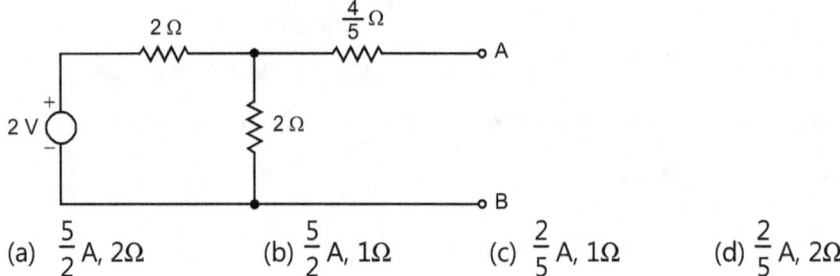

(a) $\frac{5}{2}$ A, 2Ω   (b) $\frac{5}{2}$ A, 1Ω   (c) $\frac{2}{5}$ A, 1Ω   (d) $\frac{2}{5}$ A, 2Ω

122. In the circuit shown, the value of I is

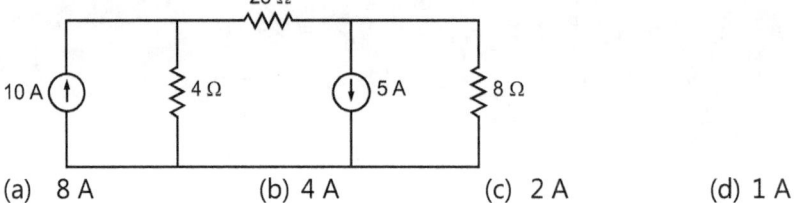

(a) 8 A   (b) 4 A   (c) 2 A   (d) 1 A

123. Norton's theorem results in a
   (a) a voltage source with an impedance in series
   (b) a current source with an impedance in parallel
   (c) current source alone
   (d) voltage source alone

124. In a circuit containing a complex impedance maximum power transfer takes place when load is
   (a) conjugate complex of the circuit impedance
   (b) equal to the complex impedance
   (c) pure resistance
   (d) none of the above

ANSWERS

1. (b)	2. (c)	3. (a)	4. (a)	5. (d)	6. (d)	7. (d)	8. (c)	9. (c)	10. (b)
11. (a)	12. (c)	13. (c)	14. (a)	15. (c)	16. (c)	17. (b)	18. (b)	19. (b)	20. (c)
21. (a)	22. (d)	23. (b)	24. (b)	25. (c)	26. (c)	27. (b)	28. (c)	29. (a)	30. (c)
31. (c)	32. (b)	33. (d)	34. (d)	35. (b)	36. (c)	37. (d)	38. (d)	39. (d)	40. (c)
41. (d)	42. (b)	43. (c)	44. (d)	45. (c)	46. (c)	47. (c)	48. (a)	49. (a)	50. (c)
51. (b)	52. (d)	53. (a)	54. (c)	55. (b)	56. (b)	57. (a)	58. (a)	59. (d)	60. (c)
61. (d)	62. (c)	63. (b)	64. (c)	65. (c)	66. (a)	67. (b)	68. (d)	69. (d)	70. (c)
71. (a)	72. (b)	73. (b)	74. (d)	75. (a)	76. (c)	77. (a)	78. (c)	79. (b)	80. (b)
81. (a)	82. (d)	83. (a)	84. (b)	85. (c)	86. (a)	87. (c)	88. (b)	89. (b)	90. (a)
91. (a)	92. (b)	93. (c)	94. (a)	95. (a)	96. (b)	97. (c)	98. (a)	99. (b)	100. (b)
101. (d)	102. (c)	103. (b)	104. (c)	105. (c)	106. (c)	107. (b)	108. (b)	109. (a)	110. (a)
111. (c)	112. (d)	113. (a)	114. (c)	115. (c)	116. (c)	117. (a)	118. (c)	119. (d)	120. (d)
121. (d)	122. (c)	123. (d)	124. (a)						

EXERCISE

1. State and prove Superposition theorem.

2. State and prove Maximum Power Transfer (MPT) as applied to DC circuit.

3. State and prove Maximum power Transfer (MPT) theorem as applied to AC circuit.

4. State and explain corollary of Maximum Power Transfer (MPT) theorem.

5. State and prove Thevenin's theorem.

6. State and prove Norton's theorem.

7. State and prove Millman's theorem.

8. State and prove dual of Millman's theorem.

9. Simplify following circuit into equivalent current source and a parallel resistor between A-B.

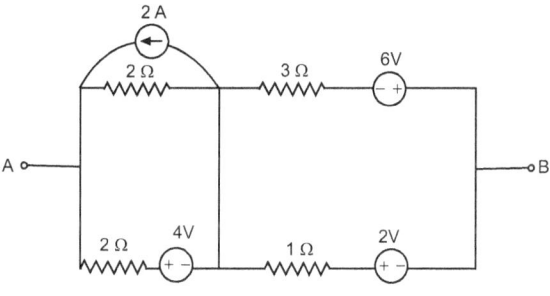

Fig. 2.141

10. Use superposition Theorem to find current in J3Ω across terminal a-b in the circuit shown.

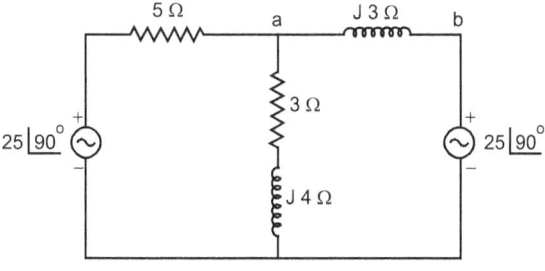

Fig. 2.142

11. Show that the equivalent Thevenin circuit consists of $R_{eq} = \dfrac{3-b}{2}$ and $V_{OC} = \dfrac{V_1}{2}[1 + a + b - ab]$ across R_L.

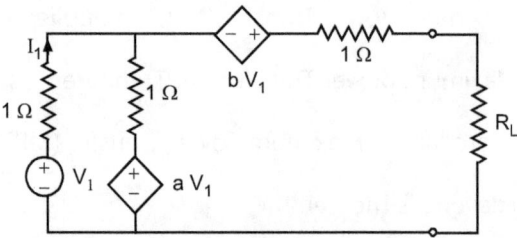

Fig. 2.143

12. For the ladder circuit shown determine R_L to be connected across a-b so that maximum power is transferred in R_L. Also determine maximum power when R_L is selected as a matched load.

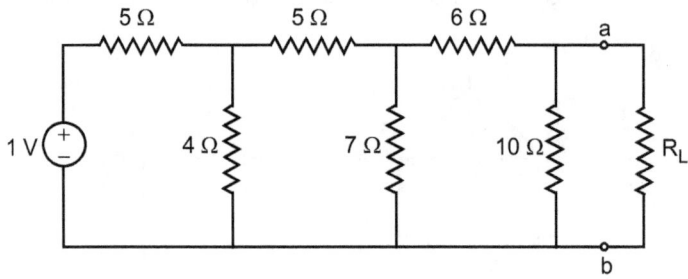

Fig. 2.144

13. What should be value of pure resistance load that is to be connected across terminals a-b in the circuit shown so that maximum power is transferred to the load? What is the maximum power.

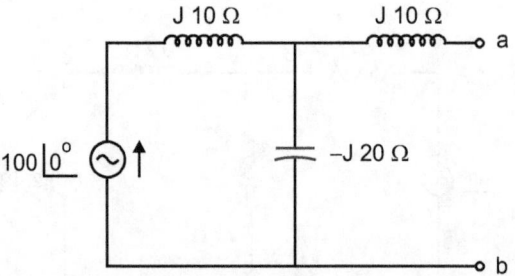

Fig. 2.145

14. In the network shown determine impedance Z_L for the maximum power transfer. Also calculate maximum power transferred to the load.

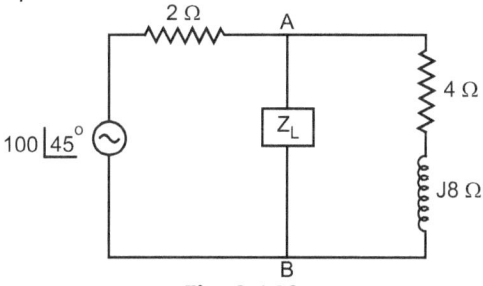

Fig. 2.146

15. Find current through capacitor. Make use of Superposition theorem

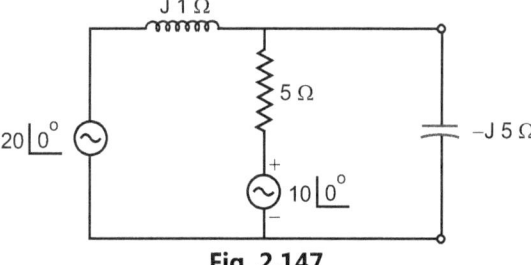

Fig. 2.147

16. Find current through 20Ω resister by (1) Superposition Theorem (2) Norton's theorem.

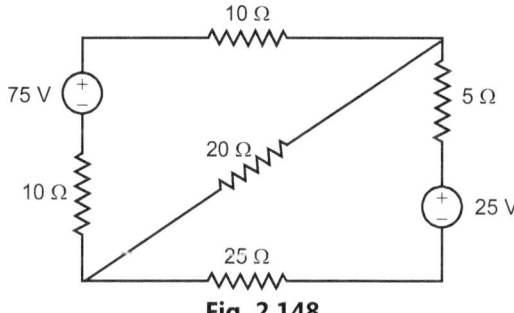

Fig. 2.148

17. Use Superposition theorem to find current through 5 ohm resistor.

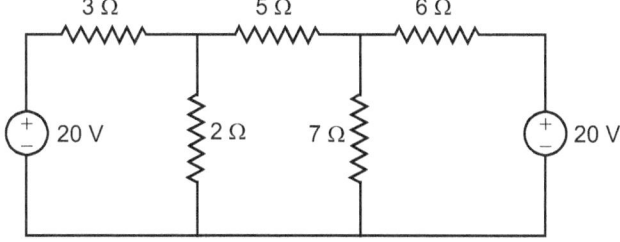

Fig. 2.149

18. Find current in resistor (R_L) across A-B by using (1) Thevenin's theorem (2) Norton's theorem.
   Also determine R_L for maximum power transfer find maximum power transferred for matched load.

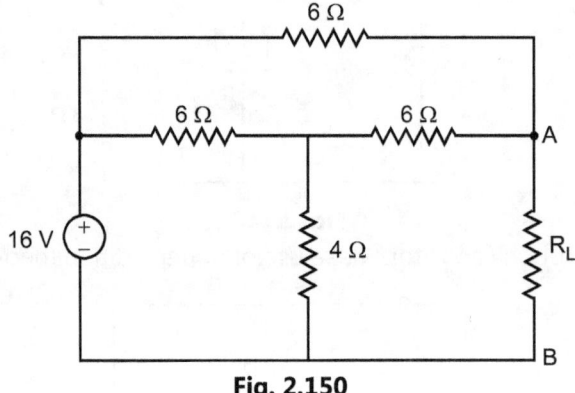

Fig. 2.150

Unit 3

TRANSIENT ANALYSIS

Contents ...
3.1 Introduction
3.2 Capacitor and its Properties
3.3 Undriven R-C Circuit
3.4 Driven R-C Circuit (Step Response of a R-C Circuit)
3.5 Inductor and its Properties
3.6 Undriven R-L Circuit
3.7 Driven R-L Circuit (Step response of R-L circuit)
3.8 Step Response of First Order Circuit
3.9 Step Response R-L-C circuit
   Multiple Choice Questions (MCQs)
   Exercise

3.1 INTRODUCTION

Suddenly applied d-c voltages are known as step voltages. Response of R-C, R-L and R-L-C circuits (To find voltages and currents) for such step voltages is the subject of this chapter. R-C and R-L circuit will give first order linear differential equations with constant coefficients, while R-L-C circuits gives second order linear differential equations with constant coefficients. Study in this chapter begin with simple R-C networks in which properties of capacitor are discussed first. Then the Driven and undriven R-C networks are discussed. Then study of R-L networks are carried out in which the properties of inductors are discussed first. Then the driven and undriven R-L networks are discussed. Finally step response of a R-L-C network with three different conditions is discussed.

[A] RESISTOR-CAPACITOR (R-C) CIRCUITS

In this section we shall discuss the properties of R-C network with capacitor initially having a voltage (V_0), and then the R-C network driven by a d-c voltage source (V), and capacitor again having a initial voltage (V_0). Before that, we shall discuss the construction and properties of the capacitor.

3.2 CAPACITOR AND ITS PROPERTIES

Capacitor is a circuit element which stores energy in electric field. In case of the resistor voltage-current relationship (V = R. I.) is linear and instantaneous. Voltage and current will exists simultaneously in resistor. But in the case of capacitor voltage is proportional to charge and not the currents. As capacitor has ability to store the charge, hence there may be voltage across it even when current is not flowing through it. Capacitor does not dissipate energy and hence called as reactive element.

Ideal capacitor (or condenser) consists of two parallel conducting plates seperated by a ideal insulator as shown in Fig. 3.1.

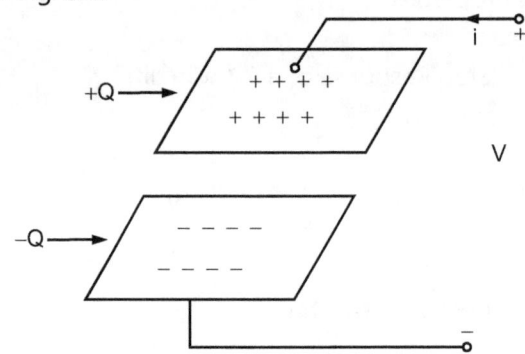

Fig. 3.1: Construction of a capacitor

As mentioned above "voltage across capacitor is proportional to charge Q on the plate".

Thus $\quad Q = C.V.\quad$ ...(3.1)

Constant of proportionality is called capacitance. Unit of the capacitor is Farad (F). Value of C depends upon geometry of conducting plates and physical properties of the insulating material. Circuit symbol of a capacitor is as shown in Fig. 3.2.

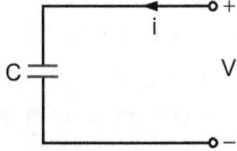

Fig. 3.2: Circuit symbol of capacitor with voltage and current conventions

Current in the capacitor (i) is time rate of change of charge. Thus

$$i = \frac{dQ}{dt} = C\frac{dV}{dt} \quad \ldots(3.2)$$

Above equation gives voltage-current relationship in a capacitor.

"Current in a capacitor is present only when the voltage across it is changing with time".

No current will flow if voltage derivative is zero. Thus "For d.c. or constant voltage $\frac{dv}{dt}$ is zero.

Hence current is zero and capacitor behaves like an open circuit.

Buildup of the voltage on capacitor due to current flowing through it is given by

$$v(t) = \frac{1}{C} \int_{-\infty}^{t} i(t)\, dt \qquad \ldots(3.3)$$

$$= \frac{1}{C} \int_{-\infty}^{0} i(t)\, dt + \frac{1}{C} \int_{0}^{1} i(t)\, dt$$

$$= \frac{1}{C} \int_{-\infty}^{0} i(t)\, dt = \frac{Q_0}{C} = V_0 \text{ is known as initial voltage on capacitor which is due to initial charge } (Q_0) \text{ on capacitor.}$$

Thus
$$v(t) = V_0 + \frac{1}{C} \int_{0}^{t} I(t)\, dt \qquad \ldots(3.4)$$

This gives capacitor charging equation.

If a capacitor with initial voltage (V_0) is discharged by a current flowing in opposite direction as shown besides in Fig. 3.3 then the discharge equation is given by

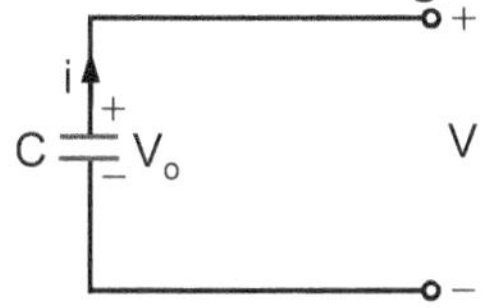

Fig. 3.3: Capacitor discharging

$$v(t) = V_0 - \frac{1}{C} \int_{0}^{t} i(t)\, dt \qquad \ldots(3.5)$$

Energy and power Relationship in a capacitor: "As capacitor is able to store charge and hence voltage in this form of storage represents storage of energy".

We have
$$p(t) = v(t)\, i(t) \text{ watts}$$

$$= V(t) \cdot C\, d\frac{v(t)}{dt}$$

$$= \frac{d}{dt}\left[\frac{1}{2} C \cdot v^2\right]$$

Since power is the time rate of change of energy, energy stored in capacitor at any instant of time is given by.

$$W_e(t) = \frac{1}{2} C v^2 \qquad \ldots(3.6)$$

Positive value of power represents power delivered to capacitor due to charging and –ve value of the power represents power delivered by the capacitor to rest of the circuits due to discharging.

Ex. 3.1: If the current waveform shown below is applied to 2µF capacitor, Find capacitor voltage $V_c(t)$ and sketch the waveform. Assume initial capacitor voltage is zero.

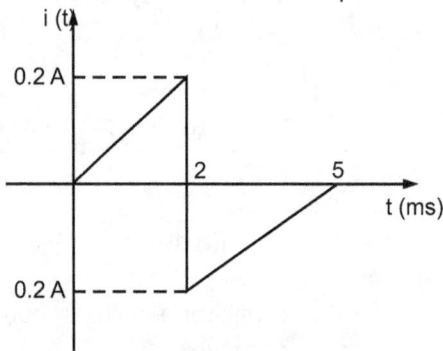

Fig. 3.4

Sol.: Given that $V_o = 0$. Hence for $t > 0$ the voltage on capacitor is given by equation (3.4) as

$$v_C(t) = \frac{1}{C} \int_0^1 i(t) \, dt$$

For $0 < t < 2$ms, $\quad i(t) = \frac{0.2}{2} \times 10^3 t = 100t$

For 2.0 ms $< t < 5.0$ ms $\quad i(t) = -0.2 + \frac{200}{3}(t-2)$

Thus for $0 < t < 2$ ms, the voltage is

$$v_c(t) = \frac{1}{2 \times 10^{-6}} \int_0^{2ms} 100 \, t \, dt = 50 \left[\frac{t^2}{2}\right]_0^{2ms}$$

At $\quad t = 2$ms, $\quad v_c(2\text{ms}) = 50 \times \frac{4 \times 10^{-6}}{2} = 100$ volts.

Also at t = 2 ms current changes from + 0.2 A to –0.2 A. Thus current changes instantaneously but the voltage on capacitor will not change at this instant and will remain at 100 V only. At t = 5 ms the voltage on capacitor is given as.

$$v(t) = 100.0 + \frac{1}{C} \int_{2ms}^{5ms} -0.2 \, dt + \frac{1}{C} \int_{2ms}^{5ms} \frac{200}{3}(t-2)$$

$$= 100 - 10^5 \, [t]_{2ms}^{5ms} + \frac{200 \times 10^6}{3 \times 2 \times 2} \times [t-2]_{2ms}^{5ms}$$

$$= 100 - 300 + 150 = -50 \text{ volts}$$

Thus required voltage waveform is as shown in below.

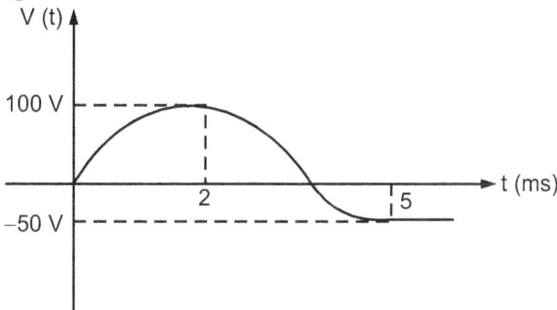

Fig. 3.5: Capacitor voltage waveform

Linearity and Superposition: An element is said to be linear if and only if superposition theorem is valid for them and vice versa.

It can be shown that superposition theorem is valid for the capacitor if and only if initial voltage (V_o) on the capacitor is zero. Other wise superposition theorem can not be applied to the capacitor. Thus for charged capacitor (For which $V_o \neq 0$) superposition theorem is not valid.

Hence capacitor is a linear element if and only if it is not charged (Initial voltage on capacitor is zero).

Series and Parallel Connection of Capacitor: Consider two capacitor C_1 and C_2 connected in parallel as shown in Fig. 3.6 (a). Voltage across the two capacitor is some.

$$i = i_1 + i_2 = C_1 \frac{dv}{dt} + C_2 \frac{dv}{dt} = (C_1 + C_2) \frac{dv}{dt}$$

If the two capacitor are to be replaced by a single capacitor of value C as shown in Fig. 3.6 (b) then

$$C = C_1 + C_2 \qquad \ldots(3.7)$$

Thus "Equivalent Capacitance of a parallel combination is given by the sum of individual capacitance" Any initial voltage on parallel capacitor will also be present on equivalent capacitor.

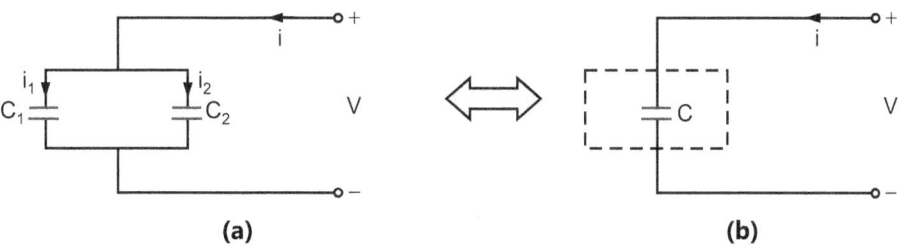

Fig. 3.6: Parallel connection of capacitor

Now consider capacitor C_1 with initial voltage V_{o1} and capacitor C_2 with initial voltage V_{o2} connected in series as shown in Fig. 3.7 (a).

We have
$$v = v_1 + v_2$$
$$= \left[\frac{1}{C_1}\int_0^t i\, dt + V_{o1}\right] + \left[\frac{1}{C_2}\int_0^t i\, dt + V_{o2}\right]$$

OR
$$= \left\{\left(\frac{1}{C_1} + \frac{1}{C_2}\right)\int_0^t i\, dt\right\} + (V_{o1} + V_{o2})$$
$$= \frac{1}{C}\int_0^t i\, dt + V_o$$

Thus equivalent capacitance (c) is given by
$$\frac{1}{C} = \frac{1}{C_1} + \frac{1}{C_2} \qquad \ldots (3.8)$$

and also
$$V_o = V_{o1} + V_{o2} \qquad \ldots (3.9)$$

Thus, "For series connection of capacitors, the reciprocal of equivalent capacitance is the sum of reciprocal of individual capacitance".

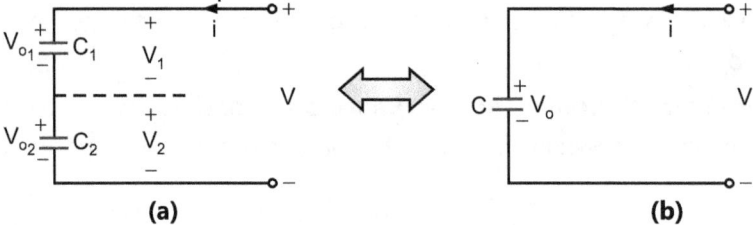

Fig. 3.7: Capacitors in parallel

3.3 UNDRIVEN R-C CIRCUIT

Consider the circuit shown in Fig. 3.8. The switch in initially on the position "a" for a long time.

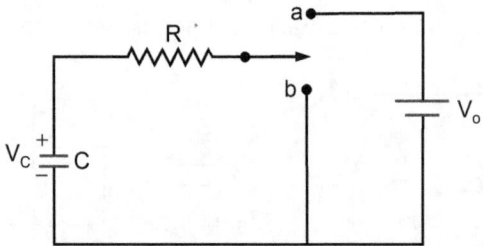

Fig. 3.8: R-C network with capacitor voltage $V_c = V_0$ at time $t = 0$

The capacitor voltage is $v_c = v_o$ volts. At $t = 0$ the switch is thrown to position "b", and circuit will be as shown below in Fig. 3.9.

Now, capacitor will discharge into resistor. Because of this discharge voltage on capacitor will reduce until it reaches to zero. We are interested to find rate at which capacitor will fall.

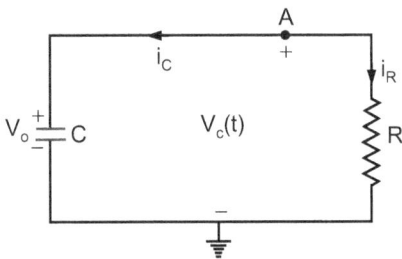

Fig. 3.9: R.C. circuit for t > 0

KCL at node 'A' gives

$$i_C + i_R = 0.$$

$$C\frac{dv_c}{dt} + \frac{v_c}{R} = 0$$

This is a first order homogeneous linear differential equation with constant coefficients.

[A linear differential equation is homogeneous if its R. H. side is zero. If R. H. side is not zero then it is a non-homogeneous LDE).

Rearranging above equation gives, $\frac{dv_c}{v_c} = -\frac{1}{RC} dt$. Integrating this equation on both sides gives.

$$\int \frac{dv_c}{v_c} = \int -\frac{1}{RC} dt$$

OR $\quad \ln v_c = -\frac{t}{RC} + K$ (constant)

Hence $\quad v_c(t) = e^{-\frac{1}{RC} + K} = e^K e^{-\frac{1}{RC}} = Ae^{-\frac{1}{RC}} \quad \ldots$(b)

Where A is a arbitrary constant whose value can be determined if we know value of v at any instant of time.

We know that at t 0, v = v_c = V_o volts.

Hence $\quad v_{c(0)} = A = V_o$ volts

Hence voltage across capacitor at any instant of time (t) > 0 given by

$$v_c(t) = V_o e^{-\frac{1}{RC}} \quad \ldots(3.10)$$

Current $i_c(t)$ through capacitor at any instant of time $(t) > 0$ is given by

$$i_c(t) = C\frac{dv_c(t)}{dt}$$

$$= -\frac{CV_o e^{-\frac{t}{RC}}}{RC}$$

Thus $$i_c(t) = -\frac{V_o}{R} e^{-\frac{t}{RC}} \qquad ...(3.11)$$

Minus sign on t (i.e., –t) indicates that the capacitor is discharging.

Waveforms for capacitor voltage [$v_c(t)$] and the current [$v_c(t)$] as given by equations (3.10) and (3.11) is as shown below in Fig. 3.10.

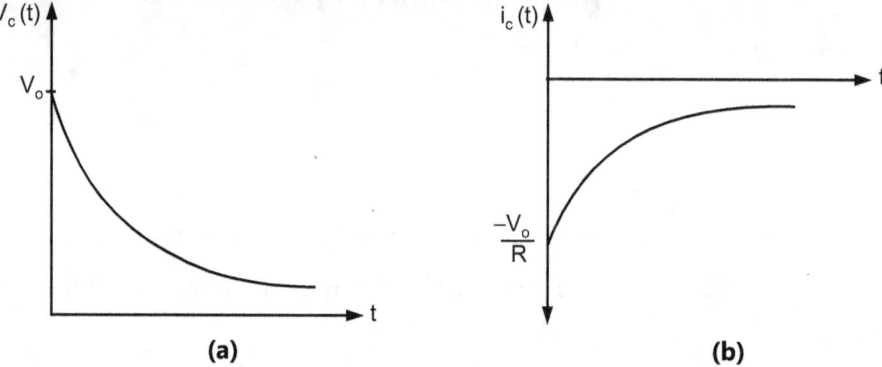

(a)   (b)

Fig. 3.10: Capacitor voltage and current waveforms

By graph it is obvious that capacitor voltage $v_c(t)$ decays exponentially becomes zero as $t \to \infty$. Rate of decays depends upon RC. Simile discharging current is maximum at $t = 0$ and decays exponentially to become zero at $t \to \infty$.

Physical explanation for this can be given as below. Initially energy stored is capacitor is $\frac{CV^2}{2}$. As the charge flows through resistor from one plate capacitor to other plate, energy is dissipated in the resistor at the rate of R_i^2. Due to this dissipation of the energy, energy stored in the capacitor is reduced hence voltage on capacitor and the current also reduces.

Time Constant (T): The product RC = T is called as Time constant c of RC circuit, and indicates how fast circuit settles down to its quiescent (steady state) value. For example when $t = T$ then by the equation (3.7) we have,

$$v_c(T) = \frac{V_o}{e} = 0.37 V_o \qquad ...(3.12)$$

Thus "Time constant (T) indicates the. time R-C circuit take in order to reduce initial voltage on capacitor (V_o) by a factor of $\frac{1}{e} = 0.37$".

Also for t = 2T, $v_c(2T) = \dfrac{V_o}{e^2}$

For t = 3T, $v_c(3T) = \dfrac{V_o}{e^3}$ and

For t = 4T, We have $v_c(4T) = \dfrac{V_o}{e^4} = 0.02\,V_o$

Thus after a time t = 4T, the voltage on capacitor reduces to 2% of initial value, hence capacitor can be assumed to be discharged completely. The waveform is as shown below in Fig. 3.11.

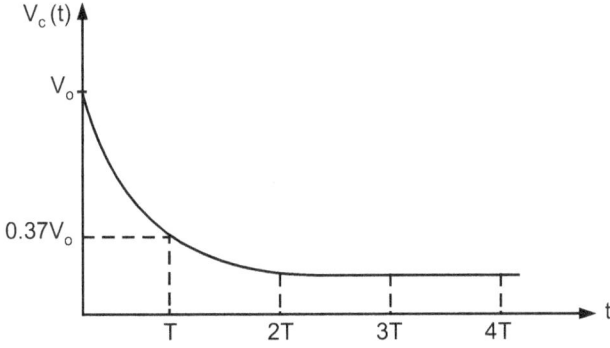

Fig. 3.11: Capacitor discharge

Ex. 3.2: In the circuit shown below find the expression for $v_2(t)$ if the switch is closed at t = 0. Find $v_2(t)$ and i(t) when t = 3.33 ms.

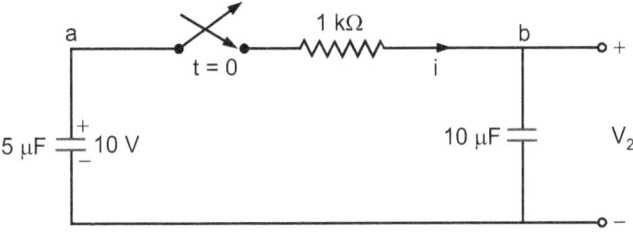

Fig. 3.12

Sol.: At t = 0 switch is closed. Then two capacitors are in series. Hence the equivalent capacitance is

$$C_{eq} = \dfrac{10 \times 5}{15} = \dfrac{10}{3}\,\mu F$$

Hence the circuit will be as shown below in Fig. 3.13.

Current i is given by $\quad i(t) = \dfrac{10}{1} \times e^{-\dfrac{t}{3.33\text{ ms}}}$ mA.

Returning to original circuit of Fig. 3.12 we have

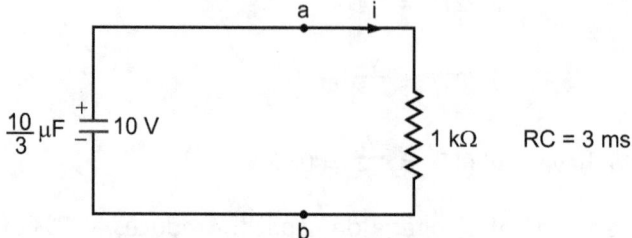

Fig. 3.13: Equivalent circuit for t > 0

$$v_2(t) = v_2(0) + \frac{1}{10\ \mu F}\int_0^t i\,.\,dt$$

$$= 0 + \frac{1}{10^{-5}}\int_0^t 10\,e^{-\frac{t}{3.3\,ms}} \times 10^{-3}\,dt$$

$$= 1000\left[e^{-\frac{t}{3.33\,mm}}\right]_0^t \times \frac{-1}{1} \times 3.33 \times 10^{-3}$$

Thus
$$v_2(t) = 3.3\left[1 - e^{-\frac{t}{3.33\,ms}}\right]\text{ volts} \qquad \ldots(a)$$

This is the required expression for voltage $v_2(t)$

$$i(t) = 10 \times 10^{-6}\frac{dv_2(t)}{dt}$$

$$= 10^{-5} \times 3.3\left(-e^{-\frac{t}{3.3\,ms}}\right) \times \frac{-1}{3.3 \times 10^{-3}}$$

$$= 10^{-2}\,e^{-\frac{t}{3.3ms}}$$

$$= 10e^{-\frac{t}{3.3ms}}\text{ mA}$$

Thus required expression for current is

$$i(t) = 10\,e^{-\frac{t}{3.3ms}}\text{ mA} \qquad \ldots(b)$$

At t = 3.3 ms, we have
$v_2(t) = 3.3\,[1 - e^{-1}] = 0.67 \times 3.3$
= **2.211 volts**
$i(t) = 10e^{-1}\,0.37 \times 10$ mA
= **3.7 mA**

3.4 DRIVEN R-C CIRCUIT (STEP RESPONSE OF A R-C CIRCUIT)

Consider a capacitor with initial voltage V_o and is connected to a battery of voltage V volts through a resistor R and in series with switch as shown below in Fig. 3.14 (a).

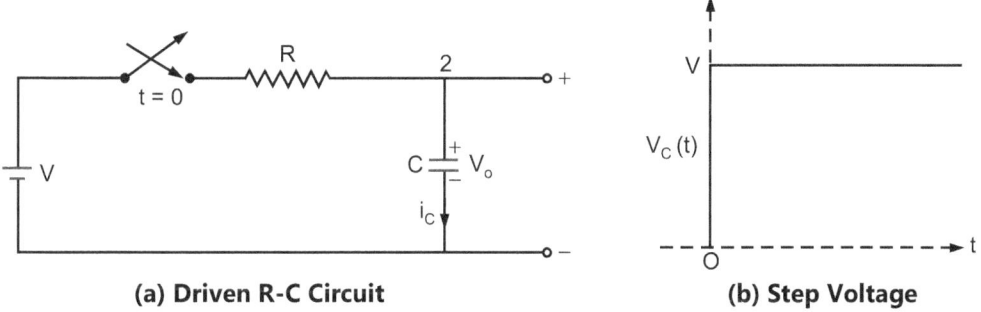

(a) Driven R-C Circuit   (b) Step Voltage

Fig. 3.14: Step response of a R-C circuit.

When switch is opened voltage applied to the R-C circuit is zero. When switch is closed at t = 0 then voltage of V volts is suddenly applied to R-C circuit. This is known as step voltage and is shown in Fig. 3.14 (b).

As long as switch is opened capacitor, will not discharge and retains its voltage V_o.

Let switch be closed at t = 0.

It $V = V_o$, then voltage across resistor is zero, which means no current will flow through R-C circuit and the capacitor maintain its voltage at Vo.

It $V > V_o$, then capacitor will be charging and capacitor voltage will increase until it reaches battery voltage V after which charging will be stopped. Thus under steady state (quiescent condition) voltage across the capacitor is the battery voltage (V). If $V < V_o$, then capacitor will be discharging until the voltage across capacitor again reaches to battery voltage.

Thus for any value of voltage V, the capacitor may charge or discharge depending upon V_n and V. For example if V_o = 5V and V = 10V, then the capacitor will go on charging until its voltage attains 10V. Alternatively V_o = 10V, V = 5V, then the capacitor will discharge until its voltage reches volts.

Thus, at any instant of time, voltage across the capacitor v_c (t) consists c a steady state component of value V and a component of delaying exponential with time constant RC.

Hence $\qquad v_c(t) = V + A e^{-\frac{1}{RC}}$ ... (3.13)

Where A is the magnitude of decaying exponential, value of which can be determined from the knowledge of initial value of v_c (t).

At t = 0 we know that $\qquad v_c(0) = V_0$

Hence $\qquad V_o = V + A e^{-0} = V + A$

OR $\qquad A = V_o - V$

Thus capacitor voltage at any time t > 0 is given

$$v_c(t) = V + (V_o - V)e^{-\frac{1}{RC}t} \quad \ldots(3.14)$$
$$= \text{(steady state value)} + \text{(Transient value)}$$

The validity of above equation can be checked as below. At t = 0 voltage on capacitor is $v_c(0) = V + (V_o - V) = V_o$, (Initial voltage). And at t → ∞ value of the capacitor voltage is V which is the steady state value.

Steady state component (Response) is also called as forced OR driven response since its value will depends upon driving force (Excitations).

Transient response will vanishes as t → ∞. But in practice, we can say that transient response vanishes after a time of T = 4T.

Alternative Proof: Alternatively equation (3.14) can be derived by considering KCL at node in Fig. 3.14 (a).

We have
$$i_c - i_R = 0$$
$$C\frac{dv_c}{dt} - \left(\frac{V - V_c}{R}\right) = 0$$

OR
$$C\frac{dv_c}{dt} + \frac{v_c}{R} = \frac{V}{R} \quad \ldots(3.15)$$

This is a non-homogeneous linear differential equation with a constant forcing function. The solution of this equation consists of two parts. (1) Complimentary solution which is obtained by making forcing function zero (Homogeneous solution) (2) Particular solution which is obtained by considering forcing function.

Homogeneous solution is obtained by making right-hand side zero. Thus we have

$$C\frac{dv_c}{dt} + \frac{v_c}{R} = 0$$

OR
$$\left(C.s. + \frac{1}{R}\right)v_c = 0$$

Hence roof of equation is $\quad s = \frac{1}{-Rc}$

Hence transient solution is

$$v_c(tr) = Ae^{-\frac{1}{RC}t}$$

Particular solution is obtain by considering the forcing function. Since forcing function is a constant, we assume a constant for forced solution.

i.e. $\quad v_c(ss) = K$

By (3.15) $\quad 0 + \frac{K}{R} = \frac{V}{R}$

Hence $\quad \boxed{K = V}$

Therefore, complete solution is given by

$$v_c(t) = v_c(tr) + v_c(ss) = Ae^{-\frac{1}{RC}} + V \qquad ...(3.16)$$

At $\quad t = 0, V(0) = V_o = A + V$

Hence $\quad A = V_o - V$

Therefore, complete solution is given by,

$$v_c(t) = V + (V_o - V)e^{-\frac{1}{RC}} \qquad ...(3.17)$$

Thus equation (3.17) is same as that of equation (3.14). Capacitor voltage as given by equation (3.14) or (3.17) is shown in Fig. 3.15 below.

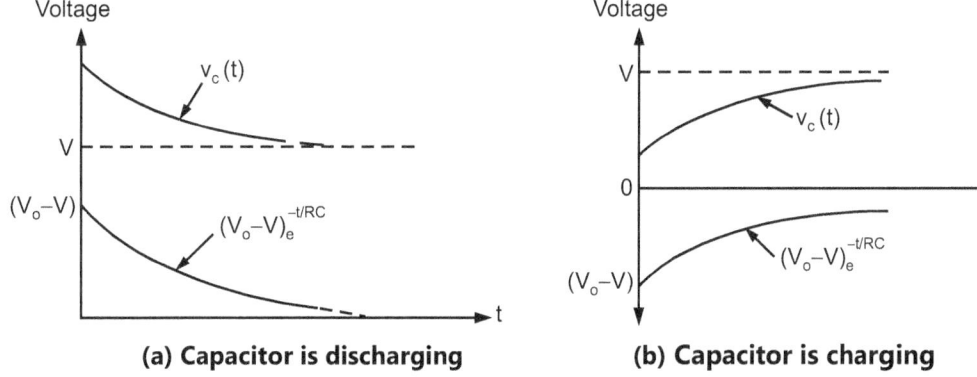

(a) **Capacitor is discharging**   (b) **Capacitor is charging**

Fig. 3.15 Capacitor voltage waveforms

If $V_o > V$, then $(V_o - V)$ is positive, capacitor will discharges from V_o to V and then remain constant at V volts as shown in 3.15 (a).

If $V_o < V$, then $(V_o - V)$ is negative. Now the capacitor actually charges and its voltage increases from initial voltage (V_o) exponetially until it will reaches battery voltage V and then it will remain constant at V volts as shown in Fig. 3.15 (b).

The current through capacitor can be obtained by following expression.

$$i_c(t) = C\frac{dv_c(t)}{dt} = C \times (V_o - V) e^{-\frac{t}{RC}} \times -\frac{1}{RC}$$

OR $\qquad i_c(t) = \left(\frac{V - V_o}{R}\right) e^{-\frac{1}{RC}} \qquad ...(3.18)$

Current as given by above expression is plotted in the waveform shown below.

If $V > V_o$ then current $i_c(t)$ is positive indicating it as a charging current as shown in Fig. 3.16 (a).

If $V_o > V$ then current $i_c(t)$ is negative indicating it as a discharging current as shown in Fig. 3.16 (b).

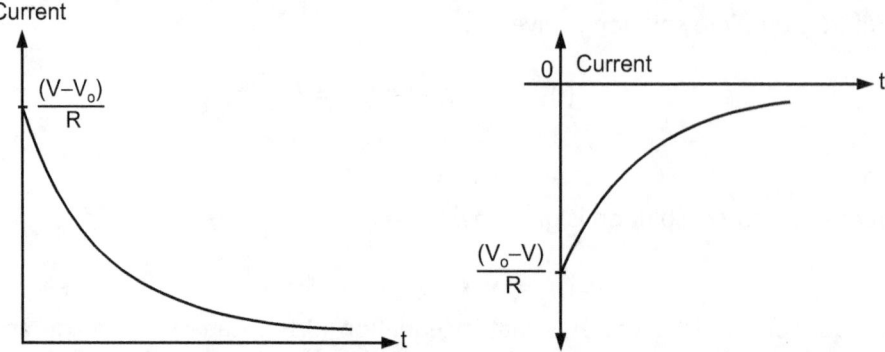

(a) $V > V_o$ (charging current) **(b)** $V_o > V$ (Discharging current)

Fig. 3.16: Capacitor current waveforms

Note: By voltage waveform it is obvious that voltage across capacitor cannot charge instantaneously. A capacitor which is charged initially will behave like a voltage source. A uncharged capacitor will initially behave like a short circuit.

Ex. 3.3: In the circuit shown below switch is closed at t = 0. Find $V_2(t)$ and $i(t)$.

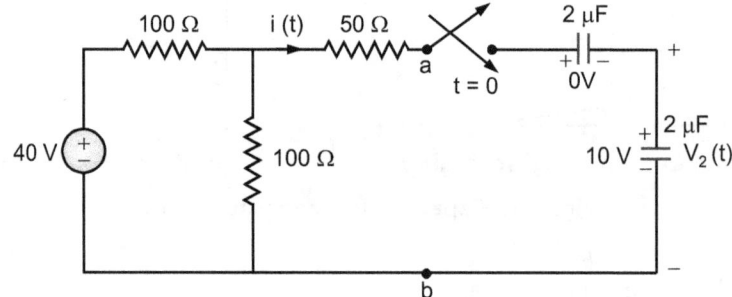

Fig. 3.17

Sol.: For t > 0 when switch is closed then thevenin equivalent at left of a –b is given by

$$V_{ab} = \frac{100 \times 40}{200} = 20 \text{ V}$$

$$R_{ab} = 50 + 100||100 = 50 + 50 = 100 \text{ }\Omega$$

Also 2μF and 2 μF are in series to give the equivalent capacitance of 1μF. The equivalent circuit for t > 0 is as shown below.

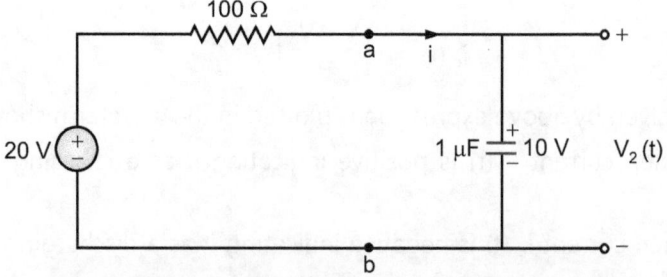

Fig. 3.18: Thevenin equivalent circuit of Fig. 3.17

Current i is given by
$$i = \left(\frac{V - V_o}{R}\right) e^{-\frac{t}{RC}}$$

OR
$$i = \left(\frac{20 - 10}{100}\right) e^{-\frac{t}{10^{-4}}} = 0.1 e^{-10^4 t} \text{ Amps.}$$

Now returning to original circuit of Fig. 3.17. We have
$$v_2(t) = V_o + \frac{1}{C} \int i \, dt = 10 + \frac{10^6}{2} \int_0^t 0.1 e^{-10^4 t} \, dt$$

$$= 10 + \frac{10^5}{2} \left[\frac{e^{-10^4 t}}{-10^4}\right]_0^t = 10 + 5 [1 - e^{-10^4 t}] \text{ volts}$$

Ex. 3.4: The switch of the circuit shown in the Fig. has been open for a long time. At t = 0 it is closed. (a) Calculate v_c at 2m sec after the switch is closed. (b) If the switch is now kept closed for a long time find v_c two milliseconds after it is suddenly opened. **[Dec. 88]**

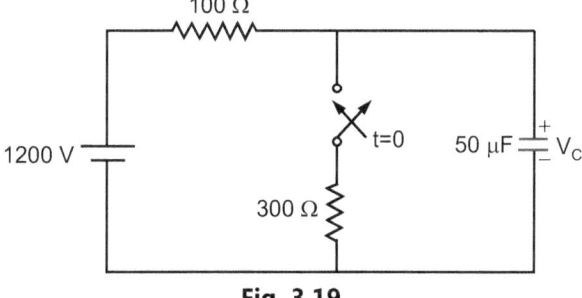

Fig. 3.19

Sol.: When switch was opened for a long time then voltage on capacitor = V_o = 1200V. For t > 0 the Thevenin equivalent circuit, will be as shown below.

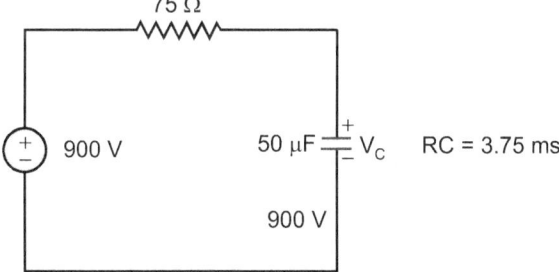

Fig. 3.20: Thevenin equivalent circuit for t > 0

where
$$V_{oc} = V_{eq} = \frac{300 \times 1200}{400} = 900 \text{ V}$$

and
$$R_{eq} = 300 \parallel 100 = 75 \, \Omega$$

The circuit is driven R.C. circuit, with initial voltage on capacitor as 1200 volts.

Using equation (3.14) we have,

$$v_c(t) = 900 + (1200 - 900) e^{-\frac{t}{3.75 \text{ ms}}}$$

$$= 900 + 300 e^{-\frac{t}{3.75 \text{ ms}}}$$

Voltage on capacitor after t = 2 ms is given by

$$v_c(2ms) = 900 + 300 e^{-\frac{2}{3.75}} - 900 + 176$$

$$= 1076 \text{ volts}$$

Ex. 3.5: The switch in the fig. has been kept open for a long time. It is closed at t = 0.
(1) Obtain an expression for $v_c(t)$ for t > 0
(2) At what time $v_c(t) = 0$ **(Dec. 89)**

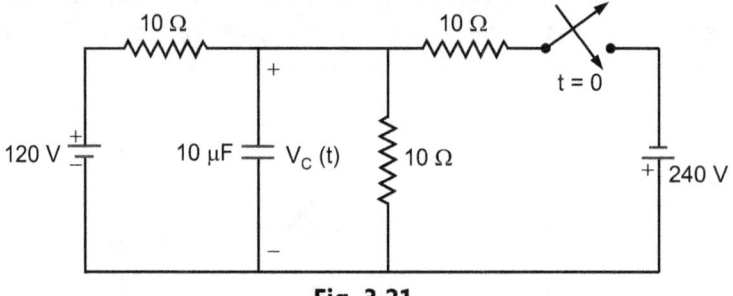

Fig. 3.21

Open circuit voltage = V_{oc}

$$= 120 \times \frac{10}{20}$$

$$= 60 \text{ V}$$

Thevenin equivalent resistance = 10 || 10 = 5Ω. Thus for t < 0, the capacitor voltage = V_o = 60 V. For t > 0, the circuit will be as shown in Fig. 3.22 (b).

Sol.: When switch is opened thevenin equivalent circuit across capacitor is as shown in Fig. 3.22 (a).

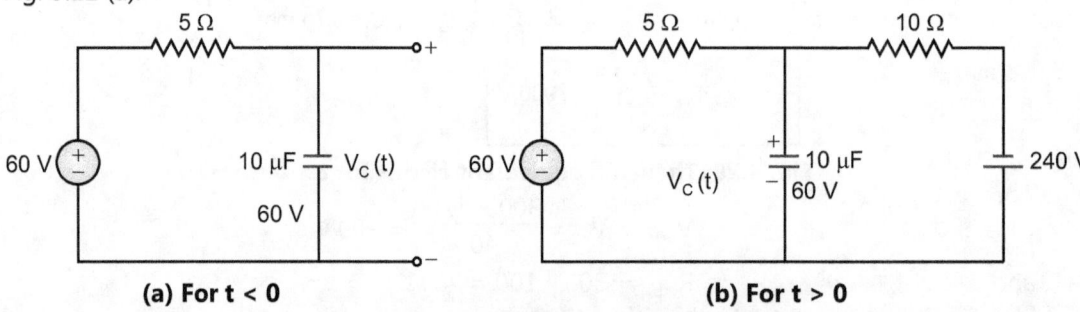

(a) For t < 0   (b) For t > 0
Fig. 3.22: Equivalent circuit of Fig. 3.21

Using source transformation the equivalent circuit can be written as shown below in Fig. 3.23.

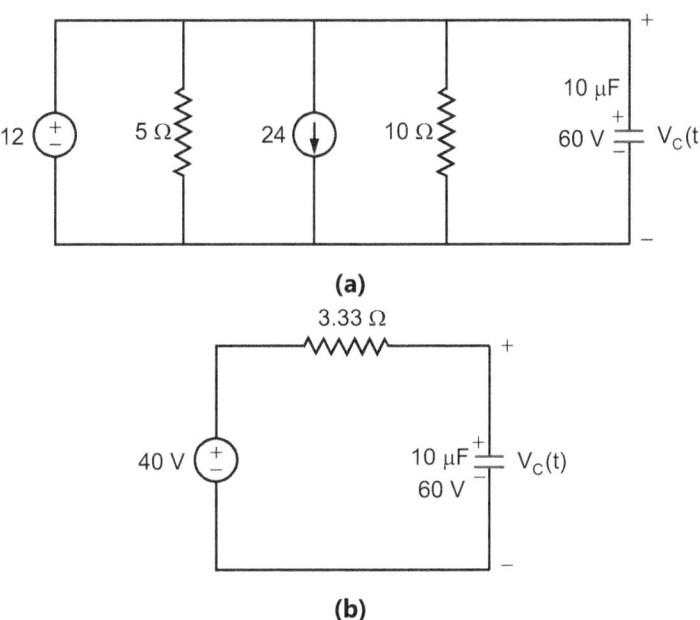

Fig. 3.23: Equivalent circuit for t > 0

Fig. 3.23 (b) is a driven R-C circuit with a battery voltage of –40V and initial capacitor voltage (V_o) of 60 V. Hence

$$V_c(t) = -40 + [60 - 40] e^{-\frac{t}{33.3 \mu sec}}$$

Thus
$$V_c(t) = -40 + 100 \, e^{-\frac{t}{33.3 \mu sec}}$$

is the required expression of the capacitor voltage.

(2) Let t_1 μsec be the time after switch is closed at t = 0, when capacitor voltages becomes zero.

Thus, $\quad -40 + 100 e^{-\frac{t_1}{33.3 \mu sec}} = 0$

Hence $\quad e^{-\frac{t_1}{33.3 \mu sec}} = 0.4$

OR $\quad -\frac{t_1}{33.3 \, \mu sec} = -0.916$

Thus $\quad t_1 = 305. \, \mu$ seconds

Ex. 3.6: At t = 1 ms in the circuit shown below, find values of (1) v_c (2) i_c (3) v_x.

[May 92]

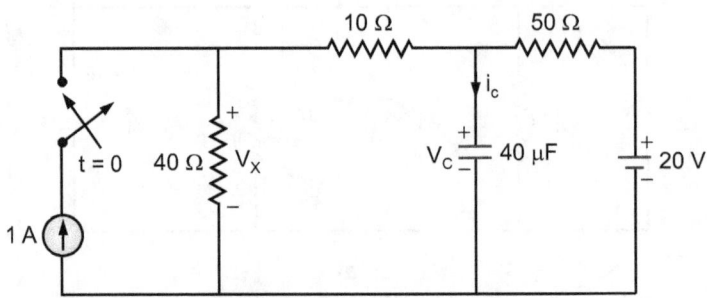

Fig. 3.24

Sol.: As switch is closed at t = 0, it means that is opened for t < 0. Thevenin equivalent for t < 0 is as shown below in Fig. 3.25 (a).

where $\qquad V_{oc} = (10 + 40)\dfrac{20}{100} = 50 \times 0.2 = 10$ V

And $\qquad R_{eq} = 50 \parallel 50 = 25\ \Omega$

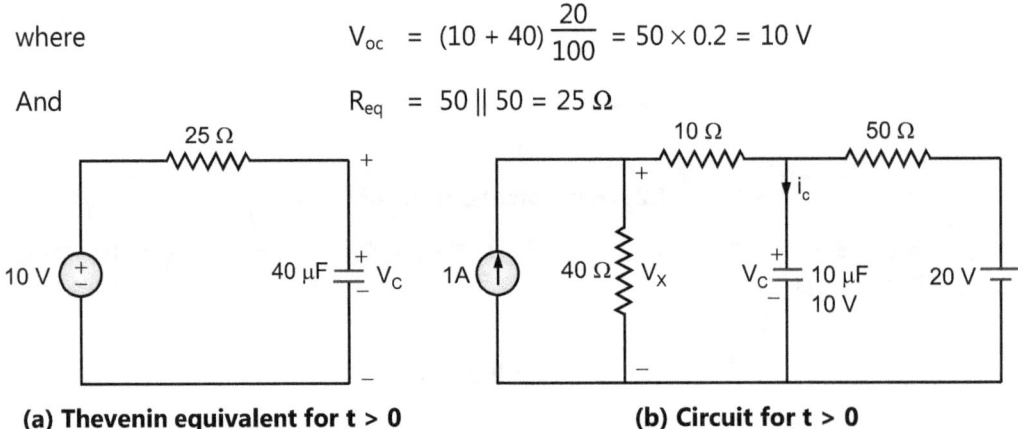

(a) Thevenin equivalent for t > 0   (b) Circuit for t > 0

Fig. 3.25

Thus for t < 0, voltage on capacitor = V_o = 10 V. Circuit for t > 0 is as shown in Fig. 3.25 (b).

This circuit can be reduced further by using source transformation as shown below in Fig. 3.26. Fig. 3.26 (b) is a driven R-C circuit with battery voltage of V = 30 V and initial voltage (V_o) = 10 V.

(1) $\qquad\qquad v_c(t) = \left[30 + (10 - 30)\, e^{-\frac{t}{1\ \text{ms}}}\right]$ volts

at $\qquad\qquad t = 1$ ms

We have Capacitor voltage = $V_c(1\text{ms}) = 30 + (-20)\, e^{-1}$

$\qquad\qquad\qquad\qquad\qquad = 30 - 7.36 = 22.64$ V

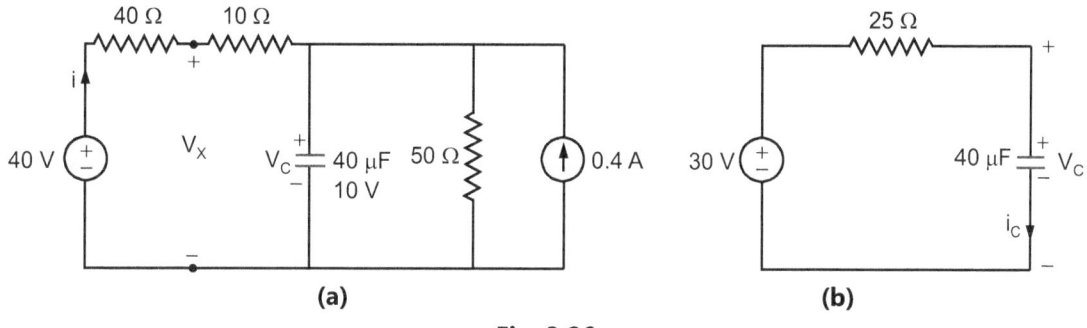

(a) (b)

Fig. 3.26

(2) $\quad i_c(t) = C\dfrac{dv_c(t)}{dt} = 40 \times 10^{-6} \times -20 \times e^{-\frac{t}{1ms}} \times -\dfrac{1}{10^{-3}}$

$= 800 \times 10^{-3} e^{-\frac{t}{1ms}}$ Amp.

$= 0.8\, e^{-\frac{t}{1ms}}$ Amps.

at t = 1 ms we have $\quad i_c(1\text{ ms}) = 0.8\, e^{-t} = 0.295$ Amp.

(3) By Fig. 3.26 (a) we have $\quad i = \left(\dfrac{40 - v_c}{50}\right)$ Amp.

Hence $\quad v_x(t) = 40 - 40\, i(i) = 40 - \dfrac{40}{50}[40 - v_c(t)]$

$= 40 - 0.8\left[40 - 30 + 20\, e^{-\frac{t}{1ms}}\right]$

$= 40 - 0.8 \times 10 - e^{-\frac{t}{1ms}}$

Thus $\quad v_x(t) = \left[32 - 16\, e^{-\frac{t}{1ms}}\right]$ volts

at t = 1msa $\quad v_x(1ms) = 32 - 16c^{-1} = $ **26.11 volts**

Ex. 3.7: The switch in the circuit shown below is closed on position 1 at t = 0 and then is moved to position 2 after one time constant. Obtain current i for t > 0. **(May 93)**

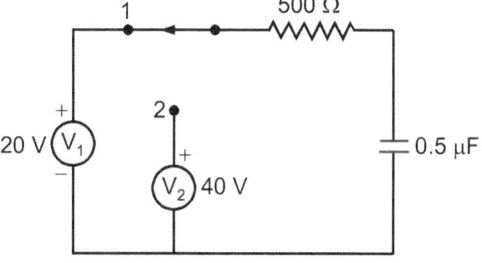

Fig. 3.27

Sol.: When switch was on position 1 for one time constant (T), then capacitor will be charged to some voltage. This voltage is given by

$$v_c(T) = 20 - 20\, e^{-\frac{RC}{RC}}$$

$$= 12.64 \text{ Volts}$$

where
$$RC = 50 \times 0.5 \times 10^{-6}$$
$$= 250 \text{ μsec.}$$

When switch is thrown to position 2 after a time of one time constant (T), then this voltage acts as a initial voltage. Thus V_o = 12.64 volts. For t > T (250 μ sec) the circuit will be as shown below in Fig. 3.28.

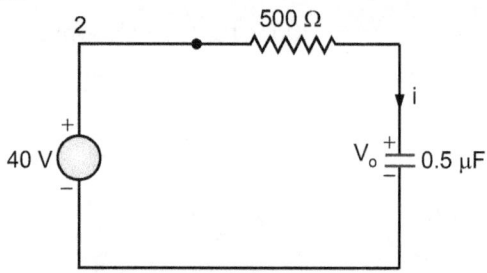

Fig. 3.28: Equivalent circuit after t > 250 μsec

From equation (3.18) we have,

$$i(t) = \left(\frac{40 - 12.64}{500}\right) e^{-\frac{t}{250\,\mu sec}}$$

$$= 0.055\, e^{-\frac{t}{250\,\mu sec}} \text{ Amps.}$$

Ex. 3.8: Find the value of $v_c(t)$ at t = 0.8 seconds in the circuit shown below. **[May 94]**

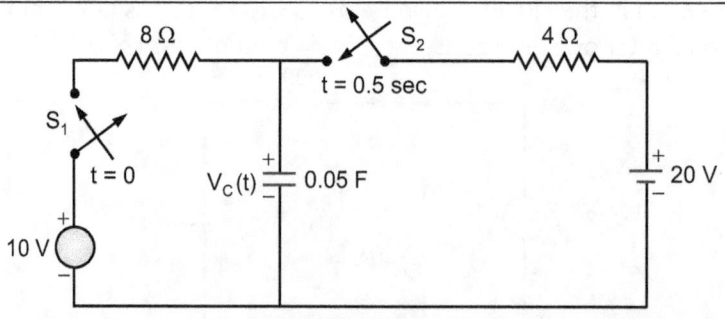

Fig. 3.29

Sol.: Initially S_1 is closed at t = 0 but S_2 is opened. Thus for 0 < t < 0.5 sec the circuit will be shown below in Fig. 3.30 (a).

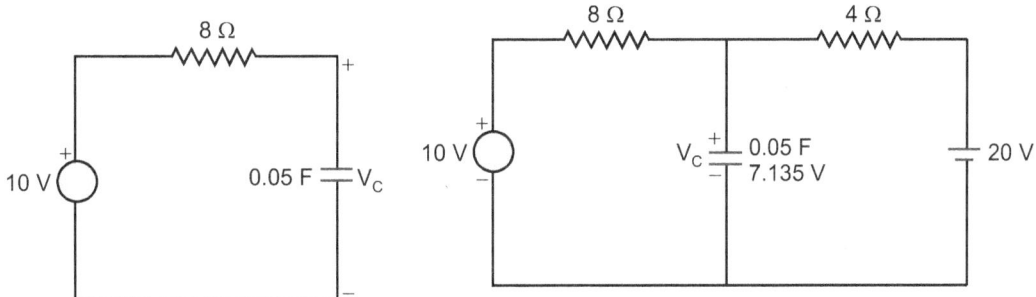

(a) Circuit for 0 < t < 0.5 sec RC = 0.4 sec   (b) Circuit for t > 0.5 sec. capacitor is having initial voltage of 7.135 V

Fig. 3.30

Capacitor voltage for 0 < t < 05 sec is given by
$$v_c(t) = 10(1 - e^{-t/RC}) = 10(1 - e^{-t/0.4}) \text{ volts}$$

at t = 0.5 sec, $v_c(0.5) = 10\left(1 - e^{-\frac{0.5}{0.4}}\right) = 7.135 \text{ volts}$

This acts as a initial voltage when switch S_2 is also closed. For t > 0.5 sec circuit is as shown in Fig. 3.30 (b).

Using source transformation the equivalent circuit will be as shown in Fig. 3.31 below.

where $R_{eq} = 4 \| 8 = \dfrac{32}{12} = 2.67 \, \Omega$

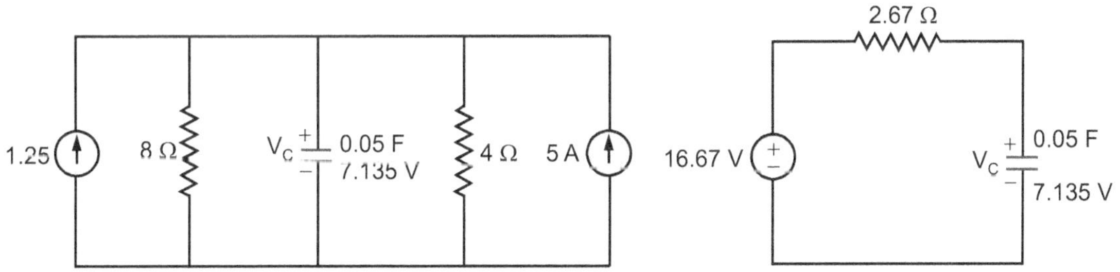

(a)   (b)

Fig. 3.31: Simplified equivalent circuit for t > 0.5 sec

$$V_{oc} = 2.67 \times 6.25$$
$$= 16.67 \text{ volts}$$

We have $RC = 2.67 \times 0.05$
$$= 0.1335 \text{ sec}$$
$$= 133.5 \text{ ms}$$

Hence by equation (3.14) or (3.17) we have

$$v_c(t) = 16.67 + (7.135 - 16.67)\, e^{\frac{-(t-0.5)}{0.1335}}$$

is the required voltage expression across capacitor.

At $\quad t = 0.8$ sec

We have $\quad v_c(0.8) = 16.67 - 9.535\, e^{-\frac{0.3}{0.1335}} = 16.67 - 1.0 = 15.67$ volts

Ex. 3.9: In the circuit shown switch (S) has been open for a long time. On closing 'S' the capacitor voltage attains a value of 80 V after 10 ms. Then switch has been closed for a long time. When 'S' opened capacitor voltage becomes 90V after half a second. Calculate values of R and C. **[Dec. 88]**

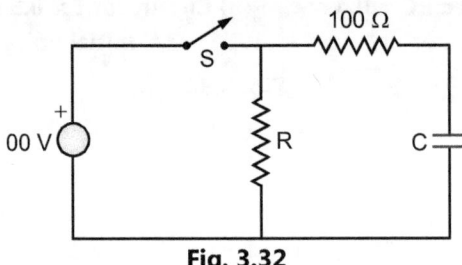

Fig. 3.32

Sol.: When switch (S) has been open for a long time then capacitor voltage is zero. Thus $V_o = 0V$. When switch (S) is closed at $t = 0$ then equivalent circuit will be as shown in Fig. 3.33.

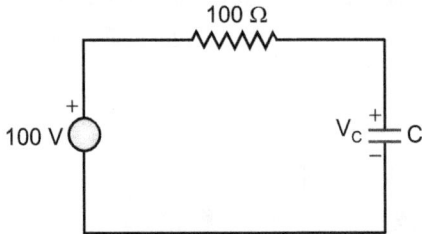

Fig. 3.33: Equivalent circuit for 0 < t < 10 m sec

Here we have resistance (R) redundant. Hence, we have

$$v_c(t) = 100 \left(1 - e^{-\frac{t}{100\,C}}\right)$$

Given that at $\quad t = 10$ ms $= 0.01$ sec, $v_c = 80V$

Thus $\quad 80 = 100 \left(1 - e^{-\frac{0.01}{100\,C}}\right)$

$e^{-\frac{0.01}{100c}} = 0.2$

Hence $\quad \boxed{C = \dfrac{0.01}{161} = 62\ \mu F}$

Unit 3 | 3.22

Now switch is closed for a long time, hence by Fig. 3.33 voltage across capacitor = 100V. Now switch is opened. The circuit will be as shown below in Fig. 3.34.

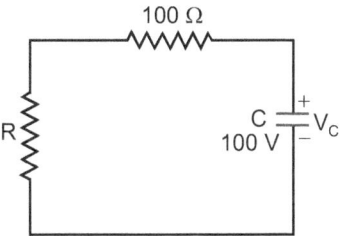

Fig. 3.34: Equivalent circuit when S is opened

This is a undriven R-C circuit. Hence by the equation (3.10) we have $v_c(t) = 100\, e^{-\frac{t}{(100 + R)C}}$. Given that after $\frac{1}{2}$ second capacitor voltage will be 90 volts. Thus.

$$90 = 100\, e^{-\frac{0.5}{(100 + R)C}}$$

OR $$-0.1 = -\frac{0.5}{(100 + R)C} = \frac{0.5}{(100 + R)\, 62 \times 10^{-6}}$$

Solving we get $(R - 100) = 80645\ \Omega$

Hence $R = 80545\ \Omega = 80.545\ K\Omega$.

Ex. 3.10: Switch in the figure is at position A for a long time. It is moved to position 'B' at t = 0. Find expression for v_c at t > 0.   **(May 88)**

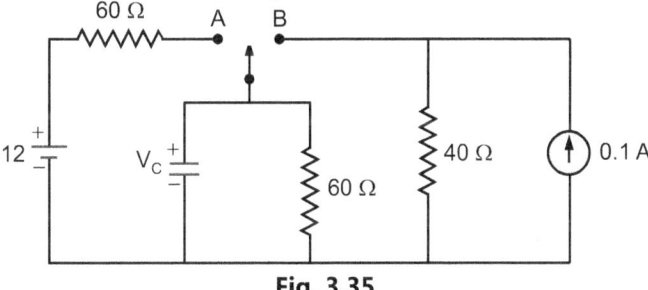

Fig. 3.35

Sol.: When switch was on position 'A' for a long time then Thevenin equivalent circuit is as shown in Fig. 3.36 (a).

Voltage on capacitor will be 6V. This will acts as a initial voltage when switch is thrown on position B.

When switch is thrown on 'B' at t = 0, then 40Ω and 60Ω are in parallel to given equivalent at resistance of $\frac{60 \times 40}{100} = 24\Omega$. This is in parallel with 0.1 A current source. Convert this into a voltage source of 2.4 × 0.1 = 2.4 volts in series with 24Ω. Thus equivalent circuit when switch is on position "B" is as shown in Fig. 3.36 (b).

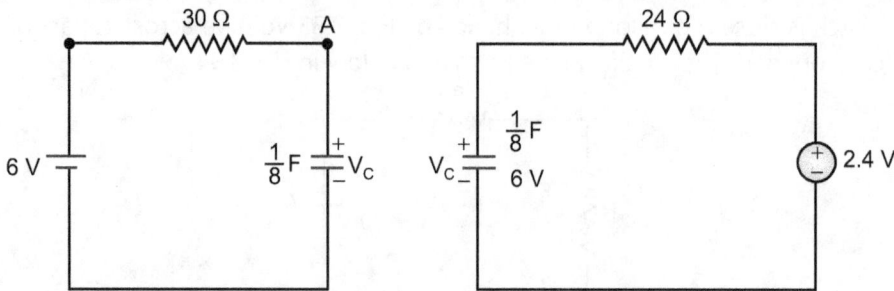

(a) Equivalent circuit when switch was on A **(b)** Equivalent circuit when switch was on B

Fig. 3.36

This is a driven R-C circuit in which a capacitor having a initial voltage of 6V is driven by a battery (V) of 2.4 volts.

Thus
$$V_c(t) = 2.4 + (6 - 2.4)\, e^{-\frac{t}{24 \times 1/8}}$$
$$= [2.4 + 3.6\, e^{-t/3}] \text{ volts}$$

This is the expression required for $t > 0$.

Ex. 3.11: In the circuit shown below switch K remains closed for a pretty long time so as to allow it to reach steady state. At $t = 0$ switch K is opened. Find out the expression for the voltage across the capacitor for $t > 0$ and determine its value at t = time constant of the circuit. **[May 90]**

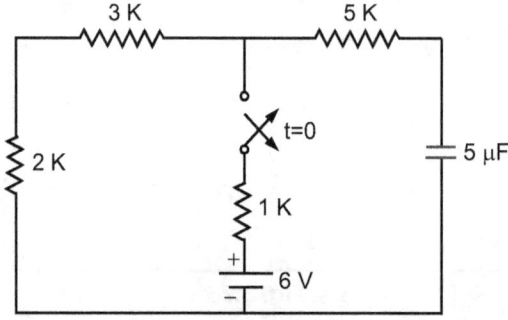

Fig. 3.37

Sol.: When switch K is closed for a long time. Then Thevenin equivalent across capacitor is as shown below in Fig. 3.38 (a).

where
$$R_{eq} = 5K + 1K \,||\, 5K$$
$$= 5.833 \text{ K}\Omega$$
$$V_{oc} = V_{eq}$$
$$= \frac{5 \times 6}{5 + 1} = 5 \text{ Volts}$$

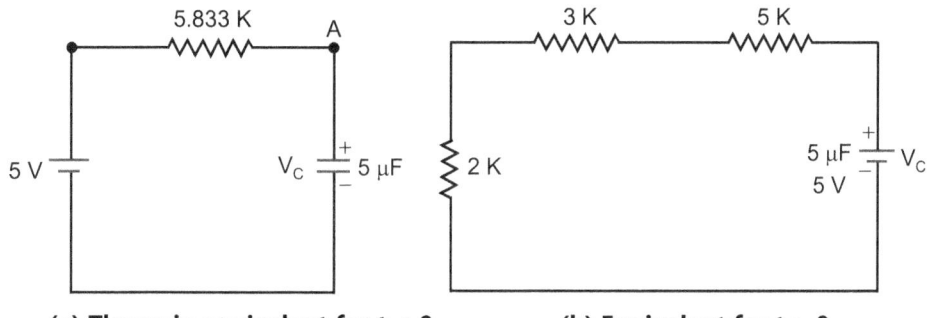

(a) Thevenin equivalent for t < 0   **(b) Equivalent for t > 0**

Fig. 3.38

Under steady state voltage on capacitor = V_o = 5V. At t = 0 switch is opened, and the equivalent of the circuit is as shown in Fig. 3.38 (b).

This is a undriven R-C circuit having a initial capacitor voltage (V_o) of 5V and a Time constant (T) of $5 \times 10^{-6} \times 10 \times 10^3 = 0.05$ sec = 50 ms

Voltage across capacitor for a time t > 0 is givenby

$$v_c(t) = 5e^{-t/RC} = 5e^{-t/0.005} = 5e^{-20t} \text{ volts}$$

At t = time constant (T) = 50 ms, we have

$$v_c(t) = 5e^{-1} = \mathbf{1.84 \text{ Volts}}$$

Ex. 3.12: Suppose that in the circuit shown in the Fig. 3.39 $v_1(0) = 10V$, and $v_2(0) = 5V$. At what time will have the voltage v (t) 0.75 V?

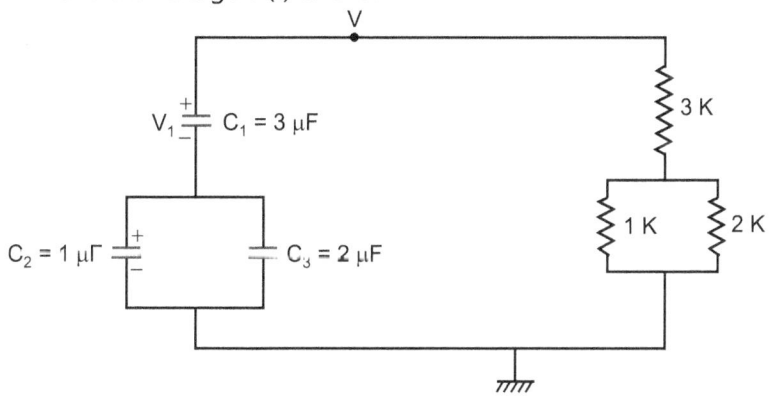

Fig. 3.39

Sol.: We have

$$R = 3k + 1k \| 2t + \frac{2}{3}k = \frac{11}{3} \text{ K}\Omega$$

$$C = 3\mu F \| 3\mu F = \frac{3}{2} \mu F$$

$$V_o = v_1(0) + v_2(0) = 10 + 5 = 15 \text{ V}$$

Hence circuit can be redrawn as shown in Fig. 3.40.

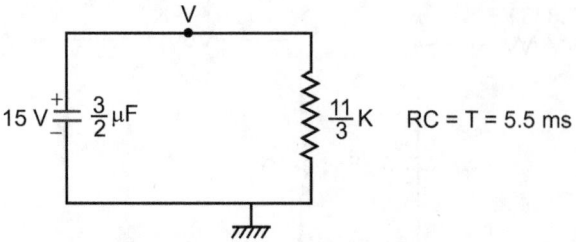

Fig. 3.40: Equivalent circuit

This is a undriven R-C circuit. Using equation (3.10) we have

$$v(t) = 15\,e^{-t/T} = 15\,e^{-t/5.5\text{ ms}}$$

Let t_1 be the time at which $v(t)$ becomes 0.75 V.

Thus $\qquad 0.75 = 15\,e^{-\frac{t_1}{5.5\text{ ms}}}$

OR $\qquad e^{-\frac{t_1}{5.5\text{ ms}}} = 0.05$

OR $\qquad -\dfrac{t_1}{5.5\text{ ms}} = \log_e(0.05) = -3.0$

Hence $\qquad t_1 = 16.5 \times 10^{-3}\text{ S} = 16.5\text{ ms}$

Thus after t_1 (16.5 ms) voltage $v(t)$ becomes 0.75 V.

Ex. 3.13: In the network shown switch K is closed at $t = 0$. The current waveforms are observed on CRO. Initial value of current measured to be 0.01 Amp. Transient appears to disappear in 0.1 secs. Find (a) value of R (b) value of C (c) equation of $i(t)$. **(Dec. 87)**

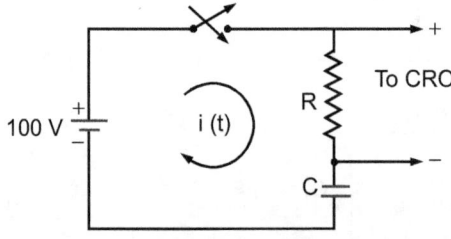

Fig. 3.41

Sol.: (a) When switch is closed at $t = 0$, the circuit will act as a driven R-C circuit. Hence current

$$i(t) = \dfrac{100}{R}\,e^{-\frac{t}{RC}}$$

Given that at $t = 0$, $\qquad i(0) = 0.01\text{ Amp.} = \dfrac{100}{R}$

Hence $\qquad R = \dfrac{100}{0.01} = 10\text{ k}\Omega$

(b) Assuming that transient disappears after a time

$$(t) = RC = 4 RC$$
$$t = 4T = 4RC$$

Thus we have, $4RC = 0.1$

$$C = \frac{0.1}{4 \times 10^4} = 2.5 \, \mu F$$

(c) As found already, the equation for i (t) is given by

$$i(t) = \frac{100}{10^4} e^{-t/T}$$

Now $T = RC = 25$ ms

Thus $i(t) = 0.01 \, e^{-40t}$ Amps

Ex. 3.14: The circuit shown in Fig. is connected by closing of switch at time t = 0.
1. What is overall time constant of the circuit?
2. Determine i (t), v_1 (t), and v_2 (t) for t > 0.
3. Sketch the three waveforms as determined in part (b).

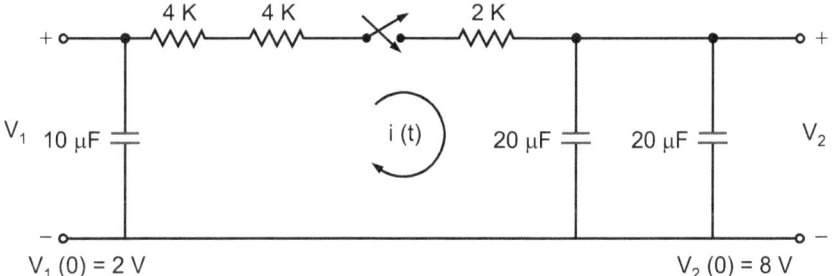

Fig. 3.42

Sol.: When switch is closed, all resistors are in series. Thus R_{eq} = 4k + 4k + 2k = 10 kΩ, 20 μF in parallel with 20 μF gives a capacitance of 40 μF. This is in series with 10 μF capacitor.

Thus $$C_{eq} = \frac{10 \times 40}{10 + 40} = 8 \mu F$$

Voltage on equivalent capacitor = V_o = 8 – 2 = 6V. The simplified equivalent equivalent circuit is as shown below.

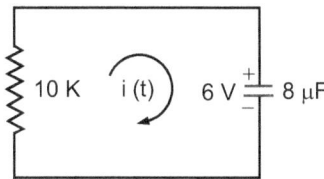

Fig. 3.43: Simplified equivalent circuit

$$i(t) = -\frac{6}{10k} e^{-\frac{t}{80ms}} = 0.6 \, e^{-12.5 \, t} \text{ mA} \qquad \ldots(a)$$

Overall time constant $(T) = 8 \times 10^{-6} \times 10^4 = 80$ ms ...(b)

When switch is closed 10 µF capacitor is charging while 40 µF capacitor is discharging.

$$v_1(t) = v_1(0) + \frac{1}{C_1} \int_i^t -I(t) \, dt$$

$$= 2 + \frac{1}{10 \times 10^{-6}} \int_0^t 0.6 \, e^{-12.5t} \, dt \cdot mA$$

$$= 2 + \frac{1}{10^{-5}} \times 0.6 \times 10^{-3} \left[\frac{e^{-12.5}}{-12.5} \right]_0^t$$

$$= 2 - 4.8 \, [e^{-12.5}]_0^t$$

$$= 6.8 - 4.8 \, e^{-12.5 \, t} \qquad \ldots(c)$$

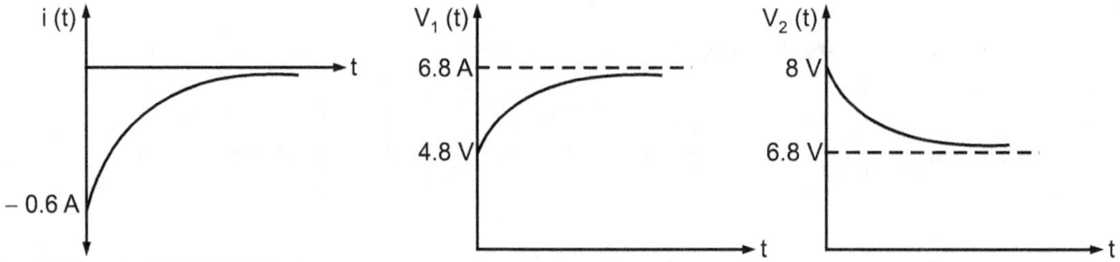

(a) Current [i (t)] waveform	(b) Waveform of $v_1(t)$	(c) Waveform of $v_2 t$

Fig. 3.44: Waveforms

$$v_2(t) = v_2(0) + \frac{1}{C_2} \int_0^t i(t) \, dt$$

$$= 8 + \frac{1}{40 \times 10^{-6}} \int_0^t -0.6 \, e^{-12.5 \, t} \text{ mA } dt$$

$$= 8 - \frac{0.6 \times 10^{-3}}{40 \times 10^{-6}} \left[\frac{e^{-12.5t}}{-12.5} \right]_0^t$$

$$= 8 + 12 \, [e^{-12.5}]_0^t$$

$$v_2(t) = 6.8 + 1.2 \, e^{-12.5 \, t} \qquad \ldots(d)$$

Waveforms for $i(t), v_1(t), v_2(t)$ are as shown in Fig. 3.44.

Ex. 3.15: In the circuit shown 10V battery is connected to the circuit by closing switch at t = 0. Assume that initially voltage on capacitor is zero. Determine expression for $v_c(t)$ and $i_c(t)$ and sketch the wave forms.

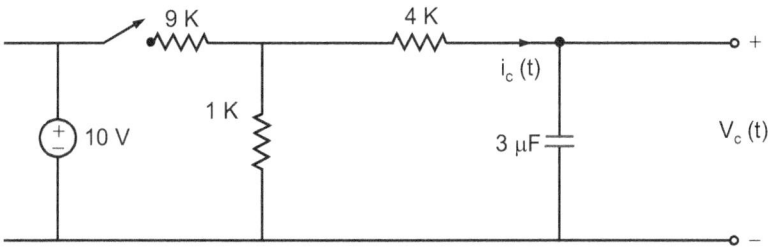

Fig. 3.45

Sol.: When switch is closed at t = 0, then for t > 0 the Thevenin equivalent circuit across capacitor is given by

$$V_{oc} = \frac{1k \times 10}{1k + 9k}$$

$$= \frac{10}{10} = 1V$$

and $R_{eq} = 4k + 9k \parallel 1k = 4k + \frac{9k}{10} = 4.9\ k\Omega$

Hence, the circuit can be redrawn as shown below.

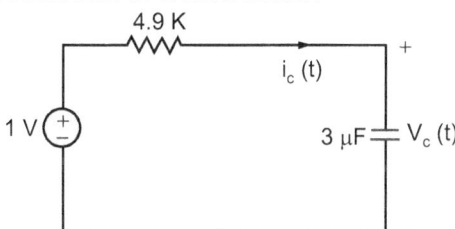

Fig. 3.46: Thevenin equivalent circuit

This is a driven R-C circuit hence,

$$v_c(t) = 1[1 - e^{-t/T}]$$

Now $T = R\text{-}C = 4.9 \times 10^3 \times 3 \times 10^3 \times 3 \times 10^{-6} = 14.7\ ms$

Hence $v_c(t) = 1\left[1 - e^{-\frac{t}{14.7\ ms}}\right]$ Volts

The voltage waveform is plotted on Fig. 3.47 (a).

Also, $i_c(t) = \left(\frac{V - V_o}{R}\right) e^{-\frac{t}{RC}} = \frac{1}{4.7k} e^{-\frac{t}{14.7\ ms}}$

OR $i_c(t) = 0.213\ e^{-\frac{t}{14.7\ ms}}$ Amps.

The current waveform is plotted in Fig. 3.47 (b).

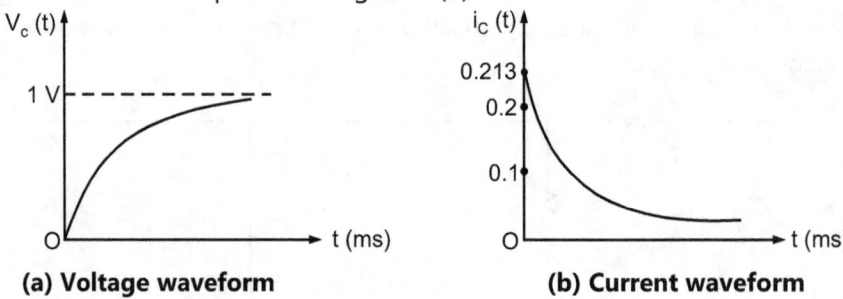

(a) Voltage waveform   (b) Current waveform

Fig. 3.47

Ex. 3.16: In the circuit shown below, the switch is closed on position 2 at t = 0 and after t = RC it is moved to position 3. Calculate the current from t = 0 to t = 4RC at the interval of 0.5 RC and roughly sketch the waveform.

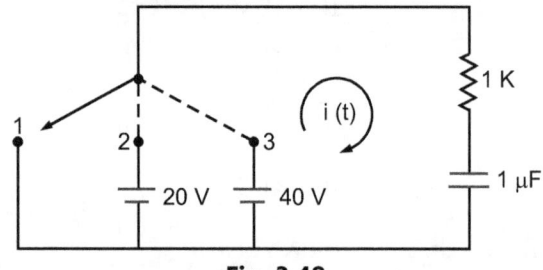

Fig. 3.48

Sol.: Initially (t < 0) switch was on position 1 and capacitor voltage was 0V.

(I) At t = 0 it is thrown an position 2. Thus for t > 0 circuit acts as a driven R-C circuit with 0V initially on capacitor.

$$v_c(t) = 20 + (0 - 20)\, e^{-t/RC}$$

We have $\quad RC = 10^3 \times 1 \times 10^{-6} = 1$ ms

$$v_c(t) = 20\left(1 - e^{-\frac{t}{1ms}}\right) \text{ volts.} \quad \ldots(a)$$

at $\quad t = RC, v_c(t = RC) = 20(1 - e^{-1}) = 12.64$ volts

Current through capacitor for t > 0 is given by

$$i_c(t) = \frac{V}{R} e^{-\frac{t}{RC}} \text{ mA}$$

at $\quad t = 0.5\, RC,$
$\quad i_c(t) = 20 e^{-.5} = 12.13$ mA

at $\quad t = 1.0\, RC, i_c = (t = RC)$
$\quad = 20\, e^{-1}$
$\quad = 7.4$ mA

(II) At t = RC, the switch was moved to position 3.

At that instant capacitor was charged with the initial voltage of 12.64 volts. The circuit will be as shown in Fig. 3.49.

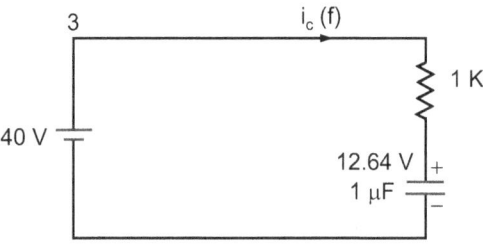

Fig. 3.49

Now current through capacitor is given by

$$i_c(t) = \left(\frac{40 - 12.64}{1}\right) e^{-\left(\frac{t-RC}{RC}\right)}$$

$$= 27.36 \, e^{-\left(\frac{t-RC}{RC}\right)} \text{ mA}$$

At t = 1.5 RC, i_c (1.5 RC) = 27.36 $e^{-0.5}$ = 16.6 mA

t = 2.0 RC, i_c (2.0 RC) = 27.36 e^{-1} = 10 mA

t = 2.5 RC, i_c (2.5 RC) = 27.36 $e^{-1.5}$ = 6.1 mA

t = 3.0 RC, i_c (3.0 RC) = 27.36 e^{-2} = 3.7 mA

t = 3.5 RC, i_c (3.5 RC) = 27.36 $e^{-2.5}$ = 2.25 mA

t = 4.0 RC, i_c (4.0 RC) = 27.36 $e^{-3.0}$ = 1.36 mA

The current waveform is plotted below in Fig. 3.50.

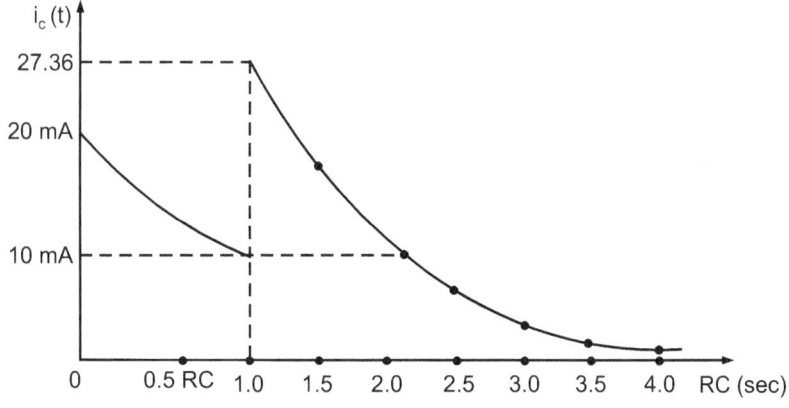

Fig. 3.50: Current waveform

[B] RESISTOR – INDUCTOR (R-L) CIRCUITS

In this section we shall discuss properties of the inductor first. Then properties of a R-L network with inductor having initial current (I_o) is discussed. Then R-L network driven by a d.c. voltage source (V) and inductor having initial current (I_o) is discussed.

3.5 INDUCTOR AND ITS PROPERTIES

Physical construction of a inductor consists of a coil of pure conducting wire, around a medium or core as shown in Fig. 3.51 below.

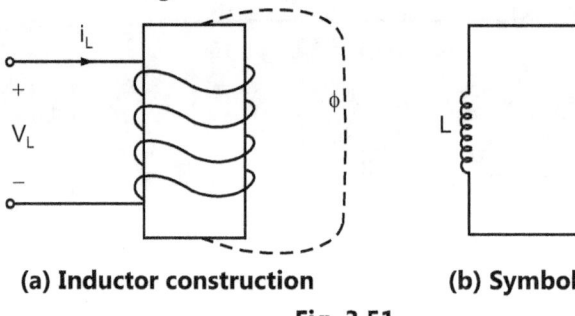

(a) Inductor construction **(b) Symbol of inductor**

Fig. 3.51

Whenever a current passes through any wire then magnetic field will be established around the wire. Magnetic flux (ϕ) is proportional to the current (i_L) flowing through it. If the wire is wound in the form of coil, then the flux due to each turn is reinforced. Hence, total magnetic flux is proportional to current and also number of turns (N).

Thus $\phi \propto Ni_L$ OR $\phi = KNi_L$ ...(3.19)

As this flux links all the N turns, Total flux linkage

$$(\lambda) = N\phi = KN^2 i_L \quad ...(3.20)$$

Ideally flux linkage (λ) is proportional to the current.

i.e. $\lambda = L i_L$ ...(3.21)

The proportionality constant (L) is called as the inductance more precisely *self inductance*,

Thus $L = KN^2$ ...(3.22)

Value of inductance [Unit is Henry (H)] is proportional to N^2.

Voltage (V_L) and Current (i_L) Relation in Inductor

$V_L - i_L$ relationship in inductor can be derived by making use of Faraday's Law of the magnetic induction. This law states that "Induced voltage in wire is equal to time rate of change of the flux linkages".

Thus, induced voltage at terminal (v_L) = $\dfrac{d\lambda}{dt}$, = $L \dfrac{di_L}{dt}$ ...(3.23)

Symbol for induced voltage (v_L) and the terminal current (i_L) is as shown in Fig. 3.51 (b).

Voltage on the inductor is present only when current through it is changing with time. Thus "under constant (or d.c.) excitation voltage across inductor is zero because current is constant. Thus for d.c. inductor acts as a short circuit".

Integrating above equation we have.

$$i_L(t) = \frac{1}{L}\int_{-\infty}^{t} v_L(t)\, dt \qquad \ldots(3.24)$$

$$= \frac{1}{L}\int_{-\infty}^{0} v_L(t)\, dt + \frac{1}{L}\int_{0}^{t} v_L(t)\, dt$$

Hence
$$i_L(t) = I_o + \frac{1}{L}\int_{0}^{t} v_L(t)\, dt \qquad \ldots(3.25)$$

I_o is called as initial current which corresponds to initial stored energy of $\frac{1}{2}L I_o^2$. By the equation (3.25) it is obvious that in inductor it takes some time to build up the current. In the inductor, current is proportional to the magnetic field and not voltage across it.

If we compare equation equations (3.23) and (3.25) with these equations of R-C circuit i.e. equations (3.2) and (3.4), then two equations are identicle if L replaces C and i and v are interchanged.

Energy and Power Relationship in Inductor

Instantaneous power in inductor $p(t) = v(t)\, i(t)$ W

OR
$$p(t) = I(t) \cdot L\frac{di(t)}{dT} = L \cdot i\frac{d}{dt} = \frac{d}{dt}\left[\frac{1}{2}Li^2\right]$$

Since, energy is obtained by integrating power.
i.e.
$$\omega = \int p \cdot dt$$

Energy stored in the inductor $= \omega_m(t) = \frac{1}{2}Li^2 \qquad \ldots(3.26)$

Positive value of $\omega(t)$ implies energy stored in inductor and negative value of $\omega m(t)$ represents energy supplied by the inductor.

Ex. 3.17: Figure shows voltage waveform applied across 100 mh inductor. As a result there is a current in the inductor. Assume initial current zero, determine expression for the current and sketch its waveform.

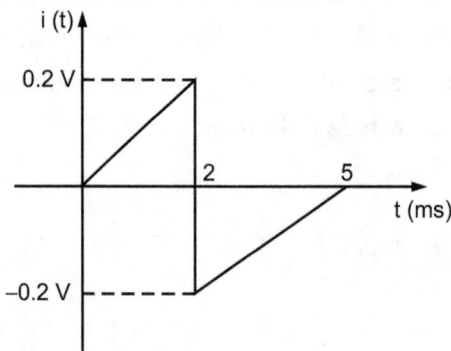

Fig. 3.52

Sol.: Current in the inductor is given by relation.

$$i_L(t) = I_o + \frac{1}{L}\int_0^t v_L \, dt$$

OR

$$i_L(t) = \frac{10^3}{100}\int_0^t v_L \, dt = 10\int_0^t v_L \, dt$$

For $0 < t < 2$ sec,

$$v_L(t) = \frac{0.2}{2} t = 0.1 t$$

Hence

$$i_L(t) = 10 \int_0^2 0.1 t = \left[\frac{t^2}{2}\right]_0^2$$

At $t = 2$ sec,

$$i_L(t) = \frac{4}{2} = 2 \text{ Amp.}$$

At $t = 2$ sec, the voltage changes from 0.2 V to -0.2 V but current cannot change at the instant.

For $2 < t < 5$ sec we have

$$v_L(t) = -0.2 + \frac{0.2}{3}[t-2] \text{ and hence we have}$$

$$i_L(t) = 2 - \frac{0.2}{L}\int_2^5 dt + \frac{0.2}{3L}\int_2^5 (t-2)\,dt$$

$$= 2 - 2\,[t]_2^5 + \frac{2}{3}\left[\frac{(t-2)^2}{2}\right]_2^t$$

At $t = 5$ sec

$$i_L(t) = 2 - 2[5-2] + \frac{2}{3} \times \frac{9}{2}$$

$$= 2 - 6 + 3 = -1 \text{ Amp.}$$

The waveform is as shown below.

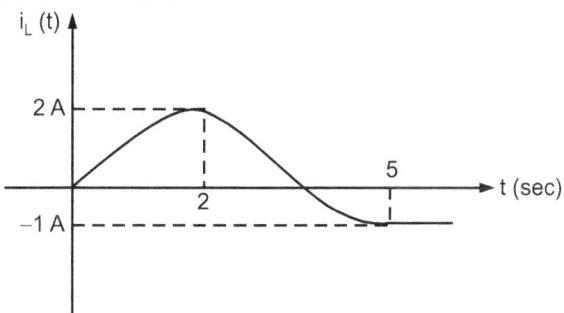

Fig. 3.53

Ex. 3.18: A current source $i_o(t)$ of waveform shown below is connected to a $\frac{1}{3}$ H inductor. Sketch the voltage $V_L(t)$ using the same co-ordinate.

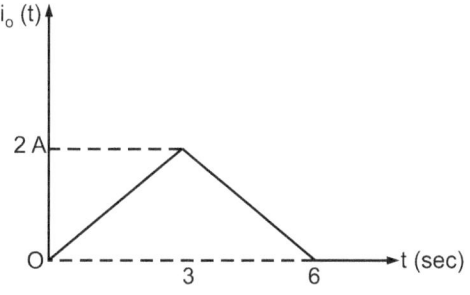

Fig. 3.54

Sol.: We have voltage across inductor is given by

$$V_L(t) = L\frac{di_L}{dt} = \frac{1}{3}\frac{d}{dt}i_L(t)$$

For $0 < t < 3$, $\dfrac{di_L}{dt} = \dfrac{2}{3}$ A/sec,

Hence in this range we have

$$V_L(t) = \frac{1}{3} \times \frac{2}{3} = \frac{2}{9} \text{ volts}$$

for $3 < t < 6$, we have

$$\frac{di_L}{dt} = \frac{2-0}{3-6} = \frac{-2}{3} \text{ A/sec}$$

Hence we have $V_L(t) = \dfrac{1}{3} \times \dfrac{-2}{3} = \dfrac{-2}{9}$ volts

The voltage waveform is as shown below.

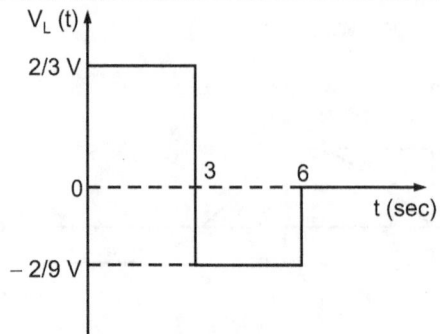

Fig. 3.55: Voltage waveforms

Linearity and Superposition: An element is said to be linear if and only if superposition theorem is valid for them and vice versa.

It can be shown that superposition theorem is valid for inductor if and only if initial current in the inductor (I_o) is zero. Otherwise superposition theorem cannot be applied. Thus, for energized inductor we cannot apply superposition theorem.

Thus, inductor acts as linear element if and only if it is not energized (Initial current in the inductor is zero).

Series and Parallel Connection of Inductors: Consider the inductor L_1 and L_2 connected in series as shown in Fig. 3.56. Current through two inductors are same.

Also
$$v = v_1 + v_2 = L_1 \frac{di}{dt} + L_2 \frac{di}{dt}$$
$$= (L_1 + L_2) \frac{di}{dt} = L_{eq} \frac{di}{dt}$$

where
$$L_{eq} = L_1 + L_2 \qquad \ldots(3.27)$$

Fig. 3.56: Inductors in series

Thus, in series connection equivalent inductance is addition of two inductance. Also any initial current present in the two inductors will also be present on equivalent inductors also.

Now consider two inductors connected in parallel as shown in Fig. 3.57. Here both the inductors are having same voltage.

Now,
$$i = i_1 + i_2 = \frac{1}{L_1}\int_0^t v\,dt + \frac{1}{L_2}\int_0^t v\,dt$$
$$= \left(\frac{1}{L_1} + \frac{1}{L_2}\right)\int_0^t v\,dt = \frac{1}{L_1}\int_0^t v\,dt$$

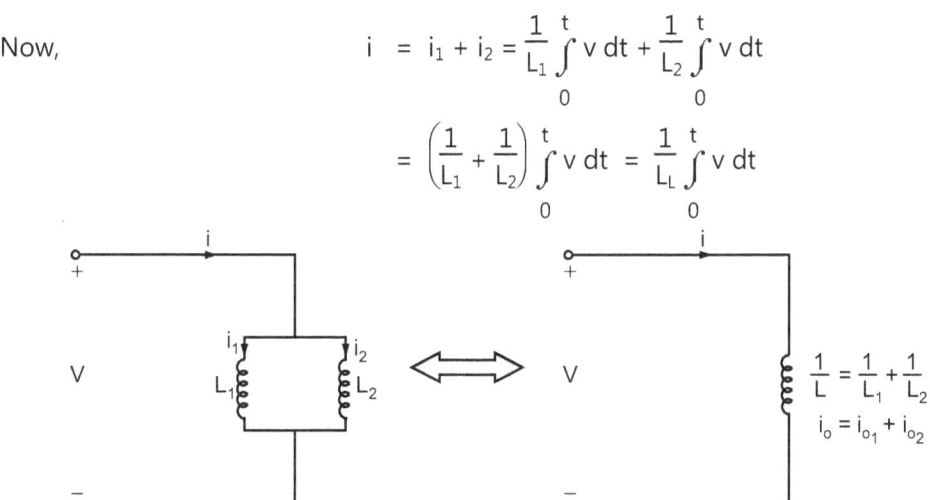

Fig. 3.57: Inductor in parallel

Thus, equivalent inductance of a parallel connected inductors is given by,

$$\frac{1}{L} = \frac{1}{L_1} + \frac{1}{L_2} \qquad \ldots(3.28)$$

If any initial current is present in individual inductor, then sum of these initial currents will be present on equivalent inductor.

3.6 UNDRIVEN R-L CIRCUIT

Consider circuit shown below in Fig. 3.58 (a).

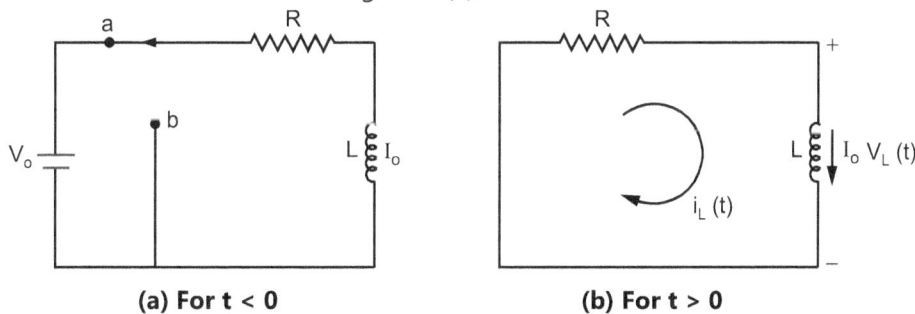

(a) For t < 0   (b) For t > 0

Fig. 3.58: Undriven circuit

Initially switch was on position 'a' for a long time. Inductor then acts as a short circuit and current through inductor = $I_0 = \dfrac{V_0}{R}$. This is known as initial current. It the switch is thrown on position 'b' at t = 0, for t > 0, the circuit will be as shown in Fig. 3.58 (b).

Now inductor current (I_o) will flow through resistor R. Hence energy stored in the inductor $\left(\frac{1}{2}LI_o^2\right)$ will be dissipated as a heat in the resistor. Because of this the initial current (I_o) will reduce. We are interested to find the rate at which inductor current reduces to zero.

KVL across the circuit of Fig. 3.58 (b) gives

$$R \cdot i_L + L\frac{di_L}{dt} = 0 \qquad \ldots(a)$$

This is a homogeneous linear differential equation. We can use *variable separable* method to solve this differential equation. Thus,

$$L\frac{di_L}{dt} = -R\, i_L \quad \text{OR} \quad \frac{di_L}{i_L} = -\frac{R}{L}dt \qquad \ldots(b)$$

Integrating equation (b) gives

$$\log_e (i_L) = -\frac{R}{L}t + K$$

Hence $\qquad i_L = e^{-\frac{R}{L}t + K} = e^{-K} e^{-\frac{R}{L}t} = Ae^{-\frac{R}{L}t}$

Thus $\qquad i_L(t) = Ae^{-\frac{R}{L}t} \qquad \ldots(c)$

Value of A can be found using initial value of $i_L(t)$.

Thus at = 0, $\qquad i_L(0) = I_o = A$

Hence $\qquad i_L(t) = I_o e^{-\frac{R}{L}t} \qquad \ldots(3.29)$

Time constant of R-L circuit: $T = \frac{L}{R}$ is known as time constant of a R-L circuit. Time constant is defined as the rate at which current (i_L) drops to $\frac{1}{e}$ or 0.37 times initial current (I_o). Current waveform is as shown below in Fig. 3.59.

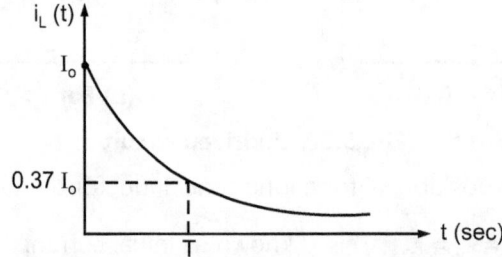

Fig. 3.59: Current waveform of undriven R-L

Voltage across inductor can be found as below.

$$v_L(t) = L\frac{di_L}{dt} = L\frac{di}{dt} = L\,I_o\,e^{-t/T} \times -\frac{1}{T} = -L\,I_o\,e^{-t/T} \times \frac{R}{L} = -RI_o\,e^{-t/T}$$

Thus $\qquad v_L(t) = -R\,I_o\,e^{-\frac{R}{L}t}$ ...(3.30)

Negative sign of $v_L(t)$ indicates that current through inductor is decreasing. Also voltage induced is maximum at $t = 0$ and is equal to $-R.\,I_o$. The waveform for voltage $v_L(t)$ is as shown blow in Fig. 3.60.

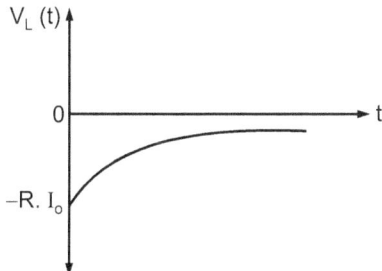

Fig. 3.60: Voltage waveform of R-L circuit

Ex. 3.19: In the circuit shown inductor is fluxed such that current i : 2 Amp. At the time $t = 0$, this inductor is connected to a resistor. If the resistor has a value of 1 kΩ and inductor a value of 50 mH. Determine the time at which current in inductor will have a value of 1 Amp.

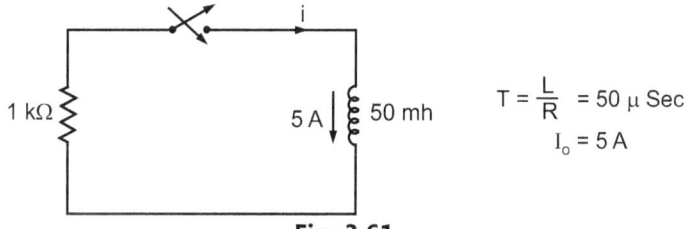

Fig. 3.61

Sol.: Given that for $t < 0$, inductor current is 5 Amp. for $t > 0$ current through inductor is given by

$$i_L(t) = I(t) = 5e^{-\frac{t_1}{T}} = 5e^{-20000\,t}$$

Let t_1 be the time after which switch is closed at $t = 0$ at which current $i(t)$ reduces to 1 Amp.

Thus $\qquad 1 = 5e^{-\frac{t_1}{T}}$

OR $\qquad e^{-\frac{t_1}{T}} = 0.2$

Hence $\qquad \frac{t_1}{T} = -1.61$

Thus $\qquad t_1 = 1.61\,T = 1.61 \times 50\,\mu\,\text{sec} = 80.5\,\mu\text{sec}.$

Thus after a time of 80.5 μ sec, the current through the inductor reduces to 1 Amp.

3.7 DRIVEN R-L CIRCUIT (STEP RESPONSE OF R-L CIRCUIT)

Consider a inductor with initial current I_o and is connected to a battery of v volts through a switch and a resistor (R) as shown below.

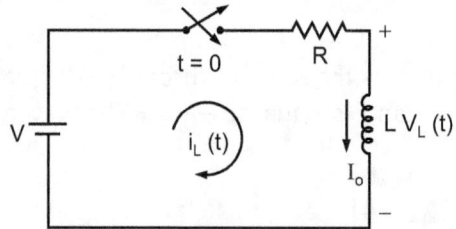

Fig. 3.62: Step response of a R-L circuit

As long as switch is opened inductor will retain its stored energy $\left[\frac{1}{2}LI_0^2\right]$. Let at t= 0 the switch is closed. Current $i_L(t)$ at any instant of time constants or two parts. (a) i_{ss}: Steady state component, (b) i_{tr}: Transient component.

If the switch is closed for a long time, then under steady state inductor is acting as a short circuit (Because current is constant).

Thus $\qquad i_{ss} = \dfrac{V}{R}$ = Steady state component

The transient condition is given by

$$i_{tr} = A e^{-t/T}$$

Thus circuit current i (t) at any time is given by

$$i_L(t) = \dfrac{V}{R} + Ae^{-\frac{R}{L}t} \qquad \ldots(a)$$

Constant 'A' is determined by initial value of current. At t = 0 we have

$$i_L(0) = I_o$$

Hence by (a) $\qquad I_o = \dfrac{V}{R} + A$

OR $\qquad A = \left(I_o - \dfrac{V}{R}\right) \qquad \ldots(3.31)$

Thus complete solution for $i_L(t)$ is

$$i_L(t) = \dfrac{V}{R} + \left(I_o - \dfrac{V}{R}\right)e^{-\frac{R}{L}t} \qquad \ldots(3.32)$$

= Steady state components + Transient component

Current wave form is as shown below in Fig. 3.63.

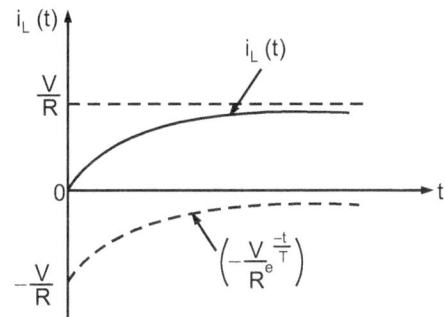

Fig. 3.63: Current waveform with $I_o = 0A$

Note: If $\frac{V}{R} > I_o$ then $i_L(t)$ is positive indicating that inductor energy is increasing.

Voltage across inductor at any instant of time is given by:

$$v_L(t) = L\frac{di_L}{dt} = L\left[\left(I_o - \frac{V}{R}\right)e^{-t/T} \times -\frac{R}{L}\right]$$

$$= -R\left(I_o - \frac{V}{R}\right)e^{-t/T}$$

Thus $\quad v_L(t) = (V - RI_o)\,e^{-Rt/L}$ ...(3.33)

Voltage waveform when $I_o = 0$ is as shown below.

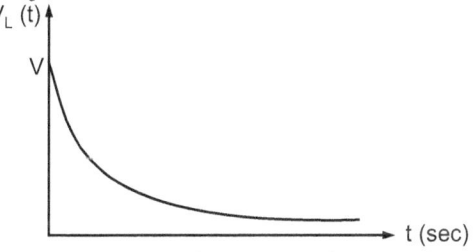

Fig. 3.64: Inductor voltage waveform with $t_o = 0$

By this waveform, it is obvious that under steady state ($t = \infty$), inductor voltage is zero. Thus inductor acts as a short circuit.

Ex. 3.20: In the circuit shown below switch is closed at $t = 0$, Determine and sketch $i_L(T)$ and $v_L(t)$ for $t > 0$.

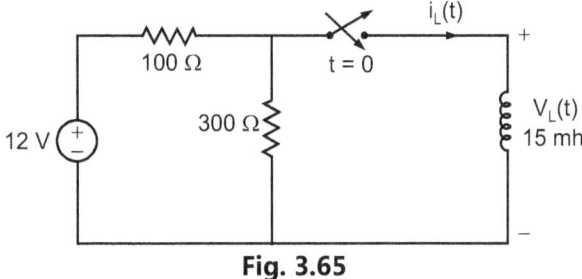

Fig. 3.65

Sol.: Switch was closed at t = 0, this means it was initially opened. Hence initial current on inductor is $I_o = 0$ Amp.

When switch was closed, for t > 0, replace the circuit by Thevenin equivalent circuit as shown below.

where $$V_{oc} = \frac{300 \times 12}{400}$$
$$= 9 \text{ volts}$$

and $$R = 300 \parallel 100$$
$$= 75 \ \Omega$$

Hence $$T = \frac{L}{R} = \frac{15 \times 10^{-3}}{75}$$
$$= 0.2 \text{ ms}$$

This is a driven R-L circuit, with initial current (I_o) is zero. Thus we have by equations. (3.32) and (3.33).

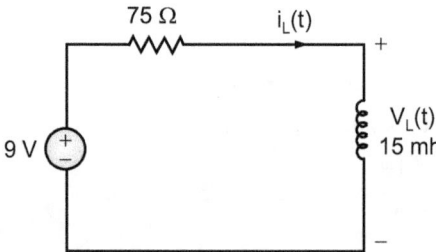

Fig. 3.66: Thevenin equivalent circuit for t > 0

$$i_L(t) = \frac{9}{75} + \left(0 - \frac{9}{75}\right) e^{-t/T}$$
$$= \frac{9}{75} [1 - e^{-5000\,t}] \text{ Amp}$$

$$v_L(t) = (9 - 0) e^{-t/T}$$
$$= 9e^{-5000\,t} \text{ volts}$$

Waveforms for voltage and currents are as shown below.

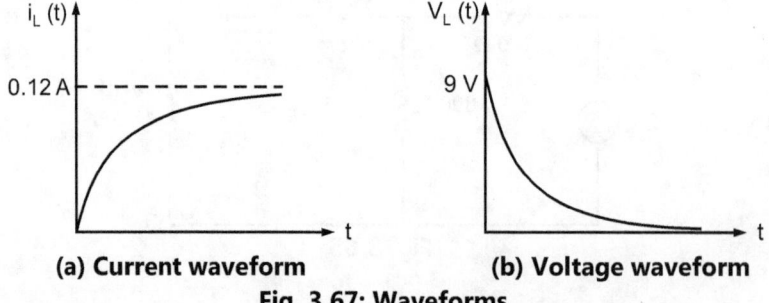

(a) Current waveform   (b) Voltage waveform

Fig. 3.67: Waveforms

Ex. 3.21: Calculate rate of change of current at
1. The instant of closing the switch.
2. When $t = T = \dfrac{L}{R}$
3. Find final steady state value of current. Circuit is switched to 200 V d.c. at $t = 0$.

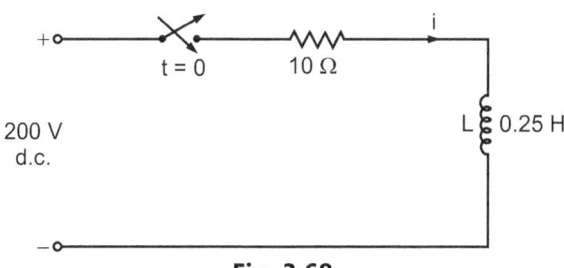

Fig. 3.68

Sol.: (a) When switch is closed at $t = 0$, the circuit acts as driven R-L circuit with initial current (I_0) as zero.

Thus
$$i(t) = \frac{V}{R} + \left(0 - \frac{V}{R}\right) e^{-\frac{R}{L}t} = \frac{V}{R}\left[1 - e^{-\frac{R}{L}t}\right]$$

Rate of change of current $= \dfrac{di}{dt} = -\dfrac{V}{R} + e^{-\frac{R}{L}t} \times \dfrac{-R}{L} = +\dfrac{V}{L} e^{-\frac{R}{L}t}$

at $t = 0$, $\dfrac{di}{dt}(0^+) = \dfrac{V}{L} = \dfrac{200}{0.25} = 100$ A/sec.

(b) at $t = T = \dfrac{L}{T} = 0.025$ sec, the rate of change of current is

$$= \frac{di}{dt}(t = T) = \frac{V}{L} e^{-1} = 100 \times \frac{1}{e} \text{ A/sec} = 26.8 \text{ Amp/sec}.$$

(c) Under steady state inductor acts as short circuit. Thus steady state value of current i

$(t = \infty) = \dfrac{V}{R} = \dfrac{200}{10} = 20$ Amp.

Ex. 3.22: Determine as a function of time the voltage across 3.2 Ω resistor and across inductor, if switch is closed at $t = 0$ and hence calculate voltage at $t = 5$ ms.

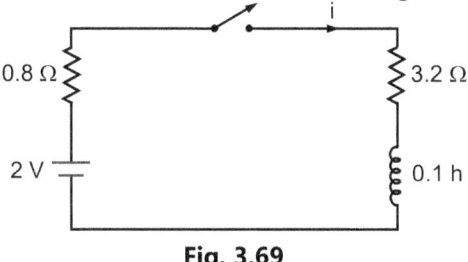

Fig. 3.69

Sol.: Assume initial current on inductor (I_o) be zero. When switch is closed at t = 0, the circuit acts as a driven R-C circuit.

Hence Loop current = $i(t) = \frac{V}{R}\left[1 - e^{-\frac{R}{L}t}\right]$

$$T = \frac{L}{R} = \frac{0.1}{4.0} = \frac{1}{40} \text{ sec.}$$

Thus $i(t) = \frac{20}{4}[1 - e^{-40t}] = 5[1 - e^{-40t}]$ Amp

1. Voltage across 3.2 Ω resistor = $V_R = 3.2 \times 5 [1 - e^{-40t}]$ volts
 = $16[1 - e^{-40t}]$ volts

This is the required expression for voltage across resistor
at t = 5 ms
We have $V_R (5 \text{ ms}) = 16[1 - e^{-40 \times 5 \times 10^{-3}}]$
 = $16[1 - e^{-0.2}] = 16[1 - 0.818]$

Thus we have V_R 5 ms = 2.9 volts

2. Voltage across inductor = $v_L = L\frac{di_L}{dt} = L \times \frac{V}{R} e^{-\frac{R}{L}t} \times \frac{R}{L}$

Thus $v_L(t) = Ve^{-\frac{R}{L}t} = 20 e^{-40t}$ volts

This is the required expression for voltage across inductor. At t = 5 ms we have v_L (5ms) = $20 e^{-0.2}$ = 16.37 volts

Ex. 3.23: The switch shown below has been closed for a long time. Find i_L for all 't' after switch is opened at t = 0.

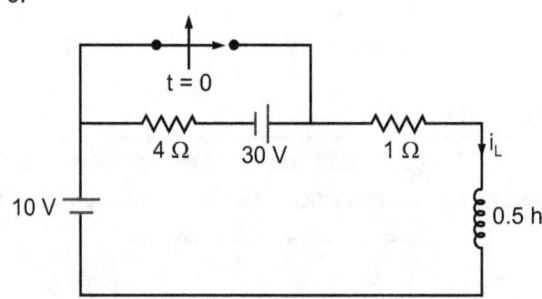

Fig. 3.70

Sol.: When switch is closed for a long time then inductor acts as a short circuit. And initial current in the inductor = $I_o = \frac{10}{1} = 10$ Amp. When switch is opened at t = 0, Then for t > 0 the circuit will be as shown below in Fig. 3.71 (a).

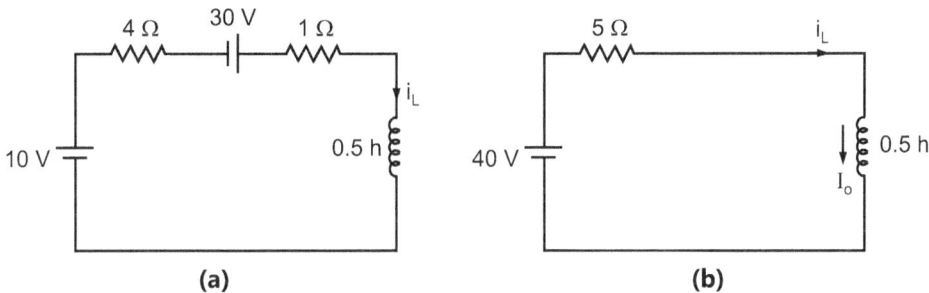

(a)   (b)

Fig. 3.71

The circuit can be simplified as shown in Fig. 3.71 (b). This is a driven R-L circuit with initial current $I_o = 10A$ and is driven by a battery of 40V.

$$i_L(t) = \frac{40}{5} + \left(10 - \frac{40}{5}\right) e^{-t/T} \text{ where } T = \frac{L}{R} = 0.1 \text{ sec}$$

OR $i_L(t) = 8 + 2e^{-10t}$

This is the required expression for current.

Ex. 3.24: The circuit shown attains steady state with switches S_1 closed and S_2 opened. The switch S_2 is closed at t 0, Determine.
1. Equation for the current for t > 0.
2. The time required for the current to reach 90% of its final value.
3. Time constant of the circuit.

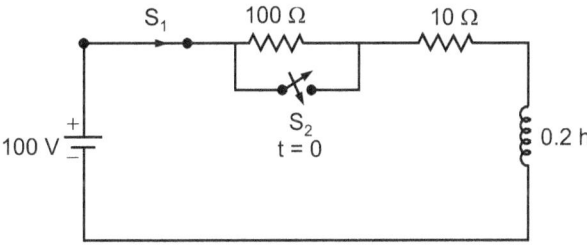

Fig. 3.72

Sol.: Initially S_2 opened, S_1 closed and steady state reached. The inductor acts as a short circuit. Initial current in the inductor = $I_o = \frac{100}{20} = 5$ Amp.

At t = 0 switch S_2 is also closed. For t > 0 the equivalent circuit is as shown below.

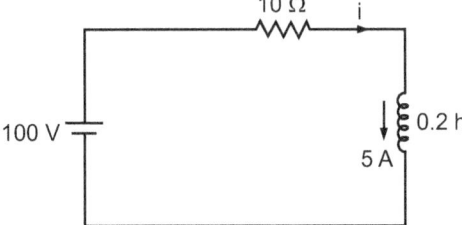

Fig. 3.73: Equivalent circuit for t > 0

This is a driven R-L circuit.

(3) Time constant of the circuit = $T = \dfrac{L}{R} = \dfrac{0.2}{10} = 20$ ms

1. Expression for current (i) can be obtained from equation (3.32). Thus,
$$i(t) = \dfrac{100}{10} + \left(5 - \dfrac{100}{10}\right) e^{-t/T} = 10 - 5 e^{-50t}$$
Hence $\quad i(t) = (10 - 5 e^{-50 t})$ Amp
is the required Expression for current.

2. Let t_1 be the time at which current reaches the 90% of final value of 10 A. Thus we have
$$9 = 10 - 5e^{-50 t_1}$$
OR $\quad 5 e^{-50 t_1} = (10 - 9) = 1$
$-50 t_1 = -1.61$ hence $t_1 = 32.2$ ms

Thus 32.2 ms after closing S_2, current in the circuit will be 90% (i.e. 9A) of final value of 10 Amp.

Ex. 3.25: In the circuit shown below switch is in open position for a long time. At t = 0. The switch is closed. Determined $i_L(t)$ at t = 5 m sec.

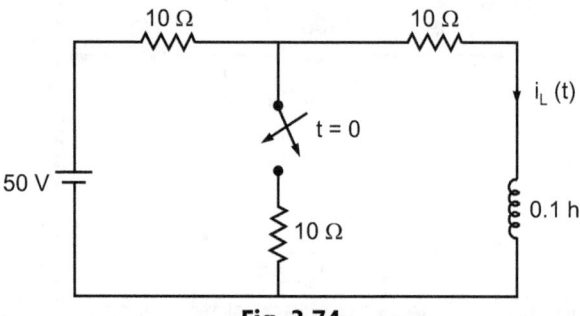

Fig. 3.74

Sol.: When switch is opened for a long time, then the inductor will act as a short circuit. Initial current in the inductor = $I_o = \dfrac{50}{20} = 2.5$ Amp.

At t = 0 switch is closed. For t > 0 Thevenin equivalent circuit will be as shown below in Fig. 3.75.

This is a driven R-L circuit with voltage source of 25V driving R-L circuit in which inductor initial current (I_o) is 2.5 Amp. Thus we have
$$i_L(t) = \dfrac{V}{R} + \left(I_o - \dfrac{V}{R}\right) e^{-t/T} = \dfrac{25}{5} + \left(2.5 - \dfrac{25}{5}\right) e^{-150 t}$$
$$= (5 - 2.5 e^{-150 t}) \text{ Amps.}$$

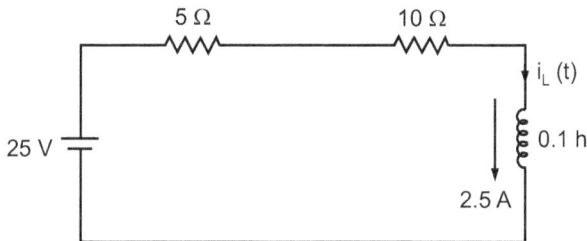

Fig. 3.75: Thevenin equivalent circuit for t > 0

This is the expression for $i_L(t)$ required. At t = 5 ms we have

$$i_L(5\text{ ms}) = 5 - 2.5\, e^{-150 \times 5 \times 10^{-3}} = (5 - 1.181)\text{ Amp} = 3.819\text{ Amp.}$$

Ex. 3.26: In the circuit shown switch is closed at t = 0. Determine current in the inductor at t = 0.1 sec. Assume I(0) = 0.

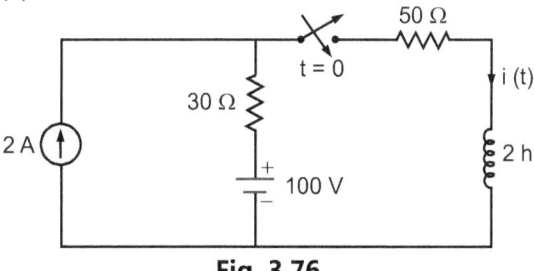

Fig. 3.76

Sol.: Before t < 0, switch was opened and inductor will not be energized. Hence initial current will be zero. for t > 0. Thevenin equivalent circuit will be as shown below.

Open circuit voltage = 100 + 2 × 30 = 160 volts

and R_{eq} = 30 + 50 = 80 Ω

This is a driven R-L circuit. Hence current i(t) is given by

$$i(t) = \frac{160}{80} + \left(0 - \frac{160}{80}\right) e^{-40t}$$

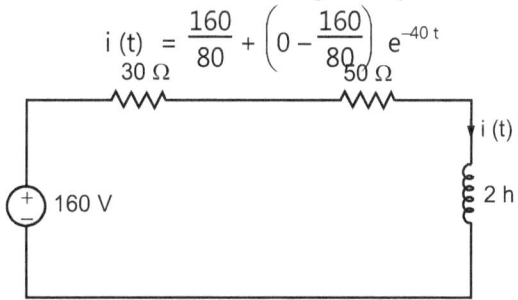

Fig. 3.77: Thevein equivalent for t ≥ 0

Thus $\quad i(t) = 2(1 - e^{-40t})$ Amp.

at $\quad$ t = 0.1 sec the inductor current is

$\quad i(0.1) = 2(1 - e^{-4}) = 2(1 - 0.0183)$

Thus $\quad i(0.1) = 1.963$ Amp.

Thus inductor current is almost equal to the steady state (maximum) current of 2 Amp.

Ex. 3.27: The switch shown below has been closed for a long time. It is opened at t = 0. Find the expression for i_L (t) at t > 0.

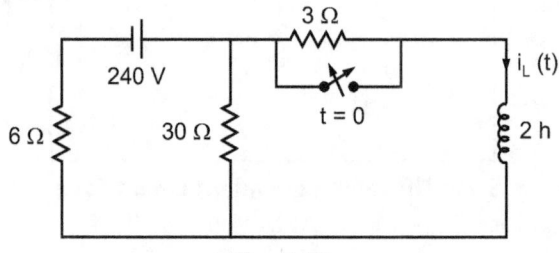

Fig. 3.78

Sol.: For t < 0 switch is closed for a long time. Hence inductor acts as a short circuit.

Current in the inductor $i_L(0) = I_o = \dfrac{240}{60}$ = 40 Amp.

Thevenin equivalent circuit for t > 0 is as shown below in Fig. 3.79.

where
$$V_{oc} = \dfrac{240 \times 30}{30 + 6}$$
$$= 200 \text{ V}$$

and
$$R_{eq} = 3 + 30 \parallel 6 = 3 + 5$$
$$= 8.0\ \Omega$$

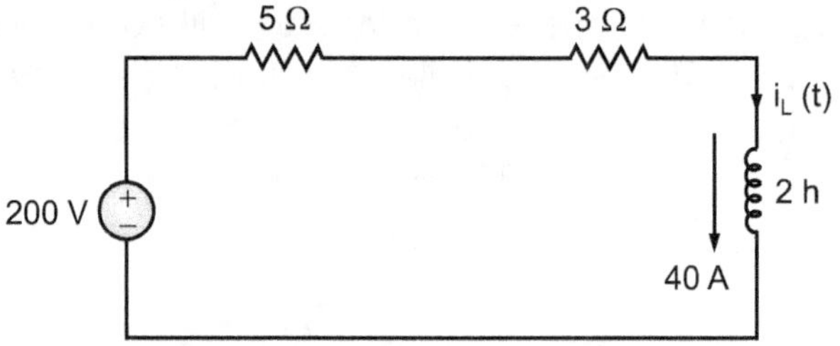

Fig. 3.79: Thevenin equivalent circuit for t > 0

This is a driven R-L circuit. Hence we have

$$i_L(t) = \dfrac{200}{8} + \left(40 - \dfrac{200}{8}\right) e^{-\dfrac{R}{L}t}$$

$$= 25 + (40 - 25)\, e^{-4t}$$

Thus $\quad i_L(t) = [25 + 15\, e^{-4t}]$ Amp.

is the required expression for the current.

Ex. 3.28: The circuit consists of a resistor and a relay of inductance L Henry. The relay is adjusted so that it is actuated when current through the coil is 0.008 Amp. The switch is closed at t = 0 and it is observed that relay is actuated at t = 0.1 sec.

Find the equation for the current i (t) and the inductance L of relay.

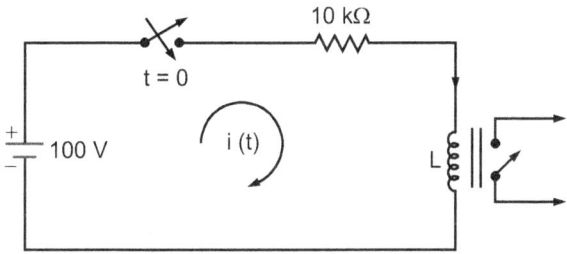

Fig. 3.80

Sol.: Initially inductor current I_o is zero.

When switch is closed at t = 0, then the current i (t) for t > 0 is given as

$$i(t) = \frac{100}{1000} + \left(0 - \frac{100}{10000}\right) e^{-t/T}$$

$$= \frac{1}{100} [1 - e^{-t/T}] \text{ Amp}$$

Given that after t = 0.1 sec current through relay is 0.08 Amp or 8 mA.

Thus $\quad\quad\quad\quad \dfrac{8}{1000} = \dfrac{1}{100}[1 - e^{-t/T}]$

OR $\quad\quad\quad\quad 0.8 = 1 - e^{-t/T}$

Hence $\quad\quad\quad e^{-t/T} = 0.2$

Hence $\quad\quad -\dfrac{0.1}{1} = \ln[0.2] = -1.61$

(a) Thus $\quad\quad T = \dfrac{0.1}{1.61} = 0.062 = \dfrac{L}{R} = \dfrac{L}{10000}$

Hence inductance of relay (L) = 620 Henry

(b) Equation of current $\quad i(t) = 0.01 [(1 - e^{-16.1\,t})]$ Amp.

Ex. 3.29: The network shown in the figure reaches a steady state with switch K opened. At t = 0 the switch K is closed. Find i (t) for the numerical values given and sketch the current waveform and indicate the value of time constant.

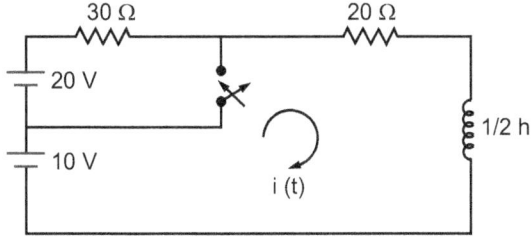

Fig. 3.81

Sol.: Initially switch was opened and steady state is reached. Then inductor acts as a shown circuit. Hence initial current in the inductor is

$$I_o = \frac{20 + 10}{30 + 20} = \frac{3}{5} \text{ Amp.}$$

For $t \geq 0$ the circuit will be as shown in Fig. 3.82 (a).

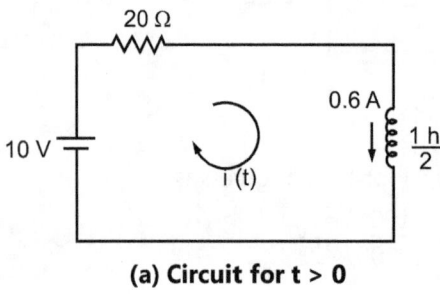

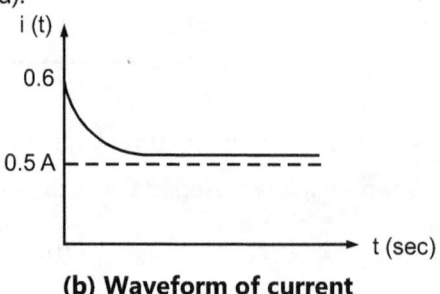

(a) Circuit for t > 0   (b) Waveform of current

Fig. 3.82

This is a driven R-L circuit with inductor having initial current of 0.6 A. Time constant of the circuit is

$$T = \frac{L}{R} = \frac{1}{40} \text{ sec.}$$

Hence current i (t) is given by equation.

$$i(t) = \frac{10}{20} + \left(0.6 - \frac{10}{20}\right) e^{-t/T}$$

Thus $i(t) = [0.5 + 0.1 \, e^{-40\,t}]$ Amps.

The current waveform is as shown in fig. 3.82 (b).

Ex. 3.30: In the circuit shown, the switch K is opened and circuit reaches a steady state. At t = 0, the switch is closed. Find the current in the inductor for t > 0. Sketch this current waveform.

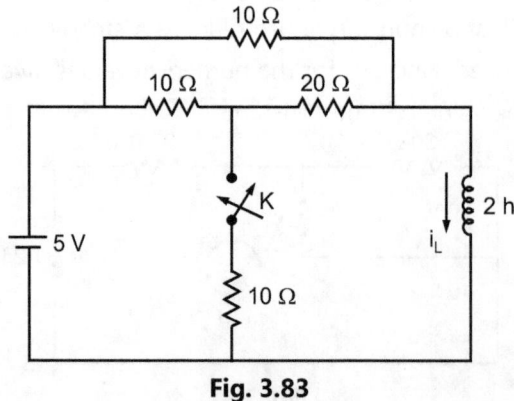

Fig. 3.83

Sol.: For t < 0 the switch was opened. Then inductor will acts as a short circuit. The current through inductor is constant and is given by.

$$I_o = \frac{5}{10\Omega \parallel 30\Omega} = \frac{5}{7.5} = \frac{2}{3} \text{ Amp.}$$

For t ≥ 0 switch is closed and inductor is carrying a initial current of $\frac{2}{3}$ Amp. Then circuit will be as shown in Fig. 3.84 (a). For the time being assume 2 Henry inductor is removed. Then Thevenin equivalent circuit is as shown in Fig. 3.84 (b). Where

$$V_{oc} = 10 \times \frac{5}{10 + 7.5} + 20 \times \frac{5}{17.5} \times \frac{10}{40}$$

$$= \frac{50}{17.5} + \frac{25}{17.5}$$

$$= 2.857 + 1.43 = 4.285 \text{ Volts}$$

and
$$R_{eq} = 10 \parallel (20 + 5) = \frac{10 \times 25}{35} = 7.143 \, \Omega$$

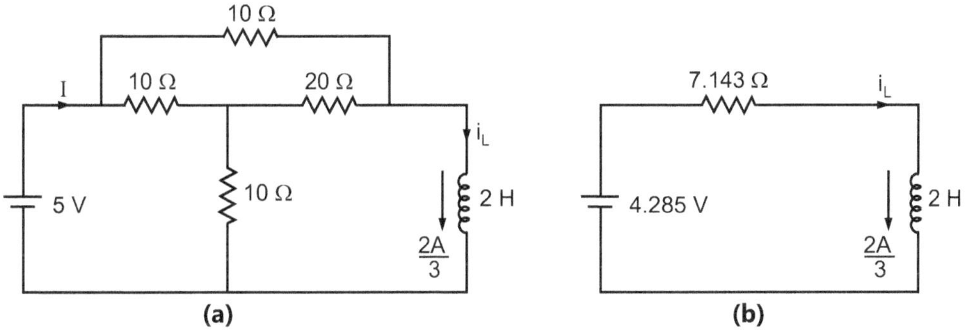

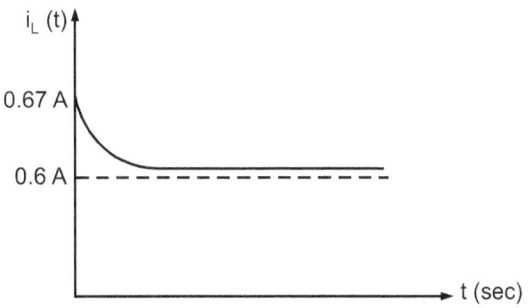

Fig. 3.84

Fig. 3.84 (b) is a driven R-L circuit with inductor having initial current $\frac{2}{3}$ A and time constant (T) = $\frac{L}{R}$ - 0.28 sec. Hence current i_L (t) through inductor is given by

Fig. 3.85: Inductor current waveform

$$i_L(t) = \frac{4.285}{7.143} + \left(\frac{2}{3} - \frac{4.285}{7.143}\right) e^{-t/0.28}$$

$$= 0.6 + [0.67 - 0.6] e^{-3.57 t}$$

Thus
$$i_L(t) = [0.6 + 0.07 e^{-3.57 t}] \text{ Amp.}$$

The current waveform is as shown below in Fig. 3.85.

Ex. 3.31: In the network shown below in Fig. 3.86 the voltmeter may be assumed ideal. If the initial value of current i_1 is 5A at t = 0 and that of i_2 is 2A at t = 0. At what time does the voltmeter reads zero voltage?

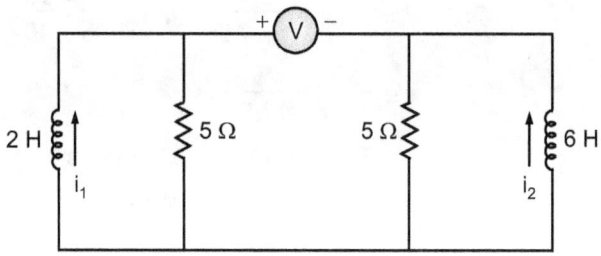

Fig. 3.86

Sol.: Given that $i_1(0) = 5A$ and $i_2(0) = 2A$.

Ideal voltmeter has infinite resistance, hence it acts as a open circuit as far as current is concerned.

Let v_1, v_2 be the node voltages as shown below which are also terminals of voltmeter.

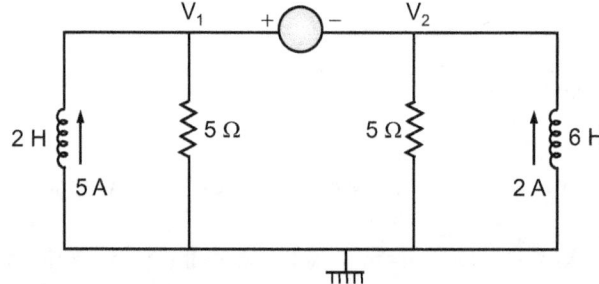

Fig. 3.87

We have, $\quad v_1 = 5 \times e^{-t/T}$

where $\quad T = \dfrac{L}{R} = \dfrac{2}{5} = 0.4$ sec

Hence $\quad v_1(t) = 25 e^{-t/T}$ volts

Also $\quad v_2(t) = 5 \times 2 e^{-t/T}$ where $T = \dfrac{L}{R} = \dfrac{6}{5} = 1.2$ sec

Hence $\quad v_2(t) = 10 e^{-t/T}$ volts

Voltmeter will read zero when $v_1 = v_2$. Let t_1 be the time after $t = 0$ at which two voltage are equal.

Thus $\quad 25 e^{-\frac{t_1}{0.4}} = 10 e^{-\frac{t_1}{1.2}}$

OR $\quad \frac{5}{2} = e^{-\frac{t_1}{1.2}} - e^{-\frac{t_1}{0.4}}$

Hence $\quad \frac{-t_1}{1.2} + \frac{t_1}{0.4} = \log_e \left(\frac{5}{2}\right)$

$= 0.916$

OR $\quad \frac{2t_1}{1.2} = 0.916$

Hece $\quad t_1 = 0.5495$

$= 550$ ms

Thus after approximately 0.55 secs, the voltmeter reads zero.

Ex. 3.32: An inductance of 0.2 H has a current of 2A following through it. If this current is reduced to zero in 10^{-4} seconds as shown below, what is the voltage induced in the inductor.

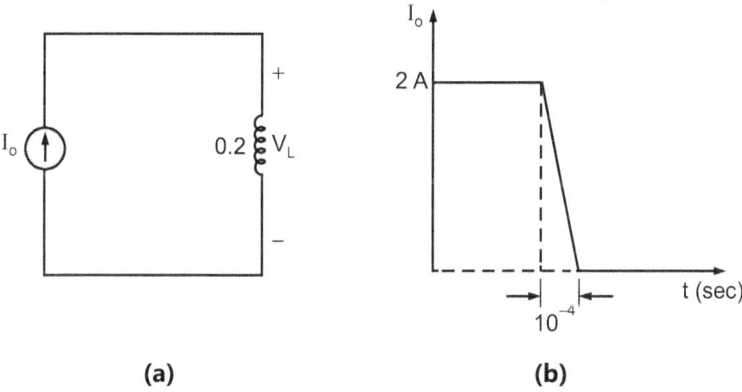

(a)   (b)

Fig. 3.88

Sol.: Voltage across inductor $(v_L) = L \frac{di}{dt}$. When the current is constant $\left[\frac{di}{dt} = 0\right]$, voltage induced is zero. When current of 2A reduces to zero in 10^{-4} seconds, then $\frac{di}{dt} = \frac{-2}{10^{-4}} = -2 \times 10^4$ A/sec.

Thus $\quad v_L = -0.2 \times 2 \times 10^4$ volts $= 4000$ volts

Voltage waveform is as shown below in Fig. 3.89.

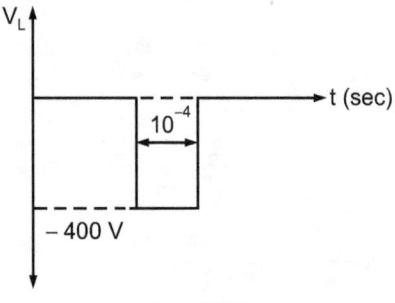

Fig. 3.89

Note: Thus we see that when a constant flowing current is reduced to zero in very short time in a inductor, then a large voltage is induced in the inductor. This principle is used in "Automobile ignition system" to generate a very high voltage needed to fire or spark the spark plug.

3.8 STEP RESPONSE OF FIRST ORDER CIRCUIT

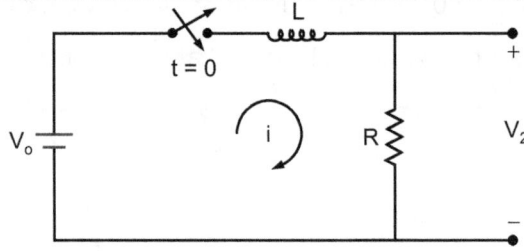

Fig. 3.90: Consider circuit

Consider circuit shown above. If at t = 0 the switch is closed, then voltage V_o is applied to the R-L circuit. V_o is the step voltage because the voltage suddenly jumps from zero to V_o.

For t ≥ 0, KVL across the loop gives:

$$Ri + L\frac{di}{dt} = V_o \ (t \geq 0)$$

As discussed earlier, this is a driven R-L circuit, hence current i (t) is given by

$$i(t) = \frac{V_o}{R}\left(1 - e^{-\frac{R}{L}t}\right)$$

Thus, output voltage v_2 (t) is given by

$$v_2(t) = V_o(1 - e^{-\sigma_1 t}) \qquad \ldots(3.34)$$

Output response is as shown below in Fig. 3.91.

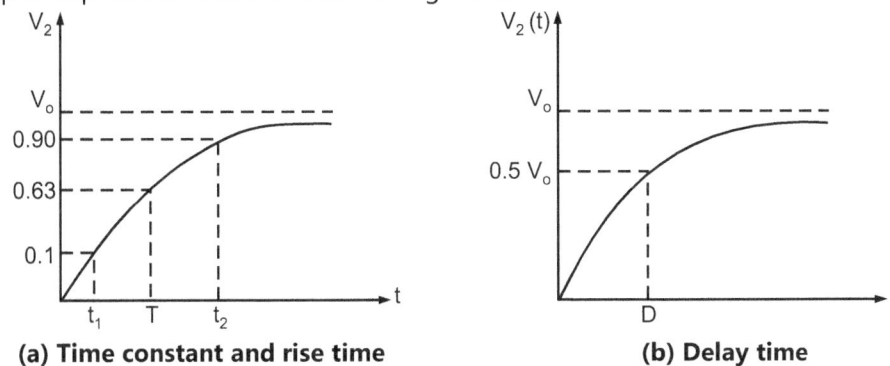

(a) Time constant and rise time (b) Delay time

Fig. 3.91: Step response of first order circuit

(a) Time constant (T): It is the time after t > 0 at which voltage reches 63% of the final value (V_o).

Thus at $\quad T = \dfrac{L}{R} = \dfrac{1}{\sigma}, \quad v_2 = V_0(1 - e^{-1}) = 0.63\, V_o$

(b) Rise Time (t_r): It is the time in which output voltage $v_2(t)$ takes to rise from 10% to the 90% of the final value (V_o).

If t_1 is the time in which output voltage $v_2(t)$ takes to reaches 10% of final value and t_2 is the time required for response to reach 90% of final value (V_o),

Then $\quad t_r = t_2 - t_1 \quad$ ...(3.35)

Now at $\quad t = t_1,\ 0.1\, V_0 = V_o\left(1 - e^{-\sigma_1 t_1}\right)$

OR $\quad t_1 = \dfrac{1}{\sigma_1} \ln\left[\dfrac{10}{9}\right]$

at $\quad t = t_2\ 0.9\, V_o = V_o\left(1 - e^{-\sigma_1 t_2}\right)$

OR $\quad t_2 = \dfrac{1}{\sigma_1} \ln(10)$

Thus $\quad t_r = t_2 - t_1 = \dfrac{1}{\sigma_1} \ln 9 = \dfrac{2.2}{\sigma_1} = 2.2\, T$

Thus $\quad t_r = 2.2\, T \quad$ ...(3.36)

(c) Delay Time (t_o): It is the time required for the output response to reach 50% of its final value.

Thus at $\quad t = t_D,$

$$v_2(t_D) = V_o\left[1 - e^{-\sigma_1 t_D}\right] = 0.5\, V_o$$

Or $\quad t_D = \dfrac{\ln 2}{\sigma_1} = \dfrac{0.692}{\sigma_1}$

$\qquad\qquad\quad = 0.692\, T$

Thus $\quad t_D = 0.7\, T$ ...(3.37)

Thus for a first order circuit delay time is 0.7 times the time constant.

[C] RESISTOR - CAPACITOR - INDUCTOR (R-L-C) CIRCUITS

Consider general form of a second order linear differential equations with constant coefficient as shown below.

$$a_o \frac{d^2 i}{dt^2} + a_1 \frac{di}{dt} + a_2 i = 0 \qquad\qquad ...(3.38)$$

Solution $i(t)$ of this equation should be such that addition of $i(t)$, its first derivative, and second derivative when multiplied by constants will give zero. Hence solution of the $i(t)$ is in the form.

$$i(t) = k\, e^{st}$$

Where k is a constant and root 's' may be real, imaginary or complex.

Thus $a_o\, s^2\, k\, e^{st} + a_1\, k\, e^{st} + a_2\, k\, e^{st} = 0$

OR $\qquad a_o\, S^2 + a_1 s + a_2 = 0 \qquad\qquad ...(3.39)$

This equation is known as characteristic (or auxiliary) equation. Two roots equations are given by.

$$S_1, S_2 = -\frac{a_1}{2a_c} \pm \frac{1}{2a_o}\sqrt{a_1^2 - 4\, a_1\, a_0} \qquad\qquad ...(3.40)$$

Two form of solution of equation is:

$$i_1 = k_1\, e^{s_1 t} \text{ and } i_2 = k_2 e^{s_2 t}$$

Then $i = i_1 + i_2$ is also solution of equation (3.39). The general form of solution of given differential equation (3.38) is:

$$i(t) = k_1\, e^{s_1 t} + k_2 e^{s_2 t} \qquad\qquad ...(3.41)$$

Roots s_1, s_2 are determined by coefficients a_0, a_1, a_2. The radical $\pm\sqrt{a_1^2 - 4 a_o a_2}$ may be zero, real, real and complex or imaginary depending upon a_o, a_1 and a_2.

Step response of a R-L-C circuit gives a second order linear differential equations with the constant coefficient solution for all four cases will be discussed.

3.9 STEP RESPONSE R-L-C CIRCUIT

When a step (d.c.) voltage is given to a R-L-C circuit, then the second order differential equations are formed. The solution of this equation depends upon the type of the roots of the equation.

Case I: When roots of equation are real and unequal consider the circuit shown below in Fig. 3.92.

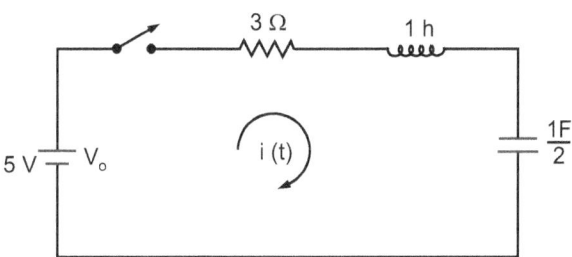

Fig. 3.92: Over damped circuit

Let switches be Open for t < 0. Capacitors and inductors are not energised. At t = 0, the switch is closed. For t > 0 the loop equation will becomes.

$$\frac{1}{C}\int i\, dt + L\frac{di}{dt} + Ri = V_o$$

OR $\qquad 2\int i\, dt + \frac{di}{dt} + 3i = 5 \qquad \ldots(1)$

Differentiating this equation gives

$$\frac{d^2 i}{dt^2} + 3\frac{di}{dt} + 2i = 0 \qquad \ldots(3.42)$$

This is a homogeneous linear differential equation (L.D.E.) of form of equation (3.38). This is also known as characteristic equation.

As before if i (t) = e^{st} is the trial solution, then equation (3.42) becomes

$$S^2 + 3.5 + 2 = 0$$

The roots of this equation are

$$S_1, S_2 = \frac{-3 \pm \sqrt{9 - 4 \times 2}}{2} = \frac{-3}{2} \pm \frac{1}{2}$$

$$= -\frac{1}{2} \text{ or } -2.$$

Thus $\qquad \boxed{S_1 = -0.5}$ and $\boxed{S_2 = -2}$

Thus two roots are *real, negative and unequal.* Hence solution will become

$$i(t) = k_1 e^{-t} + k_2 e^{-2t} \qquad \ldots(3.43)$$

Constant k_1 and k_2 are found by knowledge of the initial conditions.

At t = 0, i (t) = 0 (Because of the inductor, current cannot flow instantaneously).

Thus $\qquad 0 = k_1 + k_2 \qquad \ldots(a)$

Also by equation (1) we have at t = 0

$$0 + \frac{di}{dt} + 0 = 5$$

Hence
$$\left.\frac{di}{dt}\right|_{t=0} = 5 \text{ A/sec}$$

Differentiating equation (3.43) we have
$$\frac{di}{dt} = -k_1 e^{-t} - 2k_2 e^{-2t}$$

Also by equation (1) we have at t = − 0

At t = 0, $\left.\frac{di}{dt}\right|_{t=0} = k_1 - 2k_2 = 5$

Thus $\quad -k_1 - 2k_2 = 5 \quad\quad\quad$ ...(b)

adding (a) and (b) we have $\boxed{k_2 = -5}$

Hence $\quad\quad\quad k_1 = -k_2$
$$= +5 \text{ hence } \boxed{k_1 = 5}$$

Hence $\quad\quad\quad i(t) = 5e^{-t} - 5e^{-2t} \quad\quad\quad$ ...(3.44)

This is particular solution for the current.

Plot of the current waveform is as shown below.

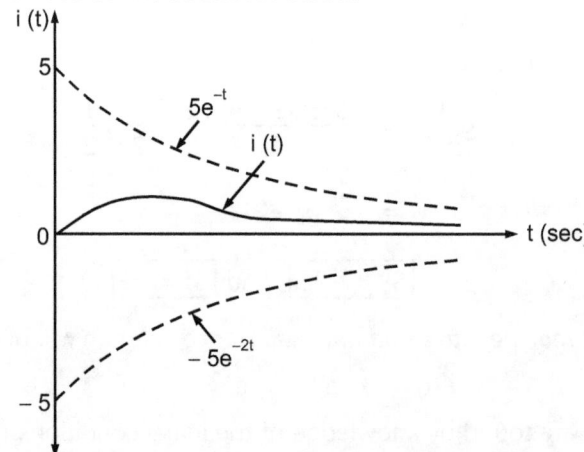

Fig. 3.93: Plot of total current and components currents waveforms

Case II: When roots of the equation are real and repeated:

Here $(a_1^2 - 4 a_0 a_2) = 0$ OR $a_1^2 = 4a_0 a_2$

For this consider circuit shown below.

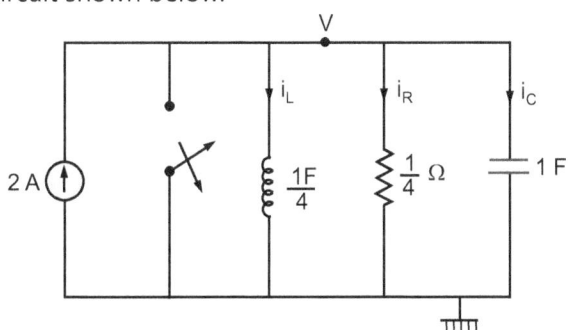

Fig. 3.94: Critically damped circuit

For t < 0, switch was closed. Hence, inductor and capacitor are unenergised. At t = 0, the switch is opened. KCL at node v gives

$$i_R + i_C + i_L = 2$$

$$4v + 1\frac{dv}{dt} + 4\int v\, dt = 2$$

Differentiating this equation gives

$$\frac{d^2v}{dt^2} + 4\frac{dv}{dt} + 4v = 0 \qquad \ldots(3.45)$$

Characteristic equation will become

$$S^2 + 4S + 4 = 0$$

Roots of the equation are

$$S_1, S_2 = \frac{-4 \pm \sqrt{16 - 4 \times 1 \times 4}}{2} = \frac{-4}{2} \pm -2$$

Thus $\boxed{S_1 = -2}$ and $\boxed{S_2 = 2}$

Thus two roots are real, negative and equal. The general solution of the equation (3.45) becomes.

$$v(t) = k_1 e^{-2t} + k_2 t e^{-2t} \qquad \ldots(3.46)$$

k_1 and k_2 are constant, which can be found by using initial conditions.

at t = 0, v(0)   = 0 + k_1
Thus $k_1 = 0$

also by (1), $\left.\frac{dv}{dt}\right|_{t=0}$ = 2 volts/sec.

Now differentiating equation (3.46), we get

$$\frac{dv}{dt} = -2k_1 e^{-2t} + k_2 [-2t\, e^{-2t} + e^{-2t}]$$

Thus at $t = 0$, $\left.\dfrac{dv}{dt}\right|_{t=0} = 0 + k_2 [0 + 1] = 2$

Thus $k_2 = 2$

Hence desired particular solution for $v(t)$ is

$$v(t) = 2t\, e^{-2t} \qquad \ldots(3.47)$$

Plot of the voltage waveform corresponding to equation (3.47) is as shown below

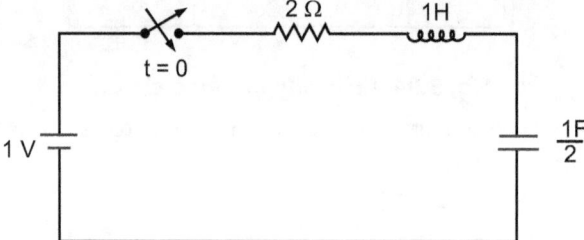

Fig. 3.95: Plot of voltage waveform for the critically damped circuit

Case III: When roots of the equation are complex: Here $(a_1^2 - 4a_0, a_2) < 0$ OR $a_1^2 = 4a_0 a_2$. For this consider circuit shown below in Fig. 3.96.

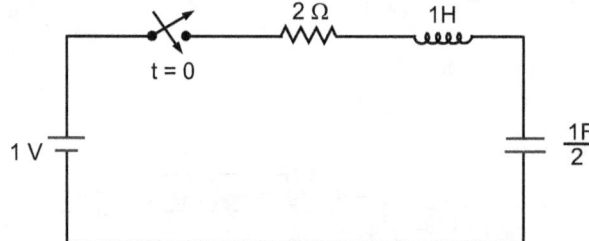

Fig. 3.96: Under-damped circuit

For $t > 0$, loop equation will be

$$2\int i(t)\, dt + 1\frac{di}{dt} + 2i(t) = 1 \qquad \ldots(1)$$

Differentiating this equation gives

$$\frac{d^2i}{dt^2} + 2\frac{di}{dt} + 2i = 0$$

The characteristic equation becomes

$$S^2 + 2S + 2 = 0 \qquad \ldots(3.48)$$

Roots of this equation are

$$S_1, S_2 = \frac{-2 \pm \sqrt{4 - 4 \times 1 \times 2}}{2 \times 1} = \frac{-2 \pm \sqrt{-4}}{2}$$

$$= -1 + J1$$

Thus $\quad S_1 = -1 + J1$ and $S_2 = -1 - J1$

With these roots, the general solution of the equation becomes

$$i(t) = k_1 e^{-S_1 t} + k_2 e^{-S_2 t}$$

$$= k_1 e^{(-1 + J1)t} + k_2 e^{(-1 - J1)t}$$

Thus $\quad i(t) = e^{-t}[k_1 e^{Jt} + k_2 e^{-Jt}] \quad \ldots(3.49)$

By using "Eulers identity" which is given as

$$e^{\pm J\omega t} = \cos \omega t \pm J \sin \omega t$$

We have $\quad e^{\pm Jt} = \cos t \pm J \sin t$

Hence equation (3.49) becomes,

$$i(t) = e^{-t}[k_1 (\cos t + J \sin t) + k_2 \cos t - J \sin t)]$$

$$= e^{-t}[(k_1 + k_2) \cos t + J(k_1 - k_2) \sin t]$$

Thus $\quad i(t) = e^{-t}[k_3 \cos t + k_4 \sin t] \quad \ldots(3.50)$

where $\quad k_3 = k_1 + k_2$ and k_4

$$= J(k_1 - k_2)$$

Value of the constant k_3 and k_4 can be using initial conditions.

At $t = 0$, we know that $i(t) = i(0) = 0 = k_3$

Also by equation (1) we have

at $\quad t = 0, \quad \left.\frac{di}{dt}\right|_{t=0} = \frac{1}{1}$

$$= 1 \text{ A/sec}$$

Now, differentiating equation (3.50) we have

$$\frac{di(t)}{dt} = \frac{d}{dt}[e^{-t} k_4 \sin t]$$

$$= k_4 [e^{-t} \cos t - e^{-t} \sin t]$$

At $t = 0$, $\quad \dfrac{di(t)}{dt} = k_4 = 1$

Thus $\quad \boxed{k_4 = 1}$

Hence, particular solution of the current is

$$i(t) = e^{-t} \sin t \quad \ldots(3.51)$$

Current waveform i (t) as given by above equation is known as *'Damped sinusoidal'* and is as shown below

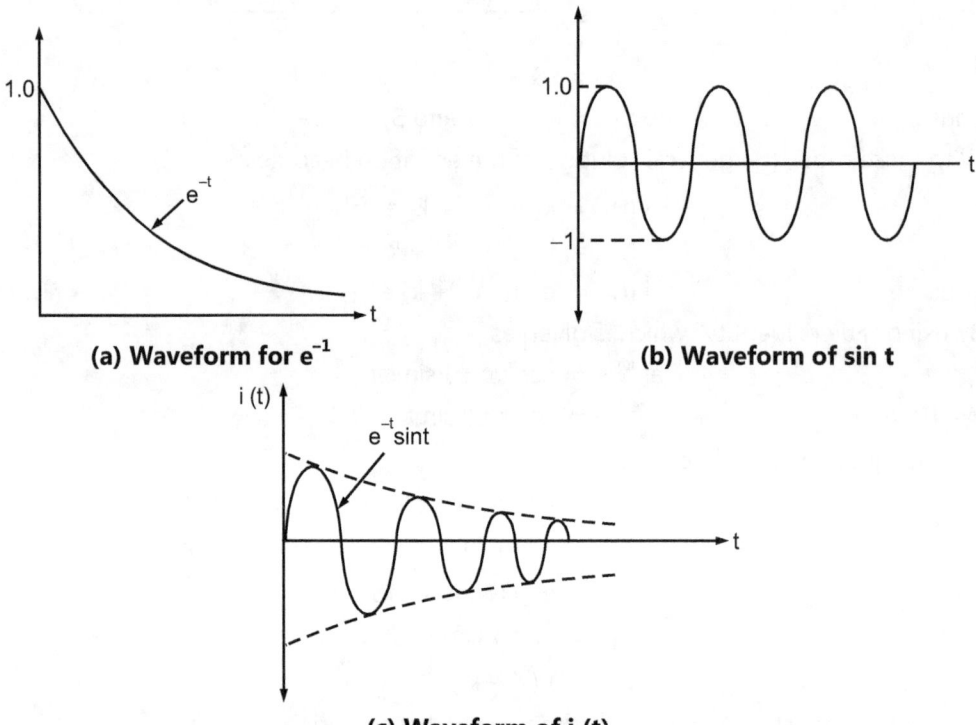

(a) Waveform for e^{-1}

(b) Waveform of sin t

(c) Waveform of i (t)

Fig. 3.97: Waveform of I (t) is a product of two waveform shown in (a) and (b)

Case IV: When roots of the equation are imaginary: This is a special case of complex root in which a_1 is zero. This corresponds to the zero resistance (R = 0) in the R-L-C circuit. Consider the circuit as shown in Fig. 3.98 below.

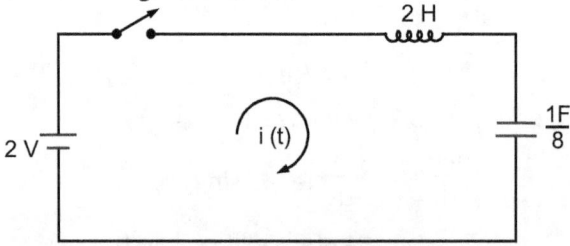

Fig. 3.98: Oscillatory circuit

When switch is closed at t = 0, then KVL across the loop gives

$$8 \int i \, dt + 2 \frac{di}{dt} = 2 \qquad \ldots(1)$$

Differentiating

$$8i + 2 \frac{d^2 i}{dt^2} = 0$$

Characteristic equation becomes
$$2S^2 + 8 = 0$$
OR
$$S^2 + 4 = 0$$

Roots of equation are $\quad S_1, S_2 = \sqrt{-4} = \pm J2$

Thus $\quad \boxed{S_1 = -S_2 = J2}$

Thus roots *are equal, and imaginary.* The solution will be
$$i(t) = k_1 e^{J2t} + k_2 e^{-J2t}$$
$$= k_1 [\cos 2t + j \sin 2t] + k [\cos 2t - J \sin 2t]$$

Thus $\quad i(t) = (k_1 + k_2) \cos 2t + J(k_1 - k_2) \sin 2t$

OR $\quad i(t) = k_3 \cos 2t + k_4 \sin 2t \quad$ ...(3.52)

where $\quad k_3 = k_1 + k_2$

and $\quad k_4 = J(k_1 - k_2)$

Constants k_3, k_4 are fond using the initial conditions.

At $t = 0$, $\quad i(0) = 0 = k_3$ thus $k_3 = 0$

Also by (1) we have $\quad \left.\dfrac{di}{dt}\right|_{t=0} = \dfrac{2}{2} = 1$ Amp/sec

Differentiating $\quad \left.\dfrac{di}{dt}\right|_{t=0} = k_4 \cdot 2 \cos 2t \Big|_{t=0} = 2k_4 = 1$

Hence equation (3.52) we have
$$k_4 = \dfrac{1}{2}$$

Thus the particular solution for the current i (t) is
$$i(t) = \dfrac{1}{2} \sin 2t \quad \text{...(3.53)}$$

Current waveform as given by (3.53) is purely sinusoidal and is given as shown in Fig. 3.99.

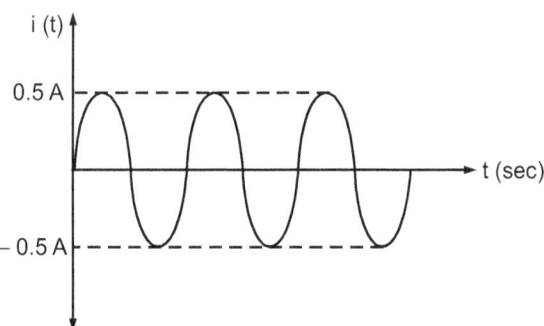

Fig. 3.99: Sinusoidal (oscillatory) waveform as represented by i (t)

Table 3.1 shown (on next page) will summerises four possible cases of the characteristic equation $a_0 S^2 + a_1 S + a_2 = 0$ where a_0, a_1 and a_2 are real and non-negative.

Ex. 3.33: In the network shown switch k is closed and steady state is reached. At t = 0, switch is opened. Find an expression for the current in the inductor $i_2(t)$.

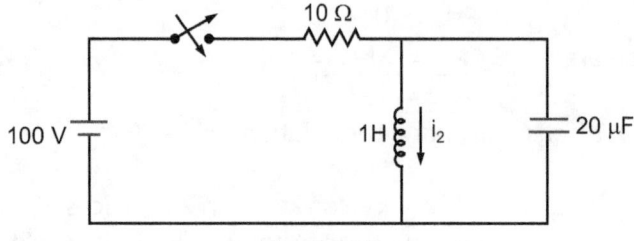

Fig. 3.100

Sol.: When switch is closed and steady state is reached (For t < 0) then inductor acts as a short circuit. Hence current through inductor is

Table 3.1: Characteristic equation is $a_0 S^2 + a_1 S + a_2 = 0$

Case	Coefficient condition	Nature of Roots	Type of circuit	Form of solution	Response
I	$a_1^2 > 4 a_0 a_2$	Negative, Real and unequal	Over damped circuit	$i = k_1 e^{S_1 t} + k_2 e^{S_2 t}$	i(t) curve rising then decaying
II	$a_1^2 = 4 a_0 a_2$	Negative, real and equal	Critical damped circuit	$i = k_1 e^{S_1 t} + k_2 t e^{S_1 t}$	i(t) curve rising then decaying
III	$a_1^2 < 4 a_0 a_2$	Complex and conjugate (Real part is negative)	Under damped circuit	$i = e^{-\delta t}[k_3 \cos \omega t + k_4 \sin \omega t]$	i(t) damped oscillation
IV	$a_1 = 0$ $a_2 \neq 0$ $a_0 \neq 0$	Conjugate imaginary	Oscillatory circuit	$i = i_2 \cos \omega t + k_2 \sin \omega t$ $S_1, S_2 = \pm J\omega$	i(t) sustained oscillation

$$i_L(0) = I_0 \frac{100}{10} = 10 \text{ Amp.}$$

For t ≥ 0 the circuit will be as shown below

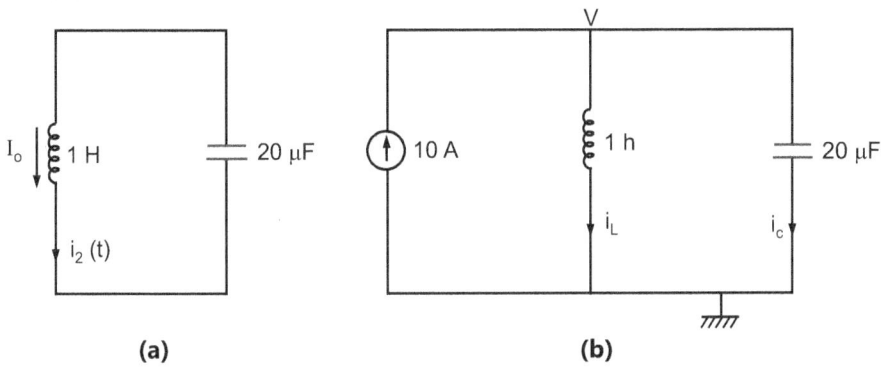

Fig. 3.101

KCL at 'v' gives $\quad i_L + i_c = -10$

$$C\frac{dv}{dt} + \frac{1}{L}\int v\, dt = -10$$

$$20 \times 10^{-6} \times \frac{dv}{dt} + \frac{1}{1}\int v\, dt = -10 \quad \ldots(a)$$

OR $\qquad 20 \times 10^{-6} \dfrac{d^2v}{dt^2} + v = 0 \quad \ldots(b)$

Hence characteristic equation is $S^2 + \dfrac{1}{20 \times 10^{-6}} = 0$

Hence $\qquad S_1, S_2 = J\, 223.6$

Thus roots are *imaginary*. Hence solution will be

$$v(t) = k_1 e^{-J\,223.6\,t} + k_2 e^{-J\,223.6t}$$
$$= (k_1 + k_2)\cos(223.6)t + J[k_2 - k_1]\sin(223.6)t$$

Hence $\qquad v(t) = k_3 \cos 223.6\,t + k_4 \sin 223.6\,t$

at t = 0, $\qquad v(0) = 0 = k_3$

Also at t = 0, $\qquad \left.\dfrac{dv}{dt}\right|_{t=0} = \dfrac{-10}{C} = -0.5 \times 10^6$ V/sec

Hence $\qquad -0.5 \times 10^6 = [k_4\, 223.6 \cos(223.6)\,t]_{t=0}$

Hence $\qquad k_4 = -2236.14$

Thus solution of v(t) is given by

$$v(t) = -2236.14 \sin(223.6)\,t$$

Hence current through inductor for t > 0 is

$$i_2(t) = \frac{1}{L}\int v(t)\,dt = \frac{-2236.1}{1}\int \sin(223.6)\,t$$

$$= \frac{-2236.1}{223.6}[-\cos(223.6)\,t] = \mathbf{10 \cos(223.6)\,t}$$

Ex. 3.34: In the circuit shown in figure circuit is not energised until at t = 0, when switch is closed. Find $v_2(t)$.

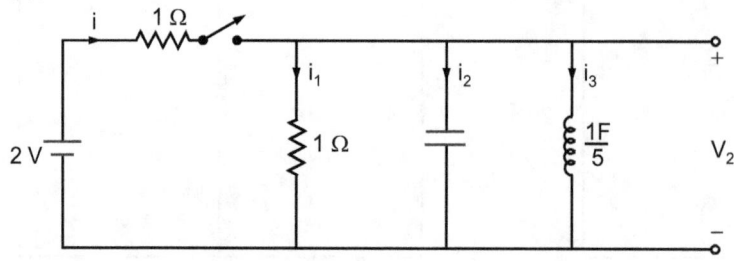

Fig. 3.102

Sol.: When switch is closed at t = 0, KCL gives

$$i_1 + i_2 + i_3 = i$$

$$\frac{v_2}{1} + 1\frac{dv_2}{dt} + 5\int v_2\, dt = \frac{2 - v_2}{1}$$

OR

$$2v_2 + \frac{dv_2}{dt} + 5\int v_2\, dt = 2 \quad \ldots(a)$$

Differentiating above equation gives

$$\frac{d^2v_2}{dt^2} + 2\frac{dv_2}{dt} + 5v_2 = 0$$

Characteristic equation is

$$S^2 + 2S + 5 = 0$$

Roots of this equation are

$$S_1, S_2 = \frac{-2 \pm \sqrt{4 - 4 \times 4}}{2} = \frac{-2 \pm J4}{2} = -1 \pm J2$$

The roots are complex. Hence solution will be

$$v_2(t) = k_1 e^{(-1+J2)t} + k_2 e^{(-1-J2)t}$$
$$= [(k_1 + k_2)\cos 2t + J(k_1 - k_2)\sin 2t]$$

OR
$$v_2(t) = e^{-t}[k_3 \cos 2t + k_4 \sin 2t) \quad \ldots(b)$$

At t = 0, $v_2(0) = 0 = k_3$ thus $\boxed{k_3 = 0}$

By (a) we have $\left.\dfrac{dv_2(t)}{dt}\right|_{t=0} = 2$

Thus $2 = k_4[2e^{-t}\cos 2t - \sin 2t\, e^{-t}]_{t=0} = 2k_4$

Hence $k_4 = 1$

Hence solution for $v_2(t)$ is $v_2(t) = e^{-t}\sin 2t$

Ex. 3.35: In the network switch is opened at t = 0. Find the current through inductor $i_2(t)$ for t ≥ 0.

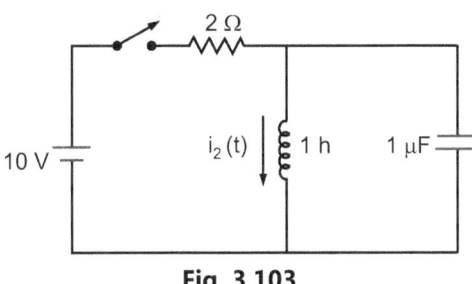

Fig. 3.103

Sol.: This problem is similar to problem (3.33). But we shall solve it by using slightly different method. For t < 0, switch was opened which means it was closed for a long time for t < 0. Then inductor acts as a short circuit and current through inductor is $I_0 = \dfrac{10}{2} = +5$ Amp.

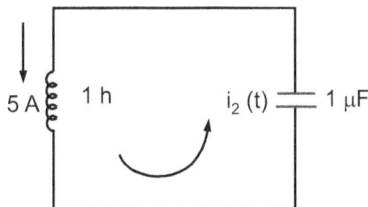

Fig. 3.104: Circuit for t > 0

For t ≥ 0 the circuit will be as shown in Fig. 3.104.

Let i2 (t) be the current in the circuit.

KVL across the loop gives.

$$\dfrac{1}{10^{-6}} \int i_2(t)\, dt + L \dfrac{di_2}{dt} = 0 \qquad \ldots(a)$$

OR $\qquad 10^6 \int i_2(t)\, dt = -\dfrac{di_2}{dt}$

Differentiating above equation gives.

$$\dfrac{d^2 i_2}{dt^2} + 10^6\, i_2(t) = 0 \qquad \ldots(b)$$

Hence, characteristic equation is

$$S^2 + 10^6 = 0 \text{ OR } S_1, S_2 = \pm J10^3$$

Hence, solution of equation (b) is in the form

$$i_2(t) = k_1 e^{-J1000\,t} + k_2 e^{+J\,1000\,t}$$
$$= (k_1 + k_2) \cos 1000\, t + J(k_1 - k_2) \sin 1000t$$

Thus $\qquad i_2(t) = k_3 \cos 1000\, t + k_4 \sin 1000\, t$

Constant k_3, and k_4 are found using initial conditions

at $t = 0$, $\quad i_2(0) = 5 = k_3$

Also by (a) $\quad \dfrac{di_2}{dt}\bigg|_{t=0} = 0 = [k_4\ 1000\cos 1000\ t]_{t=0}$

Hence $\quad \boxed{k_4 = 0}$

Thus, solution for inductor current is

$$i_2(t) = 5\cos 1000\ t$$

Ex. 3.36: In the network shown in Fig. 3.105. If $v_c(0) = 200$ V and $i_c(0) = 10$ A. Find $v_c(t)$ for $t \geq 0$. Assume $L = 2.5$ H, $R - 1\Omega$ and $C = \dfrac{1}{5}$ F.

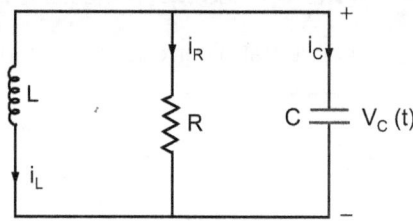

Fig. 3.105

Sol.: Applying KCL gives $i_R + i_C + i_L = 0$

$$\dfrac{v_c}{R} + C\dfrac{dv_c}{dt} + \dfrac{1}{L}\int v_c\ dt = 0$$

$$\dfrac{v_c}{1} + \dfrac{1}{5}\dfrac{dv_c}{dt} + \dfrac{1}{2.5}\int v_c\ dt = 0 \qquad \ldots(a)$$

Differentiating this equation gives

$$\dfrac{1}{5}\dfrac{d^2v_c}{dt^2} + \dfrac{dv_c}{dt} + \dfrac{v_c}{2.5} = 0$$

OR $\quad \dfrac{d^2v_c}{dt^2} + 5\dfrac{dv_c}{dt} + 2v_c = 0 \qquad \ldots(b)$

Characteristic equation is

$$(S^2 + 5S + 2)v_c = 0$$

The roots of the equation are

$$S_1, S_2 = \dfrac{-5 \pm \sqrt{25-8}}{2 \times 1} = \dfrac{-5 \pm 4.12}{2}$$

Hence solution of equation (b) is in the form

$$v_c(t) = k_1\ e^{-0.44\ t} + k_2\ e^{-4.56\ t} \qquad \ldots(c)$$

Value of k_1 and k_2 can be found using initial conditions.

At t = 0, $\quad v_c(0) = 200 = k_1 + k_2$ ...(d)

Also by (a) we have, since $i_c(0) = 10 = C\dfrac{dv_c}{dt}$

Differentiating equation (c) we get

$$\left.\dfrac{dv_c}{dt}\right|_{t=0} = -0.44\,k_1 - 4.56\,k_2 = 50 \quad ...(e)$$

Solving (d) and (c) we get

$$k_2 = 33.4 \text{ and}$$
$$k_1 = 233.4$$

Thus, solution will be $\quad v_c(t) = [233.4\,e^{-0.44\,t} - 33.4\,e^{-4.56\,t}]$ Volts

---

RECAP

1. R-C, and R-L circuits gives first order differential equation with constant coefficients.
2. Voltage and current relationship in a capacitor is given by –

$$i_c = C\dfrac{dv_c}{dt} \text{ and } v_c = V_0 + \dfrac{1}{C}\int i\,dt$$

3. Current through capacitor flows only when the voltage across it is changing, for d.c. voltage $\dfrac{dv}{dt} = 0$. Hence capacitor acts as a open circuit.

4. In a capacitor voltage cannot change instantaneously while current can change instantaneously.

5. Energy stored in capacitor is $\dfrac{1}{2}C\,v_c^2$ Where v_c is the voltage at that instant.

6. A capacitor acts as a linear element and hence superposition theorem can be applied to it, if and only if it is not initially charged ($V_0 = 0$).

7. If a capacitor (C) with initial voltage V_0 is connected to a resistor of R ohms at t = 0, then voltage across capacitor at any instant of time t ≥ 0 is given by $v_c(t) = V_0\,e^{-t/RC}$ and current through capacitor is $i_c(t) = -\dfrac{V_0}{R}\,e^{-t/T}$.

8. T = RC is called time constant of RC circuit which is time that RC circuit takes in order to reduce voltage to 0.37 time initial voltage (V_0).

9. If a capacitor (C) with initial Vo is driven by a voltage source of V volts connected to it through a resistor of R ohms at t = 0, then for any time t ≥ 0, the voltage cross capacitor = $v_c(t) = V + (V_0 - V)\,e^{-t/RC}$ and current through capacitor = $i_c(t) = (v_0 - v)\,e^{-t/RC}$ if $i_c(t)$ to +ve then capacitor charges and if $i_c(t)$ is – ve then capacitor discharges.

10. Voltage and current relationship in a inductor is given by

$$v_L = L \frac{di_L}{dt} \text{ and } i_L = I_o + \frac{1}{L} \int v_L \, dt$$

11. Voltage across inductor exists only when current through it is changing. For d.c. $\frac{di}{dt}$ is zero. Hence inductor acts as short circuit.

12. In inductor current cannot change instantaneously, while voltage can change instaneously.

13. Energy stored in an inductor is $\frac{1}{2} L i_L^2$, where i_L is the current in the inductor at that instant.

14. An inductor acts as a linear elements and hence, superposition theorem can be applied to it, if and only if it is not energised initially ($I_o = 0$)

15. If an inductor with initial current I_o (corresponding to energy stored $\left(\frac{1}{2} L \cdot I_o^2\right)$ is connected to a resistor of RΩ at t = 0, then current through Inductor at any instant of time t ≥ 0 is given by –

$$i(t) = I_o e^{-t/T} = I_o e^{-\frac{R}{L}t}$$

and the voltage across inductor is $v_L(t) = -R I_o e^{-t/T}$

16. $T = \frac{L}{R}$ is called time constant of R-L circuit which is the time R-L circuit takes in order to reduce initial current to 0.37 I_o.

17. If an inductor with initial current of Io is driven by a voltage source of V volts connected to it through a resistor of R ohms at t = 0, then for any time t ≥ 0 current through inductor is given by

$$i_L(t) = \frac{V}{R} + \left(I_o - \frac{V}{R}\right) e^{-t/T}$$

and voltage across inductor = $v_L(t) = (V - R I_o) e^{-\frac{R}{L}t}$. It $v_L(t)$ is positive the inductor is energising. If $v_L(t)$ is negative, then inductor is de-energising.

18. R-L-C circuit gives linear differential equation of second order with constant coefficients.

19. Solution of second order LDE consists of two parts complementary solution and particular integral.

20. If the input is a step voltage (d.c. voltage) then second order LDE will be having forcing function as zero. Such equation is called as the homogeneous LDE. In this case, the particular integral as zero. Complimentary solution is of four types depending upon the nature of the roots characteristic equation.

MULTIPLE CHOICE QUESTIONS (MCQs)

1. A circuit having constant source is said to be in steady state if the
   (a) currents do not change with time
   (b) voltage do not change with time
   (c) current and voltage do not change with time
   (d) current and voltage changes with time.

2. In steady state
   (a) Amplitude of sinusoid never changes
   (b) Frequency of sinusoid never changes
   (c) Amplitude and frequency of sinusoid changes
   (d) Amplitude and frequency of sinusoid never changes

3. The behaviour of the voltage or current when it is changed from one state to another state is called as
   (a) Steady state   (b) Transient state
   (c) Overdamped state   (d) Underdamped state

4. The time taken for the circuit to change from one steady state to another steady state is called as
   (a) Steady time   (b) Transient time
   (c) Response time   (d) Natural response time

5. A circuit containing storage elements which are independent of sources, the response depends upon the nature of the circuit and is called as
   (a) Transient response   (b) Steady state response
   (c) Natural response   (d) Forced response

6. The response changes with time and gets saturated after some time in a circuit called as
   (a) Transient response   (b) Steady state response
   (c) Natural response   (d) Forced response

7. The response of a circuit depends on the nature of source or sources acting in circuit this response is called as
   (a) Transient response   (b) Steady state response
   (c) Natural response   (d) Forced response

8. In a RL circuit, the time constant of a function $\frac{V}{R} e^{-\left(\frac{R}{L}\right)t}$ is the time at which the exponent of e is
   (a) zero   (b) unity
   (c) infinity   (d) none of these

9. In a RL circuit equation the steady state part is
   (a) $\frac{V}{R}\left[1 - e^{\left(-\frac{R}{L}t\right)}\right]$
   (b) $\frac{V}{R} e^{\left(-\frac{R}{L}t\right)}$
   (c) $\frac{V}{R}$
   (d) None of these

10. In a RL circuit equation, the transient part is

    (a) $\dfrac{V}{R}\left[1-e^{\left(-\frac{R}{L}t\right)}\right]$
    (b) $\dfrac{V}{R}\left[-\frac{R}{L}t\right]$
    (c) $\dfrac{V}{R}$
    (d) None of these

11. The time constant in a RL circuit is

    (a) $T = \dfrac{L}{R}$
    (b) $T = \dfrac{R}{L}$
    (c) $T = RL$
    (d) None of these

12. In a RL circuit, at a one time constant the transient term reaches ...... percent of its initial value.

    (a) 36.8
    (b) 63.2
    (c) 67.2
    (d) None of these

13. In a RL circuit, at Five time constant the transient term reaches ...... percent of its initial value.

    (a) 36.8
    (b) 13.5
    (c) 4.98
    (d) 0.67

14. In a RL circuit, the transient part reached more than ...... percent of its final value after five time constant.

    (a) 25
    (b) 50
    (c) 99
    (d) None of these

15. In a RC circuit, the time constant is

    (a) $\dfrac{R}{C}$
    (b) $\dfrac{C}{R}$
    (c) RC
    (d) None of these

16. A series RL circuit shown in Fig. Determine the current at t = 0.

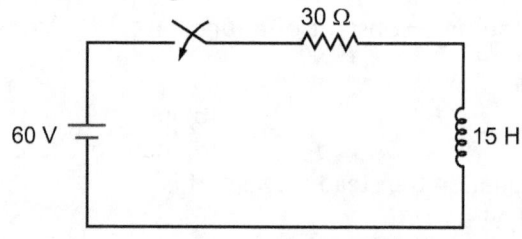

    (a) infinity
    (b) zero
    (c) $\dfrac{60}{30 + j15}$
    (d) None of these

17. A series RC circuit shown in Fig. below. Determine the current in the circuit in the circuit at t = 0.

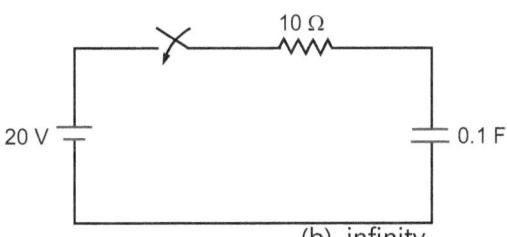

(a) zero
(b) infinity
(c) 2A
(d) $\dfrac{20}{10 - j\,0.1}$

18. In a RC circuit, the transient part in equation is
    (a) $V(1 - e^{-t/RC})$
    (b) V
    (c) $V - e^{-t/RC}$
    (d) None of these

19. In a RC circuit equation, the steady state part is
    (a) $V(1 - e^{-t/RC})$
    (b) V
    (c) $V \cdot e^{-t/RC}$
    (d) None of these

20. After a five time constant, the transient part of RC circuit reaches more than ...... its final value
    (a) 25
    (b) 50
    (c) 99
    (d) None of these

21. In the circuit shown in Fig. determine the current, when switch is closed at t = 0.

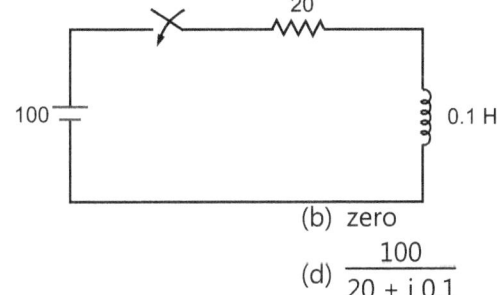

(a) inifinity
(b) zero
(c) 5
(d) $\dfrac{100}{20 + j\,0.1}$

22. In the circuit shown in Fig. determine the current when switch is S closed at t = 0.

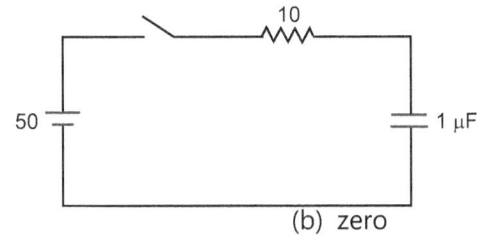

(a) infinity
(b) zero
(c) S
(d) $\dfrac{50}{10 - j1 \times 156}$

23. For the circuit shown in fig. Find the current when the switch is at position 1 t = 0.

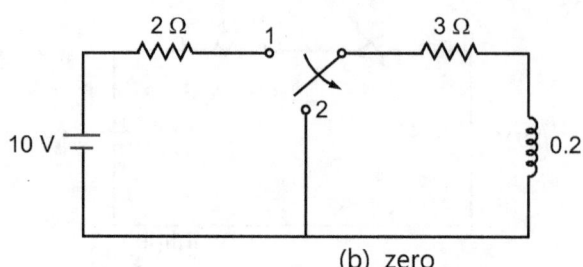

(a) infinity
(b) zero
(c) 2
(d) $\dfrac{10}{5 + j0.2}$

24. For the circuit shown in Fig. find the current at t = 0⁺, when the switch is changed to position 2.

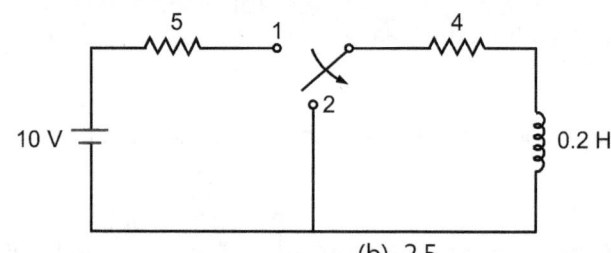

(a) 2
(b) 2.5
(c) 1.1
(d) $\dfrac{10}{9 + j\,0.2}$

25. The inductor acts as ...... for dc voltages.
    (a) open circuit
    (b) no change
    (c) no change
    (d) none of these

26. The capacitor acts as ...... for dc voltages.
    (a) short circuit
    (b) open circuit
    (c) No change
    (d) None of these

27. For the circuit shown in Fig., find the current at t = 0⁺, the switch is opened at t = 0.

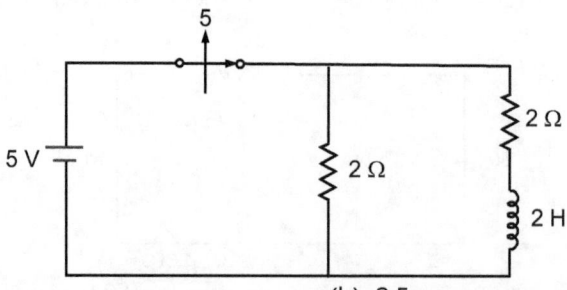

(a) 5
(b) 2.5
(c) zero
(d) none of these

28. For the circuit shown in Fig. obtain the current through 10Ω resistor, at t = 0⁻, just before switch S is opened.

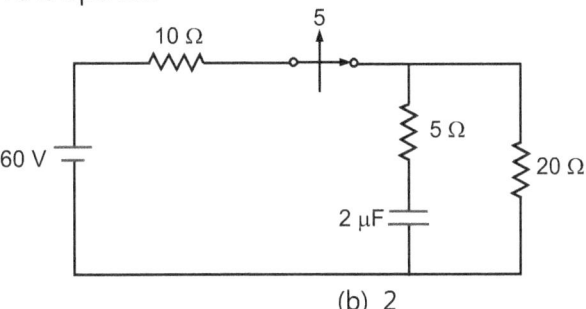

(a) 4
(b) 2
(c) zero
(d) None of these

29. For the circuit shown in Fig., find the current through the 4Ω resistor at t (0⁺). When the switch is opened at t = 0.

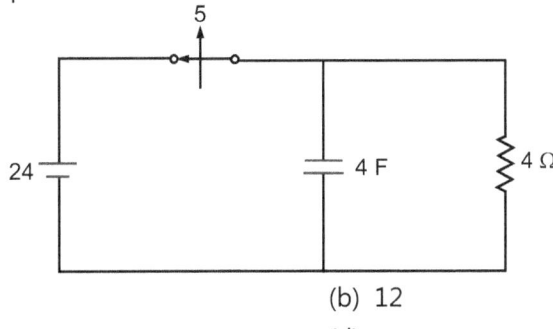

(a) 3
(b) 12
(c) 6
(d) zero

30. For the circuit shown in Fig., the switch is closed at t = 0. Find the current at t = 0⁺. Flowing in the circuit.

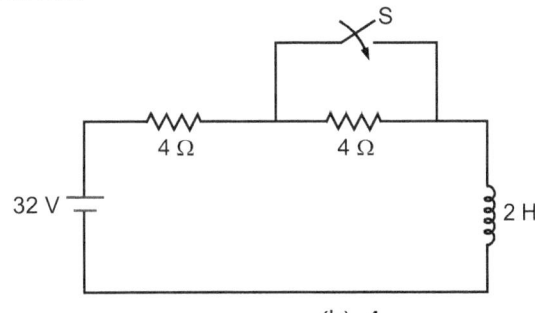

(a) 5.33
(b) 4
(c) 8
(d) zero

31. A capacitor does not allow sudden changes in
(a) voltages
(b) currents
(c) both currents and voltages
(d) None of these

32. A inductor does not allow sudden changes in
    (a) voltages
    (b) currents
    (c) both voltage and current
    (d) None of these
33. The transient response occurs in
    (a) resistive circuits
    (b) capacitive circuits
    (c) inductive circuits
    (d) both inductive and capacitive circuits
34. In Fig. the circuit which is assumed to be in steady state before the operation of the switch S. Determine the current at t = 0⁺ when switch is closed at t = 0.

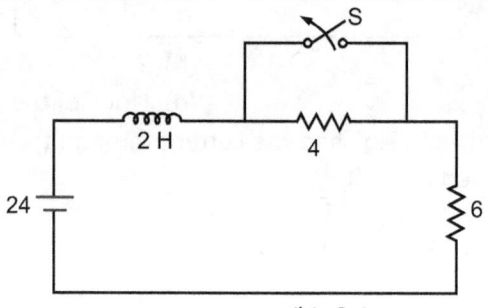

    (a) 4
    (b) 2.4
    (c) 6
    (d) None of these
35. Determine the current through the inductor at t = 0⁺ for the circuit shown in Fig.

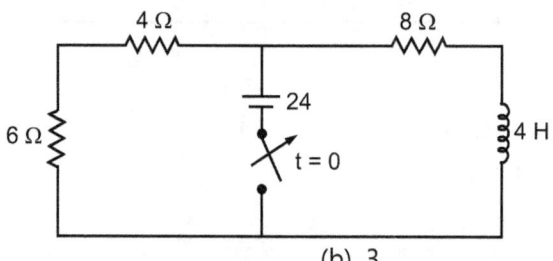

    (a) 2.4
    (b) 3
    (c) 2
    (d) None of these
36. The circuit shown in figure. The current flowing through the inductor before switching is equal to

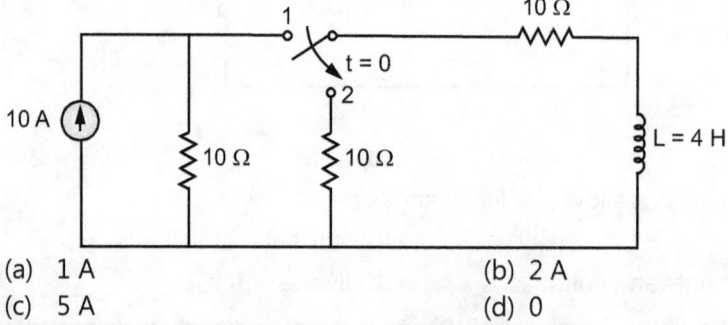

    (a) 1 A
    (b) 2 A
    (c) 5 A
    (d) 0

37. The circuit shown in figure. The voltage across inductor after switch is equal to

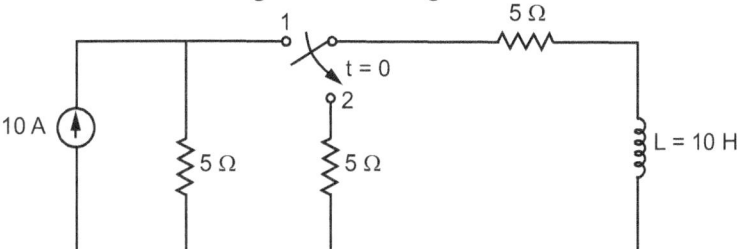

   (a) 5 V
   (b) 10 V
   (c) 15 V
   (d) none of these

38. For a suddenly applied energy source to capacitor it acts as
   (a) open circuit
   (b) short circuit
   (c) constant
   (d) no change

39. The figure shows the steady state circuit. The current through the inductor in steady state condition is equal to

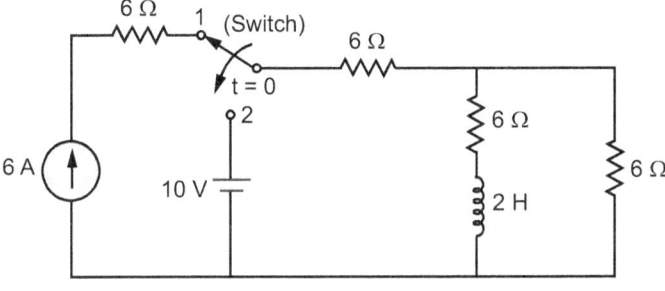

   (a) 1.33 A
   (b) 6 A
   (c) 3 A
   (d) none of these

40. The switch S showm in figure is kept open for long time and then it is closed at time t = 0. The current flowing through the capacitor at t = 0 is equal to

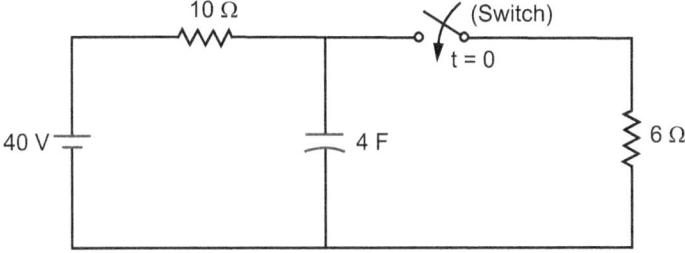

   (a) 4 A
   (b) 15 A
   (c) 3.75 A
   (d) 6.67 A

41. The correct plot of current versus time for series RL circuit is

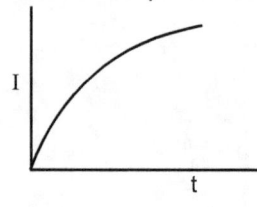
(a)

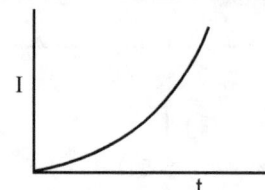
(b)

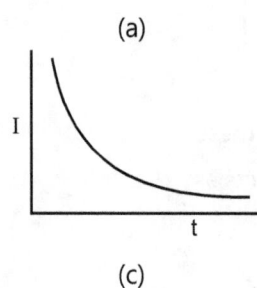
(c)

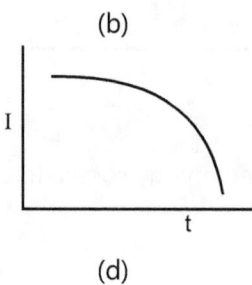
(d)

42. A coil having 10 Ω resistor and 14 H inductance is connected across a supply voltage of 140 V. The value of current at t = 0.4 sec. is equal to
   (a) 10 A
   (b) 14 A
   (c) 3.479 A
   (d) 0.783

43. For a suddenly applied voltage to inductor is equivalent to
   (a) short circuit
   (b) open circuit
   (c) constant
   (d) none of these

44. The correct plot of current versus time for RC circuit is

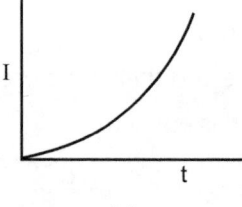
(a)

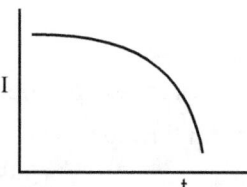
(b)

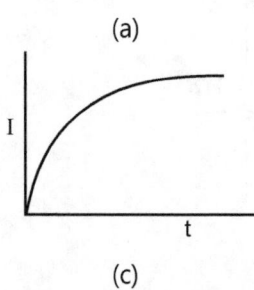
(c)

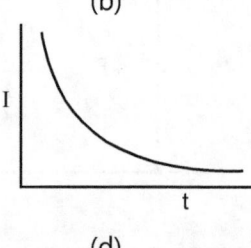
(d)

45. The current flowing through 100 Ω resistor after switch 'S' is closed at time t = 0 is equal to

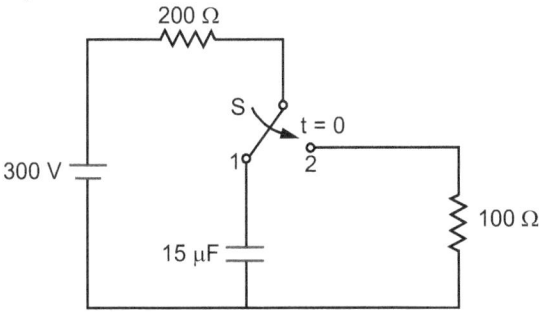

(a) 1.5 A (b) 1 A
(c) 3 A (d) none of these

46. The switch in the circuit is moved from position 1 to position 2 at t = 0 in the network shown in figure. The voltage across capacitor at t = 0^+ is equal to

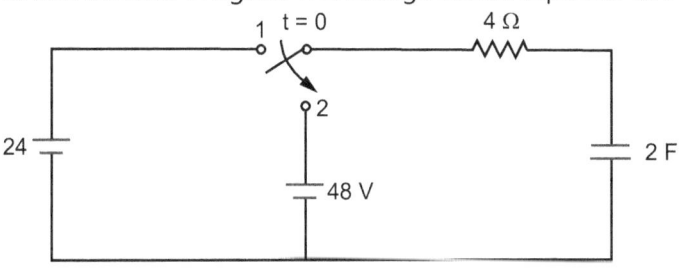

(a) 18 V (b) 24 V
(c) 04 V (d) 48 V

47. A network shown in figure, the switch is closed at t = 0. The current i at t = 0^+ is equal to

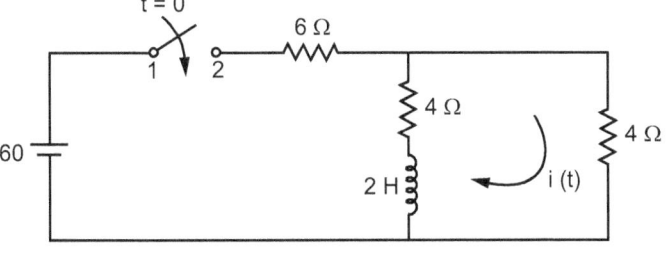

(a) 10 A (b) 7.5
(c) 7.5 A (d) none of these

48. A network shown in figure, the switch is opened at t = 0, the voltage across the capacitor at t = 0⁺ is equal to

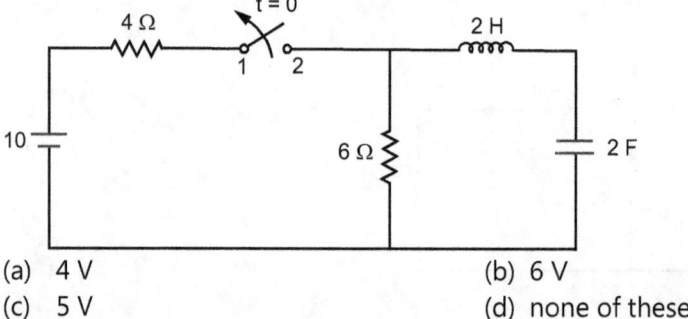

(a) 4 V (b) 6 V
(c) 5 V (d) none of these

49. A network shown in figure, the switch is moved from position 1 to position 2 at t = 0, the voltage V(t) at t = 0⁺ is equal to

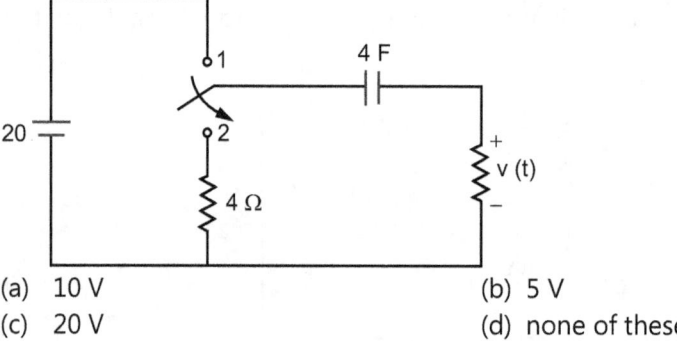

(a) 10 V (b) 5 V
(c) 20 V (d) none of these

50. In RL circuit, the time constant is equal to

(a) $\dfrac{L}{R}$ (b) $\dfrac{R}{L}$

(c) LR (d) none of these

51. A network shown in figure, the switch is initially open but closed at t = 0, steady state occurs before the operation of switch, the current i(t) at t = 0⁺ is equal to

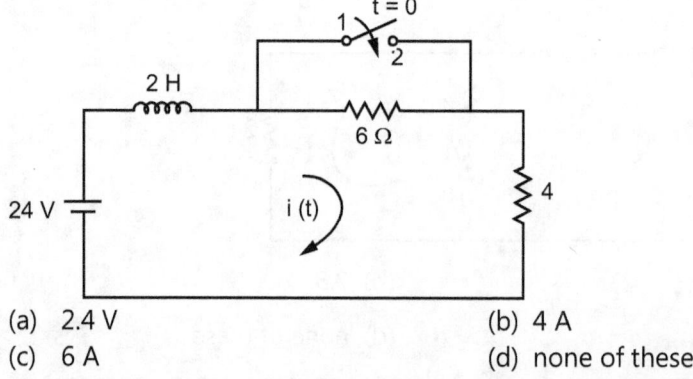

(a) 2.4 V (b) 4 A
(c) 6 A (d) none of these

52. A network shown in figure, the switch is moved from position 1 to position 2 at t = 0, the current i(t) through the inductor at t = 0⁺ is equal to

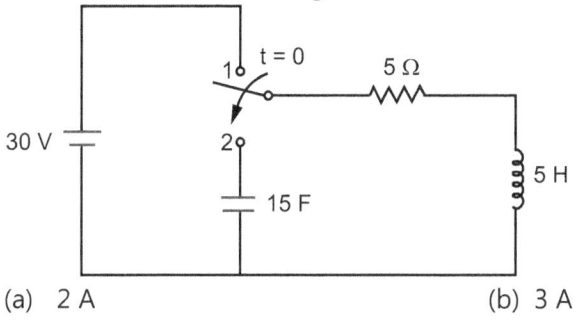

    (a) 2 A   (b) 3 A
    (c) 6 A   (d) 0 A

53. In RC network, the time constant τ is equal to
    (a) $\dfrac{R}{C}$ (b) $\dfrac{C}{R}$
    (c) RC   (d) none of these

54. In network shown in figure, the switch is closed at t = 0, the voltage V(t) at t = 0⁺ is equal to

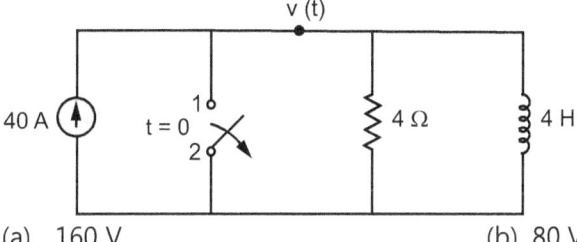

    (a) 160 V   (b) 80 V
    (c) 0 V   (d) none of these

55. A series RL circuit with R = 30 Ω of L = 30 H has a constant supply voltage V = 30 V applied to t = 0 as shown in figure. The current in an inductor is equal to

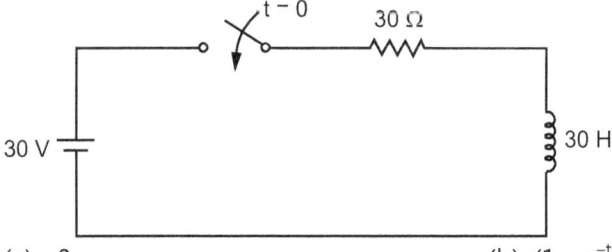

    (a) 0   (b) $(1 - e^{-t})$
    (c) $(1 - e^{-60\,t})$ (d) none of these

56. An inductor with zero initial current looks like _____ at the instant of switching.
    (a) short circuit   (b) open circuit
    (c) 1 A   (d) none of these

57. The voltage across an inductor at the instant switch is closed equal to

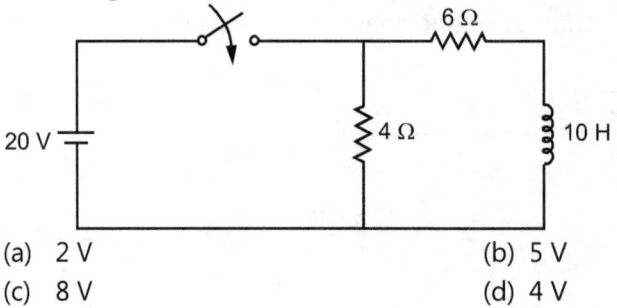

   (a) 2 V
   (b) 5 V
   (c) 8 V
   (d) 4 V

58. The circuit shown in figure. The expression of current i is equal to

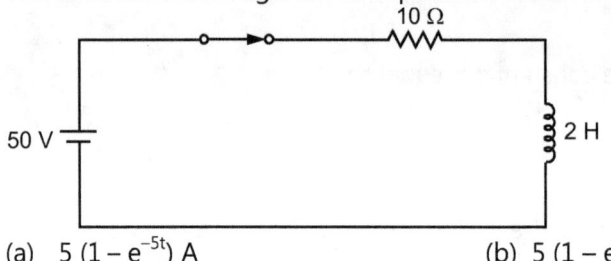

   (a) $5(1-e^{-5t})$ A
   (b) $5(1-e^{20t})$ A
   (c) $4.16(1-e^{-5t})$ A
   (d) none of these

59. The circuit is shown in figure. The switch is closed at t = 0. The current is equal to

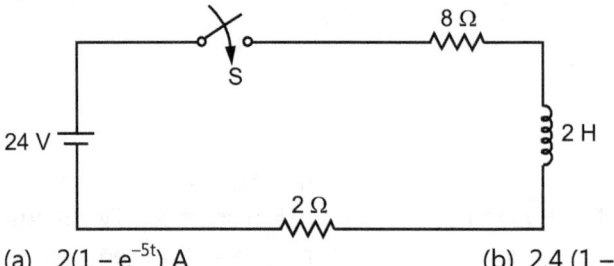

   (a) $2(1-e^{-5t})$ A
   (b) $2.4(1-e^{-5t})$ A
   (c) $3(1-e^{-2t})$ A
   (d) $3(1-e^{-5t})$ A

60. The mathematical equation for the transient behaviour of V_C for the circuit is shown in figure, when the switch is moved to position 1 equal to

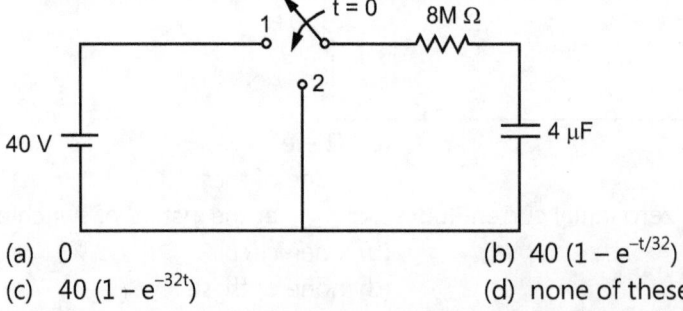

   (a) 0
   (b) $40(1-e^{-t/32})$
   (c) $40(1-e^{-32t})$
   (d) none of these

61. The mathematical expression for the transient behaviour of the voltage across the capacitor as shown in figure. If the switch is move into position 1 at t = 0 equal to

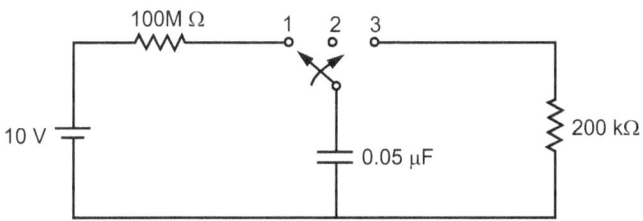

(a) $10(1-e^{-5t})$
(b) $10(1-e^{-10t})$
(c) $10(1-e^{-0.1t})$ A
(d) $10(1-e^{-t/5})$

62. The current through the capacitor if the switch is move into a position 1 at t = 0 equal to

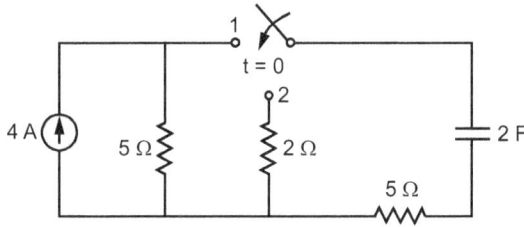

(a) $4(1-e^{-20t})$
(b) $2(1-e^{-t/2})$
(c) $2(1-e^{-t/20})$ A
(d) $4(1-e^{-2t})$

63. The circuit is shown in figure, the switch is closed at t = 0 and the initial voltage across the capacitor $V_c(0^+) = 0$. The voltage across the capacitor at t = 0 is equal to

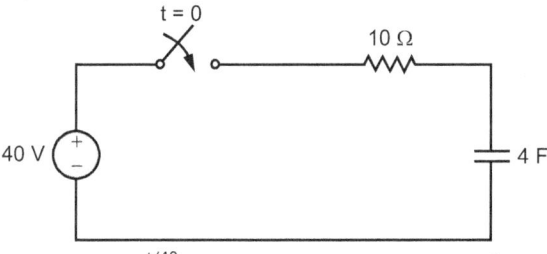

(a) $4(1-e^{-t/40})$
(b) $4(1-e^{-40\,t})$
(c) $4(1-e^{-t/2.5})$
(d) $4(1-e^{-2.5\,t})$

64. A dc voltage of 200 V is suddenly applied to a circuit consisting of a resistor of 20 Ω resistance in series with an inductor having an inductance of 0.5 H. The value of current is equal to

(a) $10(1-e^{-t/25 \times 10^{-3}})$
(b) $10(1-e^{-25 \times 10^{-3}\,t})$
(c) $10(1-e^{-10})$
(d) $10(1-e^{-t/10})$

65. A network shown in figure at t = 0, the switch is opened. The voltage at node V is equal to

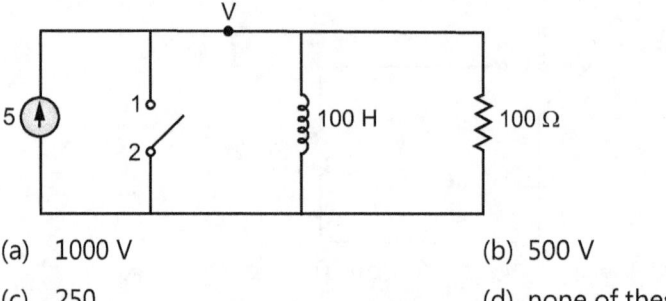

(a) 1000 V
(b) 500 V
(c) 250
(d) none of these

66. The network shown in figure, the switch is moved from the position 1 to the position 2 at t = 0, steady condition reached before switching. The current flowing through the network at t = 0^+ is equal to

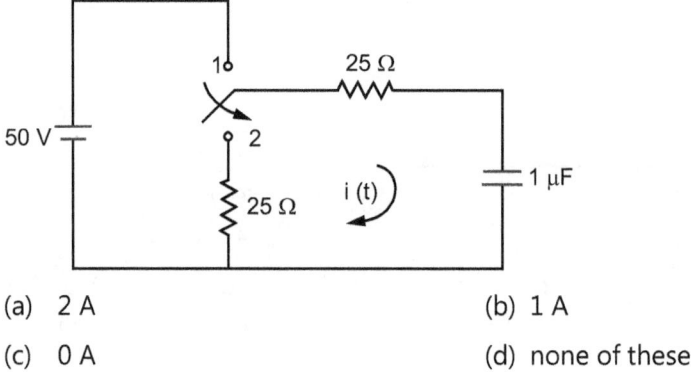

(a) 2 A
(b) 1 A
(c) 0 A
(d) none of these

67. A network is shown in figure, the switch is moved form position 1 to position 2, steady state conditions reached before switching. The current is flowing through the circuit at t = 0^+ is equal to

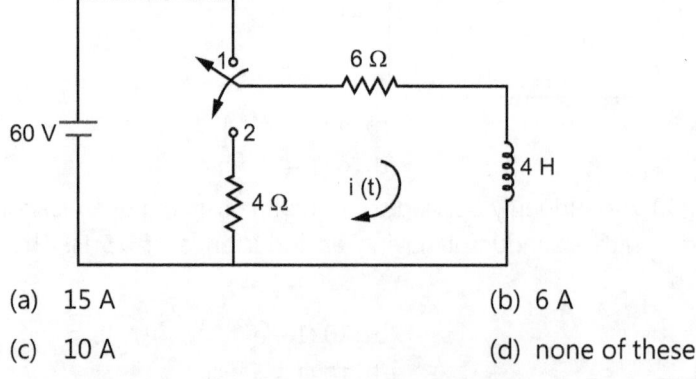

(a) 15 A
(b) 6 A
(c) 10 A
(d) none of these

68. A network shown in figure, the switch is moved from position 1 to position 2 at t = 0, steady state condition reached before switching. The current i flowing through the circuit at t = 0⁺ is equal to

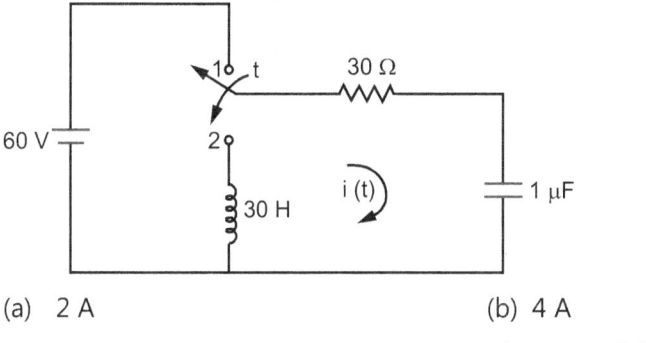

(a) 2 A (b) 4 A
(c) 0 (d) none of these

69. A network shown in figure, the switch is moved from position 1 to the position 2 at t = 0. The current i(t) at t = 0⁺ is equal to

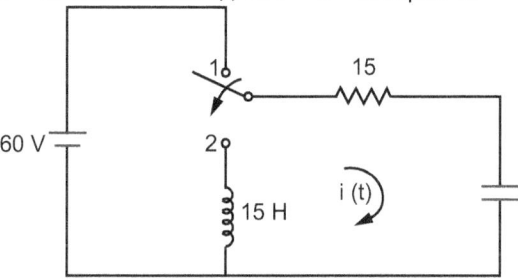

(a) 4 A (b) 2 A
(c) 0 (d) none of these

70. A network shown in figure, the switch is moved from position 1 to position 2 at t = 0, the current i(t) at t = 0⁺ is equal to

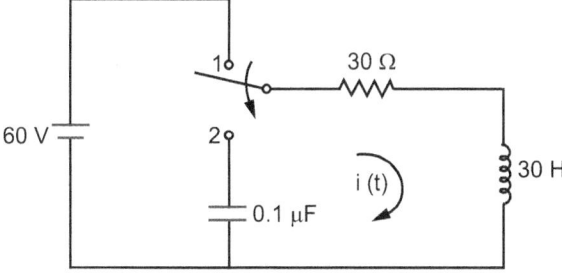

(a) 2 A (b) 1 A
(c) 0 A (d) none of these

71. A network is shown in figure, the switch is closed at t = 0, steady state condition attained at t = 0⁻. The current i(t) at t = 0⁺ is equal to

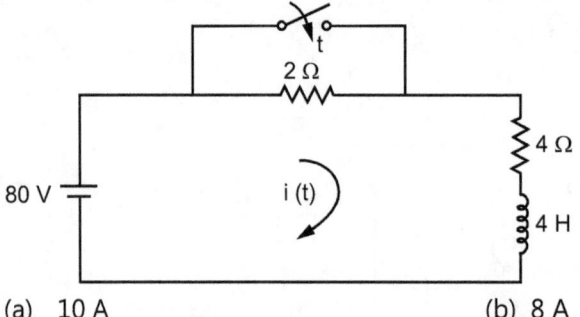

   (a) 10 A
   (b) 8 A
   (c) 13.3
   (d) none of these

72. A network is shown in figure, the switch is closed at t = 0, steady state condition previously attained. The current flowing through an inductor at t = 0⁺ is equal to

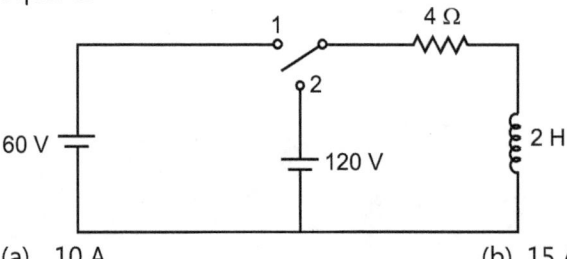

   (a) 10 A
   (b) 15 A
   (c) 20 A
   (d) 30 A

73. A resistor having a resistance of 2 Ω is connected in series with an inductor of 20 H inductance. The initial rise of current is 5 A. The voltage applied is equal to
   (a) 10 V
   (b) 2.5 V
   (c) 100 V
   (d) 50 V

74. A circuit consisting of a resistor having a resistance of 20 Ω in series with an inductor whose inductance is 4 H is fed from a 100 V dc supply. The current in the circuit is equal to
   (a) $5 \cdot e^{-5t}$
   (b) $5 \cdot e^{-t/5}$
   (c) $5(1 - e^{-5t})$
   (d) $5(1 - e^{-t/5})$

75. A circuit consisting of a 2 kΩ resistor is connected in series with an inductor of 8 mH. The input voltage applied to the circuit is 5 V and t = 4 μs. The voltage in an inductor is equal to
   (a) 5 V
   (b) 1.85
   (c) 3.35
   (d) none of these

76. A series RL circuit with R = 50 Ω and L = 10 H has 100 V input voltage applied to circuit at t = 0 by closing of a switch, the current i equal to
    (a) $4(1-e^{-5t})$
    (b) $4(1-e^{-t/5})$
    (c) $2(1-e^{-t/5})$
    (d) $2(1-e^{-5t})$

77. The current flowing through the resistor of the circuit shown in figure when the switch S is closed at t = 0 is equal to

    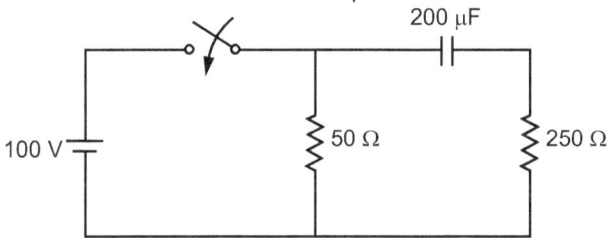

    (a) $4 \cdot e^{-0.5t}$
    (b) $2.5\, e^{-0.5t}$
    (c) $4 \cdot e^{-t/0.5}$
    (d) $2.5 \cdot e^{-t/0.5}$

78. A 20 μF capacitor is connected in series with a 50 kΩ resistor and the circuit is connected to a 20 V dc supply. The initial value of current is equal to
    (a) 4 mA
    (b) 0.4 mA
    (c) 0.147 mA
    (d) none of these

79. A capacitor is charged to 100 V and then discharged through a 50 kΩ resistor. The time constant of the circuit is 0.85. The value of the capacitor is equal to
    (a) 4 μF
    (b) 16 μF
    (c) 8 μF
    (d) none of these

80. A relay has an inductance of 100 mH and resistance of 20 Ω. It is connected to a 200 V dc supply. The final value of current is equal to
    (a) 2 A
    (b) 1 A
    (c) 10 A
    (d) none of these

81. A coil of inductance of 0.04 H and resistance 10 Ω is connected to a 120 V dc supply. The final value of current and time constant are equal to
    (a) 12 A, 4 μs
    (b) 12 A, 0.4 μs
    (c) 12 A, 4 ms
    (d) 12 A, 0.4 ms

82. The winding of an electromagnet has an inductance of 3H, a resistance of 15 Ω and 120 V applied voltage. The steady state value of current and time constant are equal to
    (a) 8 A, 45 sec.
    (b) 40 A, 45 sec.
    (c) 8 A, 5 sec.
    (d) 8 A, 0.2 sec.

8.3 A coil having an inductance of 6 H and a resistance RΩ is connected in series with a resistor of 10 Ω to a 120 V dc supply. The time constant of the circuit is 300 ms. When the steady state condition have been reached, the supply is replaced by short circuit. The resistance of the coil is equal to
(a) 4 Ω
(b) 10 Ω
(c) 6 Ω
(d) none of these

84. A circuit consisting of 5000 Ω and 20 μF elements has 100 V applied voltage at t = 0 with no initial charge at capacitor, the current is equal to
(a) $20 \cdot e^{-10t}$
(b) $20 \cdot e^{-0.1t}$
(c) $0.2\, e^{-10t}$
(d) $2 \cdot e^{-0.1t}$

85. A network is shown in figure, the switch is closed at t = 0. The current at t = 0^+ is equal to

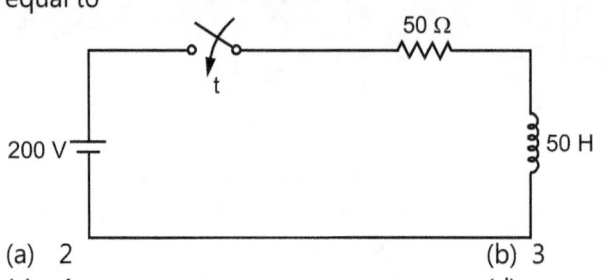

(a) 2
(b) 3
(c) 4
(d) none of these

86. A network is shown in figure, the switch is closed. Assume all initial condition as zero, the voltage across capacitor at t = 0^+ is equal to

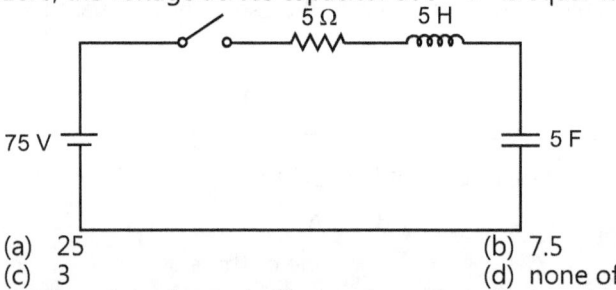

(a) 25
(b) 7.5
(c) 3
(d) none of these

87. A network is shown in figure, the switch is closed at t = 0. The voltage across the capacitor is equal to

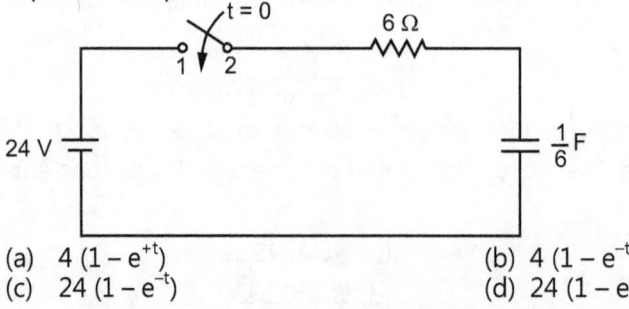

(a) $4(1-e^{+t})$
(b) $4(1-e^{-t})$
(c) $24(1-e^{-t})$
(d) $24(1-e^{+t})$

88. A network is shown in figure, the switch is closed at t = 0, the current i(t) flowing through the circuit is equal to

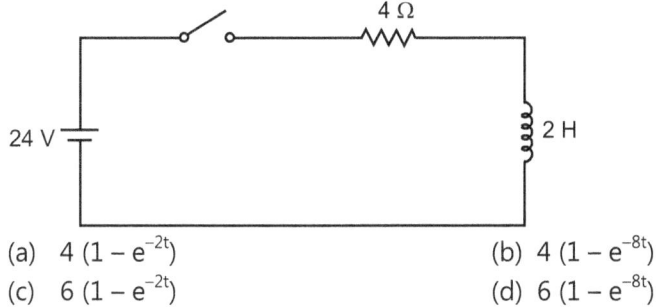

(a) $4(1-e^{-2t})$
(c) $6(1-e^{-2t})$
(b) $4(1-e^{-8t})$
(d) $6(1-e^{-8t})$

ANSWERS

1. (c)	2. (d)	3. (b)	4. (b)	5. (c)	6. (a)	7. (d)	8. (b)	9. (c)	10. (b)
11. (a)	12. (a)	13. (d)	14. (c)	15. (c)	16. (b)	17. (c)	18. (c)	19. (b)	20. (c)
21. (b)	22. (c)	23. (c)	24. (c)	25. (a)	26. (b)	27. (b)	28. (b)	29. (c)	30. (c)
31. (a)	32. (b)	33. (d)	34. (b)	35. (b)	36. (c)	37. (c)	38. (b)	39. (c)	40. (d)
41. (a)	42. (c)	43. (b)	44. (d)	45. (c)	46. (b)	47. (a)	48. (b)	49. (c)	50. (a)
51. (a)	52. (c)	53. (c)	54. (a)	55. (b)	56. (b)	57. (c)	58. (a)	59. (b)	60. (b)
61. (d)	62. (c)	63. (a)	64. (a)	65. (b)	66. (b)	67. (c)	68. (c)	69. (c)	70. ()
71. (c)	72. (b)	73. (c)	74. (a)	75. (b)	76. (d)	77. (c)	78. (b)	79. (b)	80. (c)
81. (c)	82. (d)	83. (b)	84. (c)	85. (c)	86. (d)	87. (b)	88. (c)		

EXERCISE

1. Explain various properties of a capacitor.
2. An capacitor with initial voltage V_o is connected to a resistor of value R ohms at t – 0. Derive the expression for the voltage across capacitor and current through capacitor at any time t > 0.
3. Explain various properties of an inductor.
4. An inductor with initial current I_o is connected to a resistor of R ohms at t = 0. Derive the expression for the current through inductor and voltage across inductor at any time t > 0.
5. The network shown attains steady state initially. At t = 0, switch is closed. Find $v_2(t)$ for t > 0.

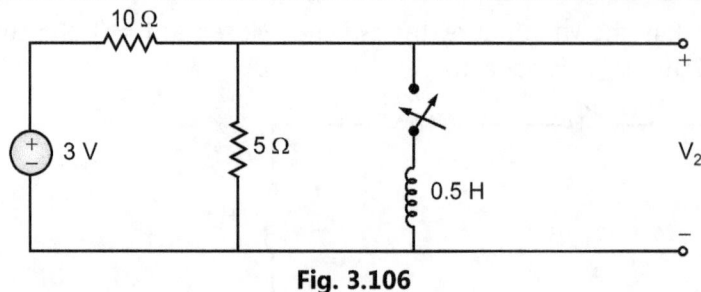

Fig. 3.106

6. Explain time constant in general. Determine the time constant of a source free R–L circuit in which the power output from inductance is 100 W at specific instant of time, and changes by 30 W after 1 sec.

7. Derive the expression for the current i(t) flowing in the circuit shown. i(0) = OA, when the switch is closed at t = 0. Show the behaviour of i(t) graphically.

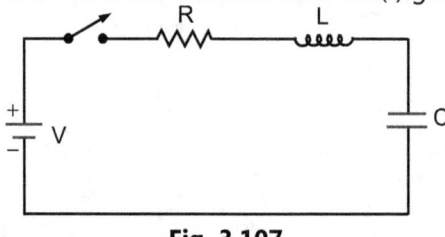

Fig. 3.107

8. In the circuit shown below, assume that the ammeter is ideal. If the initial values of voltage v_c and current i_L are 10V and 4A respectively. Determine the range of the ammeter.

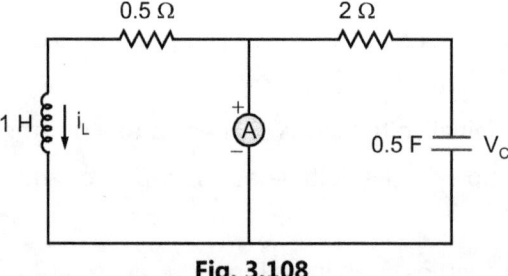

Fig. 3.108

9. A switch is closed at t = 0 connecting a Battery of V voltage with a series R-C circuit.
   (a) Determine the ratio of energy delivered to the capacitor to the total energy supplied by the source as a function of time.
   (b) Show that this ratio approaches 0.5 as t → ∞.

Unit 4

LAPLACE TRANSFORM APPLICATION TO NETWORK

Contents ...

4.1 Introduction
4.2 Laplace Transform
    4.2.1 Method of Transformation
    4.2.2 The Concept of Complex Frequency
    4.2.3 Definition of Laplace Transform
    4.2.4 Properties of Laplace Transform
        4.2.4.1 Linearity
        4.2.4.2 Real Differentiation (Differentiation with respect to Time)
        4.2.4.3 Real Integration (Integration with respect to Time)
        4.2.4.4 Differentiation by s (In the Frequency Domain)
        4.2.4.5 Complex Translation
        4.2.4.6 Real Translation (Shifting Theorem)
        4.2.4.7 Scaling
        4.2.4.8 Scalar Multiplication
        4.2.4.9 Convolution in Time Domain
        4.2.4.10 Applications of Properties of Laplace Transform To Find Laplace Transforms of Typical Functions
        4.2.4.11 The Initial-Value and Final-Value Theorems
    4.3 Inverse Laplace Transform
        4.3.1 Shifting Theorem
        4.3.2 Frequency Multiplication Theorem
        4.3.3 Partial Fraction Expansion
        4.3.4 Use of Convolution Theorem
4.4 Laplace Transform of basic R.L.C. Components
4.5 Standard Input Signals and their Laplace Transform
Multiple Choice Questions (MCQs)
Exercise

4.1 INTRODUCTION

Laplace Transformation method for solving differential equations offers a number of advantages over classical methods. The differential equations specifying performance of complicated networks are rather complex. The solution to such problems is time consuming. Laplace Transformation helps to get solution in a systematic way. This method gives total solution - the particular integral and complementary function in one operation. The initial conditions are automatically specified in the transformed equations.

In the classical methods for solving differential equations, solutions are obtained directly in the time domain. Application of Laplace Transform transforms the differential equations to the frequency domain where the independent variable is complex frequency 's'. Differentiation and integration in the time domain are transformed into algebraic operations. Thus, the solution is obtained by simple algebraic operations in the frequency domain.

4.2 LAPLACE TRANSFORM

4.2.1 Method of Transformation

Fig. 4.1 shows the philosophy of transform methods. It shows the procedure to obtain Sol. of differential equation.

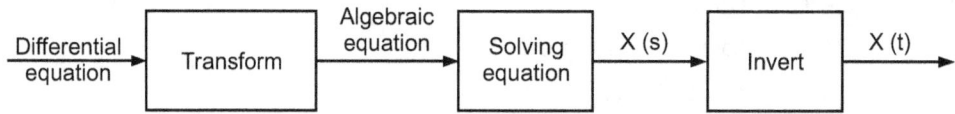

Fig. 4.1: Transform method to solve integro-differential equation

Step I: Consider the linear differential equation

$$y(x(t)) = f(t) \qquad \ldots (a)$$

where
$\quad f(t)$ = Forcing function

$\quad x(t)$ = Unknown variable

$\quad y(x(t))$ = Differential equation

Step II: Transforming both sides of equation (a),

$$T[y(x(t))] = T[f(t)] \qquad \ldots (b)$$

$$Y(X(s), s) = F(s) \qquad \ldots (c)$$

where, $X(s) = T[x(t)]$

$F(s) = T[f(t)]$

$Y(X(s), s)$ = Algebraic equation in s.

Thus, by process of transformation differential equation in time domain are changed to algebraic equations in frequency domain.

Step III: Solve equation (c) algebraically to obtain $X(s)$.

Step IV: Take inverse transformation to obtain

$$x(t) = T^{-1}[X(s)] \qquad \ldots (d)$$

4.2.2 The Concept of Complex Frequency

The solution of the differential equations for networks gives rise to time domain function in the form

$$K_n e^{S_n t} \qquad \ldots (a)$$

where, $S_n = \sigma_n + j\omega_n$

is the complex number defined as the complex frequency,

ω_n is imaginary part of complex frequency interpreted as radian frequency (radians/sec.),

σ_n is real part of complex frequency defined as neper frequency (nepers/sec.).

The radian frequency ω_n appears in time domain equations in the forms $\sin \omega_n t$ or $\cos \omega_n t$.

σ_n appears as an exponential factor $I = I_0 e^{\sigma_n t}$ such that

$$\sigma_n = \frac{1}{t} \ln \frac{I}{I_0}$$

Case I: Let $S_n = \sigma_n + j0$

The exponential function of equation (a) becomes $K_n e^{\sigma_n t}$. It is an exponential function which increases exponentially for $\sigma_n > 0$ and decays exponentially for $\sigma_n < 0$.

When $\sigma_n = 0$; $K_n e^{\sigma_n t} = K_n e^{0t} = K_n$ ... (b)

A time invariant quantity which in terms of current and voltage is described as "direct current".

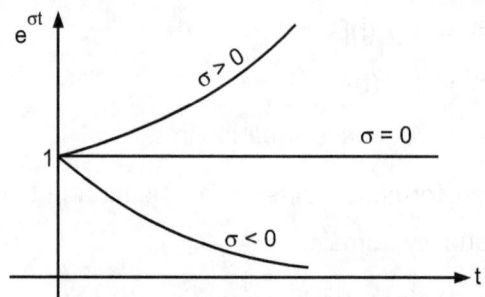

Fig. 4.2: Plot of $e^{\sigma t}$ for positive, negative and zero value of σ

Case II: Let $\quad s_n = 0 \pm j\omega_n$ (radian frequency only)

$\therefore \quad K_n e^{\pm j\omega_n t} = K_n (\cos \omega_n t \pm j \sin \omega_n t) \quad \ldots (c)$

Case III: Let $\quad s_n = \sigma_n + j\omega_n$

$$K_n e^{(\sigma_n + j\omega_n) t} = K_n e^{\sigma_n t} e^{j\omega_n t}$$

$$= K_n e^{\sigma_n t} (\cos \omega_n t + j \sin \omega_n t) \quad \ldots (d)$$

$$\text{Re}\left(e^{s_n t}\right) = e^{\sigma_n t} \cos \omega_n t \quad \ldots (4.1\,(a))$$

$$\text{Im}\left(e^{s_n t}\right) = e^{\sigma_n t} \sin \omega_n t \quad \ldots (4.1\,(b))$$

For $\sigma_n < 0$, waveform is damped sinusoid.
For $\sigma_n > 0$, oscillations increase exponentially.

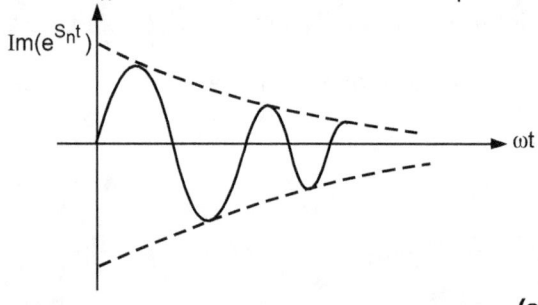 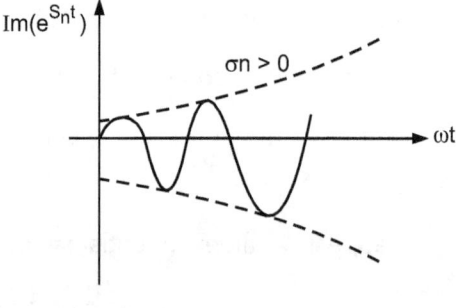

(a)

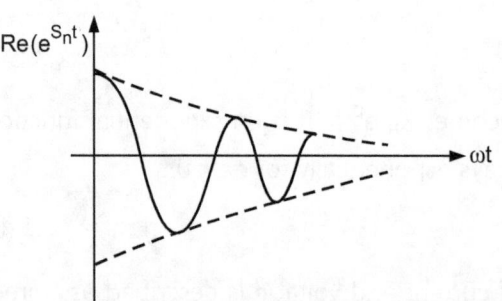 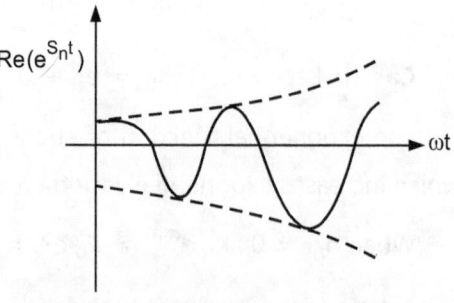

(b)

Fig. 4.3: Real and imaginary projections of rotating phasors ωt

4.2.3 Definition of Laplace Transform

The Laplace Transform of a function of time f (t) is defined as,

$$L[f(t)] = F(s) = \int_0^\infty f(t) e^{-st} dt \quad \ldots (4.2)$$

where, s is the complex frequency variable $s = \sigma + j\omega$

Thus, Laplace Transform converts general time domain function f (t) into a corresponding frequency domain representation F (s).

Ex. 4.1: Find Laplace Transform of unit step function defined as,

$$u(t) = 1; \ t \geq 0$$
$$= 0; \ t < 0$$

Sol.: $f(t) = u(t)$

∴ By definition of Laplace Transform,

$$F(s) = \int_0^\infty u(t) e^{-st} dt$$

$$= \int_0^\infty 1 \cdot e^{-st} dt = \left.\frac{e^{-st}}{-s}\right|_0^\infty$$

$$= 0 - \left(-\frac{1}{s}\right)$$

$$= \frac{1}{s}$$

∴ $$L\, u(t) = \frac{1}{s}$$

Ex. 4.2: Find Laplace Transform of $f(t) = e^{at}$.

Sol.: $f(t) e^{at} u(t)$

By definition of Laplace Transform,

$$F(s) = \int_0^\infty e^{at} e^{-st} dt$$

$$= -\left.\frac{e^{-(s-a)t}}{s-a}\right|_0^\infty$$

$$= \frac{1}{s-a}$$

∴ $$L\, e^{at} u(t) = \frac{1}{s-a}$$

4.2.4 Properties of Laplace Transform

4.2.4.1 Linearity

The transform of a finite sum of time functions is the sum of the transforms of the individual transforms.

i.e. $\quad L\left[\sum_i f_i(t)\right] = \sum_i L[f_i(t)]$

If $f_1(t)$ and $f_2(t)$ are two functions of time and a and b are constants.

Then, $L[a\, f_1(t) + b\, f_2(t)] = a\, F_1(s) + b\, F_2(s)$ ... (4.3)

where, $\quad L\, f_1(t) = F_1(s)$

and $\quad L\, f_2(t) = F_2(s)$

4.2.4.2 Real Differentiation (Differentiation with Respect to Time)

If $\quad L\, f(t) = F(s)$

then, $\quad L\left[\dfrac{d}{dt} f(t)\right] = s\, F(s) - f(0-)$ ... (4.4)

where, $f(0-)$ is the value of $f(t)$ at $t = 0-$ ($t = 0-$ is the time just before $t = 0$).

Similarly for transform of second derivative,

i.e. $\quad L\left[\dfrac{d^2}{dt^2} f(t)\right] = L\left[\dfrac{d}{dt} \cdot \dfrac{d}{dt} f(t)\right]$

$\qquad = s\left[L\dfrac{d}{dt} f(t)\right] - \dfrac{df}{dt}(0-)$

$\qquad = s\,[s\, F(s) - f(0-)] - \dfrac{df}{dt}(0-)$

$\qquad = s^2\, F(s) - s\, f(0-) - \dfrac{df}{dt}(0-)$ ... (4.5)

Hence, general expression for n^{th} derivative is,

$L\dfrac{d^n}{dt^n} f(t) = s^n\, F(s) - s^{n-1} f(0-) - s^{n-2} f'(0-) - \ldots - f^{n-1}(0-)$ ... (4.6)

where, $\quad f'(0-) = \dfrac{d}{dt} f(0-); \quad f^{n-1}(0-) = \dfrac{d^{n-1} f(0-)}{dt^{n-1}}$

This property transforms differential equations in time domain to algebraic equations in the frequency domain.

4.2.4.3 Real Integration (Integration with respect to Time)

If $L f(t) = F(s)$, then the Laplace Transform of the integral of f (t) is F (s) divided by s that is,

$$L\left[\int_0^t f(t)\, dt\right] = \frac{F(s)}{s} \qquad \ldots (4.7)$$

4.2.4.4 Differentiation by s (In the Frequency Domain)

Differentiation by s in the complex frequency domain corresponds to multiplication by t in the time domain that is,

$$L[t\, f(t)] = -\frac{d F(s)}{ds} \qquad \ldots (4.8)$$

4.2.4.5 Complex Translation

By the complex translation property if

$$F(s) = L f(t)$$

then, $\quad F(s-a) = L[e^{at} f(t)] \qquad \ldots (4.9)$

where, a is a complex number.

4.2.4.6 Real Translation (Shifting Theorem)

This theorem transforms a delayed or shifted function of time.

i.e. $\quad F(t) = f(t-a); \; t > a$

$\qquad\qquad = 0; \quad t < a$

Let $\quad L[f(t)] = F(s)$

then, the transform of the function delayed by time a is,

$$L[f(t-a)\, u(t-a)] = e^{-as} F(s) \qquad \ldots (4.10)$$

4.2.4.7 Scaling

If $\quad L f(t) = F(s)$

then, $\quad L[f(at)] = \dfrac{1}{a} F\left(\dfrac{s}{a}\right)$ where, $a > 0 \qquad \ldots (4.11)$

4.2.4.8 Scalar Multiplication

If $\quad L f(t) = F(s)$

then, $\quad L\, k\, f(t) = k\, F(s) \qquad \ldots (4.12)$

4.2.4.9 Convolution in Time Domain

If $f_1(t)$ and $f_2(t)$ are two functions which are zero for $t < 0$, the convolution theorem states that if the transform of $f_1(t)$ is $F_1(s)$ and transform of $f_2(t)$ is $F_2(s)$, then the transform of the convolution of $f_1(t)$ and $f_2(t)$ is the product of the individual transforms $F_1(s) F_2(s)$ that is,

$$L\left[\int_0^t f_1(t-u) f_2(u) \, du\right] = F_1(s) F_2(s) \qquad \ldots (4.13)$$

The integral $\int_0^t f_1(t-u) f_2(u) \, du$ is the convolution integral or folding integral and is denoted operationally as

$$\int_0^t f_1(t-u) f_2(u) \, du = f_1(t) * f_2(t) \qquad \ldots (4.14)$$

This theorem is used to find the inverse transformation.

4.2.4.10 Applications of Properties of Laplace Transform to Find Laplace Transforms of Typical Functions

Ex. 4.3:
$$f(t) = \sin \omega t = \frac{e^{j\omega t} - e^{-j\omega t}}{2j}$$

Sol.: Using property of linearity,

$$L \sin \omega t = \frac{1}{2j}\left[L\, e^{j\omega t} - L\, e^{-j\omega t}\right]$$

$$= \frac{1}{2j}\left[\frac{1}{s-j\omega} - \frac{1}{s+j\omega}\right]$$

$$= \frac{\omega}{s^2 + \omega^2}$$

Ex. 4.4:
$$f(t) = \cos \omega t = \frac{e^{j\omega t} + e^{-j\omega t}}{2}$$

Sol.:
$$L[\cos \omega t] = \frac{1}{2}\left[L\, e^{j\omega t} + L\, e^{-j\omega t}\right]$$

$$= \frac{1}{2}\left[\frac{1}{s-j\omega} + \frac{1}{s+j\omega}\right]$$

$$= \frac{s}{s^2 + \omega^2}$$

Ex. 4.5: The unit ramp function
$$f(t) = t; \quad t > 0$$
$$= 0; \quad t < 0$$

Sol.: By property of Laplace Transform,
$$L[t\,f(t)] = -\frac{dF(s)}{ds}$$

Let
$$f(t) = u(t)$$

∴
$$F(s) = L\,\omega(t) = \frac{1}{s}$$

Hence,
$$L[t\,f(t)] = -\frac{d}{ds}\left(\frac{1}{s}\right)$$
$$= \frac{1}{s^2}$$

Ex. 4.6: The unit impulse function is given by
$$\delta(t) = 1; \quad t = 0$$
$$= 0; \quad \text{for all other values of } t$$

Sol.: Unit impulse function is first derivative of a unit step function.
$$\frac{d}{dt}\omega(t) = \delta(t)$$

By property of Laplace Transform,
$$L\left[\frac{d}{dt}\omega(t)\right] = sF(s) - f(0-)$$
$$= s \cdot \frac{1}{s} - 0$$
$$= 1$$

Ex. 4.7: Find Laplace Transform of te^{-at}.

Sol.: By property of complex translation,
$$L\,e^{at}f(t) = F(s-a)$$

Let
$$f(t) = t$$

∴
$$F(s) = \frac{1}{s^2}$$

∴
$$L\,t\,e^{-at} = \frac{1}{(s+a)^2}$$

Ex. 4.8: $f(t) = t^n$

Sol.: $L(t^n) = \int_0^\infty e^{-st} t^n \, dt$

Put $st = x$

$\therefore \quad L\, t^n = \int_0^\infty e^{-x} \frac{x^n}{s^n} \cdot \frac{dx}{s}$

$= \frac{1}{s^{n+1}} \int_0^\infty e^{-x} x^n \, dx$

$= \frac{\Gamma(n+1)}{s^{n+1}}$

If n is positive integer, $\Gamma(n+1) = n!$

$\therefore \quad L(t^n) = \frac{n!}{s^{n+1}}$ \qquad if n is positive integer

---

Ex. 4.9: Find Laplace Transform of $e^{-at} \cos \omega t$.

Sol.: Let $f(t) = \cos \omega t$

$\therefore \quad F(s) = \frac{s}{s^2 + \omega^2}$

By property of complex translation,

$L\, e^{-at} \cos at = \frac{s+a}{(s+a)^2 + \omega^2}$

Ex. 4.10: Verify the convolution theorem for the pair of functions $f_1(t) = t$, $f_2(t) = e^{at}$.

Sol.: Since, $f_1(t) = t$ and $f_2(t) = e^{at}$

$F_1(s) = \frac{1}{s^2}$ and $F_2(s) = \frac{1}{s-a}$

Convolution theorem states that,

$$L\left[\int_0^t f_1(u) f_2(t-u) \, du\right] = L\left[\int_0^t f_1(t-u) \cdot f_2(u) \, du\right] = F_1(s) F_2(s)$$

Now,
$$\int_0^t f_1(u) f_2(t-u)\,du = \int_0^t u \cdot e^{a(t-u)}\,du$$

$$= \left[\frac{u}{-a} e^{a(t-u)} - \int_0^t \frac{e^{a(t-u)}}{-a} \cdot 1\,du\right] \quad \text{(Integrating by part)}$$

$$= \left[\frac{u}{-a} e^{a(t-u)} - \frac{1}{a^2} e^{a(t-u)}\right]_0^t$$

$$= \frac{1}{a^2}\left[e^{at} - at - 1\right]$$

Hence,
$$L\left\{\int_0^t f_1(u) \cdot f_2(t-u)\,du\right\} = L\left\{\frac{1}{a^2}(e^{at} - at - 1)\right\}$$

$$= \frac{1}{a^2}\left[\frac{1}{s-a} - \frac{a}{s^2} - \frac{1}{s}\right]$$

$$= \frac{1}{s^2(s-a)}$$

$$= F_1(s) \cdot F_2(s)$$

Hence, the convolution theorem for given pair of functions is verified.

4.2.4.11 The Initial-Value and Final-Value Theorems

The initial value theorem states that the initial value of the time domain function f(t) can be obtained from its Laplace transform F(s) by first multiplying the transform by s and then letting s approach infinity.

$$f(0+) = \lim_{t \to 0+} f(t) = \lim_{s \to \infty} sF(s) \qquad \ldots (4.15\,(a))$$

The above equation is valid for continuous function or at most having a step discontinuity at t = 0.

The final value theorem states that

$$\lim_{t \to \infty} f(t) = \lim_{s \to 0} sF(s) \qquad \ldots (4.15\,(b))$$

provided the poles of F(s) must not be in right half of complex frequency plane.

Table 4.1: Laplace Transforms of some typical functions

f (t)	F (s)
$\delta(t)$	1
$u(t)$	$\dfrac{1}{s}$
$t\,u(t)$	$\dfrac{1}{s^2}$
t^n	$\dfrac{n!}{s^{n+1}}$
e^{-at}	$\dfrac{1}{s+a}$
$t\,e^{-at}$	$\dfrac{1}{(s+a)^2}$
$\dfrac{t^{n-1}}{(n-1)!} e^{-at}$	$\dfrac{1}{(s+a)^n}$
$\sin \omega t$	$\dfrac{\omega}{s^2+\omega^2}$
$\cos \omega t$	$\dfrac{s}{s^2+\omega^2}$
$e^{-at} \sin \omega t$	$\dfrac{\omega}{(s+a)^2+\omega^2}$
$e^{-at} \cos \omega t$	$\dfrac{s+a}{(s+a)^2+\omega^2}$
$\cosh \alpha t$	$\dfrac{s}{s^2-\alpha^2}$
$\sinh \alpha t$	$\dfrac{\alpha}{s^2-\alpha^2}$

Table 4.2: Properties of Laplace Transform

Operation	Property
Addition	$L[a f_1(t) + b f_2(t)] = a F_1(s) + b F_2(s)$
Scalar multiplication	$L[k f(t)] = k F(s)$
Time differentiation	$L\left\{\dfrac{d f(t)}{dt}\right\} = s F(s) - f(0-)$
	$L\left\{\dfrac{d^2 f(t)}{dt^2}\right\} = s^2 F(s) - s f(0-) - f'(0-)$
	$L\left\{\dfrac{d^n f(t)}{dt^n}\right\} = s^n F(s) - s^{n-1} f(0-) - s^{n-2} f'(0-) \ldots - f^{n-1}(0-)$
Time integration	$\displaystyle\int_{0-}^{t} f(u)\, du = \dfrac{F(s)}{s}$
Complex translation	$L\, e^{at} f(t) = F(s-a)$
Shifting theorem	$L[f(t-a)\, u(t-a)] = e^{-as} F(s)$
Convolution theorem	$L\, f_1(t) * f_2(t) = F_1(s) F_2(s)$
Initial value theorem	$f(0+) = \displaystyle\lim_{s \to \infty} s F(s)$
Final value theorem	$F(\infty) = \displaystyle\lim_{s \to 0} s F(s)$

4.3 INVERSE LAPLACE TRANSFORM

If {f (t)} = F (s), then f (t) is called the inverse Laplace Transform of F (s). This relation is denoted by

$$L^{-1}\{F(s)\} = f(t) \qquad \ldots (4.16\,(a))$$

Following are some of the methods to find inverse Laplace Transform by using known Laplace transforms of elementary functions.

4.3.1 Shifting Theorem

If $\quad L^{-1}[F(s)] = f(t)$

then, $\quad L^{-1}\{F(s-a)\} = e^{at} f(t) \qquad \ldots (4.16\,(b))$

4.3.2 Frequency Multiplication Theorem

If standard transform F (s) is multiplied by s, then the inverse transform is the differentiation of f (t).

If $L^{-1}\{F(s)\} = f(t)$ and $f(0) = 0$,

Then, $L^{-1}\{s F(s)\} = \dfrac{d}{dt} f(t)$ ... (4.17)

This can be generalized as,

$$L^{-1}\{s^n F(s)\} = \dfrac{d^n}{dt^n}\{f(t)\} \quad \text{... (4.18)}$$

with conditions $f(0) = f'(0) = \ldots = f^{n-1}(0) = 0$.

Ex. 4.11: Find inverse Laplace Transform of the following:

(a) $\quad F(s) = \dfrac{1}{s+5}$

$\therefore \quad L^{-1} \dfrac{1}{s+5} = e^{-5t}$ $\left[\because L^{-1} \dfrac{1}{s+a} = e^{at}\right]$

(b) $\quad F(s) = \dfrac{2s+6}{s^2+4}$

$L^{-1} \dfrac{2s+6}{s^2+4} = L^{-1}\left[2 \cdot \dfrac{s}{s^2+4} + 3 \cdot \dfrac{2}{s^2+4}\right]$

$= 2\cos 2t + 3\sin 2t$

(c) $\quad F(s) = \dfrac{s+7}{s^2+2s+5}$

Sol.: First complete a square in the denominator.

Thus, $\quad s^2 + 2s + 5 = (s+1)^2 + (2)^2$

Hence, $\quad F(s) = \dfrac{s+7}{(s+1)^2+(2)^2} = \dfrac{s+1}{(s+1)^2+(2)^2} + 3\dfrac{2}{(s+1)^2+(2)^2}$

But $\quad L[\cos 2t] = \dfrac{s}{s^2+2^2}$ and $L[\sin 2t] = \dfrac{2}{s^2+(2)^2}$

By shifting theorem,

$L^{-1}\left\{\dfrac{s+1}{(s+1)^2+(2)^2}\right\} = e^{-t}\cos 2t$

$L^{-1}\left\{\dfrac{2}{(s+1)^2+(2)^2}\right\} = e^{-t}\sin 2t$

Thus, $L^{-1} \dfrac{s+7}{s^2+2s+5} = e^{-t}\cos 2t + 3e^{-t}\sin 2t$

4.3.3 Partial Fraction Expansion

When a network is analyzed using Laplace Transform, the final form of Sol. is a quotient of polynomial in s. Let the numerator and denominator polynomials be designated as P (s) and Q (s) respectively as,

$$I(s) = \frac{P(s)}{Q(s)} \qquad \ldots (4.19)$$

where, Q (s) = 0 is the characteristic equation.

To find out i (t) inverse Laplace Transform of I (s) should be found. For this, the transform expression for I (s) must be written as addition of simple terms.

The first step in the expansion of the quotient $\frac{P(s)}{Q(s)}$ is to check that the order of P (s) should be less than that of Q (s). If this condition is not fulfilled, P (s) should be divided by Q (s) to obtain equation of the form,

$$\frac{P(s)}{Q(s)} = A_0 + A_1 s + A_2 s^2 + \ldots\ldots B_{m-n} s^{m-n} + \frac{P_1(s)}{Q(s)} \qquad \ldots (a)$$

where, m = Order of P (s)
  n = Order of Q (s)

The second step is to factorize denominator polynomial Q (s).

$$Q(s) = a_0 s^n + a_1 s^{n-1} + \ldots\ldots + a_n \qquad \ldots (b)$$
$$= a_0 (s - s_1) \ldots\ldots (s - s_n)$$

where, $s_1, s_2, \ldots\ldots, s_n$ are n roots of the characteristic equation Q (s) = 0.

There are following three main possibilities of the roots of Q (s).

1. All the roots of Q (s) = 0 are simple and real. Then the partial fraction expansion is

$$\frac{P_1(s)}{(s - s_1)(s - s_2) \ldots\ldots (s - s_n)} = \frac{k_1}{s - s_1} + \frac{k_2}{s - s_2} + \ldots\ldots + \frac{k_n}{s - s_n} \qquad \ldots (c)$$

where, $k_1, k_2, \ldots\ldots, k_n$ are real constants called residues.

2. If the root of Q (s) = 0 is of multiplicity r, that is repeated. Then the partial function expansion for the repeated root is,

$$\frac{P_1(s)}{(s - s_1)^r} = \frac{k_{11}}{s - s_1} + \frac{k_{12}}{(s - s_1)^2} + \ldots\ldots + \frac{k_{1r}}{(s - s_1)^r} \qquad \ldots (d)$$

and there will be similar terms for every other repeated roots.

3. If two roots of Q (s) = 0 form a complex conjugate pair. Then partial fraction expansion is

$$\frac{P_1(s)}{Q_1(s)(s + \alpha + j\omega)(s + \alpha - j\omega)} = \frac{k_1}{(s + \alpha + j\omega)} + \frac{k_1^*}{(s + \alpha - j\omega)} + \ldots\ldots \qquad \ldots (e)$$

where k_1^* is complex conjugate of k_1.

Ex. 4.12: Determine the partial fraction expansion of given polynomial and determine its inverse transform.

(a) $$F(s) = \frac{7s + 2}{s^3 + 3s^2 + 2s}$$

The order of numerator polynomial is less than denominator polynomial, hence condition is satisfied.

Step I: Factorize denominator polynomial.

Hence,
$$F(s) = \frac{7s + 2}{s(s^2 + 3s + 2)}$$

$$= \frac{7s + 2}{s(s + 1)(s + 2)}$$

$$= \frac{k_1}{s} + \frac{k_2}{s + 2} + \frac{k_3}{s + 1}$$

Step II: All roots are real and simple.

$$k_1 = \frac{7s + 2}{(s + 1)(s + 2)}\bigg|_{s = 0}$$ i.e. Multiply F(s) by s and evaluate value for s = 0.

$$= \frac{2}{2}$$

$$= 1$$

$$k_2 = \frac{7s + 2}{s(s + 1)}\bigg|_{s = -2}$$ i.e. Multiply F(s) by (s + 2) and evaluate value for s = −2.

$$= \frac{-12}{2}$$

$$= -6$$

$$k_3 = \frac{7s + 2}{s(s + 2)}\bigg|_{s = -1}$$ i.e. Multiply F(s) by (s + 1) and evaluate value for s = −1.

$$= \frac{-7 + 2}{-1}$$

$$= 5$$

Hence,
$$F(s) = \frac{7s + 2}{s(s^2 + 3s + 2)}$$

$$= \frac{1}{s} - \frac{6}{s + 2} + \frac{5}{s + 1}$$

Step III: Take Inverse Laplace Transform of individual terms.

$$\therefore \quad f(t) = L^{-1} F(s)$$

$$= L^{-1} \frac{1}{s} + L^{-1} \frac{(-6)}{s+2} + L^{-1}\left(\frac{5}{s+1}\right)$$

$$= t - 6e^{-2t} + 5e^{-t}$$

(b) $\quad F(s) = \dfrac{2s+1}{s(s+1)^2(s+2)}$

$$= \frac{k_1}{s} + \frac{k_2}{(s+2)} + \frac{k_{31}}{(s+1)} + \frac{k_{32}}{(s+1)^2}$$

$$k_1 = \left.\frac{2s+1}{(s+1)^2 + (s+1)}\right|_{s=0}$$

$$= \frac{1}{2}$$

$$k_2 = \left.\frac{2s+1}{s(s+1)^2}\right|_{s=-2}$$

$$= \frac{-3}{-2}$$

$$= \frac{3}{2}$$

$$k_{31} = \left.\frac{d}{ds}\left[\frac{(s+1)^2(2s+1)}{s(s+1)^2(s+2)}\right]\right|_{s=-1}$$

$$\left[\because k_{ir-1} = \left.\frac{d}{ds}(s+s_i)^r \frac{P_1(s)}{Q(s)}\right|_{s=s_i}\right]$$

$$= \frac{d}{ds}\left[\frac{2s+1}{s(s+2)}\right]$$

$$= \left.\frac{s(s+2)\cdot 2 - (2s+1)(2s+2)}{s^2(s+2)^2}\right|_{s=-1}$$

$$= -2$$

$$k_{32} = \left.\frac{2s+1}{s(s+2)}\right|_{s=-1}$$

$$= 1$$

$$\therefore \quad F(s) = \frac{1}{2s} + \frac{3}{2(s+2)} - \frac{2}{(s+1)} + \frac{1}{(s+1)^2}$$

Taking inverse Laplace Transform,

$$f(t) = \frac{1}{2} + \frac{3}{2} e^{-2t} - 2e^{-t} + te^{-t}$$

(c) Determine partial fraction expansion for

$$F(s) = \frac{(2s + 1)}{(s^2 + 2s + 5)(s + 1)}$$

The roots of polynomial $(s^2 + 2s + 5)$ are

$$s_1, s_2 = \frac{-b \pm \sqrt{b^2 - 4ac}}{2a}$$

$$= \frac{-2 \pm \sqrt{4 - 20}}{2}$$

$$= -1 \pm j2$$

Hence,
$$F(s) = \frac{k_1}{(s + 1)} + \frac{k_2}{(s + 1 - j2)} + \frac{k_2^*}{(s + 1 + j2)}$$

where,
$$k_1 = \left.\frac{(2s + 1)}{(s^2 + 2s + 5)}\right|_{s = -1}$$

$$= \frac{-2 + 1}{1 - 2 + 5} = -\frac{1}{4}$$

$$k_2 = \left.\frac{(2s + 1)}{(s + 1)(s + 1 + j2)}\right|_{s = -1 + j2}$$

$$= \frac{2(-1 + j2) + 1}{(-1 + j2 + 1)(-1 + j2 + 1 + j2)}$$

$$= \frac{1}{8} - j\frac{1}{2}$$

$$k_2^* = \frac{1}{8} + j\frac{1}{2}$$

∴ Partial fraction expansion of F (s) is,

$$F(s) = \frac{\left(-\frac{1}{4}\right)}{s + 1} + \frac{\frac{1}{8} - j\frac{1}{2}}{s + 1 - j2} + \frac{\frac{1}{8} + j\frac{1}{2}}{s + 1 + j2}$$

4.3.4 Use of Convolution Theorem

If the function F (s) whose inverse transform is required can be expressed as product of $F_1(s) \cdot F_2(s)$, where inverse transforms of $F_1(s)$ and $F_2(s)$ are known, then convolution theorem can be used to find inverse transform.

If
$$L^{-1} F_1(s) = f_1(t)$$
$$L^{-1} F_2(s) = f_2(t)$$
and
$$F(s) = F_1(s) \cdot F_2(s)$$
Then,
$$L^{-1} F(s) = L^{-1} F_1(s) F_2(s)$$
$$= \int_0^t f_1(t-u) f_2(u) \, du \qquad \ldots (4.20)$$

(Note: $f_1(t)$ and $f_2(t)$ are interchangeable.)

Corollary: Since $L^{-1}\left(\dfrac{1}{s}\right) = 1 \cdot u(t)$

$$L^{-1} F(s) = f(t)$$

Let $F_1(s) = \dfrac{1}{s}, \quad F_2(s) = F(s)$

Hence, $L^{-1}\left[\dfrac{F(s)}{s}\right] = \int_0^t 1 \cdot f(u) \, du$

Ex. 4.13: Obtain the inverse Laplace Transform of the following using convolution theorem.

(a) $\quad F(s) = \dfrac{1}{s^2 (s+1)^2}$

Sol.: $\quad F(s) = \dfrac{1}{s^2 (s+1)^2}$

$$= \dfrac{1}{s^2} \cdot \dfrac{1}{(s+1)^2}$$

Let $\quad F_1(s) = \dfrac{1}{s^2}$

$$L^{-1} \dfrac{1}{s^2} = t$$

$$F_2(s) = \dfrac{1}{(s+1)^2}$$

$$L^{-1} \dfrac{1}{(s+1)^2} = te^{-t}$$

$$= f_1(t)$$
$$= f_2(t)$$

Using convolution theorem (equation 4.20),

$$L^{-1}\left\{\frac{1}{s^2(s+1)^2}\right\} = \int_0^t (t-u)\cdot ue^{-u}\,du$$

Now integrating by parts,

$$\int_0^t (t-u)ue^{-u}\,du = \int_0^t u(t-u)e^{-u}\,du$$

$$= \left[-(ut-u^2)e^{-u} - \int_0^t -(t-2u)e^{-u}\,du\right]_0^t$$

$$= \left\{-(ut-u^2)e^{-u} - \left[(t-2u)e^{-u} + \int e^{-u}(-2)\,du\right]\right\}_0^t$$

$$= \left[-(ut-u^2)e^{-u} - (t-2u)e^{-u} - (-2)e^{-u}\right]_0^t$$

$$= te^{-t} + 2e^{-t} - t - 2$$

(b) $\qquad F(s) = \dfrac{1}{s(s+1)}$

Sol.: $\qquad F(s) = \dfrac{1}{s(s+1)}$

Let $\qquad F_1(s) = \dfrac{1}{s} \qquad \therefore \quad f_1(t) = u(t)$

$\qquad F_2(s) = \dfrac{1}{s+1} \qquad \therefore \quad f_2(t) = e^t\,u(t)$

By convolution theorem,

$$L^{-1}F(s) = \int_0^t f_1(u)\,f_2(t-u)\,du$$

$$= \int_0^t f_1(t-u)\,f_2(u)\,du = \int_0^t 1\cdot e^{-u}\,du$$

$$= \left.\frac{e^{-u}}{-1}\right|_0^t$$

$$= -[e^{-t} - 1]$$
$$= 1 - e^{-t}$$

4.4 LAPLACE TRANSFORM OF BASIC R.L.C. COMPONENTS

(A) Resistance: Voltage and current through the resistor are related in time domain by expression

$$v_R(t) = R\, i_R(t) \quad \ldots \text{(a)}$$
or
$$i_R(t) = G\, v_R(t) \quad \ldots \text{(b)}$$

The corresponding transform equations are,

$$V_R(s) = R\, I_R(s) \quad \ldots \text{(c)}$$
$$I_R(s) = G\, V_R(s) \quad \ldots \text{(d)}$$

Thus,
$$\frac{V_R(s)}{I_R(s)} = Z_R(s) = R \quad \ldots (4.21\,(a))$$

is the transformed impedance of resistor.

$$\frac{I_R(s)}{V_R(s)} = Y_R(s) = G \quad \ldots (4.21\,(b))$$

is the transformed admittance of resistor.

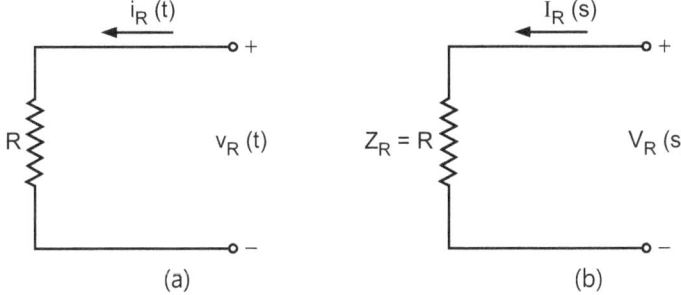

(a) (b)

Fig. 4.4: The resistor and its transformed impedance

(B) Inductance: The time domain relationship between voltage and current in an inductor is expressed as,

$$v_L(t) = L\, \frac{di_L(t)}{dt} \quad \ldots (4.22)$$

Transforming equation (4.42) in s domain,

$$V_L(s) = L\,[s\, I_L(s) - i_L(0-)] \quad \ldots (4.23)$$

where, $i_L(0-)$ is the initial current in the inductor.

Therefore,
$$I_L(s) = \frac{1}{sL}\, V(s) + \frac{i_L(0-)}{s} \quad \ldots (4.24)$$

$$I_L(s) - \frac{i_L(0-)}{s} = I_1(s) = \frac{1}{sL}\, V(s)$$

∴
$$\frac{I_1(s)}{V(s)} = \frac{1}{sL} = \text{Transformed admittance}$$

$$= Y_L(s) \quad \ldots (4.25\,(a))$$

and transformed impedance is

$$Z_L(s) = \frac{1}{Y_L(s)} = sL \qquad \ldots (4.45\,(b))$$

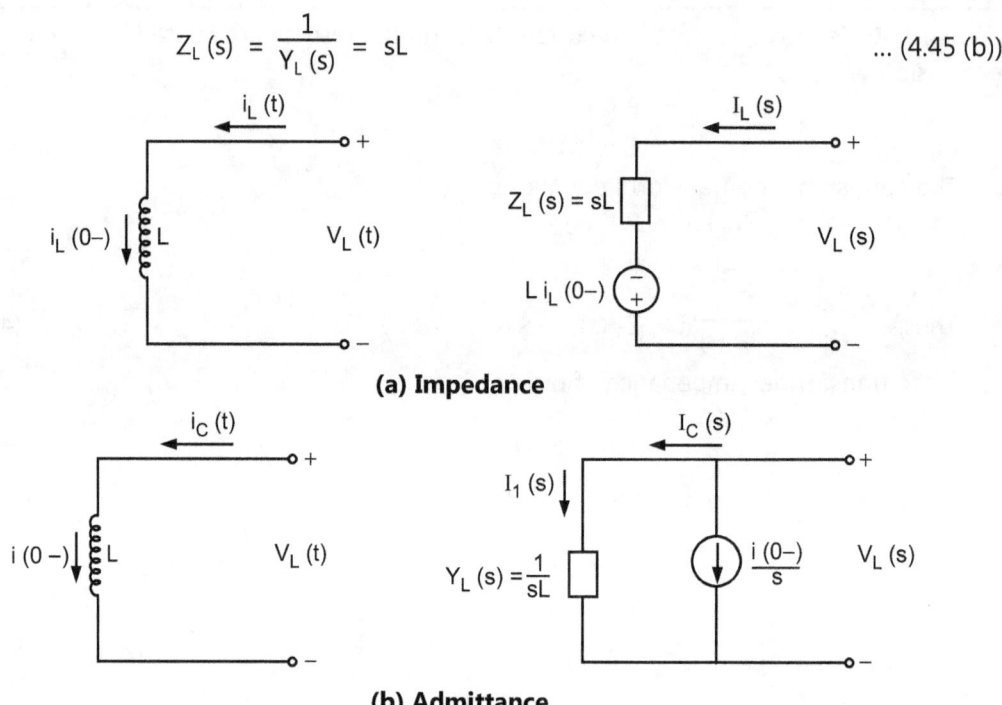

(a) Impedance

(b) Admittance

Fig. 4.5: The inductor with initial current and its transform impedance and admittance

(C) Capacitance: The time domain relationship between voltage and current for a capacitor is given by,

$$i_C(t) = C\frac{dV_C(t)}{dt}$$

$$V_C(t) = \frac{1}{C}\int_{-\infty}^{t} i_C(t)\,dt \qquad \ldots (4.26)$$

The equivalent transform equation for voltage is

$$V_C(s) = \frac{1}{C}\left[\frac{I_C(s)}{s} - \frac{q(0-)}{s}\right] \qquad \ldots (4.27)$$

where, $\dfrac{q(0-)}{C}$ (Initial voltage on the capacitor)

$$\therefore \quad \frac{1}{sC}I_C(s) = V_C(s) + \frac{V_C(0-)}{s} \qquad \ldots (e)$$

Let $V_C(s) + \dfrac{V_C(0-)}{s} = V_1(s)$

$\therefore \quad Z_C(s) = \dfrac{V_1(s)}{I_1(s)} = \dfrac{1}{sC}$ ... (4.28)

Thus, capacitor with an initial charge has an equivalent transform circuit with an impedance $\dfrac{1}{sC}$ in series with a voltage source having transform $\dfrac{-V_C(0-)}{s}$.

Similarly from equation (4.28),

$$I_C(s) = C\left[s\, V_C(s) - V_C(0-)\right]$$

$$sC\, V_C(s) = I_C(s) + C\, V_C(0-) \quad \text{... (f)}$$

Let transform current in $Y_C(s)$ be,

$$I_1(s) = I_C(s) - C\, V_C(0-)$$

$\therefore \quad Y_C(s) = \dfrac{I_1(s)}{V_C(s)} = sC$ ... (4.29)

Thus, capacitor with an initial charge has an equivalent transform representation as an admittance sC in parallel with transform current source of value $C\, v_C(0-)$.

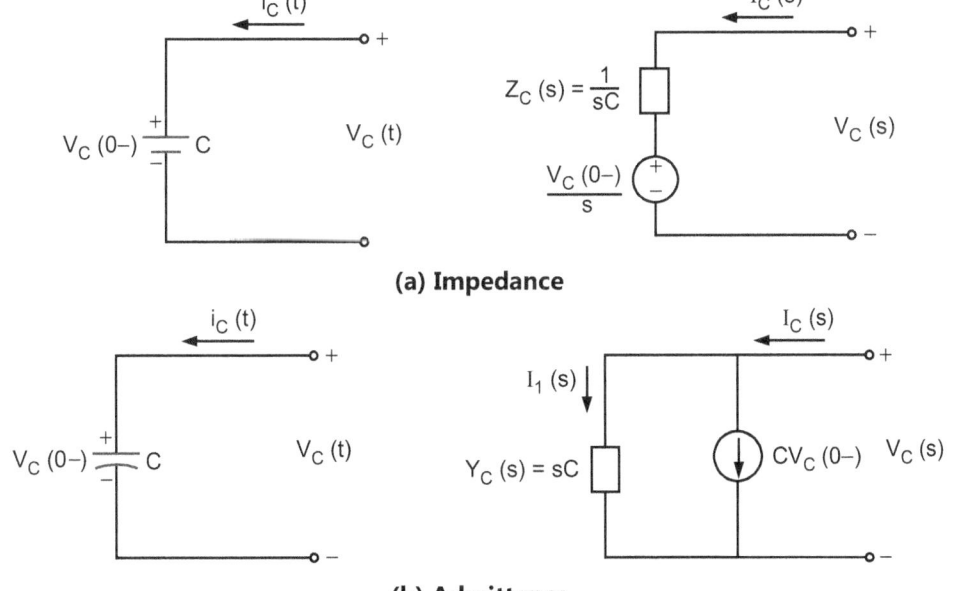

(a) Impedance

(b) Admittance

Fig. 4.6: The capacitor with initial voltage and its transform impedance and admittance

4.5 STANDARD INPUT SIGNALS AND THEIR LAPLACE TRANSFORM

Let us in this section consider some standard signals and their Laplace Transform. The functions are used in the analysis of network.

(a) Step Function:

A step function can be produced by a voltage source (V_0) and a switch in series as shown in Fig. 4.7 (a).

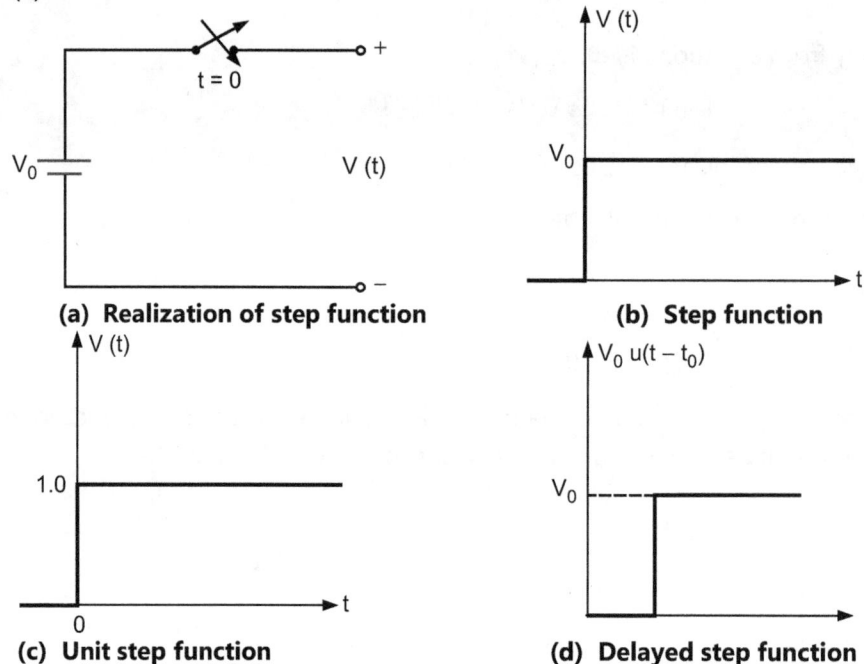

(a) Realization of step function
(b) Step function
(c) Unit step function
(d) Delayed step function

Fig. 4.7: Step functions

For $t < 0$ switch is opened. Hence, $v(t) = 0$ V. At $t = 0$ the switch is closed and hence $v(t) = V_0$ for $t \geq 0$. Thus, we have,

$$v(t) = 0 \quad \text{for } t \leq 0$$
$$ = V_0 \quad \text{for } t \geq 0 \qquad \ldots (4.30)$$

LT of unit step:

As $U(t) = 1$ for $t \geq 0$ we have,

$$L[U(t)] = \int_0^\infty e^{-st}\, dt = \left[\frac{e^{-st}}{-s}\right]_0^\infty$$

Thus, $\quad L[U(t)] = \dfrac{-1}{s}[e^{-\infty} - e^{-0}] = \dfrac{1}{s} \qquad \ldots (4.31)$

A step of magnitude k is represented as $K \cdot U(t)$.

Thus, $\quad L[K\,U(t)] = \dfrac{K}{s}$ (By scaling theorem).

A delayed step function delayed by the time t_0 with a magnitude of V_0 is shown in Fig. 4.15 (d) and is represented as $V_0 U(t - t_0)$. By shifting theorem we have,

$$L[V_0 U(t - t_0)] = V_0 \frac{e^{-st_0}}{s} \quad \ldots (4.32)$$

(b) Ramp function: An ramp function with a slope of $+ K$ is shown in Fig. 4.8 (a) and is defined as

$$f(t) = 0 \quad \text{for } t < 0$$
$$= K r(t), \quad \text{for } t \geq 0 \quad \ldots (4.33)$$

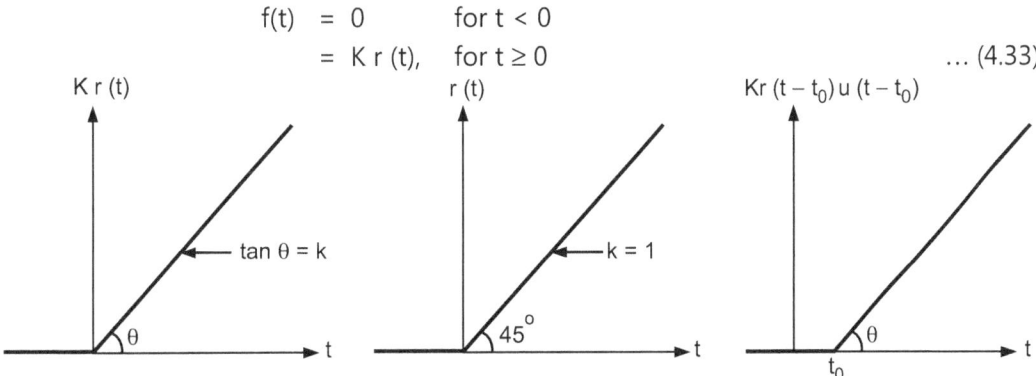

(a) Ramp function with slope k (b) Unit ramp function (k = 1) (c) Delayed ramp function
Fig. 4.8: Ramp functions

If slope (K) is unity then it is called unit ramp function and is represented by $r(t)$ where $r(t) = t \cdot U(t)$ and is shown in Fig. 4.8 (b).

An delayed ramp function delayed by a time t_0 and has a slope of $+ K$ is shown in Fig. 4.8 (c). It is given by the expression.

$$f(t) = 0 \quad \text{for } t < t_0$$
$$= K r(t - t_0) U(t - t_0) \quad \text{for } t \geq t_0$$

Laplace Transform of a Ramp function: Let $f(t) = K r(t)$.

Then, $\quad L[K r(t)] = L[Kt] \int_0^\infty K \cdot t e^{-st} dt = K \left[\frac{t e^{-st}}{-s} - \frac{e^{-st}}{s^2} \right]_0^\infty$

$$= K \left[0 - 0 - 0 + \frac{1}{s^2} \right]$$

Thus, we have $\quad L[K r(t)] = \frac{K}{s^2} \quad \ldots (4.34)$

For unit ramp $r(t)$ L.T. is $L[r(t)] = \frac{1}{s^2}$. Since, $K = 1$.

Laplace transform of delayed Ramp function: We have the delayed ramp is

$$f(t) = K r(t - t_0) U(t - t_0)$$

$$L[K r(t - t_0) U(t - t_0)] = K e^{-st} \times \frac{1}{s^2} = \frac{K}{s^2} e^{-st_0}$$

(c) Impulse Function:

Consider a pulse of unit area $\left(T \times \dfrac{1}{T} = 1\right)$ as shown in Fig. 4.9 (a). When this pulse is compressed along x-axis and stretched along y-axis keeping area unity then unit impulse function [Fig. 4.9 (b)] is formed.

Hence, mathematically unit impulse is given by,

$$\delta(t) = \lim_{T \to 0} \frac{1}{T} [U(t) - U(t - T)] \qquad \ldots (4.35)$$

Hence, unit impulse exists only at $t = 0$. The unit impulse function is also **Dirac function**.

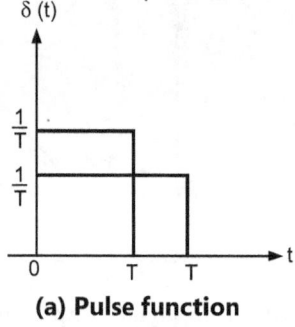
(a) Pulse function

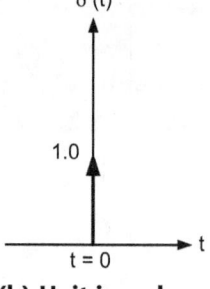
(b) Unit impulse

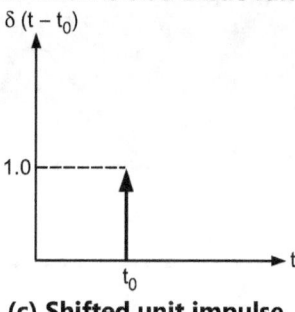
(c) Shifted unit impulse

Fig. 4.9: Impulse function

Laplace Transform of a unit impulse function $\delta(t)$:

Unit impulse function can also be represented as differential of unit step function.

i.e. $\delta(t) = \dfrac{d}{dt} U(t)$

$$L[\delta(t)] = L\left[\dfrac{d}{dt} U(t)\right] = s F(s) - f(0^-)$$

$$= s \times \dfrac{1}{s} - 0 = 1 \qquad \ldots (4.36)$$

Unit impulse shifted by t_0 is represented as $\delta(t - t_0)$.

Relation between unit step, ramp, impulse functions:

Unit impulse, ramp and step functions are shown in Fig. 4.10.

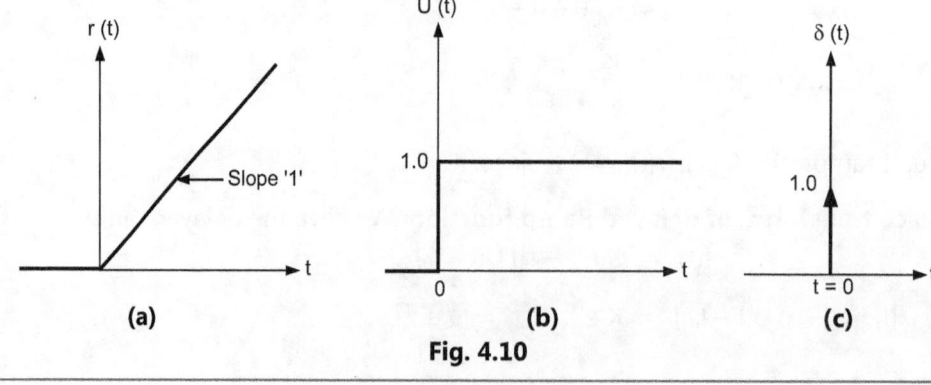

Fig. 4.10

We have unit ramp = $r(t) = t$.

$$\frac{d}{dt}[r(t)] = \frac{d}{dt}[t] = 1 = u(t) = \text{unit step}$$

$$\frac{d}{dt}[u(t)] = 1 \text{ at } t = 0 \text{ which is an unit impulse function.}$$

Thus, the relationship is:

$$r(t) \xrightarrow[\text{With respect to 't'}]{\text{Differentiate}} U(t) \xrightarrow[\text{With respect to 't'}]{\text{Differentiate}} \delta(t)$$

OR

$$\delta(t) \xrightarrow[\text{With respect to 't'}]{\text{Integrate}} U(t) \xrightarrow[\text{With respect to 't'}]{\text{Integrate}} r(t)$$

(d) Exponential function: An exponential function is shown in Fig. 4.11. It is defined by equation.

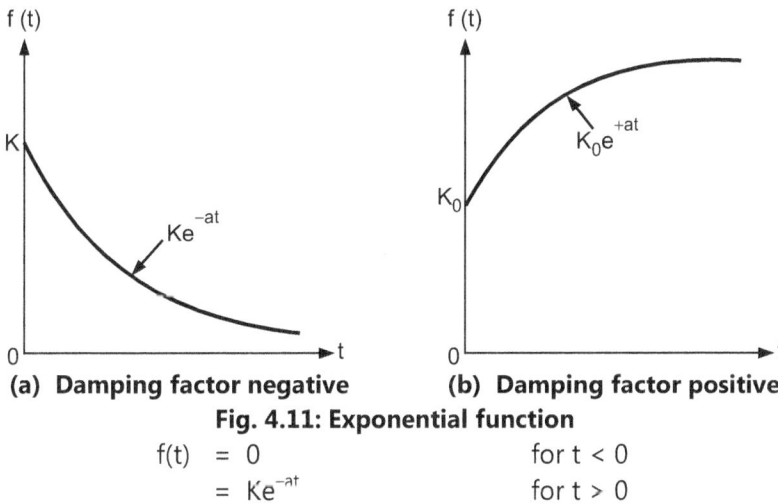

(a) Damping factor negative (b) Damping factor positive

Fig. 4.11: Exponential function

$$f(t) = 0 \quad \text{for } t < 0$$
$$= Ke^{-at} \quad \text{for } t > 0$$

Where 'a' is called damping factor and $\frac{1}{a}$ is called time constant (τ). Time constant is the time required for output to reach 37% of its the initial value (K).

L.T. Exponential function:

The L.T. of the exponential function is given by

$$L[Ke^{-at}] = \int_0^\infty Ke^{-at} e^{-st} dt = K \int_0^\infty e^{-(s+a)t} dt$$

$$= K\left[\frac{e^{-(s+a)}}{-(s+a)}\right]_0^\infty = K\left[0 + \frac{1}{s+a}\right]$$

Thus, $\quad L[Ke^{-at}] = \left[\dfrac{K}{(s+a)}\right]$ ... (4.37)

As L.T. of constant (K) is $\frac{K}{s}$. The L.T. of the function Ke^{-at} can be obtained by replacing the s by (s + a).

The exponential function with positive damping factor (+a) is shown in Fig. 4.11 (b). The equation for the function is given by:

$$f(t) = Ke^{+at} \quad \text{for } t > 0$$

Thus, $$[Ke^{+at}] = \frac{K}{(s-a)} \quad \ldots (4.38)$$

(e) Parabolic function: A parabolic function is shown in Fig. 4.12.

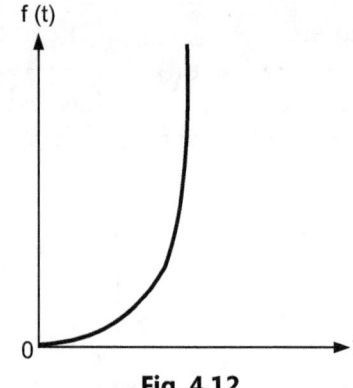

Fig. 4.12

It is mathematically represented by equation.

$$f(t) = 0 \quad \text{for } t < 0$$
$$= \frac{t^2}{2} \quad \text{for } t > 0$$

Thus, $r(t) = \frac{t^2}{2} u(t)$ represents unit parabolic function.

Laplace Transform of unit parabolic function:

$$L\left[\frac{t^2}{2} u(t)\right] = \int_0^\infty \frac{t^2}{2} e^{-st} dt = \frac{1}{2} \int_0^\infty t^2 e^{-st} dt$$

Integrating by parts using relationship of $\int v\, du = vu - \int u\, dv$ and substituting the limits we get,

$$L\left[\frac{t^2}{2} u(t)\right] = \frac{1}{s^3} \quad \ldots (4.39)$$

In general,

$$L\left[\frac{t^{n-1}}{(n-1)!} u(t)\right] = \frac{1}{s^n} \quad \ldots (4.40)$$

(f) Sine and Cosine functions: Sine and Cosine functions are shown in Fig. 4.13.

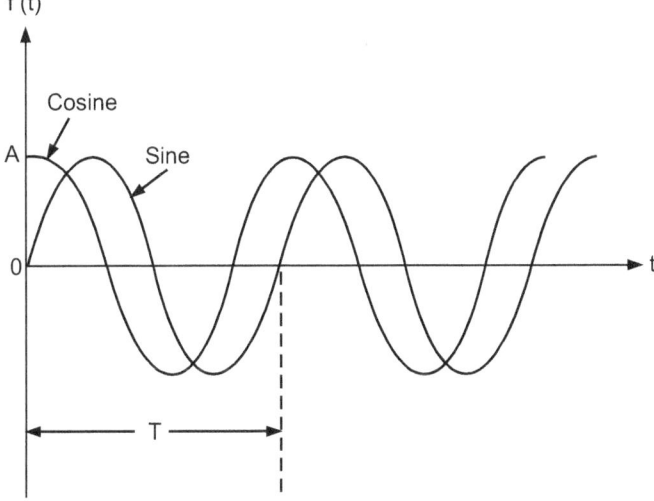

Fig. 4.13: Sine and Cosine wave

The sine wave has an amplitude of 'A' volts a period of 'T' seconds. Since, it exists for t > 0 it is mathematically represented as

$$f(t) = A \sin \omega_0 t \cdot u(t)$$

Similarly cosine function is given by

$$f_1(t) = A \cos \omega_0 t \, u(t)$$

We can express these in terms of exponential functions as

$$\sin \omega_0 t = \frac{1}{2J} [e^{J\omega_0 t} - e^{-J\omega_0 t}]$$

$$\cos \omega_0 t = \frac{1}{2} [e^{J\omega_0 t} + e^{-J\omega_0 t}]$$

L.T. of sine and cosines function:

$$L[A \sin \omega_0 t] = AL\left[\frac{1}{J2}(e^{J\omega_0 t} - e^{-J\omega_0 t})\right] = \frac{A}{J2}\left[\frac{1}{(s-J\omega_0)} - \frac{1}{(s+J\omega_0)}\right]$$

$$= \frac{A}{J2}\left[\frac{2J\omega_0}{s^2 + \omega_0^2}\right] = A\left[\frac{\omega_0}{s^2 + \omega_0^2}\right]$$

Hence, we have

$$L[A \sin \omega_0 t] = \frac{A\omega_0}{s^2 + \omega_0^2} \qquad \ldots (4.41)$$

$$L[A \cos \omega_0 t] = L\left[\frac{A}{2}(e^{J\omega_0 t} + e^{-J\omega_0 t})\right] = \frac{A}{2}\left[\frac{1}{s-J\omega_0} + \frac{1}{s+J\omega_0}\right] = A\left(\frac{s}{s^2 + \omega_0^2}\right)$$

Thus, we have

$$L[A \cos \omega_0 t] = A\left[\frac{s}{s^2 + \omega_0^2}\right] \qquad \ldots (4.42)$$

(g) Damped sinusoidal and Damped cosine functions: Damped sine and cosine functions are as shown in Fig. 4.14.

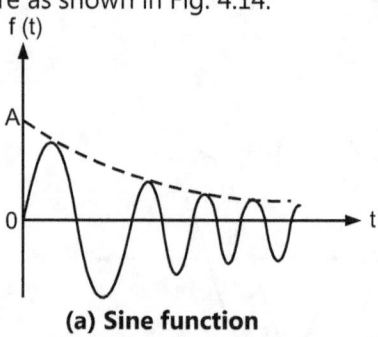

(a) Sine function

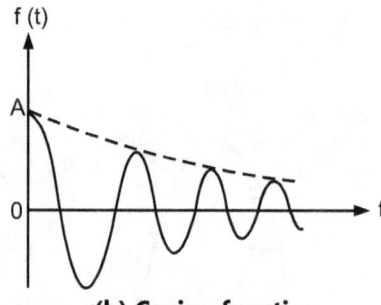

(b) Cosine function

Fig. 4.14

Sine function is mathematically represented as

$$f(t) = A e^{-at} \sin \omega_0 t \, U(t)$$

Multiplication by unit step u(t) ensures that value of the function is zero for t < 0 and the function exists for t > 0 where U(t) has unity value.

By using equation (4.14) we have,

$$L[Ae^{-at} \sin \omega_0 t] = A \frac{\omega_0}{(s+a)^2 + \omega_0^2} \qquad \ldots (4.43)$$

Cosine function shown in Fig. 4.14 (b) is mathematically represented as:

$$f_1(t) = A e^{-at} \cos \omega_0 t \, U(t)$$

$$L[Ae^{-at} \cos \omega_0 t] = A \frac{(s+a)}{(s+a)^2 + \omega_0^2} \qquad \ldots (4.44)$$

(h) Hyperbolic sine and cosine functions:

We have, $\sinh at = \frac{1}{2}[e^{at} - e^{-at}]$, $\cosh at = \frac{1}{2}[e^{at} + e^{-at}]$

Hence,
$$L[\sinh at] = \frac{1}{2}\left[\frac{1}{(s-a)} - \frac{1}{(s+a)}\right] = \frac{a}{(s^2 - a^2)} \qquad \ldots (4.45)$$

$$L[\cosh at] = \frac{1}{2}\left[\frac{1}{(s+a)} + \frac{1}{(s-a)}\right] = \frac{s}{(s^2 - a^2)} \qquad \ldots (4.46)$$

Now using complex translation theorem, the L.T. of damped sinusoid function is given by:

$$L[e^{\sigma_0 t} \sinh at] = \frac{a}{(s+\sigma_0)^2 - a^2}$$

$$L[e^{\sigma_0 t} \cosh at] = \frac{s}{(s+\sigma_0)^2 - a^2}$$

SOLVED EXAMPLES

Ex. 4.14: In the network shown in the Fig. 4.15, the switch K is moved from position a to position b at t = 0, a steady state having previously been established at position a. Solve for the current i (t) using the Laplace transformation method.

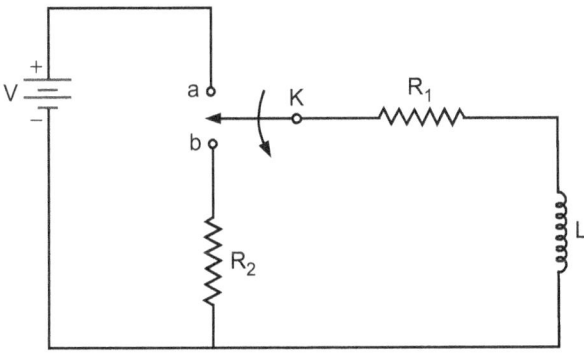

Fig. 4.15

Sol.: When switch is in position 'a', steady state is achieved and inductor L acts as S.C. in the steady state as shown in Fig. 4.15 (a).

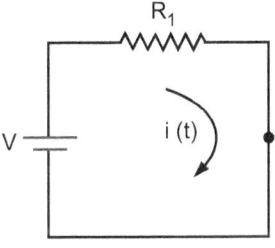

Fig. 4.15 (a)

When the switch is moved to position 'b', the circuit takes the form as shown in Fig. 4.15 (b).

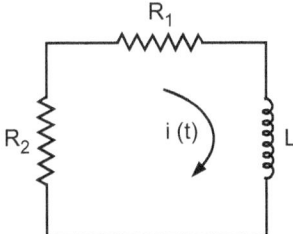   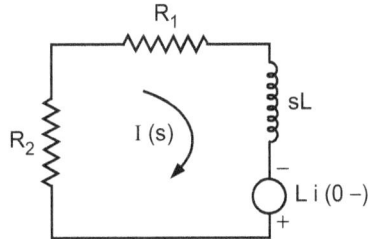

Fig. 4.15 (b): Circuit in position 'b'   **Fig. 4.15 (c): Transformed circuit**

Applying KVL to circuit in Fig. 4.15 (b),

$$(R_1 + R_2) i(t) + L \frac{d}{dt} i(t) = 0$$

Taking Laplace Transform,

$$L[sI(s) - i_L(0-)] + (R_1 + R_2)I(s) = 0$$

$$\therefore \quad L\left[sI(s) - \frac{V}{R_1}\right] + (R_1 + R_2)I(s) = 0$$

Collecting terms of I (s),

$$[sL + R_1 + R_2]I(s) = \frac{LV}{R_1}$$

$$\therefore \quad I(s) = \frac{LV}{R_1}\left(\frac{1}{sL + R_1 + R_2}\right)$$

$$= \frac{V}{R_1}\left[\frac{1}{s + \frac{(R_1 + R_2)}{L}}\right]$$

Taking Inverse Laplace Transform,

$$i(t) = \frac{V}{R_1} e^{-\left(\frac{R_1 + R_2}{L}\right)t} \quad \text{for } t \geq 0$$

Ex. 4.15: In the network shown as in Fig. 4.16 the switch K is moved from position a to position b at t = 0. A steady state current being previously established, derive the expression for current i (t).

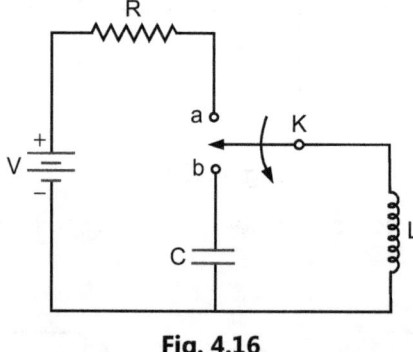

Fig. 4.16

Sol.: When switch is in position 'a', steady state is established. The inductor L acts as S.C. in the steady state.

$$i_a(t) = \frac{V}{R}$$

$$i_L(0-) = \frac{V}{R} \text{ Amp.}$$

$$V_C(0-) = 0 \text{ volts}$$

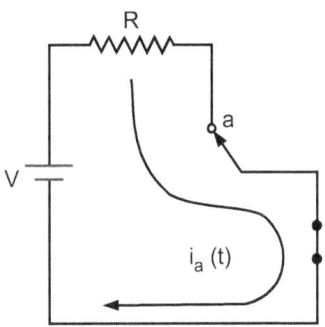

Fig. 4.16 (a)

In position 'b' circuit becomes as shown in Fig. 4.16 (b).

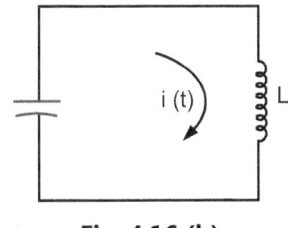   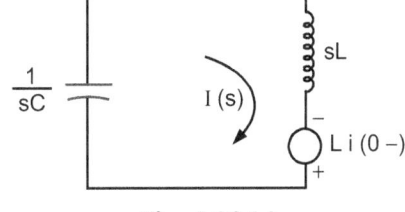

Fig. 4.16 (b)   **Fig. 4.16 (c)**

Applying KVL to circuit in Fig. 4.16 (b),

$$L\frac{di(t)}{dt} + \frac{1}{C}\int_{-\infty}^{t} i(t)\, dt = 0$$

But

$$V_C(0-) = \frac{1}{C}\int_{-\infty}^{0} i(t)\, dt = 0$$

∴

$$L\frac{di(t)}{dt} + \frac{1}{C}\int_{0}^{t} i(t)\, dt = 0$$

Taking Laplace Transform,

$$L[sI(s) - i_L(0-)] + \frac{1}{sC} I(s) = 0$$

$$I(s)\left[sL + \frac{1}{sC}\right] - L\frac{V}{R} = 0$$

$$I(s)\left(\frac{1 + s^2 LC}{sC}\right) = \frac{VL}{R}$$

Unit 4 | 4.33

$$\therefore \quad I(s) = \frac{VL}{R} \cdot \frac{sC}{1 + s^2 LC}$$

$$= \left(\frac{V}{R}\right) \cdot \frac{s}{s^2 + \frac{1}{LC}}$$

Taking Inverse Laplace Transform,

$$i(t) = \left(\frac{V}{R}\right) \cos\left(\frac{t}{\sqrt{LC}}\right) \text{ Amp}$$

Ex. 4.16: The circuit shown in Fig. 4.17 is in steady state with switch on position 1. At t = 0, it is moved to position 2. Find i (t) using Laplace Transform.

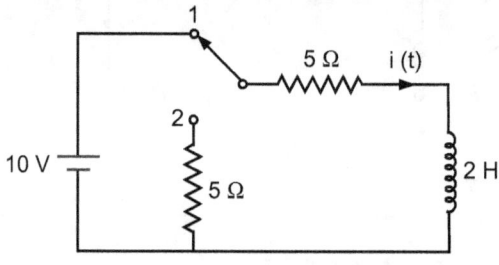

Fig. 4.17

Sol.:

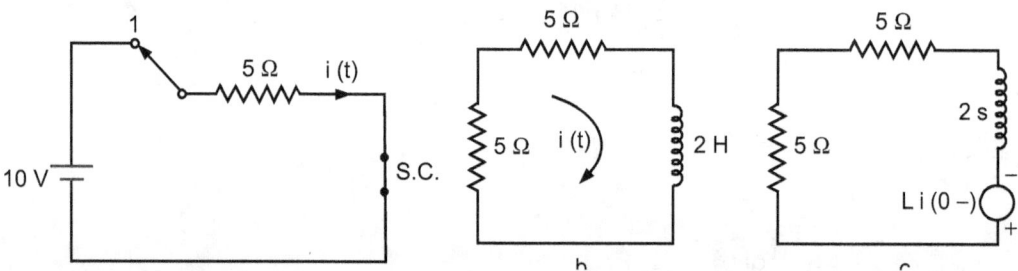

Fig. 4.17 (a): SW in position 1, steady state condition   **Fig. 4.17 (b): SW in position 2**   **Fig. 4.17 (c): Transformed circuit**

In position 1, steady state is reached, the inductor acts as short circuit as shown in Fig. 4.17 (a).

$$\therefore \quad i_L(0-) = i_L(0+) = \frac{10}{5} = 2 \text{ A}$$

In position 2, the circuit appears as shown in Fig. 4.17 (b).

Applying KVL to the circuit,

$$5\,i(t) + 5\,i(t) + 2\frac{di(t)}{dt} = 0$$

Transforming the equation,

$$5I(s) + 5I(s) + 2[sI(s) - i_L(0-)] = 0$$

$$10I(s) + 2sI(s) - 4 = 0 \qquad [\because i_L(0-) = 2A]$$

$$\therefore \quad I(s) = \frac{4}{10 + 2s}$$

$$= \frac{2}{s + 5}$$

Taking Inverse Laplace Transform of I(s),

$$i(t) = 2e^{-5t} \text{ Amp.}$$

Ex. 4.17: In the circuit shown in Fig. 4.18, find $v_a(t)$ using Laplace Transform. Assume $i_L(0-) = 2A$.

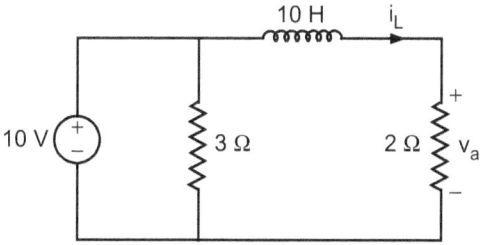

Fig. 4.18

Sol.: Applying KVL to the outer loop of circuit shown in Fig. 4.18,

$$10 = 10 \cdot \frac{di_L(t)}{dt} + 2i_L(t) \qquad \ldots (a)$$

Transform equation (a) using Laplace Transform.

Hence, transformed circuit appears as shown in Fig. 4.18 (a).

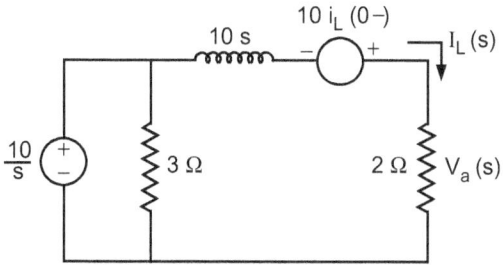

Fig. 4.18 (a)

Thus,
$$\frac{10}{s} = 10[s\,I_L(s) - 2] + 2I_L(s)$$

$$\frac{10}{s} + 20 = (10s + 2)\,I_L(s)$$

$$I_L(s) = \frac{\frac{10}{s} + 20}{10s + 2} = \frac{10 + 20s}{10s + 2}$$

$$= \frac{2s + 1}{s + 0.2} = \frac{5}{s} + \frac{3}{s + 0.2}$$

$$V_a(s) = 2\,I_L(s)$$

$$= \frac{10}{s} + \frac{6}{s + 0.2}$$

Taking Inverse Laplace Transform of $V_a(s)$,

$$V_a(t) = 10 + 6e^{-0.2t} \quad \text{volts}$$

Ex. 4.18: For the circuit shown in Fig. 4.19, solve for $i(t)$ using Laplace Transform with switch 'K' closed at $t = 0$. Assume zero initial conditions.

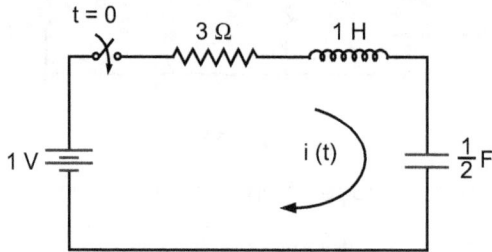

Fig. 4.19

Sol.: Applying KVL,

$$1\,u(t) = R\,i(t) + L\frac{di(t)}{dt} + \frac{1}{C}\int_{-\infty}^{t} i(t)\,dt \quad \ldots (a)$$

Taking Laplace Transform of equation (a),

$$\frac{1}{s} = R\,I(s) + sL\,I(s) + \frac{1}{sC}\,I(s)$$

$$\frac{1}{s} = 3\,I(s) + s\,I(s) + \frac{2}{s}\,I(s)$$

$$1 = (s^2 + 3s + 2)\,I(s)$$

$$\therefore \quad I(s) = \frac{1}{s^2 + 3s + 2}$$

$$= \frac{1}{(s+2)(s+1)}$$

$$= \frac{A}{s+2} + \frac{B}{s+1}$$

$$A = \frac{(s+2)}{(s+1)(s+2)}\bigg|_{s=-2} = -1$$

$$B = \frac{(s+1)}{(s+1)(s+2)}\bigg|_{s=-1} = 1$$

$$I(s) = \frac{1}{(s+1)} - \frac{1}{(s+2)}$$

Taking Inverse Laplace Transform,

$$i(t) = e^{-t} - e^{-2t} \quad \text{Amp.;} \quad t > 0$$

Ex. 4.19: For the circuit shown in Fig. 4.20, the switch S is kept in position 1 for long period to establish steady state conditions. The switch is then shifted to position 2 at t = 0. Find out the expression for current after switching the switch to position 2.

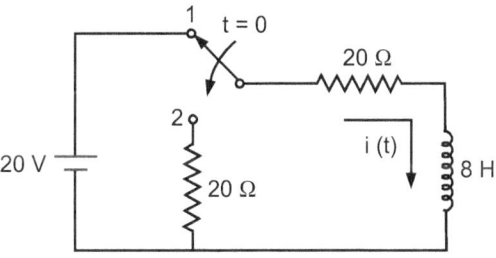

Fig. 4.20

Sol.:

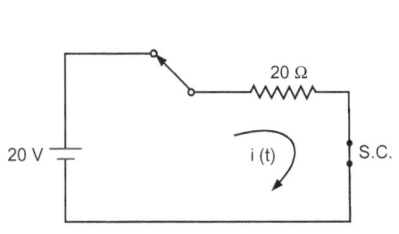

Fig. 4.20 (a): Steady state condition after SW in position 1 for long period

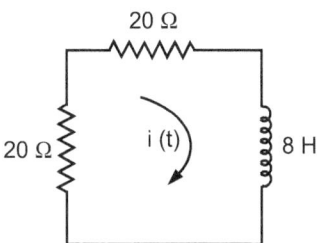

Fig. 4.20 (b): Circuit with SW in position 2

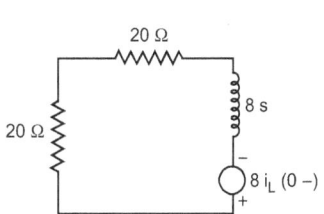

Fig. 4.20 (c): Transformed circuit

After the SW in position 1 for long period, steady state condition is established. The inductor acts as short circuit.

$$\therefore \quad i_L(0-) = \frac{20}{20} = 1 \text{ Amp.}$$

Applying KVL to circuit shown in Fig. 4.20 (b),

$$20\, i(t) + 20\, i(t) + 8\frac{di(t)}{dt} = 0$$

Taking Laplace Transform,

$$20\, I(s) + 20\, I(s) + 8\,[s\, I(s) - i_L(0-)] = 0$$

$$\therefore \quad 40\, I(s) + 8s\, I(s) - 8(1) = 0$$

$$\therefore \quad I(s) = \frac{8}{[8s + 40]}$$

$$= \frac{1}{s + 5}$$

Taking Inverse Laplace Transform,

$$i(t) = e^{-5t} \text{ Amp.}$$

Ex. 4.20: Let $V_C(0-) = 2$ V with the polarities as shown in Fig. 4.21. Write a suitable differential equation using Laplace Transform find $V_C(t)$.

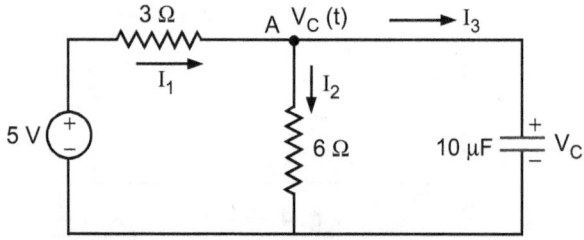

Fig. 4.21

Sol.: The node voltage at node A be $V_C(t)$. Applying KCL at node A,

$$I_1 = I_2 + I_3$$

$$\frac{5 - V_C(t)}{3} = \frac{V_C(t)}{6} + C\frac{dV_C}{dt}$$

i.e.

$$\frac{5 - V_C(t)}{3} = \frac{V_C(t)}{6} + 10 \times 10^{-6}\frac{dV_C(t)}{dt}$$

$$\frac{5}{3} - V_C(t)\left[\frac{1}{3} + \frac{1}{6}\right] = 10 \times 10^{-6}\frac{dV_C(t)}{dt}$$

Taking Laplace Transform of the above differential equation,

$$\frac{5}{3s} - \frac{1}{2} V_C(s) = 10 \times 10^{-6} [s V_C(s) - 2] \qquad [\because V_C(0-) = 2V]$$

$$\frac{5}{3s} + 20 \times 10^{-6} = V_C(s) \left[10 \times 10^{-6} s + \frac{1}{2} \right]$$

$$\frac{5 + 60 s \times 10^{-6}}{3s} = V_C(s) \left[\frac{20 \times 10^{-6} s + 1}{2} \right]$$

$$\therefore \quad V_C(s) = \frac{10 + 120 s \times 10^{-6}}{3s [1 + 20 \times 10^{-6} s]}$$

$$= \frac{\frac{10}{3} + 40 s \times 10^{-6}}{(20 \times 10^{-6}) \cdot s \cdot \left[s + \frac{1}{20 \times 10^{-6}} \right]}$$

$$= \frac{K_1}{s} + \frac{K_2}{s + \frac{1}{20 \times 10^{-6}}}$$

where,
$$K_1 = \left. \frac{\frac{10}{3} + 40s \times 10^{-6}}{20 \times 10^{-6} \left(s + \frac{1}{20 \times 10^{-6}} \right)} \right|_{s=0} = \frac{10}{3}$$

$$K_2 = \left. \frac{\frac{10}{3} + 40s \times 10^{-6}}{(20 \times 10^{-6}) s} \right|_{s = -\frac{1}{20 \times 10^{-6}}}$$

$$= -\frac{4}{3}$$

$$\therefore \quad V_C(s) = \frac{(10/3)}{s} + \frac{(-4/3)}{\left(s + \frac{1}{20 \times 10^{-6}} \right)}$$

Taking Inverse Laplace Transform of $V_C(s)$,

$$V_C(t) = \frac{10}{3} - \frac{4}{3} (e)^{-\frac{t}{20 \times 10^{-6}}} \text{ volts}$$

Ex. 4.21: After being on position 'A' for long time the switch is thrown on position 'B' at t = 0 in the circuit shown in Fig. 4.22. Find $i_L(t)$ using Laplace Transform.

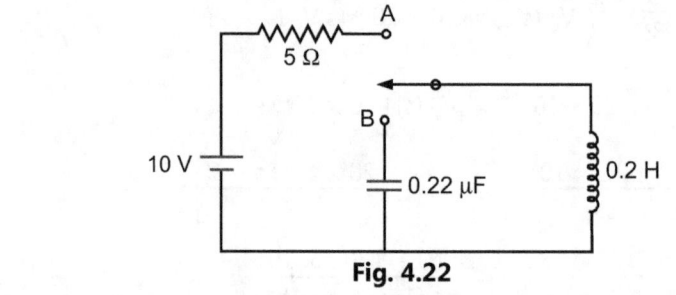

Fig. 4.22

Sol.:

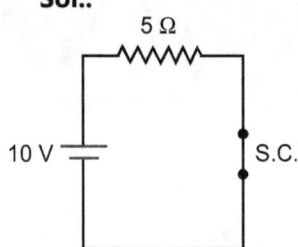 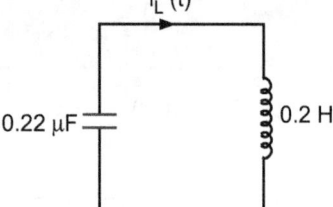 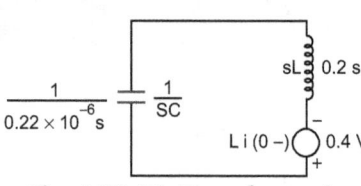

Fig. 4.22 (a): SW position A, steady state established   Fig. 4.22 (b): SW in position B   Fig. 4.22 (c): Transformed circuit

When SW is in position 'A' for a long time, steady state is achieved. The inductor acts as short circuit. Equivalent circuit appears as shown in Fig. 4.22 (a).

$$\therefore \quad i_L(0-) = \frac{10}{5} = 2 \text{ A}$$

When SW is thrown to position B [Fig. 4.22 (b)], at t = 0, applying KVL,

$$L \frac{di_L}{dt} + \frac{1}{C} \int i_L \, dt = 0$$

Transforming equation in s domain,

$$L[s I_L(s) - i_L(0-)] + \frac{1}{sC} I_L(s) = 0$$

i.e. $\quad 0.2 [s I_L(s) - 2] + \frac{1}{0.22 \times 10^{-6} s} I_L(s) = 0$

$$I_L(s) [0.044 \times 10^{-6} s^2 + 1] = 0.088 \times 10^{-6} s$$

$$I_L(s) = \frac{0.088 \times 10^{-6} s}{0.044 \times 10^{-6} \left(s^2 + \frac{1}{0.044 \times 10^{-6}}\right)} = 2 \cdot \frac{s}{s^2 + \frac{1}{0.044 \times 10^{-6}}}$$

Taking Inverse Laplace Transform,

$$i_L(t) = 2 \cos \frac{t}{0.209 \times 10^{-3}} \text{ Amp.}$$

Ex. 4.22: In the network as shown in Fig. 4.23, the switch is closed at t = 0. If the network is unenergized before the switch is closed, find expressions for $i_1(t)$ and $i_2(t)$.

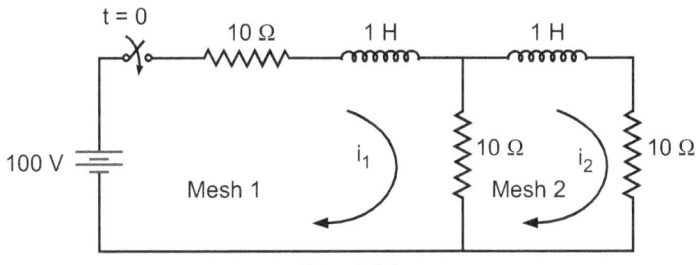

Fig. 4.23

Sol.: At t = 0, switch is closed.
Apply KVL to mesh 1 and mesh 2.

$$10\, i_1(t) + \frac{di_1(t)}{dt} + 10\,[i_1(t) - i_2(t)] = 100\, u(t)$$

$$\therefore \quad 20\, i_1(t) + \frac{di_1(t)}{dt} - 10\, i_2(t) = 100\, u(t) \qquad \ldots (a)$$

$$\frac{di_2(t)}{dt} + 10\, i_2(t) + 10\,[i_2(t) - i_1(t)] = 0$$

$$\therefore \quad 20\, i_2(t) + \frac{di_2(t)}{dt} - 10\, i_1(t) = 0 \qquad \ldots (b)$$

Transforming equations (a) and (b),

$$20\, I_1(s) - 10\, I_2(s) + s\, I_1(s) = \frac{100}{s}$$

$$-10\, I_1(s) + 20\, I_2(s) + s\, I_2(s) = 0$$

$$\therefore \quad (s + 20)\, I_1(s) - 10\, I_2(s) = \frac{100}{s} \qquad \ldots (c)$$

$$-10\, I_1(s) + (s + 20)\, I_2(s) = 0 \qquad \ldots (d)$$

Solve equations (c) and (d) simultaneously. By Cramer's rule,

$$I_1(s) = \frac{\begin{vmatrix} 100/s & -10 \\ 0 & (s+20) \end{vmatrix}}{\begin{vmatrix} s+20 & -10 \\ -10 & s+20 \end{vmatrix}} = \frac{\frac{100}{s}(s+20)}{(s^2 + 40s + 300)}$$

$$= \frac{100\,(s+20)}{s\,(s^2 + 40s + 300)}$$

$$= \frac{100\,(s+20)}{s\,(s+10)\,(s+30)}$$

By partial fraction expansion,

$$I_1(s) = \frac{A}{s} + \frac{B}{(s+10)} + \frac{C}{(s+30)}$$

where,

$$A = \left.\frac{100(s+20)s}{s(s+10)(s+30)}\right|_{s=0}$$

$$= \frac{100(20)}{10 \times 30} = \frac{20}{3} = 6.667$$

$$B = \left.\frac{100(s+20)(s+10)}{s(s+10)(s+30)}\right|_{s=-10}$$

$$= \frac{100 \times 10}{-10(20)} = -5$$

$$C = \left.\frac{100(s+20)(s+30)}{s(s+10)(s+30)}\right|_{s=-30}$$

$$= \frac{100(-10)}{-30(-20)} = -\frac{5}{3} = -1.667$$

$$\therefore \quad I_1(s) = \frac{6.667}{s} - \frac{5}{s+10} - \frac{1.667}{s+30}$$

Taking Inverse Laplace Transform,

$$i_1(t) = 6.667 - 5e^{-10t} - 1.667\,e^{-30t} \text{ Amp.}$$

Similarly,

$$I_2(s) = \frac{\begin{vmatrix} s+20 & 100/s \\ -10 & 0 \end{vmatrix}}{s^2 + 40s + 300}$$

$$= \frac{1000}{s(s+10)(s+30)}$$

The partial fraction expansion of this equation is

$$I_2(s) = \frac{K_1}{s} + \frac{K_2}{(s+10)} + \frac{K_3}{(s+30)}$$

where,

$$K_1 = \left.\frac{1000 \times s}{s(s+10)(s+30)}\right|_{s=0}$$

$$= \frac{1000}{300} = 3.333$$

$$K_2 = \left.\frac{1000\,(s+10)}{s\,(s+10)\,(s+30)}\right|_{s=-10}$$

$$= \frac{1000}{-10\,(20)} = -5$$

$$K_3 = \left.\frac{1000\,(s+30)}{s\,(s+10)\,(s+30)}\right|_{s=-30}$$

$$= \frac{1000}{-30\,(-20)} = 1.667$$

$$\therefore \quad I_2(s) = \frac{3.333}{s} - \frac{5}{s+10} + \frac{1.667}{s+30}$$

Taking Inverse Laplace Transform,

$$i_2(t) = 3.333 - 5e^{-10t} + 1.667\,e^{-30t},\ t > 0 \text{ Amp}.$$

Ex. 4.23: For the circuit shown in Fig. 4.24 solve for $i_1(t)$ and $i_2(t)$ using Laplace transform with switch closed at t = 0.

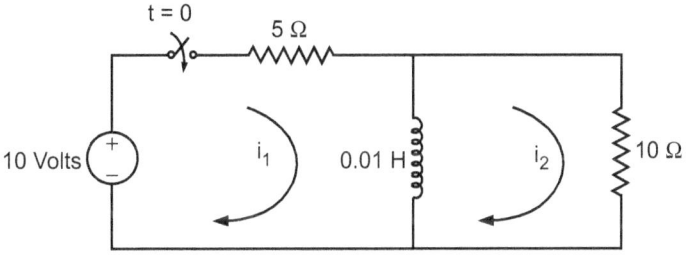

Fig. 4.24

Sol.: Assume initial values of $i_1(t)$ and $i_2(t)$ to be zero.
Applying KVL to the two loops in the circuit,

$$10\,u(t) = 5i_1(t) + 0.01\frac{d}{dt}[i_1(t) - i_2(t)]$$

$$0 = 10\,i_2(t) + 0.01\frac{d}{dt}[i_2(t) - i_1(t)]$$

Taking Laplace Transform of above set of equations.

$$\frac{10}{s} = 5I_1(s) + 0.01\,s\,[I_1(s) - I_2(s)]$$

$$\frac{10}{s} = [5 + 0.01\,s]\,I_1(s) - 0.01\,s\,I_2(s) \qquad \ldots (a)$$

$$0 = 10\,I_2(s) + 0.01\,s\,[I_2(s) - I_1(s)]$$

$$= -0.01\,s\,I_1(s) + (10 + 0.01\,s)\,I_2(s) \qquad \ldots (b)$$

By Cramer's rule, $I_1(s) = \dfrac{\begin{vmatrix} 10/s & -0.01s \\ 0 & 10+0.01s \end{vmatrix}}{\begin{vmatrix} 5+0.01s & -0.01s \\ -0.01s & 10+0.01s \end{vmatrix}}$

$= \dfrac{\dfrac{10}{s}(10+0.01s)}{(50+0.15s)} = \dfrac{\dfrac{10}{s} \times 0.01(1000+s)}{0.15\left(s+\dfrac{50}{0.15}\right)}$

$= \dfrac{2}{3} \cdot \dfrac{(1000+s)}{s(s+333.33)} = \dfrac{A}{s} + \dfrac{B}{(s+333.33)}$

where, $A = \dfrac{2}{3} \times \dfrac{1000}{333.33} = 2$

$B = \dfrac{2}{3} \times \dfrac{(1000-333.33)}{-333.33} = -\dfrac{4}{3}$

Thus, $I_1(s) = \dfrac{2}{s} - \dfrac{(4/3)}{(s+333.33)}$

Taking Inverse Laplace Transform,

$i_1(t) = 2 - \dfrac{4}{3} e^{-333.33\,t}$ Amp.; $t > 0$ Amp.

Similarly, $I_2(s) = \dfrac{\begin{vmatrix} 5+0.01s & 10/s \\ -0.01s & 0 \end{vmatrix}}{\begin{vmatrix} 5+0.01s & -0.01s \\ -0.01s & 10+0.01s \end{vmatrix}} = \dfrac{0.1}{50+0.15s} = \dfrac{2}{3} \cdot \dfrac{1}{s+333.33}$

∴ $i_2(t) = L^{-1} I_2(s) = \dfrac{2}{3} e^{-333.33\,t}$ Amp.; $t > 0$

Ex. 4.24: The switch in the Fig. 4.25 is in position 1 for a long time; it is moved to position 2 at t = 0, obtain the expression for i (t).

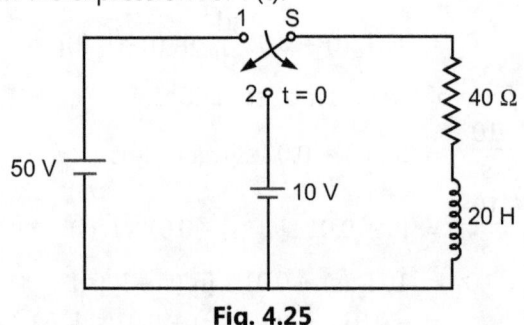

Fig. 4.25

Sol.: When switch is in position 1 for a long time, inductor acts as short circuit. [Fig. 4.25 (a)].

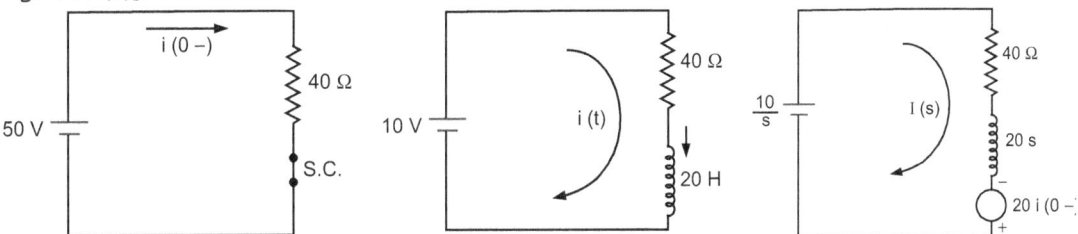

Fig. 4.25 (a): SW in position 1, steady state reached   Fig. 4.25 (b): SW in position 2   Fig. 4.25 (c): Transformed circuit

$$\therefore \quad i(0-) = \frac{50}{40} = 1.25 \text{ Amp.}$$

When SW is changed to position 2, circuit acts as shown in Fig. 4.25 (b).
Applying KVL to circuit in Fig. 4.25 (b),

$$10 \, u(t) = 40 \, i(t) + 20 \frac{di(t)}{dt}$$

Taking Laplace Transform,

$$\frac{10}{s} = 40 \, I(s) + 20 \, [s \, I(s) - i(0-)]$$

$$= (40 + 20s) \, I(s) - 25$$

$$I(s) = \frac{\frac{10}{s} + 25}{40 + 20s} = \frac{(10 + 25s)}{s \, 20 \, (s + 2)}$$

$$= \frac{25 \left(s + \frac{10}{25} \right)}{20 \, s \, (s + 2)} = \frac{1.25 \, (s + 0.4)}{s \, (s + 2)}$$

$$= \frac{A}{s} + \frac{B}{s + 2}$$

where,

$$A = \left. \frac{1.25 \, (s + 0.4)}{(s + 2)} \right|_{s = 0}$$

$$= 0.25$$

$$B = \left. \frac{1.25 \, (s + 0.4)}{s} \right|_{s = -2}$$

$$= \frac{1.25 \, (-1.6)}{(-2)} = 1$$

$$\therefore \quad I(s) = \frac{0.25}{s} + \frac{1}{s + 2}$$

$$\therefore \quad i(t) = L^{-1} \, I(s) = 0.25 + e^{-2t} \text{ Amp.} \, ; \, t > 0$$

Ex. 4.25: For the circuit shown in Fig. 4.26, determine the current i (t) for t > 0. The switch S has been closed for a long time and is opened at t = 0.

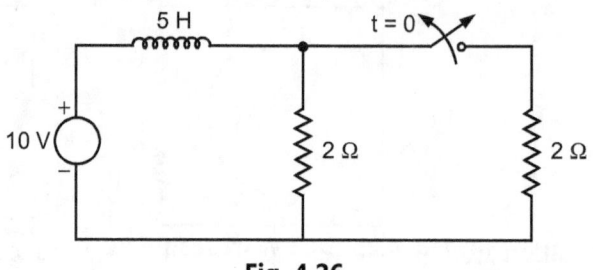

Fig. 4.26

Sol.:

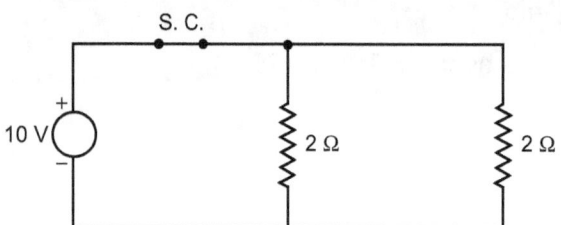

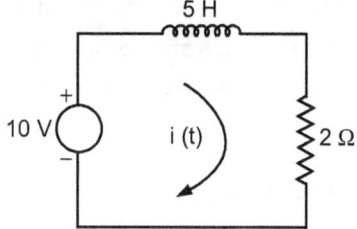

Fig. 4.26 (a): SW closed, steady state reached

Fig. 4.26 (b): SW opened at t = 0

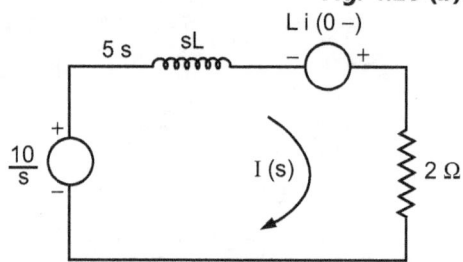

Fig. 4.26 (c): Transformed circuit

The switch has been in closed position for a long time, hence steady state has reached and inductor acts as short circuit. Hence, current through inductor.

$$\therefore \quad i(0-) = \frac{10}{2 \| 12} = \frac{10}{1} = 10 \text{ Amp.}$$

At t = 0, the SW is opened. Hence, circuit appears as shown in Fig. 4.26 (b).
Applying KVL to the circuit shown in Fig. 4.26 (b),

$$10 \, u(t) = 5\left[\frac{di(t)}{dt}\right] + 2\,i(t)$$

Transforming equation in s domain,

$$\frac{10}{s} = 5\,[s\,I(s) - i(0-)] + 2\,I(s)$$

$$= 5\,[s\,I(s) - 10] + 2\,I(s)$$

$$= (2 + 5s)\,I(s) - 50$$

$$\therefore \quad I(s) = \dfrac{\dfrac{10}{s} + 50}{2 + 5s} = \dfrac{10 + 50s}{s(2+5s)}$$

$$= \dfrac{2 + 10s}{s(s+0.4)} = \dfrac{A}{s} + \dfrac{B}{(s+0.4)}$$

where,

$$A = \dfrac{2 + 10s}{(s+0.4)}\bigg|_{s=0}$$

$$= \dfrac{2}{0.4} = 5$$

$$B = \dfrac{2 + 10s}{s}\bigg|_{s=-2/5=-0.4}$$

$$= \dfrac{2 - 4}{-0.4} = 5$$

Thus, $\quad I(s) = \dfrac{5}{s} + \dfrac{5}{s+0.4}$

$\therefore \quad i(t) = L^{-1} I(s)$

$\quad = 5 + 5e^{-0.4t}$ Amp.

Ex. 4.26: Find i(t) for t > 0 in the circuit shown in the Fig. 4.27 if the switch is opened at t = 0.

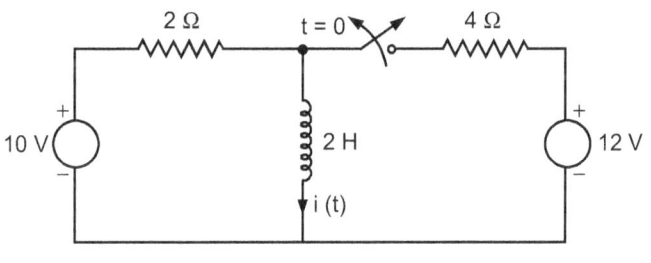

Fig. 4.27

Sol.:

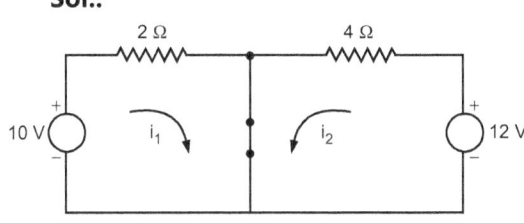

Fig. 4.27 (a): SW in closed position steady state reached

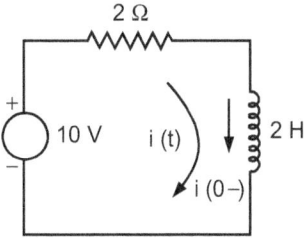

Fig. 4.27 (b): SW opened

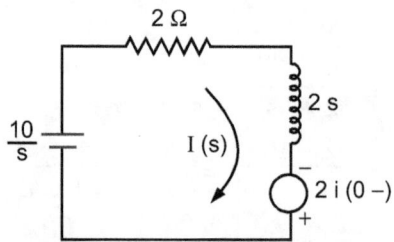

Fig. 4.27 (c): Transformed circuit

The steady state current in the inductor is

$$i(0-) = i_1(0-) + i_2(0-)$$

$$i(0-) = \frac{10}{2} + \frac{12}{4} = 8 \text{ Amp.}$$

Applying KVL to circuit in Fig. 4.27 (b),

$$10 = 2i(t) + 2\frac{di(t)}{dt}$$

Taking Laplace Transform,

$$\frac{10}{s} = 2I(s) + 2[sI(s) - i(0-)]$$

$$= [2 + 2s]I(s) - 16$$

$$\therefore \quad I(s) = \frac{\frac{10}{s} + 16}{2(s+1)} = \frac{5 + 8s}{s(s+1)}$$

$$= \frac{A}{s} + \frac{B}{s+1} = \frac{5}{s} + \frac{3}{(s+1)}$$

Taking Laplace Inverse,

$$i(t) = 5 + 3e^{-t} \text{ Amp.} ; \; t > 0 \text{ Amp.}$$

Ex. 4.27: The network shown in Fig. 4.28 reaches steady state with the switch K closed. At $t = 0$, the switch is opened. Find $i(t)$ for $t > 0$.

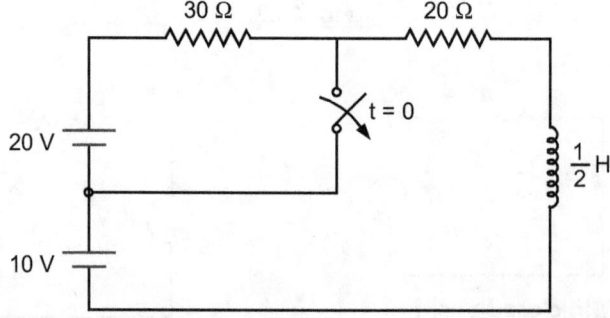

Fig. 4.28

Sol.:

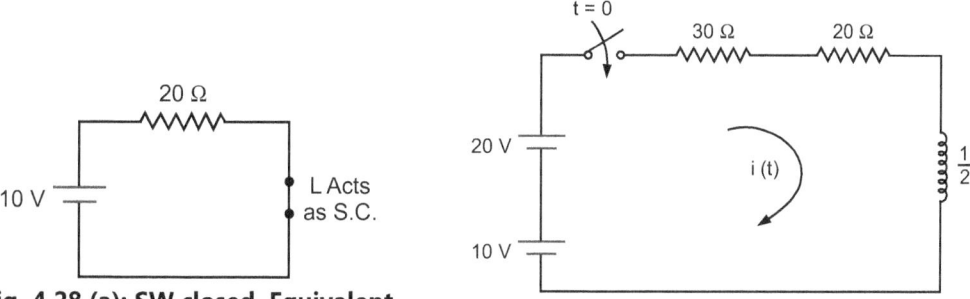

Fig. 4.28 (a): SW closed. Equivalent circuit is steady state

Fig. 4.28 (b): Equivalent circuit when SW is open

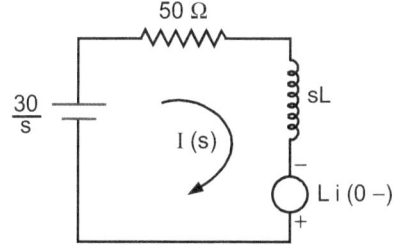

Fig. 4.28 (c): Transformed circuit

When the circuit is in closed state, before t = 0, the steady state is reached. Hence, the inductor acts as short circuit.

$$\therefore \quad i(0-) = \frac{10}{20} = 0.5 \text{ A}$$

When the switch is opened, the circuit takes the form as shown in Fig. 4.28 (b).
Applying KVL,

$$30\, u(t) = 30\, i(t) + 20\, i(t) + \frac{1}{2} \cdot \frac{di(t)}{dt}$$

Taking Laplace Transform,

$$\frac{30}{s} = 50\, I(s) + \frac{1}{2}\,[(s\, I(s) - i(0-)]$$

$$= 50\, I(s) + \frac{1}{2}\,[s\, I(s) - 0.5]$$

$$\therefore \quad \frac{30}{s} + 0.25 = \left[50 + \frac{1}{2}s\right] I(s)$$

$$\therefore \quad I(s) = \frac{(30 + 0.25\,s)}{s\left[50 + \frac{1}{2}s\right]} = \frac{2\,(30 + 0.25\,s)}{s\,(s + 100)}$$

$$= \frac{A}{s} + \frac{B}{s + 100}$$

where,

$$A = \frac{2(30 + 0.25s)s}{s(s+100)}\bigg|_{s=0}$$

$$= \frac{60}{100} = 0.6$$

$$B = \frac{20(30 + 0.25s)(s+100)}{s(s+100)}\bigg|_{s=-100}$$

$$= \frac{60 - 50}{-100} = -0.1$$

$$\therefore \quad I(s) = \frac{0.6}{s} - \frac{0.1}{s+100}$$

$$= 0.6 - 0.1\, e^{-100t} \text{ Amp.} ; \; t > 0$$

Ex. 4.28: After being on position 1 for a long time the switch is thrown on position 2 at t = 0 in the circuit shown in Fig. 4.29. Find $i_L(t)$ using Laplace Transform and sketch the waveform of $i_L(t)$.

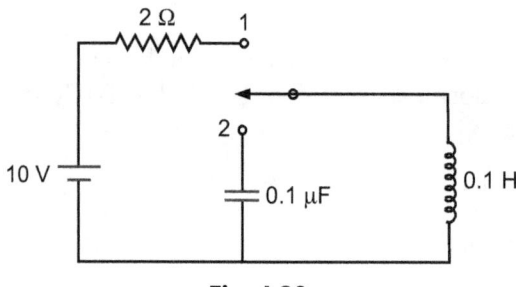

Fig. 4.29

Sol.: Circuit at time t = 0– is as shown in Fig. 4.29 (a).

$$\therefore \quad i_L(0-) = \frac{10}{2}$$

$$= 5 \text{ Amp.}$$

Fig. 4.29 (a) (2 Ω, 10 V, L Acts as S.C.)

When the switch is changed to position 2, circuit takes the form as shown in Fig. 4.29 (b).

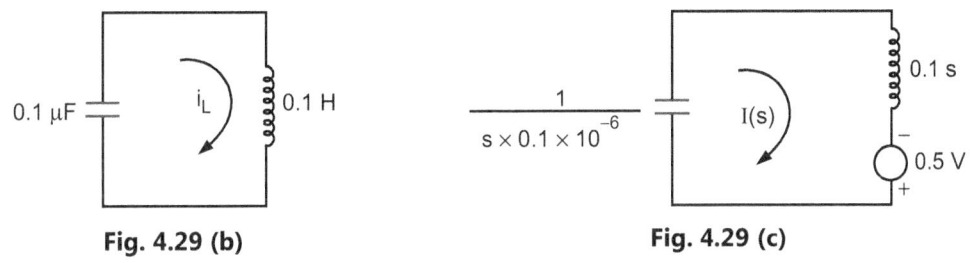

Fig. 4.29 (b) Fig. 4.29 (c)

Applying KVL,

$$\frac{1}{C}\int_{-\infty}^{t} i(t)\,dt + L\frac{di}{dt} = 0$$

i.e.

$$\frac{1}{C}\int_{0}^{t} i(t)\,dt + L\frac{di}{dt} = 0$$

(Since, initial voltage across capacitor is zero)

Transforming the equation,

$$\frac{1}{sC} I(s) + L[s I(s) - i(0-)] = 0$$

∴ $$I(s) \times \left[\frac{1}{0.1 \times 10^{-6}\,s} + 0.1\,s\right] - 0.5 = 0$$

∴ $$I(s) = \frac{0.5}{\left[\dfrac{1 + 0.01 \times 10^{-6}\,s^2}{0.1 \times 10^{-6}\,s}\right]}$$

$$= \frac{0.05 \times 10^{-6}\,s}{1 + 0.01 \times 10^{-6}\,s^2}$$

$$= \frac{0.05 \times 10^{-6}\,s}{0.01 \times 10^{-6}\left(s^2 + \dfrac{1}{0.01 \times 10^{-6}}\right)}$$

$$= 5 \times \frac{s}{s^2 + 10^8}$$

∴ $i(t) = L^{-1} I(s)$

$= 5 \cos(10^4)\,t$ Amp.

Unit 4 | 4.51

Ex. 4.29: In the circuit shown in Fig. 4.30, the switch K is thrown from position a to b at t = 0. Just before the switch is thrown to be the initial conditions are i (0–) = 2 A and V_C (0–) = 2 V. Find the current i (t). Assume L = 1 H, R = 3 Ω, C = 0.5 µF, V_1 = 5 V.

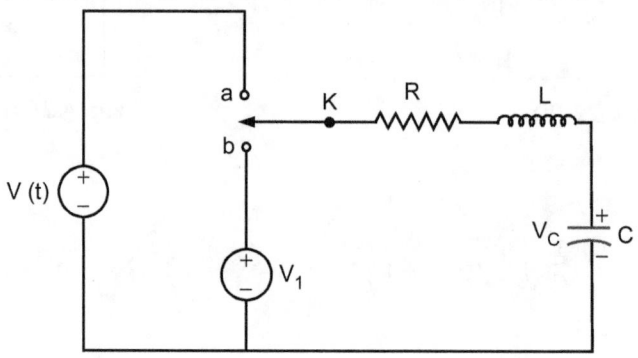

Fig. 4.30

Sol.:

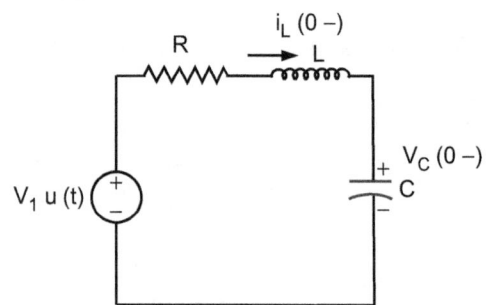

Fig. 4.30 (a): Switch in position 'b'

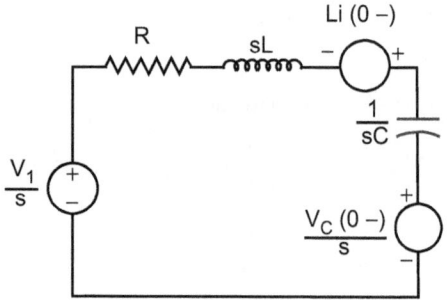

Fig. 4.30 (b): Transformed circuit

Applying KVL to circuit in Fig. 4.30 (a),

$$V_1\, u(t) = R\, i(t) + L\frac{di(t)}{dt} + \frac{1}{C}\int_{-\infty}^{t} i(t)\, dt$$

Taking Laplace Transform,

$$\frac{V_1}{s} = R\, I(s) + L\,[s\, I(s) - i(0-)] + \frac{1}{sC}\, I(s) + \frac{V_C(0-)}{s}$$

∴ $$\frac{5}{s} = 3\, I(s) + s\, I(s) - 2 + \frac{1}{s(0.5 \times 10^{-6})} + \frac{2}{5}$$

$$I(s)\left[3 + s + \frac{2 \times 10^6}{s}\right] = \frac{5}{s} - \frac{2}{s} + 2 = \frac{3}{s} + 2$$

∴ $I(s) = \dfrac{(3+2s)/s}{(s^2+3s+2\times 10^6)/s}$

$= \dfrac{3+2s}{s^2+3s+2\times 10^6}$

$= \dfrac{2(s+3/2)}{(s+3/2)^2+(2\times 10^6 - 9/4)}$

$= \dfrac{2(s+3/2)}{(s+3/2)^2+(1.414\times 10^3)^2}$

Taking Inverse Laplace Transform,

$i(t) = 2e^{-(3/2)t}\cos(1.414\times 10^3)t$ Amp.; $t>0$

Ex. 4.30: The network shown in Fig. 4.31 reaches a steady state with switch K opened. At t = 0, the switch is closed. Find i (t) for t > 0.

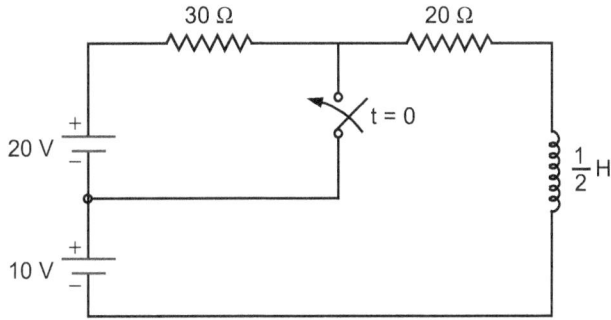

Fig. 4.31

Sol.:

$i(0-) = \dfrac{30}{50} = 0.6$ A

Fig. 4.31 (a): Switch K opened, steady state reached

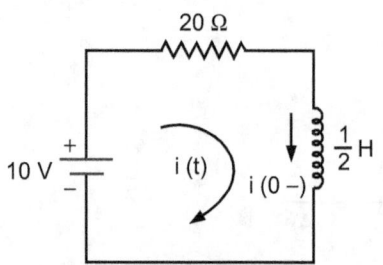
Fig. 4.31 (b): Equivalent circuit SW K closed at t = 0

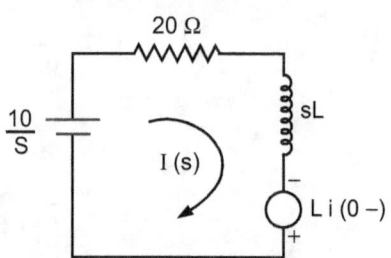
Fig. 4.31 (c): Transformed circuit

Applying KVL to circuit in Fig. 4.36 (b),

$$10 = 20\, i(t) + \frac{1}{2}\frac{di(t)}{dt}$$

Taking Laplace Transform,

$$\frac{10}{s} = 20\, I(s) + \frac{1}{2}[s\, I(s) - 0.6]$$

$$\therefore \quad \frac{10}{s} + 0.3 = I(s)\left[20 + \frac{s}{2}\right]$$

$$\therefore \quad I(s) = \frac{10 + 0.3\, s}{s(40 + s)/2}$$

$$= \frac{2(10 + 0.3\, s)}{s(40 + s)}$$

$$= \frac{A}{s} + \frac{B}{s + 40}$$

$$= \frac{0.5}{s} + \frac{0.1}{s + 40}$$

$$\therefore \quad i(t) = L^{-1} I(s) = 0.5 + 0.1\, e^{-40t} \text{ Amp.}$$

Ex. 4.31: As shown in Fig. 4.32, 10 V battery is connected to the circuit by closing the SW at t = 0. Assume that initial voltage on the capacitor is zero. Determine the expression for $V_C(t)$ and $i_C(t)$. Sketch waveforms.

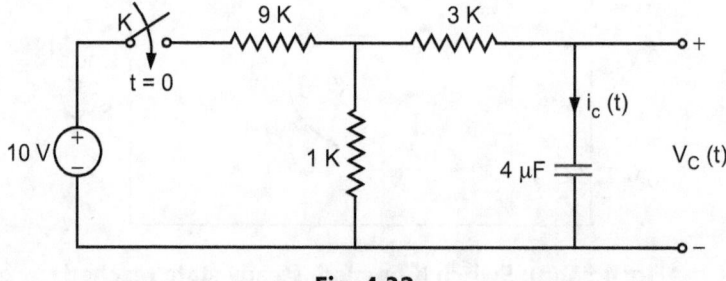
Fig. 4.32

Sol.: Convert the circuit shown in Fig. 4.32 into Thevenin's equivalent circuit as in Fig. 4.32 (a).

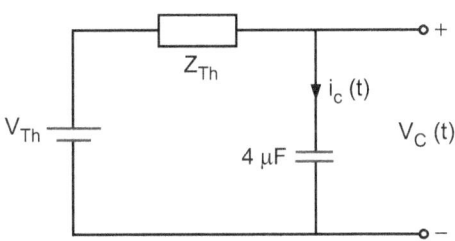

Fig. 4.32 (a): Thevenin's equivalent circuit

To find V_{Th} remove capacitor C and determine A.C. voltage between points A and B in Fig. 4.32 (b).

$$V_{Th} = V_{AB} = 10 \times \frac{1\,K}{9\,K + 1\,K} = 1 \text{ volt}$$

Fig. 4.32 (b): At t > 0

To find Z_{Th}, consider Fig. 4.32 (c)

$$\therefore \quad Z_{Th} = Z_{AB}$$
$$= 3\,K + (1\,K \parallel 9\,K)$$
$$= 3\,K + \left(\frac{1 \times 9}{1 + 9}\right) K$$
$$= 3.9 \text{ k}\Omega$$

Fig. 4.32 (c)

Reconnect capacitor of 4 µF to Thevenin's equivalent circuit.

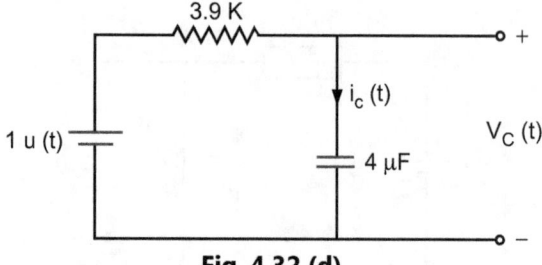

Fig. 4.32 (d)

Applying KCL to equivalent circuit in Fig. 4.32 (d),

$$1\, u(t) = 3.9\, K\, i_C(t) + \frac{1}{C}\int_{-\infty}^{t} i(t)\, dt \qquad \ldots (1)$$

Since, initial voltage across capacitor is zero,

$$V_C(0-) = \frac{1}{C}\int_{-\infty}^{0} i(t)\, dt = 0$$

Transforming equation (1),

$$\frac{1}{s} = 3.9 \times 10^3\, I_C(s) + \frac{1}{sC}\, I_C(s)$$

$$= I_C(s)\left[3.9 \times 10^3 + \frac{1}{4 \times 10^{-6}\, s}\right]$$

$$\therefore\quad I_C(s) = \frac{1/s}{\left[3.9 \times 10^3 + \dfrac{25 \times 10^4}{s}\right]} = \frac{1}{3.9 \times 10^3\left[s + \dfrac{25 \times 10^4}{3.9 \times 10^3}\right]}$$

$$= 2.564 \times 10^{-4} \times \frac{1}{(s + 64.1)}$$

$$\therefore\quad i_C(t) = 2.564 \times 10^{-4} \times e^{-64.1\, t}\ \text{Amp.}$$

Similarly,

$$V_C(s) = \frac{1}{sC}\, I(s)$$

$$\therefore\quad V_C(s) = \frac{2.564 \times 10^{-4}}{4 \times 10^{-6}\, s} \times \frac{1}{(s + 64.1)}$$

$$= \frac{64.1}{s(s + 64.1)} = \frac{A}{s} + \frac{B}{(s + 64.1)}$$

$$= \frac{1}{s} + \frac{(-1)}{s + 64.1}$$

$$\therefore\quad V_C(t) = L^{-1}\, V_C(s)$$

$$= 1 - e^{64.1\, t}\ \text{volts}$$

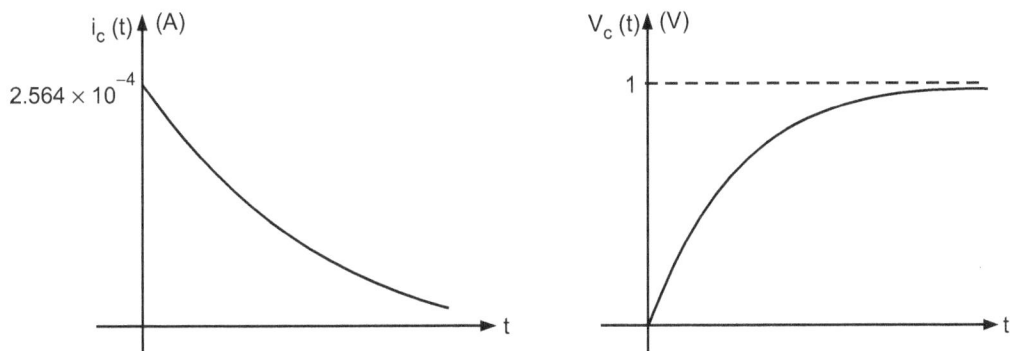

Fig. 4.32 (e): Response curves for $i_C(t)$ and $v_C(t)$

MULTIPLE CHOICE QUESTIONS (MCQs)

1. The impulse response of a causal, linear, time invariant, continuous time system is h(t). The output y(t) of the same system to an input x(t), where x(t) = 0, for t < −2 is

   (a) $\int_{-2}^{t+2} h(\tau)\, x(t-\tau)\, d\tau$

   (b) $\int_{-2}^{t-2} h(\tau)\, x(t-\tau)\, d\tau$

   (c) $\int_{0}^{t} h(\tau)\, x(t-\tau)\, d\tau$

   (d) $\int_{-2}^{t} h(\tau)\, x(t-\tau)\, d\tau$

2. On closing switch 'S', the circuit in the given figure is in steady-state. The current in the inductor after opening the switch 'S' will

   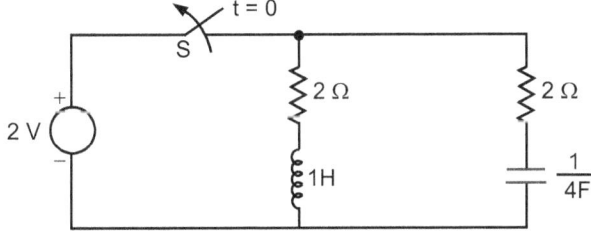

   (a) be oscillatory
   (b) consist of two decaying exponentials each with a time constant of 0.5s
   (c) decay exponentially with a time constant of 2s
   (d) decay exponentially with a time constant of 0.5s

3. The final value of $L^{-1} \dfrac{2s+1}{s^4 + 8s^3 + 16s^2 + s}$ is

   (a) infinity (b) 1
   (c) 2 (d) zero

4. The Laplace transformation method enables one to find the response of a network in the
   (a) both transient and steady states
   (b) steady state only
   (c) transient state only
   (d) transient provided sinusoidal forcing functions do not exit

5. If $x(t)$ and $\dfrac{dx(t)}{d}$ are Laplace transformable and $\lim\limits_{t \to \infty} x(t)$ exists, then $\lim\limits_{t \to \infty} x(t)$ is equal to
   (a) $\lim\limits_{s \to \infty} \dfrac{X(s)}{S}$
   (b) $\lim\limits_{s \to 0} \dfrac{X(s)}{S}$
   (c) $\lim\limits_{s \to \infty} sX(s)$
   (d) $\lim\limits_{\infty \to s} sX(s)$

6. Laplace transform of e^{at} is
   (a) $\dfrac{a}{s}$
   (b) $\dfrac{1}{(s+a)}$
   (c) $\dfrac{1}{(s-a)}$
   (d) $\dfrac{1}{s}$

7. Laplace transform of sin at is
   (a) $\dfrac{-a}{(s^2 + a^2)}$
   (b) $\dfrac{a}{(s^2 + a^2)}$
   (c) $\dfrac{-a}{(s^2 - a^2)}$
   (d) $\dfrac{a}{(s^2 - a^2)}$

8. The output of a linear system to a unit step input $u(t)$ is $t^2 e^{-2t}$. The system function $H(s)$ is
   (a) $\dfrac{2}{(s+2)^2}$
   (b) $\dfrac{2}{s^2(s+2)}$
   (c) $\dfrac{2}{(s+2)^3}$
   (d) $\dfrac{2s}{(s+2)^3}$

9. The impulse response of a system is $h(t) = \delta(t - 0.5)$. If two such systems are cascaded, then impulse response of the overall system will be
   (a) $\delta(s - 1)$
   (b) $0.55\,\delta(t - 1)$
   (c) $\delta(t - 0.25)$
   (d) $0.5\delta(t - 0.25)$

10. The double integration of a unit step function results in
    (a) a unit impulse
    (b) a unit doublet
    (c) a unit ramp function
    (d) a unit parabola

11. In the circuit shown in the given figure switch K is closed at t = 0. The circuit was initially relaxed. Which one of the following sources of v(t) will produce maximum current at t = 0^+?

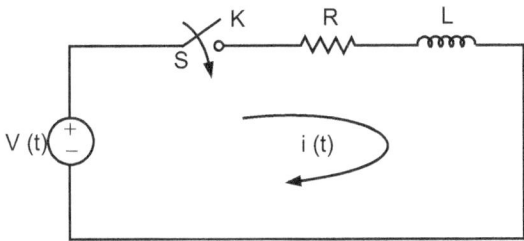

(a) unit step
(b) unit ramp
(c) unit impulse
(d) unit step plus unit ramp

12. In the given circuit, S was initially open. At time t = 0, S is closed. When the current through the inductor is 6A, the rate of change of current through the resistor is 6A/s. The value of the inductor would be

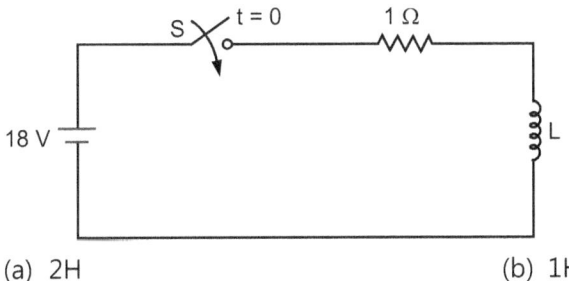

(a) 2H
(b) 1H
(c) 4H
(d) 3H

13. Which one of the following is the correct Laplace transform of the signal in the given figure?

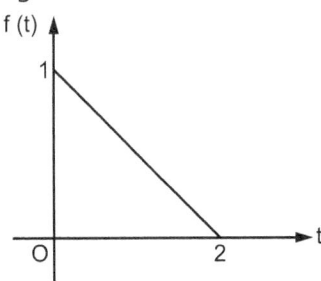

(a) $\frac{1}{T_s^2}[1 - e^{-Ts} + T_s]$
(b) $\frac{1}{T_s^2}[e^{-Ts} + 1 - T_s]$
(c) $\frac{1}{T_s^2}[e^{-Ts} - 1 + T_s]$
(d) $\frac{1}{T_s^2}[1 - e^{-Ts}(1 + T_s)]$

14. In the circuit shown in the given figure, switch 'S' is closed at time t = 0. After sometime when the current in the inductor was 6A, the rate of change of current through it was 4A/s. The value of the inductor is

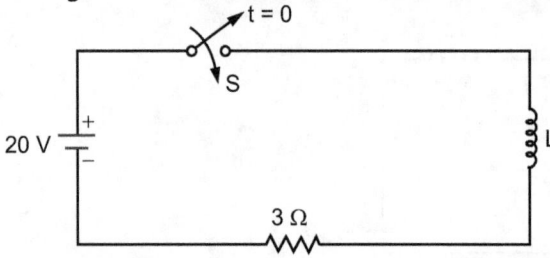

(a) 0.5 H
(b) 1.5 H
(c) 1.0 H
(d) indeterminate

15. The circuit shown in the given figure has been in the steady-state when the switch S is opened. The current I after the switch is opened in given by

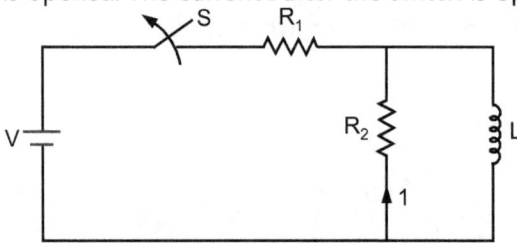

(a) $\dfrac{V}{R_1 + R_2} e^{\frac{Lt}{R_2}}$

(b) $\dfrac{V}{R_1} e^{\frac{t/L}{R_2}}$

(c) $\dfrac{VR_2}{R_1 + R_2} e^{\frac{-L(R_1 + R_2)t}{R_1 R_2}}$

(d) $\dfrac{V}{R_2} e^{-R_1 \frac{t}{L}}$

16. The output of a linear system for a unit step input is given by $t^2 e^t$. The transfer function is given by

(a) $\dfrac{2s}{(s+1)^3}$

(b) $\dfrac{s}{(s+1)^3}$

(c) $\dfrac{1}{s^2(s+1)}$

(d) $\dfrac{2}{(s+1)^2}$

17. If $h(t) = 10\, e^{-10t}\, u(t)$ and $e(t) = \sin 10t\, u(t)$ then Laplace transform of the signal

$f(t) = \int h(t-\tau)\, e(\tau)\, d\tau$ is given by

(a) $\dfrac{100}{(s+10)(s^2+100)}$

(b) $\dfrac{1}{(s+10)(s^2+100)}$

(c) $\dfrac{10}{(s+10)(s^2+100)}$

(d) $\dfrac{10(s+10)}{(s^2+100)}$

18. For the following network input impedance z(s) as s → 0 and s → ∞ are given by

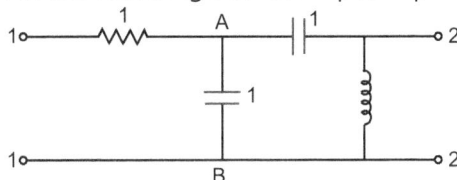

(a) $1, \dfrac{2}{3}$
(b) $\dfrac{2}{s}, 1$
(c) $\left(\dfrac{1}{2s}, 1\right)$
(d) $\dfrac{2}{s}, \dfrac{1}{s}$

19. In the circuit shown in the figure i(t) is a unit step current. The steady-state value of v(t) is

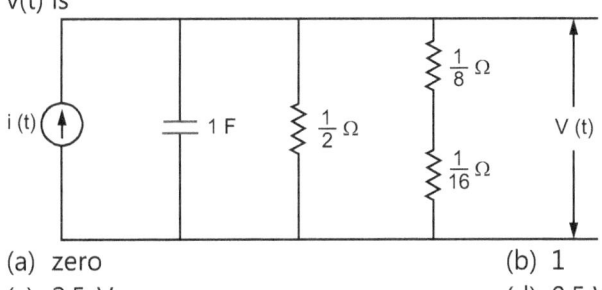

(a) zero
(b) 1
(c) 2.5 V
(d) 0.5 V

20. If x(t) and its first derivative are Laplace transformable and the Laplace transform of x(t) is X(s), Then $\lim_{t \to 0} x(t)$ is given by

(a) $\lim_{s \to 0} sX(s)$
(b) $\lim_{s \to 0} \dfrac{X(s)}{s}$
(c) $\lim_{s \to 0} sX(s)$
(d) $\lim_{s \to 0} \dfrac{X(s)}{s}$

21. If δ(t) denotes a unit, impulse, then the Laplace transform of $\dfrac{d^2\delta(t)}{dt^2}$ will be

(a) s
(b) 1
(c) s^2
(d) s^{-2}

22. The steady state current through the 1 H inductance in the circuit shown in the given figure is

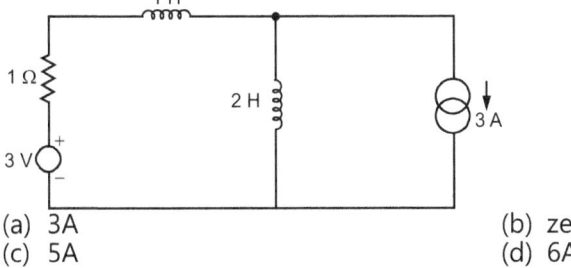

(a) 3A
(b) zero
(c) 5A
(d) 6A

23. Given the Laplace transform, $v(t) = \int_0^\infty e^{-st} v(t)\, dt$. The inverse transform v(t) is

   (a) $\int_{\sigma-j\infty}^{\sigma+j\infty} e^{st} V(s)\, ds$

   (b) $\dfrac{1}{2\pi j} \int_0^\infty e^{st} V(s)\, ds$

   (c) $\dfrac{1}{2\pi j} \int_{\sigma-j\infty}^{\sigma+j\infty} e^{st} V(s)\, ds$

   (d) $\dfrac{1}{2\pi j} \int_{\sigma-j\infty}^{\sigma+j\infty} e^{-st} V(s)\, ds$

24. Double integration of a unit step function would lead to
    (a) an impulse
    (b) a parabola
    (c) a doublet
    (d) a ramp

25. In the circuit shown in the given figure, the switch closes at t = 0. The voltage across 4 µF capacitor in ideal condition changes to

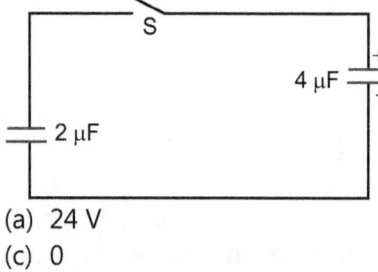

    (a) 24 V
    (b) 16 V
    (c) 0
    (d) 15 V

26. If a square wave is fed to an RC circuit then voltage across
    (a) R is square and across C is not square
    (b) both R and C are square
    (c) both R and C are not square
    (d) C is not square and across C is not square

27. A unit impulse function is obtained on differentiation of a unit
    (a) step function
    (b) ramp function
    (c) doublet
    (d) triplet

28. The Laplace transform of the waveform shown in the figure is

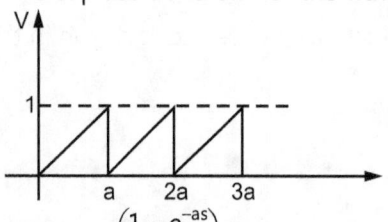

   (a) $V_{(s)} = \left(\dfrac{1-e^{-as}}{2}\right)$

   (b) $V_{(s)} = \left(\dfrac{1-e^{-as}}{2s^2} - \dfrac{e^{-as}}{s}\right)$

   (c) $V_{(s)} = \left(\dfrac{1-e^{-as}}{as^2} - \dfrac{e^{-as}}{s}\right) \dfrac{1}{(1-e^{-as})}$

   (d) $V_{(s)} = \dfrac{1}{(1-e^{as})}$

29. The Laplace transform of $\cos(\omega_0 t + \phi)$ is

(a) $\dfrac{s^2 + \omega_0^2}{s\cos\phi - \omega_0 \sin\phi}$

(b) $\dfrac{s - \omega_0 \phi}{s^2 + \omega_0^2}$

(c) $\dfrac{s^2 + \omega^2}{s\sin\phi + \omega_0 \cos\phi}$

(d) $\dfrac{s\cos\phi - \omega_0 \sin\phi}{s^2 + \omega_0^2}$

30. The Laplace transform of t^n is

(a) $\dfrac{n!}{s^{n+1}}$

(b) $\dfrac{1}{s^{2n}}$

(c) $\dfrac{n^2}{s - a}$

(d) $\dfrac{n^2}{s + a}$

31. Inverse Laplace transform of $\dfrac{s}{s^2 + \omega^2}$ is

(a) $\cosh \omega t$

(b) $\sin \omega t$

(c) $\cos \omega t$

(d) $\sinh \omega t$

32. 's' is the Laplace transform of

(a) unit step function

(b) unit doublet

(c) unit ramp function

(d) unit impulse function

33. Inverse Laplace transform of $\dfrac{10}{s^2 + 4s + 4}$ is

(a) $10 t^2 e^{-2t}$

(b) $10 e^{-2t}$

(c) $5 t^2 e^{-2t}$

(d) $10 t e^{-2t}$

34. Inverse Laplace transform of $\dfrac{7}{s^2 + 2s + 10}$

(a) $\dfrac{7}{3} e^{-t} \sin 3t$

(b) $\dfrac{7}{3} e^{-t} \cos 3t$

(c) $7 e^{-t} \sin 3t$

(d) $7 e^{-t} \cos 3t$

35. Laplace transform of unit impulse function $\delta(t - t_1)$ is

(a) $e^{t_1 s}$

(b) $e^{-t_1 s}$

(c) $2e^{-t_1 s}$

(d) 1

36. Laplace transform of unit ramp function $r(t)$ is

(a) 1

(b) s

(c) $\dfrac{1}{s^2}$

(d) $\dfrac{1}{s}$

37. The Laplace transform of function f(t) is

    (a) $\int_0^\infty f(t) e^{-st} dt$
    (b) $\int_0^\infty f(t) e^{st} dt$
    (c) $\int_{t_\infty}^{+\infty} f(t) e^{-st} dt$
    (d) $\int_{+\infty}^{-\infty} f(t) e^{st} dt$

38. Laplace transform of a unit step function is
    (a) 5
    (b) s^2
    (c) 1
    (d) $\dfrac{1}{s}$

39. Laplace transform of a unit impulse function is
    (a) s
    (b) $\dfrac{1}{s}$
    (c) 1
    (d) $\dfrac{1}{s^2}$

40. Laplace transform of shifted unit step function u(t − a) is
    (a) $\dfrac{1}{(s-a)}$
    (b) $\dfrac{1}{s}$
    (c) $e^{-at}\left(\dfrac{1}{s}\right)$
    (d) $\dfrac{1}{s-a} e^{-at}$

41. $H(s) = \dfrac{V_{(s)}}{I_{(s)}} = \dfrac{s+3}{(s+1)^2}$ i(t) is unit step. v(t) in the steady state is given by
    (a) 0
    (b) 1
    (c) 2
    (d) 3

42. The frequency at which maximum voltage results across the inductor in a series RLC circuit is

    (a) $\dfrac{1}{2\pi\sqrt{LC}}$
    (b) $\dfrac{1}{2\pi\sqrt{LC - \dfrac{C^2R^2}{2}}}$
    (c) $\dfrac{1}{2\pi\sqrt{LC - R^2}}$
    (d) $\dfrac{1}{2\pi\sqrt{\dfrac{LC - C^2R^2}{2}}}$

43. The frequency at which maximum voltage occurs across the capacitor in a series RLC circuit is

    (a) $\dfrac{1}{2\pi\sqrt{LC}}$
    (b) $\dfrac{1}{2\pi}\sqrt{\dfrac{1}{LC} - \dfrac{R^2}{2C^2}}$
    (c) $\dfrac{1}{2\pi\sqrt{LC}}\sqrt{\dfrac{R^2}{2L^2}}$
    (d) $\dfrac{1}{2\pi}\sqrt{\dfrac{1}{L^2C^2} - \dfrac{R^2}{2L}}$

44. In the network shown, the switch is opened at t = 0. Prior to that, the network was in the steady-state $V_s(t)$ At t = 0^+ is

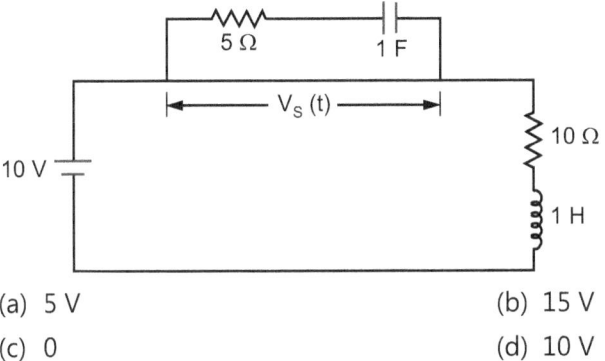

(a) 5 V
(b) 15 V
(c) 0
(d) 10 V

45. In the circuit shown i(t) is a unit step current. The steady-state value of v(t) is

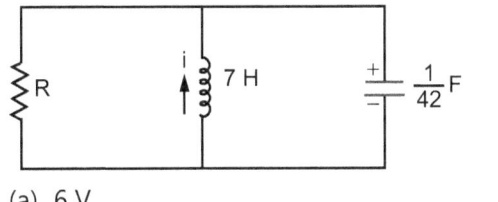

(a) 6 V
(b) 3 V
(c) 2 V
(d) 9 V

46. If $i(t) = \left(\dfrac{1}{4}\right)(1 - e^{-2t})\ u(t)$, where u(t) is a unit step voltage, then the complex frequencies associated with i(t) would include

(a) S = 0 and S = –2
(b) S = j2 and S = –j2
(c) S = 0 and S = j2
(d) S = –j2 and S = –2

47. The Laplace transform of the following voltage waveform is

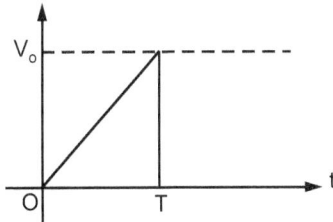

(a) $\dfrac{V_o}{T_s^2} - \dfrac{V_o}{T_s^2} e^{-sT}$

(b) $\dfrac{V_o}{T_s^2} + \dfrac{V_o}{T_s^2} e^{-sT}$

(c) $\dfrac{V_o}{T_s^2} - \dfrac{V_o}{T_s^2} e^{-sT}[1+ sT]$

(d) $\dfrac{V_o}{T_s^2} - \dfrac{V_o}{T_s} e^{-sT}$

48. The circuit shown in the given figure is steady-state with switch 'S' open. The switch is closed at t = 0. The values of $V_c(0^+)$ and $V_c(\infty)$ will be respectively.

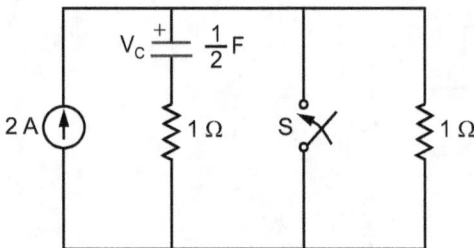

(a) 2 V, 2 V (b) 2 V, 0 V
(c) 0 V, 2 V (d) 0 V, 0 V

49. The impulse response of an R-L circuit is a
    (a) decaying exponential function
    (b) rising exponential function
    (c) parabolic function
    (d) step function

50. The sinusoidal steady-state voltage gain of the network shown in the given figure will have magnitude equal to 0.707 at an angular frequency of

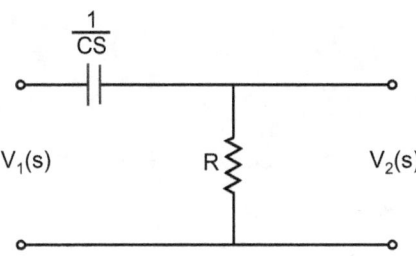

(a) zero (b) RC rad/sec
(c) 1 rad/s (d) $\dfrac{1}{RC}$ rad/sec

51. In the series RC circuit shown in figure below the voltage across C starts increasing when the d.c. source is switch on. The rate of increase of voltage across C at the instant just after the switch is closed (i.e. at t = 0^+) will be

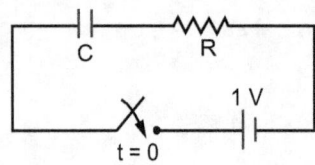

(a) RC (b) infinity
(c) $\dfrac{1}{RC}$ (d) zero

52. The impulse response of an R-L circuit is a
    (a) rising exponential function
    (b) step function
    (c) decaying exponential function
    (d) parabolic function

53. A pulse of unit amplitude and with 'a' is applied to a series RL circuit as shown in the figure. The current i(t) tends to infinity will be

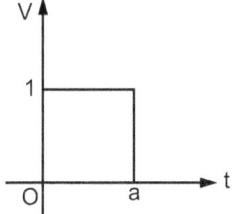
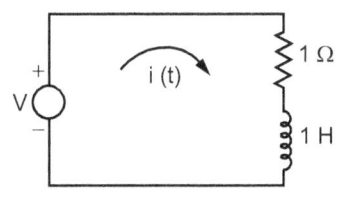

    (a) 1 A
    (b) zero
    (c) a value between zero and one depending upon the width of the pulse
    (d) infinite

54. The sinusoidal steady-state voltage gain of the network shown in figure will have magnitude equal to 0.707 at an angular frequency of

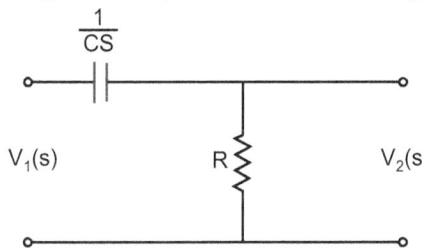

    (a) $\dfrac{1}{RC}$ rad/s
    (b) RC rad/s
    (c) zero
    (d) 1 rad/s

55. After closing the switch 'S' at t = 0, the current i(t) at any instant 't' in the network shown in the given figure will be

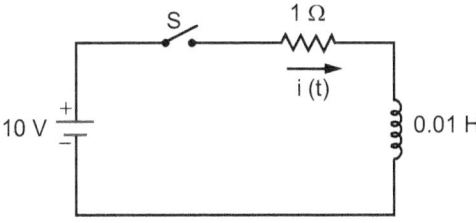

    (a) $10 - 10\,e^{-100t}$
    (b) $10 - 10\,e^{100t}$
    (c) $10 + 10\,e^{100t}$
    (d) $10 + 10\,e^{-100t}$

56. In the network shown in the given figure, if the voltage V at the time considered is 20 V then $\dfrac{dv}{dt}$ at that time will be

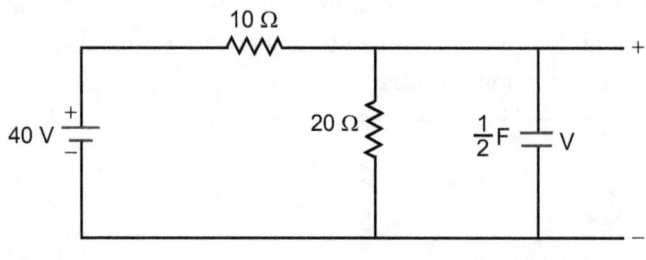

(a) $1 \dfrac{V}{s}$
(b) $2 \dfrac{V}{s}$
(c) zero
(d) $-2 \dfrac{V}{s}$

57. A system is presented by $\dfrac{dy}{dt} + 2y = 4\,u(t)$. The ramp constant in the forced response will be

(a) $3t\,u(t)$
(b) $2t\,u(t)$
(c) $t\,u(t)$
(d) $4t\,u(t)$

58. The Laplace transform of the function $i(t)$ is $I(s) = \dfrac{10s + 4}{s(s + 1)(s^2 + 4s + 5)}$. Its final value will

(a) 4
(b) $\dfrac{4}{5}$
(c) 5
(d) $\dfrac{5}{4}$

59. If the unit step response of a network is $(1 - e^{-at})$, then its unit impulse response will be

(a) $\dfrac{1}{\alpha e^{-t/\alpha}}$
(b) $(1 - \alpha)\,e^{-\alpha t}$
(c) $\alpha\, e^{-\alpha t}$
(d) $\dfrac{1}{\alpha}\,e^{-t/\alpha}$

60. The Laplace transform of $(t^2 - 2t)\,u(t - 1)$ is

(a) $\dfrac{2}{s^3}\,e^{-s} - \dfrac{1}{5}\,e^{-s}$
(b) $\dfrac{2}{s^3}\,e^{-2s} - \dfrac{2}{s^2}\,e^{-s}$
(c) $\dfrac{2}{s^3}\,e^{-s} - \dfrac{1}{s^2}\,e^{-s}$
(d) none of the above

61. The unit impulse response of a system is given as $c(t) = 4e^{-t} + 6e^{-2t}$. The step response of the same system for $t \geq 0$ is equal to
   (a) $3e^{-2t} + 4e^{-t} - 1$
   (b) $-3e^{-2t} - 4e^{-t} - 1$
   (c) $-3e^{-2t} + 4e^{-t} + 1$
   (d) $-3e^{-2t} + 4e^{-t} + 1$

62. After closing the switch 'S' at t = 0, the current i(t) at any instant 't' in the network shown in the given figure will be

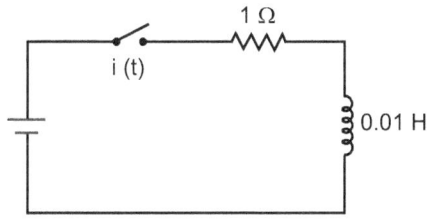

   (a) $10 + 10\, e^{-100\,t}$
   (b) $10 + 10\, e^{100\,t}$
   (c) $10 - 10\, e^{100\,t}$
   (d) $10 - 10\, e^{-100\,t}$

63. In the network shown in the figure the circuit was initially in the steady-state condition with the switch K closed. At the instant when the switch is opened, the rate of decay of current through the inductance will be

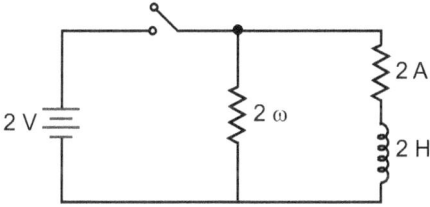

   (a) zero
   (b) 2A/S
   (c) 0.5 A/S
   (d) 1 A/S

64. In the circuit shown in figure, the switch S has been opened for long time. It is closed t = 0, for t > 0, the current flowing through the inductor will be given by

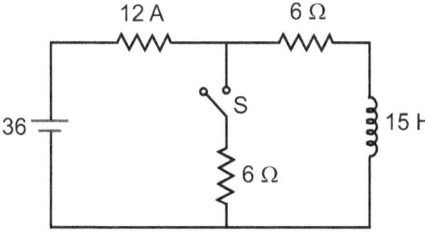

   (a) $i_L(t) = 0.8 - 1.2\, e^{-2t}$
   (b) $i_L(t) = 0.8 + 1.2\, e^{-2t}$
   (c) $i_L(t) = 1.2 - 0.8\, e^{-2t}$
   (d) $i_L(t) = 1.2 + 0.8\, e^{-2t}$

65. A periodic rectangular signal x(t) has the waveform shown in the figure. Frequency of the fifth harmonic of its spectrum is

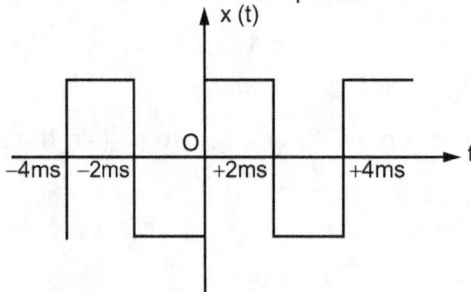

(a) 1250 Hz
(b) 200 Hz
(c) 40 Hz
(d) 250 Hz

66. In the series Rc circuit in the figure, the voltage across C starts increasing when the d.c. source is switched ON. The rate of increase of voltage across C at the instant just after the switch is closed (i.e. at t = 0⁺) will be

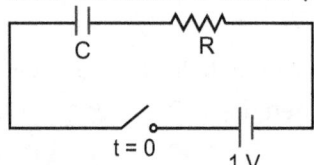

(a) RC
(b) infinity
(c) $\dfrac{1}{RC}$
(d) zero

67. The current flowing through an RL series circuits with input voltage v(t) is given in the s-domain equal to

(a) $\dfrac{V(s)}{R + SL}$
(b) $V(s) \cdot \left[R + \dfrac{1}{SL}\right]$
(c) $\dfrac{V(s)}{R + \dfrac{1}{SL}}$
(d) $V(s)(R + SL)$

68. The impedance of a 10 F capacitor in s-domain is equal to

(a) 10 s
(b) $\dfrac{10}{s}$
(c) $\dfrac{s}{10}$
(d) $\dfrac{1}{10s}$

69. If the input to a linear system of δ(t) and the output is e^{-2t} u(t), the transfer function of the system is equal to

(a) $\dfrac{s}{s + 2}$
(b) $\dfrac{s}{s - 2}$
(c) $\dfrac{1}{s - 2}$
(d) $\dfrac{1}{s + 2}$

70. In Laplace transform, the variable 's' equals (σ + jω). Which of the following represent the true nature of σ?
   1. σ has a damping effect
   2. σ is responsible for convergence of integral $\int_0^\infty F(t) \cdot e^{-st} \cdot dt$
   3. σ has a value less than zero
   Select the correct answer using the codes given below
   (a) 1 and 2
   (b) 1 and 3
   (c) 2 and 3
   (d) 1, 2 and 3

71. Which one of the following is the correct Laplace transform of the signal in the given figure

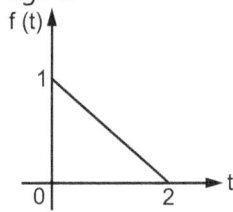

   (a) $\frac{1}{Ts^2}[1 - e^{-Ts}(1 + Ts)]$
   (b) $\frac{1}{Ts^2}[e^{-Ts} - 1 + Ts)]$
   (c) $\frac{1}{Ts^2}[e^{-Ts} + 1 - Ts)]$
   (d) $\frac{1}{Ts^2}[1 - e^{-Ts} + Ts)]$

72. Given the Laplace transform,
   $$v(t) = \int_0^\infty e^{-st} \cdot v(t) \cdot dt$$
   The inverse transform v(t) is
   (a) $\int_{\sigma-j\infty}^{\sigma+j\infty} e^{st} \cdot V(s) \cdot ds$
   (b) $\frac{1}{2\pi j}\int_0^\infty e^{st} \cdot V(s) \cdot ds$
   (c) $\frac{1}{2\pi j}\int_{\sigma-j\infty}^{\sigma+j\infty} e^{st} \cdot V(s) \cdot ds$
   (d) $\frac{1}{2\pi j}\int_{\sigma-j\infty}^{\sigma+j\infty} e^{-st} \cdot V(s) \cdot ds$

73. A unit feedback control system has a forward path transfer function equal to
   $$\frac{42.25}{s(s + 6.5)}$$
   The unit step response of this system starting from rest, will have its maximum value at a time equal to
   (a) 0 sec
   (b) infinity
   (c) 0.56 sec
   (d) 5.6 sec

74. The voltage through a resistor with current i(t) in the s-domain is equal to
   (a) R I(s)
   (b) SR I(s)
   (c) $\dfrac{R\,I(s)}{s}$
   (d) none of the above

75. For the following network input impedance Z(s) as s → 0 and s → ∞ are given by

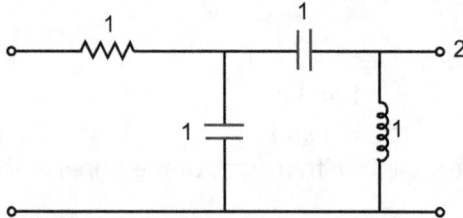

   (a) $\dfrac{1}{2s}, 1$
   (b) $\dfrac{2}{s}, 1$
   (c) $1, \dfrac{2}{s}$
   (d) $\dfrac{2}{s}, \dfrac{1}{s}$

76. The current through a series RL circuit $\dfrac{1}{4} \cdot e^{-t/2}$ when excited by a unit impulse voltage. The values of R and L are respectively
   (a) 8, 4
   (b) 2, 4
   (c) 4, 2
   (d) 1, 4

77. If x(t) is the linear input to a linear network whose impulse response h(t) is known, then assuming that the impulse applied at t = λ the output response y(t) will be
   (a) y(t) = x(t) * h(t)
   (b) y(t) = x(t − λ) * h(t)
   (c) y(t) = x(λ) * h(t − λ)
   (d) y(t) = x(t + λ) * h(t − λ)

ANSWERS

1. (d)	2. (c)	3. (b)	4. (a)	5. (c)	6. (c)	7. (b)	8. (d)	9. (a)	10. d)
11. (c)	12. (a)	13. (c)	14. (a)	15. (b)	16. (b)	17. (c)	18. (c)	19. (d)	20. (a)
21. (c)	22. (a)	23. (c)	24. (b)	25. (a)	26. (c)	27. (a)	28. (c)	29. (d)	30. (a)
31. (c)	32. (b)	33. (d)	34. (a)	35. (b)	36. (c)	37. (a)	38. (d)	39. (c)	40. (c)
41. (d)	42. (b)	43. (b)	44. (d)	45. (c)	46. (a)	47. (c)	48. (b)	49. (a)	50. (d)
51. (c)	52. (c)	53. (b)	54. (a)	55. (a)	56. (b)	57. (b)	58. (b)	59. (c)	60. (a)
61. (c)	62. (d)	63. (b)	64. (d)	65. (a)	66. (c)	67. (a)	68. (d)	69. (d)	70. (a)
71. (b)	72. (c)	73. (b)	74. (a)	75. (a)	76. (b)	77. (c)			

EXERCISE

1. Define and explain complex frequency variable (s).
2. Define Laplace Transform of a functiojn f(t).
3. Distinguish between 'time domain analysis' and 'Frequency domain analysis'.
4. Explain what is meant by 'Convolution integral'.
5. Explain how convolution theorem can be used to find Inverse Laplace Transform of a given function F(s).
6. Explain following input signals and obtain their Laplace transform :
   (a) Unit step
   (b) Unit ramp
   (c) Unit impulse
   (d) Sinusoidal
   (e) Exponential
   (f) Hyperbolic
   (g) Gate.
7. Obtain the transform of the following circuit elements :
   (a) Resistor
   (b) Inductor
   (c) Charged capacitor.
8. Explain following theorems on Laplace Transform
   (a) Shifting
   (b) Linearity
   (c) Scaling
   (d) Convolution
   (e) Initial value
   (f) Final value.

9. Find inverse L.T. of the following functions :

(a) $\dfrac{3}{s(s^2 + 6s + 9)}$

(b) $\dfrac{2s}{(s^2 + 4)(s + 5)}$

(c) $\dfrac{1}{s(s^2 - a^2)}$

(d) $\dfrac{s^2 + 7s^2 + 14s + 11}{s^3 + 6s^2 + 11s + 16}$

(e) $\dfrac{s^2 + 3s^2 + 3s + 2}{s^2 + 2s + 2}$

(f) $\dfrac{(s + 1)}{s^2(s^2 + 4s + 4)}$

(g) $\dfrac{s^4 + 10s^2 + 9}{s^3 + 4s}$

(h) $\dfrac{2(s^2 + 4s + 3)}{(s^2 + 8s + 12)}$

10. In the circuit switch 'K' is closed and steady state conditions reached. At t = 0 switch opened obtain expression for current through inductor and plot it.

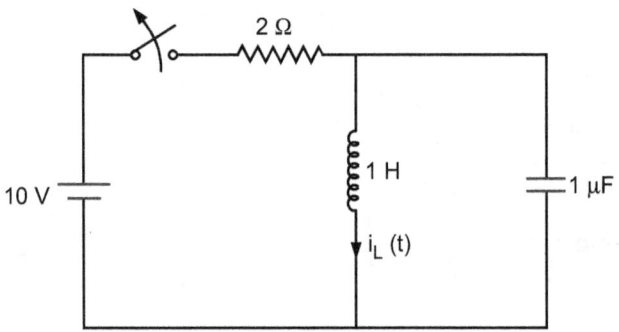

Fig. 4.33

(**Ans.** 5 cos 1000 t)

11. In the circuit switch has been open for a long time at t = 0 it is closed. Find voltage across capacitor V(t).

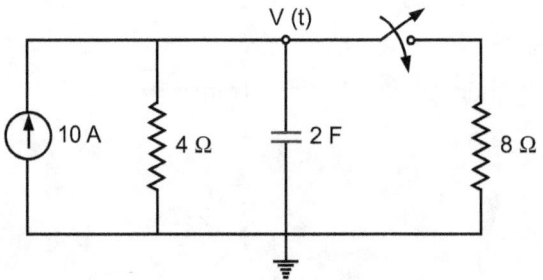

Fig. 4.34

(**Ans.** 40 u (f) = $\dfrac{40}{3}$ u(t) [1 – 3e$^{-3/16}$])

12. In the circuit shown find current through inductor if V(t) = 5 U(t).

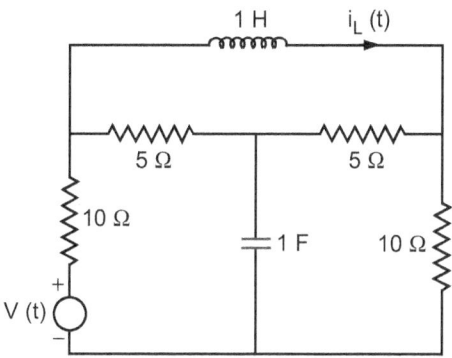

Fig. 4.35

13. Initially circuit is not energised at t = 0 both switches closed using superposition theorem find current in inductor use L.T.

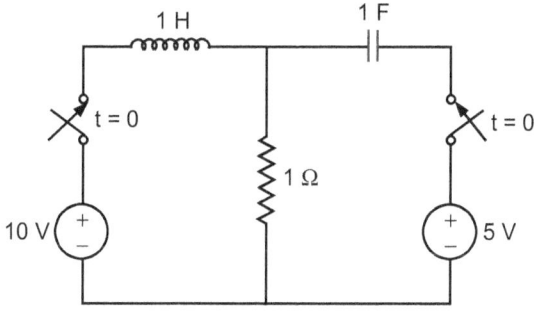

Fig. 4.36

14. For the circuit shown determine response V(t) when input i(t) is (1) impulse function, (2) unit step function.

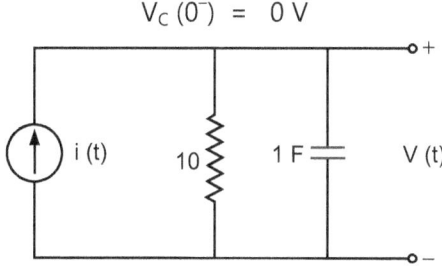

Fig. 4.37

(**Ans.** (1) e^{-t}, (2) $1 - e^{-t}$)

15. Assume unit impulse current find differential equation relating v(t) and i(t).

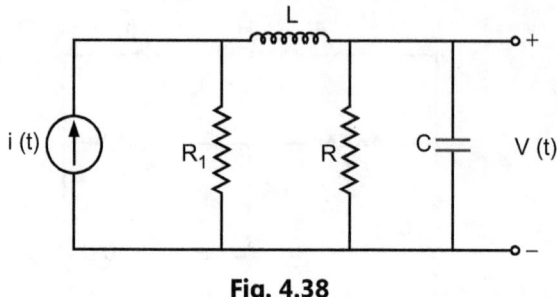

Fig. 4.38

Unit 5

TWO PORT NETWORK AND FILTERS

Contents ...

5.1 Introduction
    5.1.1 Four Terminal Network
    5.1.2 Port
    5.1.3 One Port Network
    5.1.4 Two Port Network
    5.1.5 Multiport Network
5.2 Characterization of Two Port Network
5.3 Open Circuit Impedance or Z-Parameter
    5.3.1 Condition for Reciprocity and Symmetry
5.4 Short-Circuit Admittance of Y-Parameters
    5.4.1 Condition for Symmetry and Reciprocity
5.5 Transmission or ABCD Parameters
    5.5.1 Condition for Symmetry and Reciprocity
5.6 Hybrid Parameters or h-Parameters
    5.6.1 Condition for Symmetry and Reciprocity
5.7 Interrelationships between the Parameters
    5.7.1 Z-parameter in Terms of Other Parameters
5.8 Instantaneous Power
5.9 Maximum Average Power Transfer
5.10 Effective or RMS Value
5.11 Power Factor
5.12 Complex Power
5.13 Power Factor Correction
5.14 Problem in Optimizing Power
5.15 Energy Storage
5.16 Insertion Loss
5.17 Introduction of Filters
5.18 Passive Filters
    5.18.1 Basic Definitions
    5.18.2 Classification of Passive Filters
    5.18.3 Ideal and a Practical Filter
5.19 Filter Fundamentals
    5.19.1 Logical Thinking
    5.19.2 Mathematical Analysis

5.20 m Derived Low Pass Filter
    5.20.1 Operation of m-derived LPF
    5.20.2 Reactance Curves
    5.20.3 f_∞ and f_c in m derived LPF
    5.20.4 Derivation of f_∞ and m for a m derived LPF
    5.20.5 π Section
5.21 m Derived High Pass Filter
    5.21.1 Operation of m Derived HPF
    5.21.2 Reactance Curves
    5.21.3 F_∞ and F_C in m Derived HPF
    5.21.4 Deviation of F_∞ and m for am derived LPF
    5.21.5 π Section
5.22 Summary of m Derived Filters
5.23 Solved Numericals on m Derived Filters
5.24 Disadvantages of m Derived Filters
5.25 Termination with m Derived Half Sections
    5.25.1 Necessity of m-derived Half Sections
    5.25.1 m Derived Half Sections (T type)
    5.25.3 m Derived Half Section (π Type)
    5.25.4 Characteristics Impedance of a m Derived Half Section
    5.25.5 Terminating a T and a π Section Filter Network
5.26 Summary of m Derived Terminating Half Sections
5.27 Composite Filter
5.28 Solved Numericals on Composite Filters
5.29 Summary on Filters
    5.29.1 Constant K Prototype Filters
    5.29.2 m Derived Filters
    5.29.3 m Derived Terminating Half Sections
    Exercise

5.1 INTRODUCTION

A network containing two pairs of terminals is called as two port network. One of them is input port other one is output port. In total there are 4 variables. Taking two variables as independent and expressing other two variables in terms of these independent variables gives rise to six types of parameters. In this chapter we are going to study only 4 types of parameters viz z-parameter, y-parameter. H-parameter and ABCD parameters in detail. No detailed study is carried out about inverse transmission parameters and g-parameters.

Parameters of a network represents characteristic of that particular network. For example, H-parameters are extensively used to define characteristic of a transistor such as its input impedance, output impedance. Reverse voltage gain, current gain etc. By knowing parameter we can judge suitability of a particular network to some applications. Thus parameters represents electrical characteristic (quality) of a particular network.

In addition to defining various types of parameters, and calculation of parameters of various network, effect on parameters, when various networks are inter-connected is also studied in this chapter. Also characteristic of gyrator, transformer and negative impedance converters is studied.

5.1.1 Four-Terminal Network

Every network has some external terminals. One for entry and other for exit.

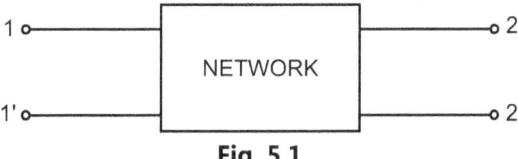

Fig. 5.1

A network having four such terminals is called as four terminal network.

5.1.2 Port

A pair of terminals at which an electrical signal may enter or leave a network is called as a port.

5.1.3 One Port Network

A network having only one pair of terminals is called as one port network.

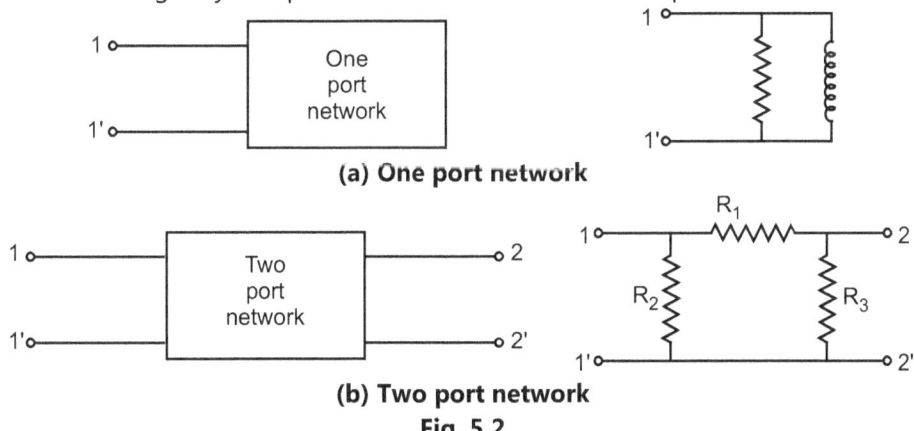

(a) One port network

(b) Two port network

Fig. 5.2

5.1.4 Two Port Network

A network having two pairs of terminals is called as two port network.

By analogy with transmission networks, one of the port (normally the port labelled with 1-1') is called as **input port.** While the other (labelled as 2-2') is called as **output port.**

5.1.5 Multiport Network

A network having multiple such ports is called as multiport network.

e.g.

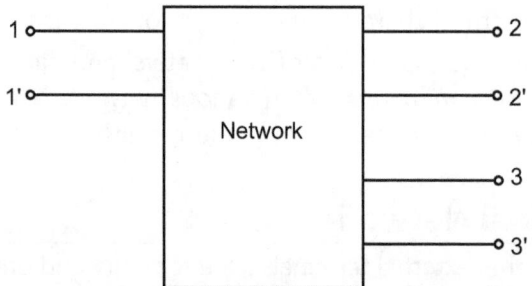

Fig. 5.3: 6-Terminal three port network

5.2 CHARACTERIZATION OF TWO PORT NETWORK

In the two port networks as shown in Fig. 5.4, we see four variables identified - two voltages (V_1 and V_2) and two currents (I_1 and I_2).

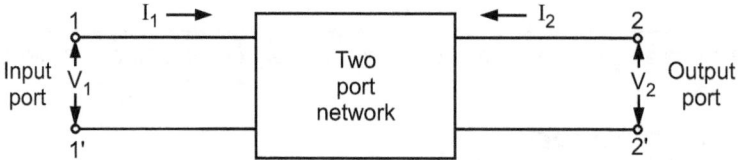

Fig. 5.4: Two port network

Here we assume that -
- There are other voltages and currents that might be identified inside the box. But they are not considered here for analysis.
- The box showing two port network is perfectly **linear** and **time invariant.**
- Only dependent sources may be present inside the box, no independent source is allowed.
- The direction of currents I_1 and I_2 is inside as shown in Fig. 5.4.

Here we assume that the variables V_1 and I_1 at input port and V_2 and I_2 at output port are transformed quantities. In order to describe the relationships among the port voltages and currents, as many linear equations are required as there are ports.

Thus, for a two port network, two linear equations are required among the four variables.

Out of the four variables - two are **independent** variables and remaining two are **dependent** i.e. by specifying any two we can calculate remaining two.

Here there are six possible ways of selecting two independent variables out of four variables.

These six combinations and their different network parameters names are indicated in the Table 5.1.

Table 5.1

Network Parameter	Variable Dependent	Variable Independent	Equation giving dependent variable
Open-circuit impedance (Z)	V_1, V_2	I_1, I_2	$\begin{bmatrix} V_1 \\ V_2 \end{bmatrix} = \begin{bmatrix} Z_{11} & Z_{12} \\ Z_{21} & Z_{22} \end{bmatrix} \begin{bmatrix} I_1 \\ I_2 \end{bmatrix}$
Short-circuit admittance (Y)	I_1, I_2	V_1, V_2	$\begin{bmatrix} I_1 \\ I_2 \end{bmatrix} = \begin{bmatrix} Y_{11} & Y_{12} \\ Y_{21} & Y_{22} \end{bmatrix} \begin{bmatrix} V_1 \\ V_2 \end{bmatrix}$
Transmission parameters (T) (A, B, C, D)	V_1, I_1	V_2, I_2	$\begin{bmatrix} V_1 \\ I_1 \end{bmatrix} = \begin{bmatrix} A & B \\ C & D \end{bmatrix} \begin{bmatrix} V_2 \\ -I_2 \end{bmatrix}$
Hybrid parameter (h)	V_1, I_2	V_2, I_1	$\begin{bmatrix} V_1 \\ I_2 \end{bmatrix} = \begin{bmatrix} h_{11} & h_{12} \\ h_{21} & h_{22} \end{bmatrix} \begin{bmatrix} I_1 \\ V_2 \end{bmatrix}$
Inverse transmission (T') (A', B', C', D')	V_2, I_2	V_1, I_1	$\begin{bmatrix} V_2 \\ I_2 \end{bmatrix} = \begin{bmatrix} A' & B' \\ C' & D' \end{bmatrix} \begin{bmatrix} V_1 \\ -I_1 \end{bmatrix}$
Inverse hybrid (g)	I_1, V_2	V_1, I_2	$\begin{bmatrix} I_1 \\ V_2 \end{bmatrix} = \begin{bmatrix} g_{11} & g_{12} \\ g_{21} & g_{22} \end{bmatrix} \begin{bmatrix} V_1 \\ I_2 \end{bmatrix}$

5.3 OPEN CIRCUIT IMPEDANCE OR Z-PARAMETER

In Z-parameter, voltages V_1 and V_2 are expressed in terms of current of I_1 and I_2.

$$(V_1, V_2) = f(I_1, I_2)$$

$$[V] = [Z][I]$$

$$\begin{bmatrix} V_1 \\ V_2 \end{bmatrix} = \begin{bmatrix} Z_{11} & Z_{12} \\ Z_{21} & Z_{22} \end{bmatrix} \begin{bmatrix} I_1 \\ I_2 \end{bmatrix}$$

∴ Z-parameter equations are

$$\left. \begin{array}{l} V_1 = Z_{11} I_1 + Z_{12} I_2 \\ V_2 = Z_{21} I_1 + Z_{22} I_2 \end{array} \right\} \quad \ldots (5.1)$$

To calculate the values of Z_{11}, Z_{12}, Z_{21} and Z_{22}, we have to make either $I_1 = 0$ or $I_2 = 0$. Thus we will get,

(i) When $I_2 = 0$, output is open circuited,

$$Z_{11} = \left[\frac{V_1}{I_1}\right]_{I_2 = 0} \quad \ldots \text{(a)}$$

$$Z_{21} = \left[\frac{V_2}{I_1}\right]_{I_2 = 0} \quad \ldots \text{(b)}$$

(ii) When $I_1 = 0$, input is open circuited,

$$Z_{12} = \left[\frac{V_1}{I_2}\right]_{I_1 = 0} \quad \ldots \text{(c)}$$

$$Z_{22} = \left[\frac{V_2}{I_2}\right]_{I_1 = 0} \quad \ldots \text{(d)}$$

where,
Z_{11} = Open circuit during point impedance
Z_{22} = Open circuit output impedance
Z_{12} = Open circuit forward transfer impedance
Z_{21} = Open circuit reverse transfer impedance

As per the conditions, $I_1 = 0$ or $I_2 = 0$ implies open circuit at port 1 or port 2. These parameters are called as **open-circuit parameters.**

The equivalent circuit for Z-parameters is as shown in Fig. 5.5.

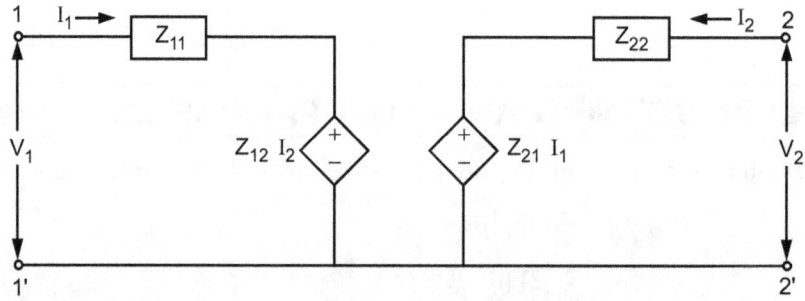

Fig. 5.5: Equivalent two port network in terms of Z-parameters

5.3.1 Condition for Reciprocity and Symmetry

(A) Symmetry condition:

The network is said to be symmetrical if impedance measured from one port with other port open circuit is equal to the impedance measured at other port with first port open circuited.

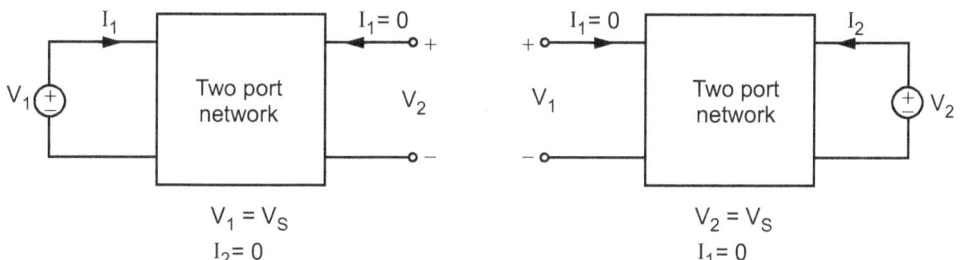

Fig. 5.6

To prove the condition of symmetry, let us consider,

Case I: $\quad V_1 = V_s \brace I_2 = 0$ ... (a)

From equation (5.1), $\quad V_1 = Z_{11} I_1 + Z_{12} I_2$

$\quad V_2 = Z_{21} I_1 + Z_{22} I_2$

Putting equation (a) in equation (5.1),

$$V_s = Z_{11} I_1$$

$\therefore \quad \boxed{Z_{11} = \dfrac{V_s}{I_1}}$ ... (b)

Case II: $\quad V_2 = V_s \brace I_1 = 0$ ... (c)

Putting equation (c) in equation (5.1),

$$V_s = Z_{22} I_2$$

$\therefore \quad \boxed{Z_{22} = \dfrac{V_s}{I_2}}$ ... (d)

As per symmetry condition,

$$\text{Input impedance} = \text{Output impedance}$$

$$\dfrac{V_s}{I_1} = \dfrac{V_s}{I_2}$$

$\therefore \quad \boxed{Z_{11} = Z_{22}}$ ... (5.2)

is the condition for symmetry.

(B) Reciprocity Condition:

A network is said to be reciprocal, if the ratio of voltage at one port to the current at other port is same to the ratio, if position of voltage and current are interchanged.

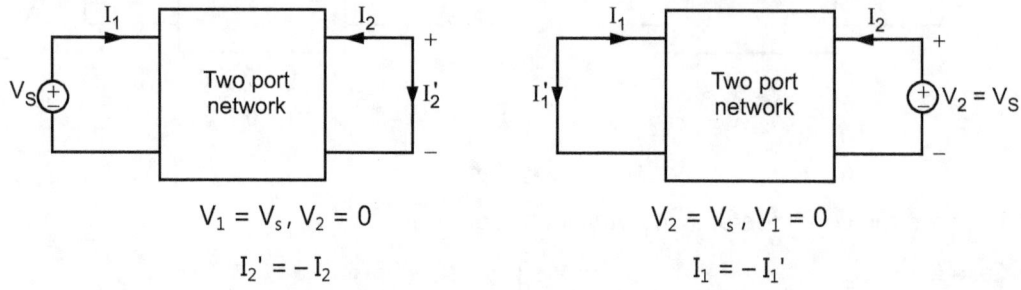

$$V_1 = V_s, V_2 = 0 \qquad\qquad V_2 = V_s, V_1 = 0$$
$$I_2' = -I_2 \qquad\qquad I_1 = -I_1'$$

Fig. 5.7

For reciprocal network, $\boxed{\dfrac{V_s}{I_1} = \dfrac{V_s}{I_2}}$ ... (e)

For Z-parameter:

Case I: $\qquad V_1 = V_s, V_2 = 0$

$\qquad\qquad\qquad I_2 = -I_2'$

Putting these values in equation (5.1),

$$V_s = Z_{11} I_1 + Z_{12} (-I_2') \qquad \text{... (f)}$$

and $\qquad\quad 0 = Z_{21} I_1 + Z_{22} (-I_2')$

$\therefore \qquad Z_{21} I_1 = Z_{22} I_2'$

$\therefore \qquad I_1 = \dfrac{Z_{22}}{Z_{21}} \cdot I_2' \qquad \text{... (g)}$

Putting in equation (f),

$$V_s = Z_{11} \left(\dfrac{Z_{22}}{Z_{21}}\right) I_2' - Z_{12} (I_2')$$

$$V_s = \dfrac{Z_{11} Z_{22}}{Z_{21}} \cdot I_2' - Z_{12} I_2'$$

$$= I_2' \left(\dfrac{Z_{11} Z_{22} - Z_{12} Z_{21}}{Z_{21}}\right)$$

$$\boxed{\dfrac{V_s}{I_2'} = \left(\dfrac{Z_{11} Z_{22} - Z_{12} Z_{21}}{Z_{21}}\right)} \qquad \text{... (h)}$$

Case II: $V_2 = V_s$, $V_1 = 0$

$$I_1 = -I_1'$$

Putting these values in equation (5.1),

$$0 = Z_{11}(-I_1') + Z_{12} I_2 \quad \ldots \text{(i)}$$
$$V_s = Z_{21}(-I_1') + Z_{22} I_2 \quad \ldots \text{(j)}$$

From equation (i),

$$\boxed{I_2 = \frac{Z_{11}}{Z_{12}} \cdot I_1'} \quad \ldots \text{(k)}$$

Putting in equation (j),

$$V_s = Z_{21}(-I_1') + Z_{22}\left(\frac{Z_{11}}{Z_{12}}\right) I_1'$$

$$\therefore \quad \boxed{\frac{V_s}{I_1'} = \frac{Z_{11} Z_{22} - Z_{12} Z_{21}}{Z_{12}}} \quad \ldots (l)$$

From reciprocity condition,

$$\frac{V_s}{I_2'} = \frac{V_s}{I_1'}$$

$$\therefore \quad \frac{Z_{11} Z_{22} - Z_{12} Z_{21}}{Z_{21}} = \frac{Z_{11} Z_{22} - Z_{12} Z_{21}}{Z_{12}}$$

$$\therefore \quad \boxed{Z_{21} = Z_{12}} \quad \ldots (5.3)$$

is the condition for reciprocity.

Ex. 5.1: Find the Z-parameters of the network shown in Fig. 5.8 and draw its equivalent circuit.

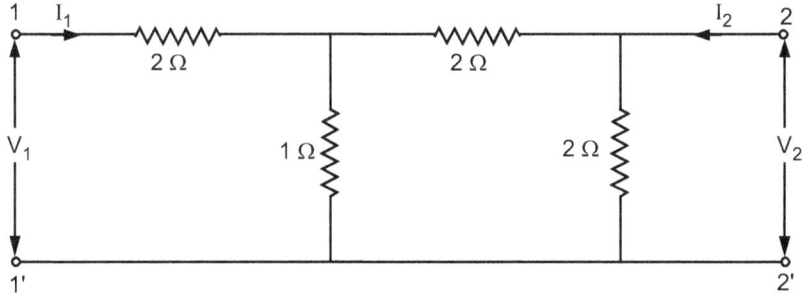

Fig. 5.8 (a)

Sol.: From definitions,

(a) $I_2 = 0$

Output terminals 2 - 2' open circuit.

$\therefore \quad Z_{11} = \left[\dfrac{V_1}{I_1}\right]_{I_2 = 0}$ and $Z_{21} = \left[\dfrac{V_2}{I_1}\right]_{I_2 = 0}$

Let us consider that a V_1 volt source is applied as input to 1 - 1'.

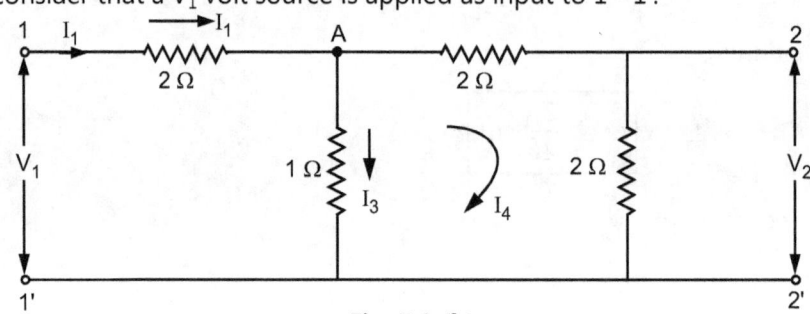

Fig. 5.8 (b)

By applying KCL at point A,

$$I_1 = I_3 + I_4$$

By current divider rule,

$$I_4 = \left(\dfrac{1}{1+4}\right) I_1$$

$\therefore \quad \boxed{I_4 = \dfrac{1}{5} I_1}$ ... (a)

and

$$I_3 = \dfrac{4}{(1+4)} I_1$$

$\therefore \quad \boxed{I_3 = \dfrac{4}{5} I_1}$ ... (b)

But

$$I_4 = \dfrac{V_2}{2}$$

$\therefore$ Putting into equation (a),

$$\dfrac{V_2}{2} = \dfrac{I_1}{5}$$

$\therefore \quad \dfrac{V_2}{I_1} = \dfrac{2}{5}$

$\therefore \quad Z_{21} = \left[\dfrac{V_2}{I_1}\right]_{I_2 = 0} = \dfrac{2}{5} \Omega$

$\therefore \quad \boxed{Z_{21} = \dfrac{2}{5} \Omega}$

Now by applying KVL to input loop,

$$-2I_1 - I_3 + V_1 = 0$$
$$\therefore \quad V_1 = 2I_1 + I_3$$

But,
$$I_3 = \frac{4}{5} I_1$$

From equation (5.1)

$$\therefore \quad V_1 = 2I_1 + \frac{4}{5} I_1$$

$$V_1 = I_1 \left(2 + \frac{4}{5}\right)$$

$$\frac{V_1}{I_1} = \frac{14}{5}$$

$$\therefore \quad \boxed{Z_{11} = \frac{14}{5} \, \Omega}$$

(b) Now make $I_1 = 0$

Input terminals 1 - 1' open circuit.

$$\therefore \quad Z_{12} = \left[\frac{V_1}{I_2}\right]_{I_1 = 0}$$

$$Z_{22} = \left[\frac{V_2}{I_2}\right]_{I_1 = 0}$$

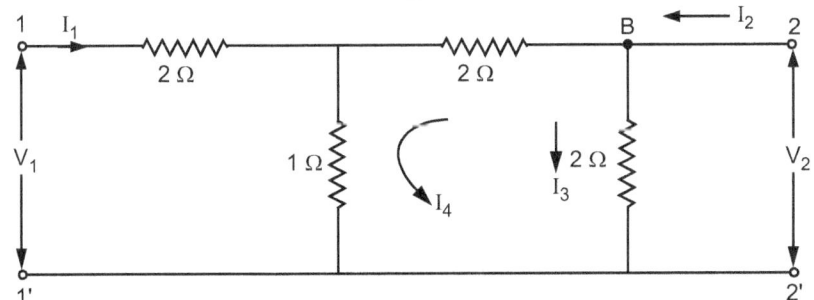

Fig. 5.8 (c)

By KCL at point B, $\quad I_2 = I_3 + I_4$

By current divider rule, $\quad I_4 = \dfrac{2 I_2}{(2 + 3)}$

$$I_4 = \frac{2}{5} I_2 \qquad \ldots \text{(c)}$$

and
$$I_3 = \frac{3 \times I_2}{(3+2)}$$
$$I_3 = \frac{3}{5} I_2 \quad \ldots (d)$$

But
$$I_4 = \frac{V_1}{1}$$
$$I_4 = V_1$$

∴
$$V_1 = \frac{2}{5} I_2 \quad \ldots \text{From equation (c)}$$
$$\frac{V_1}{I_2} = \frac{2}{5}$$

∴
$$\boxed{Z_{12} = \frac{2}{5} \Omega}$$

By applying KVL to output side,
$$V_2 = 2 I_3$$
$$= 2 \times \frac{3}{5} I_2 \quad \ldots \text{From equation (d)}$$

∴
$$\frac{V_2}{I_2} = \frac{6}{5} \Omega$$

∴
$$\boxed{Z_{22} = \frac{6}{5} \Omega}$$

∴ Z-parameters are:
$$[Z] = \begin{bmatrix} \frac{14}{5} & \frac{2}{5} \\ \frac{2}{5} & \frac{6}{5} \end{bmatrix} \Omega$$

Equivalent circuit for Z-parameters is

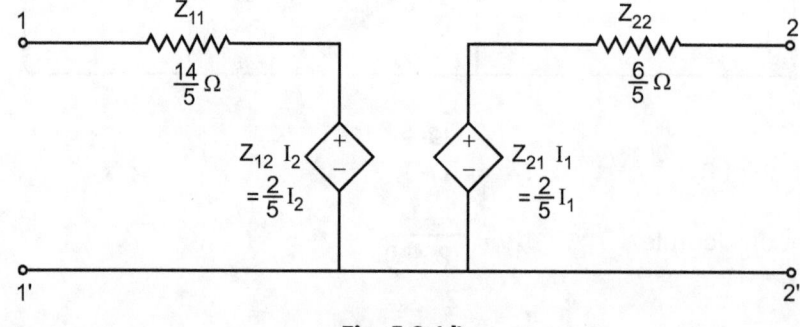

Fig. 5.8 (d)

5.4 SHORT-CIRCUIT ADMITTANCE OR Y-PARAMETERS

In Y-parameter, currents I_1 and I_2 are expressed in terms of voltage V_1 and V_2.

$$(I_1, I_2) = f(V_1, V_2)$$
$$[I] = [Y][V]$$

or
$$\begin{bmatrix} I_1 \\ I_2 \end{bmatrix} = \begin{bmatrix} Y_{11} & Y_{12} \\ Y_{21} & Y_{22} \end{bmatrix} \begin{bmatrix} V_1 \\ V_2 \end{bmatrix}$$

Y-parameter equation is

$$\left. \begin{array}{l} I_1 = Y_{11} V_1 + Y_{12} V_2 \\ I_2 = Y_{21} V_1 + Y_{22} V_2 \end{array} \right\} \qquad \ldots (5.4)$$

To calculate Y_{11}, Y_{12}, Y_{21} and Y_{22}, we have to make either $V_1 = 0$ or $V_2 = 0$

Case I: $V_2 = 0$, i.e. output is short-circuited.

(i) Driving point admittance,
$$Y_{11} = \left[\frac{I_1}{V_1} \right]_{V_2 = 0}$$

(ii) Forward transfer admittance,
$$Y_{21} = \left[\frac{I_2}{V_1} \right]_{V_2 = 0}$$

Case II: $V_1 = 0$ i.e. input is short circuited.

(iii) Output driving point admittance,
$$Y_{22} = \left[\frac{I_2}{V_2} \right]_{V_1 = 0}$$

(iv) Reverse transfer admittance:
$$Y_{12} = \left[\frac{I_1}{V_2} \right]_{V_1 = 0}$$

As $V_1 = 0$ or $V_2 = 0$, input or output are short circuited. Hence it is called as **short circuit admittance parameters**.

The equivalent circuit for Y-parameter is shown in Fig. 5.9.

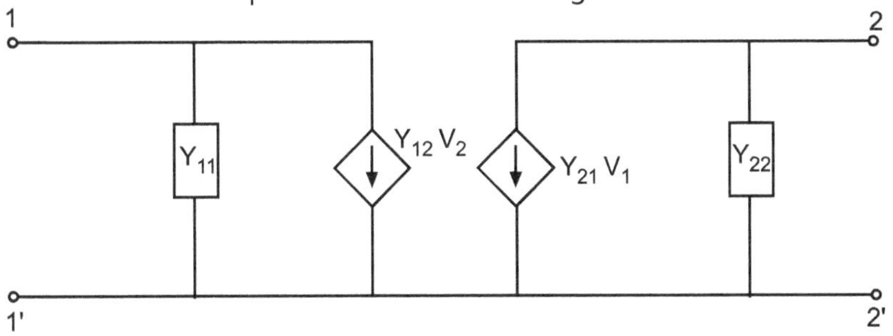

Fig. 5.9: Y-Parameters equivalent circuit

5.4.1 Condition for Symmetry and Reciprocity

(A) Symmetry Condition:
Similar to Z-parameters, Refer Fig. 5.6.

Case I: $\quad V_1 = V_s$
$\quad I_2 = 0$

From equation (5.14),

$$I_1 = Y_{11} V_s + Y_{12} V_2 \quad \ldots (a)$$
$$0 = Y_{21} V_s + Y_{22} V_2 \quad \ldots (b)$$

$\therefore \quad V_2 = -\dfrac{Y_{21}}{Y_{22}} V_s$

Putting in equation (5.15 a),

$$I_1 = Y_{11} V_s + Y_{12}\left(-\dfrac{Y_{21}}{Y_{22}}\right) V_s$$

$$I_1 = V_s\left[Y_{11} - \dfrac{Y_{12} Y_{21}}{Y_{22}}\right]$$

$$\boxed{\dfrac{V_s}{I_1} = \dfrac{Y_{22}}{Y_{11} Y_{22} - Y_{12} Y_{21}}} \quad \ldots (c)$$

Case II: $\quad V_2 = V_s$
and $\quad I_1 = 0$

$\therefore$ From equation (5.4),

$$0 = Y_{11} V_1 + Y_{12} V_s \quad \ldots (d)$$
$$I_2 = Y_{21} V_1 + Y_{22} V_s \quad \ldots (e)$$

$$V_1 = -\dfrac{Y_{12}}{Y_{11}} \cdot V_s$$

Putting in equation (e),

$$I_2 = Y_{21}\left(-\dfrac{Y_{12}}{Y_{11}}\right) V_s + Y_{22} V_s$$

$$I_2 = V_s\left[-\dfrac{Y_{21} Y_{12}}{Y_{11}} + Y_{22}\right]$$

$$\boxed{\dfrac{V_s}{I_2} = \dfrac{Y_{11}}{Y_{11} Y_{22} - Y_{21} Y_{12}}} \quad \ldots (f)$$

NETWORK ANALYSIS (P.U.) (S.E. ELECTRICAL) — TWO PORT NETWORK AND FILTERS

But by symmetry condition,

$$\frac{V_s}{I_1} = \frac{V_s}{I_2}$$

$$\frac{Y_{22}}{Y_{11}Y_{22} - Y_{21}Y_{12}} = \frac{Y_{11}}{Y_{11}Y_{22} - Y_{21}Y_{12}}$$

$$\therefore \boxed{Y_{22} = Y_{11}} \qquad \ldots (5.5)$$

That is the condition for symmetry.

Ex. 5.2: Find y-parameters for the 'T' network shown. Is this a symmetrical and reciprocal network?

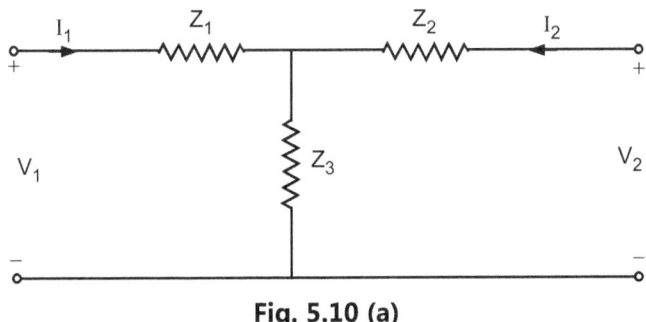

Fig. 5.10 (a)

Sol.: Step I: With $V_2 = 0$ we have,

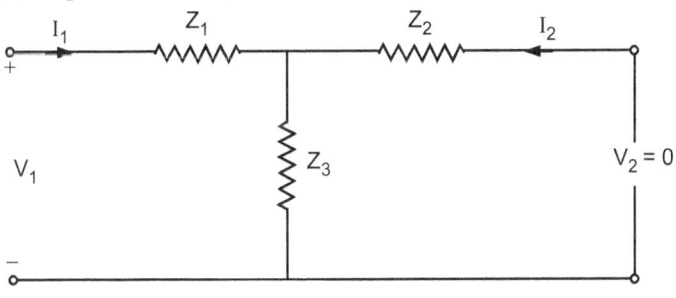

Fig. 5.10 (b)

$$I_1 = \frac{I_1}{Z_1 + \dfrac{Z_2 Z_3}{Z_2 + Z_3}} = \frac{V_1 (Z_2 + Z_3)}{Z_1 Z_2 + Z_2 Z_3 + Z_3 Z_1}$$

$$\therefore Y_{11} = \frac{I_1}{V_1} = \frac{Z_2 + Z_3}{Z_1 Z_2 + Z_2 Z_3 + Z_3 Z_1} \qquad \ldots (a)$$

$$I_2 = -I_1 \times \frac{Z_3}{Z_2 + Z_3}$$

$$= -\frac{Z_3 V_1}{Z_1 Z_2 + Z_2 Z_3 + Z_3 Z_1} \qquad \ldots (b)$$

Step II: With $V_1 = 0$.

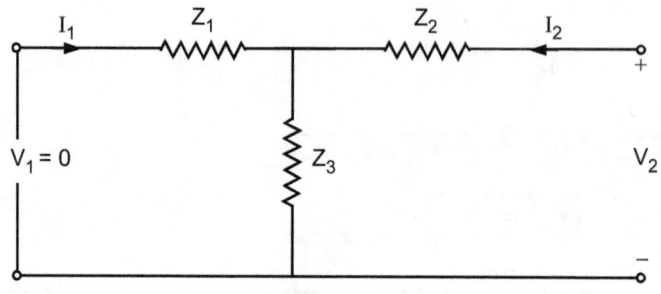

Fig. 5.10 (c)

$$I_2 = \frac{V_2}{Z_2 + \dfrac{Z_1 Z_3}{Z_1 + Z_3}} = \frac{(Z_1 + Z_3) V_2}{(Z_1 Z_3 + Z_1 Z_2 + Z_2 Z_3)}$$

$$Y_{22} = \frac{I_2}{V_2} = \frac{Z_1 + Z_3}{Z_1 Z_3 + Z_1 Z_2 + Z_2 Z_3} \qquad \ldots (c)$$

$$I_1 = -I_2 \times \frac{Z_3}{Z_1 + Z_3} = \frac{Z_3 V_2}{Z_1 Z_3 + Z_2 Z_3 + Z_1 Z_2}$$

$$\therefore \quad Y_{12} = \frac{I_1}{V_2} = -\frac{Z_3}{Z_1 Z_3 + Z_2 Z_3 + Z_1 Z_2} \qquad \ldots (d)$$

Since $Y_{11} \neq Y_{22}$ network is not symmetrical

$Y_{12} = Y_{21}$ network is reciprocal.

(B) Reciprocity Condition:

Similar to Z-parameters,

Case I: $\qquad V_1 = V_s, V_2 = 0$

$\qquad\qquad\qquad I_2 = -I_2'$

Putting these values in equation (5.4),

$$I_1 = Y_{11} V_s + 0$$
$$-I_2' = Y_{21} V_s + 0$$
$$I_1 = Y_{11} V_s$$

and $\qquad \boxed{\dfrac{V_s}{I_2'} = \dfrac{-1}{Y_{21}}} \qquad \ldots (a)$

Case II: $\qquad V_2 = V_s, V_1 = 0$

$\qquad\qquad\qquad I_1 = -I_1'$

Putting in equation (5.14),

$$-I_1' = Y_{12} V_s$$
$$I_2 = Y_{21} V_s$$

$$\boxed{\frac{V_s}{I_1'} = \frac{-1}{Y_{12}}} \quad \ldots \text{(b)}$$

But by reciprocity condition,

$$\frac{V_s}{I_2'} = \frac{V_s}{I_1'}$$

∴ $\quad Y_{21} = Y_{12}$ or $\boxed{Y_{12} = Y_{21}}$ ... (5.6)

This is the condition for reciprocity.

5.5 TRANSMISSION OR ABCD PARAMETERS

In transmission or ABCD or chain parameters, voltage V_1 and current I_1 at input port is expressed in terms of voltage V_2 and current I_2 at output port.

$$V_1 = f(V_2, -I_2)$$
$$I_1 = f(V_2, -I_2)$$

Transmission parameters are generally used in the analysis of power transmission line, the input port is called as sending end and the output port is receiving end.

Here variable used is $-I_2$ instead of I_2. Negative sign indicates that current I_2 is considered outward i.e. leaving port 2 - 2'.

In matrix form,

$$\begin{bmatrix} V_1 \\ I_1 \end{bmatrix} = \begin{bmatrix} A & B \\ C & D \end{bmatrix} \begin{bmatrix} V_2 \\ -I_2 \end{bmatrix} \quad \ldots \text{(5.7)}$$

∴ ABCD parameter equations are

$$\left. \begin{array}{l} V_1 = AV_2 + B(-I_2) \\ I_1 = CV_2 + D(-I_2) \end{array} \right\} \quad \ldots \text{(5.8)}$$

∴ To calculate ABCD parameters, we have to make either $V_2 = 0$ or $I_2 = 0$.

Case I: $I_2 = 0$ i.e. output port 2 - 2' is open circuited.

(i) $\quad A = \left[\dfrac{V_1}{V_2} \right]_{I_2 = 0}$

i.e. the reverse voltage ratio with receiving i.e. output port open circuited.

(ii) $$C = \left[\frac{I_1}{V_2}\right]_{I_2 = 0}$$

i.e. transfer admittance.

Case II: $V_2 = 0$ i.e. output or receiving end is short-circuited.

(iii) $$B = \left[\frac{V_1}{-I_2}\right]_{V_2 = 0}$$

i.e. transfer impedance with output short-circuited.

(iv) $$D = \left[\frac{I_1}{-I_2}\right]_{V_2 = 0}$$

i.e. reverse current ratio.

5.5.1 Condition for Symmetry and Reciprocity

(A) Symmetry Condition:

Similar to Z-parameters, refer Fig. 5.6.

Case I: $\quad V_1 = V_s, I_2 = 0$

From equation (5.7),

$$V_s = AV_2 \quad \ldots (a)$$
$$I_1 = CV_2 \quad \ldots (b)$$

$\therefore \quad V_2 = \dfrac{I_1}{C}$

Putting in equation (a), we get

$$V_s = \frac{A}{C} I_1$$

$\therefore \quad \dfrac{V_s}{I_1} = \dfrac{A}{C} \quad \ldots (c)$

Case II: $\quad V_2 = V_s, I_1 = 0$

Putting in equation (5.7),

$$V_1 = AV_s + B(-I_2)$$
$$0 = CV_s + D(-I_2)$$

$\therefore \quad CV_s = DI_2$

$\therefore \quad \dfrac{V_s}{I_2} = \dfrac{D}{C} \quad \ldots (d)$

But from symmetry condition,
$$\frac{V_s}{I_1} = \frac{V_s}{I_2}$$

∴ $$\frac{A}{C} = \frac{D}{C}$$

∴ $$\boxed{A = D}$$ ... (5.9)

Symmetry condition.

(B) Reciprocity Condition:

Similar to Z-parameters,

Case I: $V_1 = V_s$, $V_2 = 0$

and $I_2' = I_2$

From equation (5.7),
$$V_s = B\, I_2'$$

∴ $$\frac{V_s}{I_2'} = B$$ ... (e)

Case II: $V_2 = V_s$, $V_1 = 0$ and $I_1' = -I_1$

∴ Equation (5.7) becomes,
$$0 = AV_s + B(-I_2)$$ ... (f)
$$-I_1' = CV_s + D(-I_2)$$ ... (g)

∴ From equation (f), we get
$$I_2 = \frac{A}{B} \cdot V_s$$

Putting this in equation (g) gives
$$-I_1' = CV_s + D\left(-\frac{A}{B} \cdot V_s\right)$$

$$-I_1' = V_s\left(C - \frac{AD}{B}\right)$$

$$-I_1' = V_s\left(\frac{BC - AD}{B}\right)$$

$$\frac{V_s}{I_1'} = \frac{B}{AD - BC}$$

∴ From reciprocity condition,
$$\frac{V_s}{I_1'} = \frac{V_s}{I_2'}$$

$$\frac{B}{AD - BC} = B$$

∴ $$\boxed{AD - BC = 1}$$ Condition of reciprocity ... (5.10)

Ex. 5.3: Find ABCD parameters for the given R-C network.

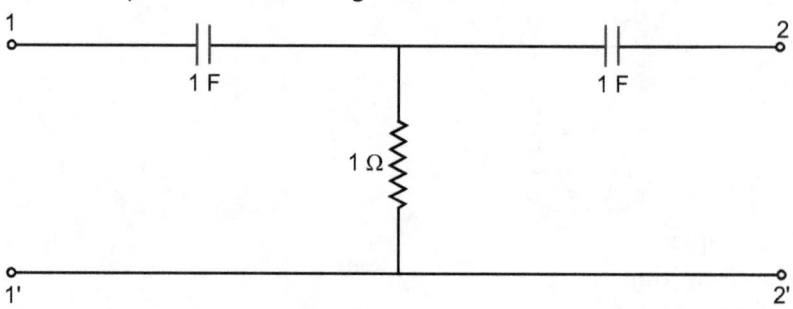

Fig. 5.11

Sol.: ABCD parameter equations are

$$V_1 = AV_2 + B(-I_2)$$
$$I_1 = CV_2 + D(-I_2)$$

Case I: $I_2 = 0$ i.e. output is open circuited.

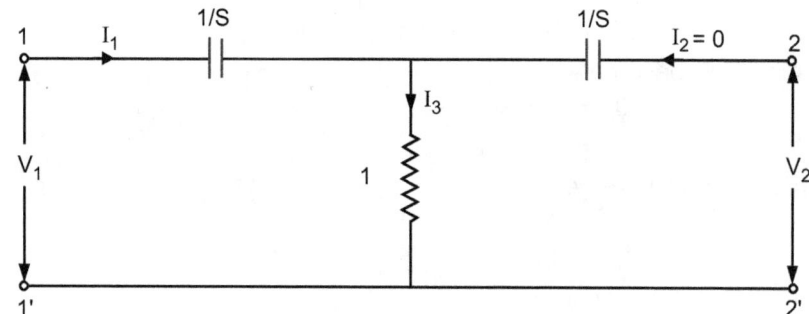

Fig. 5.11 (a): S-domain representation

∴ $$I_1 = \frac{V_1}{1 + \frac{1}{S}} = V_1 \cdot \frac{s}{s+1}$$

But, $$V_2 = I_1 \times 1\,\Omega$$

∴ $$A = \left[\frac{V_1}{V_2}\right]_{I_2 = 0} = \frac{\frac{s+1}{s} \cdot I_1}{I_1}$$

∴ $$\boxed{A = \frac{s+1}{s}}$$

and $$C = \left[\frac{I_1}{V_2}\right]_{I_2 = 0} = 1$$

∴ $$\boxed{C = 1}$$

Case II: $V_2 = 0$ i.e. output is short-circuited.

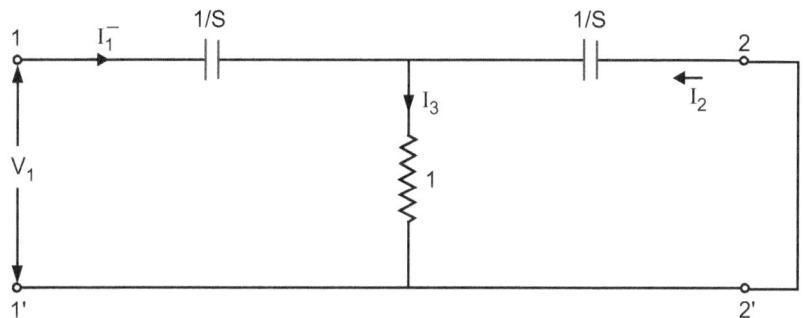

Fig. 5.11 (b)

$$V_2 = 0$$

$$\therefore \quad I_3 = -I_2 \cdot \frac{1}{S}$$

$$I_1 = I_3 - I_2$$

$$= -\frac{I_2}{S} - I_2$$

$$I_1 = -I_2 \left[\frac{s+1}{S}\right]$$

$$\therefore \quad D = \left[-\frac{I_1}{I_2}\right]_{V_2 = 0}$$

$$\therefore \quad \boxed{D = \frac{s+1}{s}}$$

Now, $\quad V_1 = I_1 \cdot \frac{1}{S} + I_3 = -I_2 \cdot \frac{s+1}{s^2} - I_2 \cdot \frac{1}{S}$

$$= -I_2 \left[\frac{2s+1}{s^2}\right]$$

$$\therefore \quad B = \left[-\frac{V_1}{I_2}\right]_{V_2 = 0}$$

$$\therefore \quad \boxed{B = \frac{2s+1}{s^2}}$$

$\therefore \quad$ ABCD parameters are

$$[T] = \begin{bmatrix} \frac{s+1}{s} & \frac{2s+1}{s^2} \\ 1 & \frac{s+1}{s} \end{bmatrix}$$

5.6 HYBRID PARAMETERS OR h-PARAMETERS

The hybrid or h-parameters are used in constructing models of transistors. The parameter of transistor cannot be measured by short-circuit admittance or open circuit impedance parameter individually. Therefore, the combination of both short-circuit admittance and open-circuit impedance is called as hybrid or h-parameter.

In h-parameters, voltage at input port V_1 and the current of the output port I_2, are expressed in terms of the current at the input port I_1 and voltage at output port V_2.

$$(V_1, I_2) = f(I_1, V_2)$$

or

$$V_1 = f(I_1, V_2)$$
$$I_2 = f(I_1, V_2)$$

In matrix form,

$$\begin{bmatrix} V_1 \\ I_2 \end{bmatrix} = \begin{bmatrix} h_{11} & h_{12} \\ -h_{21} & h_{22} \end{bmatrix} \begin{bmatrix} I_1 \\ V_2 \end{bmatrix} \quad \ldots (5.11)$$

h-parameter equations are

$$\left. \begin{array}{l} V_1 = h_{11} I_1 + h_{12} V_2 \\ I_2 = h_{21} I_1 + h_{22} V_2 \end{array} \right\} \quad \ldots (5.12)$$

To calculate h-parameters,

Case I: $V_2 = 0$ i.e. output is short-circuited.

$\therefore$
$$h_{11} = \left[\frac{V_1}{I_1} \right]_{V_2 = 0}$$

which is input impedance with output short-circuited.

$$h_{21} = \left[\frac{I_2}{I_1} \right]_{V_2 = 0}$$

which is forward current gain.

Case II: $I_1 = 0$

$$h_{12} = \left[\frac{V_1}{V_2} \right]_{I_1 = 0}$$

Which is reverse voltage gain with input open-circuited.

$$h_{22} = \left[\frac{I_2}{V_2} \right]_{I_1 = 0}$$

Which is output admittance ($\mho$).

The equivalent circuit for h-parameters are shown in Fig. 5.12.

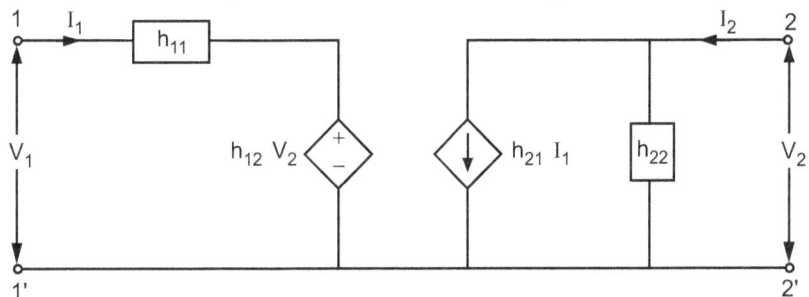

Fig. 5.12: h-parameters equivalent circuit

5.6.1 Condition for Symmetry and Reciprocity

(A) Symmetry Condition:

Similar to Z-parameters. Refer to Fig. 5.6.

Case I: $\quad V_1 = V_s, I_2 = 0$

From equation (5.12),

$$V_s = h_{11} I_1 + h_{12} V_2 \quad \ldots (a)$$

and

$$0 = h_{21} I_1 + h_{22} V_2 \quad \ldots (b)$$

$\therefore \quad -h_{22} V_2 = h_{21} I_1$

$$V_2 = -\frac{h_{21}}{h_{22}} \cdot I_1$$

Substituting value of V_2 in equation (a) gives

$$V_s = h_{11} I_1 + h_{12} \left[\frac{-h_{21}}{h_{22}} \right] I_1$$

$$V_s = \left[h_{11} - \frac{h_{12} h_{21}}{h_{22}} \right] I_1$$

$$\frac{V_s}{I_1} = \frac{h_{11} h_{22} - h_{12} h_{21}}{h_{22}} \quad \ldots (c)$$

Case II: $\quad V_2 = V_s$ and $I_1 = 0$

$$V_1 = h_{12} V_s \quad \ldots (d)$$

$$I_2 = h_{22} V_s \quad \ldots (e)$$

$$\frac{V_s}{I_2} = \frac{1}{h_{22}} \quad \ldots (f)$$

From symmetry condition,

$$\frac{V_s}{I_1} = \frac{V_s}{I_2}$$

$$\frac{h_{11} h_{22} - h_{12} h_{21}}{h_{22}} = \frac{1}{h_{22}}$$

$$\therefore \boxed{h_{11} h_{22} - h_{12} h_{21} = 1} \qquad \ldots (5.13)$$

which is condition of symmetry.

(B) Reciprocity Condition:

Similar to Z-parameter.

Case I: $\qquad V_1 = V_s, V_2 = 0$

and $\qquad I_2' = -I_2$

From equation (5.10),

$$V_s = h_{11} I_1 \qquad \ldots (g)$$

and $\qquad -I_2' = h_{21} I_1$

$$\therefore \quad I_1 = \frac{-1}{h_{21}} \cdot I_2'$$

Putting in equation (g), we get

$$V_s = \frac{-h_{11}}{h_{21}} \cdot I_2'$$

$$\therefore \quad \frac{V_s}{I_2'} = \frac{-h_{11}}{h_{21}} \qquad \ldots (h)$$

Case II: $\qquad V_2 = V_s, V_1 = 0$

$$I_1' = -I_1$$

Putting in equation (5.10),

$$0 = -h_{11} I_1' + h_{12} V_s \qquad \ldots (i)$$

and $\qquad I_2 = -h_{21} I_1' + h_{22} V_s \qquad \ldots (j)$

$$\therefore \quad I_1' = \frac{h_{12}}{h_{11}} V_s$$

$$\therefore \quad \frac{V_s}{I_1'} = \frac{h_{11}}{h_{12}} \qquad \ldots (k)$$

By reciprocity condition,

$$\frac{V_s}{I_2'} = \frac{V_s}{I_1'}$$

$$-\frac{h_{11}}{h_{21}} = \frac{h_{11}}{h_{12}}$$

∴ $\boxed{h_{12} = -h_{21}}$ ... (5.14)

Reciprocity condition for h-parameters.

Ex. 5.4: The hybrid parameters of the network shown in Fig. 5.13 are $h_{11} = 2\ \Omega$, $h_{12} = 4$, $h_{21} = -5$, $h_{22} = 2$ ℧.

Determine the supply voltage V_s if the power dissipated in the load resistor $R_L = 4\ \Omega$ is 25 W and $R_s = 2\ \Omega$.

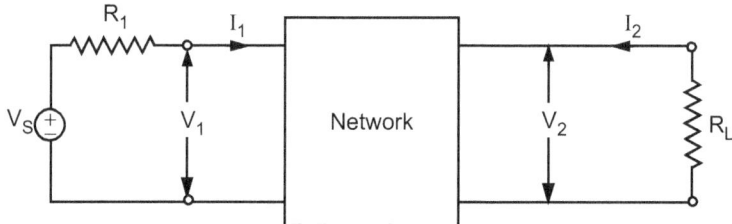

Fig. 5.13

The h-parameter equations are

$$V_1 = 2 I_1 + 4 V_2$$
$$I_2 = -5 I_1 + 2 V_2$$

Now power dissipated in R_L is

$$P_L = \frac{V_2^2}{R_L} = 25 \text{ watts}$$

∴ $V_2 = 10$ V

But $V_2 = -I_2 R_L$

∴ $I_2 = -2.5$ A

Putting these values in h-parameter equation,

$$V_1 = 2 I_1 + 40$$

and $-2.5 = -5 I_1 + 20$

Solving these two equations,

$$I_1 = 4.5 \text{ A}$$
and
$$V_1 = 49 \text{ V}$$

Since,
$$I_1 = \frac{V_s - V_1}{2}$$

$$4.5 = \frac{V_s - 49}{2}$$

$$9 = V_s - 49$$

$$\therefore \quad V_s = 58 \text{ V}$$

$\therefore$ The supply voltage is $V_s = 58$ V

5.7 INTERRELATIONSHIPS BETWEEN THE PARAMETERS

Uptil now, we have studied four different parameters. Each has its own utility and is suited for certain specific application. But, we often find it necessary to convert from one set of parameters to another. Through simple mathematical manipulation, it is possible to convert from any one set to any of the remaining set.

5.7.1 Z-Parameter in Terms of Other Parameters

Let us first rewrite the equations of Z-parameters.

$$\left.\begin{aligned} V_1 &= Z_{11} I_1 + Z_{12} I_2 \\ V_2 &= Z_{21} I_1 + Z_{22} I_2 \end{aligned}\right\} \quad \ldots \text{(a)}$$

(A) Z-Parameters in Terms of Y-Parameters

Now equations for Y-parameters are

$$\left.\begin{aligned} I_1 &= Y_{11} V_1 + Y_{12} V_2 \\ I_2 &= Y_{21} V_1 + Y_{22} V_2 \end{aligned}\right\} \quad \ldots \text{(b)}$$

i.e.
$$\begin{bmatrix} I_1 \\ I_2 \end{bmatrix} = \begin{bmatrix} Y_{11} & Y_{12} \\ Y_{21} & Y_{22} \end{bmatrix} \begin{bmatrix} V_1 \\ V_2 \end{bmatrix}$$

Let us solve this equation simultaneously for V_1 and V_2 from (b)

By Cramer's rule,
$$V_1 = \frac{\begin{vmatrix} I_1 & Y_{12} \\ I_2 & Y_{22} \end{vmatrix}}{\begin{vmatrix} Y_{11} & Y_{12} \\ Y_{21} & Y_{22} \end{vmatrix}} = \frac{Y_{22} I_1 - Y_{12} I_2}{Y_{11} Y_{22} - Y_{12} Y_{21}}$$

$$V_1 = \frac{Y_{22}}{Y_{11} Y_{22} - Y_{12} Y_{21}} I_1 - \frac{Y_{12}}{Y_{11} Y_{22} - Y_{12} Y_{21}} I_2$$

Let $D_y = Y_{11} Y_{22} - Y_{12} Y_{21}$

$$V_1 = \frac{Y_{22}}{D_y} I_1 - \frac{Y_{12}}{D_y} I_2 \qquad \ldots (c)$$

and

$$V_2 = \frac{\begin{vmatrix} Y_{11} & I_1 \\ Y_{21} & I_2 \end{vmatrix}}{\begin{vmatrix} Y_{11} & Y_{12} \\ Y_{21} & Y_{22} \end{vmatrix}} = \frac{Y_{11} I_2 - y_{21} I_1}{Y_{11} Y_{22} - Y_{12} Y_{21}}$$

$\therefore$

$$V_2 = \frac{Y_{11}}{D_y} I_2 - \frac{Y_{21}}{D_y} I_1$$

$$V_2 = \frac{-Y_{21}}{D_y} I_1 + \frac{Y_{11}}{D_y} I_2 \qquad \ldots (d)$$

Comparing equations (c) and (d) with Z-parameter equations, we get

$$Z_{11} = \frac{Y_{22}}{D_y}, \; Z_{12} = \frac{-Y_{12}}{D_y}$$

$$Z_{21} = \frac{-Y_{21}}{D_y}, \; Z_{22} = \frac{Y_{11}}{D_y}$$

$$[Z] = \begin{bmatrix} \dfrac{Y_{22}}{D_y} & \dfrac{-Y_{12}}{D_y} \\ \dfrac{-Y_{21}}{D_y} & \dfrac{Y_{11}}{D_y} \end{bmatrix} \qquad \ldots (5.15)$$

Thus Z-parameters matrix is obtained by inverse of y-parameters matrix. Similarly it can be proved that y-parameters matrix is obtained by inverse of z-parameters matrix.

(B) Z-Parameters in Terms of h-Parameters

The h-parameter equations are

$$V_1 = h_{11} I_1 + h_{12} V_2 \qquad \ldots (e)$$
$$I_2 = h_{21} I_1 + h_{22} V_2 \qquad \ldots (f)$$

$\therefore \qquad h_{22} V_2 = I_2 - h_{21} I_2$

$$V_2 = \frac{1}{h_{22}} I_2 - \frac{h_{21}}{h_{22}} I_1$$

$$V_2 = \frac{-h_{21}}{h_{22}} I_1 + \frac{1}{h_{22}} I_2 \qquad \ldots (g)$$

Putting this value in equation (e), we get

$$V_1 = h_{11} I_1 + h_{12} \left[\frac{1}{h_{22}} I_2 - \frac{h_{21}}{h_{22}} I_1 \right]$$

$$V_1 = h_{11} I_1 + \frac{h_{12}}{h_{22}} I_2 - \frac{h_{12} h_{21}}{h_{22}} I_1$$

$$V_1 = \left[h_{11} - \frac{h_{12} h_{21}}{h_{22}} \right] I_1 + \frac{h_{12}}{h_{22}} I_2$$

$$V_1 = \frac{h_{11} h_{22} - h_{12} h_{21}}{h_{22}} I_1 + \frac{h_{12}}{h_{22}} I_2 \quad \ldots \text{(h)}$$

Comparing this equation with Z-parameter equation,

$$\boxed{Z_{11} = \frac{h_{11} h_{22} - h_{12} h_{21}}{h_{22}}} \qquad \boxed{Z_{12} = \frac{h_{12}}{h_{22}}}$$

Comparing equation (g) with Z-parameter equation.

$$\boxed{Z_{21} = -\frac{h_{21}}{h_{22}}} \quad \text{and} \quad \boxed{Z_{22} = \frac{1}{h_{22}}}$$

$$\therefore \quad [Z] = \begin{bmatrix} \dfrac{Dh}{h_{22}} & \dfrac{h_{12}}{h_{22}} \\ \dfrac{-h_{21}}{h_{22}} & \dfrac{1}{h_{22}} \end{bmatrix} \quad \ldots \text{(5.16)}$$

(C) Z-Parameters in Terms of ABCD Parameters

ABCD parameter equations are

$$V_1 = AV_2 + B(-I_2) \quad \ldots \text{(i)}$$
$$I_1 = CV_2 + D(-I_2) \quad \ldots \text{(j)}$$

From equation (j), we get,

$$CV_2 = I_1 + DI_2$$

$$V_2 = \left(\frac{1}{C}\right) I_1 + \left(\frac{D}{C}\right) I_2 \quad \ldots \text{(κ)}$$

Comparing equation with Z-parameter equation,

$$\boxed{Z_{21} = \frac{1}{C}} \qquad \boxed{Z_{22} = \frac{D}{C}}$$

Putting value of V_2 in equation (j), we get

$$V_1 = A \left[\frac{1}{C} I_1 + \frac{D}{C} I_2 \right] + B(-I_2)$$

$$V_1 = \frac{A}{C} I_1 + \frac{AD}{C} I_2 - BI_2$$

$$V_1 = \frac{A}{C} I_1 + \left[\frac{AD}{C} - B\right] I_2$$

$$V_1 = \frac{A}{C} I_1 + \frac{AD - BC}{C} I_2 \qquad \ldots (l)$$

Comparing with Z-parameter equation,

$$\boxed{Z_{11} = \frac{A}{C}} \qquad \boxed{Z_{12} = \frac{AD - BC}{C}}$$

$$\therefore \quad [Z] = \begin{bmatrix} \dfrac{A}{C} & \dfrac{AD - BC}{C} \\ \dfrac{1}{C} & \dfrac{D}{C} \end{bmatrix} \qquad \ldots (5.17)$$

In similar manner, we can express any one parameter in terms of remaining other parameters.

Table 5.2 gives the summary of all relationships between different sets of parameters. In this table matrices placed in each rows are equivalent. The equivalent table involves determinants Dz, Dy, Dh, ΔT, etc. where

$$Dz = Z_{11} Z_{22} - Z_{12} Z_{21}$$
$$Dy = Y_{11} Y_{22} - Y_{12} Y_{21}$$
$$Dh = h_{11} h_{22} - h_{12} h_{21}$$
$$\Delta T = AD - BC, \text{ etc.}$$

Table 5.2: Interrelationship between parameters

[Z]	[Y]	[T]	[h]
$\begin{bmatrix} Z_{11} & Z_{12} \\ Z_{21} & Z_{22} \end{bmatrix}$	$\begin{bmatrix} \dfrac{Y_{22}}{Dy} & \dfrac{-Y_{12}}{Dy} \\ \dfrac{-Y_{21}}{Dy} & \dfrac{Y_{11}}{Dy} \end{bmatrix}$	$\begin{bmatrix} \dfrac{A}{C} & \dfrac{DT}{C} \\ \dfrac{1}{C} & \dfrac{D}{C} \end{bmatrix}$	$\begin{bmatrix} \dfrac{Dh}{h_{22}} & \dfrac{h_{12}}{h_{22}} \\ \dfrac{-h_{21}}{h_{22}} & \dfrac{1}{h_{22}} \end{bmatrix}$
$\begin{bmatrix} \dfrac{Z_{22}}{Dz} & \dfrac{-Z_{12}}{Dz} \\ \dfrac{-Z_{21}}{Dz} & \dfrac{Z_{11}}{Dz} \end{bmatrix}$	$\begin{bmatrix} Y_{11} & Y_{12} \\ Y_{21} & Y_{22} \end{bmatrix}$	$\begin{bmatrix} \dfrac{D}{B} & \dfrac{-DT}{B} \\ \dfrac{-1}{B} & \dfrac{A}{B} \end{bmatrix}$	$\begin{bmatrix} \dfrac{1}{h_{11}} & \dfrac{-h_{12}}{h_{11}} \\ \dfrac{h_{21}}{h_{11}} & \dfrac{Dh}{h_{11}} \end{bmatrix}$
$\begin{bmatrix} \dfrac{Z_{11}}{Z_{21}} & \dfrac{Dz}{Z_{21}} \\ \dfrac{1}{Z_{21}} & \dfrac{Z_{22}}{Z_{21}} \end{bmatrix}$	$\begin{bmatrix} \dfrac{-Y_{22}}{Y_{21}} & \dfrac{-1}{Y_{21}} \\ \dfrac{-Dy}{Y_{21}} & \dfrac{-Y_{11}}{Y_{21}} \end{bmatrix}$	$\begin{bmatrix} A & B \\ C & D \end{bmatrix}$	$\begin{bmatrix} \dfrac{-Dh}{h_{21}} & \dfrac{-h_{11}}{h_{21}} \\ \dfrac{-h_{22}}{h_{21}} & \dfrac{-1}{h_{21}} \end{bmatrix}$
$\begin{bmatrix} \dfrac{Dz}{Z_{22}} & \dfrac{Z_{21}}{Z_{22}} \\ \dfrac{-Z_{21}}{Z_{22}} & \dfrac{1}{Z_{22}} \end{bmatrix}$	$\begin{bmatrix} \dfrac{1}{Y_{11}} & \dfrac{-Y_{12}}{Y_{11}} \\ \dfrac{Y_{21}}{Y_{11}} & \dfrac{Dy}{Y_{11}} \end{bmatrix}$	$\begin{bmatrix} \dfrac{B}{D} & \dfrac{DT}{D} \\ \dfrac{-1}{D} & \dfrac{C}{D} \end{bmatrix}$	$\begin{bmatrix} h_{11} & h_{12} \\ h_{21} & h_{22} \end{bmatrix}$

Table 5.3 gives the summary for condition of symmetry and reciprocity for different parameters.

Table 5.3: Condition for symmetry and reciprocity

Parameter	Condition of symmetry	Condition of reciprocity
[Z]	$Z_{11} = Z_{22}$	$Z_{12} = Z_{21}$
[Y]	$Y_{11} = Y_{22}$	$Y_{12} = Y_{21}$
{ABCD} or [T]	A = D	AD − BC = 1
[h]	$h_{11} h_{22} - h_{12} h_{21} = 1$	$h_{12} = -h_{21}$

SOLVED EXAMPLES OF PARAMETERS

Ex. 5.5: Find Z-parameters of the network shown in Fig. 5.14 (a).

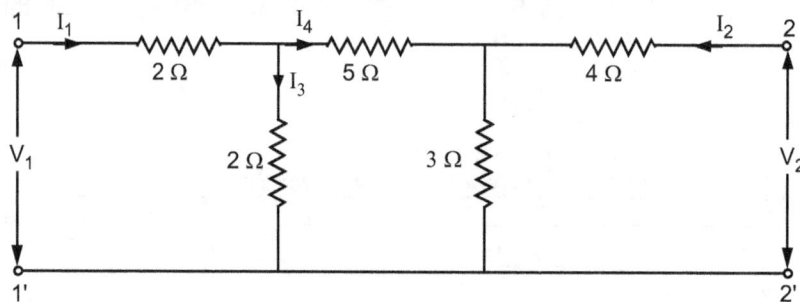

Fig. 5.14 (a)

Sol.: Z-parameter equations are

$$V_1 = Z_{11} I_1 + Z_{12} I_2$$
$$V_2 = Z_{21} I_1 + Z_{22} I_2$$

Case I: $I_2 = 0$, output 2 - 2' open circuited.

$$I_1 = I_3 + I_4$$

$$I_4 = \left(\frac{2}{2+8}\right) I_1 = \frac{1}{5} I_1$$

and

$$I_3 = \frac{8 I_1}{2+8} = \frac{4}{5} I_1$$

But

$$I_4 = \frac{V_2}{3}$$

∴

$$\frac{V_2}{3} = \frac{I_1}{5}$$

$$\therefore \quad \frac{V_2}{I_1} = \frac{3}{5}$$

$$\therefore \quad Z_{21} = \left[\frac{V_2}{I_1}\right]_{I_2 = 0} = \frac{3}{5} \, \Omega$$

By applying KVL to input loop,

$$-2I_1 - 2I_3 + V_1 = 0$$

$$V_1 = 2(I_1 + I_3)$$

But

$$I_3 = \frac{4}{5} I_1$$

$$V_1 = 2\left(I_1 + \frac{4}{5} I_1\right)$$

$$V_1 = 2I_1\left(\frac{9}{5}\right)$$

$$\frac{V_1}{I_1} = \frac{18}{5}$$

$$\therefore \quad \boxed{Z_{11} = \frac{V_1}{I_1} = \frac{18}{5} = 3.6 \, \Omega}$$

Case II: $I_1 = 0$, Input 1 - 1' is open circuited.

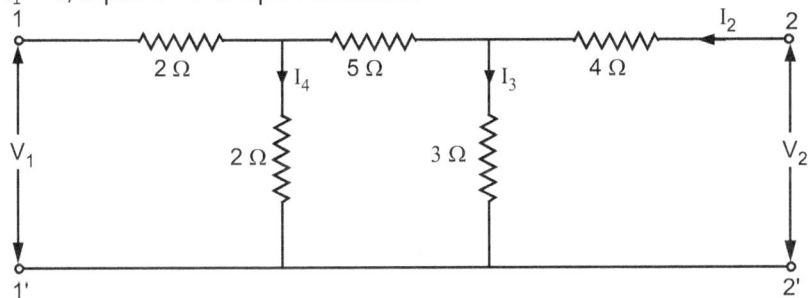

Fig. 5.14 (b)

$$I_2 = I_3 + I_4$$

$$I_3 = \frac{7 I_2}{(3 + 7)} = \frac{7}{10} I_2$$

and

$$I_4 = \frac{3 I_2}{7 + 3} = \frac{3}{10} I_2$$

By applying KVL to output loop,

$$-4 I_2 - 3 I_3 + V_2 = 0$$

$$V_2 = 4 I_2 + 3 I_3$$

$$= 4 I_2 + 3 \times \frac{7}{10} I_2$$

$$V_2 = I_2\left[4 + \frac{21}{10}\right]$$

$$Z_{22} = \frac{V_2}{I_2} = \frac{40 + 21}{10}$$

$$= \frac{61}{10} = 6.1$$

∴ $\boxed{Z_{22} = 6.1\ \Omega}$

$$V_1 = 2\,I_4$$

$$I_4 = \frac{V_1}{2}$$

But $I_4 = \frac{3}{10}\,I_2 = \frac{V_1}{2}$

$$\frac{V_1}{I_2} = \frac{6}{10} = 0.6$$

∴ $\boxed{Z_{12} = 0.6\ \Omega}$

∴ $[Z] = \begin{bmatrix} 3.6 & 0.6 \\ 0.6 & 6.1 \end{bmatrix}$ (ohms)

Ex. 5.6: Find transmission parameters of the following network shown in Fig. 5.15.

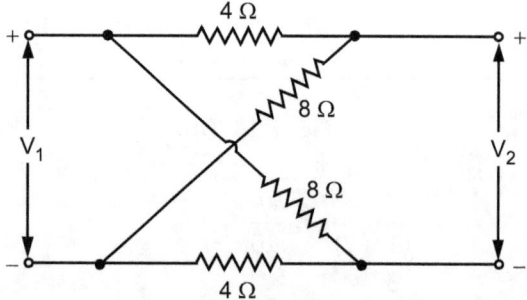

Fig. 5.15

Sol.: Transmission parameters or ABCD parameters are given by equations:

$$V_1 = AV_2 + B(-I_2)$$
$$I_1 = CV_2 + D(-I_2)$$

The network shown in Fig. 5.15 can be redrawn as:

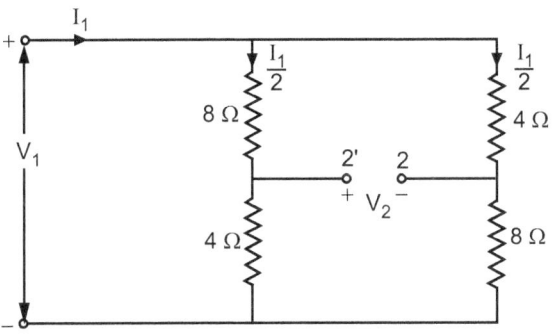

Fig. 5.15 (a)

Case I: Let $I_2 = 0$ i.e. 2 - 2' is open-circuited.

Voltage at terminal 2 is

$$V' = 8\left(\frac{I_1}{2}\right) = 4I_1$$

Voltage at terminal 2' is

$$V'' = 4\left(\frac{I_1}{2}\right) = 2I_1$$

$$V_2 = V' - V''$$
$$= 4I_1 - 2I_1$$

∴ $\quad V_2 = 2I_1$ ... (a)

∴ $\quad \boxed{C = \left[\dfrac{I_1}{V_2}\right]_{I_2 = 0} = \dfrac{1}{2}\,\mho}$

Now, $\quad V_1 = I_1\,[(8 + 4) \parallel (8 + 4)]$

$\quad V_1 = I_1\,[12 \parallel 12]$

∴ $\quad V_1 = I_1 \times 6$ ... (b)

Dividing equation (b) by equation (a),

$$\frac{V_1}{V_2} = \frac{6I_1}{2I_1} = 3$$

∴ $\quad \boxed{A = \left[\dfrac{V_1}{V_2}\right]_{I_2 = 0} = 3}$

Case II: Let $V_2 = 0$. The circuit is shown in Fig. 5.15 (b).

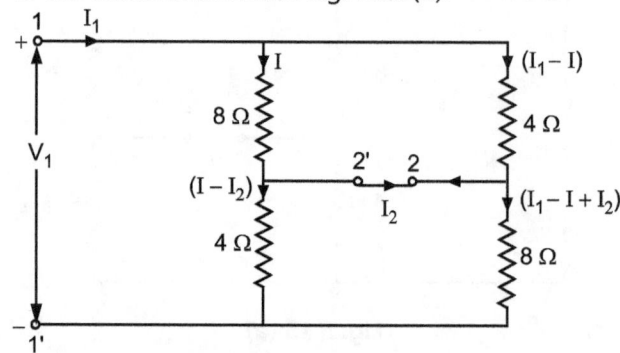

Fig. 5.15 (b)

Consider a closed path 1 - 2 - 2' - 1' - 1.
$$V_1 = 4(I_1 - I) + 4(I - I_2)$$
$$V_1 = 4I_1 - 4I + 4I - 4I_2$$
$$V_1 = 4I_1 + 4(-I_2) \quad \ldots (c)$$

Consider a closed path 1 - 2' - 2 - 1' - 1.
$$V_1 = 8I + 8(I_1 - I + I_2)$$
$$V_1 = 8I_1 + 8I_2$$
$$V_1 = 8I_1 - 8(-I_2) \quad \ldots (d)$$

Let us solve for I_2.
$$V_1 = 16(-I_2)$$
$$B = \left[\frac{V_1}{-I_2}\right]_{V_2 = 0} = 16 \, \Omega$$
$$D = \left[\frac{I_1}{-I_2}\right]_{V_2 = 0} = 3 \, \Omega$$

$$\therefore \quad [T] = \begin{bmatrix} 3 & 16 \, \Omega \\ 1/2 \, \mho & 3 \end{bmatrix}$$

Ex. 5.7: Determine Y-parameters of the network shown in Fig. 5.16.

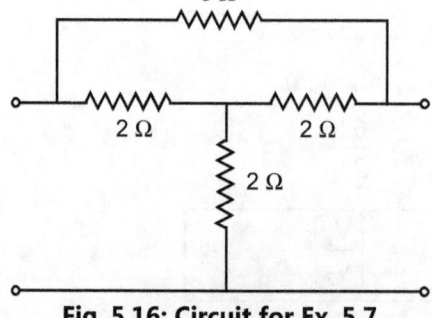

Fig. 5.16: Circuit for Ex. 5.7

Sol.: The given network can be considered as parallel connection of two networks shown in Fig. 5.16 (a) and 5.16 (b).

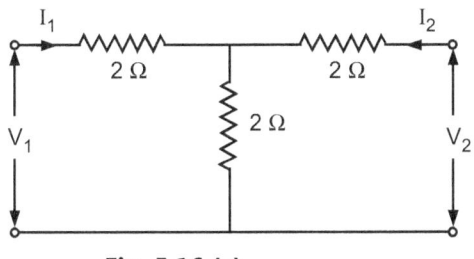

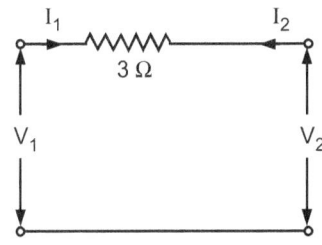

Fig. 5.16 (a)   **Fig. 5.16 (b)**

Now, for Fig. 5.16 (a), Y-parameters can be written as

With $V_2 = 0$, $I_1 = \dfrac{V_1}{3}$

$\therefore$ $Y_{11} = \left[\dfrac{I_1}{V_1}\right]_{V_2 = 0} = \dfrac{1}{3}$ ℧

and $I_2 = -\left(\dfrac{2}{4}\right) I_1 = \dfrac{-V_1}{6}$

$\therefore$ $Y_{21} = \left[\dfrac{I_2}{V_1}\right]_{V_2 = 0} = -\dfrac{1}{6}$ ℧

As network is symmetric and reciprocal,

$$Y_{12} = Y_{21} = -\dfrac{1}{6} \text{ ℧}$$

$$Y_{22} = Y_{11} = \dfrac{1}{3} \text{ ℧}$$

Similarly Y-parameters of Fig. 5.16 (b) can be written as

$$Y_{11} = Y_{22} = \dfrac{1}{3} \text{ ℧}$$

$$Y_{12} = Y_{21} = -\dfrac{1}{3} \text{ ℧}$$

Here, these two networks are connected in parallel.

The overall Y-parameters of the combination can be written as:

$$[Y] = \begin{bmatrix} \dfrac{1}{3} & -\dfrac{1}{6} \\ -\dfrac{1}{6} & \dfrac{1}{3} \end{bmatrix} + \begin{bmatrix} \dfrac{1}{3} & -\dfrac{1}{3} \\ -\dfrac{1}{3} & \dfrac{1}{3} \end{bmatrix} = \begin{bmatrix} \dfrac{2}{3} & -\dfrac{1}{2} \\ -\dfrac{1}{2} & \dfrac{2}{3} \end{bmatrix} \text{ (mho)}$$

Ex. 5.8: Find open-circuit impedance parameters of the circuit containing a controlled source shown in Fig. 5.17. Also find out its Y-parameters.

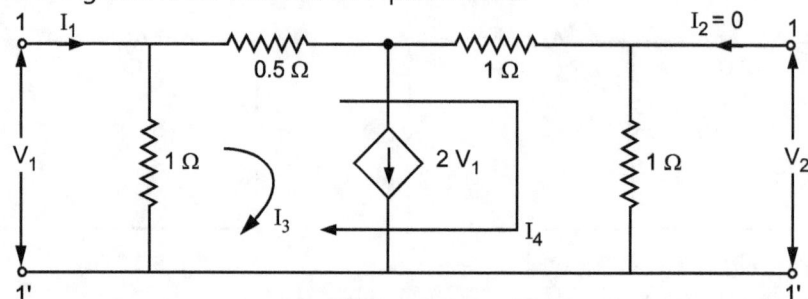

Fig. 5.17: Circuit for Ex. 5.8

Sol.: For Z-parameters:
Case I: Port 2 - 2' is open-circuited.

i.e. $I_2 = 0$
and $I_3 = 2V_1$
Now, $V_1 = (I_1 - I_3) \times 1$
∴ $V_1 = I_1 - 2V_1$
∴ $3V_1 = I_1$
∴ $\dfrac{V_1}{I_1} = \dfrac{1}{3}$

∴ $Z_{11} = \left[\dfrac{V_1}{I_1}\right]_{I_2=0} = \dfrac{1}{3}\ \Omega$

Again, by KVL,
$1.5\, I_4 + 0.5\, I_3 + V_2 = V_1$
or $1.5\,(2V_2) + 0.5\, I_3 + V_2 = V_1$
or $3V_2 + 0.5\,(2V_1) + V_2 = V_1$
∴ $4V_2 = 0$
∴ $V_2 = 0$

∴ $Z_{21} = \left[\dfrac{V_2}{I_1}\right]_{I_2=0} = 0\ \Omega$

Case II: $I_1 = 0$, the circuit is shown in Fig. 5.17 (a).

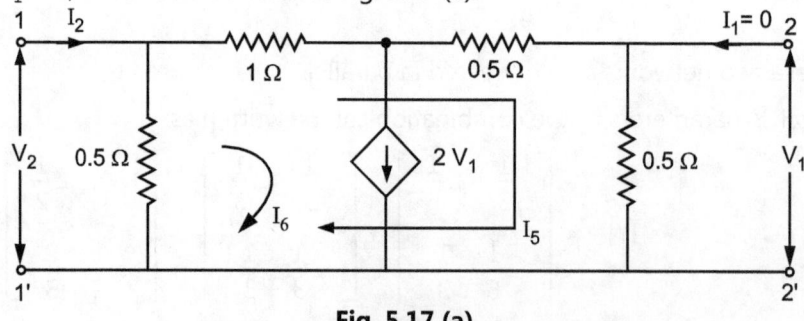

Fig. 5.17 (a)

For this circuit, $I_6 = 2V_1$
and $1 \times I_5 = V_1$
By KVL,
$(I_2 - I_6 - I_5) \times 0.5 = V_2$
and $I_6 \times 1 + I_5 (2.5) = V_2$
Thus, $(I_2 - I_5 - I_6) \times 0.5 = I_6 + 2.5 I_5$
$\therefore$ $I_2 = 3 I_6 + 6 I_5$

Putting the values of I_5 and I_6,

$I_2 = 6V_1 + 6V_1 = 12 V_1$

$\therefore$ $Z_{12} = \left[\dfrac{V_1}{I_2}\right]_{I_1 = 0} = \dfrac{1}{12} \, \Omega$

and $I_6 + 2.5 I_5 = V_2$
or $2V_1 + 2.5 V_1 = V_2$
$\therefore$ $4.5 V_1 = V_2$

But $V_1 = \dfrac{I_2}{12}$

$\therefore$ $4.5 \left(\dfrac{I_2}{12}\right) = V_2$

$\therefore$ $Z_{22} = \left[\dfrac{V_2}{I_2}\right]_{I_1 = 0} = \dfrac{4.5}{12} = \dfrac{3}{8} \, \Omega$

$\therefore$ Z-parameters are $[Z] = \begin{bmatrix} 1/3 & 1/12 \\ 0 & 3/8 \end{bmatrix} \Omega$

From conversion table, $Y_{11} = \dfrac{Z_{22}}{Dz}$

$Dz = Z_{11} Z_{22} - Z_{12} Z_{21} = \dfrac{1}{8}$

$\therefore$ $Y_{11} = \dfrac{3/8}{1/8} = 3 \, \mho$

$Y_{21} = \dfrac{-Z_{21}}{Dz} = 0$

$Y_{12} = \dfrac{-Z_{12}}{Dz} = -\dfrac{2}{3} \, \mho$

$Y_{22} = \dfrac{Z_{11}}{Dz} = \dfrac{8}{3} \, \mho$

$\therefore$ Y-parameters are $[Y] = \begin{bmatrix} 3 & -2/3 \\ 0 & 8/3 \end{bmatrix} \mho$

Ex. 5.9: Find hybrid parameters for the two port network shown in Fig. 5.18.

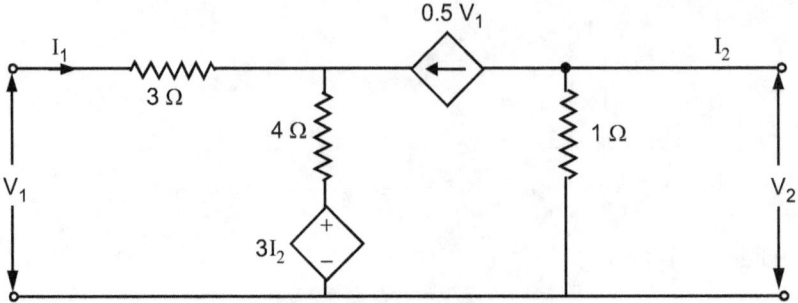

Fig. 5.18: Circuit for Ex. 5.9

Sol.: For h-parameters:

Case I: $V_2 = 0$ i.e. output port is short-circuited.

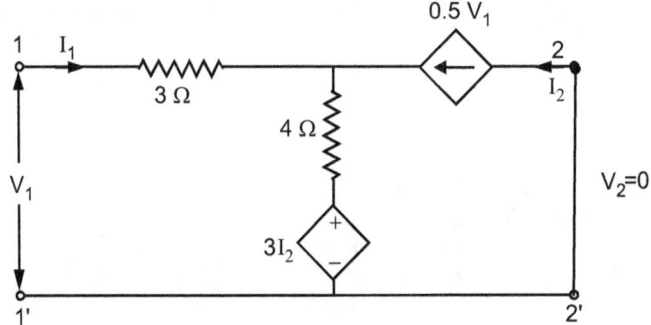

Fig. 5.18 (a)

By KVL, we get, $\quad V_1 = 3 I_1 + 4 (I_1 + I_2) + 3 I_2$

and $\quad I_2 = 0.5 V_1$

Putting value of I_2 in equation of V_1, we get,

$$V_1 = 3 I_1 + 4 (I_1 + 0.5 V_1) + 3 (0.5 V_1)$$

∴ $\quad V_1 = 7 I_1 + 3.5 V_1$

∴ $\quad \dfrac{V_1}{I_1} = \dfrac{7}{-2.5} = -2.8$

∴ $\quad h_{11} = \left[\dfrac{V_1}{I_1}\right]_{V_2 = 0} = -2.8 \, \Omega$

But, $\quad V_1 = -2.8 \, I_1$

and $\quad I_2 = 0.5 V_1$

∴ $\quad I_2 = (0.5)(-2.8 \, I_1)$

$$h_{21} = \left[\dfrac{I_2}{I_1}\right]_{V_2 = 0} = -1.4$$

Case II: $I_1 = 0$ i.e. input is open-circuited.

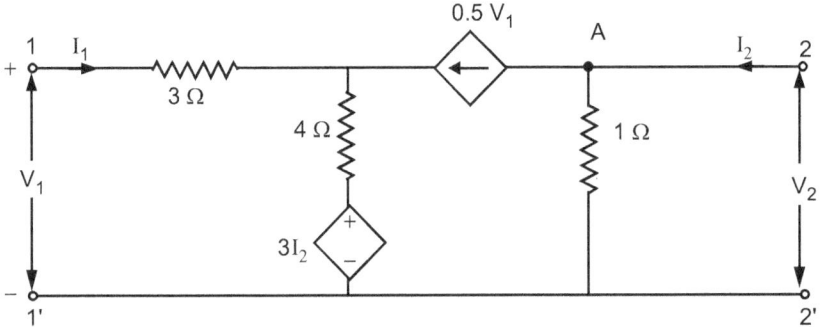

Fig. 5.18 (b)

Applying KCL at node A,

$$I_2 = \frac{V_2}{1} + 0.5 V_1 \quad \text{... (a)}$$

But $\quad V_1 = 4(0.5 V_1) + 3 I_2$

∴ $\quad V_1 = 2 V_1 + 3 I_2$

or $\quad -V_1 = 3 I_2 \quad \text{... (b)}$

Thus, $\quad I_2 = V_2 + 0.5(-3 I_2)$

∴ $\quad 2.5 I_2 = V_2$

∴ $\quad h_{22} = \left[\frac{I_2}{V_2}\right]_{I_1 = 0} = 0.4 \; \mho$

Also putting equation (a) in equation (b),

$$-V_1 = 3(V_2 + 0.5 V_1)$$

$$-V_1 - 1.5 V_1 = 3 V_2$$

$$-2.5 V_1 = 3 V_2$$

∴ $\quad \dfrac{V_1}{V_2} = \dfrac{3}{-2.5}$

∴ $\quad h_{12} = \left[\dfrac{V_1}{V_2}\right]_{I_1 = 0} = -1.2$

∴ The h-parameters for the given network are

$$[h] = \begin{bmatrix} -2.8 \; \Omega & -1.2 \\ -1.4 & 0.4 \; \mho \end{bmatrix}$$

Ex. 5.10: Obtain Z and Y parameters for the circuit shown in Fig. 5.19.

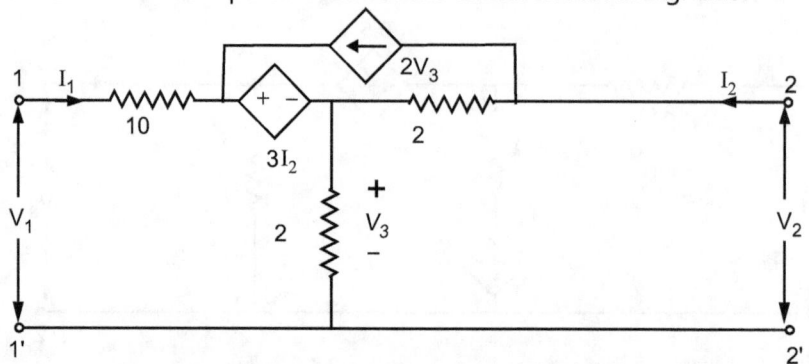

Fig. 5.19: Circuit for Ex. 5.10

Sol.: To find Z-parameters:
Case I: $I_2 = 0$, i.e. output is open-circuited.
As $I_2 = 0$, dependent source $3 I_2$ will be shorted.

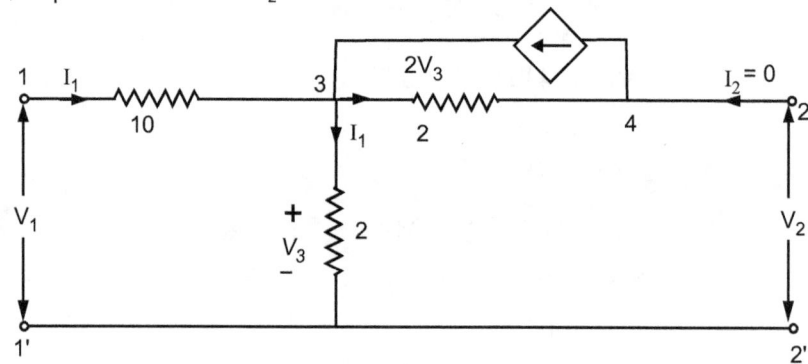

Fig. 5.19 (a)

Applying KVL to 1 - 3 - 1' - 1,
$$10 I_1 + 2 I_1 = V_1$$
$$12 I_1 = V_1$$

∴ $$\frac{V_1}{I_1} = 12$$

∴ $$Z_{11} = \left[\frac{V_1}{I_1}\right]_{I_2 = 0} = 12 \, \Omega$$

Now, by KVL to loop 2 - 4 - 3 - 2' - 2,
$$-2 (2 V_3) + 2 I_1 = V_2$$
But, $$V_3 = 2 I_1$$
∴ $$-2 [2 (2 I_1)] + 2 I_1 = V_2$$
$$-8 I_1 + 2 I_1 = V_2$$
$$-6 I_1 = V_2$$

∴ $$Z_{21} = \left[\frac{V_2}{I_1}\right]_{I_2 = 0} = -6 \, \Omega$$

Case II: $I_1 = 0$ i.e. input port is open circuited.

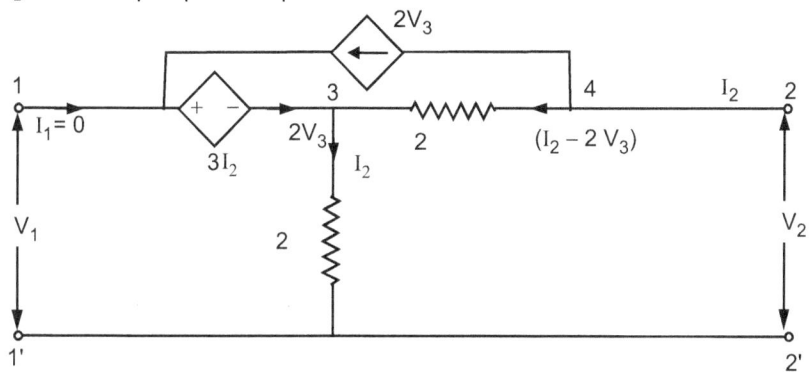

Fig. 5.19 (b)

As $I_1 = 0$, no current flows through 10 Ω resistor.

Current flowing through 2 Ω resistor is $(I_2 - 2V_3)$.

Applying KVL to 2 - 4 - 3 - 2' - 2,

$$(I_2 - 2V_3) \times 2 + 2I_2 = V_2$$

But, $V_3 = 2I_2$

∴ $(I_2 - 4I_2) \times 2 + 2I_2 = V_2$

∴ $-4I_2 = V_2$

∴ $Z_{22} = \left[\dfrac{V_2}{I_2}\right]_{I_1 = 0} = -4\,\Omega$

Applying KVL to 1 - 3 - 1' - 1,

$$3I_2 + 2I_2 = V_1$$

∴ $5I_2 = V_1$

∴ $Z_{12} = \left[\dfrac{V_1}{I_2}\right]_{I_1 = 0} = 5\,\Omega$

∴ Overall Z-parameters are given as

$$[Z] = \begin{bmatrix} 12 & 5 \\ -6 & -4 \end{bmatrix} \text{ (ohms)}$$

From conversion table,

$$Y_{11} = \dfrac{Z_{22}}{Dz} = \dfrac{Z_{22}}{Z_{11}Z_{22} - Z_{12}Z_{21}}$$

$$= \dfrac{-4}{12 \times (-4) - 5 \times (-6)}$$

∴ $Y_{11} = \dfrac{-4}{-18} = \dfrac{2}{9}\ \mho$

$Y_{12} = \dfrac{-Z_{12}}{Dz} = \dfrac{-5}{-18} = \dfrac{5}{18}\ \mho$

$Y_{21} = \dfrac{-Z_{21}}{Dz} = \dfrac{6}{-18} = -\dfrac{1}{3}\ \mho$

$Y_{22} = \dfrac{Z_{11}}{Dz} = \dfrac{12}{-18} = \dfrac{-4}{6}\ \mho$

∴ Overall Y-parameters are given by

$$[Y] = \begin{bmatrix} 2/9 & 5/18 \\ -1/3 & -4/6 \end{bmatrix}\ \text{(mho)}$$

Ex. 5.11: For the transformer with turn ratio 1 : n, find ABCD parameters.

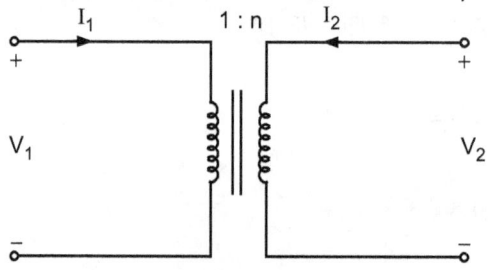

Fig. 5.20: Circuit for Ex. 5.11

Sol.: For ideal transformer,

$$\dfrac{V_1}{V_2} = -\dfrac{I_2}{I_1} = \dfrac{1}{n} \qquad \ldots (1)$$

ABCD parameters are given by equation

$$V_1 = AV_2 - BI_2 \qquad \ldots (2)$$
$$I_1 = CV_2 - DI_2 \qquad \ldots (3)$$

With $I_2 = 0$, $V_1 = AV_2$

Also, $V_1 = \dfrac{V_2}{n}$

Hence, $A = \dfrac{1}{n},\ B = 0$

With $V_2 = 0$, $V_1 = 0$, hence, $I_1 = -nI_2$

Also, $I_1 = -DI_2$

Hence, $C = 0,\ D = n$

Hence ABCD parameters are $\begin{bmatrix} 1/n & 0 \\ 0 & n \end{bmatrix}$

5.8 INSTANTANEOUS POWER

The instantaneous power absorbed by an element is the product of the element's terminal voltage and the current through the element:

$$p(t) = v(t)\, i(t)$$

In steady state condition:

$$v(t) = V_{max} \cos(\omega t + \theta_v)$$
$$i(t) = I_{max} \cos(\omega t + \theta_i)$$

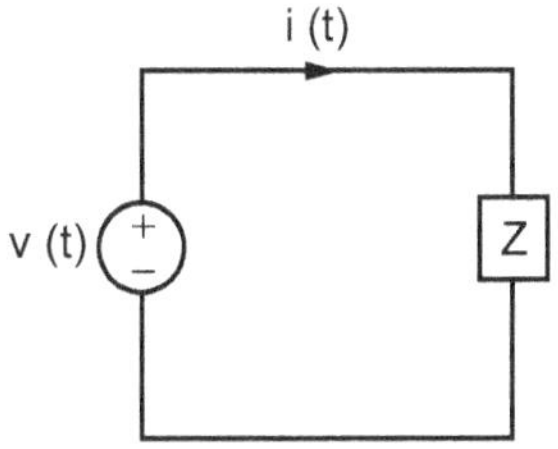

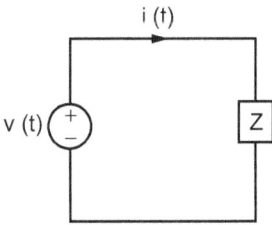

Fig. 5.21

$$p(t) = V_{max} I_{max} \cos(\omega t + \theta_v) \cos(\omega t + \theta_i)$$

$$\cos \phi_1 \cos \phi_2 = \frac{1}{2}[\cos(\phi_1 - \phi_2) + \cos(\phi_1 + \phi_2)]$$

Therefore, under steady state condition, the instantaneous power is:

$$p(t) = \frac{V_{max} I_{max}}{2}\left[\underbrace{\cos(\theta_v - \theta_i)}_{\text{constant}} + \underbrace{\cos(2\omega t + \theta_v + \theta_i)}_{\text{Changes with time and twice the frequency}}\right]$$

... (5.18)

Ex. 5.12: Assume: $v(t) = 4 \cos(\omega t + 60°)$, $Z = 2 \angle 30°\ \Omega$. Find $i(t)$, $p(t)$.

Fig. 5.22

Sol.: $I = \dfrac{V}{Z} = \dfrac{4 \angle 60°}{2 \angle 30°} = 2 \angle 30°\ A$

$i(t) = 2 \cos(\omega t + 30°)$ (A)

$V_{max} = 4,\ \theta_v = 60°$

$I_{max} = 2$, $\theta_i = 30°$

$$p(t) = \frac{V_{max} I_{max}}{2} [\cos(\theta_v - \theta_i) + \cos(2\omega t + \theta_v + \theta_i)]$$

$p(t) = 4\cos 30° + 4\cos(2\omega t + 90°)$

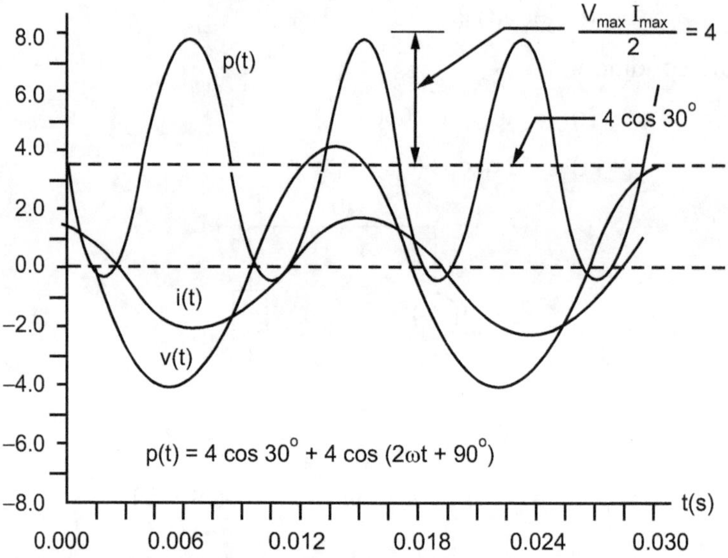

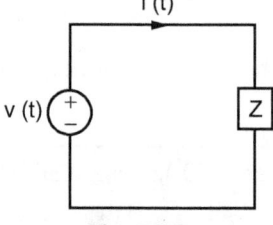

Fig. 5.22 (a)

Ex. 5.13: If $v(t) = 160\cos(50t)$ and $i(t) = -20\sin(50t - 30°)$

Fig. 5.23

1. Find the instantaneous power.
2. Why do you think that the instantaneous power is positive for some part of the cycle and negative for the rest of the cycle?

Sol.: Considering the "cos" term as a reference, then

$i(t) = -20\sin(50t - 30°) = 20\cos(50t - 30° + 180° - 90°)$

$i(t) = 20\cos(50t + 60°)$

$p(t) = v(t)\,i(t) = (160)(20)\cos(50t)\cos(50t + 60°)$

$p(t) = \frac{V_{max} I_{max}}{2}[\cos(\theta_v - \theta_t) + \cos(2\omega t + \theta_v + \theta_t)]$

OR

$$p(t) = 1600 [\cos(100t + 60°) + \cos(60°)] \text{ W}$$

$$p(t) = 800 + 1600 \cos(100t + 60°) \text{ W}$$

$$p(t) = \begin{cases} > 0 & \text{The power is absorbed by the load} \\ & \text{The power is transferred from} \\ & \text{the source to the circuit} \\ < 0 & \text{The power is absorbed by the source} \\ & \text{The power is transferred from} \\ & \text{the load to the source} \end{cases}$$

$$p(t) = \frac{V_{max} I_{max}}{2} [\cos(\theta_v - \theta_t) + \cos(2\omega t + \theta_v + \theta_i)]$$

The instantaneous power has a constant term and a sinusoidal term at twice the frequency.

The quantity in brackets fluctuates between:

and
- A minimum value of $\cos(\theta_v - \theta_i) - 1$
- A maximum value of $\cos(\theta_v - \theta_i) + 1$

This fluctuation of power delivered to the load has certain disadvantages.

An electric motor, for example, operates by receiving electric power and transmitting mechanical (rotational) power at its shaft. If the electric power is delivered to the motor in spurts, the motor is likely to vibrate.

In order to run satisfactorily, a physically larger motor will be needed, with a larger shaft and flywheel, to provide inertia than would be the case if the delivered power were constant.

This problem is solved using three-phase system.

5.8.1 Average Power

The instantaneous power changes with time and it is therefore difficult to measure. The average power is more convenient to measure. For sinusoidal signals or any other periodic signal we compute average power over one period using the following relation:

$$P = \frac{1}{T} \int_{t_o}^{t_o + T} p(t) \, dt$$

This period is:

$$T = \frac{2\pi}{\omega}$$

The instantaneous power:

$$p(t) = \frac{V_{max} I_{max}}{2} [\cos(\theta_v - \theta_t) + \cos(2\omega t + \theta_v + \theta_t)]$$

Integrating the instantaneous power and dividing by one period, we get:

$$P = \frac{V_{max} I_{max}}{2} \cos(\theta_v - \theta_t) \text{ watts} \quad \ldots (5.19)$$

The average power is measured in watts.

For Purely Resistive Loads

The voltage and current are in phase

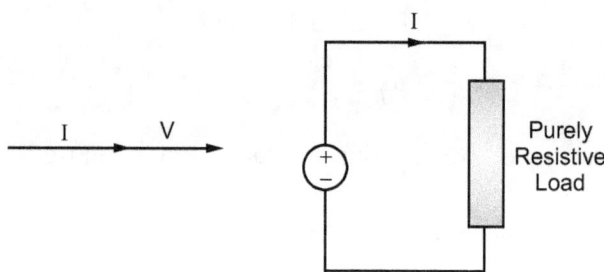

Fig. 5.24

$$P = \frac{V_M I_M}{2} \cos(\theta_v - \theta_t)$$

$$\theta_v = \theta_i \Rightarrow P = \frac{1}{2} V_M I_M = \frac{1}{2} \frac{V_M^2}{R} = \frac{1}{2} R I_M^2$$

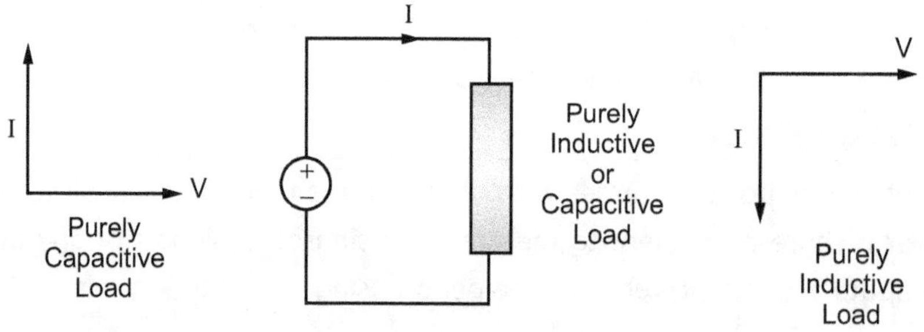

Fig. 5.25

$$\theta_v - \theta_i = \pm 90° \Rightarrow P = 0$$

Note:

1. Because purely reactive impedance absorb no average power, they are often called loss less elements. The purely reactive network operates in a mode in which it stores energy over one part of the period and release it over another.

2. The constant term of the instantaneous power is equal to the average power.

Ex. 5.14: Find the average power absorbed by the load impedance.

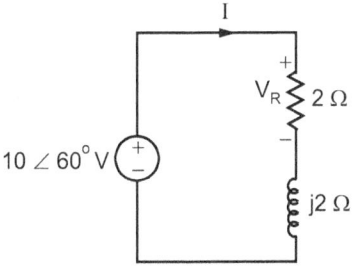

Fig. 5.26

Sol.:
$$P = \frac{V_{max} I_{max}}{2} \cos(\theta_v - \theta_i)$$

$$I = \frac{10 \angle 60°}{2 + j2} = \frac{10 \angle 60°}{2\sqrt{2} \angle 45°} = 3.53 \angle 15° \text{ (A)}$$

$V_{max} = 10$, $I_{max} = 3.53$, $\theta_v = 60°$, $\theta_i = 15°$

$$P = \frac{35.3}{2} \cos(45°) = 12.5 \text{ W}$$

Since inductor does not absorb power one can use voltages and currents across the resistive part:

$$V_R = \frac{2}{2+j2} 10 \angle 60° = 7.06 \angle 15° \text{(V)}$$

$$P = \frac{1}{2} 7.06 \times 3.53 \text{ W}$$

$$P = 12.461 \text{ W}$$

Ex. 5.15: Determine the average power absorbed by each element, the total average power absorbed and the average power supplied by the source.

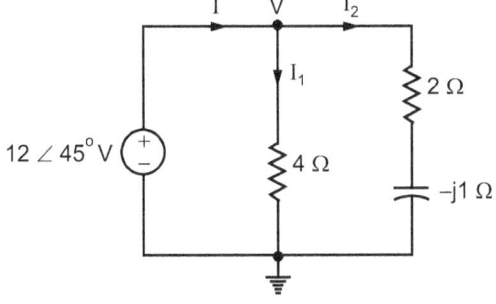

Fig. 5.27

Sol.: For the 4 ohm resistor, voltage and current are in phase:

$\theta_v = \theta_i$

$$P = \frac{1}{2} V_{max} I_{max} = \frac{1}{2} \frac{V_{max}^2}{R} = \frac{1}{2} R I_{max}^2$$

$$I_1 = \frac{12 \angle 45°}{4} = 3 \angle 45° \text{ (A)}$$

$$P_{4\Omega} = \frac{1}{2} 12 \times 3 = 18 \text{ W}$$

For the 2 ohm resistor,

$$I_2 = \frac{12 \angle 45°}{2 - j1} = \frac{12 \angle 45°}{\sqrt{5} \angle -26.37°} = 5.36 \angle 71.57° \text{ (A)}$$

$$P_{2\Omega} = \frac{1}{2} \times 2 \times 5.36^2 \text{ (W)} = 28.7 \text{ W}$$

For the – j1 ohm reactance

$$P_{(-j1)} = \frac{V_{max} I_{max}}{2} \cos(\theta_v - \theta_t)$$

$\theta_v - \theta_i = -90°$ Purely capacitive load

$P_{(-j1\Omega)} = 0$

The total average power absorbed:

$P_{absorbed} = 18 + 28.7 = 46.7 \text{ W}$

The average power supplied by the source

$$P = \frac{V_{max} I_{max}}{2} \cos(\theta_v - \theta_t)$$

$I = I_1 + I_2 = 3 \angle 45° + 5.36 \angle 71.57°$

$I = 8.15 \angle 62.10° \text{ (A)}$

$$P_{supplied} = \frac{1}{2} 12 \times 8.15 \times \cos(45° - 62.10°)$$

$P_{supplied} = 46.7 \text{W} \Rightarrow P_{supplied} = P_{absorbed}$

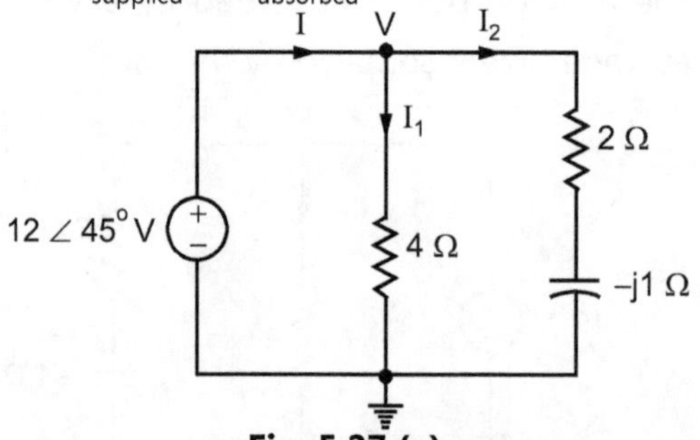

Fig. 5.27 (a)

Note: This rule is correct for ideal systems. For practical systems we have to consider system losses.

$P_{supplied} = P_{absorbed} + P_{losses}$

5.8.1.1 The Passive Sign Convention

Current direction and voltage polarity play a major role in determining the sign of the power.

Passive sign convention is satisfied when the current enters the positive polarity of the voltage

$$p = + iv$$

The element is absorbed power.

If the current enters the negative terminals, then passive sign convention is not satisfied

$$p = - iv$$

The element is supplying power.

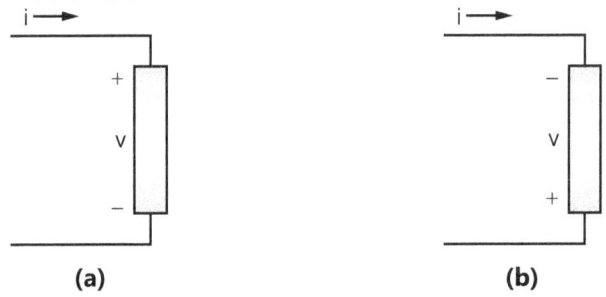

Fig. 5.28

5.9 MAXIMUM AVERAGE POWER TRANSFER

To obtain the maximum average power transferred from a source to a load, the load impedance should be chosen equal to the conjugate of the Thevenin equivalent impedance representing the reminder of the network.

Consider the network shown in the Fig. 5.29. The average power at the load side of the network is:

$$P_L = \frac{1}{2} | V_L || I_L | \cos (\theta_{V_L} - \theta_{I_L}) \qquad \ldots (a)$$

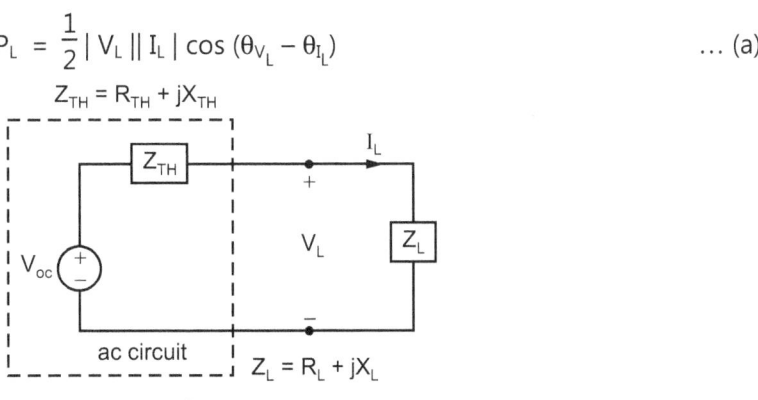

Fig. 5.29

The load voltage and its magnitude are:

$$V_L = \frac{Z_L}{Z_L + Z_{TH}} V_{OC} \qquad |V_L| = \left|\frac{Z_L}{Z_L + Z_{TH}}\right| |V_{OC}| \qquad \ldots (5.20\text{ (a)})$$

or

$$|V_L| = \frac{\sqrt{R_L^2 + X_L^2}}{\sqrt{(R_{TH} + R_L)^2 + (X_{TH} + X_L)^2}} |V_{OC}| \qquad \ldots (5.20\text{ (b)})$$

The load current and its magnitude are:

$$I_L = \frac{V_{OC}}{Z_L + Z_{TH}}, \qquad |I_L| = \frac{|V_{OC}|}{|Z_L + Z_{TH}|} \qquad \ldots (5.21\text{ (a)})$$

or

$$|I_L| = \frac{|V_{OC}|}{\sqrt{(R_{TH} + R_L)^2 + (X_{TH} + X_L)^2}} \qquad \ldots (5.21\text{(b)})$$

The load impedance is:

$$Z_L = R_L + jX_L$$

And the angle of the load impedance is:

$$\theta_{V_L} - \theta_{I_L} = \theta_{Z_L}$$

$$\cos(\theta_{V_L} - \theta_{I_L}) = \frac{R_L}{\sqrt{R_L^2 + X_L^2}} \qquad \ldots (b)$$

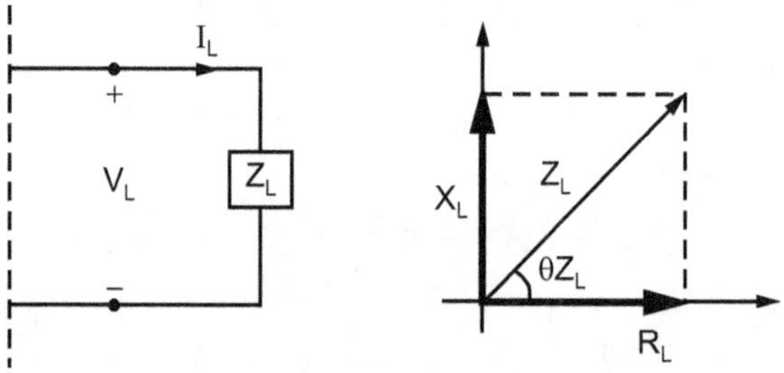

Fig. 5.30

Substituting equations (5.20 (b)), (5.21 (a)) and (5.21 (b)) into equation (a), we get:

$$P_L = \frac{1}{2}|V_L||I_L|\cos(\theta_{V_L} - \theta_{I_L})$$

$$P_L = \frac{\sqrt{R_L^2 + X_L^2}|V_{OC}|}{\sqrt{(R_{TH} + R_L)^2 + (X_{TH} + X_L)^2}} \cdot \frac{|V_{OC}|}{\sqrt{(R_{TH} + R_L)^2 + (X_{TH} + X_L)^2}} \cdot \frac{R_L}{\sqrt{R_L^2 + X_L^2}}$$

$$P_L = \frac{1}{2}\frac{|V_{OC}|^2 R_L}{(R_{TH} + R_L)^2 + (X_L + X_{TH})^2} \qquad \ldots (5.22)$$

Note: The quantity, $(X_L + X_{TH})$ absorbed no power, any non-zero value of this quantity will reduce the power. Hence we can eliminate this term by selecting

$$X_L = -X_{TH} \qquad \ldots (c)$$

Therefore, the expression for the average power is modified to:

$$P_L = \frac{1}{2}\frac{|V_{OC}|^2 R_L}{2(R_L + R_{TH})^2} \qquad \ldots (d)$$

This expression is similar to the average power of a resistive circuit, where:

R_L gives maximum average power at $\frac{\partial P_L}{\partial R_L} = 0$.

which is valid at: $R_L = R_{TH}$ ... (e)

Therefore, the maximum average power will be transferred from the source to the load at the following condition:

$$\begin{aligned}X_L &= -X_{TH} \\ R_L &= R_{TH}\end{aligned} \Rightarrow Z_L = R_{TH} - jX_{TH} \Rightarrow Z_L^{opt} = Z_{TH}^*$$

Under maximum power transfer

$$X_L = -X_{TH}$$

$$R_L = R_{TH}$$

$$I_L = \frac{V_{OC}}{Z_L + Z_{TH}}$$

$$|I_L| = \frac{|V_{OC}|}{\sqrt{(R_{TH} + R_L)^2 + (X_{TH} + X_L)^2}}$$

OR $\quad |I_L| = \dfrac{|V_{OC}|}{2R_{TH}}$

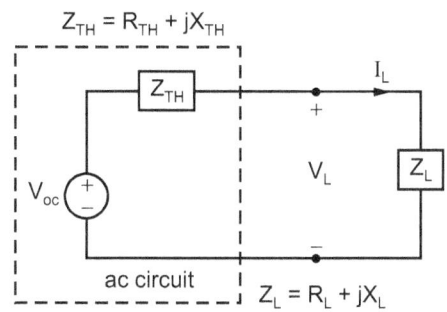

Fig. 5.31

The maximum average power transferred to the load is:

$$P_L^{max} = \frac{1}{2}|I_L|^2 R_L$$

OR $$P_L^{max} = \frac{1}{2}\left(\frac{|V_{OC}|^2}{4R_{TH}}\right) \qquad \ldots (5.23)$$

Ex. 5.16: Find: Z_L, for maximum average power transferred from the source to the laod.

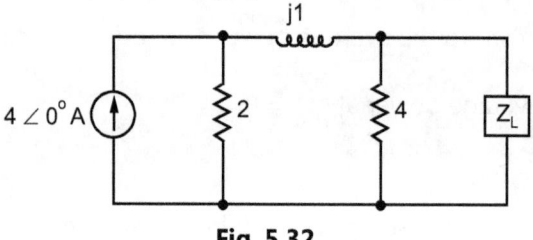

Fig. 5.32

Sol.: The maximum average power will be transferred from the source to the load at the following condition:

$$Z_L = R_{TH} - jX_{TH}$$

Remove the load and determine the Thevenin equivalent of remaining circuit

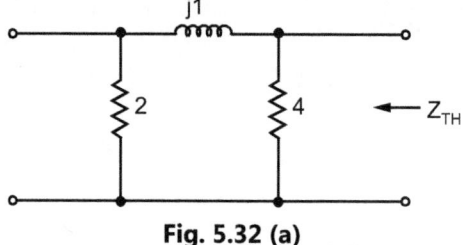

Fig. 5.32 (a)

$$Z_{TH} = 4 \parallel (2 + j1) = \frac{8 + j4}{6 + j1}$$

$$= \frac{8 + j4}{6 + j1} = \frac{8.94 \angle 26.57°}{6.08 \angle 9.64°}$$

$$Z_{TH} = 1.47 \angle 16.93° \, \Omega$$

Under maximum average power transfer:

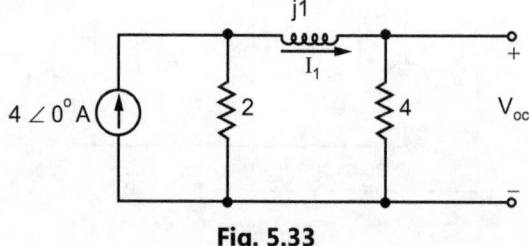

Fig. 5.33

$$Z_L = R_{TH} - jX_{TH}$$

$$Z_L^{opt} = Z_{TH}^* = 1.47 \angle -16.93° = 1.41 - j\,0.43\ \Omega$$

$$V_{OC} = 4 \times \frac{2}{2+4+j1}\ 4 \angle 0°$$

$$= \frac{32 \angle 0°}{6.08 \angle 9.64°} = 5.26 \angle -9.64°$$

The maximum average power transferred is:

$$P_L^{max} = \frac{1}{2}\left(\frac{|V_{OC}|^2}{4R_{TH}}\right)$$

$$P_L^{max} = \frac{1}{2} \times \frac{5.26^2}{4 \times 1.41} = 2.45\ (W)$$

Ex. 5.17: Find the maximum average power transferred from the source to the load.

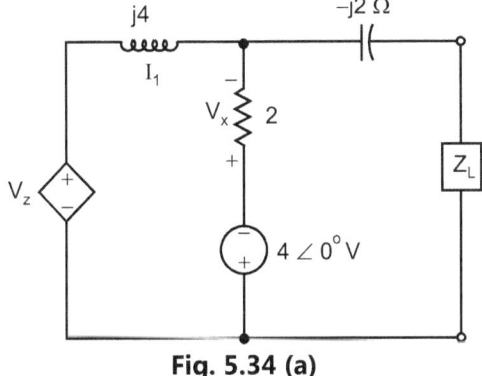

Fig. 5.34 (a)

Sol.: The maximum average power will be transferred from the source to the load at the following condition:

$$Z_L^{opt} = Z_{TH}^*$$

Circuit with dependent sources: $Z_{TH} = \dfrac{V_{OC}}{I_{SC}}$

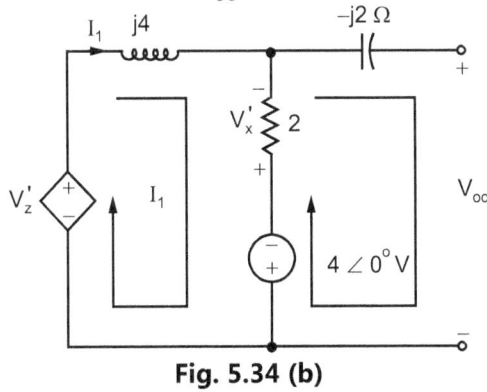

Fig. 5.34 (b)

First: find the open circuit voltage:

Loop 1: $4\angle 0° = -V_x' + (2 + j4) I_1$

$$V_x' = -2I_1$$

$$4\angle 0° = (4 + j4) I_1$$
$$= (4\sqrt{2} \angle 45°) I_1$$
$$I_1 = \frac{4\angle 0°}{4\sqrt{2} \angle 45°}$$
$$= 0.707 \angle -45° \text{ (A)}$$

Loop 2: $V_{OC} = 2I_1 - 4\angle 0° = 1 - j1 - 4$
$$= 3 - j1 = \sqrt{10} \angle -161.5°$$

Next: Find the short circuit current

Loop 1: $-V_x'' + j4I + 2(I - I_{SC}) - 4\angle 0° = 0$ ... (1)

Loop 2: $4\angle 0° + 2(I_{SC} - I) - j2I_{SC} = 0$ ... (2)

Controlling variable

$$V_x'' = 2(I_{SC} - I) \qquad \ldots (3)$$

Substitute for V_x'' and rearrange the two equations

$$(4 + j4) I - 4I_{SC} = 4 \qquad \ldots (4)$$
$$-2I + (2 - j2) I_{SC} = -4 \Rightarrow I = (1 - j1) I_{SC} + 2 \qquad \ldots (5)$$

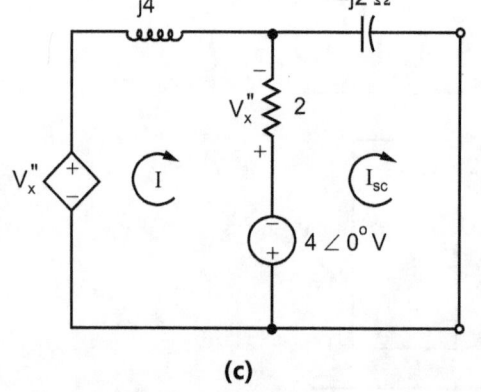 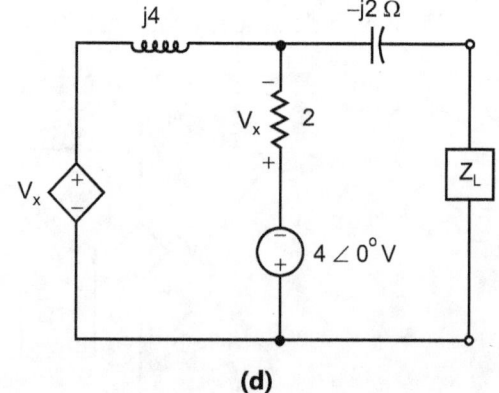

(c)   (d)

Fig. 5.34

Substitute equation (5) into equation (4)

$$4(1 + j)[(1 - j)I_{SC} + 2] - 4I_{SC} = 4$$

$$I_{SC} = -1 - j2(A) = \sqrt{5} \angle -116.57°$$

$$Z_{TH} = \frac{V_{OC}}{I_{SC}} = \frac{\sqrt{10} \angle -161.5°}{\sqrt{5} \angle -116.57°}$$

$$Z_{TH} = \sqrt{2} \angle -45° = 1 - j1\Omega \Rightarrow Z_L^{opt} = 1 + j1\Omega$$

$$P_L^{max} = \frac{1}{2} \times \frac{(\sqrt{10}^2)}{4 \times 1} = 1.25 \text{ (W)}$$

5.10 EFFECTIVE OR RMS VALUE

The **effective value** is introduced as a means of measuring the effectiveness of a source in delivering power to a resistive load. The **effective value** of a varying current source is the equivalent constant (dc) current that delivers the same average power as given by the varying current source.

For the resistive load shown in Fig. 5.35.

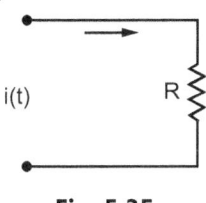

Fig. 5.35

The instantaneous power is :

$$p(t) = i^2(t)R$$

If current is periodic with period T, then the average power is :

$$P_{av} = \frac{1}{T} \int_{t_o}^{t_o + T} p(t) \, dt \qquad \ldots (5.24)$$

If current is constant dc (I_{dc}) then, the power is :

$$P_{dc} = RI_{dc}^2 = RI_{eff}^2 \qquad \ldots (5.25)$$

The effective value of ac current is the equivalent dc value that supplies the same average power.

$$p_{dc} = p_{av}$$

Substituting, eq. (1) and eq. (2).

$$RI_{eff}^2 = \frac{1}{T} \int_{t_0}^{t_0+T} Ri^2(t)\, dt$$

$$RI_{eff}^2 = R\left[\frac{1}{t} \int_{t_0}^{t_0+T} i^2(t)\, dt\right]$$

$$I_{eff}^2 = \frac{1}{T} \int_{t_0}^{t_0+T} i^2(t)\, dt$$

$$I_{eff} = \sqrt{\frac{1}{T} \int_{t_0}^{t_0+T} i^2(t)\, dt} = I_{rms}$$

Effective Value = RMS (Root Mean Square)

Ex. 5.18: Compute the rms value of the voltage waveform

$$v(t) = \begin{cases} 4t & 0 < t \le 1 \\ 0 & 1 < t \le 2 \\ -4(t-2) & 2 < t \le 3 \end{cases}$$

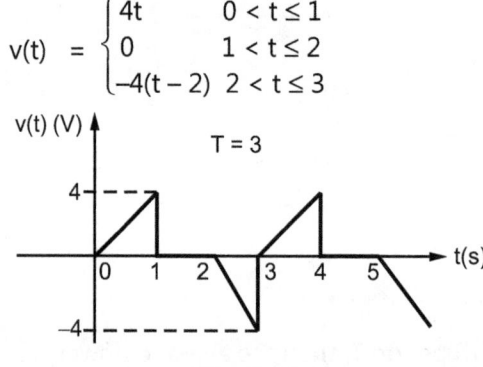

Fig. 5.36

Sol. :

$$\int_0^T v^2(t)\, dt = \int_0^1 (4t)^2\, dt + \int_1^2 (0)^2\, dt + \int_2^3 (-4(t-2))^2\, dt$$

$$= \int_0^1 10t^2\, dt + \int_2^3 (16t^2 - 64t + 64)\, dt$$

$$\int_0^T v^2(t)dt = \left[\frac{16t^3}{3}\right]_0^1 + \left[\frac{16t^3}{3} - \frac{64t^2}{2} + 64t\right]_2^3$$

$$= \left[\frac{16}{3}\right] + \left[\frac{16 \times 27}{3} - \frac{64 \times 9}{2} + 64 \times 3\right]$$

$$- \left[\frac{16 \times 8}{3} - \frac{64 \times 4}{2} + 64 \times 2\right] = 10.66$$

$$V_{rms} = \sqrt{\frac{1}{T} \int_{t_o}^{t_o + T} v^2(t)\, dt}$$

or $V_{rms} = \sqrt{\frac{1}{3} \cdot 10.66} = 1.89 \text{ (V)}$

Note : If the current in a resistor R is composed of a sum of sinusoidal waves of different frequencies, the power absorbed by the resistor can be expressed as :

$$P = (I_{1\,rms}^2 + I_{2\,rms}^2 + \ldots + I_{n\,rms}^2)\, R$$

or $P = (I_{rms}^2)_T\, R$

$$(I_{2\,rms}^2)_T = (I_{1\,rms}^2 + I_{2\,rms}^2 + \ldots + I_{n\,rms}^2)$$

The (rms) value of the total current is :

$$(I_{rms})_T = \sqrt{I_{1\,rms}^2 + I_{2\,rms}^2 + \ldots + I_{n\,rms}^2} \qquad \ldots(5.26)$$

Ex. 5.19: Compute the rms value of the current waveform and use it to determine the average power supplied to the resistor.

$$i(t) = I_m \cos(wt - \theta)$$

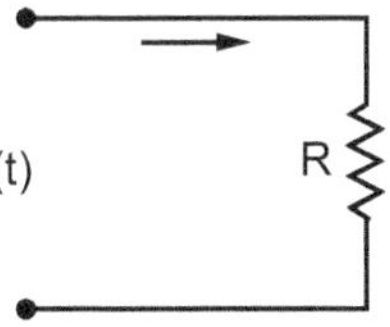

Fig. 5.37

Sol.:

$$I_{rms} = \sqrt{\frac{1}{T} \int_{t_o}^{t_o + T} I_m^2 \cos^2(wt - \theta)\, dt}$$

or
$$I_{rms} = \sqrt{\frac{I_m^2}{T} \int_{t_o}^{t_o+T} \left[\frac{1}{2} + \frac{1}{2}\cos(2wt - 2\theta)\right] dt}$$

$$I_{rms} = \sqrt{\frac{I_m^2}{T} \left[\int_{t_o}^{t_o+T} \frac{1}{2} dt + \int_{t_o}^{t_o+T} \frac{1}{2}\cos(2wt - 2\theta) dt\right]}$$

or
$$I_{rms} = \sqrt{\frac{I_m^2}{2T} \left[\int_{t_o}^{t_o+T} 1 dt + \int_{t_o}^{t_o+T} \cos(2wt - 2\theta) dt\right]}$$

$$= \sqrt{\frac{I_m^2}{2T} [t]_{t_o}^{t_o+T}} = \sqrt{\frac{I_m^2}{2T} T}$$

$$I_{rms} = \frac{I_m}{\sqrt{2}}$$

and
$$P_{av} = RI_{rms}^2 = R\left(\frac{I_m}{\sqrt{2}}\right)^2 = \frac{1}{2} I_m^2 R$$

Ex. 5.20 : Determine the RMS value for the following waveforms.

Sol.:

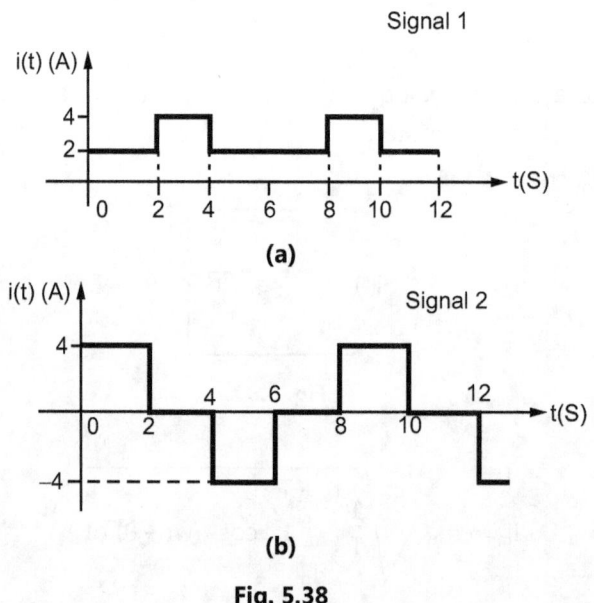

(a)

(b)

Fig. 5.38

Signal 1:
$$I_{rms} = \sqrt{\frac{1}{6}\left[\int_0^2 4\,dt + \int_2^4 16\,dt + \int_4^6 4\,dt\right]}$$

$$I_{rms} = \sqrt{\frac{8 + 32 + 8}{6}} = \sqrt{8}$$

Signal 2:
$$I_{rms} = \sqrt{\frac{1}{8}\left[\int_0^2 16\,dt + \int_6^4 16\,dt\right]} = \sqrt{8}$$

5.11 POWER FACTOR

The **power factor** is a very important quantity. Its important comes from the economic impact it has on industrial users of large amounts of power. The **power factor (pf)** is defined as the ratio of the **average power** to apparent power.

$$P_{av} = V_{rms} I_{rms} \cos(\theta_v - \theta_i) \text{ (W)}$$
$$P_{apparent} = V_{rms} I_{rms} \text{ (VA)}$$
$$pf = \frac{P_{av}}{P_{apparent}} = \cos(\theta_v - \theta_i) = \cos\theta_z$$
$$\theta_v - \theta_t = \theta_z$$
$$P_{av} = V_{rms} \times I_{rms} \times pf \qquad \ldots(5.27)$$

1. **For Resistive load**

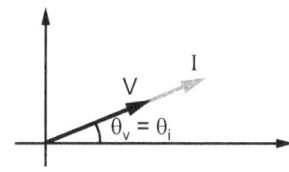

Fig. 5.39 (a)

Current and voltage are in phase
$$\theta_z = \theta_v - \theta_i$$
$$\theta_z = 0°$$
$$pf = 1.0$$

2. **For inductive load**

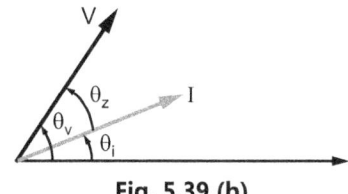

Fig. 5.39 (b)

3. For capacitive load

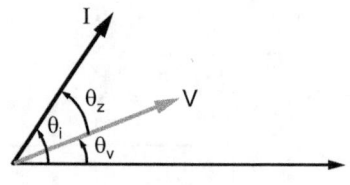

Fig. 5.39 (c)

Current lags the voltage

Inductive load

$\theta_z = \theta_v - \theta_i$

$0° < \theta_z < 90°$

$0 < pf < 1.0$

pf is lagging

Current lags the voltage

Capacitive load

$\theta_z = \theta_v - \theta_i$

$-90 < \theta_z < 0°$

$0 < pf < 1.0$

pf is leading

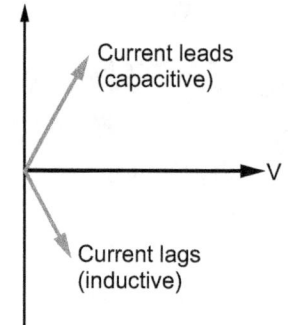

Fig. 5.39 (d)

Therefore, in general :

$$pf = \frac{P_{av}}{P_{apparent}} = \cos(\theta_v - \theta_i) = \cos \theta_z$$

pf	θ_z	Load
0	−90°	pure capacitive
0 < pf < 1	−90° < θ_z < 0°	leading or capacitive
1	0°	resistive
0 < pf < 1	0° < θ_z < 90°	lagging or inductive
0	90°	pure inductive

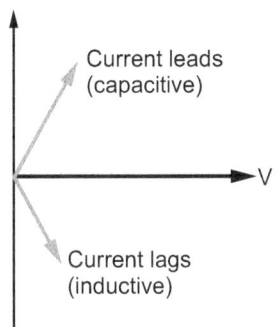

Fig. 5.39 (e)

Note :

1. If p.f. = 0.8 lag and $\theta_v = 45°$

$$\cos(\theta_v - \theta_i) = \cos\theta_z$$
$$\theta_z = \cos^{-1}(pf) = 36.87°$$
$$\theta_z - \theta_i = \theta_z \Rightarrow \theta_v > \theta_i$$
$$45 - \theta_i = 36.87°$$
$$\theta_i = 45 - 36.87 = 8.13°$$

2. If p.f. = 0.8 leading and $\theta_v = 45°$

$$\cos(\theta_v - \theta_i) = \cos\theta_z$$
$$\theta_z = \cos^{-1}(pf) = 36.87°$$
$$\theta_v - \theta_i = -\theta_z \Rightarrow \theta_v < \theta_i$$
$$45 - \theta_i = -36.87°$$
$$\theta_i = 45 - (-36.87) = 81.87°$$

Ex. 5.21: Find the power supplied by the source. Determine how it changes if the power factor is changed to 0.9.

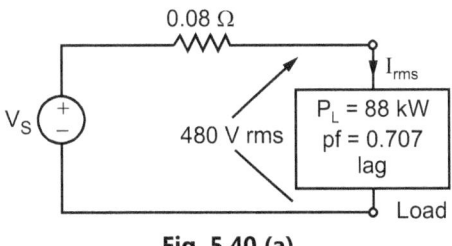

Fig. 5.40 (a)

Sol.:

1. The generated power

$$P = V_{rms} \times I_{rms} \times pf$$

At pf = 0.707 lagging

$$I_{rms} = \frac{88 \times 10^3 \text{ (W)}}{480 \times 0.707} = 259.3 \text{ (A) rms}$$

$$P_{losses} = I_{rms}^2 R = 259.3^2 \times 0.08$$

$$P_{losses} = 5.378 \text{ kW}$$

$$P_{source} = P_{losses} + 88,000 \text{ (W)}$$

$$P_{source} = 93.378 \text{ (kW)}$$

At pf = 0.90 lagging

$$I_{rms} = \frac{88,000}{480 \times 0.9} = 203.7 \text{ (A) rms}$$

$$P_{losses} = I_{rms}^2 R = 203.7^2 \times 0.08$$

$$P_{losses} = 3.32 \text{ kW} \quad \text{losses are reduced}$$

$$P_{source} = P_{losses} + 88,000 \text{ (W)}$$

$$P_{source} = 91.32 \text{ (kW)}$$

2. The generated voltage

At pf = 0.707 lagging

$$pf = \cos\theta_z$$
$$0.707 = \cos(\theta_v - \theta_i)$$
$$45° = (0° - \theta_i)$$
$$\theta_i = -45°$$
$$I_{rms} = 2593 \angle -45° \text{ (A) rms}$$

At pf = 0.707 lagging

$$pf = \cos\theta_z$$
$$0.90 = \cos(\theta_v - \theta_i)$$
$$25.8° = (0° - \theta_i)$$
$$\theta_i = -25.8°$$
$$I_{rms} = 203.7 \angle -25.8°$$

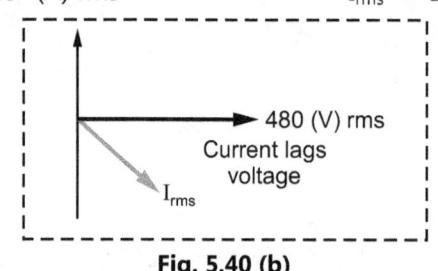

Fig. 5.40 (b)

$$V_{S_{rms}} = 0.08 I_{rms} + V_L$$
$$= 0.08 \times 259.3 \angle -45° + 480 \angle 0°$$
$$= 495 \angle -1.7° \text{ (V)}$$

$$V_S = 14.47 - j7.09 + 480$$
$$= 494 \angle -0.82°$$

Notes :
1. The previous example clearly indicates the economic impact of the load's power factor. A low power factor at the load means that the utility generators must be capable of carrying more current at a constant voltage, and they must also supply for higher line losses than would be required if the load's power factor were high.
2. The power factor is the cosine of the phase difference voltage and current. It is also the cosine of the load-impedance angle.
3. The apparent power (i 3.n VA) is the product of the rms values of voltage and current. Leading power factor means that current leads the voltage and lagging power factor means current lagging the voltage.

5.12 COMPLEX POWER

The complex power is an important element in power analysis because it contains all the information related to the power used by a load. The complex power S (in VA) is the product of the rms voltage phasor and the complex conjugate of the rms current phasor. Consider the circuit shown in the Fig. 5.14 (a) the complex power is defined to be

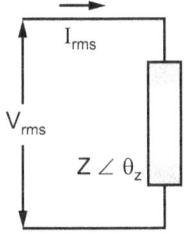

Fig. 5.41 (a)

$$S = V_{rms} I_{rms}^*$$
$$S = V_{rms} \angle \theta_v° \times [I_{rms} \angle \theta_i°]^*$$
$$S = V_{rms} I_{rms} \angle \theta_v - \theta_i$$
$$S = V_{rms} I_{rms} \cos(\theta_v - \theta_i) + jV_{rms} I_{rms} \sin(\theta_v - \theta_i)$$

$\underbrace{\phantom{V_{rms} I_{rms} \cos(\theta_v - \theta_i)}}_{\text{Active Power}}$ $\underbrace{\phantom{jV_{rms} I_{rms} \sin(\theta_v - \theta_i)}}_{\text{Reactive Power}}$

Active Power (P) $= V_{rms} I_{rms} \cos(\theta_v - \theta_i)$ (watt)
Reactive Power (Q) $= V_{rms} I_{rms} \sin(\theta_v - \theta_i)$ (VAR)

OR, the complex power is

$$S = P + JQ \quad \text{(VA)} \qquad \ldots (5.28)$$

Using the load impedance,

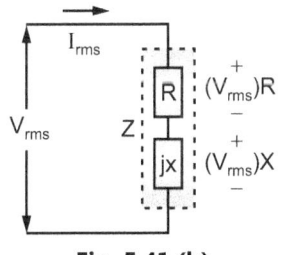

Fig. 5.41 (b)

$$Z = R + jX$$
$$S = V_{rms} I_{rms}^* \quad \text{(VA)}$$
$$V_{rms} = ZI_{rms}$$
$$S = (ZI_{rms}) I_{rms}^*$$
$$S = Z |I_{rms}|^2$$

$$S = (R + jX) |I_{rms}|^2 \qquad |I_{rms}| = \frac{|(V_{rms})_R|}{R}$$

$$S = (R + jX) |I_{rms}|^2 \qquad |I_{rms}| = \frac{|(V_{rms})_X|}{X}$$

$$S = P + jQ$$

$$P = R |I_{rms}|^2 \text{ (watt)} \qquad P = \frac{|(V_{rms})_R|^2}{R} \text{ (watt)}$$

$$Q = X |I_{rms}|^2 \text{ (VAR)} \qquad Q = \frac{|(V_{rms})_X|^2}{X} \text{ (VAR)}$$

The complex Power relations could be summarized as:

$$S = V_{rms} I_{rms}^* \text{ (VA)}$$

$$S = |V_{rms}| |I_{rms}| \angle (\theta_v - \theta_i) \text{ (VA)}$$

$$S = |S| \angle (\theta_v - \theta_i) \text{ (VA)}$$

$$|S| = |V_{rms}| |I_{rms}| = \text{Apparent Power (VA)}$$

$$S = \underbrace{V_{rms} I_{rms} \cos(\theta_v - \theta_i)}_{\text{Active Power}} \pm j \underbrace{V_{rms} I_{rms} \sin(\theta_v - \theta_i)}_{\text{Reactive Power}} \text{ (VA)}$$

$$S = P \pm jQ \text{ (VA)}$$

$$P = \text{Re}\{S\} = |S| \cos(\theta_v - \theta_i) = R |I_{rms}|^2 \text{ (Watt)} \qquad \ldots(5.29)$$

$$Q = \text{Im}\{S\} = |S| \sin(\theta_v - \theta_i) = X |I_{rms}|^2 \text{ (VAR)} \qquad \ldots(5.30)$$

$$pf = \cos(\theta_v - \theta_i) = \cos(\theta_Z)$$

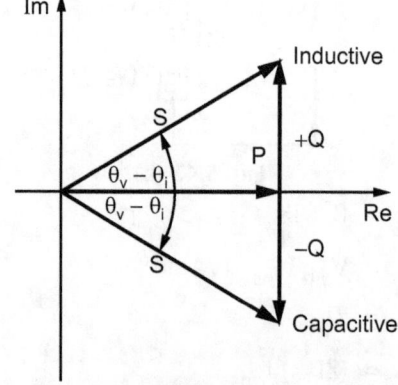

Fig. 5.41 (c)

Ex. 5.22: For the network shown, determine the load complex power, voltage and power factor at the source side.

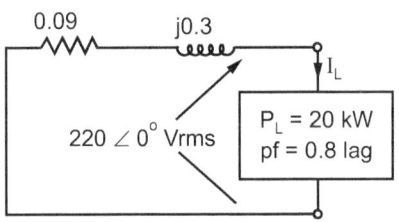

Fig. 5.42 (a)

Sol.:

$$P = \text{Re}\{S\} = |S| \cos(\theta_v - \theta_i) = |S| \times pf$$

$$\therefore \quad |S_L| = \frac{P_L}{pf} = \frac{20}{0.8} = 25 \text{ kVA}$$

$$pf = \cos(\theta_v - \theta_i) = \cos(\theta_z) = 0.8$$

$$\theta_z = 36.87$$

$$Q_L = |S| \sin(\theta_v - \theta_i)$$

$$Q_L = |25| \sin(36.87) = 15 \text{ kVAR}$$

$$S_L = 20 + j15 = 25 \angle 36.87° \text{ Inductive load}$$

> **Note :** p.f. = 0.8 lag and $\theta_v = 0°$
> $$\cos(\theta_v - \theta_i) = \cos\theta_z$$
> $$\theta_z = \cos^{-1}(pf) = 36.87°$$
> $$\theta_v - \theta_t = \theta_z \Rightarrow \theta_v > \theta_i$$
> $$0 - \theta_i = 36.87°$$
> $$\theta_i = 0 - 36,87 = -36.87°$$

The complex power is

$$S_L = V_L I_L^*$$

$$I_L = \left[\frac{S_L}{V_L}\right]^* = \left[\frac{25000 \angle 36.87°}{220 \angle 0°}\right]^* = 113.64 \angle -36.86° \text{ (A)}$$

Fig. 5.42 (b)

$V_S = (0.09 + j0.3) I_L + 220 \angle 0°$

$V_S = (0.09 + j0.3)(90.91 - j68.18) + 220$ (V)

$V_S = 248.63 + j21.14 = 249.53 \angle 4.86°$

$pf_{source} = \cos(\theta_V^{source} - \theta_i^{source})$

$pf_{source} = \cos(4.86 - (-36.86))$

$pf_{source} = \cos(41.72°) = 0.746$ Lag

Note : $pf_{source} = 0.746$ lag and $pf_{load} = 0.8$ lag

Ex. 5.23 : Compute the average power flow between networks. Determine which network is the source.

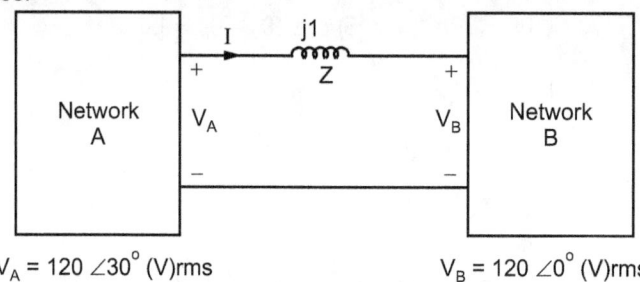

$V_A = 120 \angle 30°$ (V)rms $V_B = 120 \angle 0°$ (V)rms

Fig. 5.43

Sol.: $I = \dfrac{V_A - V_B}{Z} = \dfrac{120 \angle 30° - 120 \angle 0°}{j1} = 60 + j16.08 = 62.12 \angle 15°$ (A) rms

Using the Passive Sign Convention, the power received by A is:

$S_A = V_A (-I)^* = 120 \angle 30° \times 62.12 \angle -195° = 7454 \angle -165°$ A

$P_A = 7545 \cos(165°) = -7200$ (W) Supplying power

$S_B = V_B (I^*) = 120 \angle 0° \times 62.12 \angle -15° = 7454 \angle -15°$ VA

$P_B = 7,454 \cos(-15°) = 7.200$ (W) Absorbing Power

Network A supplies 7.2 kW average power to Network B

5.12.1 The Power Triangle

It is a standard practice to represent S, P and Q in the form of a triangle, known as power triangle.

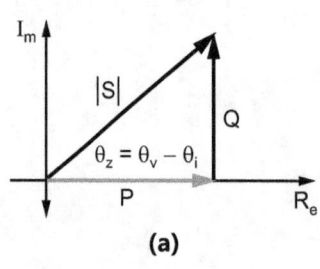

(a)   (b)

Fig. 5.44

The power triangle has four items, the **apparent power, real power, reactive power and the power factor angle**. Given two of these items, the other two can easily be obtained.

For the power triangle, when $|S|$ lies in the first quadrant, we have an inductive load and a lagging power factor.

When $|S|$ lies in the fourth quadrant, we have a capacitive load and leading power factor.

The **Reactive Power** Q is transferred back and forth between the load and the source. It represents a loss less interchange between the load and the source.

$$Q \begin{cases} = 0 & \text{Resistive Load, Unity pf} \\ < 0 & \text{Capacitive Load, Leading pf} \\ > 0 & \text{Inductive Load, Lagging pf} \end{cases}$$

5.13 POWER FACTOR CORRECTION

Most of the industrial and domestic loads are inductive and operate at a low lagging power factor. A low power factor at the load means higher line losses in the system. The process of increasing the power factor without changing the loads or altering the voltage or the current to the original load is known as power factor correction.

Typical Industrial Loads

Without a capacitor:

$$S_{old} = P_{old} + jQ_{old}$$
$$= |S_{old}| \angle \theta_{old}$$
$$pf_{old} = \cos(\theta_{old})$$

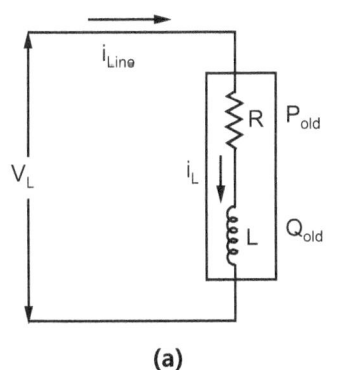

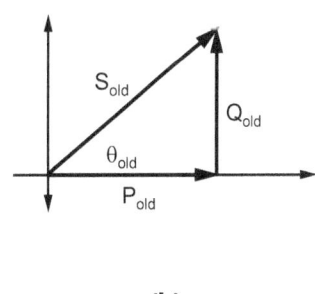

(a) (b)

Fig. 5.45

The load's power factor is improved or corrected by the deliberately installing a capacitor in parallel with the load.

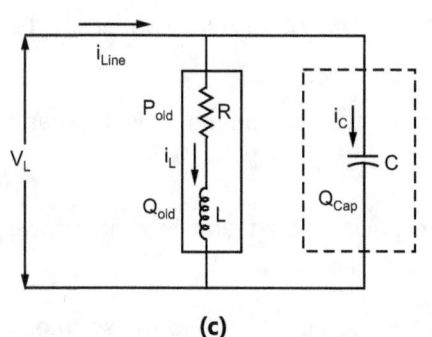

With a capacitor:

$$S_{new} = S_{old} + S_{capacitor}$$
$$= P_{old} + jQ_{old} - jQ_{cap}$$
$$= |S_{new}| \angle \theta_{new}$$
$$pf_{new} = \cos(\theta_{new})$$

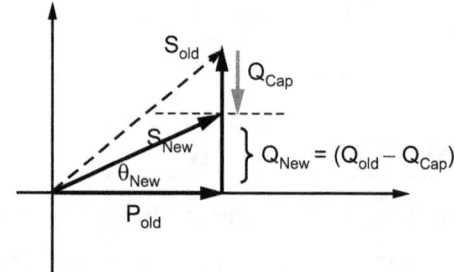

(c)   (d)

Fig. 5.45

Installing a capacitor in parallel with the load, then

Fig. 5.45 (e)

$$V_L = \frac{1}{j\omega C} I_C$$

$$|Q_{cap}| = |V_L||I_C| \sin(-90)$$

$$= |V_L|^2 \omega C$$

$$C = \frac{Q_{cap}}{|V_L|^2 \omega}$$

$$Q_{new} = (Q_{old} - Q_{cap})$$

$$\tan(\theta_{new}) = \frac{Q_{old} - Q_{cap}}{P_{old}}$$

$$Q_{cap} = Q_{old} - P_{old} \tan(\theta_{new}) \text{ and } \theta_{new} = \cos^{-1}(pf_{new})$$

$$\therefore \quad C = \frac{Q_{old} - P_{old} \tan(\theta_{new})}{|V_L|^2 \omega} \quad \ldots (5.31)$$

Ex. 5.24: What value of capacitance must be placed in parallel with the 18 kW load in the network in order to raise the power factor of this load of 0.9 lagging?

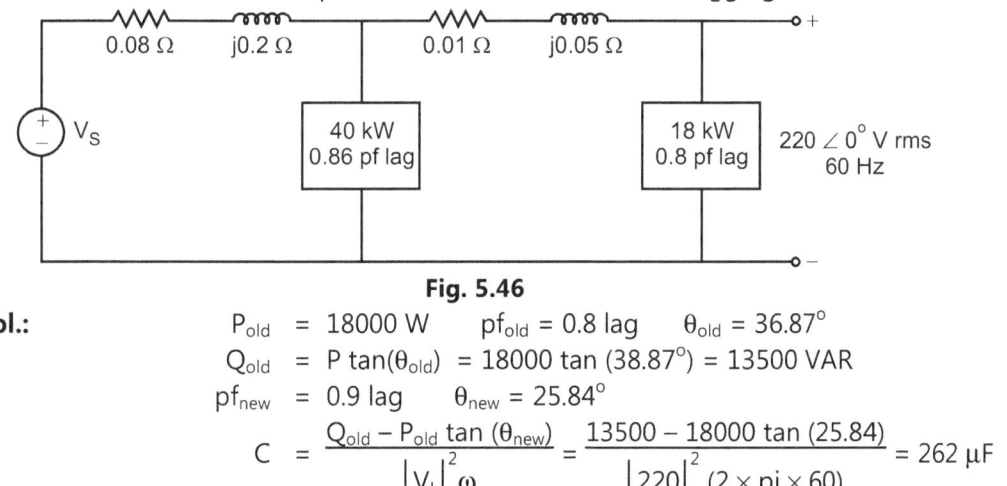

Fig. 5.46

Sol.:
$P_{old} = 18000$ W $\quad pf_{old} = 0.8$ lag $\quad \theta_{old} = 36.87°$
$Q_{old} = P \tan(\theta_{old}) = 18000 \tan(38.87°) = 13500$ VAR
$pf_{new} = 0.9$ lag $\quad \theta_{new} = 25.84°$

$$\therefore \quad C = \frac{Q_{old} - P_{old} \tan(\theta_{new})}{|V_L|^2 \omega} = \frac{13500 - 18000 \tan(25.84)}{|220|^2 (2 \times pi \times 60)} = 262 \ \mu F$$

Ex. 5.25: A industrial load consumes 44 kW at 0.82 pf lagging from a $220 \angle 0°$ V rms, 60 Hz line. A bank of capacitors totaling 900 µF is available. If these capacitors are placed in parallel with the load, what is the new complex power and new power factor of the total load?

Sol.:

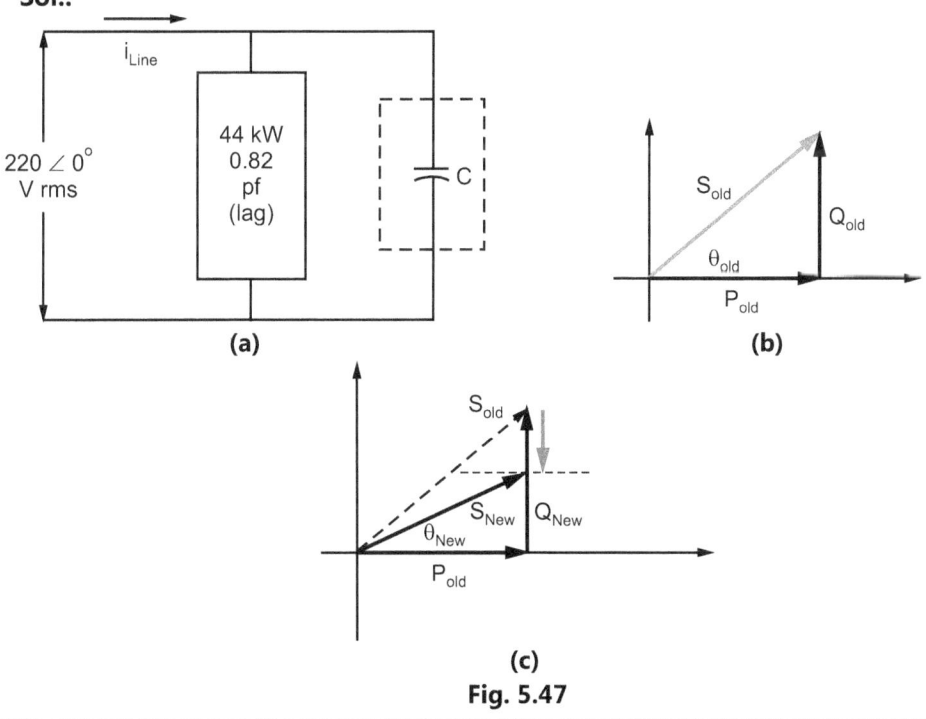

Fig. 5.47

$$S_{cap} = Q_{cap} = -j|V_L|^2 \omega C$$

$$Q_{cap} = -(220)^2 (377)(900 \times 10^{-6}) = -j\,16.422 \text{ kVAR}$$

Using the old power triangle:

$$S_{old} = P + jP \tan(\cos^{-1}(Pf_{old}))" = 44000 + j30712 \text{ VA}$$

$$S_{new} = S_{old} + Q_{cap} = (P_{old} + JQ_{old}) - jQ_{cap}$$

$$S_{new} = (44000 + j30712) - j16220 = 44000 + j14289 \text{ VA}$$

$$\theta_{new} = \tan^{-1}\left(\frac{14289}{44000}\right) = 18°$$

and

$$pf_{new} = \cos(18°) = 0.95 \text{ lag}$$

5.14 PROBLEM IN OPTIMIZING POWER TRANSFER

The transmission of electric power from the source to the load is performed in one loop circuit, and despite its simplicity there are many unsolved problems related to it. They result from the fact that in the energy transporting process there are two signals involved the voltage and current, and they can produce the same power with various, sometimes unpredictable, waveforms. Applying some quality criteria we can find the optimal wave shape of the voltage and current signals. The power quality discipline usually deals with this crucial problem. Let us consider a simple one loop circuit depicted in Fig. 5.48.

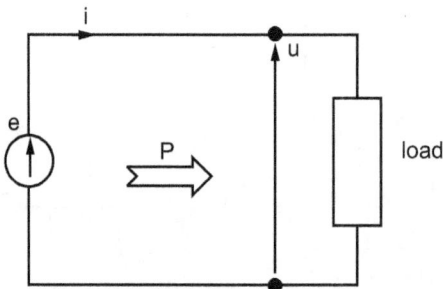

Fig. 5.48: The power transfer circuit

Such a circuit serves to transport power from the source e to the receiver. The problem, which seems to be easy, is to find such a signal i to assure a given prescribed power P and it can be solved only by means of optimization technique.

The source power equation

$$P = (e, i)$$

Obviously leads to an abundance of solutions since there is an infinite amount of such signals e and i which lead to the same dot product, equal to active power P.

The average power in a resistor is given by:

$$P = \frac{1}{T}\int_0^T v(t)\, i(t)\, dt$$

$$= \frac{1}{T}\int_0^T \frac{v^2(t)}{R}\, dt = \frac{1}{R}\frac{1}{T}\int_0^T v^2(t)\, dt$$

$$= \frac{V_{rms}^2}{R} \qquad \ldots (5.32)$$

where : $V_{rms} = \sqrt{\frac{1}{T}\int_0^T v^2(t)\, dt}$

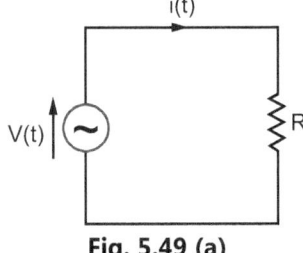

Fig. 5.49 (a)

The root-mean-square voltage V_{rms} determines the power dissipated in a circuit

$$P = \frac{V_{rms}^2}{R} \qquad \ldots (5.33)$$

There is a similar expression for the power dissipated when the current I_{rms} flows through a circuit:

$$P = R I_{rms}^2 \qquad \ldots (5.34)$$

These expressions apply to any waveform

The rms value of sinusoid of amplitude (peak) value v_0:

$$V_{rms} = \sqrt{\frac{1}{T}\int_0^T v^2(t)\, dt} = \sqrt{\frac{1}{T}\int_0^T v_0^2 \cos^2(\omega t)\, dt}$$

$$= \sqrt{v_0^2 \frac{1}{T}\int_0^T \frac{1}{2} + \frac{1}{2}\cos(2\omega t)\, dt} \qquad \text{Averages to zero over a complete cycle: } T = 2\pi/w$$

$$= \sqrt{\frac{v_0^2}{2}} = \frac{v_0}{\sqrt{2}}$$

Square wave of amplitude $\pm v_0$:

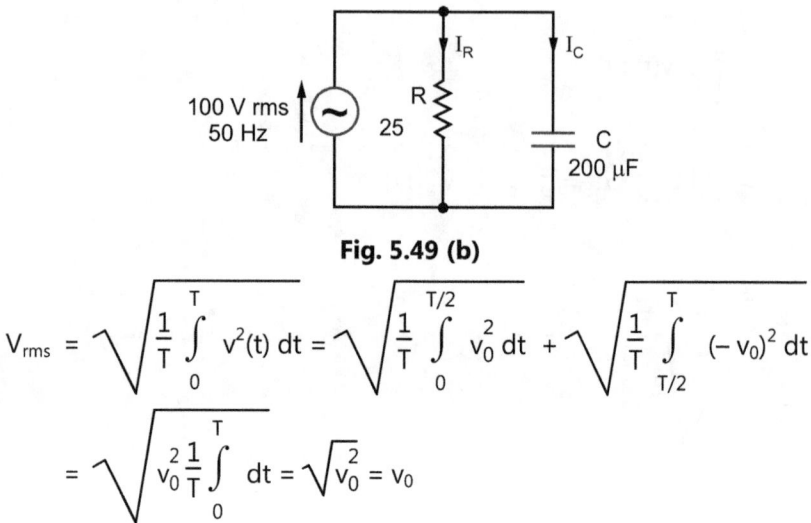

Fig. 5.49 (b)

$$V_{rms} = \sqrt{\frac{1}{T}\int_0^T v^2(t)\,dt} = \sqrt{\frac{1}{T}\int_0^{T/2} v_0^2\,dt} + \sqrt{\frac{1}{T}\int_{T/2}^T (-v_0)^2\,dt}$$

$$= \sqrt{v_0^2 \frac{1}{T}\int_0^T dt} = \sqrt{v_0^2} = v_0$$

The ratio between the peak voltage and the rms voltage is known as the crest factor:

$$cf = \frac{V_{peak}}{V_{rms}}$$

For a sinusoidal the cresh factor is $\sqrt{2}$; for a square wave the crest factor is 1.

For audio signals the crest factor depends on the source but is commonly 2 or higher.

150 W of audio into 4 Ω loudspeakers would therefore require peak voltages of 50 V or greater.

Power in a Reactive Load

Capacitors and inductors store energy, but do not dissipate power

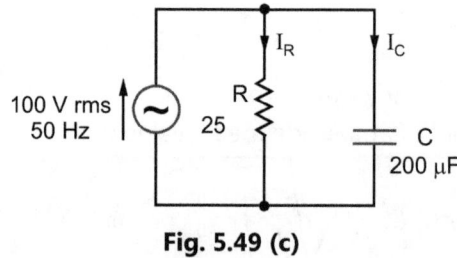

Fig. 5.49 (c)

$$I_R = \frac{100}{25} = 4A$$

$$I_C = \frac{100}{|Z_C|} = 100 \times 2\pi \times 50 \times 200 \times 10^{-6}\,A = 6.28\,A$$

$$P = \frac{100^2}{25} = 400\,W$$

5.14.1 rms Voltages and Currents

Power expressed in terms of rms voltages and currents:

$$P = \frac{1}{2} V_o i_o \cos\phi = \frac{1}{2} V_{rms}\sqrt{2}\, I_{rms}\sqrt{2} \cos\phi$$

$$= V_{rms} I_{rms} \cos\phi \;(W)$$

$$P = \frac{V_{rms}^2}{|Z|} \cos\phi$$

$$P = I_{rms}^2 |Z| \cos\phi \qquad \ldots (5.35)$$

Ex. 5.26: Determine the average power dissipated in the circuit

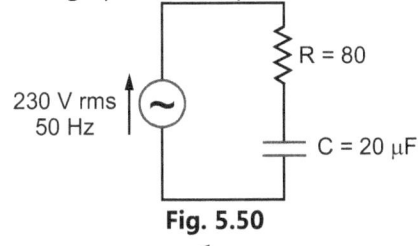

Fig. 5.50

$$Z = R + \frac{1}{j\omega C} = 80 + \frac{1}{j2\pi \times 50 \times 20 \times 10^{-6}}$$

$$= 80 - j159.2 \;\Omega$$

$$= 178.1 \angle -1.105\;(-63.3°)\;\Omega$$

$$P = \frac{V_{rms}^2}{|Z|} \cos\phi = \frac{230^2}{178.1} \cos -1.105 = 133.4 \;W$$

Ex. 5.27: Determine the average power dissipated in the circuit.

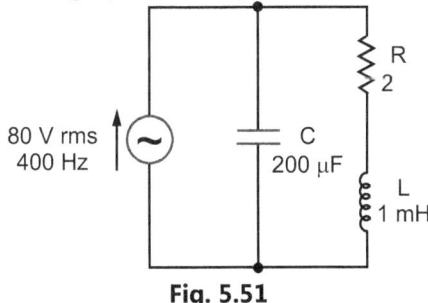

Fig. 5.51

The driving-point impedance of this circuit at 400 Hz (calculated previously) is:

$$Z = 3.091\;\Omega \angle -0.9282$$

$$P = \frac{V_{rms}^2}{|Z|} \cos\phi = \frac{80^2}{3.091} \cos -0.9283$$

$$= 1241 \;W$$

Electrical Energy

Electrical energy = Power × Time

If the power is measured in watts and the time in seconds then the unit of energy is watt-seconds or joules. If the power is measured in kilowatts and the time in hours then the unit of energy is kilowatt-hours, often called the unit of electricity. The electricity meter in the home records the number of kilowatt-hours used and is thus an energy meter.

5.15 ENERGY STORAGE

Reactive components (capacitors and inductors) do not dissipate power when an ac voltage or current is applied.

Power is dissipated only in resistors.

Instead reactive components store energy.

During an ac cycle reactive components alternately store energy and then release it.

Over a complete ac cycle there is not net change in energy stored and therefore no power dissipation.

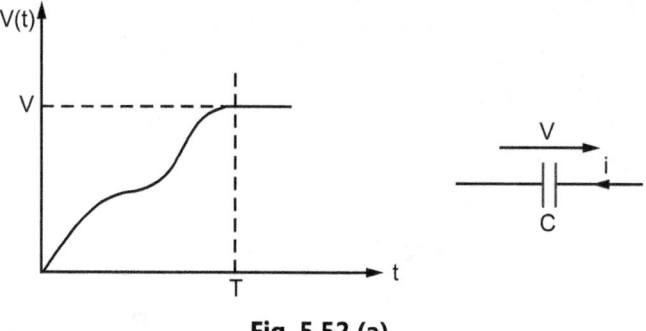

Fig. 5.52 (a)

The voltage across a capacitor is increased from zero to V produced a stored energy E:

$$E = \int_0^T v(t)\,i(t)\,dt$$

$$= \int_0^T v(t)\, C \frac{dv}{dt}\, dt$$

$$= C \int_0^V V\,dv \qquad\qquad i = C\frac{dv}{dt}$$

$$E = \frac{1}{2}CV^2$$

Ex. 5.28: Calculate the energy storage in an electronic flash capacitor of 1000 μF charged to 400 V.

$$E = \frac{1}{2}CV^2 = \frac{1}{2} \times 1000 \times 10^{-6} \times 400^2$$
$$= 80 \text{ J}$$

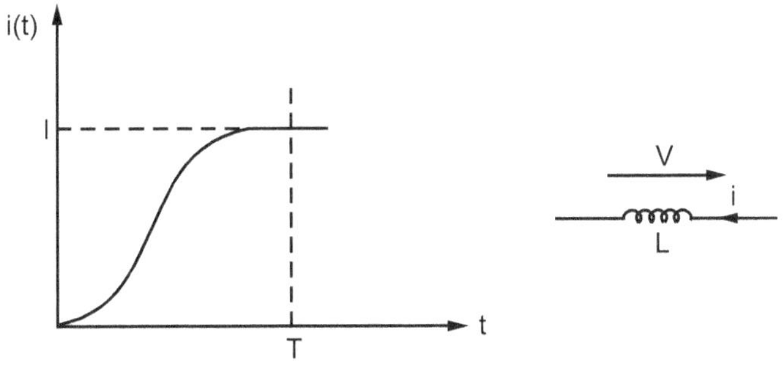

Fig. 5.52 (b)

The current in an inductor is increase from zero to I producing a store energy E.

$$E = \int_0^T v(t)\, i(t)\, dt = \int_0^T L\frac{di}{dt} i(t)\, dt$$

$$= L \int_0^I i\, di \qquad\qquad v = L\frac{di}{dt}$$

$$E = \frac{1}{2}LI^2$$

Ex. 5.29: Calculate the energy storage in a 2 mH inductor carrying a current of 10 A

$$E = \frac{1}{2}Li^2$$
$$= \frac{1}{2} \times 2 \times 10^{-3} \times 10^2$$
$$= 0.1 \text{ J}$$

5.16 INSERTION LOSS

Insertion loss varies with frequency. It is determined by the electrical configuration, source/load impedances and component values. As a result of the nature of ceramic dielectric materials, capacitance change (and therefore insertion loss) may be affected by applied voltage, temperature and the age of the part. Insertion loss can also be affected by load current due to ferrite saturation

Insertion Loss = $10 * \log(P_o/P_i)$
where P_o = Power Out
and P_i = Power In

There are 3 main causes of Insertion Loss in transmission line: Reflected losses, Dielectric losses and Copper losses. Reflected losses are those losses caused by the VSWR of the connector. Dielectric losses are those losses caused by the power dissipated in the dielectric materials (Teflon, rexolite, delrin, etc.). Copper losses are those losses caused by the power dissipated due to the conducting surfaces of the connector. It is a function of the material and plating used.

Electrical Configuration

A number of different electrical configurations are available in feed through filters, including the common types shown below. A single element filter (a capacitor or an inductor) theoretically provides an insertion loss characteristic of 20dB per decade, a dual element filter (capacitor/inductor) 40dB per decade whilst a triple element filter (Pi or T configuration) theoretically yields 60dB per decade. In practise, the insertion loss curves do not exactly match the predictions, and the datasheets should be consulted for the realistic figure. The choice of electrical configuration is made primarily on the source and load impedances and may also be influenced by the level of attenuation required at various frequencies

Insertion loss figures are normally published for a 50Ω source and 50Ω load circuit. In practise the impedance values will probably be very different, which could result in either an increase or reduction in insertion loss. The electrical configuration of the filter (the capacitor/inductor combination) should be chosen to optimise the filter performance for that particular source/load impedance situation.

Load current

For filters which include ferrite inductors, the insertion loss under load current may be less than that with no load. This is because the ferrite material saturates with current. The reduction in insertion loss depends on the current and the characteristics of the particular ferrite material. In extreme cases the ferrite will become ineffective and insertion loss will appear to be the same as for a C filter.

5.17 INTRODUCTION OF FILTERS

- Concept of "Filters" is very common in our day-to-day life. We use filters at many places. e.g. Paper filter is used to remove unwanted constituents such as suspended particles in water.
  Example: Breathing masks (Filters) are used when driving in a very polluted city, etc.
- These are all the examples of mechanical filters. Similarly electrical filters do exists and are used to remove unwanted constituents such as noise or some frequency band from a electrical signal.
- An electronic filter is an electronic circuit which performs signal processing functions, specifically to remove unwanted frequency components from the signal to enhance the wanted ones or both.

- An electronic filter may also be sometimes used in circuits with sinusoidal sources of constant frequency. Ex. L, C, LC filters used for ripple rejection in the various power supplies, just after the rectifier circuits. Filter are very commonly used in telephones, TV, radioreceivers and almost in every electronic circuit. Any electronic filters can roughly be classified as under:

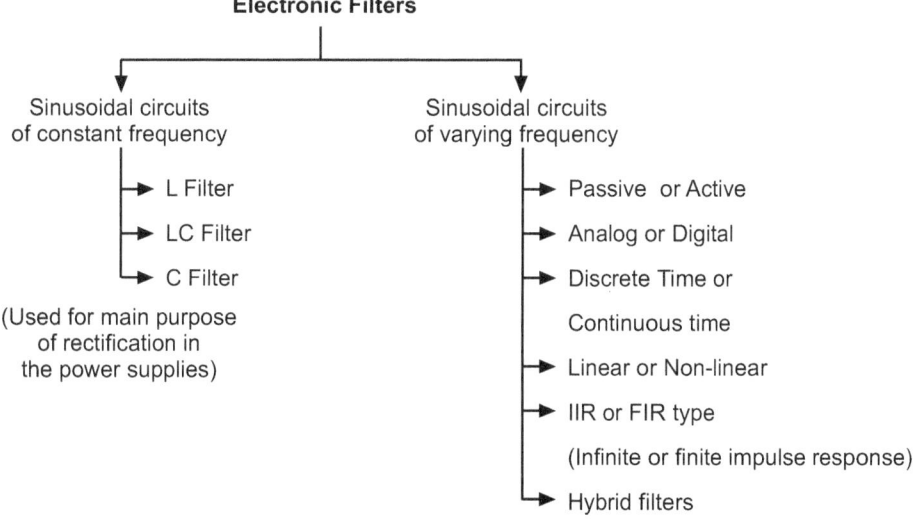

Fig. 5.53: Classification of Electronic Filters

In this chapter we will concentrate only on PASSIVE filters and analyse the effect on the o/p voltage due to the variation in the source frequency.

5.18 PASSIVE FILTERS

- Passive filters are the oldest forms of the electronic filters, which incorporates passive devices like resistors, capacitors and inductors.
- A passive filter does not have any active components like transistors or op-amps.
- Thus the output signal in case of passive filters can never have more power or amplitude than the applied that signal.
- Moreover use of inductors in the passive filters, make the circuit bulky and costly.
- The only advantage of using passive circuits is that they do not require additional power supplies for their operation.

    [op/amps need V_{cc}, V_{ee} supply for their operation. Even transistors have to be biased by V_{cc}, I_B etc. before their operation].

5.18.1 Basic Definitions

Let us now understand the basic terms associated with any filter circuit.

(a) Frequency Response:
- Filter networks are designed to separate different. Frequency bands available in an alternating input signal. Thus, when analyzing the filter network, we actually analyse the effect on voltage and current in different frequency bands, due to variation in the source frequency.
- That means we learn the response of the filter circuit (in terms of voltage, gain or current) to the changing i/p frequency. This is called as the frequency response of the circuit.

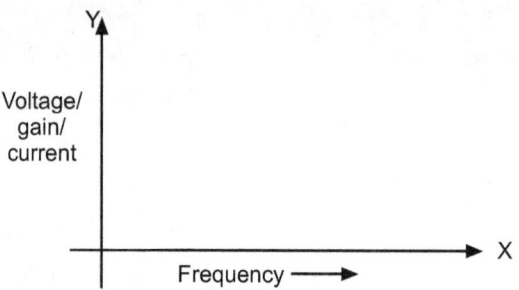

Fig. 5.54: Frequency Response: Plot of frequency Vs. Circuit parameter

- And the analysis of this behaviour is called as frequency response analysis.

(b) Cut-off Frequency:
- Speaking in terms of network filters, the cut-off frequency can loosely be defined as the frequency can loosely be defined as the frequency after which the circuit will show change in its behaviour and the response. It is the frequency which indicates the change in the band (pass band to stop band or vice versa) of the filter, thus separates the bands.
- It is actually the frequency at which the voltage gain equals 0.707 of its maximum value.
- This cut-off frequency is also referred to as the half power frequency because the load power is half of its maximum value at the this frequency.
- The output power is half of the maximum at the cut-off frequencies because:
  When the voltage gain is 0.707 of the maximum value, the output voltage is 0.707 of the maximum value. Now power = $\frac{(\text{Voltage})^2}{\text{Resistance}}$.
  So, when you square 0.707 we have 0.5 and so load power is half of its maximum value at the cut-off frequencies.
- Depending on the type of filter, the circuit may have one or two cut-off frequencies.
- Cut-off frequency is also referred as corner frequency.

(c) Pass Band:

- We have kept on defining a filter as the circuit which freely passes the desired band of the frequencies, while suppresses other band of frequencies. [Frequency discriminators].

- But in reality filters are not actually or physically separating the frequencies. It is the output voltage or current of the filter which prominently differs at different frequencies, thus enabling us to separate them.

- Thus, the pass band is defined as the range of frequencies for which the filter circuit responses to the input signal giving an considerable. Voltage at the output.

- In short it may be defined as the range of frequencies over which attenuation by the filter is zero, or the range of frequencies over which signals are passed from the input to the output.

(d) Stop Band or Attenuation Band:

- As the name indicates, a stop band can similarly be defined as the range of frequencies over which the filter circuit does not respond to the i/p signal giving almost no voltage at the output.

- In short it may be defined as the range of frequencies over which attenuation by the filter is infinite, or the range of frequencies over which the signals are blocked from input to the output.

- Depending on the type of the filter, the circuit may have one or two pass and stop bands.

Practically, we have one more band existing in the response of the filter circuit i.e. Transition Band. We will see this when discussing the ideal and practical filter.

5.18.2 Classification of Passive Filters

There are different types of filters existing in the electronics world. They are:

1. Low Pass Filter
2. High Pass Filter
3. Band Pass Filter
4. Band Stop Filter
5. All Pass Filter

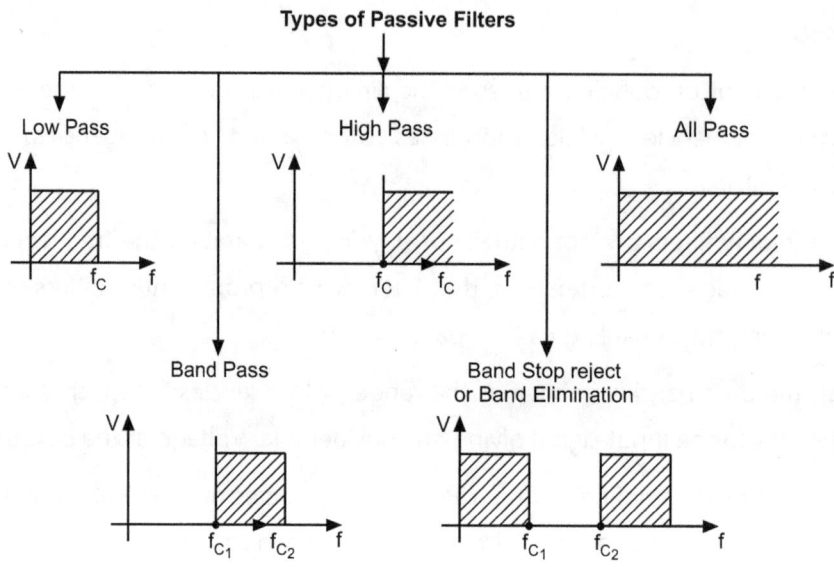

Fig. 5.55: Types of Passive Filters

1. Low Pass Filter:

A low pass filter is a circuit which responses to all the frequencies below the cut-off (f_c) frequency which attenuates or blocks the frequencies higher than the cut-off frequency. Thus, we say that low frequency signals are passed from input to the output with ideally zero and practically less attenuation. Signals falling in the band of frequencies ($0 < f < f_c$) have their magnitude ideally equal to the signal and are known as passband. Input voltage outside this band ($f_c < f < \infty$) of frequencies have their magnitude attenuated by the circuit. This band of frequencies is known as **stop band**.

Table 5.4: Low Pass Filter:

A filter that passes the frequencies lower than the cut-off frequency

Band	Frequency Range	O/P Voltage Ideal	Ideal Attenuation
Pass Band	$0 < f \leq f_c$	$V_{out} = V_{in}$	0
Stop Band	$f_c < f \leq \infty$	$V_{out} = 0$	∞

2. High Pass Filter:

- A High pass filter is a circuit which responses to all the frequencies above the cut-off (f_c). Frequency which attenuates or blocks the frequencies lower than the cut-off frequency.
- Thus, we Say that high frequency signals are passed from input to the output with ideally zero and practically less attenuation.

- Signals falling in this band of frequencies ($f_c < f$) have their magnitude ideally equal to the input signal and are known as **pass band**.
- Input voltage outside this band of frequencies ($0 < f < f_c$) have their magnitudes attenuated by the circuit. This band of frequencies is known as **stop band**.

3. **Band Pass Filter:**
   - A Band pass filter responses only to a particular band of frequencies and blocks the frequencies higher and lower than the desired hand.
   - It is a circuit with two cut-off frequencies f_L and f_H and has two stop hands.
   - The frequencies below f_L and above f_H are completely attenuated.
   - Only the frequencies between f_L and f_H are passed to the output.
   - This band of frequencies where ($f_L \leq f \leq f_H$) V_{out} is ideally equal to V_{in} is called as **pass band**.
   - The two bands of frequencies ($f < f_L$ and $f > f_H$) i.e. below the lower cut-off and above the higher cut-off are **stop band** frequencies.

4. **Band Stop Filter:**
   - A Band stop filter rejects or blocks a particular band of frequencies and passes all the frequencies higher and lower than this band.
   - It is a circuit with two cut-off frequencies f_L and f_H and it has two pass bands.
   - The frequencies between f_L and f_H are completely blocked or attenuated by the circuit and the frequencies less than f_L and higher than f_H are passed to the output.
   - These band of frequencies where in ideally $V_{out} = V_{in}$ [$f \leq f_L$ and $f \geq f_H$] is **stop band** frequency. [$V_{out} = 0$].
   - This filter is also called as **Band Stop** or **elimination** filter.

5. **All Pass Filter:**
   - All pass filter is a circuit with no stop band and has only a pass band. Because of it passes all the frequencies between zero and infinity.
   - It is strange that it still has to be called as filter. Since it zero attenuation for all the frequencies.
   - The reason it is so called is because of the effect it has on the phase of the signals passing thorough it.
   - This filter is useful when we want to produce a certain amount of phases shift for the signal being filtered without changing the amplitude.

We will however restrict our discussion and scope of analysis to only first four types of filters namely LPF, HPF, BPF, BSF. So let just summarise them:

Filter	Band	Frequency Range	Ideal output voltage	Ideal Attenuation	Ideal frequency Responses
Low Pass	Pass	$0 < f \leq f_c$	$V_{out} = V_{in}$	0	
	Stop	$f_c < f < \infty$	$V_{out} = 0$	∞	
High Pass	Pass	$f \leq f_c < \infty$	$V_{out} = V_{in}$	0	
	Stop	$0 < f < f_c$	$V_{out} = 0$	∞	
Band Pass	Pass	$f_L < f \leq f_H$	$V_{out} = V_{in}$	0	
	Stop	$0 < f < f_L$	$V_{out} = 0$	∞	
	Stop	$f_H < f < \infty$	$V_{out} = 0$	∞	
Band Stop	Pass	$0 < f < f_L$	$V_{out} = V_{in}$	0	
	Pass	$f_H < f < \infty$	$V_{out} = 0$	0	
	Stop	$f_L < f < f_H$	$V_{out} = 0$	∞	

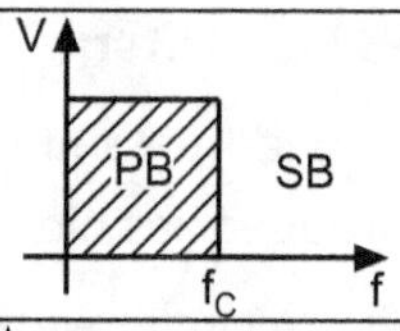

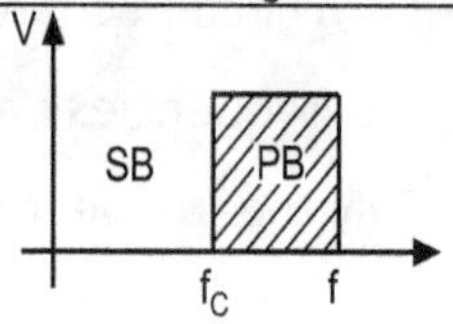

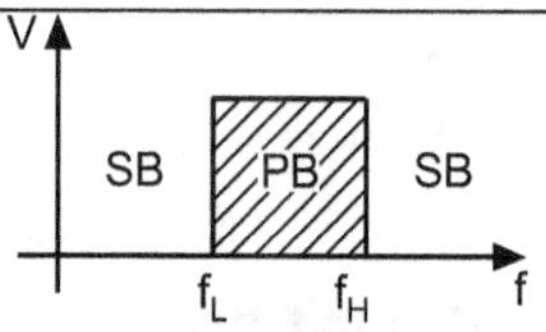

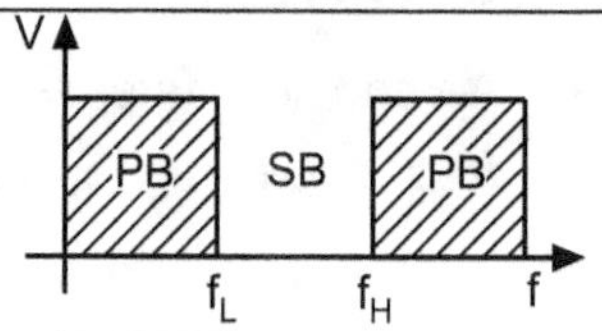

PB: Pass Band, SB: Stop Band

Fig. 5.56: Summary of Passive Filter

Low Pass   : Passes the frequencies lower than the f_C.
High Pass : Passes the frequencies higher than the f_C.
Band Pass : Passes a band of frequencies between f_L and f_H.
Band Stop : Stops / Rejects a band of frequencies between f_L and f_H.

We have discussed one way of classifying the passive filters i.e. based on their functionality. Now each of these filters can be further classified as follows:

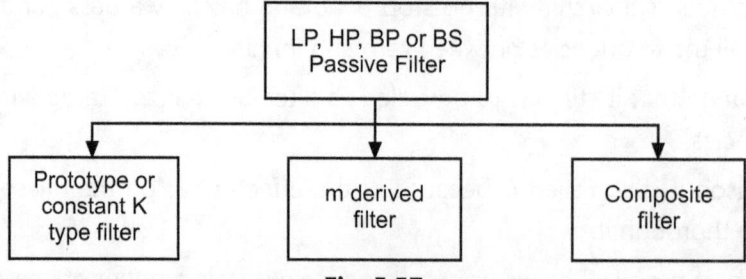

Fig. 5.57

We will be covering each of this type of filter in this chapter but at a later stage.

5.18.3 Ideal and a Practical Filter

You must have noticed that it all the discussions we had, there were always some terms like ideal and practical, may be related to voltages at the output or to the values of attenuation or frequency responses.

Now, let us understand these terms, considering an example.

Assume that you are on the sixth floor of a building and you want to reach the ground floor. Now this movement should ideally take absolutely no time. But practically even if you use an elevator with highest speed and latest technology it will still take some time (may be in ms) to reach the ground floor. So we need to understand that there is always some time elapsed in the change over of the states. No change can be sudden or instant. It will always take some time. That is the reason even the clock signal which ideally is drawn as in Fig. 5.58 (a) will in actual (practically) be as shown in Fig. 5.58 (b).

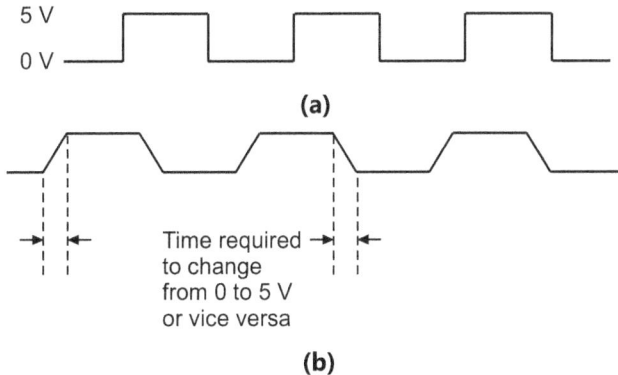

Fig. 5.58: Ideal and Practical Clock

- Now let us relate this concept with the filters.

  A filter circuit has two bands, pass band and stop hand, following each other.

	Attenuation	V_{out}
Pass band	0	V_{in}
Stop band	∞	0

- Thus, it must now be clear that when the band changes from pass band to stop band, attenuation changes from 0 to ∞ and V_{out} change from V_{in} to 0.

- So this change over cannot be instant or sudden, as expected ideally. Practically it is gradual and takes time.

- As will be discussed in the point of filter fundamentals, filter is made up of reactive elements like inductors and capacitors, which oppose the change in current and voltage respectively. So change of voltage and current from 0 to maximum value cannot be instant.

- So an ideal frequency response, say for low pass filter is as shown in Fig. 5.59 (a) and a practical frequency curve would be as in Fig. 5.59 (b).

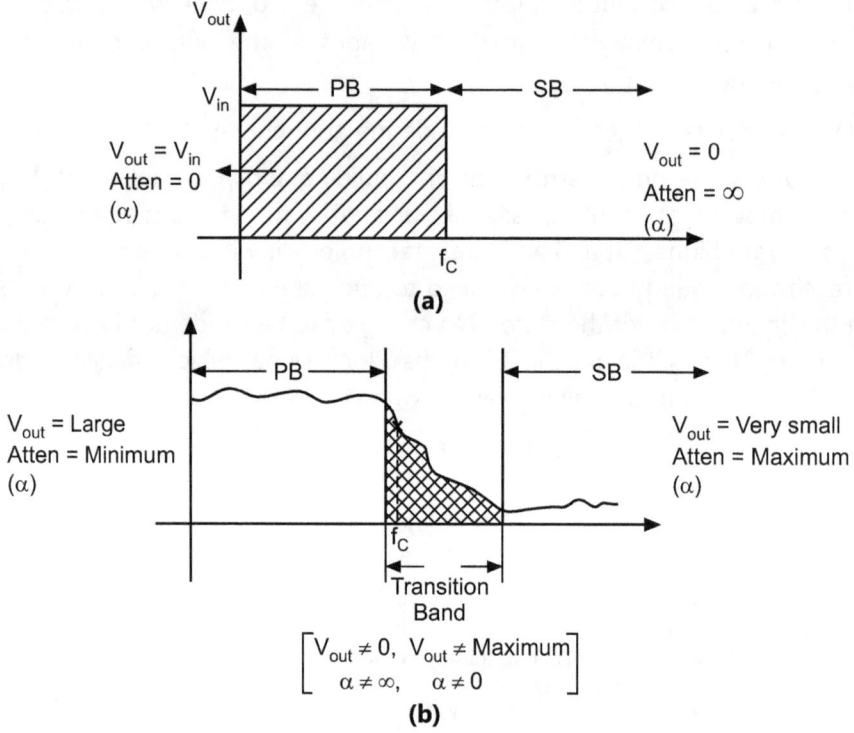

Fig. 5.59: Ideal and Practical Frequency Response (LPF)

- As seen in the diagram, the roll-off region between the pass band and the stop band, where V_{out} is neither zero nor equal to V_{in} and even the attenuation is neither infinity nor-zero, is called as transition band.
- This transition band does not exist in the ideal response for a filter. It is sometimes called a **brick wall response**, because the right edge of the rectangle looks like a brick wall.

Summary:

Ideal frequency curves or response of any filter differ from the practical response in three ways:

	Ideal Filter Response	Practical Filter Response
1.	Attenuation α is zero in pass band infinite in stop band	Attenuation α is minimum is pass band maximum in stop band
2.	Output voltage is equal to V_{in} in pass band 0 is stop band	Output voltage is maximum ($\neq V_{in}$) in PB very less ($\neq 0$) in SB
3.	There exists no transition band in ideal response (vertical transition)	There exists a transition band in practical response.

5.19 FILTER FUNDAMENTALS

- We have discussed about the pass and the stop bands which every filter must have.
- Let us now discuss about the:
- Type of component [R, L or C] required to build any filter circuit.
- Necessary conditions which these components should satisfy so that filter operates in both bands.
- Frequency range of these bands.

  Filters are realized using symmetrical T or π sections as shown in Fig. 5.60.

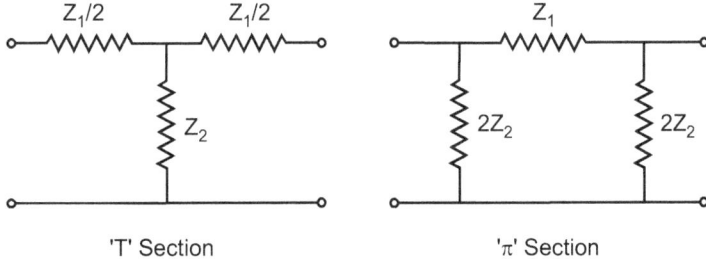

Fig. 5.60: Symmetrical T and π Sections

- Now, as we are discussing passive filters in this chapter, so obviously we have to choose between R, L and C as the values of Z_1 and Z_2.
- So the possible combinations would be having a filter circuit consisting of

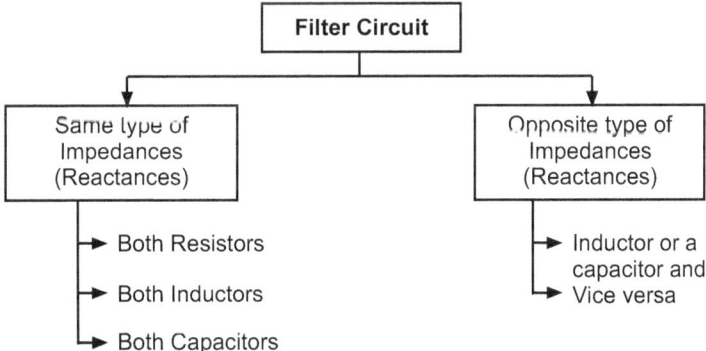

Fig. 5.61

- Before giving mathematical treatment or any analysis of all these possibilities, to reach a conclusion about the combination of Z_1 and Z_2, let us just logically think about the possible combination.

5.19.1 Logical Thinking

- Passive implementations of linear filters are based on combinations of the passive components resistors (R), Inductors (L) and Capacitors (C).
- This filter must have a pass and a stop band at high or low frequency depending on the type of the filter.
- So, naturally you must have the filter circuit components conducting at low and high frequencies.
- Possibility of having Z_1 and Z_2 both as resistors must be completely ruled out because the response of any filter depends on the frequency. So the component used to build filter must be frequency dependent. Resistors on their own have no frequency selective properties. Nor do their value depend on frequency. So we cannot have this frequency independent component to build a frequency dependent circuit.
- Now let us think about the components which are dependent on frequency. Reactances of inductor and a capacitor depend on frequency. Their behaviour can be summarized as:

		High Frequency	Low Frequency
Inductors ($j\omega L$)	Reactance (αf)	Very high	Very low
	Operation	Block signal	Pass signal
Capacitors $\left(\dfrac{1}{j\omega c}\right)$	Reactance $\left(\alpha \dfrac{1}{f}\right)$	Very low	Very high
	Operation	Pass signal	Block signal

- So now, with a conclusion of using L and C as the Z_1 and Z_2 components let us again think of the same possibility i.e. selecting Z_1 and Z_2 both as 'L' or selecting Z_1 and Z_2 both as 'C'. [Same type of reactance].
- If we build a filter with only inductors i.e. Z_1 and Z_2 both as inductors, then as clear from the summary table above, we will have a filter which will pass the lower frequencies and will block the higher frequencies.
- So with this combination a filter will always have a passband at lower freuqnices and a stop band at higher frequencies. Thus making it impossible to have pass band at higher frequencies which is desired for High pass and Band pass filters.
- The same will be the case if Z_1 and Z_2 both are capacitors. With this combination you will end up with a filter having a stop band at lower frequencies and pass band at higher frequencies, thus leaving no scope to design and low pass or a band stop filter, in which pass band is required at low frequencies as well.

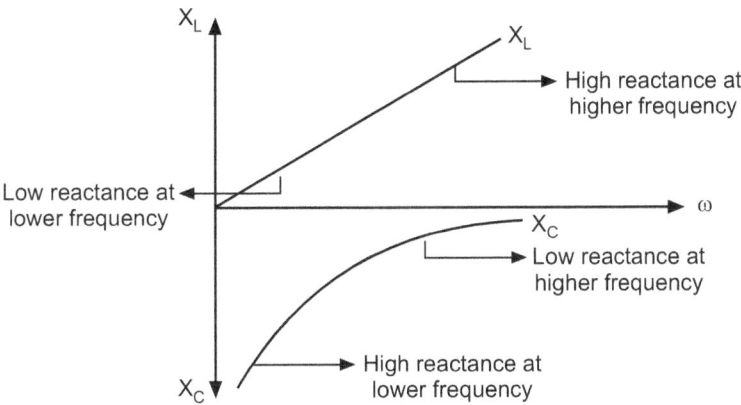

Fig. 5.62: Reactance Curves of L and C

- So we just cannot have a filter circuit having
    - Z_1 and Z_2 both as Resistors
    - Z_1 and Z_2 both as Capacitor
    - Z_1 and Z_2 both as Inductor
- So the only choice we are left when selecting frequency dependent components for filters is having Z_1 and Z_2 as opposite type of reactances.
- So any filter can be build using Z_1 and Z_2 as L and C. With this combination we will have one component, inductor for filter circuit conducting (passing the signal) at lower frequency and one component, capacitor conducting at high frequency.
- So with the various combinations of L and C we can design any time of filter.
- Now, let us mathematically understand and also verify the necessity of having Z_1 and Z_2 as opposite type of reactances.

5.19.2 Mathematical Analysis

- Before we start with mathematical analysis let us revise the hyperbolic trigonometry without going into any details.
- Hyperbolic functions simply the writing of certain exponential relations and knowledge of their limits is useful.
- sinh, cosh, tanh are the hyperbolic functions that are normally used.
- The values of these functions at the limits $\mu = 0$, $\mu = \infty$ are

Table 5.5

Hyperbolic Function	$\mu = 0$	$\mu = \infty$
$\sinh \mu$	0	∞
$\cosh \mu$	1	∞
$\tanh \mu$	0	1

For complex angles, where $\mu = a + jb$, the expressions are:
$$\sinh(a + jb) = \sinh a \cosh jb + \cosh a \sinh jb$$
$$= \sinh a \cos b + j \cosh a \sin b$$

We will need these theory as we move into deeper filter fundamentals.

- A filter is made up of symmetrical T or π sections.
- The propagation constant 'γ' (gama) is one important property of the symmetrical networks.
- This property is a function of frequency and so can supply the information on the ability of the filter to perform as desired.

$$\gamma = \alpha + j\beta$$

γ is imaginary	$\alpha = 0$	$I_{out} = I_{in}$	No attenuation only phase shift (Pass Band)
γ is real and positive	$\alpha \neq 0$ $\alpha = +\text{ve value}$	$I_{out} < I_{in}$	Attenuation occurred Attenuation/Stop band

$$\sinh \frac{\gamma}{2} = \sqrt{\frac{Z_1}{4Z_2}} \qquad \ldots(a)$$

$$\sinh \frac{\gamma}{2} = \sinh \left(\frac{\alpha}{2} + j\frac{\beta}{2}\right)$$

$$\sinh \frac{\gamma}{2} = \sinh \frac{\alpha}{2} \cos \frac{\beta}{2} + j \cosh \frac{\alpha}{2} \cdot \sin \frac{\beta}{2} \qquad \ldots(b)$$

A filter must have both the bands irrespective of the type of filter, both i.e. a pass and a stop band will exist in it. So for constructing a filter circuit γ must accordingly have both imaginary as well as real and positive values.

Case I: Z_1 and Z_2 Are the same type of reactance

- Let us start our analysis thinking that Z_1 and Z_2 can be same type of reactances.

If Z_1 and Z_2 both are:

(i) Resistors

then, $\quad \dfrac{Z_1}{4Z_2} = \dfrac{R_1}{4R_2}$ = Real and positive ratio

(ii) Inductors

then, $\quad \dfrac{Z_1}{4Z_2} = \dfrac{j\omega L_1}{j\omega L_2}$ = Real and positive ratio

(iii) Capacitors

then, $\dfrac{Z_1}{4Z_2} = \dfrac{\dfrac{1}{j\omega C_1}}{\dfrac{1}{j\omega C_2}}$ = Real and positive ratio

Thus, in any case, when Z_1 and Z_2 are of the same type,

$$\left|\dfrac{Z_1}{4Z_2}\right| > 0 \quad \text{Real and a positive ratio}$$

∴ $\sinh\dfrac{\gamma}{2}$ must be real and positive.

∴ From equation (b)

(i) $\sinh\dfrac{\alpha}{2}\cos\dfrac{\beta}{2} = \sqrt{\dfrac{Z_1}{4Z_2}}$ ... (5.36 (a))

...must be simultaneously satisfied

(ii) $\cosh\dfrac{\alpha}{2}\sin\dfrac{\beta}{2} = 0$ ... (5.36 (b))

From equation (ii)

$$\sin\dfrac{\beta}{2} = 0 \quad \ldots \because \cosh\dfrac{\alpha}{2} \neq 0 \text{ minimum value of cosh is '1'}$$

∴ $\boxed{\beta = n\pi}$ ... (5.37)

If $\sin\dfrac{\beta}{2} = 0$

then $\cos\dfrac{\beta}{2} = 1 \quad \ldots \because \sin^2 x + \cos^2 x = 1$

So equation (i) becomes

$$\sinh\dfrac{\alpha}{2} = \sqrt{\dfrac{Z_1}{4Z_2}}$$

$$\boxed{\alpha = 2\sinh^{-1}\sqrt{\dfrac{Z_1}{4Z_2}}} \quad \ldots (5.38)$$

Thus if the reactances are of the same type then γ will always be positive and thus only and only a stop band will exists in such a filter circuit.

Case II: Z_1 and Z_2 are opposite type of reactances

When Z_1 and Z_2 are L and C, then

If $Z_1 = L$ and $Z_2 = C$
$$\frac{Z_1}{4Z_2} = \frac{j\omega L}{\frac{1}{j\omega C}} = j^2 \omega^2 LC = -\omega^2 LC$$

OR

If $Z_1 = C$ and $Z_2 = L$
$$\frac{Z_1}{4Z_2} = \frac{\frac{1}{j\omega C}}{j\omega L} = \frac{1}{j^2 \omega^2 LC} = -\frac{1}{\omega^2 LC}$$

So, $\frac{Z_1}{4Z_2}$ is negative.

$\therefore$ $\sinh\frac{\gamma}{2}$ must be negative.

So, from equation (b)

(i) $\sinh\frac{\alpha}{2} \cos\frac{\beta}{2} = 0$

(ii) $\cosh\frac{\alpha}{2} \sin\frac{\beta}{2} = \sqrt{\frac{Z_1}{4Z_2}}$

...must be simultaneously satisfied

Let us start with two condition possible in (a) part.

$\sinh\frac{\alpha}{2} = 0$ and $\cos\frac{\beta}{2} = 0$

Condition I:

$$\sinh\frac{\alpha}{2} = 0$$

$\therefore$ $\boxed{\alpha = 0}$ ... (5.39)

(i) and (ii) must be simultaneously satisfied.

If as per (a), $\alpha = 0$, then $\cosh\frac{a}{2}$ in (b) will be '1' ($\cosh 0 = 1$).

$\therefore$ $\beta \neq 0$

$\therefore$ $\sin\frac{\beta}{2} = \sqrt{\frac{Z_1}{4Z_2}}$

$$\boxed{\beta = 2\sin^{-1}\sqrt{\frac{Z_1}{4Z_2}}}$$ ...(5.40)

Condition II:

If
$$\cos\frac{\beta}{2} = 0$$

∴
$$\sin\frac{\beta}{2} = 1 \qquad (\because \cos^2 A + \sin^2 A = 1)$$

$$\boxed{\beta = (2n-1)\pi} \qquad \ldots(5.41)$$

(i) and (ii) must be simultaneously satisfied, so if as per equation (i)
$$\sin\frac{\beta}{2} = 1$$

then, as per (ii)
$$\cosh\frac{\alpha}{2} = \sqrt{\frac{Z_1}{4Z_2}}$$

$$\boxed{\alpha = 2\cosh^{-1}\sqrt{\frac{Z_1}{4Z_2}}} \qquad \ldots(5.42)$$

Condition I Leads to a passband or region of zero attenuation.

$$\alpha = 0$$

$$\beta = 2\sin^{-1}\sqrt{\frac{Z_1}{4Z_2}}$$

The band is limited by the upper limit of sine, so it is required that

$$-1 < \frac{Z_1}{4Z_2} < 0$$

Thus, the cut-off frequencies would be

$$\frac{Z_1}{4Z_2} = 0 \quad \text{or} \quad \boxed{Z_1 = 0} \qquad \ldots(5.43)$$

$$\frac{Z_1}{4Z_2} = 1 \quad \text{or} \quad \boxed{Z_1 = -4Z_2} \qquad \ldots(5.44)$$

To conclude, let us understand that the pass band ($\alpha = 0$) for a filter circuit with the reactances of different type would exist when

$$\frac{Z_1}{4Z_2} = 0 \text{ to } -1$$

i.e. between, $Z_1 = 0$ and $Z_1 = -4Z_2$

The phase angle in this band would be

$$\beta = 2\sin^{-1}\sqrt{\frac{Z_1}{4Z_2}} \qquad \ldots (5.45\,(a))$$

Condition II Leads to a stop band or an attenuation band ($\alpha \neq 0$)

$$\alpha = 2\cosh^{-1}\sqrt{\frac{Z_1}{4Z_2}} \qquad \ldots (5.45\,(b))$$

Even this band will naturally be limited by the upper limit of cosh. As this upper limit for cosh is ∞ we would say,

$$\frac{Z_1}{4Z_2} < -1$$

5.20 m DERIVED LOW PASS FILTER

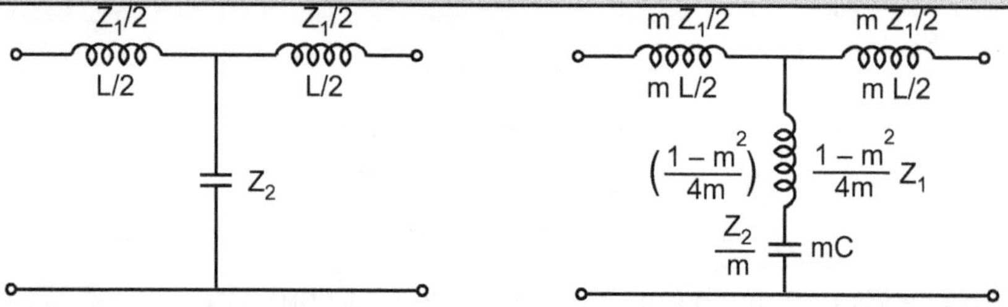

(a) Prototype LPF (T section)
(b) m derived LPF (T Section)

Fig. 5.63

- In the very last section we have seen that Z_2' in case of m derived section is a series combination of two impedances.

$$\frac{1-m^2}{4m}Z_1 \quad \text{and} \quad \frac{Z_2}{m}$$

- **Note:** When an impedance of a condenser is divided by m then its capacitance must be multiplied by m.
- Now let us clearly understand that how such a small modification in the circuit will give us infinite attenuation near cut-off frequency or how do we get zero output voltage near f_c in case of m derived LPF.

5.20.1 Operation of m Derived LPF

- As is clear from the Fig. 5.63 (b) shunt arm of m derived section is a series resonant circuit. [L in series with C].
- In a series resonant circuit i.e. in a circuit when inductive and capacitive reactances are in series the reactances cancel each other at resonant frequency.
- So, at this resonant frequency, the shunt arm appears as a short circuit on the network.
- As shown in Fig. 5.64 the short circuit provides ground path to the input signal, thereby making $V_{out} = 0V$ and thus attenuation is very high [as ideally expected] at this resonant frequency.

- This frequency of infinite or very high attenuation is called f_∞.

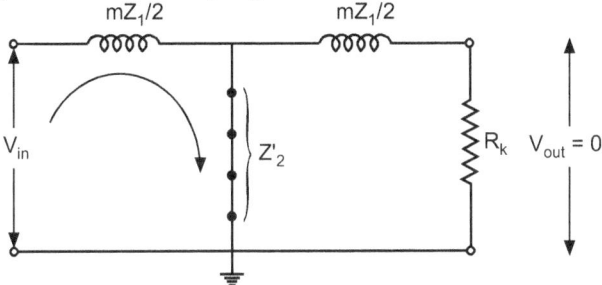

Fig. 5.64: An Approximate Model of m Derived LPF at f_∞, Where Shunt Arm Appears as Short circuit bypassing The Load

5.20.2 Reactance Curves

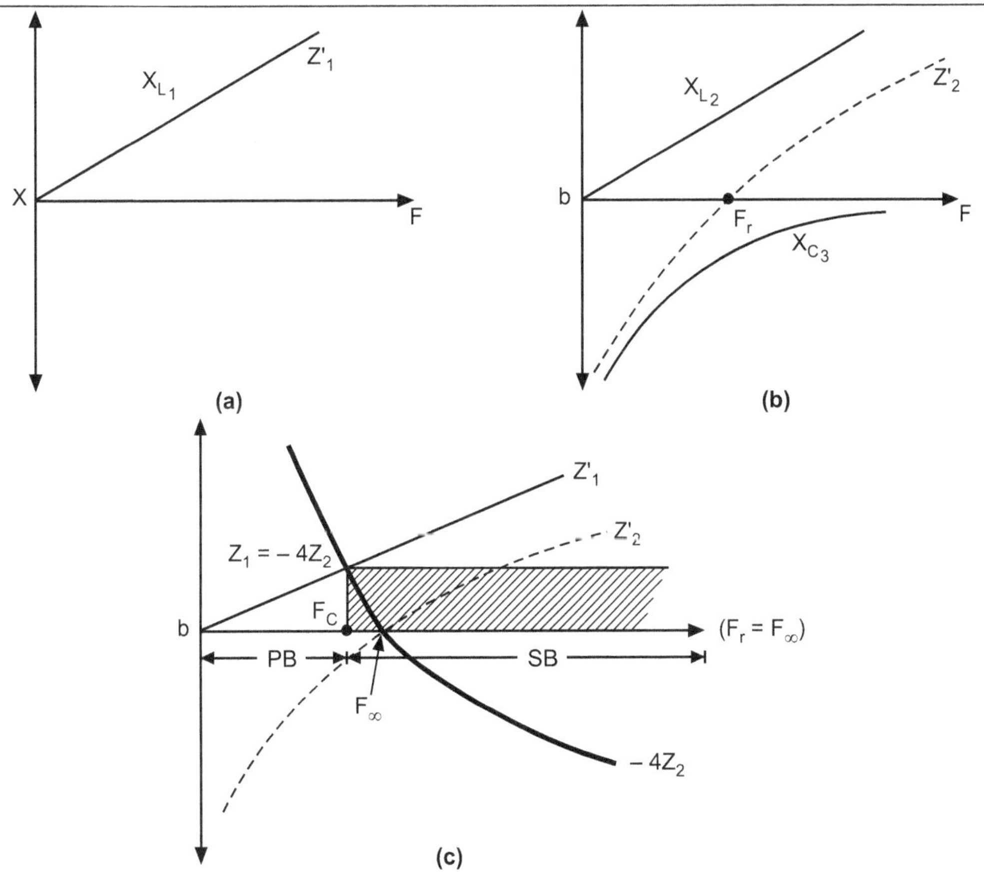

Fig. 5.65: Reactance plots of (a) series arm (b) shunt arm

(c) reactance curve indicating PB and SB of m derived

Here,

$$Z_1' = \text{series arm having inductor } L_1$$

$$Z_2' = \text{shunt arm having inductor } L_2 \text{ capacitor C}$$

- Fig. 5.65 (a) is a plot of x_L against f. Fig. 5.65 (b) shows the plot of the individual components L_2 and C and also plot of Z_2' as a series resonating circuit.
- 'f_r' in Fig. 5.65 (b) is a resonating frequency at which $X_{L2} = X_C$.
  i.e. Reactances of inductor and capacitor present in the shunt arm of the m derived filter are equal, thus making it act as a short circuit at f_r.
- Fig. 5.65 (c) shows the reactance curves of Z_1' and Z_2' to indicate a pass band between the frequencies of which $Z_1' = -4 Z_2'$ and $Z_1' = 0$.
- f_C and f_r are shown. f_r as discussed earlier is nothing but f_∞ i.e. the frequency at which shunt arm will act as short circuit making $V_{out} = 0$.
- **Note:** f_C and f_∞ are two different frequencies close to each other. This observation needs an explanation.

5.20.3 f_∞ and f_C in m Derived LPF

- We have designed m derived filters with an objective to have very high attenuation at cut-off frequency (f_C).
- To achieve this, a inductor is added in shunt arm making it function as series resonant circuit resonating at frequency f_∞ (i.e. f_r).
- At this frequency, f_∞, $V_{out} = 0$ and thus attenuation is very very high.
- Ideally we want this operation, this behaviour at f_C i.e. cut-off frequency.
- Practically we achieve it to f_∞ and not at f_C. f_∞ can be chosen arbitrarily close to f_C so the α near f_C is made high.
- We might end up thinking that why is f_∞ not made same as f_C.
- There are two reasons justifying that f_∞ and f_C can never be the same frequencies. $f_\infty \neq f_C$. And f_∞ will always and always be higher than f_C, in case of m derived LPF.

  1. At f_C we must have $Z_1' = -4 Z_2'$.

     AT f_∞ we must have $Z_2' = 0$.

     It is impossible to achieve or satisfy both these conditions at very same frequency. So f_C can never be equal to f_∞. They have to be two different frequencies.

2. Below f_C, Z_2' is capacitive.

   Below f_∞, Z_2' is capacitive

   Above f_∞, Z_2' is inductive.

   So, if f_∞ is below f_C than these conditions will not be met. So f_∞ is always higher than f_C.

5.20.4 Derivations of f_∞ and m for a m Derived LPF

The shunt arm of m derived LPF (T section) resonates of frequency f_∞ (f_r).

$$f_r = \frac{1}{2\pi\sqrt{LC}} \quad \text{... expression for } f_r \text{ series reasonance}$$

Here,

$$f_\infty = \frac{1}{2\pi\sqrt{\left(\frac{1-m^2}{4m}\right)L(mC)}}$$

$$f_\infty = \frac{1}{\pi\sqrt{(1-m^2)LC}} \quad \text{... (a)}$$

But, for a low pass filter

$$f_C = \frac{1}{\pi\sqrt{LC}} \quad \text{... (b)}$$

∴ Substituting equation (b) in (a)

$$\boxed{f_\infty = \frac{f_C}{\sqrt{(1-m^2)}}} \quad \text{... (5.46)}$$

Simplifying equation (5.90) we have

$$\sqrt{1-m^2} = \frac{f_C}{f_\infty}$$

$$1 - m^2 = \left(\frac{f_C}{f_\infty}\right)^2$$

$$\boxed{m = \sqrt{1 - \left(\frac{f_C}{f_\infty}\right)^2}} \quad \text{... (5.47)}$$

This equation determines the value of m to be used for a particular f_∞.

5.20.5 π-Section

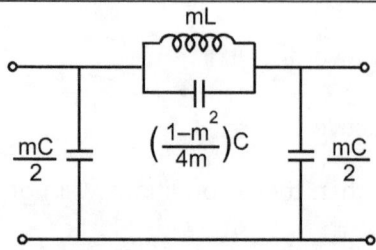

Fig. 5.66: m derived LPF π Section

5.21 m DERIVED HIGH PASS FILTER

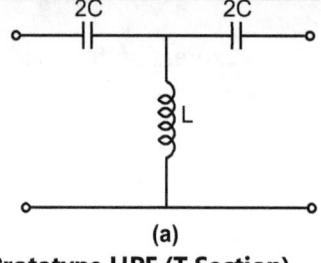
(a)
(a) Prototype HPF (T Section)

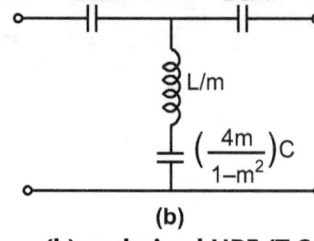
(b)
(b) m derived HPF (T Section)

Fig. 5.67

- Z_2' in case of m derived section in a series combination of two impedances.

$$\frac{1-m^2}{4m} Z_1 \text{ and } \frac{Z_2}{m}$$

Here Z_1 is a capacitor (C)

Here Z_2 is an inductor (L)

∴ Z_2' is $\frac{L}{M}$ in series with $\frac{4m}{1-m^2}$ C.

- Note: When a impedance of a condenser is divided by m then its capacitance should be multiplied by m.

5.21.1 Operation of m Derived HPF

- It is clear From the Fig. 5.67 (b) shunt arm of m derived section is a series resonant circuit [L in series with C].
- In a series resonant circuit i.e. in a circuit when inductive and capacitive reactances are in series the reactances can cell each other at resonant frequency.
- So at this resonant frequency, the shunt arm appears as a short circuit on the network.

- As shown in Fig. 5.68, this short circuit provides ground path to the input signal thereby making $V_{out} = 0V$ and thus the attenuation is very very high [as ideally expected] at this resonant frequency.
- This frequency of infinite or very high attenuation is called f_∞.

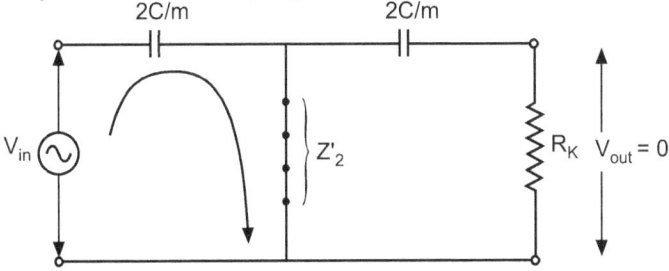

Fig. 5.68: An approximate model at f_∞, where shunt arm appears as short circuit (bypassing the load)

5.21.2 Reactance Curves

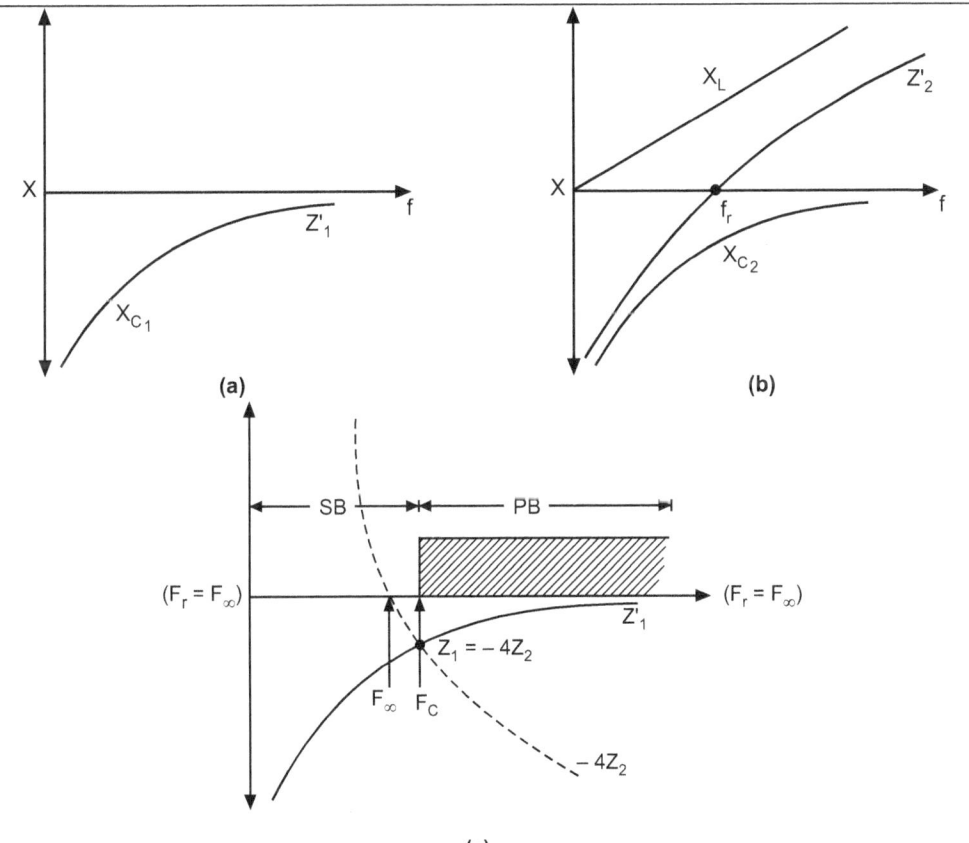

Fig. 5.69: Reactance plots of (a) series arm (b) shunt arm (c) reactance curve indicate PB, SB

Here, Z_1' = Series arm having capacitor (C_1)

Z_2' = Shunt arm having inductor (L), capacitor (C_2)

- Fig. 5.69 (a) is a plot of X_{C_1} against f and 5.69 (b) shows the plot of the individual components L and C_2 and also plot of Z_2' as a series resonating circuit.
- f_r is Fig. 5.69 (b) is a resonating frequency at which

$$X_L = X_{C_2}$$

i.e. reactances of inductor and capacitor present in the shunt arm of m derived filter are equal, thus making it act as a short circuit at f_r.

- Fig. 5.69 (c) shows the reactance curves of Z_1' and Z_2' to indicate a pass band between the frequencies at which $Z_1' = -4Z_2'$ and $Z_1' = 0$.
- f_r and f_∞ are indicated. f_r as already discussed is nothing but f_∞, i.e. the frequency at which shunt arm will act as short circuit making $V_{out} = 0$.
- f_C and f_∞ are two different frequencies close to each other.

5.21.3 f_∞ and f_C in m Derived HPF

1. At f_C, we must have

$$Z_1' = -4Z_2'$$

   At f_∞, we must have

$$Z_2' = 0$$

2. It is impossible to achieve or satisfy both these conditions at very same frequency. So f_C can never be equal to f_∞. They have to be two different frequencies.

   Above f_C Z_2' is inductive

   Below f_∞ Z_2' is capacitive

   Above f_∞ Z_2' is inductive

   So, if f_∞ is shifted above f_C, than these conditions will not be satisfied. So f_∞ is always lower than f_C.

5.21.4 Derivations of f_∞ and m for a m Derived LPF

The shunt arm of m-derived HPF (T section) resonates at frequency f_∞ i.e. f_r.

$$f_\infty = \frac{1}{2\pi \sqrt{\left(\frac{L}{m}\right)\left(\frac{4m}{1-m^2}\right)C}}$$

$$f_\infty = \frac{1}{2\pi \sqrt{\frac{4LC}{(1-m^2)}}}$$

Substituting value of f_C in the equation for f_∞.

$$\boxed{f_\infty = f_C \sqrt{(1-m^2)}} \qquad \ldots (5.48)$$

Simplifying equation (5.92)

$$\frac{f_\infty}{f_C} = \sqrt{1-m^2}$$

$$\left(\frac{f_\infty}{f_C}\right)^2 = 1-m^2$$

$$m^2 = 1 - \left(\frac{f_\infty}{f_C}\right)^2$$

$$\boxed{m = \sqrt{1 - \left(\frac{f_\infty}{f_C}\right)^2}} \qquad \ldots (5.49)$$

This equation determines the value of m to be used for a particular f_∞.

5.21.5 π Section

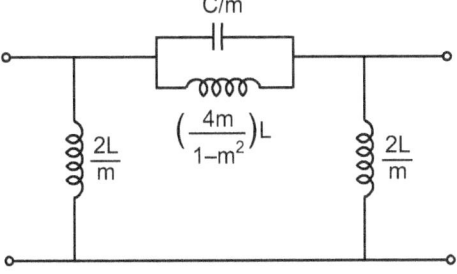

Fig. 5.70: m derived π section for a HPF

5.22 SUMMARY OF m DERIVED FILTERS

	m-derived LPF	m derived HPF
T section filter	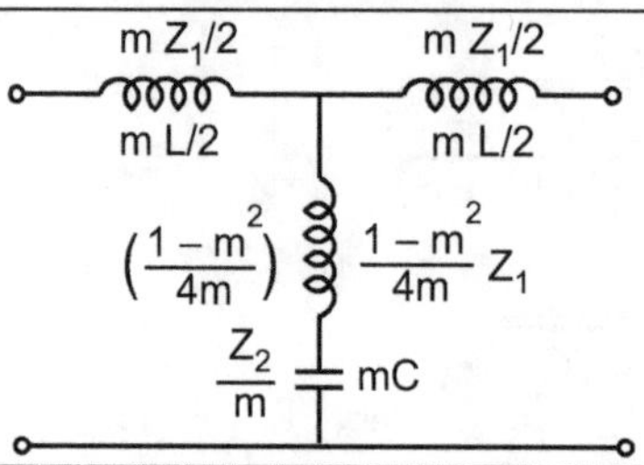 Series: $mZ_1/2$, $mL/2$ — $mZ_1/2$, $mL/2$; Shunt: $\left(\dfrac{1-m^2}{4m}\right)Z_1 = \dfrac{1-m^2}{4m}Z_1$, $\dfrac{Z_2}{m} = mC$	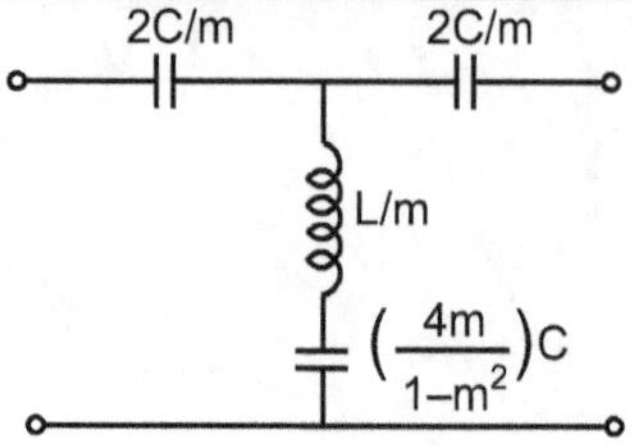 Series: $2C/m$, $2C/m$; Shunt: L/m, $\left(\dfrac{4m}{1-m^2}\right)C$
π section filter	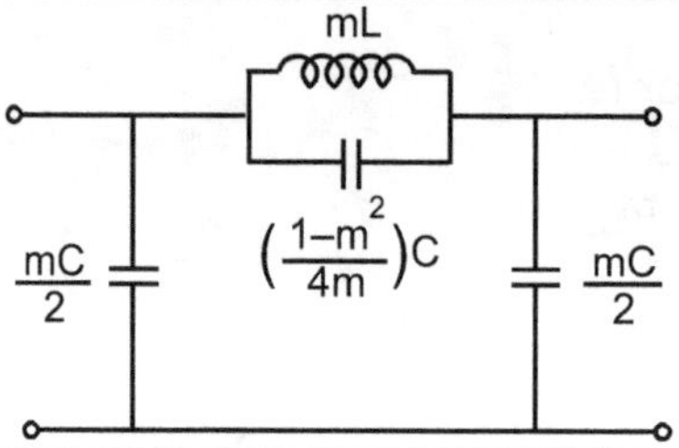 Series: mL, $\left(\dfrac{1-m^2}{4m}\right)C$; Shunt: $\dfrac{mC}{2}$, $\dfrac{mC}{2}$	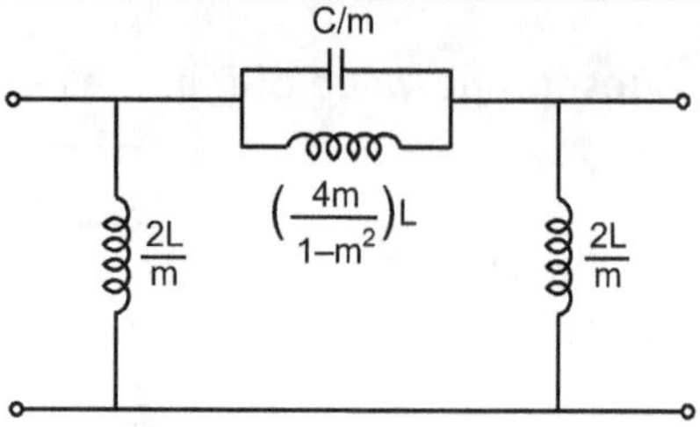 Series: C/m, $\left(\dfrac{4m}{1-m^2}\right)L$; Shunt: $\dfrac{2L}{m}$, $\dfrac{2L}{m}$
f_∞	$f_\infty = \dfrac{f_C}{\sqrt{1-m^2}}$	$f_\infty = f_C\sqrt{1-m^2}$
m	$m = \sqrt{1-\left(\dfrac{f_C}{f_\infty}\right)^2}$	$m = \sqrt{1-\left(\dfrac{f_\infty}{f_C}\right)^2}$
Relation in f_∞ and f_C	$f_\infty > f_C$	$f_\infty < f_C$

Fig. 5.117

5.23 SOLVED NUMERICALS ON m DERIVED FILTERS

Ex. 5.30: Design a m-derived low pas filter to match a line having characteristic impedance of 500 Ω and to pass signals upto 1 kHz with infinite attenuation at 1.2 kHz.

Sol.: Given $R_0 = 500$ Ω, $f_C = 1$ kHz, $f_\infty = 1.2$ kHz.

1. **Design of prototype low pass filter section (T Type)**

    Using design equations,

    $$L = \frac{R_0}{(\pi f_C)}$$

    $$L = \frac{500}{\pi \times 1000}$$

    $$\boxed{L = 159.155 \text{ mH}}$$

$$C = \frac{1}{(\pi f_C) R_0}$$

$$C = \frac{1}{(\pi \times 1000)(500)}$$

$$\boxed{C = 0.6366 \ \mu F}$$

Thus, prototype low pass filter (T type) is as shown in the Fig. 5.71 (a).

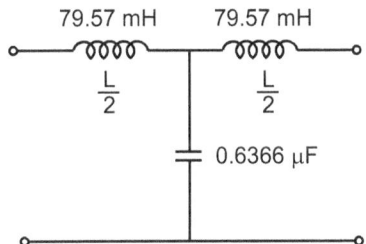

Fig. 5.71 (a)

2. **Design of m-derived low pass filter:**

   The value of m is given by,

   $$m = \sqrt{1 - \left(\frac{f_c}{f_\infty}\right)^2}$$

   $$m = \sqrt{1 - \left(\frac{1000}{1200}\right)^2}$$

   $$\boxed{m = 0.552}$$

   The elements in the series and shunt arms of m-derived filter section are given by,

   $$\frac{mL}{2} = \frac{(0.5527)(159.155 \times 10^{-3})}{2}$$

   $$\boxed{\frac{mL}{2} = 43.976 \ mH}$$

   $$mC = (0.5527)(0.6366 \times 10^{-6})$$

   $$\boxed{mL = 0.3518 \ \mu F}$$

   $$\left(\frac{1 - m^2}{4m}\right) L = \left[\frac{1 - (0.5527)^2}{4(0.5527)}\right] (159.133 \times 10^{-3})$$

   $$\boxed{\left(\frac{1 - m^2}{4m}\right) L = 50 \ mH}$$

Hence m-derived low pass filter is as shown in the Fig. 5.71 (b).

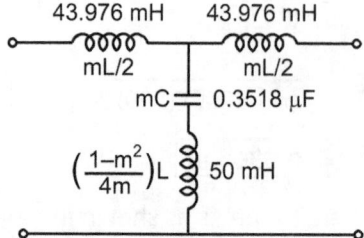

Fig. 5.71 (b): m-derived low pass filter T type section

Ex. 5.31: Design m-derived LPF having cut-off frequency of 5 kHz and impedance of 600 Ω. The frequency of infinite attenuation is 1.25 times the cut-off frequency.

Sol.: Given: $R_0 = 600\ \Omega$, $f_C = 5$ kHz, $f_\infty = (1.25 \times 5) = 6.25$ kHz.

$$L = \frac{R_0}{\pi f_C} = \frac{600}{\pi \times 5 \times 10^3}$$

$$\boxed{L = 38.197\ \text{mH}}$$

$$C = \frac{1}{(\pi f_C)\ R_0} = \frac{1}{\pi \times 5 \times 10^3 \times 600}$$

$$\boxed{C = 0.106\ \mu F}$$

For m derived LPF m is given by,

$$m = \sqrt{1 - \left(\frac{f_C}{f_\infty}\right)^2} = \sqrt{1 - \left(\frac{5 \times 10^3}{6.25 \times 10^3}\right)^2}$$

$$\boxed{m = 0.6}$$

The actual values of components in series and shunt arms of m-derived filter are

$$\frac{mL}{2} = \frac{0.6 \times 38.197 \times 10^{-3}}{2}$$

$$\boxed{\frac{mL}{2} = 11.459\ \text{mH}}$$

$$mC = 0.6\ (0.106 \times 10^{-6})$$

$$\boxed{mC = 0.0636\ \mu F}$$

$$\left(\frac{1-m^2}{4m}\right) L = \left(\frac{1-(0.6)^2}{4(0.6)}\right)(38.197 \times 10^{-3})$$

$$\boxed{\left(\frac{1-m^2}{4m}\right) L = 10.18\ \text{mH}}$$

∴ The low pass filter is as shown below in Fig. 5.72.

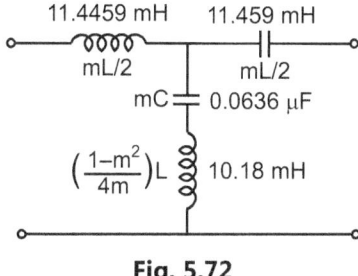

Fig. 5.72

Ex. 5.32: Design an m-derived lowpass T-section filter to have termination of 600 Ω resistance. The cut-off frequency is 1.8 kHz and finite attenuation occurs at 2 kHz.

Sol.: Given $R_0 = 600\ \Omega$, $f_C = 1.8$ kHz, $f_\infty = 2$ kHz

1. **Design of prototype lowpass filter section:**

   Using design equations,

   $$L = \frac{R_0}{\pi f_C} = \frac{600}{\pi \times 1.8 \times 10^3}$$

   $$\boxed{L = 106.1\ \text{mH}}$$

   $$C = \frac{1}{(\pi f_C) R_0} = \frac{1}{(\pi \times 1.8 \times 10^3 \times 600)}$$

   $$\boxed{C = 0.2947\ \mu F}$$

   Hence prototype T section is low pass filter is as shown in the Fig. 5.73 (a).

   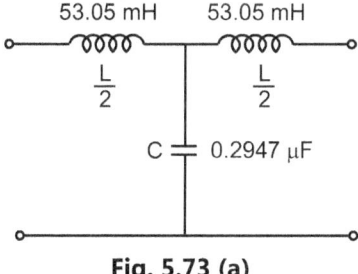

   Fig. 5.73 (a)

2. **Design of m-derived lowpass filter:**

   $$m = \sqrt{1 - \left(\frac{f_C}{f_\infty}\right)^2}$$

   $$= \sqrt{1 - \left(\frac{1800}{2000}\right)^2}$$

   $$\boxed{m = 0.4358}$$

Thus the elements in series and shunt arms of m-derived sections are as follows:

$$\frac{mL}{2} = \frac{(0.4358)(106.1 \times 10^{-3})}{2}$$

$$\boxed{\frac{mL}{2} = 23.12 \text{ mH}}$$

$$mC = (0.4358)(0.2947 \times 10^{-6})$$

$$\boxed{mC = 0.1284 \text{ μF}}$$

$$\left(\frac{1-m^2}{4m}\right)L = \left[\frac{1-(0.4358)^2}{4(0.4358)}\right] \times (106.1 \times 10^{-3})$$

$$\boxed{\left(\frac{1-m^2}{4m}\right)L = 49.305 \text{ mH}}$$

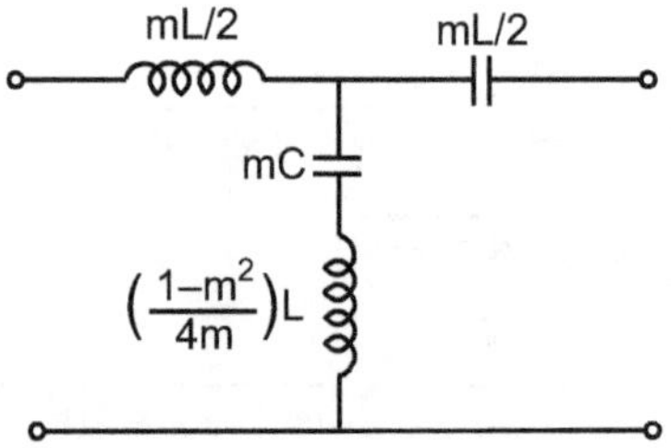

Fig. 5.73 (b)

Ex. 5.33: Design a composite high pass filter to operate into a load of 600 Ω and have a cut-off frequency of 1.2 kHz. The filter is to have one constant k-section and one m-derived section with an infinite attenuation at 1.1 kHz.

Sol.: Given $R_0 = 600$ Ω, $f_C = 1.2$ kHz $= 1200$ Hz, $f_\infty = 1.1$ kHz $= 1100$ Hz.

1. **Design of constant – k high pass filter:**

   Using design equations, values of L and C are given by,

   $$L = \frac{R_0}{4\pi f_C} = \frac{600}{4 \times \pi \times 1200}$$

   $$\boxed{L = 39.788 \text{ mH}}$$

   $$C = \frac{1}{(4\pi f_C) R_0} = \frac{1}{4 \times \pi \times 1200 \times 600}$$

   $$\boxed{C = 0.11 \text{ μF}}$$

Hence constant-k type T-section of high pass filter is as shown in the Fig. 5.74 (a).

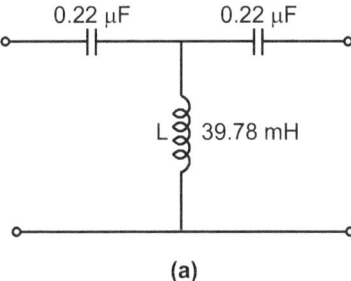

(a)

2. **Design of m-derived high pass filter:**

$$m = \sqrt{1 - \left(\frac{f_\infty}{f_c}\right)^2} = \sqrt{1 - \left(\frac{1100}{1200}\right)^2} = 0.399 \approx$$

$$\boxed{m = 0.4}$$

Hence the elements of m-derived high pass filter are given by,

$$\frac{2C}{m} = \frac{2 \times 0.11 \times 10^{-6}}{0.4}$$

$$\boxed{\frac{2C}{m} = 0.55 \ \mu F}$$

$$\frac{L}{m} = \frac{39.788 \times 10^{-3}}{0.4}$$

$$\boxed{\frac{L}{m} = 99.47 \ mH}$$

$$\frac{4m}{1-m^2} C = \left[\frac{4 \times 0.4}{1 - (0.4)^2}\right] \times 0.11 \times 10^{-6}$$

$$\boxed{\frac{4m}{1-m^2} C = 0.209 \ \mu F}$$

Hence m-derived high pass filter is shown in the Fig. 5.74 (b).

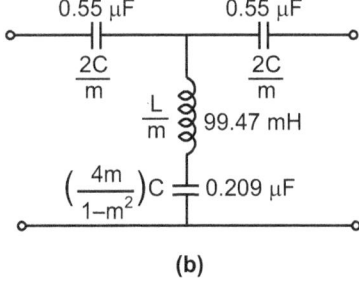

(b)

Fig. 5.74 (b)

Thus, the complete composite filter consisting one constant-k section and one m-derived section is as shown in the Fig. 5.74 (c).

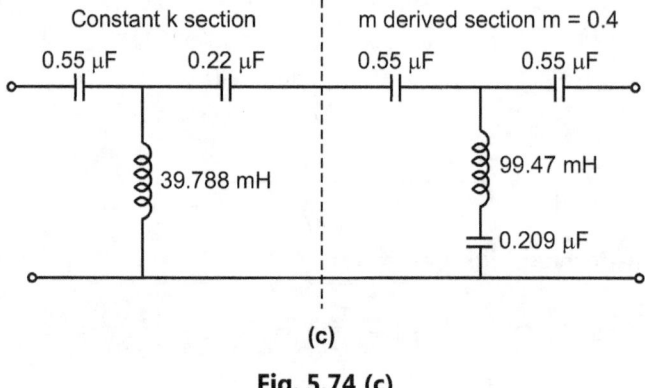

(c)

Fig. 5.74 (c)

5.24 DISADVANTAGES OF m DERIVED FILTER

- In constant k or prototype section, sharp rise in attenuation in the stop band was a limitation.

  i.e.   In LPF, high α was needed in stop band after f_C.

  In HPF, high α was needed in stop band before f_C.

  and this was not achieved.

- So a m-derived. Filter was designed which gave very very high attenuation at frequency f_∞, very close but not equal to f_C.

- Thus, at f_∞ (which is located in stop band in LPF and HPF) the rise in the attenuation is very sharp.

- But the limitation is that this increase in α is only at f_∞. After f_∞ the value of α again decreases.

- Ideally α should be very large (infinite) throughout the stop band for any filter. But in the case of m derived filters the desired high attenuation is only at one frequency in stop band. It does not last for the entire stop band as actually expected and is clear. From Fig. 5.75.

- The reason for such a behaviour of $\propto$ is because of f_∞, the shunt arm of LPF and HPF acts as good as a short circuit. X_L cancels X_C at f_∞, which is the resonating frequency.

  But if we recollect the concepts of resonance, it is very clear that only at resonating frequency, $x_L = x_C$ i.e. only the resonance the total reactance is zero. In series resonance for any frequency above or below f_r, there is some reactance existing (may be inductive or capacitive respectively), so the output will not be completely zero. A finite voltage will appear across the load.

- The attenuation α is said to be infinite or very large only when V_{out} is zero. So, in case of m derived filter this is achieved only at f_∞, value of α drops for other frequencies in stop band.
- This happens to be a major limitation in m derived filters.
- However, this limitation can be overcomed by two ways:
    1. Use of composite filter
    2. Use as many m derived sections as desired to:
        - Produce a high attenuation over the entire stop band.
        - Supress the signal components at only at some particular frequencies.

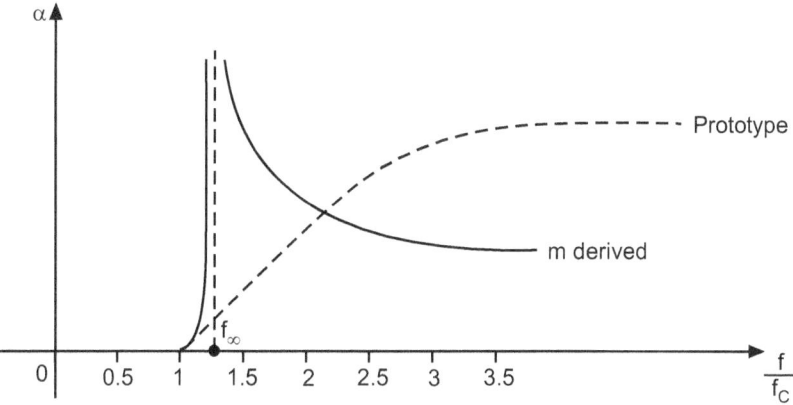

Fig. 5.75: Variation of α in prototype and m derived section

5.25 TERMINATION WITH m DERIVED HALF SECTIONS

5.25.1 Necessity of m-Derived Half Sections

- Let us revise the theorem of maximum power transfer, which was studied in chapter 1.
- "In an active network, maximum power transfer to the load takes place when the load impedance is equivalent to impedance of the network as viewed from the terminals of the load".
- In case of filter we occasionally have to cascade some T or π filter sections of constant k filters or of m derived or sometimes even a constant k with m derived filter (This will be discussed in the next section and this cascade connection has to be placed between the source and the load. So impedance matching at various points is a crucial requirement. For maximum power transfer.

- In chapter 5, reactance L sections were designed that would transform a given resistance to a more desired valued.
- But this L section will solve the problem of satisfactorily terminating a section or matching the impedance only at one particular frequency.
- Now, all the filters consists of frequency dependent components, whose reactances change with frequency.
- So, obviously in this case we will need a L-section, whose characteristics will change with frequency in such a way that filter is approximately matched to its load at all frequencies over the pass band.
- Zobel discovered m derived half sections which has the property of:

    (i) Constant impedance almost over the entire pass band.

    (ii) Matching a T filter with a π filter and vice versa.

We have studied m derived filters of T and π type. They are reproduced here in Fig. 5.76 for reference.

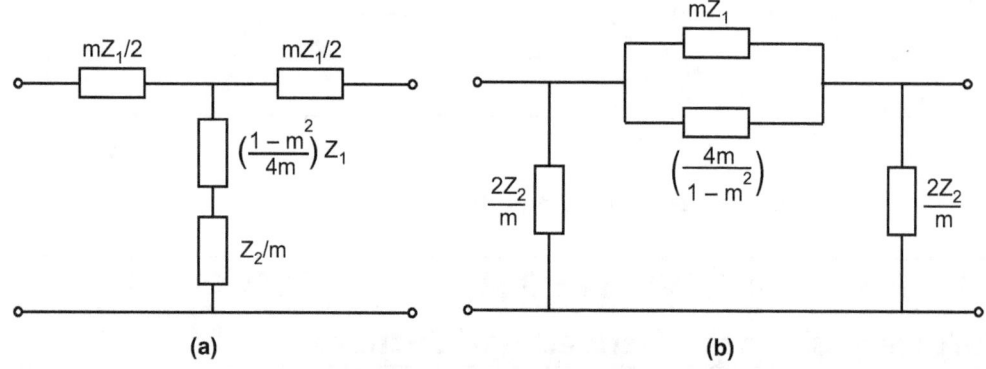

Fig. 5.76: m derived T and π type filters

5.25.2 m Derived Half Sections (T Type)

- Let us now analyse one of these types to verify the above stated properties.
- Consider the m derived T filter as shown in Fig. 5.76 (a). This 'T' type m derived filter can be split in two half sections i.e. m-derived half section as shown in Fig. 5.76 (a) and (b).
- These half sections are asymmetrical network. So let us start our analysis with the calculation of image impedances for a one of these half sections say Fig. 5.77 (b).

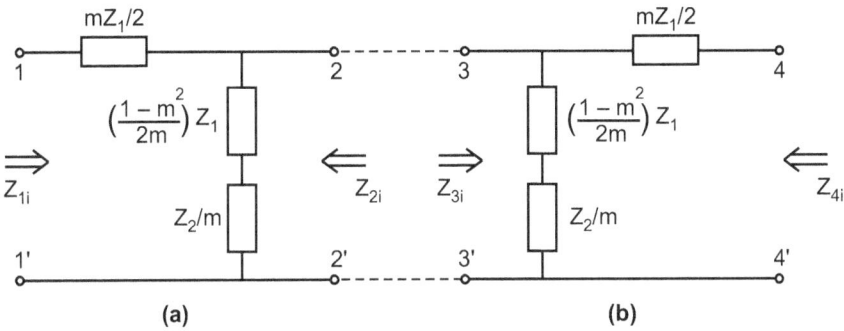

Fig. 5.77: m-derived half sections of a m-derived T section

- Image impedance at a port x is defined as:

$$Z_{xi} = \sqrt{Z_{xoc} Z_{xsc}}$$

- Now, let us find the image impedance at port 3-3'

$$Z_{3i} = \sqrt{Z_{3oc} Z_{3sc}}$$

- Open circuiting and short circuiting the terminal 4-4 of Fig. 5.77 (b) gives

$$Z_{3oc} = \left(\frac{1-m^2}{2m}\right) Z_1 + \frac{2Z_2}{m}$$

$$Z_{3sc} = \left(\frac{mZ_1}{2}\right) \parallel \left[\left(\frac{1-m^2}{2m}\right) Z_1 + \frac{2Z_2}{m}\right]$$

$$= \frac{\left[\left(\frac{1-m^2}{2m}\right) Z_1 + \frac{2Z_2}{m}\right] \frac{mZ_1}{2}}{\left(\frac{1-m^2}{2m}\right) Z_1 + \frac{2Z_2}{m} + \frac{mZ_1}{2}}$$

Thus, equation $Z_{3i} = \sqrt{Z_{30Z} \cdot Z_{3sc}}$ becomes

$$Z_{3i} = \sqrt{\left[\left(\frac{1-m^2}{2m}\right) Z_1 + \frac{2Z_2}{m}\right] \frac{\left[\left(\frac{1-m^2}{2m}\right) Z_1 + \frac{2Z_2}{m}\right] \frac{mZ_1}{2}}{\frac{1-m^2}{2m} Z_1 + \frac{2Z_2}{m} + \frac{mZ_1}{2}}}$$

$$Z_{3i} = \sqrt{\frac{\left[\left(\frac{1-m^2}{2m}\right) Z_1 + \frac{2Z_2}{m}\right]^2 \frac{mZ_1}{2}}{\left(\frac{1-m^2}{2m}\right) Z_1 + \frac{2Z_2}{m} + \frac{mZ_1}{2}}}$$

which on simplification gives

$$Z_{3i} = \left[1 + (1 - m^2)\frac{Z_1}{4Z_2}\right]\sqrt{\frac{Z_1 Z_2}{1 + \frac{Z_1}{4Z_2}}}$$

$$\boxed{Z_{3i} = M \cdot Z_{0\pi}} \qquad \ldots (5.50\,(a))$$

where

$$Z_{0\pi} = \sqrt{\frac{Z_1 Z_2}{1 + \frac{Z_1}{4Z_2}}}$$

$$M = \left[1 - (1 - m^2)\frac{Z_1}{4Z_2}\right]$$

Similarly, now let us find the image impedance at port 4-4'.

$$Z_{4i} = \sqrt{Z_{4oc} \cdot Z_{4sc}}$$

Open circuiting and short circuiting the terminal 3-3' of Fig. 5.77 (a) gives

$$Z_{4oc} = \left(\frac{1 - m^2}{2m}\right) Z_1 + \frac{2Z_2}{m} + \frac{mZ_1}{2}$$

$$Z_{4sc} = \frac{m Z_1}{2}$$

Equation $Z_{4i} = \sqrt{Z_{4oc} Z_{4sc}}$ becomes

$$Z_{4i} = \sqrt{\left[\left(\frac{1 - m^2}{2m}\right) Z_1 + \frac{2Z_2}{m} + \frac{mZ_1}{2}\right]\left[\frac{mZ_1}{2}\right]}$$

$$Z_{4i} = \sqrt{Z_1 Z_2 + \frac{Z_1^2}{4} - \frac{Z_1^2 m^2}{4} + \frac{m^2 Z_2^2}{4}}$$

$$\boxed{Z_{4i} = \sqrt{\frac{Z_1^2}{4} + Z_1 Z_2} = Z_{0T}} \qquad \ldots(5.50(b))$$

It is very clear from equation (5.49) that the image impedance Z_{3i} is a function of $Z_{0\pi}$ modified by a factor M where,

$$M = 1 + (1 - m^2)\frac{Z_1}{4Z_2}$$

Similarly, equation (5.50 (a)) indicates that the image impedance at terminal 4-4' is equal to Z_{0T}, i.e. characteristics impedance of symmetrical T network.

Let us know discuss about the m derived half section in Fig. 5.77 (a).

$$Z_{1i} = \sqrt{Z_{1oc} \cdot Z_{25c}}$$
$$Z_{2i} = \sqrt{Z_{2oc} \cdot Z_{25c}}$$

Using the similar mathematical treatment and by the same reasoning, we have

$$\boxed{Z_{1i} = Z_{0T}} \qquad \ldots(5.51)$$

$$\boxed{Z_{2i} = M' Z_{0\pi}} \quad \text{i.e. modified } Z_{0\pi} \qquad \ldots (5.52)$$

where M' is a function of 'm'.

Fig. 5.78 compares a half section with m derived section and the difference is very clear.

Prototype Half Section (T type)	m Derived Half Section (T type)
T n/w (circuit diagrams)	(a) and (b) circuit diagrams
Image impedances $Z_{1i} = Z_{0T}$ $Z_{2i} = Z_{0\pi}$ $Z_{3i} = Z_{0\pi}$ $Z_{4i} = Z_{0T}$	**Image impedances** $Z_{1i} = Z_{0T}$ $Z_{2i} = M' Z_{0\pi}$ $Z_{3i} = M Z_{0\pi}$ $Z_{4i} = Z_{0T}$ M and M' depend on 'm'.

Fig. 5.78: Comparison of prototype half section with m derived half section

Image impedances at port 2-2' and 3-3' are both function of $Z_{0\pi}$ but modified values which depend on 'm' and thus has the possibility of variation of impedance with value of m. The image impedance at port 1-1' and 4-4' of the m derived half sections is equal to Z_{0T}. Thus, it can be used for matching the characteristic of a symmetrical T network.

5.25.3 m Derived Half Section (π Type)

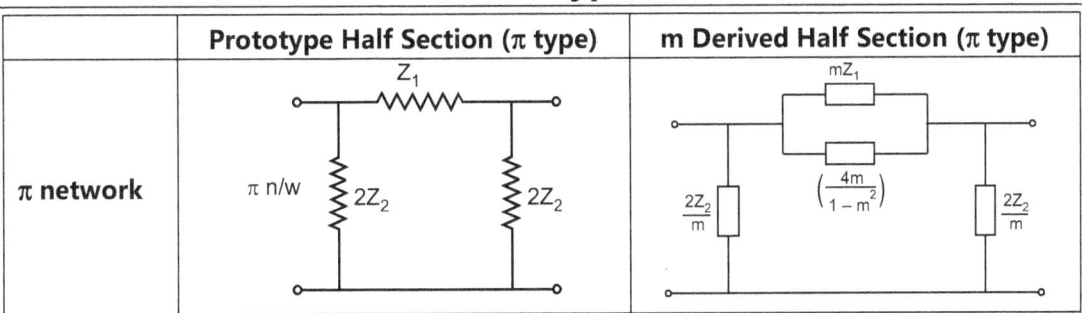

	Prototype Half Section (π type)	m Derived Half Section (π type)
π network	π n/w	

contd. ...

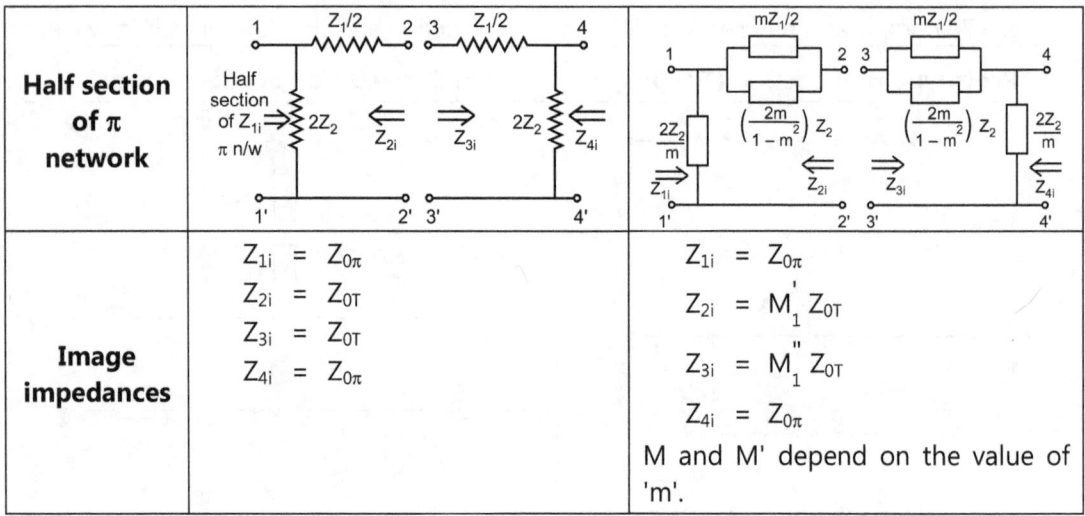

Fig. 5.79: Comparison of a Prototype and a m Derived Half Section

- Consider a m derived π filter of Fig. 5.76 (b). The image impedances of the m derived half sections can be derived in a very similar way to m derived half sections of a T network, derived in Section 5.25.2.
- These results are summarized in the comparison in above Fig. 5.79.
- All the explanations of section 5.25.2 are applicable to these derivations also. So, as clear from the comparison table, the image impedances Z_{1i} and Z_{4i} are equal to the characteristic impedance $Z_{0\pi}$ of a symmetrical π network and thus can be used for matching purpose.
- Image impedances Z_{2i} and Z_{3i} are both function of Z_{0T} but again modified by a factor which depends on m and thus to have possibility of variation of image impedance with value of m.

Thus, **m derived half sections** of m derived T and π network, also known as **terminating half sections** are normally added to the design of any filter to provide uniform termination and matching characteristics.

5.25.4 Characteristics Impedance of a m-Derived Half Section

We have derived the equations and also plotted the graphs of characteristics impedance for T and π sections of prototype low pass, high pass, band pass and band stop filter. These equation and plots of a LPF are reproduced here for our reference.

For a LPF

$$Z_{0T} = R_K \sqrt{1 - \left(\frac{f}{f_C}\right)^2}$$

$$Z_{0T} = \frac{R_K}{\sqrt{1 - \left(\frac{f}{f_C}\right)^2}}$$

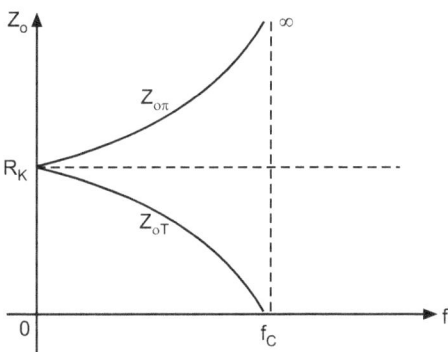

Fig. 5.80: Characteristics Impedance of a Prototype LPF

- As already discussed and also clear from Fig. 5.80, characteristics impedance of T and π section, Z_{0T} and $Z_{0\pi}$ varies between R_K and ∞. This applies to all the prototype filters.
- The curves show that the characteristic impedance of neither section T or π is sufficiently constant over the pass band that any load will give a satisfactory impedance match.
- One of the reason to design m derived half section was to eliminate this drawback.
- So, we derived the equations for the image impedances of m derived half section.
- As seen in Sections 5.25.2 and 5.25.3, image impedance Z_{2i} and Z_{3i} of both T and π type half sections, were function of $Z_{0\pi}$ and Z_{0T} respectively, modified by values M and M'.
- These values (M and M') are dependent on 'm'. The variation of these image impedances is plotted over the pass band for the several values of m.
- This variation of Z_{2i} and Z_{3i} of m derived half section over the pass band for various values of m is plotted in Fig. 5.81.

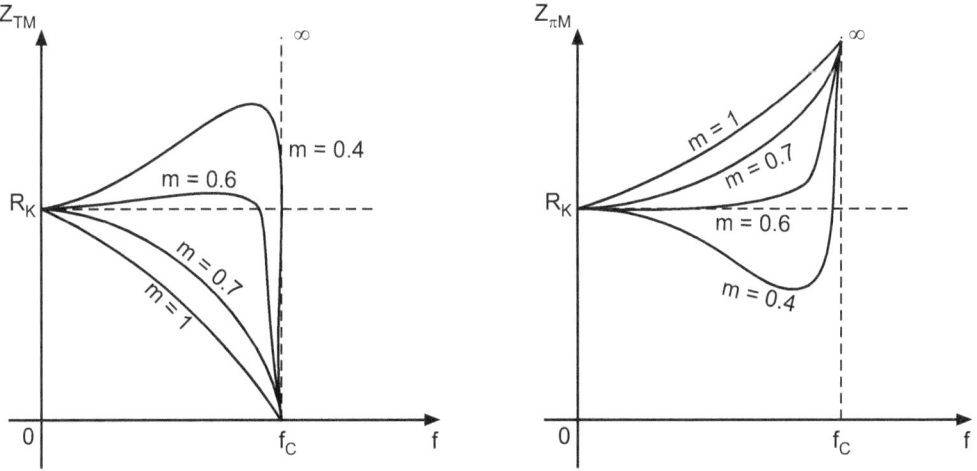

Fig. 5.81: Variation of Z_i of m Derived T and π Sections of a Prototype LPF

- It is observed that for m = 0.6, the image impedance equals the design impedance R_K over most of the pass band.

- The performed experiments say that, with m = 0.6 for a half section, a nearly constant value of $Z_i = R_K$ is obtained over 85 percentage of the pass band.

- Thus, impedance is constant in pass band and is equal to R_K i.e. design impedance. Therefore, a source impedance equal to R_K can be matched satisfactorily on an image basis at the corresponding terminal over most of the pass band.

- A similar variation with m can be developed for the high pass filter. Even in this case using m = 0.6, will give similarly satisfactory matching of impedances.

- So always, when m derived terminating half sections are used m must be equal to 0.6.

- These terminating half sections are also referred to as L section.

- **Note:** We have studied m derived filters which are used to obtain large attenuation and m derived half sections (terminating half sections) which are used for proper termination and matching. Value of m in m derived filters will depend on f_∞ i.e. frequency of infinite attenuation. We have also derived the formula for calculating the value of m in case of LPF and HPF. But value of m in m derived terminating half sections is fixed and will always be selected as 0.6. Let us not get confused in these two things.

5.25.5 Terminating a T and a π Section Filter Network

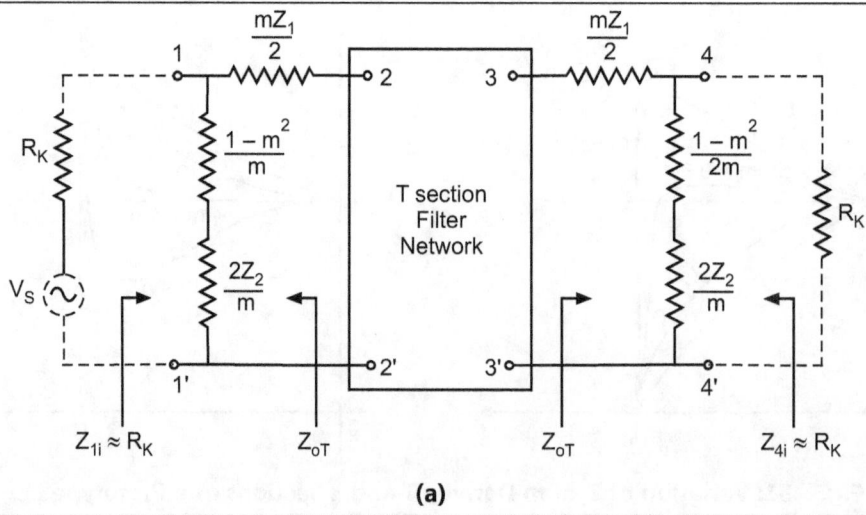

(a)

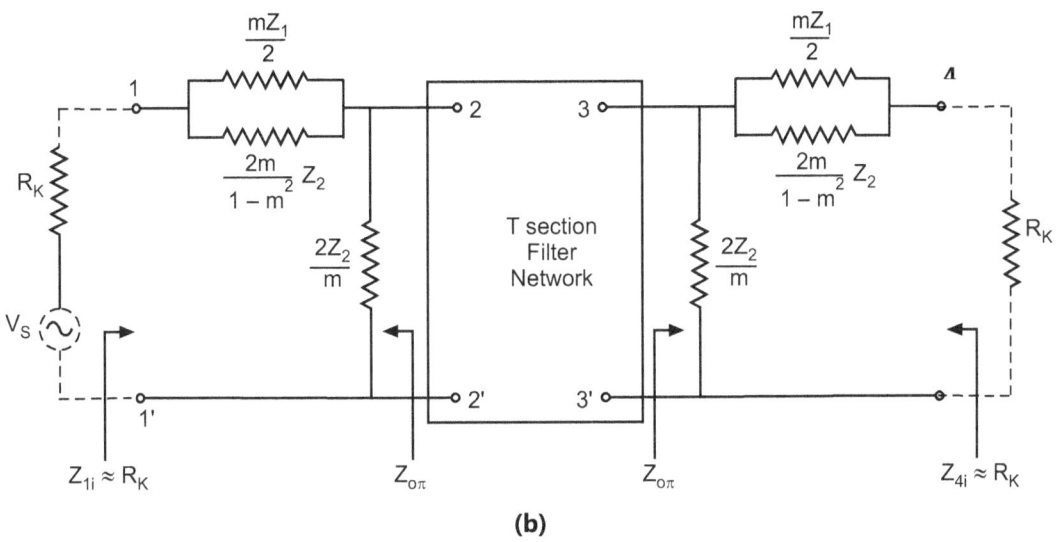

Fig. 5.82: Use of m Derived Terminating Half Sections [L Sections] to Terminate

(a) A T Section Filter

(b) A π Section Filter

Value of m should be 0.6

- Proper termination of any circuit is required to achieve maximum transfer of power.
- Fig. 5.82 (a) and (b) shows a general arrangement to use a m derived terminating half sections between the source and load.
- We have studied that image impedance at one of the terminals of these half section is almost constant and is equal to R_K and at another terminal impedance is = Z_{0T} or $Z_{0\pi}$.
- So, a generator of internal impedance R_K may be connected to the terminals 1-1' and a satisfactory image impedance match can be obtained over 85% of the pass band.
- Likewise, a load of value R_K may be connected to the 4-4 terminals.
- Prototype and m derived T or π sections, designed with design impedance R_K can be inserted between 2-2' and 3-3'.
- Maximum power will be transferred over atleast 85% of the pass band, because the overall characteristics impedance of the above discussed assembly will be almost constant with a satisfactory impedance match between all the connected sections.
- Thus, depending upon the designed filter section, an appropriate m derived half section with m = 0.6 must be used to achieve satisfactory impedance matching and thus transfer maximum power from source to the load.

5.26 SUMMARY OF m DERIVED TERMINATING HALF SECTIONS

	m derived T Section	m derived π Section
m derived Filter Section	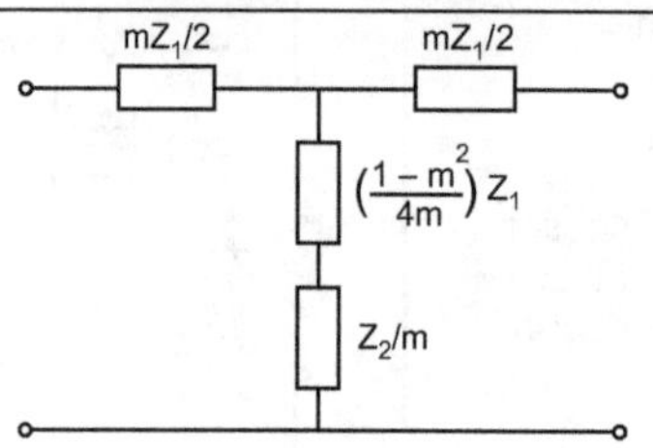 Series arm: $mZ_1/2$, $mZ_1/2$; Shunt arm: $\left(\dfrac{1-m^2}{4m}\right)Z_1$ in series with Z_2/m	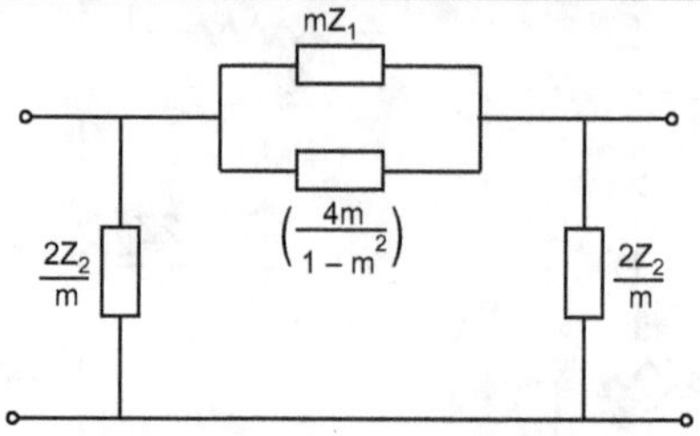 Series arm: mZ_1; Shunt arms: $2Z_2/m$, $\left(\dfrac{4m}{1-m^2}\right)$, $2Z_2/m$
Terminating half Section (L Section)	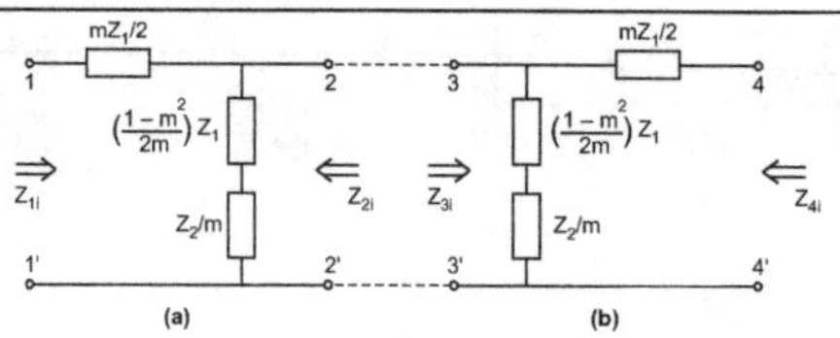 (a) and (b) sections with $mZ_1/2$, $\left(\dfrac{1-m^2}{2m}\right)Z_1$, Z_2/m	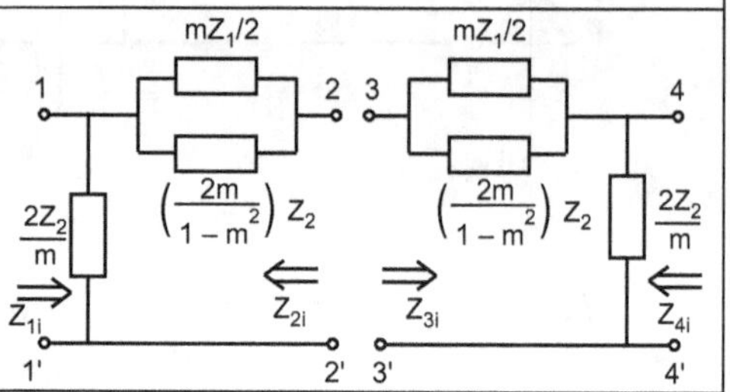 Sections with $mZ_1/2$, $2Z_2/m$, $\left(\dfrac{2m}{1-m^2}\right)Z_2$
Image Impedance	$Z_{1i} = Z_{0T}$ $Z_{2i} = M'\, Z_{0\pi} \approx R_K$ (For m = 0.6) $Z_{3i} = M\, Z_{0\pi} \approx R_K$ (From m = 0.6) $Z_{4i} = Z_{0T}$	$Z_{1i} = Z_{0\pi}$ $Z_{2i} = M_1'\, Z_{0T} \approx R_K$ (For m = 0.6) $Z_{3i} = M_2''\, Z_{0T} \approx R_K$ (From m = 0.6) $Z_{4i} = Z_{0\pi}$

Fig. 5.83

5.27 COMPOSITE FILTER

- In this unit of filters, we started our discussion with prototype filters. We realized that the attenuation characteristics is not very sharp in the attenuation band as it is ideally expected. Due to this it was very difficult to distinguish the frequencies after and before cut-off frequency.

- So, to overcome this drawback in prototype filters, we designed m derived filters which gave very large attenuation at a frequency f_∞, very close to f_C. But even m derived filters had a limitation. It was observed that in the stop band though α is very high at f_∞, it drastically reduces after f_∞ in case of LPF and before f_∞ in case of HPF.

- Constant k or prototype filter is a good choice if high attenuation is needed in deeper stop band, at frequencies far away from f_0.

- Similarly a m-derived filter should be a preferable choice if very high attenuation is needed at a frequency close to f_c.

- But none of these filters are ideal filters because none of them give you high attenuation through out the stop band as ideally desired.
- So a wise choice is to use a prototype section in series with a m derived section. As indicated in Fig. 5.84. This assembly would definitely give appreciably high attenuation through out the stop band.
- Such a combination along with terminating half sections is called as a composite filter.

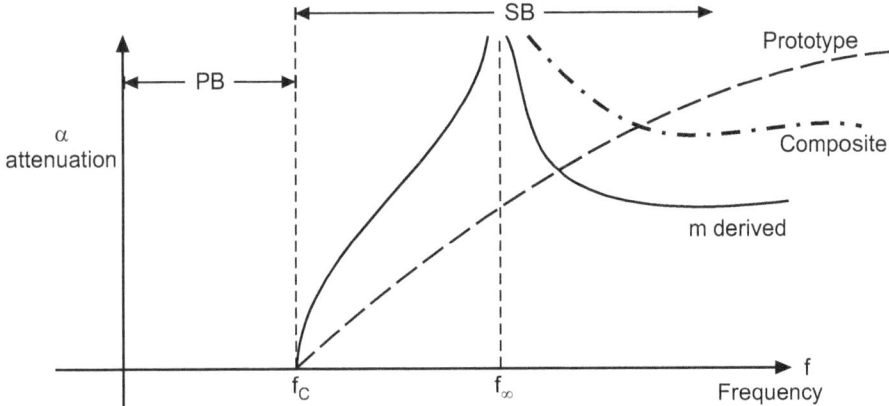

Fig. 5.84: Variation of α in Constant k, m Derived and Composite Filter

- Thus a general block schematic of the composite filter will have:
  1. One or more prototype sections.
  2. One or more m derived sections
  3. Terminating half sections (with m = 0.6).
- Thus to summarize.

	Filter	Attenuation Near f_c	Attenuation after f_c
1.	Constant K	Very low	Very high
2.	m derived	Very high	Low
3.	Composite	High	High

- The block schematic of composite filter is shown in Fig. 5.85.

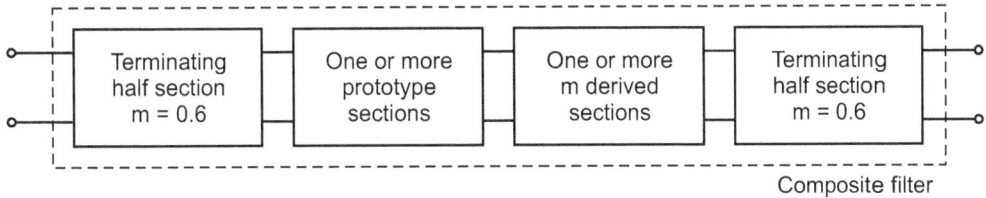

Fig. 5.85: Block Schematic of the Composite Filter

- Terminating half sections with m = 0.6 are inserted to achieve proper impedance matching and constant characteristics impedance through out the pass band.

- If it is desired to have very large attenuation at few particular frequencies in the stop band, corresponding number of m derived filter section must be used in cascade with the desired value of f_∞.
- In cases, where an impedance match is not important, the attenuation may be built-up near cut-off by cascading or connecting a number of constant k prototype sections in series.
- Thus, the number of various sections in any composite filter would totally depend on the desired attenuation characteristics.
- In any case, design impedance R_K, the cut-off frequency f_C and infinite frequency f_∞ are some important design specification in a composite filter.

5.28 SOLVED NUMERICALS ON COMPOSITE FILTERS

Ex. 5.34: Design a composite low pass filter to work into 500 Ω resistance with cut-off at 1000 Hz. It should have very high attenuation at 1065, 1250 and ∞ kHz.

Given: f_C = 1000 Hz, $f_{\infty 1}$ = 1065, $f_{\infty 2}$ = 1250 Hz, $f_{\infty 3}$ = ∞, R_k = 500 Ω.

Sol.: (i) Prototype Section:

$$L = \frac{R_K}{\pi f_C}$$

$$= \frac{500}{\pi \times 1000}$$

$$L = 159 \text{ mH}$$

$$\boxed{\frac{L}{2} = 0.079 \text{ H}}$$

$$C = \frac{1}{\pi f_C R}$$

$$= \frac{1}{\pi \times 1000 \times 500}$$

$$\boxed{C = 0.636 \text{ }\mu F}$$

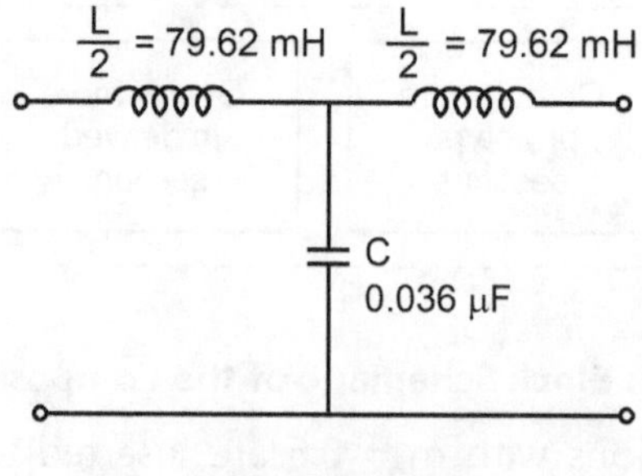

$\frac{L}{2}$ = 79.62 mH $\frac{L}{2}$ = 79.62 mH

C = 0.036 µF

Fig. 5.86 (a)

(ii) m derived section

We know, $m = \sqrt{1 - \left(\dfrac{f_c}{f_\infty}\right)^2}$

(a) For $\quad f_\infty = \infty$ (infinity) Hz

$\boxed{m = 1}$, which is nothing but the prototype as shown above in Fig. 5.133 (a)

(b) For $\quad f_\infty = 1065$ Hz

$$m = \sqrt{1 - \left(\dfrac{1000}{1065}\right)^2}$$

$\boxed{m = 0.344}$

$\left(\dfrac{1-m^2}{4m}\right)L = \left[\dfrac{1 - 0.344^2}{4 \times 0.344}\right] 159$

$\boxed{\left(\dfrac{1-m^2}{4m}\right)L = 101.9 \text{ mH}}$

$mC = 0.344 \times 0.636 \text{ μF}$

$\boxed{mC = 0.219 \text{ μF}}$

$\dfrac{mL}{2} = 0.344 \times \dfrac{0.0795}{2}$

$\boxed{\dfrac{mL}{2} = 0.0273 \text{ H}}$

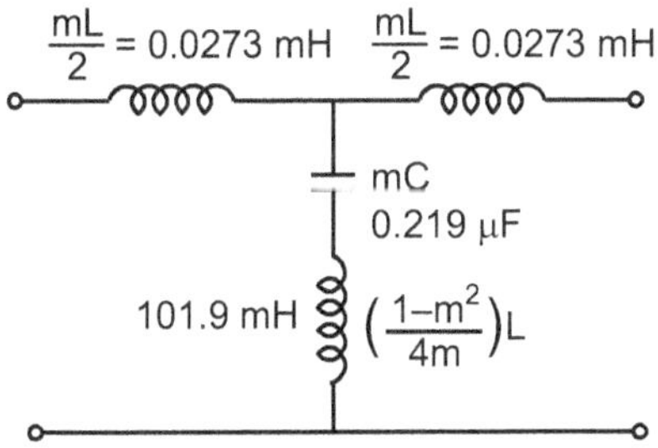

$\dfrac{mL}{2} = 0.0273 \text{ mH} \qquad \dfrac{mL}{2} = 0.0273 \text{ mH}$

mC 0.219 μF

101.9 mH $\left(\dfrac{1-m^2}{4m}\right)L$

Fig. 5.86 (b)

(c) For $\quad f_\infty = 1250$ Hz

$$m = \sqrt{1 - \left(\dfrac{1000}{1250}\right)^2}$$

$\boxed{m = 0.6}$

Now since m = 0.6, this section can be used as a terminating half-section. Therefore series and shunt arms of the terminating sections are:

$$\frac{mL}{2} = 0.6 \times 0.0785$$

$$\boxed{\frac{mL}{2} = 0.0477 \text{ H}}$$

$$= \boxed{47.7 \text{ mH}}$$

$$\frac{mC}{2} = 0.6 \times \frac{0.6366}{2}$$

$$\boxed{\frac{mC}{2} = 0.1909 \text{ μF}}$$

$$\left(\frac{1-m^2}{2m}\right)L = \left[\frac{1-(0.6)^2}{2(0.6)}\right]0.1591$$

$$\boxed{\left(\frac{1-m^2}{2m}\right) = 84.8 \text{ H}}$$

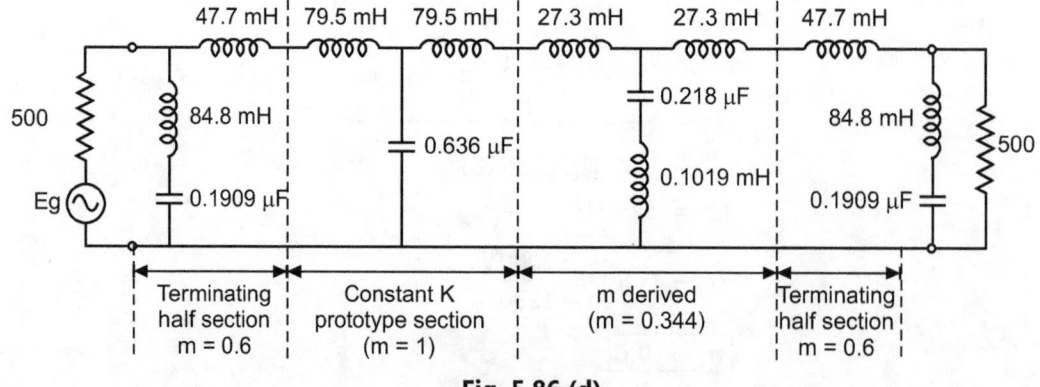

Fig. 5.86 (c)

(iii) Composite filter: The designed constant k type, n-derived filter section and terminating half-sections are all connected in cascade to form a composite low pass filter.

Fig. 5.86 (d)

The series inductors can be added to the circuit can be simplified to obtain equivalent composite filter as:

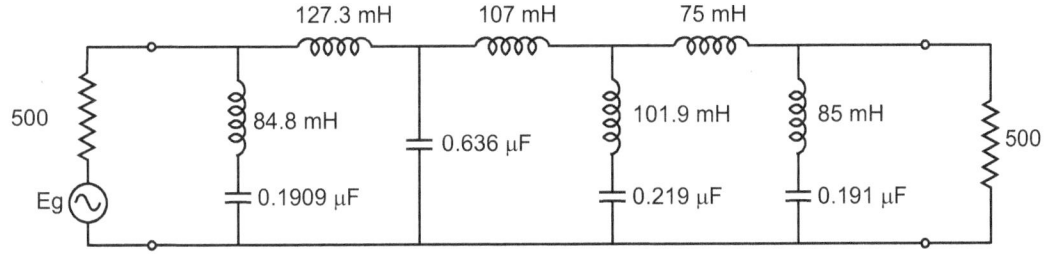

Fig. 5.86 (e)

Ex. 5.35: Design a composite high pass filter work into 1000 Ω resistance with cut-off frequency of 1000 Hz and with high attenuation of 800 Hz and 950 Hz.

Given: R_K = 1000 Ω
           f_C = 1 kHz
           $f_{\infty 1}$ = 800 Hz
           $f_{\infty 2}$ = 950 Hz

Sol.: (i) Design of prototype section

$$L = \frac{R_K}{4\pi f_C}$$

$$= \frac{1000}{4\pi \times 1000}$$

$$\boxed{L = 79 \text{ mH}}$$

$$C = \frac{1}{4\pi R_K f_C}$$

$$= \frac{1}{4\pi \times 1000 \times 1000}$$

$$\boxed{C = 0.0795 \text{ μF}}$$

$$\boxed{2C = 0.159 \text{ μF}}$$

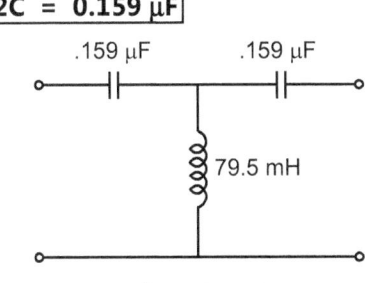

Fig. 5.87 (a)

(ii) Design of m derived section

We have $\quad m = \sqrt{1 - \left(\dfrac{f_\infty}{f_c}\right)^2}$

(a) $\quad f_\infty = 800$ Hz

$$m = \sqrt{1 - \left(\dfrac{800}{1000}\right)^2}$$

$$\boxed{m = 0.6}$$

Thus, this can be used as a terminating half section. Therefore, the series and the shunt elements are:

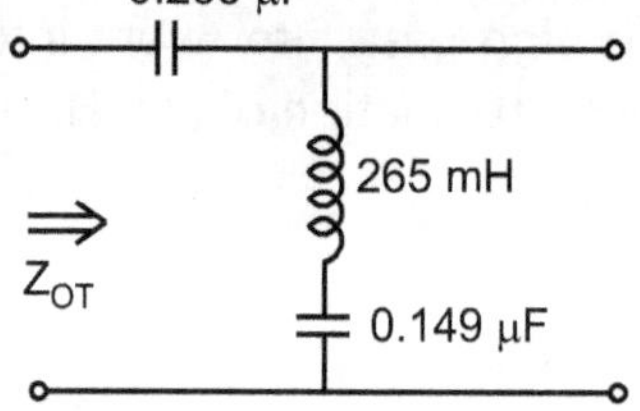

[Circuit diagram: Z_{OT} with 0.265 μF series capacitor, 265 mH inductor, and 0.149 μF shunt capacitor]

Fig. 5.87 (b)

$$\dfrac{2C}{m} = \dfrac{0.159}{0.6} = 0.265 \; \mu F$$

$$\dfrac{2L}{m} = \dfrac{79.5 \times 2}{0.6} = 265.0 \; mH$$

$$\left(\dfrac{2m}{1-m^2}\right)C = \dfrac{2 \times 0.6}{(1-0.36)} \times 0.0795 = 0.149 \; \mu F$$

(b) $\quad f_\infty = 950$ Hz

$$m = \sqrt{1 - \left(\dfrac{f_\infty}{f_c}\right)^2} = \sqrt{1 - \left(\dfrac{950}{1000}\right)^2}$$

$$\boxed{m = 0.312}$$

Components are:

$$\dfrac{2C}{m} = \dfrac{2 \times 0.0795}{0.312}$$

$$= \dfrac{0.159}{0.3} = 0.51 \; \mu F$$

$$\dfrac{L}{m} = \dfrac{0.0795}{0.312} = 25.5 \; mH$$

$$\left(\dfrac{4m}{1-m^2}\right)C = \left[\dfrac{4 \times 0.312}{1-0.097}\right] \times 0.0795 = 0.11 \; \mu F$$

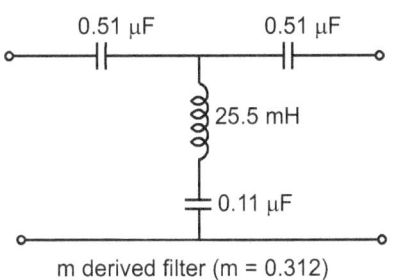

m derived filter (m = 0.312)

Fig. 5.87 (c)

(iii) Composite HPF is as shown in Fig. 5.87 (c).

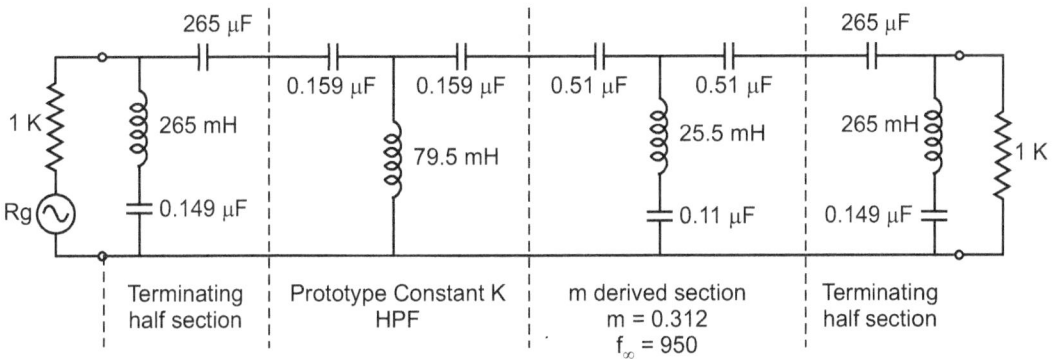

Fig. 5.87 (d)

The designed constant k type, m derived filter section and terminating half sections are all connected in cascade to form a composite high pass filter.

Capacitors in series can be combined and the simplified composite filter is as shown in Fig. 5.87 (e)

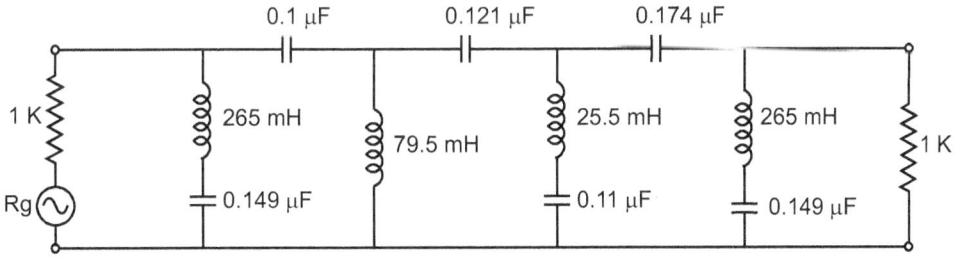

Fig. 5.87 (e)

Note: In both the above problems 5.34 and 5.35, at one of the frequency of high (infinite) attenuation m is equal to 0.6. Hence, this is used for the terminating half section. But in case if at infinite attenuation m ≠ 0.6 then m derived half-section is to be separately designed with m = 0.6.

5.29 SUMMARY OF FILTERS

5.29.1 Constant K Prototype Filters

Filter → Parameter ↓	LPF	HPF
Circuit diagram	T-section: series $L/2$, $L/2$ with shunt C. π-section: series L with shunt $C/2$, $C/2$.	T-section: series $2C$, $2C$ with shunt L. π-section: series C with shunt $2L$, $2L$.
Design impedance	$R_K = \sqrt{\dfrac{L}{C}}$	$R_K = \sqrt{\dfrac{L}{C}}$
Equation for f_C	$f_C = \dfrac{1}{\pi\sqrt{LC}}$	$f_L = \dfrac{1}{4\pi\sqrt{LC}}$
Equation for α	$\alpha = 2\cosh^{-1}\left(\dfrac{f}{f_C}\right)$	$\alpha = 2\cosh^{-1}\left(\dfrac{f_C}{f}\right)$
Equation for β	$\beta = 2\sin^{-1}\left(\dfrac{f}{f_C}\right)$	$\beta = 2\sin^{-1}\left(\dfrac{f_C}{f}\right)$
Equation for Z_0	$Z_{0T} = R_K\sqrt{1-\left(\dfrac{f}{f_C}\right)^2}$ $Z_{0\pi} = \dfrac{R_K}{\sqrt{1-\left(\dfrac{f}{f_C}\right)^2}}$	$Z_{0T} = R_K\sqrt{1-\left(\dfrac{f}{f_C}\right)^2}$ $Z_{0\pi} = \dfrac{R_K}{\sqrt{1-\left(\dfrac{f}{f_C}\right)^2}}$
Design equation	$L = \dfrac{R_K}{\pi f_C}$ $C = \dfrac{1}{\pi f_C R_K}$	$L = \dfrac{R_K}{4\pi f_C}$ $C = \dfrac{1}{4\pi f_C R_K}$

... contd.

	Band Pass Filter	Band Stop Filter
Ideal frequency response	V vs f: PB then SB, boundary at f_C	V vs f: SB then PB, boundary at f_C
Circuit diagram	Series arm: $L_1/2$, $2C_1$ — $2C_1$, $L_1/2$; Shunt arm: $L_2 \parallel C_2$. Alternate: Series L_1–C_1; Shunt $C_2/2 \parallel 2L_2$ on each side.	Series arm: $L_1/2$ — $L_1/2$ with $2C_1$ shunt between, shunt arm L_2 series C_2. Alternate: Series $L_1 \parallel C_1$; Shunt $2L_2$ with $C_2/2$ each side.
Design impedance	$R_K = \sqrt{\dfrac{L_1}{C_2}} = \sqrt{\dfrac{L_2}{C_1}}$ $L_1 C_1 = L_2 C_2 = \dfrac{1}{\omega_0^2}$	$R_K = \sqrt{\dfrac{L_1}{C_2}} = \sqrt{\dfrac{L_2}{C_1}}$ $L_1 C_1 = L_2 C_2 = \dfrac{1}{\omega_0^2}$
Equation for f_C	$f_0 = \sqrt{f_1 f_2}$ $f_0 = f_r = f_{ar}$	$f_0 = \sqrt{f_1 f_2}$ $f_0 = f_r = f_{ar}$
Design equation	$C_1 = \dfrac{(f_2 - f_1)}{4\pi R_K f_1 f_2}$ $L_1 = \dfrac{R_K}{\pi(f_2 - f_1)}$ $C_2 = \dfrac{1}{\pi R_K (f_2 - f_1)}$ $L_2 = \dfrac{R_K (f_2 - f_1)}{4\pi f_1 f_2}$ $f_0 = \dfrac{1}{2\pi\sqrt{L_1 C_1}} = \dfrac{1}{2\pi\sqrt{L_2 C_2}}$	$C_1 = \dfrac{1}{4\pi R_K (f_2 - f_1)}$ $L_1 = \dfrac{R_K (f_2 - f_1)}{\pi f_1 f_2}$ $C_2 = \dfrac{(f_2 - f_1)}{\pi R_K (f_1 f_2)}$ $L_2 = \dfrac{R_K}{4\pi (f_2 - f_1)}$ $f_0 = \dfrac{1}{2\pi\sqrt{L_1 C_1}} = \dfrac{1}{2\pi\sqrt{L_2 C_2}}$

contd. ...

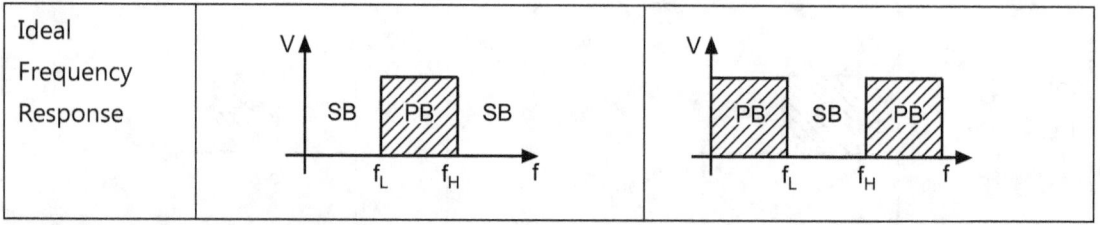

5.29.2 m Derived Filters

	m-derived LPF	m derived HPF
T section filter	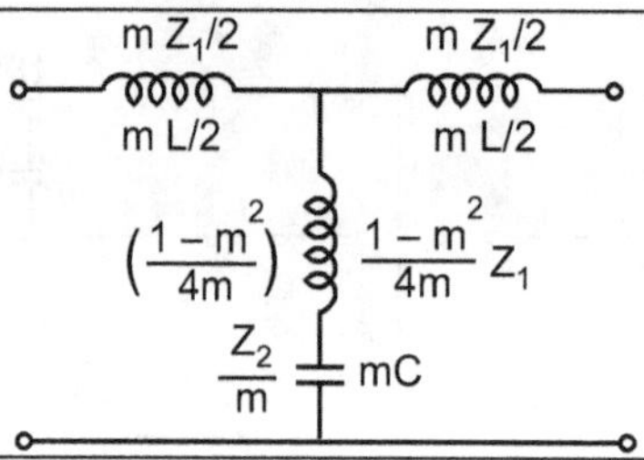	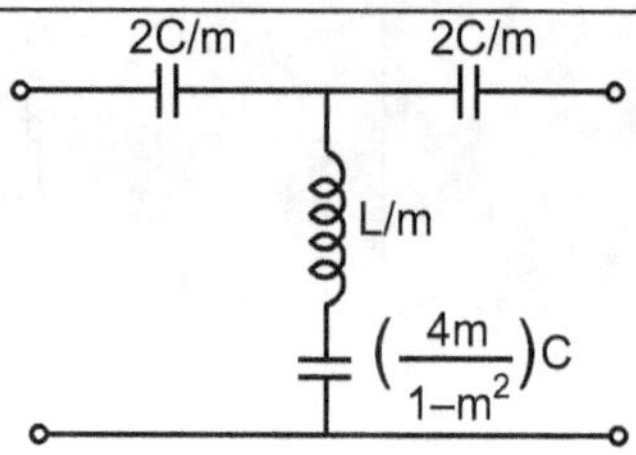
π section filter	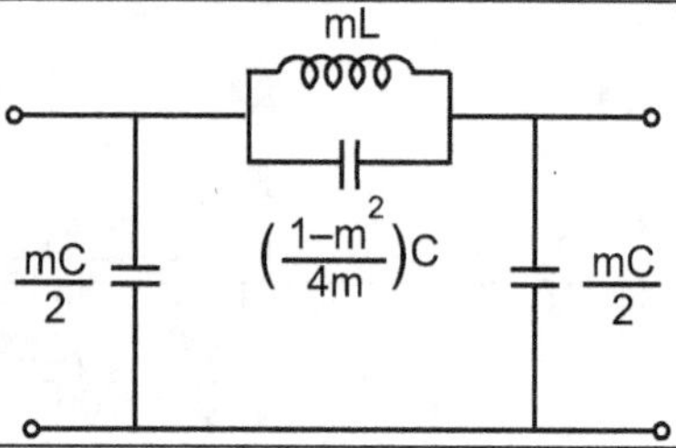	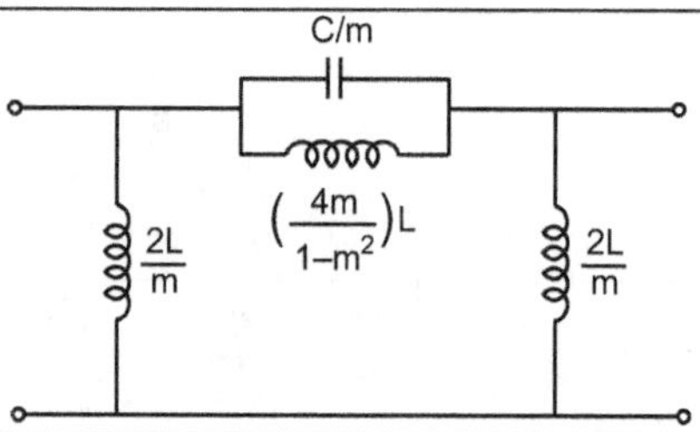
f_∞	$f_\infty = \dfrac{f_C}{\sqrt{1-m^2}}$	$f_\infty = f_C\sqrt{1-m^2}$
m	$m = \sqrt{1-\left(\dfrac{f_C}{f_\infty}\right)^2}$	$m = \sqrt{1-\left(\dfrac{f_\infty}{f_C}\right)^2}$
Relation in f_∞ and f_C	$f_\infty > f_C$	$f_\infty < f_C$

5.29.3 m Derived Terminating Half Sections

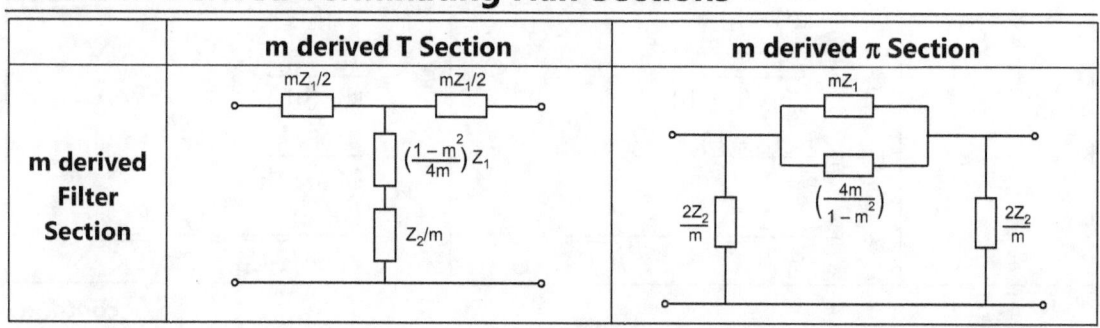

contd. ...

Terminating half Section (L Section)	(figures showing m-derived L-section half sections (a) and (b))
Image Impedance	$Z_{1i} = Z_{0T}$ $Z_{2i} = M' Z_{0\pi} \approx R_K$ (For m = 0.6) $Z_{3i} = M Z_{0\pi} \approx R_K$ (From m = 0.6) $Z_{4i} = Z_{0T}$	$Z_{1i} = Z_{0\pi}$ $Z_{2i} = M_1' Z_{0T} \approx R_K$ (For m = 0.6) $Z_{3i} = M_2'' Z_{0T} \approx R_K$ (From m = 0.6) $Z_{4i} = Z_{0\pi}$

EXERCISE

1. Sketch the reactance curves for a constant k T section and a π section of a F low and a high pass filter.

2. In a band pass filter resonating and an antiresonating frequency must be same. Justify with the help of reactance curves.

3. Prove that resonant frequency f_0 is the geometric mean of two cut-off frequencies f_1 and f_2.

4. What are the disadvantages of a prototype filter ? How are they corrected in the m derived filter ?

5. Why is a m derived half section used as terminating section in a filter ? Explain why is m = 0.6 used in terminating half sections.

6. Explain the disadvantages of a m derived filter. How are they corrected in a composite filter.

7. Define open circuit impedance parameters. Obtain the equivalent circuit in terms of Z-parameters.

8. Define short circuit admittance parameters. Obtain the equivalent circuit in terms of Y-parameters.

9. Define hybrid parameters. Obtain the equivalent circuit in terms of h-parameters. Explain why h-parameters are used for transistors.

10. Define Transmission (ABCD) parameters. Explain why ABCD parameters are also known as T-parameters.

11. Establish the relationship between Z and Y parameters.

12. What is the symmetrical network reciprocal network? Give relationship between parameters for symmetrical and reciprocal network.

13. Show that when two or more networks are cascaded, then their overall T-parameters is the multiplication of T-parameter matrix of individual networks.

14. Show that when two networks are series-series connected, then overall Z-parameter matrix is the addition of Z-parameters of the individual networks.

15. For the network shown below obtain Z and h parameters.

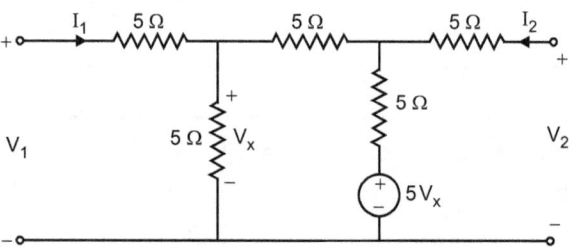

Fig. 5.88: Circuit for Q. 9

16. Show that for the network given, following equation holds good.

$$\begin{bmatrix} V_2 \\ I_2 \end{bmatrix} = \begin{bmatrix} 1.5 & 6.5 \\ 0.25 & 1.25 \end{bmatrix} \begin{bmatrix} V_1 \\ -I_1 \end{bmatrix}$$

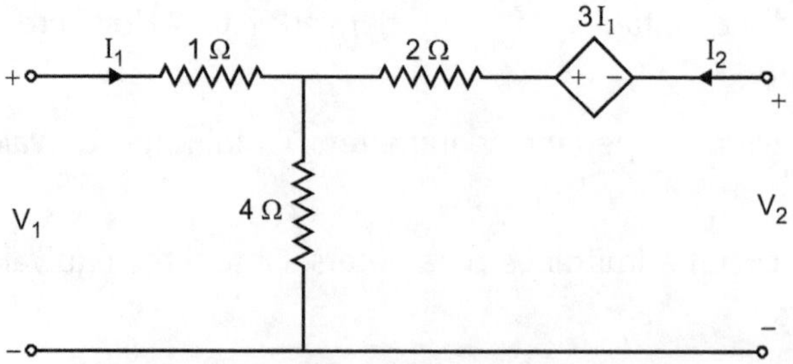

Fig. 5.89: Circuit for Q.10

17. Determine $\frac{V_2}{I}$ in terms of R_1, R_2 and Z-parameters of network.

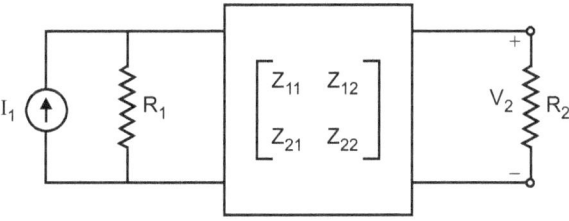

Fig. 5.90: Circuit for Q.17

18. Find Z and Y parameters.

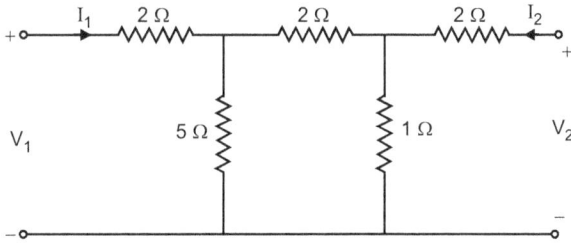

Fig 5.91: Circuit for Q.18

19. Show that ABCD parameters of the network is

$$\begin{bmatrix} A & B \\ C & D \end{bmatrix} = \begin{bmatrix} \left(\frac{1+s^2}{s^2}\right) & \left(\frac{1+2s^2}{s^3}\right) \\ \frac{1}{s} & \left(\frac{s^2+1}{s^2}\right) \end{bmatrix}$$

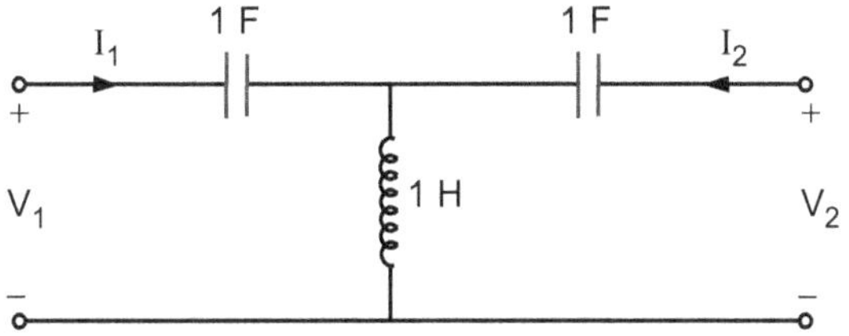

Fig. 5.92: Circuit for Q.19

20. For the bridged T, R-C network, determine Z and Y parameters.

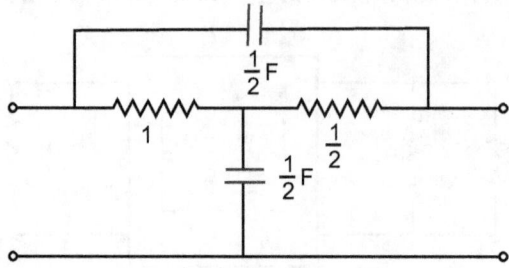

Fig. 5.93: Circuit for Q.20

Unit 6

NETWORK FUNCTIONS

Contents ...

6.1 System Function or Network Functions

6.2 Poles and Zeros

6.3 Necessary Conditions for Transfer Function and Driving Point Function

6.4 Circuit with Active Devices

6.5 Time Domain Behaviour from Pole-Zero Plot

6.6 Magnitude and Phase (Frequency Domain) Response from Pole-Zero Plot

6.7 Pole Position and Stability

6.8 Parallel Resonating Circuit

    6.8.1 Antiresonating Frequency

    6.8.2 Reactance Curves

    6.8.3 Impedance of Parallel Resonance Circuit

    6.8.4 Currents in Antiresonant Circuits

    6.8.5 Bandwidth of Antiresonant Circuit

    6.8.6 General Case: Resistance present in both the Branches

    6.8.7 Applications of Parallel RCL Circuit

    6.8.8 Summary of Parallel Resonant Circuit

    6.8.9 Important Formulae

6.9 Numericals on Parallel Resonant Circuits

    Exercise

6.1 SYSTEM FUNCTION OR NETWORK FUNCTIONS

A network function $F(s)$ is a function of 's' relating transform of voltage and currents. The network may contain passive component dependent sources, **but must not contain any independence energy sources and initial conditions**.

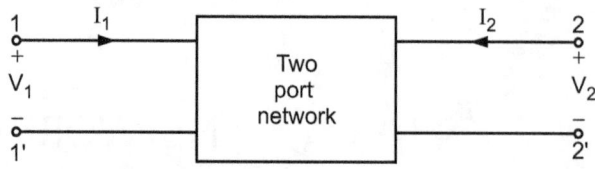

Fig. 6.1

In a linear network (system), excitation e (t) and response r (t) are related by linear differential equations. But when Laplace transform is used, then relation between E (s) and R (s) is algebraic.

Thus, $\quad R(s) = F(s) E(s) \quad$ ... (6.1)

F (s) is called system function. It assume many forms depending on whether excitation E (s) is voltage or current and response (R) is voltage or current.

Driving Point Functions: If excitation and response are measured at same pair of terminals, then it is called driving point function.

$$Z_{11}(s) = \frac{V_1(s)}{I_1(s)} \quad \text{... (a)}$$

is a driving point impedance function.

$$Z_{22}(s) = \frac{V_2(s)}{I_2(s)} \quad \text{... (b)}$$

is also driving point impedance function.

Thus, Z_{11} (s), Z_{22} (s) are transform impedances which are ratio of voltage transform to current transform at a port.

Similarly, $\quad Y_{22}(s) = \dfrac{I_2(s)}{V_2(s)}$

and $\quad Y_{11}(s) = \dfrac{I_1(s)}{V_1(s)}$

are transform admittances. Here they are called driving point admittance function.

Transfer Functions: If excitation and response are measured at separate terminal pairs, then it is called transfer function. For two port network, there are four types of transfer function.

Voltage transfer function, $\quad G_{21}(s) = \dfrac{V_2(s)}{V_1(s)} \quad$ ... (c)

Current transfer function, $\quad \alpha_{21}(s) = \dfrac{I_2(s)}{I_1(s)} \quad$ ... (d)

Transfer impedance function, $\quad Z_{21}(s) = \dfrac{V_2(s)}{I_1(s)} \quad$ ... (e)

Transfer admittance function, $\quad Y_{21}(s) = \dfrac{I_2(s)}{V_1(s)} \quad$ ... (f)

Following examples explain various types of network functions.

This is series R–L–C circuit which has only one port. Driving point impedance function for this is

$$Z(s) = R_1 + L_1 s + \frac{1}{C_1 s}$$

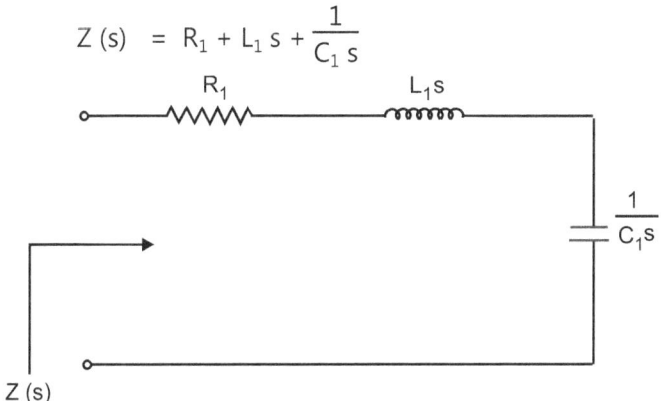

Fig. 6.2: One-port network

For this network, driving point admittance function is

$$Y(s) = Cs + \frac{1}{(R + sL)}$$

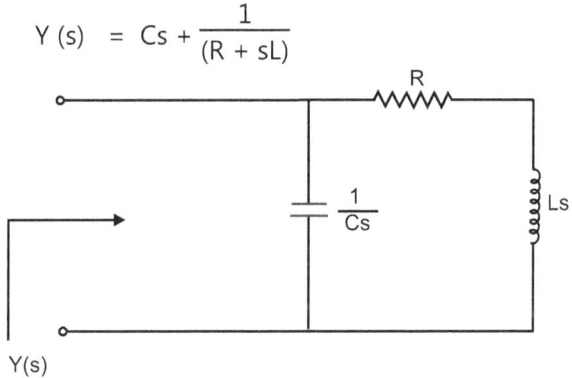

Fig. 6.3: One-port network

Thus for one port network only driving point impedance and admittance functions are define. Also $Z(s) = \frac{1}{Y(s)}$. But transfer functions are not defined.

Now consider two port network shown in Fig. 6.4.

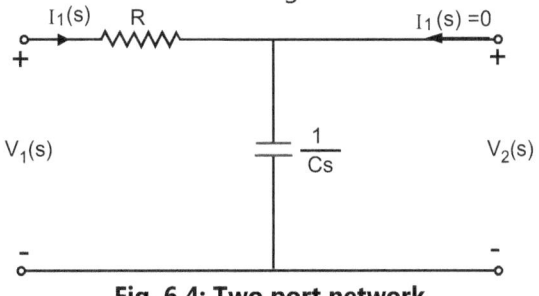

Fig. 6.4: Two port network

Driving point impedance function is

$$Z_{11}(s) = \frac{V_1(s)}{I_1(s)}$$

$$= R + \frac{1}{sC}$$

Transfer impedance function

$$Z_{21}(s) = \frac{V_2(s)}{I_1(s)}$$

$$= \frac{1}{sC}$$

Voltage ratio transfer function,

$$G_{21}(s) = \frac{\frac{1}{Cs} \cdot I_1(s)}{\left(R + \frac{1}{Cs}\right) I_1(s)}$$

i.e. $$G_{21}(s) = \frac{1}{1 + RCS}$$

Current ratio transfer function,

$$\alpha_{21}(s) = \frac{I_2(s)}{I_1(s)} = 0$$

Impedance functions and admittance functions together are called as immittance functions. For one port networks,

$$Z(s) = \frac{1}{Y(s)},$$

While for two port networks, usually,

$$Z_{12}(s) \neq \frac{1}{Y_{12}(s)}$$

In general, all network functions are the ratio of polynomial in s. The general form is

$$F(s) = \frac{p(s)}{q(s)}$$

$$= \frac{a_0 s^n + a_1 s^{n-1} + \ldots + a_n}{b_0 s^m + b_1 s^{m-1} + \ldots + b_m} \quad \ldots (6.2)$$

where 'n' is the degree of numerator polynomial and 'm' is the degree of denominator polynomial.

6.2 POLES AND ZEROS

As said above, in general network function F (s) is ratio of two polynomials of 's' and is written as

$$F(s) = \frac{p(s)}{q(s)} = \frac{a_0 s^n + a_1 s^{n-1} + \ldots + a_n}{b_0 s^m + b_1 s^{m-1} + \ldots + b_m} \quad \ldots (6.3)$$

where a, b are coefficients with real positive value with p (s) having 'n' roots, q (s) having 'm' roots.

Hence F (s) is rewritten as

$$F(s) = H \cdot \frac{(s - Z_1)(s - Z_2) \ldots (s - Z_n)}{(s - P_1)(s - P_2) \ldots (s - P_m)} \quad \ldots (6.4)$$

where $H = \dfrac{a_0}{b_0}$ is a constant.

Zeros: When $s = Z_1, Z_2, Z_3, \ldots, Z_n$ then network function F (s) = 0. **Hence complex frequencies, at which network function F (s) vanishes, are called as zeros of network function.** Roots of numerator polynomial p (s) are zeros of network functions.

Poles: When $s = P_1, P_2, \ldots, P_m$, then network function F (s) = ∞. **Hence complex frequencies at which value of network function F (s) becomes infinite are called as poles of network function.** Roots of denominator polynomial q (s) are poles of network functions.

Significance of Poles and Zeros:

Poles and zeros together with scale factor (H) completely specifies a network function. When two or more poles or zeros have same value then those poles or zeros are said to be repeated. Poles or zeros which are not at s = 0 or ∞ are said to be finite poles or zeros. For any rational network function, if poles and zeros at 0 and at ∞ are taken into account in addition to finite poles and zeros. Then,

Total number of poles = Total number of zeros

Poles and zeros are critical frequencies because at poles network function becomes '∞' while at zero network function becomes 0. At any other frequency network function has finite non-zero value. For example, if

$$Z_{11}(s) = \frac{V_1(s)}{I_1(s)}$$

then a pole of Z_{11} (s) implies zero current for finite value of driving voltage i.e. it signifies a open circuit. While zeros of Z_{11} (s) implies zero voltage V_1 (s) for finite value of driving point current i.e. it signifies a short circuit.

Representation of Poles and Zeros:

Poles and zeros are represented on a complex 's' plane. Poles are marked 'X' while zeros are marked as '0'.

For example, if $F(s) = \dfrac{s^2(s+4)}{(s+1)(s^2+4s+5)}$

then, $F(s) = \dfrac{s^2(s+4)}{(s+1)(s+2+j1)(s+2-j1)}$

This is represented as

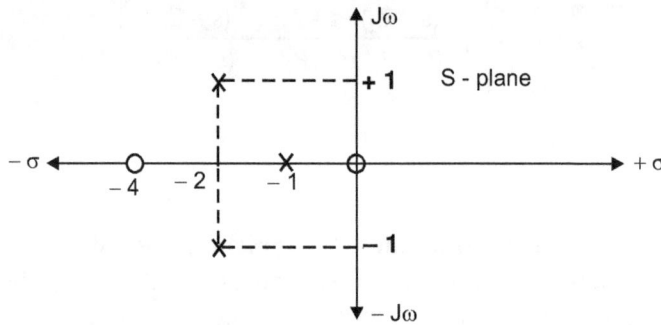

Fig. 6.5: Pole - zero locations

Note that there are two zeros at origin. Also complex poles and zeros always occur in conjugate.

6.3 NECESSARY CONDITIONS FOR TRANSFER FUNCTION AND DRIVING POINT FUNCTION

When given network is dissipationless (loss less) then network has only imaginary poles and zeros.

A network function having poles and zeros, which are real or complex, is stable if real part of poles and zeros are negative i.e. poles and zeros are lying in left half of s-plane.

Necessary condition for driving point function:

1. Coefficient in polynomial p(s) and q(s) of $F(s) = \dfrac{p(s)}{q(s)}$ must be real and positive.
2. Complex and imaginary poles and zeros occur in conjugate.
3. Polynomial p(s), q(s) must not have missing terms between highest and lowest degree unless all even or odd terms missing.
4. Real part of all poles and zeros must be negative and not positive. If real part is zero, then pole and zero must be simple.
5. p(s) and q(s) must differ at most by one in highest or lowest degree.

Necessary condition for transfer function:

For a given network function F (s) to be a transfer function,
1. Coefficients in polynomials p (s) and q (s) must be real and those of q (s) must be positive.
2. Imaginary or complex poles and zeros are conjugate.
3. Real part of poles must be negative. If it is zero, then it must be simple pole.
4. Polynomial q (s) must not have any missing term between highest and lowest degree unless all even or odd terms missing.
5. Polynomial p (s) may have terms missing between highest and lowest degree and some coefficient may be negative.
6. Degree of p (s) may be as small as zero independent of degree of q (s).
7. For G_{21} and α_{12}, p (s) and q (s) must have same highest degree.
8. For Z_{21} and Y_{21} highest degree of p (s) is greater than q (s) by unity.

SOLVED EXAMPLES

Ex. 6.1: Poles and zeros plot of a voltage transfer function is as shown. D.C. gain is 10. Find transfer function.

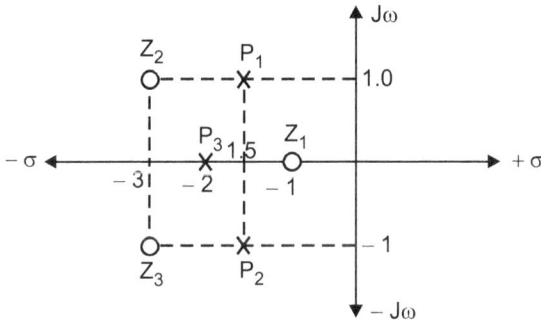

Fig. 6.6: Pole-zero plot for Ex. 6.1

Sol.: Zeros are at
$Z_1 = -1$
$Z_2 = -3 + j1$
$Z_3 = -3 - j1$

Poles are at
$P_1 = -1.5 + j1$
$P_2 = -1.5 - j1$
$P_3 = -2$

Hence transfer function is

$$T(s) = K \frac{(s+1)(s+3+j1)(s+3-j1)}{(s+2)(s+1.5+j1)(s+1.5-j1)}$$

$$= K \frac{(s+1)(s^2+6s+10)}{(s+2)(s^2+3s+3.25)}$$

Since d.c. gain is 10, i.e. T (s) = 10 for d.c. (s = 0),

∴ $\quad 10 = \dfrac{K \times 1 \times 10}{2 \times 3.25}$

∴ $\quad K = 6.5$

Hence required transfer function is

$$T(s) = \dfrac{6.5\,(s+1)\,(s^2+6s+10)}{(s+2)\,(s^2+3s+3.25)}$$

Ex. 6.2: For the network shown determine transfer function $Y_{21}(s)$ and plot the pole-zeros of $Y_{21}(s)$.

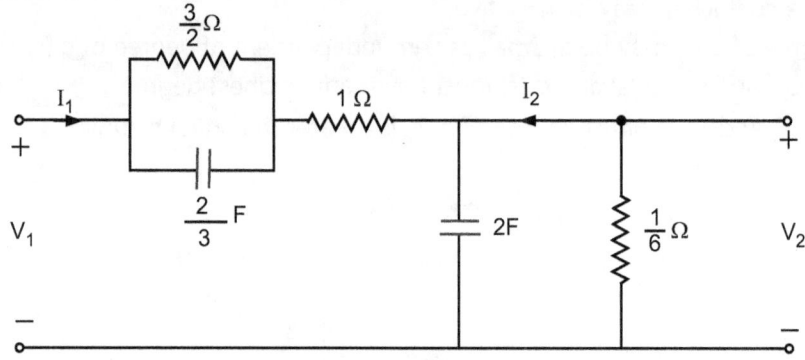

Fig. 6.7: Circuit for Ex. 6.2

Sol.: Transformed circuit of the network given is

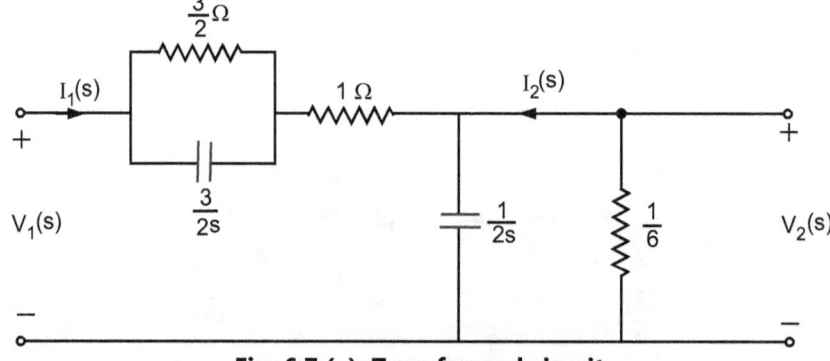

Fig. 6.7 (a): Transformed circuit

Now, $\quad Y_{21}(s) = \dfrac{I_2(s)}{V_1(s)}$

$$V_2(s) = \dfrac{\dfrac{1}{2s} \times \dfrac{1}{6}}{\dfrac{1}{2s} + \dfrac{1}{6}} \times I_1(s)$$

$$= \dfrac{1}{6+2s} \times I_1(s)$$

Chp 6 | 6.8

$$V_1(s) = \frac{I_1(s)}{6+2s} + \left(\frac{\frac{3}{2} \times \frac{3}{2s}}{\frac{3}{2} + \frac{3}{2s}} + 1\right) I_1(s)$$

$$= \frac{I_1(s)}{6+2s} + \left(\frac{9}{6s+6} + 1\right) I_1(s)$$

$$= \frac{I_1(s)}{6+2s} + \frac{s+2.5}{(s+1)} I_1(s)$$

$$= \frac{I_1(s)}{1} \left[\frac{0.5}{(s+3)} + \frac{s+2.5}{(s+1)}\right]$$

$$= I_1(s) \left[\frac{0.5 + 0.5s + s^2 + 5.5s + 7.5}{(s+1)(s+3)}\right]$$

$$= I_1(s) \left[\frac{s^2 + 6s + 8}{(s+1)(s+3)}\right]$$

$$= I_1(s) \left[\frac{(s+4)(s+2)}{(s+1)(s+3)}\right]$$

Also,
$$I_2(s) = -6V_2(s) = -6 \times \frac{I_1(s)}{2(s+3)}$$

$$= -3 \times \frac{I_1(s)}{(s+3)}$$

$$Y_{21}(s) = \frac{I_2(s)}{V_1(s)} = -\frac{3}{(s+3)} \times \frac{(s+1)(s+3)}{(s+4)(s+2)}$$

$$= -3 \times \frac{(s+1)}{(s+4)(s+2)}$$

Pole-zero plot is shown below.

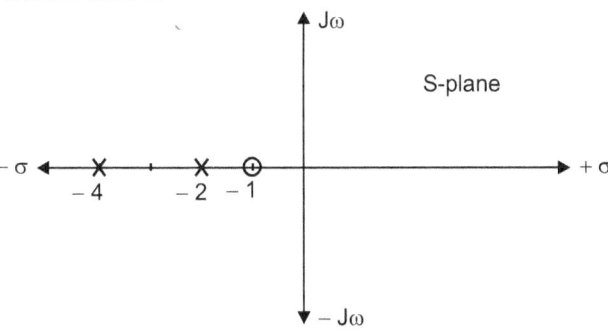

Fig. 6.7 (b): Pole-zero plot

Ex. 6.3: For the network determine voltage ratio $\dfrac{V_2}{V_1}$, current ratio $\dfrac{I_2}{I_1}$ and transfer impedance $\dfrac{V_2}{I_1}$.

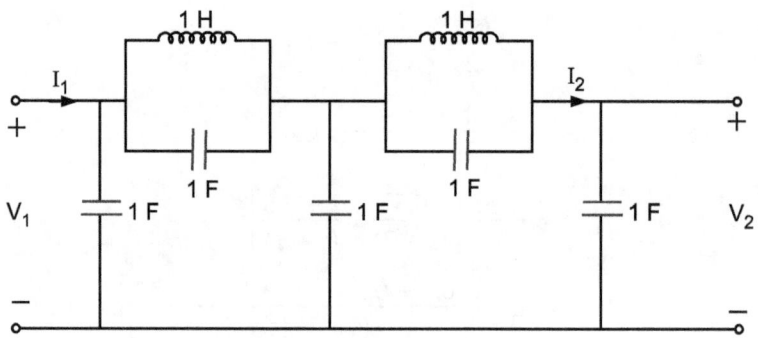

Fig. 6.8: Circuit for Ex. 6.3

Sol.: Transformed circuit is as shown below.

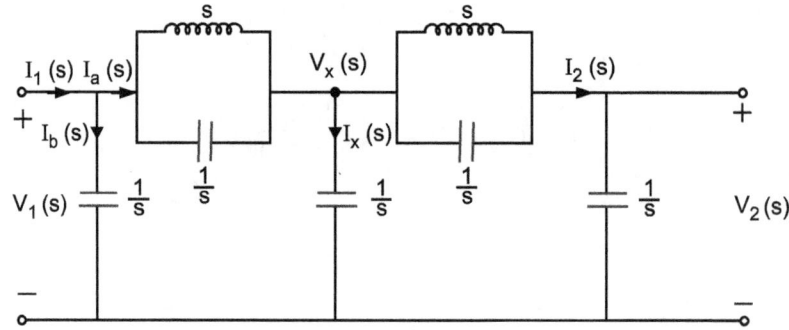

Fig. 6.8 (a): Transformed circuit

We have, $V_2(s) \times s = I_2(s)$

$$V_x(s) = V_2(s) + \left[\dfrac{s \times \dfrac{1}{s}}{s + \dfrac{1}{s}}\right] I_2(s)$$

$$= V_2(s) + \dfrac{s}{s^2 + 1} \times s \cdot V_2(s)$$

$$= V_2(s)\left[1 + \dfrac{s^2}{s^2 + 1}\right]$$

$$= V_2(s)\left[\dfrac{1 + 2s^2}{1 + s^2}\right]$$

$$I_x(s) = sV_x(s) = s\left[\frac{1+2s^2}{1+s^2}\right]V_2(s)$$

$$I_a(s) = I_x(s) + I_2(s)$$

$$= \left[\frac{s(1+2s^2)}{1+s^2} + s\right]V_2(s)$$

$$= \left[\frac{s^3 + s + s + 2s^3}{(1+s^2)}\right]V_2(s)$$

$$= \frac{3s^3 + 2s}{(1+s^2)} \times V_2(s)$$

$$\therefore \quad I_a(s) = \frac{s(2+3s^2)}{(1+s^2)} \times V_2(s)$$

$$V_1(s) = V_x(s) + \left[\frac{s}{s^2+1}\right] \times I_a(s)$$

$$V_1(s) = V_2(s)\left[\frac{(1+2s^2)}{(1+s^2)} + \frac{s^2(3s^2+2)}{(1+s^2)^2}\right] \quad \ldots (2)$$

$$I_1(s) = I_a(s) + I_b(s)$$

$$= V_2(s)\left[\frac{s(3s^2+2)}{1+s^2}\right] + sV_1(s)$$

$$= V_2(s)\left[\frac{s(3s^2+2)}{(1+s^2)} + \frac{s(1+2s^2)}{(a+s^2)} + \frac{s^3(2+3s^2)}{(1+s^2)^2}\right]$$

$$I_1(s) = V_2(s)\left[\frac{s(3s^2+2)(1+s^2) + s(1+2s^2)(1+s^2) + s^3(2+3s^2)}{(1+s^2)^2}\right]$$

$$I_1(s) = V_2(s)\left[\frac{3s^5 + 5s^3 + 2s + 2s^5 + 3s^3 + s + 3s^5 + 2s^3}{(1+s^2)^2}\right] \quad \ldots (3)$$

Hence by (1), (2) and (3), we have,

$$\frac{V_2(s)}{V_1(s)} = \frac{(1+s^2)^2}{3s^4 + 2s^2 + 2s^4 + 3s^2 + 1} = \frac{(1+s^2)^2}{5s^4 + 5s^2 + 1}$$

$$\frac{I_2(s)}{I_1(s)} = \frac{s(1+s^2)^2}{8s^5 + 10s^3 + 3s}$$

$$\frac{V_2(s)}{I_1(s)} = \frac{(1+s^2)^2}{(8s^5 + 10s^3 + 3s)}$$

Ex. 6.4: Find ratio $\dfrac{V_2}{V_1}$ for the circuit shown in Fig. 6.9.

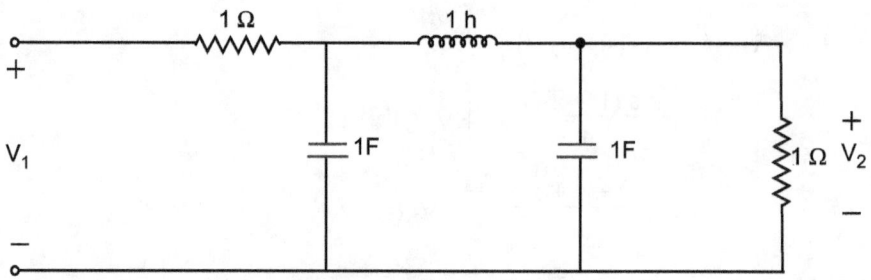

Fig. 6.9: Circuit for Ex. 6.4

Sol.: Transformed circuit is shown below.

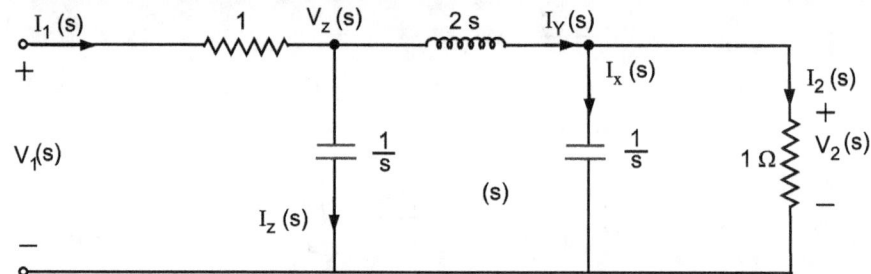

Fig. 6.9 (a): Transformed circuit

Now,
$$I_2(s) = V_2(s)$$
$$I_x(s) = sV_2(s)$$
$$I_y(s) = I_x(s) + I_2(s) = V_2(s)[1+s]$$
$$V_z(s) = V_2(s) + 2s \times I_y(s) = V_2(s)[1 + 2s(s+1)]$$
$$I_z(s) = sV_z(s) = V_2(s) \cdot s[1 + 2s(s+1)]$$
$$I_1(s) = I_z(s) + I_y(s)$$
$$= V_2(s)\left[1 + s + s[1 + 2s(s+1)]\right]$$
$$= V_2(s)[1 + s + s + 2s^3 + 2s^2]$$
$$= V_2(s)[2s^3 + 2s^2 + 2s + 1]$$
$$V_1(s) = V_z(s) + V_2(s)[2s^3 + 2s^2 + 2s + 1]$$
$$= V_2(s)[1 + 2s^2 + 2s + 2s^3 + 2s^2 + 2s + 1]$$
$$= V_2(s)[2s^3 + 4s^2 + 4s + 2]$$

$$\dfrac{V_2(s)}{V_1(s)} = \dfrac{1}{2s^3 + 4s^2 + 4s + 2}$$

Ex. 6.5: (1) For the network shown with port 2 open, show that input impedance at port '1' is 1 Ω.

(2) Find voltage ratio transfer function.

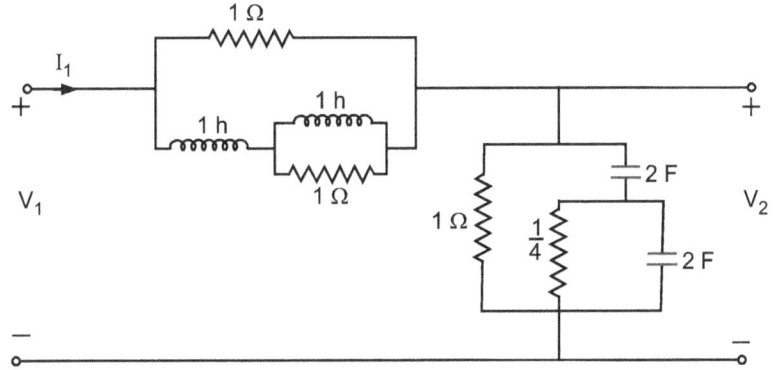

Fig. 6.10: Circuit for Ex. 6.5

Sol.: Transformed circuit will be

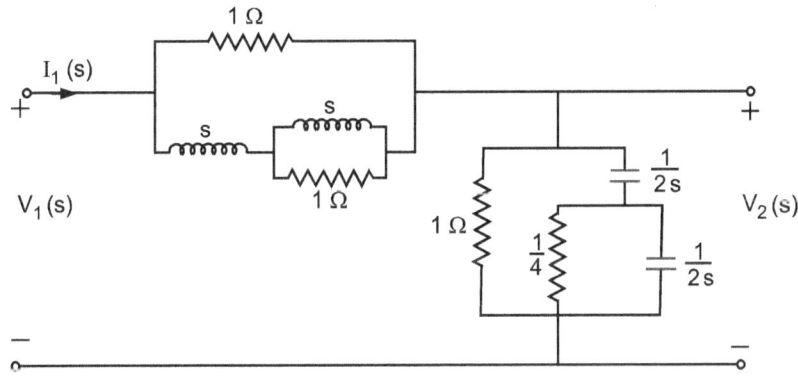

Fig. 6.10 (a): Transformed circuit

The circuit can be written as

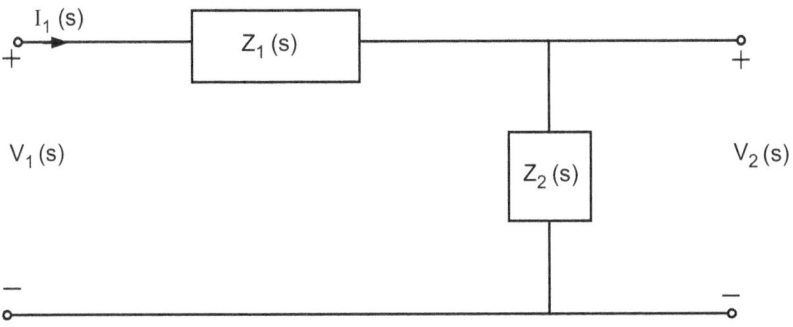

Fig. 6.10 (b): Simplified circuit

$$Z_1(s) = 1 \| s + \frac{s}{s+1} = 1 \| \left(\frac{s^2 + 2s}{s+1}\right)$$

$$= \frac{\left(\frac{s^2+2s}{s+1}\right)}{\left(\frac{s^2+2s}{s+1}+1\right)} = \frac{s^2+2s}{s^2+3s+1}$$

$$Z_2(s) = 1 \| \left(\frac{1}{2s} + \frac{1}{2s+4}\right) = 1 \| \left(\frac{4s+4}{2s \times (2s+4)}\right)$$

$$= \frac{1 \times \frac{(s+1) \times 2}{(2s^2+4s)}}{1 + \frac{2(s+1)}{2s^2+4s}} = \frac{(s+1)\,2}{(2s^2+4s)+2(s+1)}$$

$$= \frac{2(s+1)}{2(s^2+3s+1)} = \frac{s+1}{(s^2+3s+1)}$$

(1) Hence input impedance at port '1' is

$$Z_{in} = Z_1(s) + Z_2(s)$$

$$= \frac{s^2+2s}{s^2+3s+1} + \frac{(s+1)}{(s^2+3s+1)}$$

$$= \frac{s^2+3s+1}{s^2+3s+1} = 1\,\Omega$$

(2) Voltage ratio transfer function

$$= \frac{V_2(s)}{V_1(s)} = \frac{Z_2(s)}{Z_2(s)+Z_1(s)} = \frac{Z_2(s)}{1} = \frac{(s+1)}{(s^2+3s+1)}$$

Ex. 6.6: Show that with $Z_a \times Z_b = R_o^2$ in the bridged 'T' network,

$$\frac{V_2}{V_1} = \frac{1}{1 + \frac{Z_a}{R_o}}$$

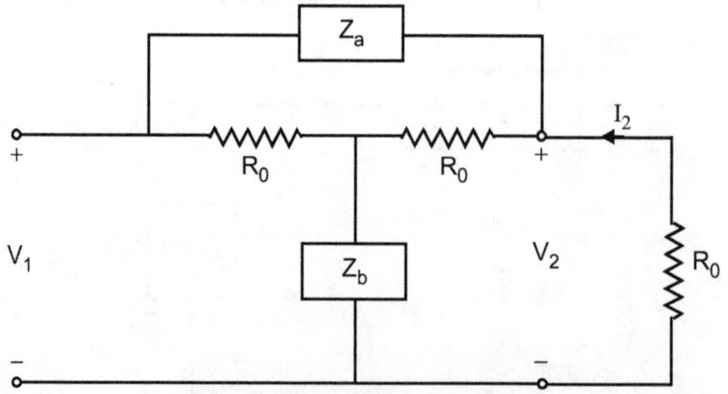

Fig. 6.11: Circuit for Ex. 6.6

Sol.: Converting 'T' network into π network, the given circuit can be written as

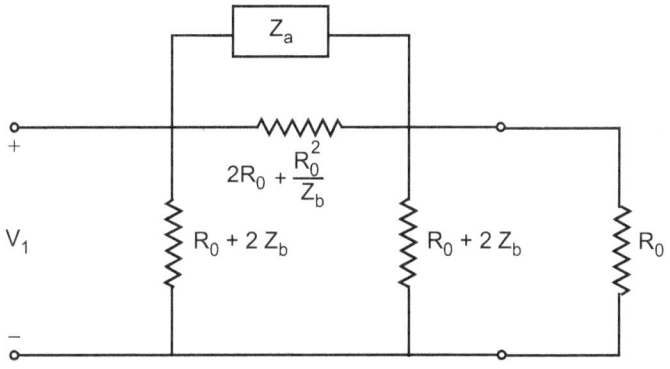

Fig. 6.11 (a): Equivalent circuit

Let
$$Z_2 = R_0 \parallel (R_0 + 2Z_b)$$
$$= \frac{R_0 (R_0 + 2Z_b)}{2(Z_b + R_0)}$$

$$Z_1 = Z_a \parallel (2R_0 + Z_a)$$
$$= \frac{Z_a (2R_0 + Z_a)}{(2R_0 + 2Z_a)}$$

$$= \frac{Z_a (Z_a + 2R_0)}{2(R_0 + Z_a)} \qquad \text{where } Z_a = \frac{R_0^2}{Z_b}$$

$$\therefore V_2(s) = \frac{Z_2}{Z_1 + Z_2} V_1(s)$$

$$\therefore \frac{V_2(s)}{V_1(s)} = \frac{Z_2}{Z_1 + Z_2}$$

$$\therefore \frac{V_2(s)}{V_1(s)} = \frac{1}{1 + \frac{Z_1}{Z_2}}$$

$$= \frac{1}{1 + \frac{Z_a (Z_a + 2R_0)(Z_b + R_0)}{R_0 (R_0 + Z_a)(R_0 + 2Z_b)}}$$

$$= \frac{1}{1 + \frac{Z_a}{Z_0} \cdot \frac{(Z_a \times Z_b + 2R_0^2 + R_0 Z_a + 2Z_b R_0)}{(R_0^2 + 2Z_a Z_b + R_0 Z_a + 2Z_b R_0)}} \qquad (\because Z_a Z_b = R_0^2)$$

$$= \frac{1}{1 + \frac{Z_a}{Z_0}} \quad \text{hence proof.}$$

Ex. 6.7: For the bridge 'T' network shown calculate following network functions.

(1) $Z_{11}(s)$, (2) $Z_{22}(s)$, (3) $Z_{12}(s)$, (4) $G_{21}(s)$, (5) $\alpha_{21}(s)$

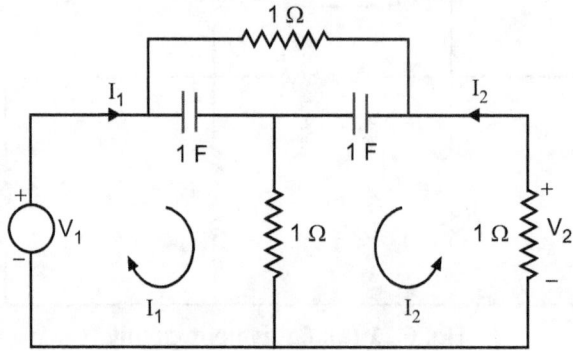

Fig. 6.12: Circuit for Ex. 6.7

Sol.: Transformed circuit is as shown in Fig. 6.12.

KVL across $I_1(s)$ is

$$\left(1 + \frac{1}{s}\right) \times I_1(s) + 1 \cdot I_2(s) - \frac{1}{s} I_3(s) = V_1(s)$$

KVL across $I_2(s)$ is

$$I_1(s) + \left(2 + \frac{1}{s}\right) I_2(s) + \frac{1}{s} I_3(s) = 0$$

KVL across $I_3(s)$ is

$$-\frac{1}{s} I_1(s) + \frac{1}{s} I_2(s) + \left(1 + \frac{2}{s}\right) I_3(s) = 0$$

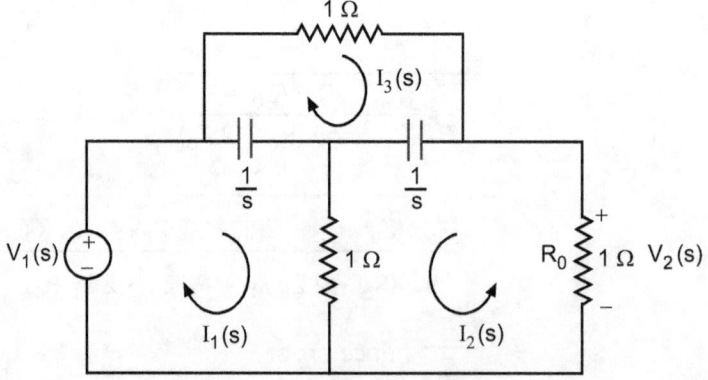

Fig. 6.12 (a): Transformed circuit

Solving for $I_2(s)$ and $I_1(s)$

$$\Delta = \begin{vmatrix} \left(1+\dfrac{1}{s}\right) & 1 & -\dfrac{1}{s} \\ 1 & \left(2+\dfrac{1}{s}\right) & +\dfrac{1}{s} \\ -\dfrac{1}{s} & \dfrac{1}{s} & \left(1+\dfrac{2}{s}\right) \end{vmatrix}$$

$$\Delta = \left(1+\dfrac{1}{s}\right)\left[\left(2+\dfrac{1}{s}\right)+\left(1+\dfrac{2}{s}\right)-\dfrac{1}{s^2}\right] - 1\left(1+\dfrac{2}{s}\right) - \dfrac{1}{s^2} - \dfrac{1}{s^2}\left(2+\dfrac{1}{s}\right) - \dfrac{1}{s^2}$$

$$= \left(1+\dfrac{1}{s}\right)\left[2+\dfrac{4}{s}+\dfrac{1}{s}+\dfrac{2}{s^2}-\dfrac{1}{s^2}\right] - 1 - \dfrac{2}{s} - \dfrac{1}{s^2} - \dfrac{1}{s^3} - \dfrac{2}{s^2} - \dfrac{1}{s^2}$$

$$= \dfrac{2}{1}+\dfrac{5}{s}+\dfrac{1}{s^2}+\dfrac{2}{s}+\dfrac{5}{s^2}+\dfrac{1}{s^3} - 1 - \dfrac{1}{s^3} - \dfrac{2}{s^2} - \dfrac{2}{s} - \dfrac{2}{s^2}$$

$$= 1 + \dfrac{2}{s^2} + \dfrac{5}{s}$$

$$= \dfrac{(s^2+5s+2)}{s^2}$$

$$\Delta_1 = \begin{vmatrix} 2+\dfrac{1}{s} & \dfrac{1}{s} \\ \dfrac{1}{s} & \left(1+\dfrac{2}{s}\right) \end{vmatrix}$$

$$= \left(2+\dfrac{1}{s}\right)\left(1+\dfrac{2}{s}\right) - \dfrac{1}{s^2} = \dfrac{2s^2+5s+1}{s^2}$$

$$\Delta_2 = \begin{vmatrix} 1 & \dfrac{1}{s} \\ -\dfrac{1}{s} & \left(1+\dfrac{2}{s}\right) \end{vmatrix}$$

$$= 1 + \dfrac{2}{s} + \dfrac{1}{s^2} = \dfrac{s^2+2s+1}{s^2}$$

$\therefore \qquad I_1(s) = \dfrac{\Delta_1}{\Delta} V_1(s)$

Hence, $\quad Z_{11}(s) = \dfrac{V_1(s)}{I_1(s)} = \dfrac{\Delta}{\Delta_1} = \dfrac{s^2 + 5s + 2}{2s^2 + 5s + 1}$

$V_2(s) = -R_0 I_2(s)$ But $R_0 = 1$

$\quad\quad\quad = -1 \cdot \dfrac{\Delta_2}{\Delta} V_1(s)$

Hence, $\quad G_{21}(s) = \dfrac{V_2(s)}{V_1(s)} = -\dfrac{s^2 + 2s + 1}{s^2 + 5s + 2}$ ... Ans.

$\alpha_{21}(s) = \dfrac{I_2(s)}{I_1(s)} = \dfrac{\Delta_2}{\Delta_1} = \dfrac{s^2 + 2s + 1}{2s^2 + 5s + 1}$

$Z_{12}(s) = \dfrac{V_1(s)}{I_2(s)} = \dfrac{\Delta}{\Delta_2} = \dfrac{s^2 + 5s + 2}{s^2 + 2s + 1} = Z_{12}(s)$

Ex. 6.8: Find impedance function $\dfrac{V(s)}{I(s)}$ of the network.

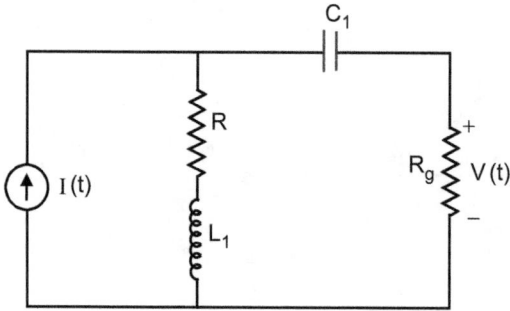

Fig. 6.13: Circuit for Ex. 6.8

Sol.: Transformed circuit is

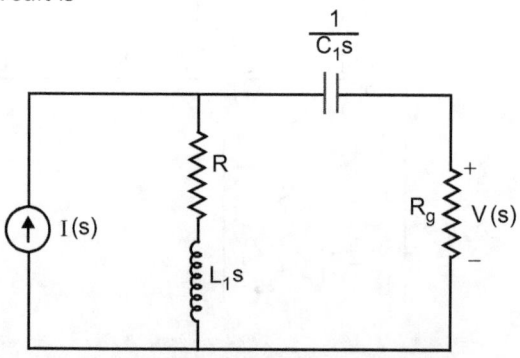

Fig. 6.13 (a): Transformed circuit

Using current divider current through resistor R_g is given by

$$\dfrac{I(s) \times (R + sL_1)}{(R + R_g) + L_1 s + \dfrac{1}{C_1 s}}$$

Hence, voltage, $V(s) = \dfrac{R_g(R + sL_1)\, I(s)}{(R + R_g) + \left(sL_1 + \dfrac{1}{C_1 s}\right)}$

∴ Impedance function $\dfrac{V(s)}{I(s)} = \dfrac{R_g(R + sL_1)}{(R + R_g) + \left[L_1 s + \dfrac{1}{C_1 s}\right]}$

Ex. 6.9: Write nodal equation for R.C. ladder network and determine function $\dfrac{V_o}{V_i}$.

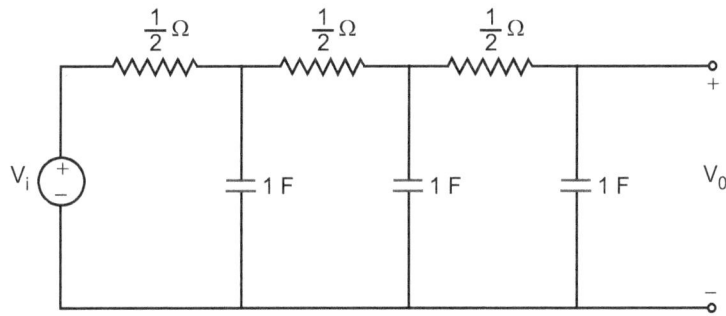

Fig. 6.14: Circuit for Ex. 6.9

Sol.: Transformed circuit is

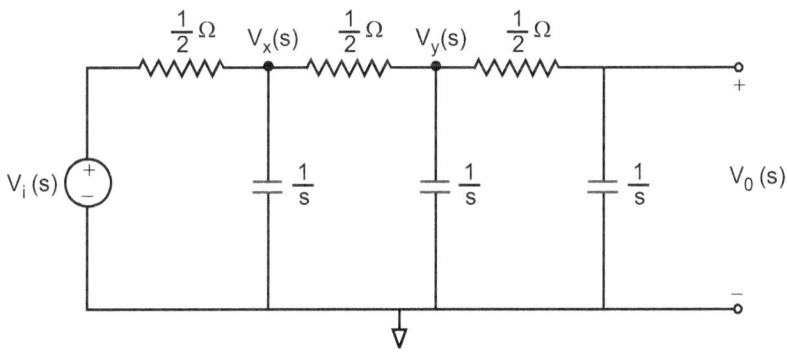

Fig. 6.14 (a): Transformed circuit

Let $V_x(s)$, $V_y(s)$ be unknown node voltages. KCL at $V_x(s)$ gives

$$\dfrac{V_i(s) - V_x(s)}{\tfrac{1}{2}} = \dfrac{V_s(s)}{\tfrac{1}{s}} + \dfrac{V_x(s) - V_y(s)}{\tfrac{1}{2}}$$

or
$2V_i(s) = 2V_x(s) + sV_x(s) + 2V_x(s) - 2V_y(s)$

$2V_i(s) = V_x(s)(4 + s) - 2V_y(s)$ ... (1)

KCL at $V_y(s)$ gives

$$2[V_y(s) - V_x(s)] + sV_y(s) + \frac{2s\,V_y(s)}{s+2} = 0$$

$$\Rightarrow V_y(s)\left[2 + s + \frac{2s}{s+2}\right] = 2V_x(s) \qquad \ldots (2)$$

Substitute $V_x(s)$ from (2) in equation (1),

$$2V_i(s) = (4+s)\left[1 + \frac{s}{2} + \frac{s}{s+2}\right]V_y(s) - 2V_y(s)$$

$$= V_y(s)\left[(4+s)\left(1 + \frac{s}{2} + \frac{s}{s+2}\right) - 2\right]$$

$$\Rightarrow 2V_i(s) = V_y(s)\left[4 + 2s + \frac{4s}{s+2} + s + \frac{s^2}{2} + \frac{s^2}{s+2} - 2\right]$$

$$= V_y(s)\left[\frac{4(s+2) + 6s(s+2) + 2(s^2+4s) + s^2(s+2)}{2(s+2)}\right]$$

$$= V_y(s)\left[\frac{4s + 8 + 6s^2 + 12s + 2s^2 + 8s + s^3 + 2s}{(s+2)2}\right]$$

$$= V_y(s)\left[\frac{s^3 + 8s^2 + 26s + 8}{(s+2)2}\right]$$

$$\therefore V_y(s) = \frac{4(s+2)}{(s^3 + 8s^2 + 26s + 8)} \times V_i(s)$$

Now using voltage divider relation,

$$V_o(s) = \frac{\frac{1}{s}V_y(s)}{\frac{1}{s} + \frac{1}{2}} = \frac{2V_y(s)}{(s+2)}$$

$$= \frac{8V_i(s)}{s^3 + 8s^2 + 26s + 8}$$

Hence, $\dfrac{V_o(s)}{V_i(s)} = \dfrac{8}{s^3 + 8s^2 + 26s + 8}$ ... **Ans.**

6.4 CIRCUIT WITH ACTIVE DEVICES

So far we have studied system functions of the circuit containing only R, L, C elements. But circuit can contain voltage or current source whose value depends upon voltage across or current through some other part of circuit. These are called controlled sources.

They are of four types which are shown below in Fig. 6.15 with their symbols.

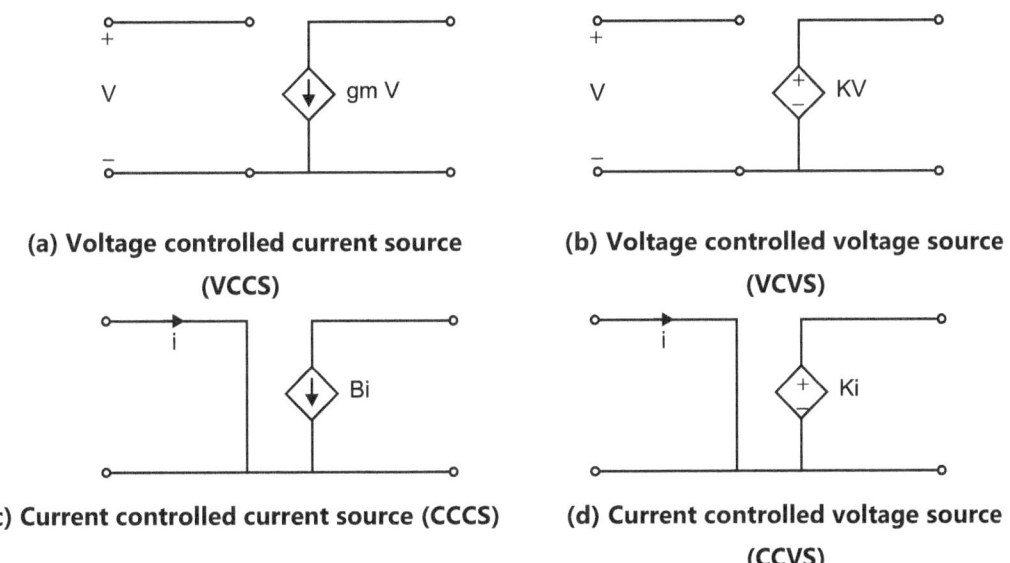

(a) Voltage controlled current source (VCCS)

(b) Voltage controlled voltage source (VCVS)

(c) Current controlled current source (CCCS)

(d) Current controlled voltage source (CCVS)

Fig. 6.15: Controlled sources

Operational amplifier is another active device. Transfer function of which is obtained assuming following ideal characteristic:

1. Input impedance (r_i) is infinity.
2. Output impedance (r_o) is zero.
3. Open loop gain (A) is infinity.
4. Inverting and non-inverting inputs are virtual short.

Ex. 6.10: For the circuit find voltage ratio $\dfrac{V_o}{V_i}$ and plot pole-zero on S-plane.

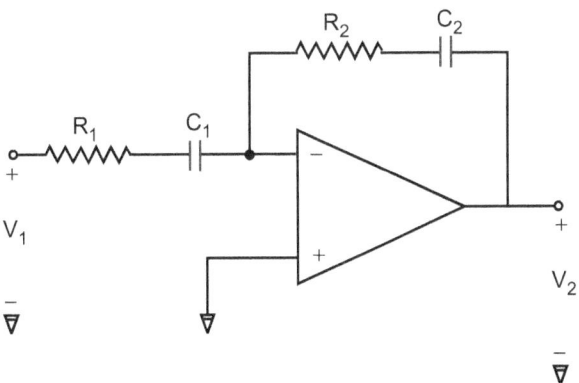

Fig. 6.16: Circuit for Ex. 6.10

Sol.: If $\quad Z_1(s) = R_1 + \dfrac{1}{C_1 s} = \dfrac{1 + R_1 C_1 s}{C_1 s}$

and $\quad Z_2(s) = R_2 + \dfrac{1}{C_2 s} = \dfrac{1 + R_2 C_2 s}{C_2 s}$

Pole-zero plot if $R_1 C_1 > R_2 C_2$ is shown in Fig. 6.16 (a).

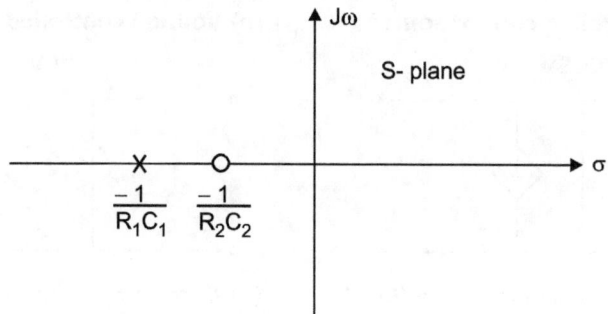

Fig. 6.16 (a) Pole-zero plot

Then, $\quad \dfrac{V_2(s)}{V_1(s)} = -\dfrac{Z_2(s)}{Z_1(s)}$

$$= -\dfrac{C_1}{C_2} \cdot \dfrac{(1 + R_2 C_2 s)}{(1 + R_1 C_1 s)}$$

There is zero at $\quad s = -\dfrac{1}{R_2 C_2}$

Plot at $\quad s = -\dfrac{1}{R_1 C_1}$

Ex. 6.11: Find transfer function $\dfrac{V_2(s)}{V_1(s)}$ and plot pole-zero.

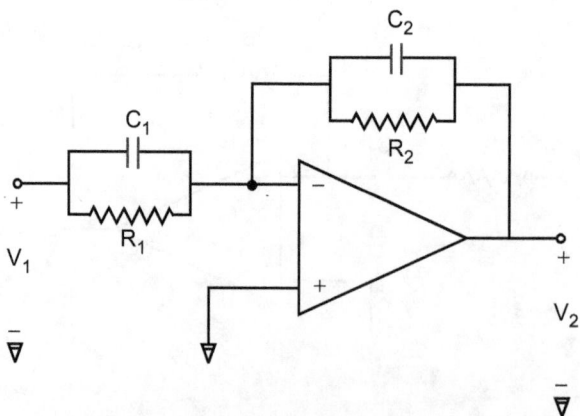

Fig. 6.17: Circuit for Ex. 6.11

Sol.: Here
$$Z_1(s) = R_1 \| \frac{1}{C_1 s} = \frac{R_1 \times \frac{1}{C_1 s}}{R_1 + \frac{1}{C_1 s}} = \frac{R_1}{1 + R_1 C_1 s}$$

$$Z_2(s) = R_2 \| \frac{1}{C_2 s} = \frac{R_2}{1 + R_2 C_2 s}$$

Hence,
$$\frac{V_2(s)}{V_1(s)} = \frac{Z_2(s)}{Z_1(s)} = \frac{-R_2}{R_1} \cdot \frac{(1 + R_1 C_1 s)}{(1 + R_2 C_2 s)}$$

the zero is at $s = -\dfrac{1}{R_1 C_1}$

Pole is at $s = -\dfrac{1}{R_2 C_2}$

Pole-zero plot if $R_1 C_1 > R_2 C_2$ is

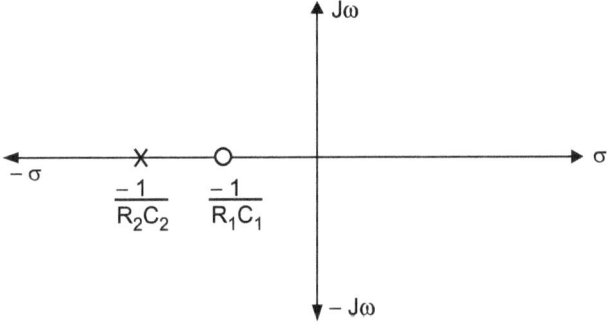

Fig. 6.17 (a)

Ex. 6.12: Find transfer function $T(s) = \dfrac{V_2(s)}{V_1(s)}$ and plot pole-zero diagram.

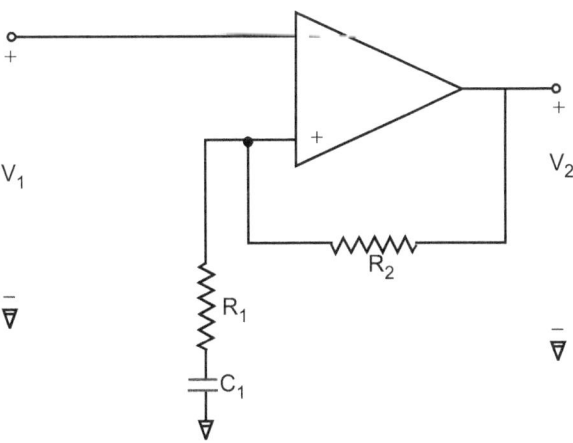

Fig. 6.18: Circuit for Ex. 6.12

Sol.: If $Z_1(s) = R_1 + \dfrac{1}{C_1 s} = \dfrac{1 + R_1 C_1 s}{C_1 s}$

Then since this is non-inverting amplifier,

$$T(s) = \dfrac{V_2(s)}{V_1(s)} = 1 + \dfrac{R_2}{Z_1(s)} = 1 + \dfrac{R_2 C_1 s}{(1 + R_1 C_1 s)} = \dfrac{1 + (R_1 C_1 + R_2 C_1) s}{1 + R_1 C_1 s}$$

Zero is at $\quad s = -\dfrac{1}{R_1 C_1 + R_2 C_1}$

Pole is at $\quad s = -\dfrac{1}{R_1 C_1}$

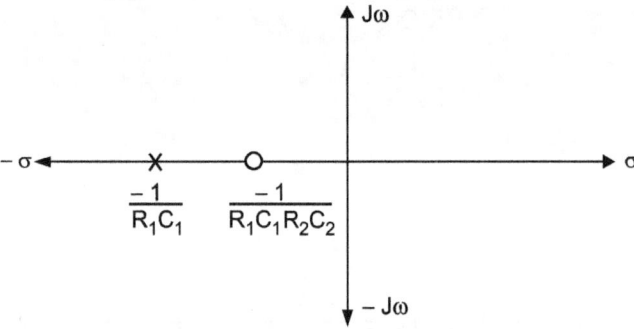

Fig. 6.18 (a): Pole-zero plot

Since input impedance of OP-AMP is ideally infinite and output impedance is zero, there is absolutely no loading from one stage to other stage when OP-AMPs are cascaded. Hence for cascaded OP-AMPs overall transfer function is multiplication transfer function of individual stage.

Following example explains this.

Ex. 6.13: For the cascaded OP-AMP find overall transfer function

$$T(s) = \dfrac{V_2(s)}{V_1(s)}$$

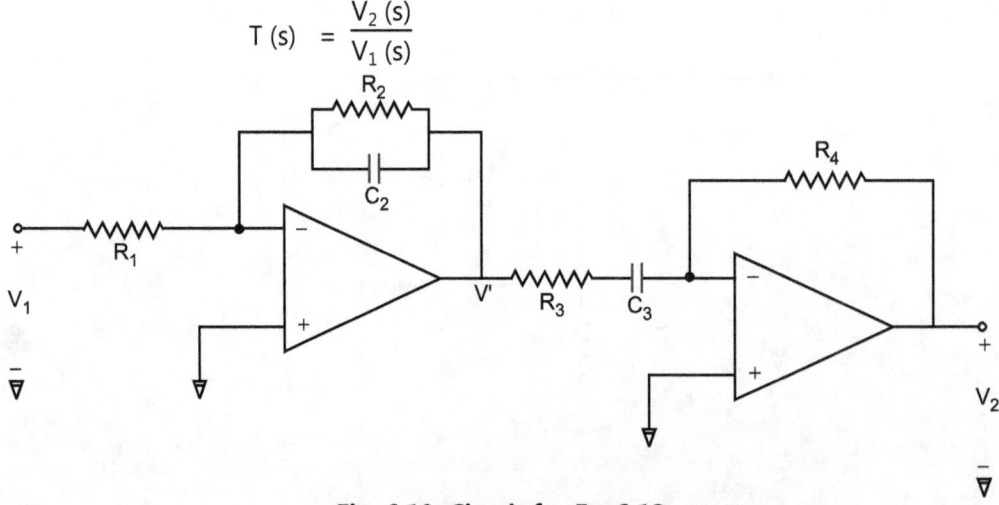

Fig. 6.19: Circuit for Ex. 6.13

Sol.: Let $T_1(s)$ be transfer function of first OP-AMP.

i.e. $$T_1(s) = \frac{V'(s)}{V_1(s)}$$

$$= -\frac{\left(\dfrac{R_2 \times \dfrac{1}{C_2 s}}{R_2 + \dfrac{1}{C_2 s}}\right)}{R_1}$$

$$= \frac{-R_2/R_1}{1 + R_2 C_2 s}$$

Let $T_2(s)$ be transfer function of second OP-AMP.

$$T_2(s) = \frac{V_2(s)}{V'(s)}$$

$$= -\frac{R_4}{R_3 + \dfrac{1}{C_3 s}} = -\frac{R_4 C_3 s}{1 + R_3 C_3 s}$$

Hence overall transfer function $T(s)$ is

$$T(s) = T_1(s) \times T_2(s)$$

$$= \frac{R_2}{R_1} \cdot \frac{R_4 C_3 s}{(1 + R_2 C_2 s)(1 + R_3 C_3 s)}$$

6.5 TIME DOMAIN BEHAVIOUR FROM POLE-ZERO PLOT

Time domain behaviour of a system can be determined from pole-zero plot of the system function on S-plane.

For example, let a driving voltage $V(s)$ be applied to a network having a impedance $Z(s)$ then,

Current, $$I(s) = \frac{V(s)}{Z(s)} = \frac{P(s)}{q(s)} = F(s)$$

where $$\frac{P(s)}{q(s)} = \frac{H(s - Z_1)(s - Z_2) \ldots (s - Z_n)}{(s - P_1)(s - P_2) \ldots (s - P_m)} \quad \ldots m > n$$

$$= \frac{K_1}{(s - P_1)} + \frac{K_2}{(s - P_2)} + \ldots$$

K_1 and K_2 etc. are called residue at P_1 and P_2 etc.

The poles determine the time domain behaviour of $i(t)$. Scale factor H and zeros together with poles determine magnitude of each term of $i(t)$.

Graphical method for determination of residue:

Let
$$F(s) = \frac{K_1}{(s - P_1)} + \frac{K_2}{(s - P_2)} + \ldots + \frac{K_m}{(s - P_m)} \quad \ldots (1)$$

Then residue K_i is given by

$$K_i = [(s - P_i) F(s)]_{s \to P_i} = H \frac{(P_i - Z_1)(P_i - Z_2) \ldots (P_i - Z_n)}{(P_i - P_1)(P_i - P_2) \ldots (P_i - P_m)} \quad \ldots (2)$$

From complex plane (s) point of view, equation (2) interprets that "Each term $(P_i - Z_i)$ represents a vector drawn from Z_i to pole in question i.e. P_i.

Also each term $(P_i - P_k)$, $i \neq k$, represents vector drawn from other poles to pole in question i.e. P_i.

Hence,
$$K_i = \frac{\text{Product of vectors from each zero to } P_i}{\text{Product of vectors from other poles to } P_i} \times H$$

For example: Given pole-zero diagram as below:

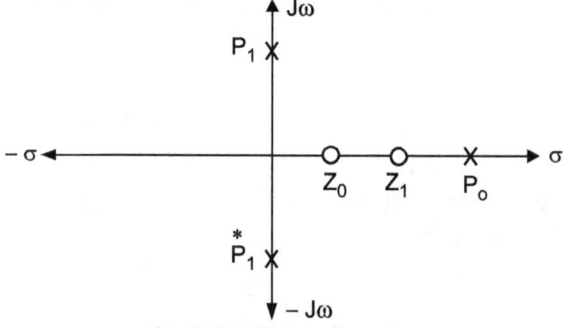

Fig. 6.20: Pole-zero plot

Now function representing above pole-zero plot is

$$F(s) = \frac{H(s + Z_0)(s + Z_1)}{(s + P_0)(s - P_1)(s - P_1^*)}$$

$$= \frac{K_0}{(s + P_0)} + \frac{K_1}{(s - P_1)} + \frac{K_1^*}{P_1^*}$$

Now to find residue at P_1:

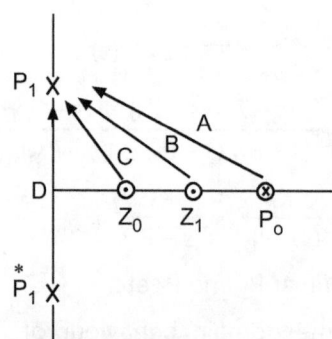

Fig. 6.20 (a): Residue at P_1

$$K_1 = \frac{CB}{AD} \times H$$

i.e. $$K_1 = \frac{(\text{Vector from } Z_0 \text{ to } P_1)(\text{Vector from } Z_1 \text{ to } P_1)}{(\text{Vector from } P_0 \text{ to } P_1)(\text{Vector from } P_1^* \text{ to } P_1)} \times H$$

Note: Graphical method can be used if poles are simple and complex. But it cannot be used when there are multiple (repeated) poles.

Ex. 6.14: Voltage transform V (s) of a network is given by

$$V(s) = \frac{4s}{(s+2)(s^2+2s+2)}$$

Plot its poles and zeros. Calculate residue at poles graphically, Hence find V (t).

Sol.: Pole-zero plot is as shown in Fig. 6.21 below.

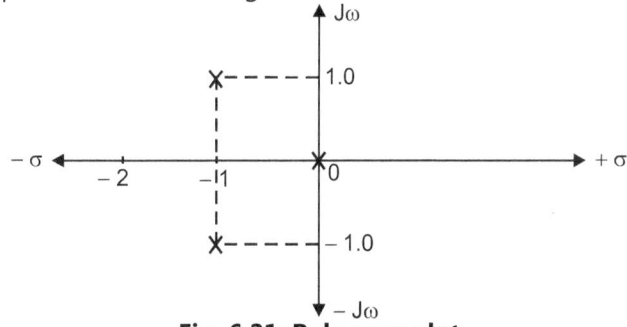

Fig. 6.21: Pole-zero plot

$$V(s) = \frac{4s}{(s+2)(s+1+j1)(s+1-j1)}$$

$$= \frac{K_0}{(s+2)} + \frac{K_1}{(s+1+j1)} + \frac{K_1^*}{(s+1-j1)}$$

(a) Residue at s = – 2 is K_0

$$K_0 = \frac{4 \times 2 \angle -180°}{\sqrt{2} \angle -135° \times \sqrt{2} \angle +135°}$$

$$= \frac{4 \times 2}{2} \angle -180° = -4$$

Fig. 6.21 (a): Residue at s = – 2

Chp 6 | 6.27

(b) Residue at $s = -1 - j1$ is K_1

$$K_1 = \frac{4 \times \sqrt{2} \angle 135°}{\sqrt{2} \angle 45° \times 2 \angle +90°} = 2 \angle 0° = 2$$

(c) Residue at $s = -1 - 1 + j1$ is K_1^*

$$K_1^* = \frac{4 \times \sqrt{2} \angle -135°}{\sqrt{2} \angle 45° \times 2 \angle -90°} = \frac{4}{2} \angle 0° = 2$$

Hence given function is

$$V(s) = \frac{-4}{(s+2)} + \frac{2}{(s+1+j1)} + \frac{2}{s+1-j1}$$

$$= \frac{-4}{s+2} + 2\left[\frac{2s+2}{(s+1)^2+1}\right] = \frac{-4}{(s+2)} + \frac{4(s+1)}{(s+1)^2+1}$$

Hence, $V(t) = -4e^{-2t} + 4e^{-t}\sin t$

$$= 4\left[e^{-t}\sin t - e^{-2t}\right]$$

Ex. 6.15: Graphically determine residue at poles of the following function

$$F(s) = \frac{s^2+4}{(s+2)(s^2+9)}$$

Sol.: Given F (s) can be written as

$$F(s) = \frac{s^2+4}{(s+2)(s+j3)(s-j3)} = \frac{(s+j2)(s-j2)}{(s+2)(s+j3)(s-j3)}$$

$$= \frac{K_0}{s+2} + \frac{K_1}{(s+j3)} + \frac{K_1^*}{(s-j3)}$$

(a) To find residue at $s = -2$, plot is

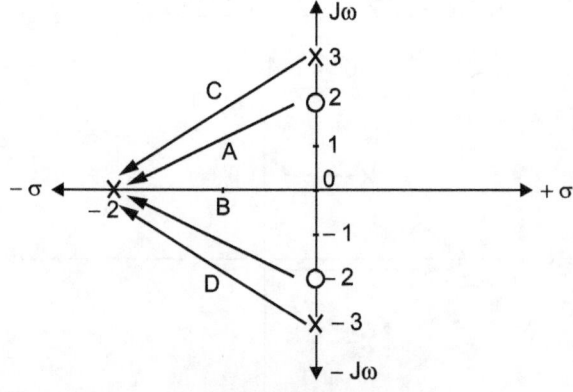

Fig. 6.22: Residue K_0

$$K_0 = \frac{AB}{CD}$$

$$A = \sqrt{8} \angle 225°$$
$$B = \sqrt{8} \angle 135°$$
$$C = \sqrt{13} \angle 236.4°$$
$$D = \sqrt{13} \angle 123.7°$$

$$\therefore K_0 = \frac{\sqrt{8} \angle 225° \times \sqrt{8} \angle 135°}{\sqrt{13} \angle 236.4° \times \sqrt{13} \angle 123.7°}$$

$$= \frac{8}{13} \angle 360° - 360°$$

$$= \frac{8}{13}$$

(b) To find residue at s = j3.

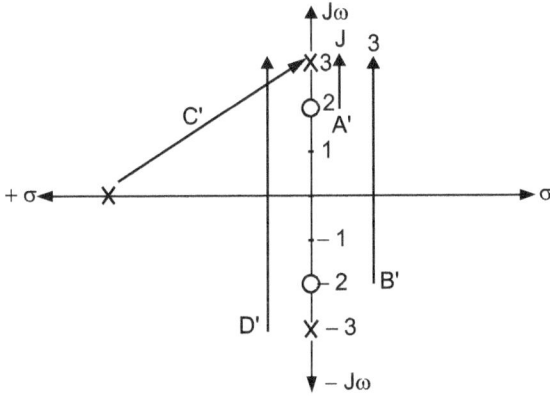

Fig. 6.22 (a): Residue K_1

$$K_1 = \frac{A'B'}{C'D'}$$

$$= \frac{1 \angle 90° \times 5 \angle 90°}{\sqrt{13} \angle 56.31° \times 6 \angle 90°}$$

$$= \frac{5}{\sqrt{13} \times 6} \angle 33.69°$$

$$= 0.231 \angle 33.7°$$

$$= 0.192 + j\, 0.128$$

(c) Similarly residue at s = − j3 can be found out which is complex conjugate of K_1.

i.e. $\quad K_1^* = 0.231 \angle -33.7°$

$$= 0.192 - j\, 0.128$$

Ex. 6.16: Find residue of the pole frequency using pole-zero plot of following function:

$$F(s) = \frac{(s+1)(s+4)}{(s+2)(s+5)}$$

Sol.: Given:
$$F(s) = \frac{s^2 + 5s + 4}{s^2 + 7s + 10}$$

Since numerator degree is equal to denominator degree, divide by numerator by denominator before PEE carried out.

$$F(s) = 1 - \frac{(2s+6)}{(s+2)(s+5)}$$

$$= 1 - \left[\frac{K_0}{(s+2)} + \frac{K_1}{(s+5)} \right] 2$$

Pole-zero plot of function

$$F_1(s) = \frac{s+3}{(s+2)(s+5)} \text{ is as shown below.}$$

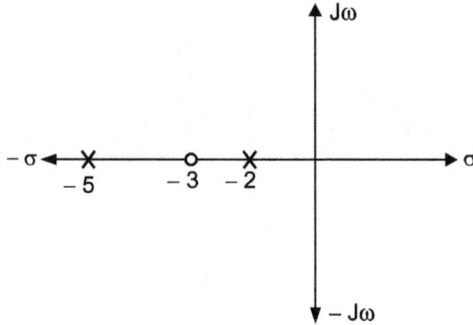

Fig. 6.23: Pole-zero plot

Residue at pole $s = -2$ is

$$K_0 = 2 \cdot \frac{A}{B} = \frac{2\angle 0}{3\angle 0} = \frac{2}{3}$$

Fig. 6.23 (a): Residue K_0

Residue at pole s = −5 is

$$K_1 = 2 \cdot \frac{A'}{B'} = \frac{2 \times 2 \angle 180°}{3 \angle 180°} = \frac{4}{3}$$

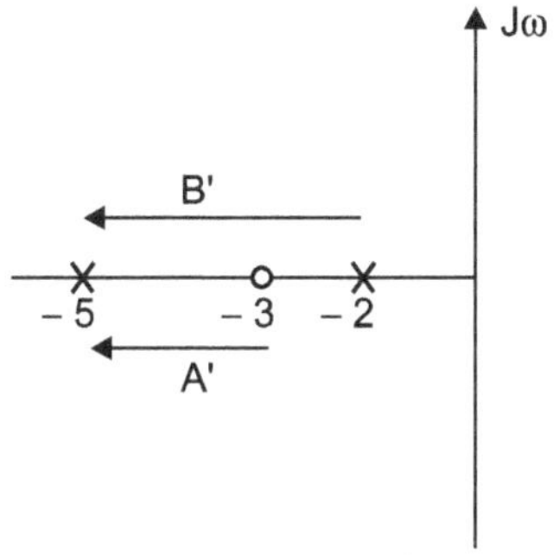

Fig. 6.23 (b): Residue K_1

Hence given function is

$$F(s) = 1 - \left[\frac{2}{3(s+2)} + \frac{4}{3(s+5)}\right]$$

$$= 1 - \frac{2}{3(s+2)} - \frac{4}{3(s+5)}$$

Taking inverse L-T gives,

$$f(t) = U(t) - \frac{2}{3} e^{-2t} - \frac{4}{3} e^{-5t}$$

6.6 MAGNITUDE AND PHASE (FREQUENCY DOMAIN) RESPONSE FROM POLE-ZERO PLOT

Let $F(s) = \dfrac{P(s)}{q(s)}$ be any network function.

F (s) can be written as

$$F(s) = \frac{H(s - Z_1)(s - Z_2) \ldots (s - Z_n)}{(s - P_1)(s - P_2) \ldots (s - P_m)}$$

At s = jω, we have,

$$F(j\omega) = \frac{P(j\omega)}{q(j\omega)}$$

$$= H \frac{(j\omega - Z_1)(j\omega - Z_2) \ldots (j\omega - Z_n)}{(j\omega - P_1)(j\omega - P_2) \ldots (j\omega - P_m)}$$

is the frequency response of the network. This consists of two parts.

(a) $|F(j\omega)|$ versus 'ω' is magnitude (amplitude) response.

(b) $e^{j\phi(\omega)} = \angle \phi(\omega)$ versus 'ω' gives phase response.

For various values of 'ω' phase response and amplitude response can be plotted as a graph. If this plot is straight line (Asymptotic), then this plot is called as Bodes plot.

Ex. 6.17: For function $F(s) = \dfrac{s}{s+10}$, find phase and magnitude response.

Sol.: We have, $\qquad F(j\omega) = \dfrac{j\omega}{j\omega + 10}$

(a) Magnitude plot:

$$|F(j\omega)| = \dfrac{\omega}{\sqrt{100 + \omega^2}}$$

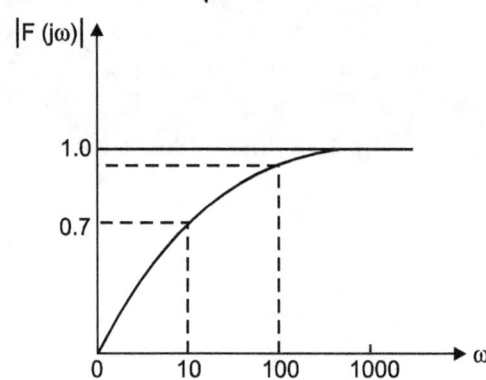

Fig. 6.24: Magnitude plot

At $\omega = 0$, $\qquad |F(j\omega)| = 0$

At $\omega = 10$, $\qquad |F(j\omega)| = 0.707$

At $\omega = 100$, $\qquad |F(j\omega)| = 0.995$

At $\omega = 1000$, $\qquad |F(j\omega)| = 1.0$

(b) Phase plot: $\qquad F(j\omega) = \phi(j\omega)$ versus 'ω'

gives phase plot.

We have, $\qquad \phi(j\omega) = \tan^{-1}\left(\dfrac{\omega}{0}\right) - \tan^{-1}\left(\dfrac{\omega}{10}\right)$

$\qquad\qquad\qquad\qquad = 90° - \tan^{-1}\left(\dfrac{\omega}{10}\right)$

For $\omega = 0$, $\qquad \phi(j0) = 90°$

$\omega = 10$, $\qquad \phi(j10) = 45°$

$\omega = 100$, $\qquad \phi(j100) = 5.7°$

$\omega = 1000$, $\qquad \phi(j1000) = 0°$

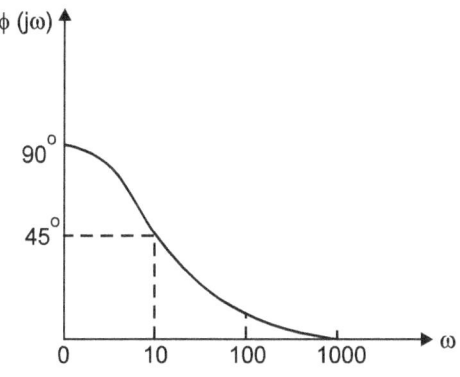

Fig. 6.24 (a): Phase plot

Ex. 6.18: Find magnitude of phase response for

$$F(s) = \frac{s+10}{s-10}$$

Sol.:

$$F(j\omega) = \frac{10+j\omega}{j\omega-10}$$

(a) Magnitude of F (jω) is given by

$$|F(j\omega)| = \frac{\sqrt{100+\omega^2}}{\sqrt{100+\omega^2}}$$

For all 'ω' magnitude is unity, hence its plot is

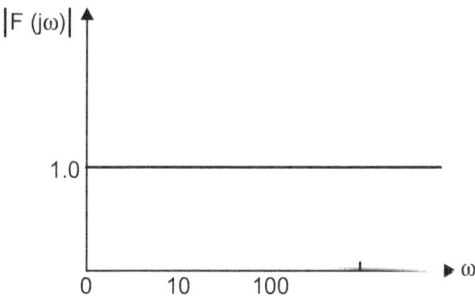

Fig. 6.25: Magnitude plot

(b) Phase response of F (jω):

$$\phi(j\omega) = \tan^{-1}\left(-\frac{\omega}{10}\right) + \tan^{-1}\left(-\frac{\omega}{10}\right)$$

$$= 2\tan^{-1}\left(-\frac{\omega}{10}\right)$$

For ω = 0,   φ (j0) = 0°
ω = 10,   φ (j10) = 90°
ω = 100,   φ (j100) = 168.6°
ω = 1000,   φ (1000) = 178.9°

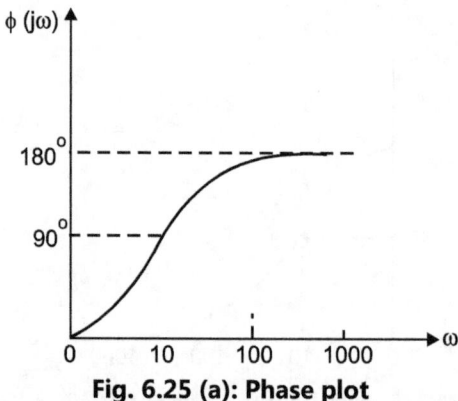

Fig. 6.25 (a): Phase plot

When amplitude and phase of a system function is to be calculated at a particular frequency then pole-zero plot can be used. Following two examples illustrate how to find this.

Ex. 6.19: Evaluate amplitude and phase of the network function $F(s) = \dfrac{4s}{s^2 + 2s + 2}$ from pole-zero plots at $s = j0$, $s = j2$.

Sol.: Pole-zero plot is as shown below in Fig. 6.26.

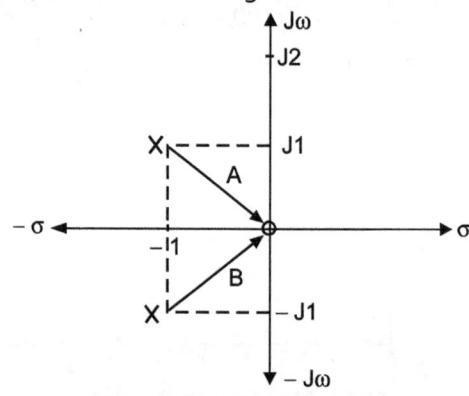

Fig. 6.26: Pole-zero plot

$$F(s) = \dfrac{4s}{(s + 1 + j1)(s + 1 - j1)}$$

(a) At $s = j0$, $\;F(j0) = 4 \times \dfrac{\text{Product of vectors from all zeros to } j0}{\text{Product of vectors from all poles to } j0}$

$$= \dfrac{4 \times 0 \angle 0°}{A \times B} = \dfrac{4 \times 0 \angle 0°}{\sqrt{2} \angle -45° \times \sqrt{2} \angle +45°}$$

$$= 0 \angle 0°$$

Hence at $s = j0$, magnitude and phase are '0'.

(b) At s = j2, $F(j2) = \dfrac{\text{Product of vectors from all zeros to j2}}{\text{Product of vectors from all poles to j2}}$

$$= \dfrac{2 \angle 90°}{\sqrt{2} \angle 45° \times \sqrt{10} \angle \tan^{-1}(3)} = 0.447 \angle -26.56°$$

Hence, at s = j2, Magnitude = 0.447, Phase = − 26.56°

Ex. 6.20: Using pole-zero plot, find magnitude and phase of the function

$$F(s) = \dfrac{(s+1)(s+3)}{s(s+2)}$$

at s = − 4 and s = j4.

Sol.: Pole-zero plot is as shown besides in Fig. 6.27.

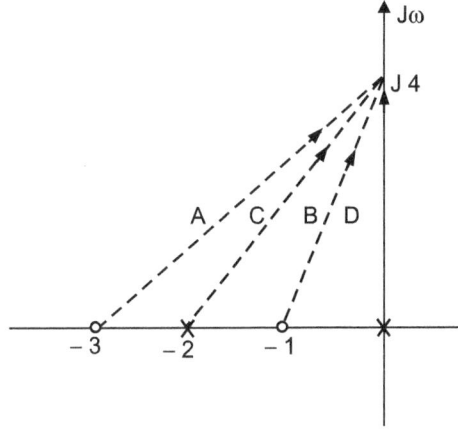

Fig. 6.27: Pole-zero plot

(a) At s = j4, we have,

$$F(j4) = \dfrac{\text{Product of vectors from all zeros to j4}}{\text{Product of vectors from all poles to j4}}$$

$$= \dfrac{A \cdot B}{C \cdot D} = \dfrac{5 \angle 53.13° \times \sqrt{17} \angle 76°}{\sqrt{20} \angle 63.4° \times 4 \angle 90°}$$

$$= 1.15 \angle -24.3°$$

Hence at s = j4, Magnitude = 1.15, Phase = − 24.3°.

(b) At s = − 4, we have,

$$F(-4) = \dfrac{1 \angle 180° \times 3 \angle 180°}{4 \angle 180° \times 2 \angle 180°}$$

$$= \dfrac{3}{8} \angle 0°$$

Hence at = s = − j4, Magnitude = $\dfrac{3}{8}$, Phase = 0°.

Ex. 6.21: For the network shown, find the driving point function Z (s). Plot the poles and zeros of Z (s) on S-plane.

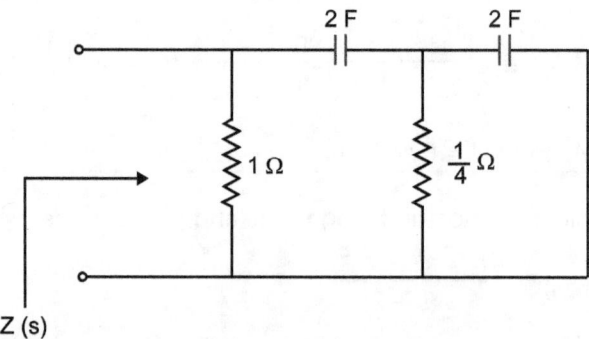

Fig. 6.28: Circuit for Ex. 6.21

Sol.: The transformed circuit is shown below in Fig. 6.28 (a).

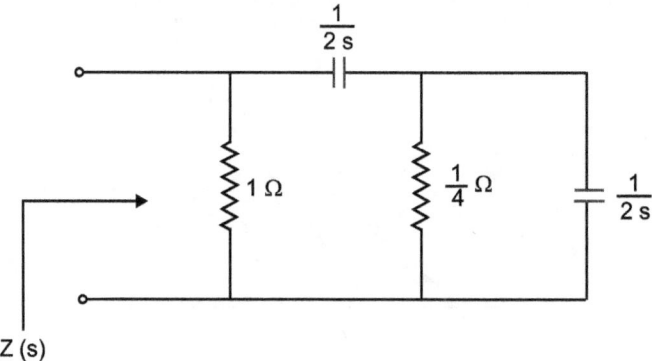

Fig. 6.28 (a): Transformed circuit

$$Z(s) = 1\,\Omega \parallel \left[\frac{1}{2s} + \frac{1}{2s} \parallel \frac{1}{4} \right]$$

$$= 1\,\Omega \parallel \left[\frac{1}{2s} + \frac{1/8s}{\frac{1}{2s} + \frac{1}{4}} \right] = 1\,\Omega \parallel \left[\frac{1}{2s} + \frac{1}{2s + 4} \right]$$

$$= 1\,\Omega \parallel \left[\frac{2s + 4 + 2s}{2s(2s + 4)} \right] = 1\,\Omega \parallel \left[\frac{4s + 4}{2s(2s + 4)} \right]$$

$$= 1\,\Omega \parallel \frac{s + 1}{(s^2 + 2s)} = \frac{1 \times \frac{s + 1}{s^2 + 2s}}{1 + \frac{s + 1}{s^2 + 2s}} = \frac{s + 1}{(s^2 + 3s + 1)}$$

Thus, $\quad Z(s) = \dfrac{P(s)}{q(s)} = \dfrac{s + 1}{(s^2 + 3s + 1)}$

The zeros are given by P (s) = 0 i.e. s = – 1.
Poles are given by equation q (s) = $s^2 + 3s + 1 = 0$

Thus using quadratic equation formula, we get,

$$s = \frac{-3 \pm \sqrt{9-4}}{2} = \frac{-3 \pm \sqrt{5}}{2}$$

Thus poles at $s_1 = 2.618$ and $s_2 = -0.3819$.

The pole-zero plot is shown below.

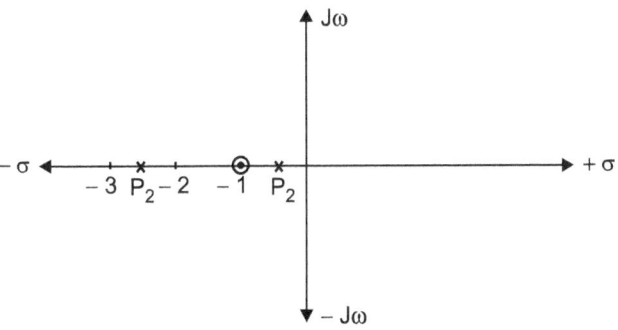

Fig. 6.28 (b): Pole-zero plot

Ex. 6.22: Find input impedance $Z_{in}(s)$ and plot its poles and zeros of the circuit.

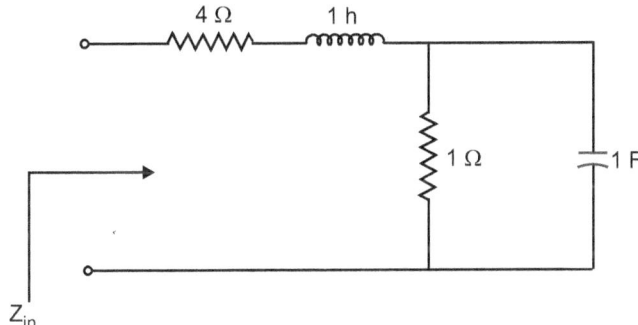

Fig. 6.29: Circuit for Ex. 6.22

Sol.: The transformed circuit is shown below.

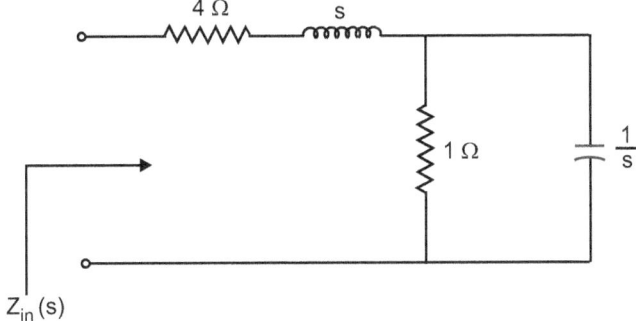

Fig. 6.29 (a): Transformed circuit

$$Z_{in}(s) = 4 + s + \left[(1\,\Omega) \| \left(\frac{1}{s}\right)\right] = (s+4) + \left[\frac{1 \times \frac{1}{s}}{1 + \frac{1}{s}}\right] = (s+4) + \frac{1}{(s+1)}$$

$$= \frac{(s+4)(s+1)+1}{(s+1)} = \frac{s^2 + 5s + 5}{(s+1)} = \frac{N(s)}{D(s)}$$

The poles are given by $D(s) = (s+1) = 0$ i.e. at $s_1 = -1$.

The zeros are given by $N(s) = s^2 + 5s + 5 = 0$

This is a quadratic equation. The roots are

$$s = \frac{-5 \pm \sqrt{(5)^2 - 4 \times 5}}{2 \times 1} = -2.5 \pm 1.118$$

Thus zeros are at $s_1 = -1.38$ and $s_2 = -3.618$.

The pole-zero plot is shown below in Fig. 6.29 (b).

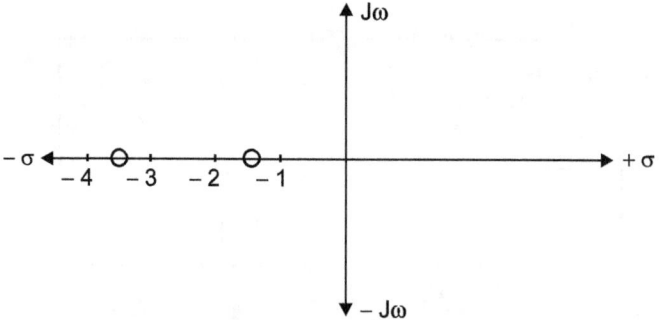

Fig. 6.29 (b): Pole-zero plot

Ex. 6.23: Find $Z(s) = \frac{V_1}{I_1}$ and $T(s) = \frac{V_2}{V_1}$ for the network shown in the Fig. 6.30.

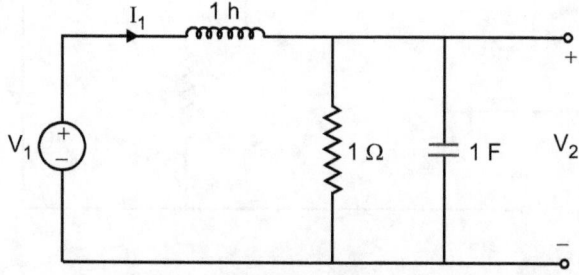

Fig. 6.30: Circuit for Ex. 6.23

Sol.: The transformed circuit is shown below in Fig. 6.30 (a).

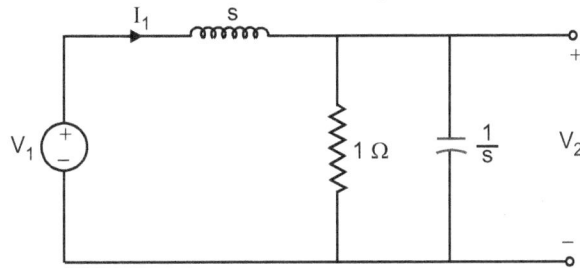

Fig. 6.30 (a): Transformed circuit

Let $\quad Z_1(s) = 1\,\Omega \parallel \dfrac{1}{s} = \dfrac{1 \times \dfrac{1}{s}}{1 + \dfrac{1}{s}} = \dfrac{1}{(s+1)}$

Then, $\quad I_1 = \dfrac{V_1}{s + Z(s)} = \dfrac{V_1}{s + \dfrac{1}{(s+1)}} = \dfrac{(s+1)\,V_1}{(s^2 + s + 1)}$

Thus, $\quad Z(s) = \dfrac{V_1}{I_1} = \dfrac{s^2 + s + 1}{(s+1)}$

Also by voltage divider relation, we get,

$$V_2 = \dfrac{Z_1(s) \cdot V_1}{Z_1(s) + s} = \dfrac{\dfrac{1}{s+1} \cdot V_1}{\left(\dfrac{1}{s+1}\right) + s} = \dfrac{V_1}{(s^2 + s + 1)}$$

Thus, $\quad T(s) = \dfrac{V_2}{V_1} = \dfrac{1}{(s^2 + s + 1)}$

Ex. 6.24: For the circuit shown, find input admittance $Y_{in}(s)$ and hence obtain equivalent inductance of the circuit.

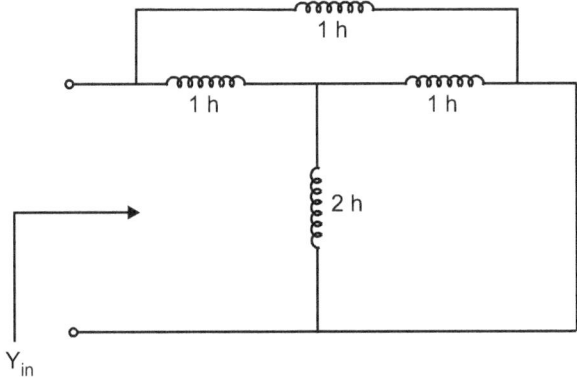

Fig. 6.31: Circuit for Ex. 6.24

Sol.: The transformed circuit is shown below in Fig. 6.31 (a).

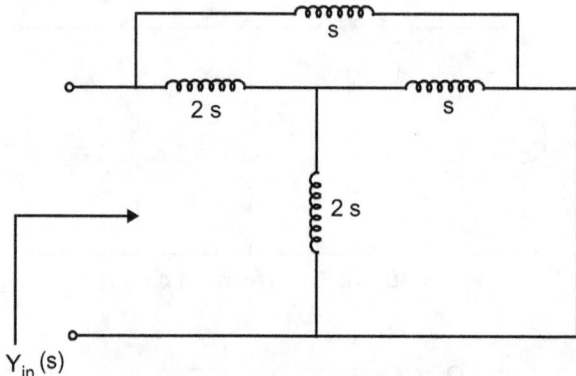

Fig. 6.31 (a): Transformed circuit

The equivalent circuits are as shown below in Fig. 6.31 (b).

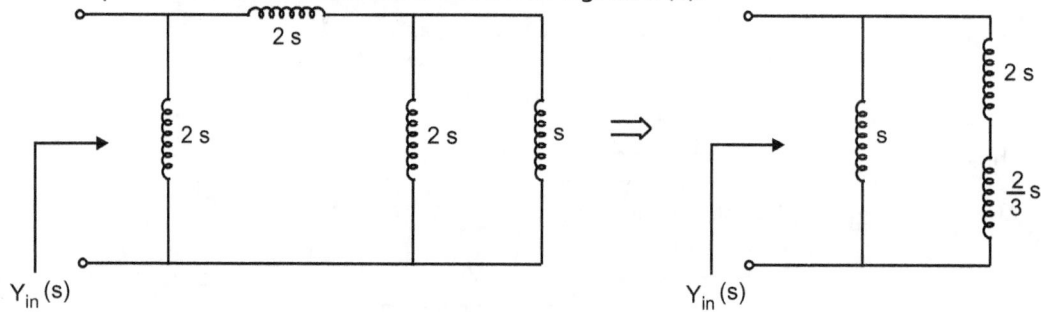

Fig. 6.31 (b): Equivalent circuits

Thus the resultant admittance will be

$$Y_{in}(s) = \frac{1}{s} + \left(2s + \frac{2s}{3}\right) = \frac{1}{s} + \frac{3}{8s} = \frac{8+3}{8s} = \frac{11}{8s} \text{ mho}$$

Hence, $L_{eq} = \frac{8}{11}$ Henry, is the equivalent inductance.

Ex. 6.25: For the network shown, find the expression for the following network functions $\frac{V_2}{V_1}, \frac{I_2}{I_1}, \frac{V_2}{I_1}$ and $\frac{I_2}{V_1}$.

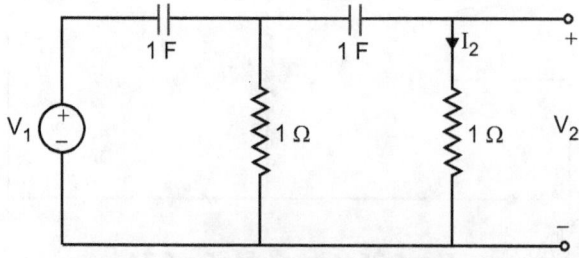

Fig. 6.32: Circuit for Ex. 6.25

Sol.: The transformed circuit is shown below in Fig. 6.32 (a).

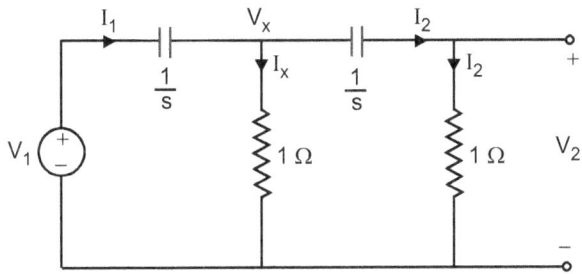

Fig. 6.32 (a): Transformed circuit

$$I_2 = \frac{V_2}{1} = V_2 \qquad \ldots (a)$$

$$V_x = V_2 + \frac{1}{s} I_2 = V_2 + \frac{V_2}{s}$$

$$= \left(\frac{s+1}{s}\right) V_2 \qquad \ldots (b)$$

$$I_x = \frac{V_x}{1} = \left(\frac{s+1}{s}\right) V_2$$

Thus, $\qquad I_1 = I_x + I_2 = V_2 \left(\frac{s+1}{s}\right) + V_2$

$$= \left(\frac{2s+1}{s}\right) V_2 \qquad \ldots (c)$$

Hence, $\qquad V_1 = \frac{I_1}{s} + V_x = \left(\frac{2s+1}{s^2}\right) V_2 + \left(\frac{s+1}{s}\right) V_2$

$$V_1 = V_2 \left[\frac{(2s+1) + s(s+1)}{s^2}\right]$$

$$= \left[\frac{s^2 + 3s + 1}{s^2}\right] V_2 \qquad \ldots (d)$$

Thus, $\qquad \dfrac{V_2}{V_1} = \dfrac{s^2}{s^2 + 3s + 1}, \quad \dfrac{V_2}{I_2} = \dfrac{s}{(2s+1)}$

$$\frac{I_2}{V_1} = \frac{V_2}{\left(\frac{s^2+3s+1}{s^2}\right) V_2} = \frac{s^2}{(s^2+3s+1)}$$

$$\frac{I_2}{I_1} = \frac{V_2}{\left(\frac{2s+1}{s}\right) V_2} = \frac{s}{(2s+1)}$$

Ex. 6.26: Find driving point impedance and driving point admittance of the circuit shown.

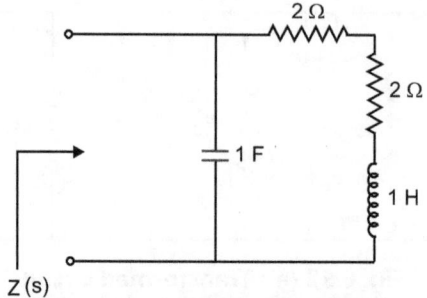

Fig. 6.33: Circuit for Ex. 6.26

Sol.: The transformed circuit is shown below in Fig. 6.33 (a).

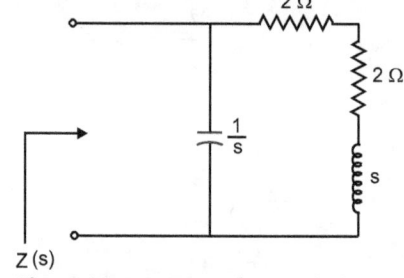

Fig. 6.33 (a): Transformed circuit

Let $Z_1(s) = (2 + 2 + s) = (4 + s)$

Then, $Z(s) = \dfrac{1}{s} \| Z_1(s) = \dfrac{1}{s} \| (4 + s)$

$$Z(s) = \dfrac{\dfrac{1}{s} \times (s+4)}{(s+4) + \dfrac{1}{s}} = \dfrac{s+4}{(s^2 + 4s + 1)} = \text{Driving point impedance.}$$

Hence, $Y(s) = \dfrac{s^2 + 4s + 1}{(s+4)} = $ Driving point admittance

Ex. 6.27: Determine $\dfrac{V_2}{I_1}$ and $\dfrac{V_2}{V_1}$ for the circuit shown in Fig. 6.34.

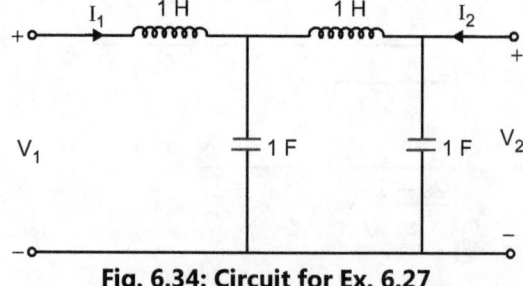

Fig. 6.34: Circuit for Ex. 6.27

Sol.: The transformed circuit is shown below in Fig. 6.34 (a).

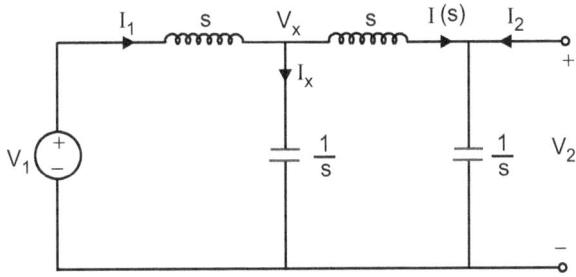

Fig. 6.34 (a): Transformed circuit

With output open ($I_2 = 0$), we have,

$$I(s) = \frac{V_2}{1/s} = sV_2$$

$$V_x = sI(s) + V_2 = s^2 V_2 + V_2 = V_2(s^2 + 1)$$

$$I_x = sV_x = s(s^2 + 1)V_2 = (s^3 + s)V_2$$

$$I_1 = I_x + I(s) = (s^3 + s)V_2 + sV_2 = V_2(s^3 + 2s)$$

$$V_1 = sI_1 + V_x = s(s^3 + 2s)V_2 + (s^2 + 1)V_2$$

$$= V_2(s^4 + 2s^2 + s^2 + 1) = V_2(s^4 + 3s^2 + 1)$$

Thus, $\dfrac{V_2}{V_1} = \dfrac{1}{(s^4 + 3s^2 + 1)}$

$$\frac{V_2}{I_1} = \frac{V_2}{V_2(s^3 + 2s)} = \frac{1}{(s^3 + 2s)} = \frac{1}{s(s^2 + 2)}$$

Ex. 6.28: Find the input impedance and plot its poles and zeros of the circuit shown below in Fig. 6.35.

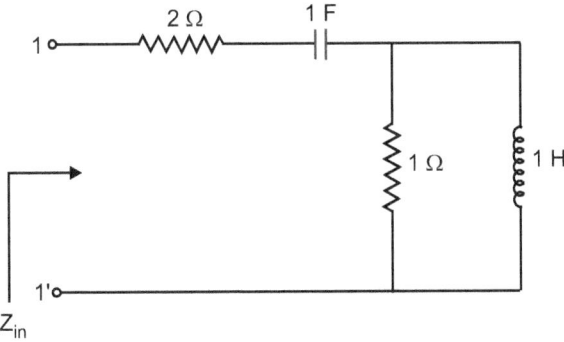

Fig. 6.35: Circuit for Ex. 6.28

Sol.: The transformed circuit is shown below in Fig. 6.35 (a).

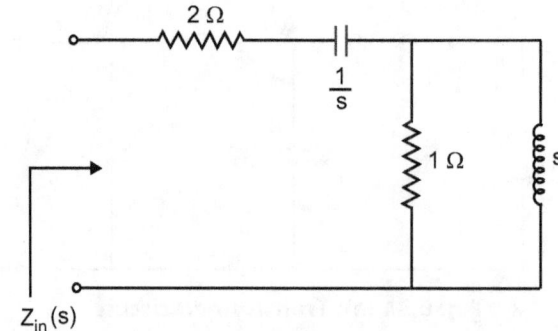

Fig. 6.35 (a): Transformed circuit

$$Z_{in}(s) = \left[2 + \frac{1}{s}\right] + 1 \parallel s = 2 + \frac{1}{s} + \frac{s}{(s+1)}$$

$$= \frac{2s(s+1)(s+1) + s^2}{s(s+1)}$$

$$= \frac{3s^2 + 2s + s + s^2}{s(s+1)} = \frac{3s^2 + 3s + 1}{s(s+1)}$$

The pole is at $s = -1$ and $s = 0$.

Zeros are given by equation $3s^2 + 3s + 1 = 0$. This is an quadratic equation, the roots of which are

$$s = \frac{-3 \pm \sqrt{9 - 4 \times 3}}{6} = \frac{-3 \pm j\sqrt{3}}{6} = -\frac{1}{2} \pm j\frac{\sqrt{3}}{6}$$

Thus, $s_1 = -\frac{1}{2} + j\frac{\sqrt{3}}{6}$ and $s_2 = -\frac{1}{2} - j\frac{\sqrt{3}}{6}$

The pole-zero plot is shown below.

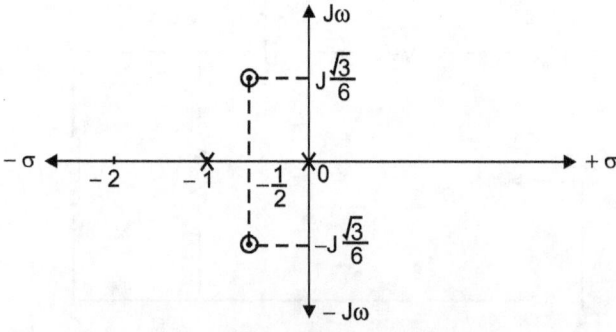

Fig. 6.35 (b): Pole-zero plot

Ex. 6.29: Find the input impedance $Z_{in}(s)$ and plot its poles and zeros for the circuit shown in Fig. 6.36.

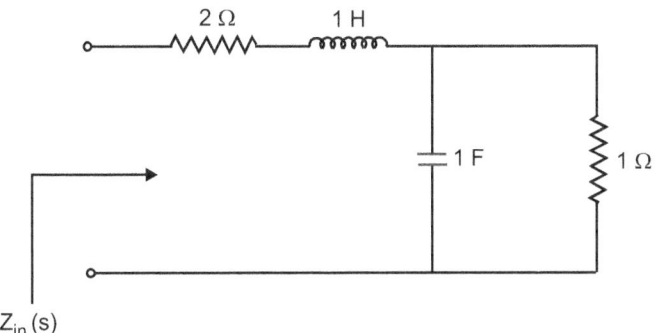

Fig. 6.36: Circuit for Ex. 6.29

Sol.: The transformed circuit is shown below in Fig. 6.36 (a).

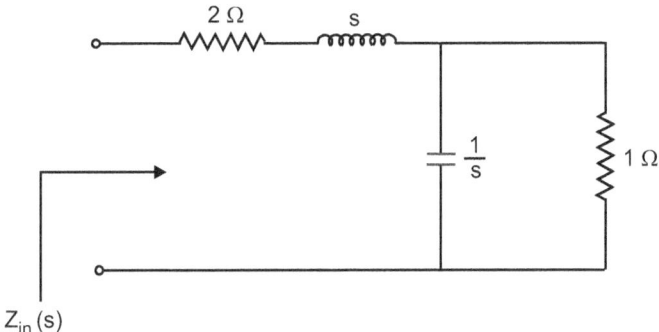

Fig. 6.36 (a): Transformed circuit

Now, $\quad 1 \| \dfrac{1}{s} = \dfrac{1/s}{1 + \dfrac{1}{s}} = \dfrac{1}{(s+1)}$

$$Z_{in}(s) = 2 + s + \dfrac{1}{(s+1)} = \dfrac{2(s+1) + s(s+1) + 1}{(s+1)} = \dfrac{s^2 + 3s + 3}{(s+1)}$$

Thus pole is at $s = -1$.

The zeros are obtained from equation $s^2 + 3s + 3 = 0$

Solving this quadratic equation gives

$$s = \dfrac{-3 \pm \sqrt{9 - 4 \times 3}}{2 \times 1} = \dfrac{-3 \pm \sqrt{-3}}{2} = -\dfrac{3}{2} \pm j\dfrac{\sqrt{3}}{2}$$

Thus poles are at $s_1 = -\dfrac{3}{2} + j\dfrac{\sqrt{3}}{2}$ and $s_2 = -\dfrac{3}{2} - j\dfrac{\sqrt{3}}{2}$.

The plot is as shown below in Fig. 6.36 (b).

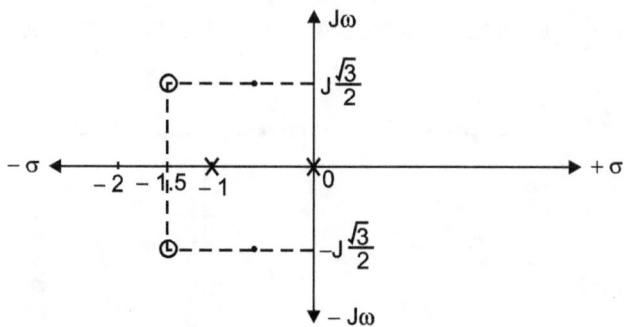

Fig. 6.36 (b): Pole-zero plot

Ex. 6.30: For the network shown, find the expression for the following network functions $\dfrac{V_2}{V_1}$, $\dfrac{I_2}{I_1}$ and $\dfrac{V_2}{I_1}$.

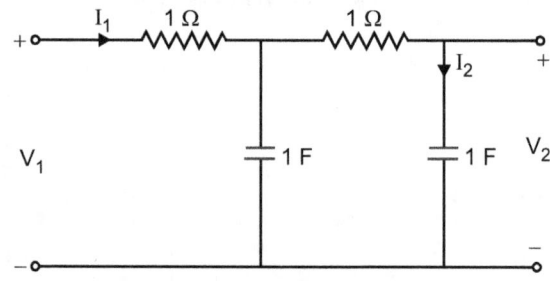

Fig. 6.37: Circuit for Ex. 6.30

Sol.: The transformed circuit is shown below in Fig. 6.37 (a).

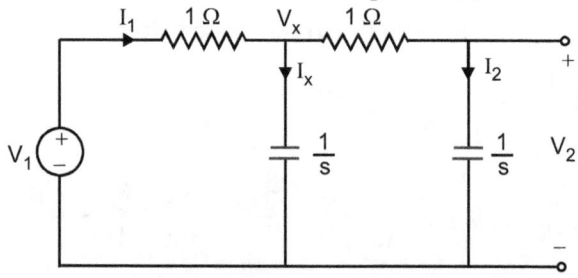

Fig. 6.37 (a): Transformed circuit

We have,
$$I_2 = \frac{V_2}{1/s} = sV_2$$

$$V_x = 1 \times I_2 + V_2 = sV_2 + V_2 = (s+1)V_2$$

$$I_x = \frac{V_x}{1/s} = sV_x = s(s+1)V_2$$

$$I_1 = I_x + I_2 = s(s+1)V_2 + V_2 = V_2(s^2 + 2s)$$

$$V_1 = I_1 \times 1 + V_x = V_2(s^2 + 2s) + (s+1)V_2 = V_2(s^2 + 3s + 1)$$

Thus,
$$\frac{V_2}{V_1} = \frac{1}{s^2 + 3s + 1}$$

$$\frac{I_2}{I_1} = \frac{sV_2}{V_2(s^2 + 2s)} = \frac{s}{(s^2 + 2s)} = \frac{1}{(s+2)}$$

$$\frac{V_2}{I_1} = \frac{V_2}{V_2(s^2 + 2s)} = \frac{1}{s(s+2)}$$

Ex. 6.31: Find the driving point impedance of the circuit shown below in Fig. 6.38.

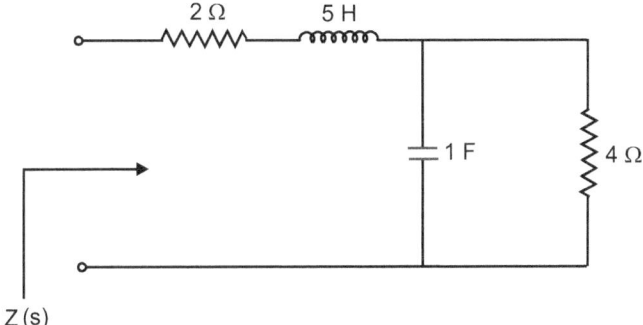

Fig. 6.38: Circuit for Ex. 6.31

Sol.: The transformed circuit is shown below in Fig. 6.38 (a).

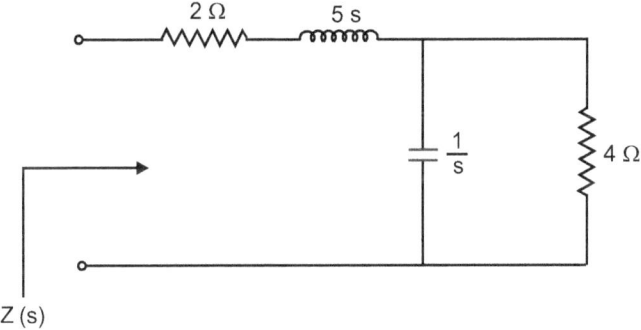

Fig. 6.38 (a): Transformed circuit

We have, $Z_1(s) = \dfrac{1}{s} \| 4 = \dfrac{4/s}{\left(4 + \dfrac{1}{s}\right)} = \dfrac{4}{(4s + 1)}$

$Z(s)$ = Driving point impedance = $2 + 5s + Z_1(s)$

$= 2 + 5s + \dfrac{4}{(4s+1)} = \dfrac{(2+5s)(4s+1) + 4}{(4s+1)}$

$= \dfrac{20s^2 + 8s + 5s + 2 + 4}{(4s+1)} = \dfrac{20s^2 + 13s + 6}{(4s+1)}$

Ex. 6.32: Write driving point impedance Z (s) of the circuit shown in Fig. 6.39. Locate the poles and zeros of Z (s) on S-plane.

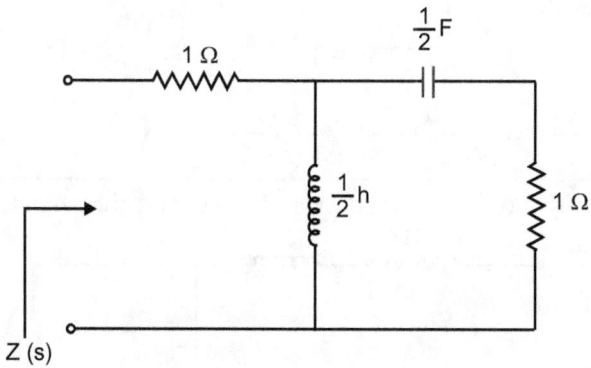

Fig. 6.39: Circuit for Ex. 6.32

Sol.: The transformed circuit is shown below in Fig. 6.39 (a).

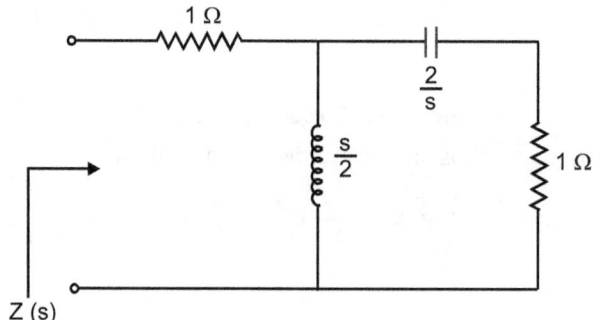

Fig. 6.39 (a): Transformed circuit

Now, let $\quad Z_1(s) = \dfrac{s}{2} \parallel \left(1 + \dfrac{2}{s}\right) = \dfrac{s}{2} \parallel \dfrac{2+s}{s}$

$$= \dfrac{\dfrac{s}{2} \times \dfrac{(s+2)}{s}}{\dfrac{s}{2} + \dfrac{s+2}{s}} = \dfrac{\dfrac{s(s+2)}{2s}}{\dfrac{s^2+2s+4}{2s}} = \dfrac{s(s+2)}{(s^2+2s+4)}$$

Then driving point impedance,

$$Z(s) = 1 + Z_1(s) = 1 + \dfrac{s(s+2)}{s^2+2s+4}$$

$$= \dfrac{(s^2+2s+4) + s^2+2s}{(s^2+2s+4)}$$

Thus, $Z(s) = \dfrac{P(s)}{q(s)} = s\left[\dfrac{s^2 + 2s + 2}{s^2 + 2s + 4}\right]$

$= 2\left[\dfrac{(s + 1 + j1)(s + 1 - j1)}{(s + 1 + j\sqrt{3})(s + 1 - j\sqrt{3})}\right]$

Thus poles are at $s_1 = -1 + j\sqrt{3}$ and $s_2 = -1 - j\sqrt{3}$

Zeros are at $s_3 = -1 + j1$ and $s_4 = -1 - j1$

The pole-zero plot of Z (s) is shown below in Fig. 6.39 (b). It consists of two complex poles and zeros each.

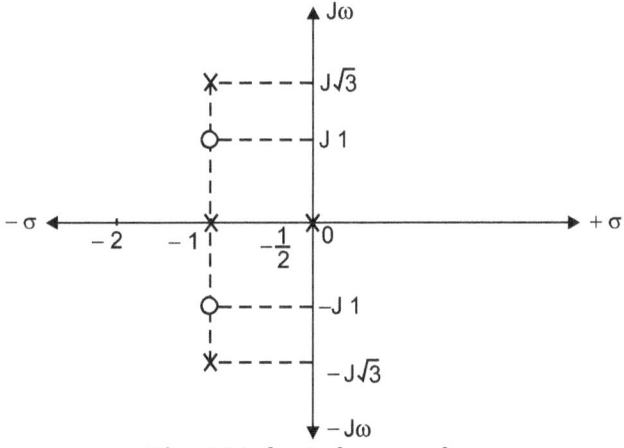

Fig. 6.39 (b): Pole-zero plot

Ex. 6.33: Find $V_2(s)$ in the circuit shown. Use superposition theorem and Laplace transform method.

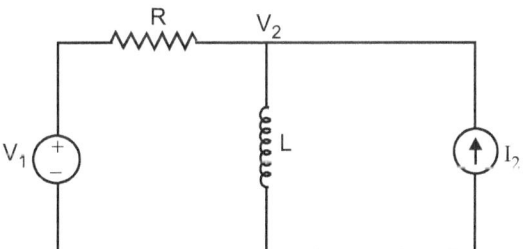

Fig. 6.40: Circuit for Ex. 6.33

Sol.: The transformed circuit is shown below in Fig. 6.40 (a).

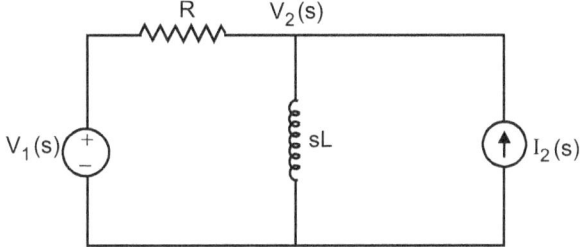

Fig. 6.40 (a): Transformed circuit

Step I: With $V_1(s)$ only considered, circuit is as shown in Fig. 6.40 (b).

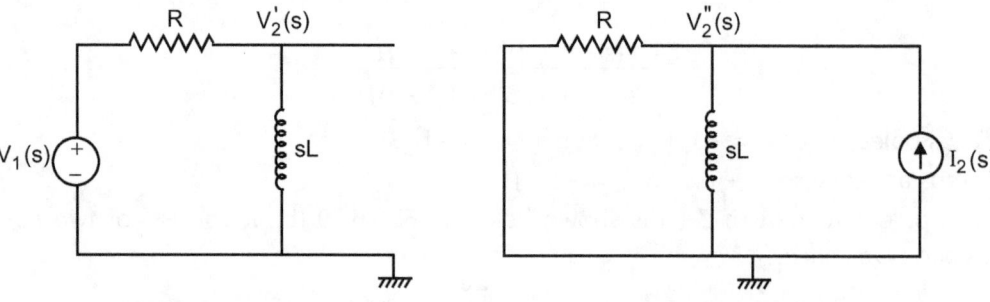

Fig. 6.40 (b)   Fig. 6.40 (c)

$$V_2'(s) = V_1(s) \times \frac{sL}{sL+R} = \frac{sL}{R+sL} \times V_1(s) \qquad \ldots (a)$$

Step II: With only $I_2(s)$ considered, the circuit is as shown in Fig. 6.106 (c).

$$V_2''(s) = I_2(s) \times sL \parallel R = \frac{sRL}{sL+R} \times I_2(s) \qquad \ldots (b)$$

Step III: By superposition theorem, we have,

$$V_2(s) = V_2'(s) + V_2''(s) = \frac{sL}{R+sL}[V_1(s) + RI_2(s)]$$

Ex. 6.34: Find $Z = \dfrac{V_1}{I_1}$ and $T(s) = \dfrac{V_2}{V_1}$ for the circuit shown in Fig. 6.41.

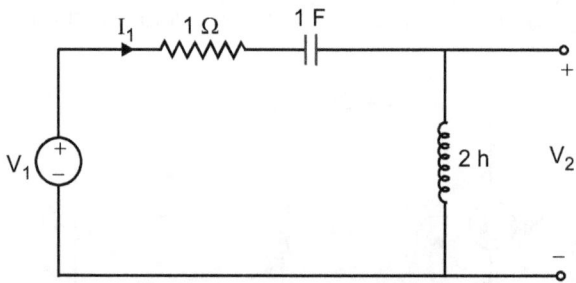

Fig. 6.41: Circuit for Ex. 6.33

Sol.: The transformed circuit is shown below in Fig. 6.41 (a).

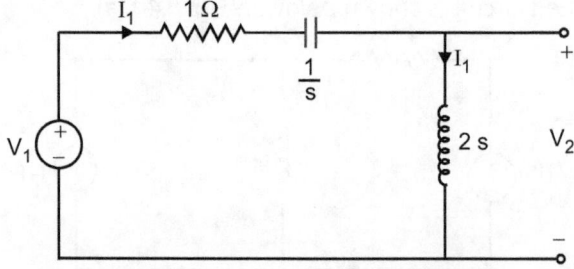

Fig. 6.41 (a): Transformed circuit

We have, $I_1 = \dfrac{V_1}{1 + \dfrac{1}{s} + 2s} = \dfrac{sV_1}{(2s^2 + s + 1)}$

Thus, $\dfrac{V_1}{I_1} = \dfrac{(2s^2 + s + 1)}{s}$

$V_2 = 2s\, I_1 = 2s^2 \times \dfrac{V_1}{(2s^2 + s + 1)}$

Thus, $T(s) = \dfrac{V_2}{V_1} = \dfrac{2s^2}{(2s^2 + s + 1)}$

Ex. 6.35: Determine $V(s)$ in the circuit shown. Assume zero initial conditions. Use Laplace transform method.

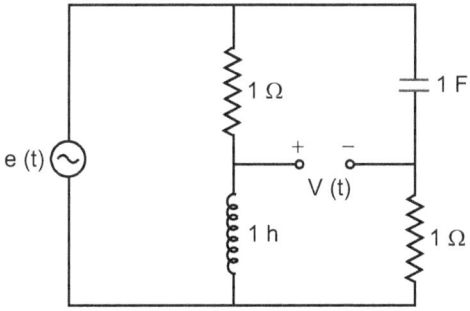

Fig. 6.42: Circuit for Ex. 6.34

Sol.: The transformed circuit is shown below in Fig. 6.42 (a).

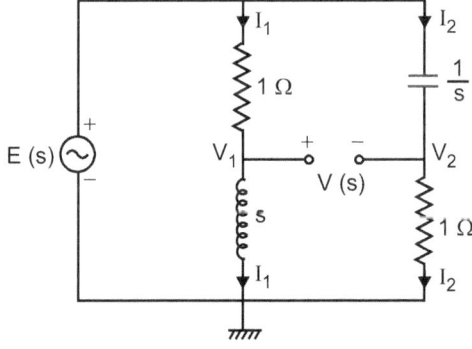

Fig. 6.42 (a): Transformed circuit

$I_1 = \dfrac{E(s)}{(1 + s)}$ Thus, $V_1 = sI_1 = \dfrac{sE(s)}{(s + 1)}$

$I_2 = \dfrac{E(s)}{\left(1 + \dfrac{1}{s}\right)} = \dfrac{sE(s)}{s + 1}$ Thus, $V_2 = 1 \times I_2 = \dfrac{sE(s)}{(s + 1)}$

Hence, $V(s) = V_1 - V_2 = \dfrac{sE(s)}{(s + 1)} - \dfrac{sE(s)}{(s + 1)} = 0$

Ex. 6.36: Find driving point impedance and driving point admittance for the circuit shown in Fig. 6.43.

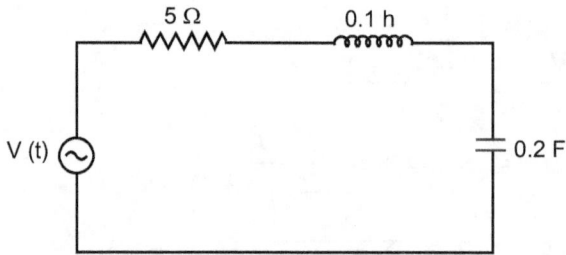

Fig. 6.43: Circuit for Ex. 6.36

Sol.: The transformed circuit is shown below in Fig. 6.43 (a).

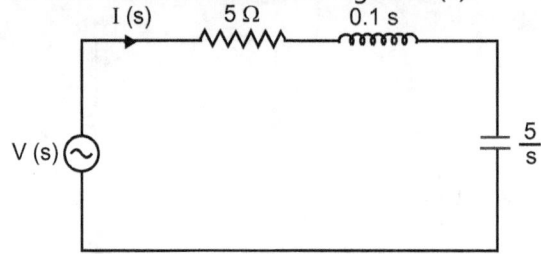

Fig. 6.43 (a): Transformed circuit

Driving point impedance,

$$[Z(s)] = \frac{V(s)}{I(s)} = 5 + 0.2s + \frac{5}{s} = \frac{s^2 + 50s + 50}{10s}$$

Driving point admittance,

$$[Y(s)] = \frac{I(s)}{V(s)} = \frac{10s}{s^2 + 50s + 50}$$

Ex. 6.37: For the network function draw pole-zero plot and obtain time response i(t).

$$I(s) = \frac{2s}{(s+1)(s+2)}$$

Sol.: The zero is at s = 0.
Poles are at s = – 1 and s = – 2.
The pole-zero plot is shown below in Fig. 6.44.

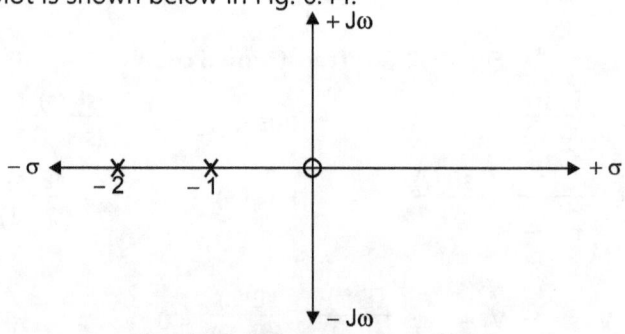

Fig. 6.44: Pole-zero plot of I (s)

$$I(s) = \frac{2s}{(s+1)(s+2)} = \frac{K_1}{(s+1)} + \frac{K_2}{(s+2)}$$

$$K_1 = \left[(s+1)I(s)\right]_{s \to -1} = \left[\frac{2s}{(s+2)}\right]_{s \to -1} = \frac{-2}{(-1+2)} = -2$$

$$K_2 = \left[(s+2)I(s)\right]_{s \to -2} = \left[\frac{2s}{(s+1)}\right]_{s \to -2} = \frac{-4}{(-2+1)} = 4$$

Thus,
$$I(s) = \frac{-2}{(s+1)} + \frac{4}{(s+2)}$$

$$i(t) = L^{-1}[I(s)] = -2e^{-t} + 4e^{-2t}$$

Ex. 6.38: Draw the pole-zero plot of following function:

$$H(s) = \frac{s^2 + 4}{s^2 + 6s + 4}$$

Sol.: The function can be written as

$$H(s) = \frac{(s + j2)(s - j2)}{(s + 0.764)(s + 5.236)}$$

The zeros are at $s_1 = j2$ and $s_2 = j2$.

The poles are at $s_3 = -0.764$ and $s_4 = -5.236$.

The pole-zero plot is shown below.

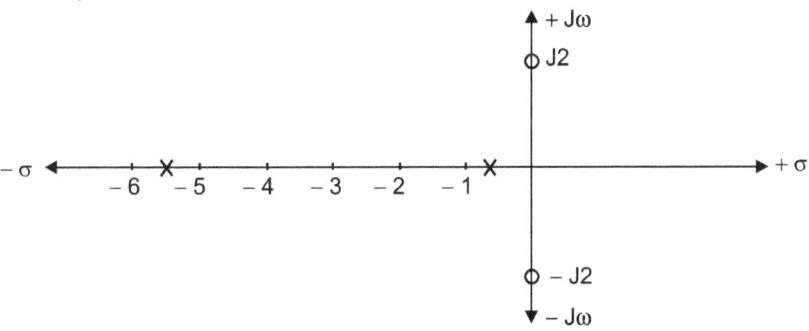

Fig. 6.45: Pole-zero plot

Ex. 6.39: For the given network function, draw the pole-zero plot and hence obtain the time domain response.

$$V(s) = \frac{5(s+5)}{(s+2)(s+7)}$$

Sol.: The zero is at $s = -5$.

The poles are at $s_1 = -2$ and $s_2 = -7$.

The pole-zero plot is shown below in Fig. 6.46.

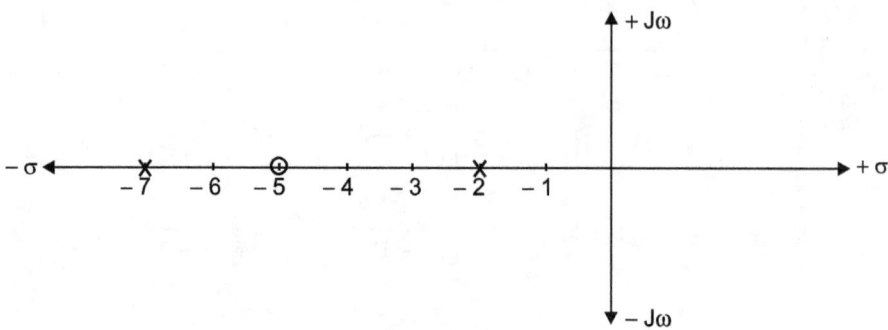

Fig. 6.46: Pole-zero plot

We have,
$$V(s) = \frac{5(s+5)}{(s+2)(s+7)} = \frac{k_0}{(s+2)} + \frac{k_1}{(s+7)}$$

$$K_0 = [(s+2)V(s)]_{s \to -2} = \left[\frac{5(s+5)}{(s+7)}\right]_{s \to -2} = 5\left(\frac{3}{5}\right) = 3$$

$$K_1 = [(s+7)V(s)]_{s \to -7} = \left[\frac{5(s+5)}{(s+2)}\right]_{s \to -7} = \frac{5 \times -2}{-5} = 2$$

Thus,
$$V(s) = \frac{3}{(s+2)} + \frac{2}{(s+7)}$$

$$V(t) = 3e^{-2t} + 2e^{-7t}$$

Ex. 6.40: Determine the voltage ratio transfer function $\frac{V_2}{V_1}$ for the circuit shown in Fig. 6.46.

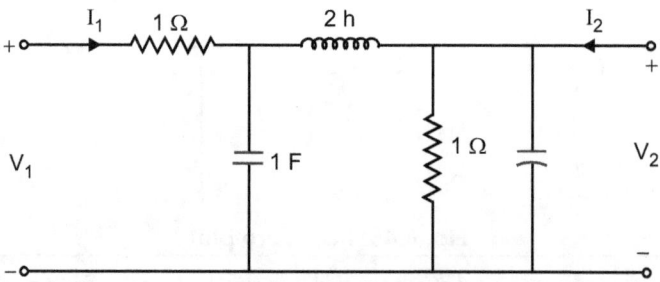

Fig. 6.46: Circuit for Ex. 6.40

Sol.: Output open i.e. $I_2 = 0$, the voltage ratio transfer function is given by

$$T(s) = \frac{V_2}{V_1}$$

$$= \frac{1}{2s^3 + 4s^2 + 4s + 2}$$

6.7 POLE POSITION AND STABILITY

Most important requirement of any system is stability. An unstable system usually is considered as a useless system.

Stability of the system can be classified as absolute stability and relative stability. **Absolute stability** is the condition where the system is stable or unstable. It is like yes or no type answer. Once a system is confirmed to be stable, then **relative stability** of the system determines degree of the stability.

As defined earlier, a system is said to be stable if bounded input excitation the output (response) does not go on increasing indefinitely.

Impulse response of the system can be used to determine the system stability.

A stable system is one in which impulse response will approach zero for sufficiently large time.

An unstable system is one in which impulse response grows without bound. i.e. it approaches to infinity for sufficient large time.

In marginally stable system, impulse response approaches a constant non-zero value or a constant amplitude oscillation for a sufficient large time.

The pole position and system stability is very closely related. The necessary and sufficient condition for the system to be stable is that the roots of the characteristic equation of the system must lie on negative half of the S-plane. Thus, if $T(s) = \dfrac{N(s)}{D(s)}$ is the transfer function, then roots of $D(s) = 0$ must lie on the negative half of S-plane. For any root (pole) on right half of S-plane the system will be unstable.

Let us now consider the relationship between pole positions and the corresponding impulse responses.

(a) **Poles on the negative real axis:** Consider a simple pole on negative real axis.

i.e. $$F(s) = \dfrac{K}{(s+a)}$$

The corresponding impulse response is given by
$$f(t) = L^{-1}[F(s)] = Ke^{-at}$$

For large t, f(t) approaches to zero as shown in the Fig. 6.47. Thus it is a stable system.
Suppose we have multiple poles in the system. For example, consider
$$F(s) = \dfrac{K}{(s+a)^r}$$

Then the response will be
$$f(t) = K t^r e^{-at}$$

This also approaches to zero as $t \to \infty$. Hence this is a stable system.

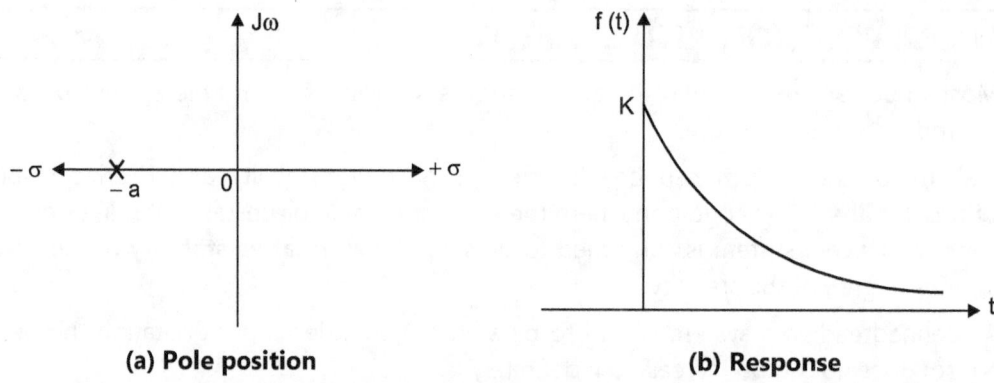

(a) Pole position   (b) Response

Fig. 6.47: Poles on negative real axis and its response

Thus for all poles lying on the negative real axis, the system is stable.

(b) Complex poles on left half of S-plane: Consider an F (s) with poles at $s = -\sigma_1 \pm j\beta_1$ as in Fig. 6.48.

$$F(s) = \frac{K_1}{(s + \sigma_1 - j\beta_1)} \pm \frac{K_2}{(s + \sigma_1 + j\beta_1)}$$

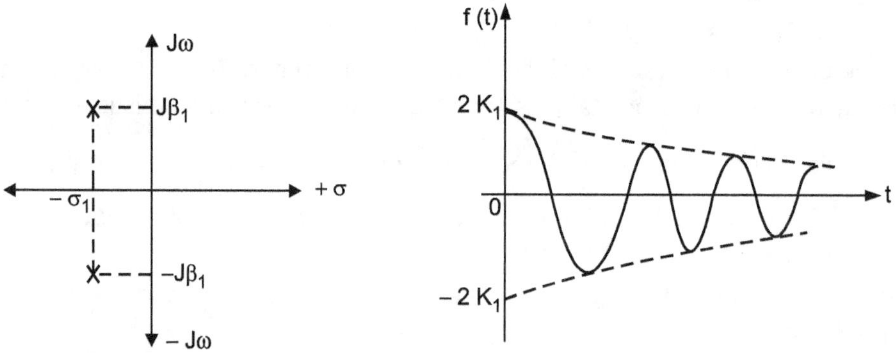

(a) Pole positions   (b) Response

Fig. 6.48: Complex poles on left half of S-plane and its response

The corresponding time response is given by

$$f(t) = L^{-1}[F(s)] = L^{-1}\left[\frac{2K_1(s + \alpha_1)}{(s + \alpha_1)^2 + \beta_1^2}\right]$$

As t approaches infinity f (t) becomes zero. Thus the system becomes stable.

For multiple order of poles on left half of the S-plan, the response will be of the form

$$f(t) = 2t_1 \, t^r \, e^{-\alpha_1 t} \cos \beta_1 t$$

This also approaches to zero as $t \to \infty$.

Thus **"For all complex poles lying on left half of S-plane, the system is stable"**.

(c) Poles on positive real axis: Consider a function in which pole is on right half of S-plane i.e.

$$F(s) = \frac{K}{(s-a)}$$

Then response will be

$$f(t) = Ke^{+at}$$

This response increases exponentially to infinity as $t \to \infty$. Thus the system is unstable. If there are multiple order of poles on +ve real axis, the system becomes more unstable.

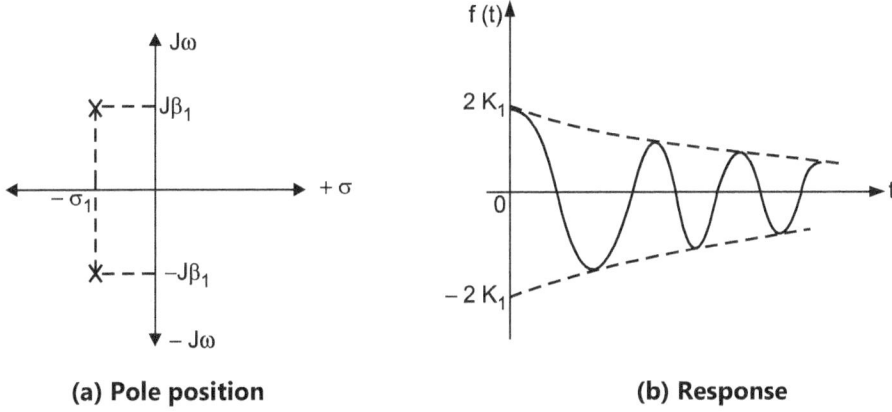

(a) Pole position   (b) Response

Fig. 6.49: Simple pole on positive real axis and its response

Thus "If the system has any pole on right half of S-plane then it is an unstable system".

(d) Complex poles on the right half of S-plane: Consider a system with complex poles at $s = \alpha_1 + j\beta_1$. i.e.

$$F(s) = \frac{K_1}{(s - \alpha_1 + j\beta_1)} + \frac{K_1}{(s - \alpha_1 - j\beta_1)}$$

The time response is given by

$$f(t) = L^{-1}[F(s)] = L^{-1}\left[\frac{2K_1(s - \alpha_1)}{(s - \alpha_1)^2 + \beta_1^2}\right] = 2K_1 e^{\alpha_1 t} \cos \beta_1 t$$

Thus, $f(t)$ increases exponentially with damped oscillations as $t \to \infty$ as shown in Fig. 6.50.

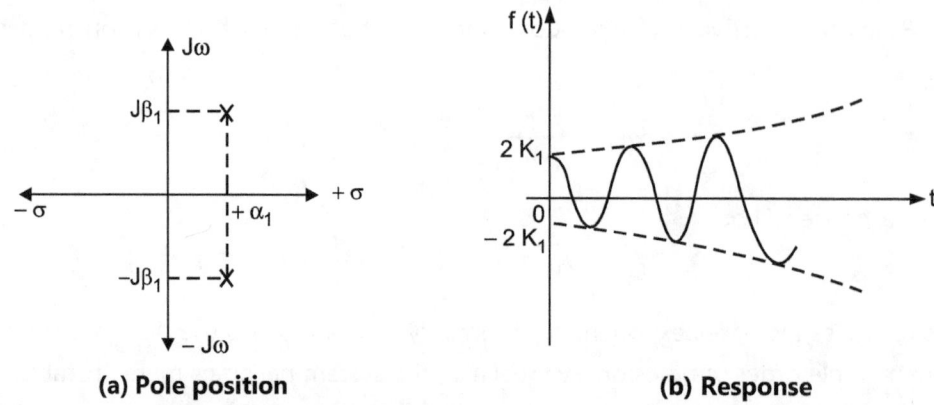

(a) Pole position (b) Response

Fig. 6.50: Complex poles on +ve real axis and its response

Thus "**If the system has complex poles on right half of S-plane i.e. on +ve real axis then the system is an unstable system**".

(e) Pole at the origin: Consider a system with the poles at origin. i.e. $F(s) = \dfrac{K}{s}$. Now the time domain response is given by

$$f(t) = L^{-1}[F(s)] = L^{-1}\left[\dfrac{K}{s}\right] = K\,u(t)$$

Thus, as $t \to \infty$, $f(t)$ remains constant at K. Hence it is a stable system.

Suppose there are multiple poles at the origin. If $F_1(s) = \dfrac{K}{s^2}$, then time response will be given by

$$f_1(t) = K\,t\,u(t)$$

This shows that if $t \to \infty$, then $f(t) \to \infty$ and hence it is a unstable system.

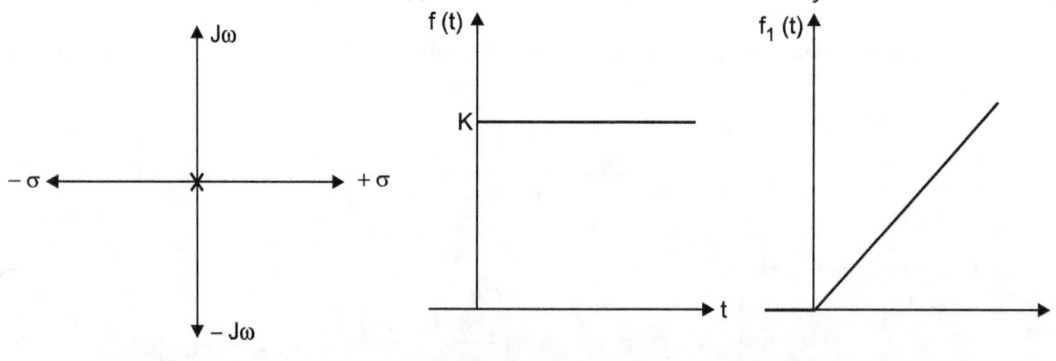

(a) Single pole   (b) Single pole response   (c) Multiple pole response

Fig. 6.51: Single and multiple pole at origin and its response

Thus "**If there is single pole at origin, then the system is stable. If there are multiple poles at origin, then the system is unstable**".

6.8 PARALLEL RESONATING CIRCUIT

Consider circuit shown in Fig. 6.52.

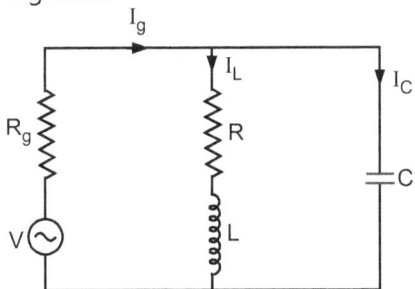

Fig. 6.52: A parallel resonating circuit

- We have consider R_g i.e. the internal generator resistance in this circuit. Moreover, the capacitor is connected in parallel to an inductor and it is assumed to be a lossless element and hence its resistance is negligible. R in this case is the sum of the resistance of inductor and any other load resistance connected externally.
- This circuit is connected to the voltage source of V volts and generator resistance R_g ohms.
- It is also called as an antiresonating circuit.

6.8.1 Antiresonating Frequency

The admittance of the capacitive branch of the circuit is
$$Y_C = j\omega C$$
and that of the inductive branch is
$$Y_L = \frac{1}{R + j\omega L} = \frac{R - j\omega L}{R^2 + \omega^2 L^2}$$

Thus, Y i.e. total admittance
$$Y = Y_C + Y_L$$
$$Y = \frac{R - j\omega L}{R^2 + \omega^2 L^2} + j\omega C$$
$$Y = \frac{R}{R^2 + \omega^2 L^2} - j\left[\frac{\omega L}{R^2 + \omega^2 L^2} - \omega C\right]$$

- For antiresonance, the circuit must have unity power factor, therefore the j term must be zero. So setting the reactive term equal to zero at ω_{ar} i.e. antiresonant frequency.

∴ At $\omega = \omega_{ar}$

$$\frac{\omega_{ar} L}{R^2 + \omega_{ar}^2 L^2} - \omega_{ar} C = 0$$

$$\boxed{R^2 + \omega_{ar}^2 L^2 = \frac{L}{C}} \quad \ldots (6.5)$$

This equation will be used in Section 6.7.3.

$$\omega_{ar}^2 = \left(\frac{L}{C} - R^2\right)\frac{1}{L^2}$$

$$\omega_{ar}^2 = \left(\frac{1}{LC} - \frac{R^2}{L^2}\right)$$

$$\boxed{f_{ar} = \frac{1}{2\pi}\sqrt{\frac{1}{LC} - \frac{R^2}{L^2}}} \quad \ldots (6.6)$$

f_{ar}, gives the frequency of resonance in a parallel R_{LC} circuit.

$$f_{ar} = \frac{1}{2\pi}\sqrt{\frac{1}{LC}}\sqrt{1 - \frac{1}{Q^2}}$$

$$\boxed{f_{ar} = f_r \sqrt{1 - \frac{1}{Q^2}}} \quad \ldots (6.7)$$

$$\boxed{\omega_{ar}^2 LC = 1 - \frac{1}{Q^2}} \quad \ldots (6.8)$$

which can be written as

$$\omega_{ar} L = \frac{1}{\omega_{ar} C}\left(1 - \frac{1}{Q^2}\right)$$

to give

$$\boxed{X_L = X_C \left(1 - \frac{1}{Q^2}\right)} \quad \ldots (6.9)$$

Equation 6.7 gives the expression for the antiresonating frequency. Equations 6.7, 6.8, 6.9 are the modified versions and need careful understanding.

Comments on Equations 6.5, 6.6, 6.7 and 6.8.

1. In series resonant circuit,

$$f_r = \frac{1}{2\pi\sqrt{LC}}$$

and thus resonance was possible for all the values of resistance present. In contrast to this, as clear from equation 6.6 in an antiresonant circuit, resonance is possible only when $\frac{1}{LC} > \frac{R^2}{L^2}$.

i.e. Resonance is impossible for all the values of R that makes

$$\frac{R^2}{L^2} > \frac{1}{LC}$$

This is clear from equation 6.6.

2. Equation 6.7 indicates that the antiresonant frequency, differs from that of a series resonant circuit with the same circuit elements only by the factor $\sqrt{1-\frac{1}{Q^2}}$.

   If Q > 10 then error < 10% and $f_{ar} = f_r$.

   Another point indicated by equation 6.7 is that it shows the antiresonance is impossible for circuits with values of Q less than unity.

3. Equations 6.8 and 6.9 shows another interesting fact. We define resonance as a condition of a circuit when $X_L = X_C$ and unity power factor is achieved. But in an antiresonant circuit at f_{ar} the reactances of inductive and capacitive branches are not quite equal as they were incase of series resonating circuit.

6.8.2 Reactance Curves

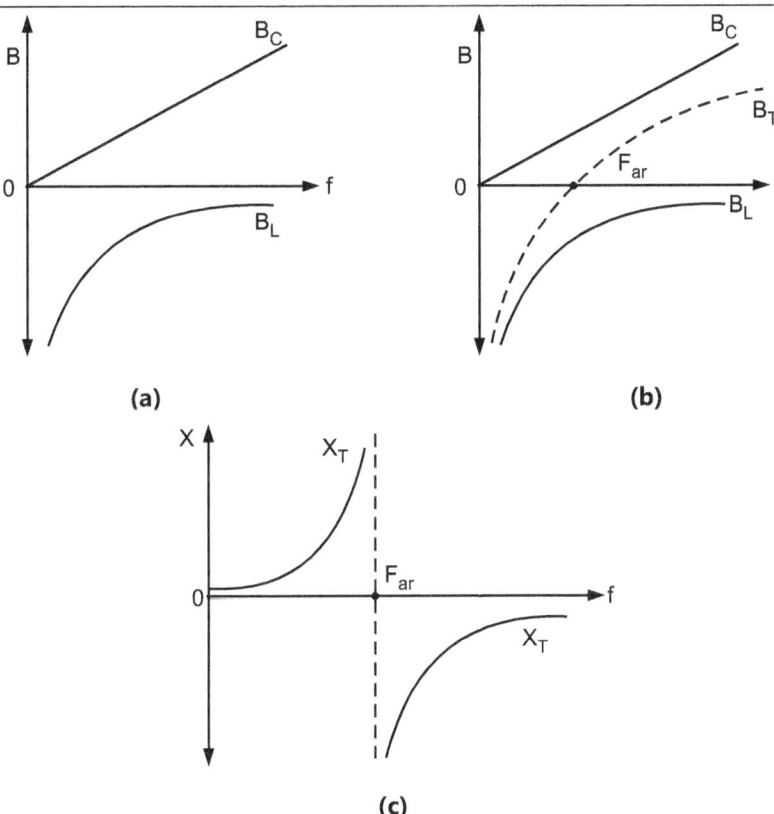

Fig. 6.53: (a) Suspectance Vs Frequency plot for L and C, (b) Total Suspectance B_T Vs Frequency, (c) X_T plotted as reciprocal of B_T

- Inductive reactance is a linear positive function of frequency and is plotted as a straight line through origin. Capacitive reactance similarly, is plotted as a negative hyperbola the reason being it is an inverse negative function of frequency.

- In case of parallel resonating circuit we plot the susceptances, thus inductive susceptance is plotted as hyperbolic negative and capacitive susceptance is plotted as a linear positive plot.
- These plots are shown in Fig. 6.53 (a) and (b). Fig. 6.53 (c) shows the plot of total reactance X_T plotted as a reciprocal of total susceptance. Thus, at antiresonating frequency f_{ar}, susceptance B_T was zero and so X_T is therefore infinity. Below f_{ar}, B_T is capacitive and thus X_T is inductive. Similarly X_T is capacitive above f_{ar}. Even this is very contradictory to the reactance plot of series resonance.

6.8.3 Impedance of Parallel Resonance Circuit

The admittance of the capacitive branch of the circuit is

$$Y_C = j\omega C$$

Similarly,

$$Y_L = \frac{1}{R + j\omega L}$$

$$= \frac{R - j\omega L}{R^2 + \omega^2 L^2}$$

∴ Total admittance Y is

$$Y = \frac{R - j\omega L}{R^2 + \omega^2 L^2} + j\omega C$$

∴ $$Y = \frac{R}{R^2 + \omega^2 L^2} - j\left(\frac{\omega L}{R^2 + \omega^2 L^2} - \omega C\right)$$

(a) Impedance at antiresonating frequency:

With the condition of unity power factor imposed, admittance at f_{ar} is

$$Y_{ar} = \frac{R}{R^2 + \omega_{ar}^2 L^2}$$

∴ Antiresonant impedance is

∴ $$Z_{ar} = R_{ar} = \frac{R^2 + \omega_{ar}^2 L^2}{R}$$

$$Z_{ar} = R + \frac{\omega_{ar}^2 L^2}{R}$$

$$\boxed{Z_{ar} = R\left(1 + Q_{war}^2\right)} \qquad \ldots (6.10)$$

For the circuit with very high value of Q.

$$\boxed{Z_{ar} = R \cdot Q_{ar}^2} \qquad \ldots \text{high Q values}$$

This equation gives Z_{ar} in terms of Q_{ar}. Recollect equation which we saw in Section 6.8.1. The equation is

$$R^2 + \omega_{ar}^2 L = \frac{L}{C}$$

Using this result in the equation

$$Z_{ar} = R + \frac{\omega_{ar}^2 L^2}{R}$$

i.e.
$$Z_{ar} = \frac{R^2 + \omega_{ar}^2 L^2}{R}$$

Gives,
$$\boxed{Z_{ar} = \frac{L}{CR}}$$ ...(6.11)

This equation gives the expression for Z_{ar} in terms of circuit components.

(b) The impedance of parallel resonant circuit near resonance:

The impedance of parallel resonant circuit at any frequency is given by,

$$Z = (R + j\omega L) \parallel \left(\frac{1}{j\omega C}\right)$$

$$Z = \frac{(R + j\omega L) \times \frac{1}{j\omega C}}{R + j\omega L + \frac{1}{j\omega C}}$$

$$Z = \frac{R\left(1 + \frac{j\omega L}{R}\right)\left(\frac{1}{j\omega C}\right)}{R\left[1 + \frac{j\omega L}{R}\left(1 - \frac{1}{\omega^2 LC}\right)\right]}$$

$$Z = \frac{R\left(1 + \frac{j\omega L}{R}\right)\left(\frac{1}{j\omega C}\right)}{R\left[1 + \frac{j\omega L}{R}\left(1 - \frac{1}{\omega^2 LC}\right)\right]}$$

$$Z = \frac{\frac{L}{RC} + \frac{1}{j\omega C}}{1 + \frac{j\omega L}{R}\left(1 - \frac{1}{\omega^2 LC}\right)}$$ ...(6.12)

Above equation gives general expression for the impedance of a parallel resonant circuit at any frequency ω.

Let δ be the fractional deviation

$$\delta = \frac{f - f_{ar}}{f_{ar}}$$

$$= \frac{\omega - \omega_{ar}}{\omega_{ar}} = \frac{\omega}{\omega_{ar}} - 1$$

$$\boxed{(1 + \delta) = \frac{\omega}{\omega_{ar}}} \text{ or } \boxed{\frac{\omega_{ar}}{\omega} = \frac{1}{(1 + \delta)}}$$

Now let us consider the terms in the denominator of equation 6.12.

$$\frac{\omega L}{R} = \frac{\omega_{ar} L}{R} \cdot \frac{\omega}{\omega_{ar}} = Q(1 + \delta)$$

$$\frac{1}{\omega^2 LC} = \frac{\omega_{ar}^2}{\omega^2} \times \frac{1}{\omega_{ar}^2 LC}$$

$$= \frac{1}{(1+\delta)^2} \qquad \ldots \text{when Q is high } \omega_{ar}^2 LC = 1$$

Substituting these values in equation 6.12.

$$Z = \frac{\dfrac{L}{CR}\left(1 + \dfrac{R}{j\omega L}\right)}{1 + j\dfrac{\omega L}{R}\left(1 - \dfrac{1}{\omega^2 LC}\right)}$$

$$Z = \frac{L}{CR} \cdot \frac{1 - j\dfrac{1}{Q_0(1+\delta)}}{1 + jQ(1+\delta)\left[1 + \dfrac{1}{(1+\delta)^2}\right]}$$

$$Z = \frac{L}{CR} \cdot \frac{1 - j\dfrac{1}{\theta(1+\delta)}}{1 + jQ\left[\dfrac{1 + \delta^2 + 2\delta - 1}{(1+\delta)}\right]}$$

$$Z = \frac{L}{CR} \cdot \frac{1 - j\dfrac{1}{Q(1+\delta)}}{1 + jQ\delta\dfrac{(2+\delta)}{(1+\delta)}} \qquad \ldots (6.13)$$

At antiresonating frequency

$$Z_{ar} = \frac{L}{CR}$$

and $\delta \ll 1$. Therefore, neglecting it.
Substituting in equation 6.13.

$$Z = Z_{ar} \frac{1 - j\dfrac{1}{Q}}{1 + jQ\delta \cdot 2}$$

$\dfrac{1}{Q}$ is $\ll 1$. Therefore, neglecting it.

$$\boxed{Z = \frac{Z_{ar}}{1 + j2\delta Q}} \qquad \ldots (6.14)$$

Equation (6.14) gives the value of impedance near resonance.

6.8.4 Currents in Antiresonant Circuits

At antiresonance, the power delivered by the generator to the circuit of Fig. 6.52.
$$P = I_g^2 R_{ar}$$
Power dissipated in the parallel circuit assuming negligible capacitor losses is
$$P = I_L^2 R$$
This power is equal to the power supplied by the generator, since there are no other power dissipating elements in the circuit.

∴ Input power = Delivered power
$$I_g^2 R_{ar} = I_L^2 R$$
$$\frac{I_g^2}{I_L^2} = \frac{R}{R_{ar}}$$

Now,
$$R_{ar} = \frac{L}{CR}$$
$$\frac{I_g^2}{I_L^2} = \frac{R}{\frac{L}{CR}}$$
$$\frac{I_g^2}{I_L^2} = \frac{CR^2}{L}$$
$$I_L^2 = \frac{L}{CR^2} I_g^2$$

As
$$Q = \frac{\omega L}{R} = \frac{1}{R}\sqrt{\frac{L}{C}} \quad \ldots \quad \omega_{ar} = \frac{1}{\sqrt{LC}}$$
$$I_L^2 = Q^2 I_g^2$$
$$\boxed{I_L = Q I_g} \qquad \ldots (6.15)$$

At antiresonance:
Now current flowing through the capacitor is given by
$$I_C = \frac{V}{X_C} = \frac{V}{\left(\frac{1}{\omega_{ar}C}\right)}$$
$$I_C = \omega_{ar} C \cdot V$$
$$I_C = \omega_{ar} C [I_g \times Z_{ar}]$$
$$I_C = \omega_{ar} C I_g \left(\frac{L}{CR}\right)$$
$$I_C = \left(\frac{\omega_{ar} L}{R}\right) I_g$$
$$\boxed{I_C = Q I_g} \qquad \ldots (6.16)$$

Equations (6.15) and (6.16) show that at f_{ar}, the currents through the inductor and the capacitor are amplified by a factor Q.
- Recollect the equation (6.6), which we saw in Section 6.8.1.
  At antiresonance,
  $$X_L = X_C \left(1 - \frac{1}{Q^2}\right)$$
  i.e. the reactances of inductive and capacitive branches are not quite equal to units power factor.
- The current will always depend on reactance. So if reactances are not equal, the currents will obviously not be equal.
  At antiresonance
  $$\frac{I_C}{I_L} = \sqrt{1 - \frac{1}{Q^2}}$$
  This is the ratio of magnitude of the currents in the capacitive branch to the inductive branch at unity power factor.
- The two currents are thus not equal if the resistance is appreciable, approaching equality as R is decreased.
- Higher the value of Q, the higher will I_C and I_L be and I_g will be low.
- At infinite Q, currents I_C and I_L will be infinite and I_g will be zero.

6.8.5 Bandwidth of Antiresonant Circuit

- We have already defined bandwidth for resonating circuits.
- Let us derive equation for bandwidth of a parallel resonant circuit shown in Fig. 6.54 (a).

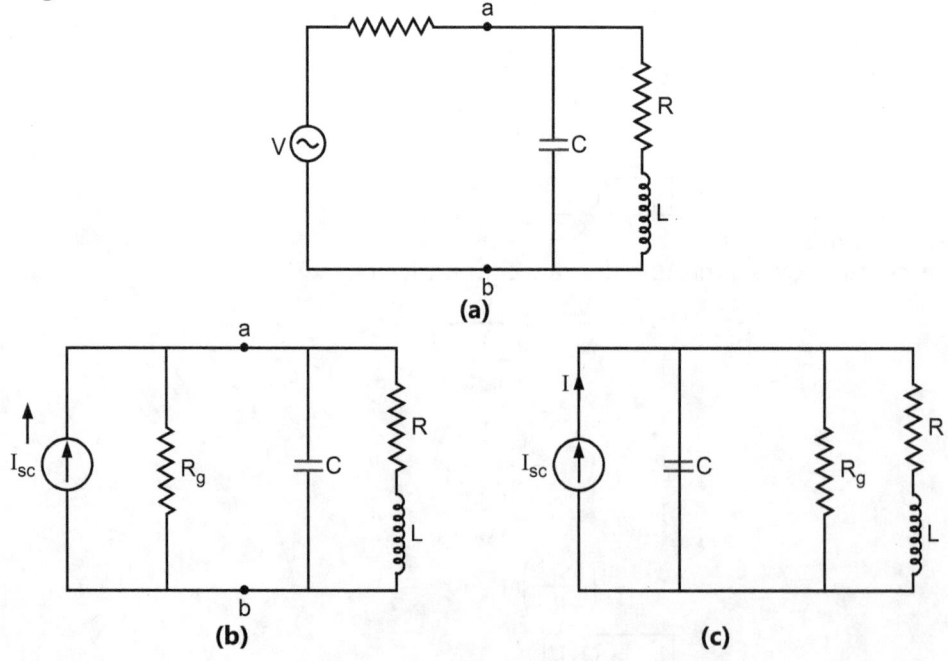

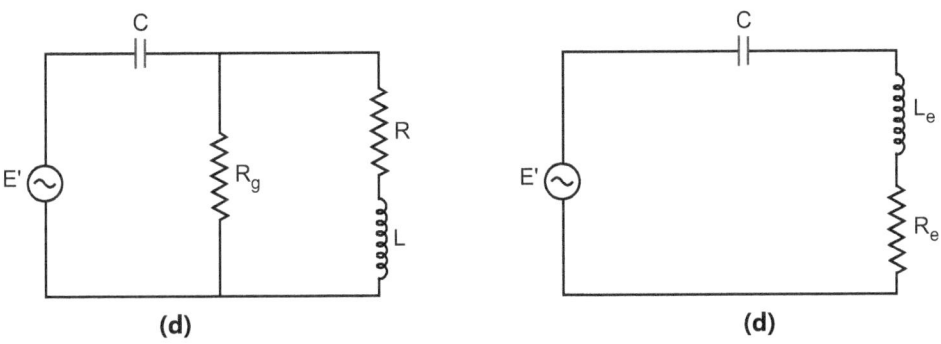

Fig. 6.54 (a) Parallel RLC circuit connected to a generator of internal resistance R_g

(b), (c), (d) Successive steps in reduction of (a) to (e)

(e) Series RLC equivalent of a

- Using voltage source transformation the circuit in Fig. 6.54 (a) is transformed to one in Fig. 6.54 (b). Since, all the branches are now in parallel we can interchange the positions of R_g and C. Using current source transformation circuit in Fig. 6.54 (c) can be drawn as in Fig. 6.54 (d). Finally, Fig. 6.54 (e) shows an equivalent of series RLC circuit the parallel RLC circuit in Fig. 6.54 (a) where

$$(R_e + X_{Le}) = R_g \parallel (X_L + R)$$

- Now, in the equivalent series RLC circuit capacitor C is the internal impedance of a new generator E'.
- Let us now analyse Fig. 6.54 (e) where we have,

$$Z_e = R_e + L_e = R_g \parallel (L + R)$$
$$Z_e = R_g \parallel (j\omega L + R)$$
$$Z_e = \frac{R_g \times (j\omega L + R)}{R_g + R + j\omega L}$$

After rationalizing,

$$Z_e = \frac{R_g (j\omega L + R)(R_g + R - j\omega L)}{(R_g + R + j\omega L)(R_g + R - j\omega L)}$$

$$Z_e = \frac{(j\omega L R_g + R_g R)(R_g + R - j\omega L)}{(R_g + R)^2 + \omega^2 L^2}$$

$$Z_e = \frac{\begin{array}{l} R_g^2 R + R_g R^2 - j\omega L R_g R + j\omega L R_g^2 \\ + j\omega L R_g R + \omega^2 L_g^2 \end{array}}{(R_g + R)^2 + \omega^2 L^2}$$

$$Z_e = \frac{R_g^2 R + R_g R^2 + j\omega L R_g^2 + \omega^2 L^2 R_g}{(R_g + R)^2 + \omega^2 L^2}$$

$$Z_e = (R_e + X_{Le}) = \frac{R_g^2 R + R_g R^2 + R_g \omega^2 L^2 + j\omega L R_g^2}{(R_g + R)^2 + \omega^2 L^2}$$

Form which we have,

$$R_e = \frac{R_g^2 R + R_g R^2 + R_g \omega^2 L^2}{(R_g + R)^2 + \omega^2 L^2}$$

$$\omega L_e = \frac{\omega L R_g^2}{(R_g + R)^2 + \omega^2 L^2}$$

It has been shown that bandwidth of a series resonant circuit is given as

$$BW = \frac{f_r}{Q}$$

The parallel RLC circuit is proved to be equivalent to a series resonant circuit.

$$\therefore \quad \text{BW of parallel RLC circuit} = \frac{f_{ar}}{Q}$$

where, $\quad Q$ must be $= \dfrac{\omega L_e}{R_e}$

$$\therefore \quad \text{Bandwidth (BW)} = \Delta f$$
$$= f_2 - f_1$$

$$\Delta f = \frac{f_{ar}}{Q}$$

$$\Delta f = \frac{f_{ar}}{\frac{\omega L_e}{R_e}}$$

$$\Delta f = f_{ar} \cdot \frac{R_e}{\omega L_e}$$

$$\Delta f = \left(\frac{R_g R^2 + R R_g^2 + R_g \omega^2 L^2}{\omega L R_g^2}\right) f_{ar}$$

$$\Delta f = \left(\frac{R}{\omega L} + \frac{R_g(R^2 + \omega^2 L^2)}{\omega L R_g^2}\right) f_{ar}$$

$$\Delta f = \left[\frac{1}{Q} + \frac{R^2\left(1 + \frac{\omega^2 L^2}{R^2}\right)}{\omega L R_g}\right] f_{ar}$$

$$\Delta f = \left[\frac{1}{Q} + \frac{R^2}{\omega L R_g}\left(\frac{R_{ar}}{R}\right)\right] f_{ar}$$

... equation (6.11) is section 6.8.3

$$Z_{ar} = R(1 + Q^2)$$

$$\Delta f = \left[\frac{1}{Q} + \frac{R \cdot R_{ar}}{\omega L R_g}\right] f_{ar}$$

$$\boxed{\Delta f = \frac{f_{ar}}{Q}\left[1 + \frac{R_{ar}}{R_g}\right]} \quad \ldots(6.17)$$

- If it is desired to match the impedances, as to obtain the greatest possible power delivery from generator to load, then $R_g = R_{ar}$.

  ∴ Bandwidth for matched condition will be

$$\Delta f = \frac{2}{Q} f_{ar} \qquad \ldots(6.18)$$

- Above equation (6.17), can be modified slightly to explain the factors effecting bandwidth.

  We have $\quad \Delta f = \dfrac{f_{ar}}{Q}\left(1 + \dfrac{R_{ar}}{R_g}\right)$

  But $\quad R_{ar} = \dfrac{L}{CR}$

$$\Delta f = \frac{f_{ar}}{Q}\left(1 + \frac{L}{CR\, R_g}\right) \qquad \ldots(6.19)$$

Equations (6.17), (6.18) and (6.19) are the expressions of BW in terms of Q, R_{ar} and R_g and must be closely understood so need further clarification.

Comments on Bandwidth and Selectivity:

1. Equation (6.17) shows that as seen in series RLC circuit, even in parallel circuit the bandwidth is inversely proportional to the Q of the original parallel circuit modified by a factor dependent on R_g.

   Q of original parallel circuit $= \dfrac{\omega L}{R}$

   Q of equivalent series RLC circuit $= \dfrac{\omega L_e}{R_e}$

2. Equation 6.17, also shows that for smaller bandwidth or greater selectivity of the antiresonant circuit a generator of a very high internal resistance R_g, should be used. Thus, in case of parallel RLC circuit R_g must be of a very high value. This is indicated in Fig. 6.55.

3. Equation 6.18, indicates that for a matched conditions $R_g = R_{ar}$ [to have maximum power transfer]. Since, R_g must be high for high selectivity R_{ar} must also be very high for maximum power transfer in the circuit.

4. Equation 6.19, shows that L must be small and C must be large for designing a circuit with high frequency selectivity i.e. circuit with less bandwidth. But doing this will lower the value of Z_{ar} and R_{ar}.

   ∴ $\quad Z_{ar} = R_{ar} = \dfrac{L}{CR}$

   Lowering the value of R_{ar} is highly undesirable if maximum power is needed to be transferred. So the designer must go for some engineering compromise between selectivity and maximum power to be transferred in a parallel resonating circuit.

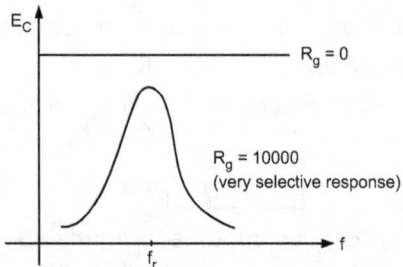

Fig. 6.55: Frequency response indicating effect of internal resistance R_g

6.8.6 General Case: Resistance present in both the Branches

Let the capacitor be lossy hence there will be resistances in both the branches as shown in Fig. 6.56.

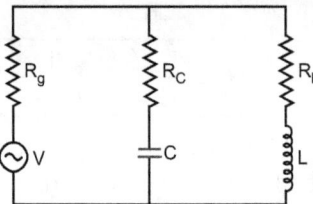

Fig. 6.56: Antiresonant circuit with resistance in both the branches

In this case, admittance Y_L of an inductive branch is

$$Y_L = \frac{1}{R_1 + j\omega L}$$

$$Y_L = \frac{R_1 - j\omega L}{R_1^2 + \omega^2 L^2}$$

Similarly, admittance Y_C of a capacitive branch is

$$Y_C = \frac{1}{R_2 - \dfrac{j}{\omega C}}$$

$$Y_C = \frac{R_2 + \dfrac{j}{\omega C}}{R_2^2 + \dfrac{1}{\omega^2 C^2}}$$

Total admittance $Y_T = Y_C + Y_L$

$$Y_T = \frac{R_1 - j\omega L}{R_1^2 + \omega^2 L^2} + \frac{R_2 + \dfrac{j}{\omega C}}{R_2^2 + \dfrac{1}{\omega^2 C^2}}$$

$$Y_T = \frac{R_1}{R_1^2 + \omega^2 L^2} + \frac{R_2}{R_2^2 + \dfrac{1}{\omega^2 C^2}} - j\left(\frac{\omega L}{R_1^2 + \omega^2 L^2} - \frac{\dfrac{1}{\omega C}}{R_2^2 + \dfrac{1}{\omega^2 C^2}}\right) \quad \ldots(6.20)$$

For antiresonant condition, unity power factor must be achieved. Therefore, the reactive term must be zero, thus at $\omega = \omega_{ar}$.

$$\omega_{ar} L \left[R_2^2 + \frac{1}{\omega_{ar}^2 C^2} \right] - \frac{1}{\omega_{ar} C} \left[R_1^2 + \omega_{ar}^2 L^2 \right] = 0$$

$$\omega_{ar} L R_2^2 + \frac{L}{\omega_{ar} C^2} = \frac{R_1^2}{\omega_{ar} C} + \frac{\omega_{ar} L^2}{C}$$

$$\omega_{ar}^2 R_2^2 C^2 L + L = R_1^2 C + \omega_{ar}^2 L^2 C$$

$$\omega_{ar}^2 LC \left(R_2^2 C - L \right) = C R_1^2 - L$$

$$\omega_{ar}^2 = \frac{1}{LC} \left[\frac{C R_1^2 - L}{R_2^2 C - L} \right]$$

$$\boxed{f_{ar} = \frac{1}{2\pi} \sqrt{\frac{1}{LC} \left(\frac{L - R_1^2 C}{L - R_2^2 C} \right)}} \qquad \ldots (6.21)$$

- Equation 6.21 gives the expression for f_{ar} when resistance is present in both the branches of the antiresonant circuit.
- If $R_2 = 0$, then the circuit will be same as in Fig. 6.37, and f_{ar} will be

$$f_{ar} = \frac{1}{2\pi} \sqrt{\frac{1}{LC} \left(1 - R_1^2 \frac{C}{L} \right)}$$

which is same as the one derived earlier.

(a) Antiresonance at all Frequencies:

- If two resistances R_1 and R_2 are equal and is $\sqrt{\frac{L}{C}}$

i.e. $\qquad R_1 = R_2 = \sqrt{\frac{L}{C}}$

Then the reactance associated with J terms in above Y_T equation 6.20, is

$$\frac{\omega L}{R_1^2 + \omega^2 L^2} - \frac{\frac{1}{\omega C}}{R_2^2 + \frac{1}{\omega^2 C^2}} = \frac{\omega L}{\frac{L}{C} + \omega^2 L^2} - \frac{\frac{1}{\omega C}}{\frac{L}{C} + \frac{1}{\omega^2 C^2}}$$

$$= \frac{\omega C}{1 + \omega^2 CL} - \frac{\omega C}{1 + \omega^2 CL} = 0$$

Thus, the reactance term is zero. The total admittance will be given by

$$Y_T = \frac{\sqrt{\frac{L}{C}}}{\frac{L}{C} + \omega^2 L^2} + \frac{\sqrt{\frac{L}{C}}}{\frac{L}{C} + \frac{1}{\omega^2 C^2}}$$

$$Y_T = \frac{\sqrt{\frac{L}{C}} \times C}{L(1 + \omega^2 LC)} + \frac{\sqrt{\frac{L}{C}} \times \omega^2 C^2}{C(1 + \omega^2 LC)}$$

$$Y_T = \sqrt{\frac{L}{C}}$$

The impedance $= \dfrac{1}{Y_T} = \sqrt{\dfrac{L}{C}} = R_1 = R_2$.

Thus, at all the frequencies impedance of the parallel circuit is

$$\boxed{Z = \sqrt{\frac{L}{C}}}$$

when $\quad R_1 = R_2 = \sqrt{\dfrac{L}{C}}$

So we say, the circuit is antiresonant at all the frequencies and thus the circuit is purely resistance (unity power factor) at all the frequencies.

(b) Variable Phase Angle Circuit:

Consider the circuit as shown in Fig. 6.57.

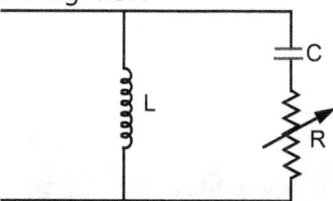

Fig. 6.57: Variable phase and constant impedance circuit

Impedance of the circuit is

$$Z = j\omega L \parallel \left(R - \frac{j}{\omega C} \right)$$

$$Z = \frac{j\omega L \cdot \left(R - \frac{j}{\omega C} \right)}{j\omega L + R - \frac{j}{\omega C}}$$

If at a given frequency ω,

$$\omega L = \frac{2}{\omega C}$$

Then,

$$Z = \frac{j\left(\dfrac{2}{\omega C}\right)\left(R - \dfrac{j}{\omega C}\right)}{R + \dfrac{2j}{\omega C} - \dfrac{j}{\omega C}}$$

$$Z = \frac{2}{\omega C} \angle 90° - 2\tan^{-1}\left(\frac{1}{\omega RC}\right)$$

As R is varied then the impedance magnitude $\left(\dfrac{2}{\omega C}\right)$ is constant but phase angle varies from $+30°$ at $R = \infty$ to $-90°$ at $R = 0$.

6.8.7 Applications of Parallel RCL Circuit

1. Parallel RLC circuit or an antiresonant circuit is used to achieve impedance transformation.

Impedance transformation is necessary to match the resistances of the generator and load in all the applications for the maximum power transfer. To mention a few applications, where impedance transform is required are radio transmitters and common emitter amplifier.

When a radio transmitter having output impedance of the order of few kilo ohms is coupled with an antenna having very small resistance (75 Ω – typical value) there is a mismatch, hence maximum power cannot be transferred.

Parallel resonant circuit offer a purely resistive impedance at antiresonance. At antiresonance

$$Z_{ar} = \frac{L}{CR_L}$$

R_L is negligible

$$Z_{ar} = \frac{L}{C}$$

∴ Thus, Z_{ar} depends on ratio $\dfrac{L}{C}$, so by varying the ratio $\dfrac{L}{C}$, the value of Z_{ar} can be varied.

2. Currents through the inductor and a capacitor are Q times the supplied current at antiresonance

$$I_L = QI$$
$$I_C = QI$$

Antiresonant circuit can be used as current amplifier.

6.8.8 Summary of Parallel Resonant Circuit

The characteristics of a parallel resonance are given as:
1. At antiresonance, the input impedance is maximum or the input admittance is minimum.
2. An antiresonance, circuit is purely resistive and hence the power factor is unity. Current is minimum at f_{ar}
3. The circuit is capacitive for frequencies above f_{ar}, (i.e. $f > f_{ar}$). It is inductive for frequency below f_{ar} (i.e. $f < f_{ar}$).

4. At antiresonance, parallel RLC circuit acts as a current amplifier where $I_L = QI$ and $I_C = QI$.

5. Quality factor is given as:

$$Q = \frac{R}{\omega_{ar} L} = \omega_{ar} CR$$

6. The resonant frequency is given

$$f_{ar} = \frac{1}{2\pi} \sqrt{\frac{1}{LC} - \frac{R^2}{L^2}} = f_r \sqrt{1 - \frac{1}{Q^2}}$$

Antiresonance is possible when $\frac{1}{LC} > \frac{R^2}{L^2}$.

7. R_g, generator resistance must be very high for high selectivity in the parallel RLC circuit.

8. Bandwidth $= \frac{f_{ar}}{a}\left[1 + \frac{Z_{ar}}{R_g}\right]$. $f_{ar} = \sqrt{f_1 f_2}$

9. $f_{ar} = \sqrt{f_1 f_2}$ above f_1 and f_2 are half power frequencies and f_{ar} is geometric mean of f_1 and f_2.

6.8.9 Important Formulae

		Parallel RLC Circuit
1.	Diagram	
2.	Resonating frequency	$f_{ar} = \frac{1}{2\pi}\sqrt{\frac{1}{LC} - \frac{R^2}{L^2}}$ $f_{ar} = f_r\sqrt{1 - \frac{1}{Q^2}}$
3.	Quality factor	$Q = \frac{\omega_{ar} L}{C}$ $Q = \frac{1}{\omega_{ar} CR}$
4.	Reactancy type	Above f_{ar} : Capacitive At f_{ar} : Resistive Below f_{ar} : Inductive

5. Impedance	$Z_{ar} = \dfrac{L}{C R_L}$
	$= R(1 + Q^2)$ ... at F_{ar}
	$Z = \dfrac{Z_{ar}}{1 + j\,2\,\delta\,Q}$ ...near f_{ar}
6. Voltage or current at resonance	$I_C = Q \cdot I$ $I_L = Q \cdot I$
7. Bandwidth	$BW = \dfrac{f_{ar}}{Q}\left[1 + \dfrac{R_{ar}}{R_g}\right]$ $R_{ar} = Z_{ar}$

6.9 NUMERICALS ON PARALLEL RESONANT CIRCUITS

Ex. 6.41: Find the bandwidth of the antiresonant circuit with the following conditions:

(i) Q of the circuits inductive branch is 100.

(ii) Frequency of unity power factors is 1 MHz.

(iii) Value of inductance = 100 µH.

(iv) Internal resistance of generator is 10 kΩ.

Sol.: Given: Q of inductive branch = 100, f_r = 1 MHz, L = 100 µH, R_g = 10 kΩ.

To calculate: BW =

To calculate bandwidth

$$BW = \dfrac{f_{ar}}{Q}\left[1 + \dfrac{Z_{ar}}{R_g}\right]$$

$$= f_{ar}\left[1 + \dfrac{1}{C R_L \cdot R_g}\right]$$

Let us calculate BW. We need to calculate C, R_L.

(i) To calculate capacitance value:

$$f_{ar} = \dfrac{1}{2\pi\sqrt{LC}}\sqrt{1 - \dfrac{1}{Q^2}}$$

$$1 \times 10^6 = \dfrac{1}{2\pi\sqrt{100 \times 10^{-6}}\sqrt{C}}\sqrt{1 - \dfrac{1}{100^2}}$$

$$C = \dfrac{1}{(2\pi)^2 (100 \times 10^{-6})(1 \times 10^6)^2}\sqrt{1 - \dfrac{1}{100^2}}$$

$$\boxed{C = 0.2533 \text{ nF}}$$

(ii) To calculate value of R_L:

$$Q = \frac{\omega_r L}{R}$$

$\therefore \quad 100 = \dfrac{2 \times \pi \times 1 \times 10^6 \times 100 \times 10^{-6}}{R}$

$\boxed{R = 6.2831 \ \Omega}$

(iii) To calculate Z_{ar}:

$$Z_{ar} = \frac{L}{CR_L} = \frac{100 \times 10^{-6}}{0.2533 \times 10^{-9} \times 6.2831} = 62.833 \text{ k}\Omega$$

$\boxed{Z_{ar} = 62.833 \text{ k}\Omega}$

(iv) To calculate bandwidth:

$$BW = \frac{f_{ar}}{Q}\left[1 + \frac{Z_{ar}}{R_g}\right]$$

$$BW = \frac{1 \times 10^6}{100}\left[1 + \frac{62.833 \times 10^3}{10 \times 10^3}\right]$$

$\boxed{BW = 72.833 \text{ kHz}}$

Ans.:

$\boxed{BW = 72.833 \text{ kHz}}$

In this example, Z_{ar} can alternatively be calculated using $Z_{ar} = R_L(1 + Q^2) = 6.2831$ $(1 + 100^2) = 62.83$ kΩ. So no need to calculate value of C.

Ex. 6.42: For a parallel resonant circuit:
(i) Specify the value of the circuit capacitor.
(ii) Calculate the resistance of the circuit at parallel resonance.
(iii) What is the absolute bandwidth of the resonant circuit?
(iv) What is the bandwidth of the circuit when it is matched with the generator impedance?

Assume Q = 75, L = 120 µH and the resonating frequency of 1 MHz.

Sol.: Given: L = 120 µH, Q = 75, $f_{ar} = 1 \times 10^6$ Hz.
To calculate: C, R_L, Z_{ar}, BW, BW when $R_g = Z_{ar}$.

(i) To calculate value of capacitor:

$$f_{ar} = \frac{1}{2\pi\sqrt{LC}}\sqrt{1 + \frac{1}{Q^2}}$$

$$1 \times 10^6 = \frac{1}{2\pi\sqrt{120 \times 10^{-6}}\sqrt{C}}\sqrt{1 - \frac{1}{75^2}}$$

$$C = \frac{1}{(2\pi \times 1 \times 10^6)^2 (120 \times 10^{-6})}\left[1 - \frac{1}{75^2}\right]$$

$\boxed{C = 208.9 \text{ pF}}$

(ii) Resistance of coil, R_{coil}:

$$Q = \frac{\omega_{ar} L}{R}$$

$$75 = \frac{2 \times \pi \times 1 \times 10^6 \times 120 \times 10^{-6}}{R}$$

$$\boxed{R_L = 10.05 \, \Omega}$$

(iii) The resistance of circuit at resonance:

i.e. Z_{ar} or R_{ar}

$$Z_{ar} = \frac{1}{CR_L}$$

or

$$Z_{ar} = R_L (1 + Q^2)$$

$$Z_{ar} = \frac{120 \times 10^{-6}}{(208.9 \times 10^{-12})(10.05)}$$

$$\boxed{Z_{ar} = 57.157 \, k\Omega}$$

(iv) Absolute bandwidth is given by:

$$BW = \frac{f_{ar}}{Q} = \frac{1 \times 10^6}{75}$$

$$\boxed{BW = 13.33 \, k\Omega}$$

(v) When it is matched condition $R_g = Z_{ar}$:

$$\therefore \quad BW = \frac{f_{ar}}{Q}\left[1 + \frac{Z_{ar}}{R_g}\right]$$

$$\therefore \quad BW = 2\frac{f_{ar}}{Q}$$

$$= 26.66 \, k\Omega$$

$$\boxed{BW = 26.66 \, k\Omega}$$

Ans.:

$$\begin{array}{|l|}
\hline
C = 208.9 \, pF \\
R_L = 10.05 \, \Omega \\
Z_{ar} = 57.157 \, k\Omega \\
BW = 13.33 \, k\Omega \\
BW = 26.66 \, k\Omega \\
\text{when matched condition} \\
\hline
\end{array}$$

Ex. 6.43: In the circuit shown in Fig. 6.58 the inductance of 0.1 H having Q factor of 5 is in parallel with capacitor. Determine the value of capacitance and coil resistance at resonant frequency of 500 rad/sec.

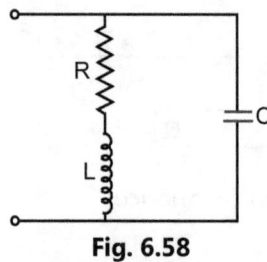

Fig. 6.58

Sol.: Given: f_r = 500 rad/sec., L = 0.1 H, Q = 5.

(i) To calculate R_L:

$$Q = \frac{\omega_{ar} L}{R}$$

$$5 = \frac{500 \times 0.1}{R}$$

$$\boxed{R_L = 10 \, \Omega}$$

(ii) To calculate value of capacitance:

$$f_{ar} = \frac{1}{2\pi} \sqrt{\frac{1}{LC} - \frac{R_L^2}{L^2}}$$

$$\omega_{ar}^2 = \left(\frac{1}{LC} - \frac{R_L^2}{L^2}\right)$$

$$500^2 = \frac{1}{(0.1) C} - \frac{10^2}{(0.1)^2}$$

$$\frac{1}{0.1 \, C} = 250000 + 10000$$

$$C = 38.46 \times 10^{-6} \, F$$

$$\boxed{C = 38.46 \, \mu F}$$

Ans.:

$$\boxed{\begin{array}{l} R_L = 10 \, \Omega \\ C = 38.46 \, \mu F \end{array}}$$

Ex. 6.44: A parallel resonant circuit has a coil of 150 μH with Q of 60 and resonated at 1 MHz.
  (i) Specify the value of required capacitor.
  (ii) What is the circuit impedance at resonance?
  (iii) What is the resistance of inductor?
  (iv) If Q is reduced to 4 by adding additional series resistance, then how much resistance is needed?

Sol.: Given: L = 150 µH, Q = 60, f_{ar} = 1 MHz.

To calculate C, R_L, Z_{ar}, New Q, New f_{ar}.

(i) The value of capacitance:

$$f_{ar} = \frac{1}{2\pi\sqrt{LC}}\sqrt{1-\frac{1}{Q^2}}$$

$$1 \times 10^6 = \frac{1}{2\pi\sqrt{150 \times 10^{-6}}\sqrt{C}}\sqrt{1-\frac{1}{60^2}}$$

$$C = \frac{1}{(2\pi \times 1 \times 10^6)^2 \cdot (150 \times 10^{-6})}\left[1-\frac{1}{3600}\right]$$

$$C = 168.821 \times 10^{-12} \text{ F}$$

$$\boxed{C = 168.82 \text{ pF}}$$

(ii) The resistance of coil:

$$Q = \frac{\omega_{ar} L}{R_L}$$

$$60 = \frac{2\pi \times 1 \times 10^6 \times 150 \times 10^{-6}}{R_L}$$

$$\boxed{R_L = 15.7 \ \Omega}$$

(iii) The impedance of the parallel circuit:

$$Z_{ar} = \frac{L}{CR_L} = \frac{150 \times 10^{-6}}{168.82 \times 10^{-12} \times 15.7}$$

$$\boxed{Z_{ar} = 56.593 \text{ k}\Omega}$$

(iv) New quality factor can be expressed in terms of additional resistance:

$$Q' = \frac{\omega'_{ar} L}{(R_L + R')}$$

We will thus, need to calculate ω'_{ar}.

∴ $$f'_{ar} = \frac{1}{2\pi\sqrt{LC}}\sqrt{1-\frac{1}{Q^2}}$$

$$f'_{ar} = \frac{1}{2\pi\sqrt{150 \times 10^{-6} \times 168.82 \times 10^{-12}}}\sqrt{1-\frac{1}{4^2}}$$

$$\boxed{f'_{ar} = 968.385 \text{ kHz}}$$

∴ $$Q' = \frac{\omega'_{ar} L}{(R_L + R')}$$

where R' is the additional resistance to be added.

$$(R_L + R') = \frac{2\pi f'_{ar} L}{Q'}$$

$$(15.7 + R') = \frac{2\pi \times 968.385 \times 10^3}{4}$$

$$\boxed{R' = 212.417 \ \Omega}$$

Ans.:

$$\boxed{\begin{array}{l} C = 168.82 \text{ pF} \\ R_L = 15.7 \ \Omega \\ Z_{ar} = 56.593 \text{ k}\Omega \\ R' = 212.47 \ \Omega \end{array}}$$

Ex. 6.45: Two impedances $Z_1 = 20 + 10j$ and $Z_2 = 10 - 30j$ are connected in parallel and this combination is connected in series with $Z_3 = 30 + XJ$. Find the value of X which will produce resonance.

Sol.:

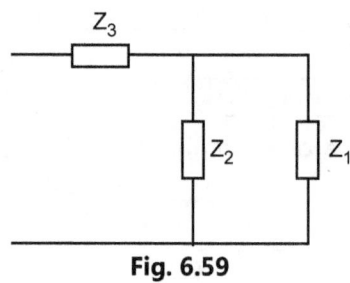

Fig. 6.59

Given:
$$Z_1 = 20 + 10j$$
$$Z_2 = 10 - 30j$$
$$Z_3 = 30 + XJ$$

To calculate X:

(i) To find the total impedance:

$$Z_T = Z_3 + (Z_1 \| Z_2) = Z_3 + \frac{Z_1 Z_2}{Z_1 + Z_2}$$

$$Z = Z_3 + \frac{Z_1 Z_2}{Z_1 + Z_2}$$

$$Z = (30 + jX) + \frac{(20 + j10)(10 - j30)}{(20 + j10) + (10 - j30)}$$

$$Z = 30 + jX + \frac{200 + j100 + j600 + 300}{30 - j20}$$

$$Z = 30 + jX + \frac{500 - j500}{30 - j20}$$

$$Z = 30 + jX + \frac{[500(1-j)][30+j20]}{30^2 + 20^2}$$

$$Z = 30 + jX + \frac{500}{1300}[30+j20-30j+20]$$

$$Z = 30 + jX + \frac{5}{13}[50-j10]$$

$$Z = 30 + \frac{250}{13} + j\left[X - \frac{50}{13}\right]$$

To circuit will resonate, if imaginary part is zero.

∴ $\quad X - \dfrac{50}{13} = 0$

$$X = \frac{50}{13}$$

$\boxed{X = 3.846\ \Omega}$

Ans.:

$$\boxed{X = 3.846\ \Omega}$$

Ex. 6.46: From the basics obtain the expression for the resonance frequency in the circuit shown in Fig. 6.60.

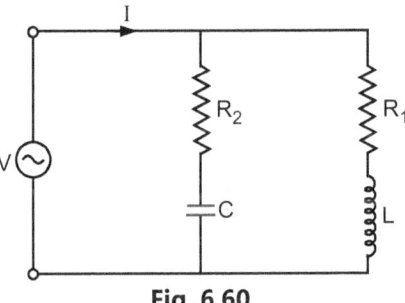

Fig. 6.60

Sol.: The two branches connected in parallel will produce resonance when the resultant current through combination i.e. I, is in phase with voltage V. The condition of parallel resonance is that the impedance of the parallel combination is purely resistive.

The admittance of branch containing:

L is:

$$Y_L = \frac{1}{R_1 + j\omega L}$$

$$= \frac{R_1 - j\omega L}{(R_1 + j\omega L)(R_1 - j\omega L)}$$

$$Y_L = \frac{R_1 - jX_L}{R_1^2 + X_L^2}$$

where, $\quad X_L = \omega L$

The admittance of branch containing C is

$$Y_C = \dfrac{1}{R_2 - \dfrac{j}{\omega C}} = \dfrac{R_2 + jX_C}{R_2^2 + X_C^2}$$

Total admittance Y is given by

$$Y = Y_L + Y_C$$

$$Y = \dfrac{R_1 + jX_C}{R_1^2 + X_L^2} + \dfrac{R_2 + jX_C}{R_2^2 + X_C^2}$$

$$Y = \left(\dfrac{R_1}{R_1^2 + X_L^2} + \dfrac{R_2}{R_2^2 + X_C^2}\right) + \left(\dfrac{X_C}{R_2^2 + X_C^2} - \dfrac{X_L}{R_1^2 + X_L^2}\right)$$

At resonance, we have unity power factor is zero condition

$$\therefore \quad \dfrac{X_C}{R_2^2 + X_C^2} - \dfrac{X_L}{R_1^2 + X_L^2} = 0$$

$$\dfrac{X_C}{R_2^2 + X_C^2} = \dfrac{X_L}{R_1^2 + X_L^2}$$

$$\dfrac{\dfrac{1}{\omega_{ar} C}}{R_2^2 + \left(\dfrac{1}{\omega_{ar} C}\right)^2} = \dfrac{\omega_{ar} L}{R_1^2 + \omega_{ar}^2 L^2}$$

$$\therefore \quad R_1^2 + \omega_{ar}^2 L^2 = \omega_{ar}^2 LC\left(R_2^2 + \dfrac{1}{\omega_{ar}^2 C^2}\right)$$

$$R_1^2 + \omega_{ar}^2 L^2 = \omega_{ar}^2 LC R_2^2 + \dfrac{L}{C}$$

$$\omega_{ar}^2 (L^2 - LCR_2^2) = \dfrac{L}{C} - R_1^2$$

$$(LC)\,\omega_{ar}^2 = \dfrac{\dfrac{L}{C} + R_1^2}{\dfrac{L}{C} - R_2^2}$$

$$\omega_{ar} = \dfrac{1}{\sqrt{LC}} \sqrt{\dfrac{R_1^2 - \dfrac{L}{C}}{R_2^2 - \dfrac{L}{C}}}$$

$$\boxed{f_{ar} = \dfrac{1}{2\pi\sqrt{LC}} \sqrt{\dfrac{R_1^2 - \dfrac{L}{C}}{R_2^2 - \dfrac{L}{C}}}}$$

where, f_{ar} : Antiresonating frequency
R_1 : Ohmic resistance of coil
R_2 : Leakage and dielectric loss resistance of capacitor

Ex. 6.47: In the circuit of Fig. 6.61 calculate resonant frequency (ω_{ar}). If R_1 is increased what is the maximum value of R_1 for which there is a resonant frequency?

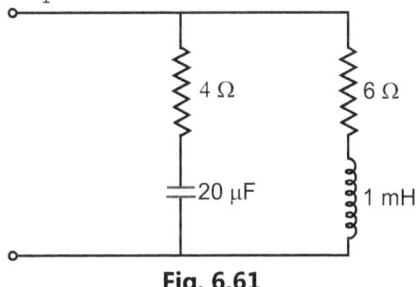

Fig. 6.61

Sol.: $R_2 = R_L = 6\,\Omega$, $R_1 = R_C = 4\,\Omega$, $L = 1$ mH, $C = 20$ μF.
To calculate: ω_{ar} and maximum value of R_L

(i) To calculate ω_{ar}:
In case when resistance is present in both the branches:

$$\omega_{ar} = \frac{1}{\sqrt{LC}}\sqrt{\frac{R_L^2 - \frac{L}{C}}{R_C^2 - \frac{L}{C}}} = \frac{1}{\sqrt{1\times 10^{-3}\times 20\times 10^{-6}}}\sqrt{\frac{6^2 - \frac{1\times 10^{-3}}{20\times 10^{-6}}}{4^2 - \frac{1\times 10^{-3}}{20\times 10^{-6}}}}$$

$$= \frac{1}{\sqrt{20\times 10^{-9}}}\sqrt{\frac{36-50}{16-50}}$$

$$\boxed{\omega_{ar} = 2911.62 \text{ rad/sec.}}$$

(ii) To calculate $R_{1\,(max)}$ i.e. R_C maximum:

$$\omega_{ar} = \frac{1}{\sqrt{LC}}\sqrt{\frac{R_L^2 - \frac{L}{C}}{R_C^2 - \frac{L}{C}}}$$

So if $R_C^2 = \frac{L}{C}$, then denominator = 0 and $\omega_{ar} = \infty$

Therefore, maximum value should be selected as follows:

$$R_C = R_1 = \sqrt{\frac{L}{C}}$$

$$R_C = R_1 = \sqrt{\frac{10^{-3}}{20\times 10^{-6}}}$$

$$R_C = \sqrt{50}$$

$$R_C = 7.071\,\Omega$$

At this value of R_C, $f_{ar} = \infty$.

∴ Maximum value of R_C must be less than 7

∴ $\boxed{R_{C\,(max)} < 7}$

Ans.:

$$\boxed{\begin{array}{l} \omega_{ar} = 2911.62 \text{ rad/sec.} \\ \text{Maximum value } R_C = 7\,\Omega \end{array}}$$

Ex. 6.48: Find exact resonant frequency of the network shown in Fig. 6.62. Also find 'Q_0' at that frequency.

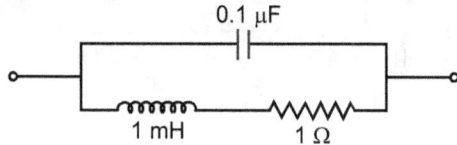

Fig. 6.62

Sol.: Given: C = 0.1 μF, L = 1 mH, R = 10 Ω. To calculate f_{ar}, Q.

(i) To calculate f_{ar}:

$$f_{ar} = \frac{1}{2\pi} \sqrt{\frac{1}{LC} - \frac{R^2 L}{L^2}}$$

$$= \frac{1}{2\pi} \sqrt{\frac{1}{1 \times 10^{-3} \times 0.1 \times 10^{-6}} - \frac{10 \times 10 \times 1 \times 10^{-3}}{(1 \times 10^{-3})^2}}$$

$\boxed{f_{ar} = 15.835 \text{ kHz}}$

(ii) To calculate Q:

$$Q = \frac{\omega_{ar} L}{R}$$

$$Q = \frac{2 \times \pi \times 15.83 \times 10^3 \times 1 \times 10^{-3}}{10}$$

Q = 9.95

$\boxed{Q \approx 10}$

Ans.:

$$\boxed{\begin{array}{l} f_{ar} = 15.83 \text{ kHz} \\ Q = 10 \end{array}}$$

Ex. 6.49: Find 'R_L' for resonance circuit of Fig. 6.63. Comment on R_L obtained.

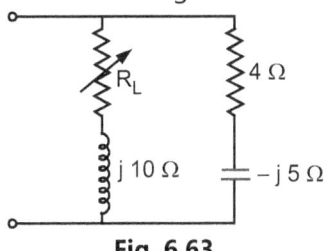

Fig. 6.63

Sol.: For the resonance, the susceptance in admittance must be zero.

$$Y = \frac{1}{R + j10} + \frac{1}{4 - j5}$$

$$Y = \frac{R - j10}{R^2 + 100} + \frac{4 + j5}{(4)^2 + 5^2}$$

$$Y = \frac{R - j10}{R^2 + 100} + \frac{4 + j5}{41}$$

$$Y = \left[\frac{R}{R^2 + 100} + \frac{4}{41}\right] + j\left[\frac{5}{41} - \frac{10}{R^2 + 100}\right]$$

Susceptance part must be zero.

$$\frac{5}{41} - \frac{10}{R^2 + 100} = 0$$

$$\frac{5}{41} = \frac{10}{R^2 + 100}$$

$$5R^2 + 500 = 410$$

$$R^2 = -\frac{90}{5} = -18$$

Ans.:

$$\boxed{R = \sqrt{18}\ \Omega}$$

Thus, for resonance, value of R is negative i.e. R is imaginary. This clearly shows that in the circuit, resonance is impossible for positive values of R.

Ex. 6.50: Find the value of 'L' for which the circuit in Fig. 6.64 is resonant at a frequency of ω_0 = 1000 rad/sec.

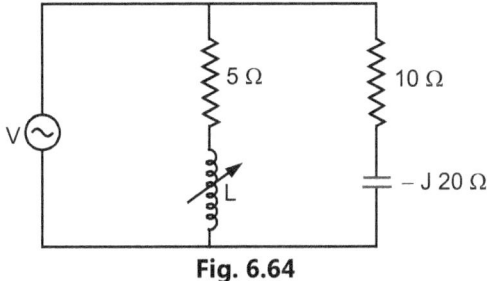

Fig. 6.64

Sol.: Given: $R_L = 5$, $R_C = 10$, $C = -j20\ \Omega$.

To calculate:

Let the reactance offered by the inductance is jX_L. Then the total admittance of parallel resonant circuit looking from source side is given by

$$Y_T = Y_L + Y_C$$

$$Y_T = \frac{1}{5 + jX_L} + \frac{1}{10 - j20}$$

$$Y_T = \frac{5 - jX_L}{5^2 + X_L^2} + \frac{10 + j20}{10^2 + 20^2}$$

$$Y_T = \frac{5}{25 + X_L^2} - \frac{jX_L}{25 + X_L^2} + \frac{10}{500} + \frac{j20}{500}$$

$$Y_T = \left[\frac{5}{25 + X_L^2} + \frac{10}{500}\right] + j\left[\frac{20}{500} - \frac{X_L}{25 + X_L^2}\right]$$

To have resonance, the imaginary term must be zero. Hence, to obtain the condition of resonance, equate susceptance to zero.

$$\frac{20}{500} - \frac{X_L}{25 + X_L^2} = 0$$

$$\frac{X_L}{25 + X_L^2} = \frac{1}{25}$$

$$X_L^2 - 25 X_L + 25 = 0$$

Solving quadratic equation for X_L,

$$X_L = \frac{+25 \pm \sqrt{25^2 - 4 \times 25 \times 1}}{2}$$

$$X_L = \frac{25 \pm \sqrt{0.525}}{2}$$

$$X_L = \frac{25 \pm 22.9128}{2}$$

X_L = 23.9564 Ω

or X_L = 1.0436

But $X_L = \omega L$

$\therefore$ ωL = 23.9564 Ω or 1.0436

ω = 1000 rad/sec.

$\therefore$ $\boxed{L = 23.9564\ \text{mH or}\ 1.0436\ \text{mH}}$

Ans.:

Value of L = 23.9564 mH or 1.0436 mH

Ex. 6.51: A parallel resonant circuit has fixed 'C' and variable 'L'. The 'Q' of inductor is 5 and it is constant. Find the value of L and C for a circuit independence of 100 + j0 at f = 1.5 MHz. What is the bandwidth?

Sol.: Given: $Q = 5$, $f_{ar} = 1.5$ MHz, $Z_{ar} = 100 + j0$.

To calculate L, C, BW.

(i) To calculate R_L:

$$Z_{ar} = R(1 + Q^2) = R_Q^2$$

$$100 = R_L \cdot 25$$

$$\boxed{R_L = 4\,\Omega}$$

(ii) To calculate L:

$$Q = \frac{\omega_{ar} L}{R}$$

$$5 = \frac{2 \times \pi \times f_{ar} \times L}{4}$$

$$L = \frac{20}{2 \times \pi \times 1.5 \times 10^6}$$

$$\boxed{L = 2.122\ \mu H}$$

(iii) To calculate C:

$$f_{ar} = \frac{1}{2\pi\sqrt{LC}}\sqrt{1 - \frac{1}{Q^2}}$$

$$1.5 \times 10^6 = \frac{1}{2\pi\sqrt{2.122 \times 10^{-6} \times C}}\sqrt{1 - \frac{1}{5^2}}$$

$$\boxed{C = 5.0931\ nF}$$

(iv) To calculate BW:

$$BW = \frac{f_{ar}}{Q} = \frac{1.5 \times 10^6}{5}$$

$$\boxed{BW = 300\ kHz}$$

Ans.:

R_L	= 4 Ω
L	= 2.122 μH
C	= 5.0931 nF
BW	= 300 kHz

Ex. 6.52: A parallel resonant circuit has coil of 100 mH with Q = 50. It is resonant at 0.7 MHz.

Find: (i) Value of capacitor (ii) Resistance in series with coil (iii) Circuit impedance at resonance.

Sol.: Given: L = 100 mH, Q = 50, f_{ar} = 0.7 MHz.

To calculate: C =?, R_S =?, Z_{ar} =?

(i) To calculate the capacitor value:

$$f_{ar} = \frac{1}{2\pi\sqrt{LC}} \sqrt{1 - \frac{1}{Q^2}}$$

$$0.7 \times 10^6 = \frac{1}{2\pi\sqrt{100 \times 10^{-3} \times C}} \sqrt{1 - \frac{1}{50^2}}$$

$$C = 5.1684 \times 10^{-13} \text{ F}$$

$$\boxed{C = 0.5168 \text{ pF}}$$

(ii) To calculate R_L:

$$Q = \frac{\omega_{ar} L}{R}$$

$$50 = \frac{2 \times \pi \times 0.7 \times 10^6 \times 100 \times 10^{-3}}{R}$$

$$\boxed{R = 8.796 \text{ k}\Omega}$$

(iii) Circuit impedance at resonance:

$$Z_{ar} = \frac{L}{CR_L} = \frac{100 \times 10^{-3}}{0.5168 \times 10^{-12} \times 8.796 \times 10^3}$$

$$\boxed{Z_{ar} = 21.998 \text{ M}\Omega}$$

Ans.:

$$\boxed{\begin{aligned} C &= 0.5168 \text{ pF} \\ r &= 8.796 \text{ k}\Omega \\ Z_{ar} &= 21.99 \text{ M}\Omega \end{aligned}}$$

Ex. 6.53: A parallel resonant circuit has fixed 'C' and variable 'L'. The Q of inductor is 4 and constant. Find the values of 'L' and 'C' of a circuit impedance of 1000 + j0.0 at f_{ar} = 2.4 MHz. What is the bandwidth?

Sol.: Given: Q = 4, Z_{ar} = 1000 + j0 Ω, f_{ar} = 2.4 MHz.

To calculate: BW, L, C.

(i) To calculate value of L:

$$Z_{ar} = R_L (1 + Q^2)$$
$$1000 = R_L (1 + 4^2)$$
$$R_L = \frac{1000}{7} = 58.82 \text{ }\Omega$$

Now, Z_{ar} can also be expressed as

$$Z_{ar} = \frac{L}{CR_L}$$

$$1000 = \frac{L}{C \times 58.82}$$

$$\boxed{\frac{L}{C} = 58.82 \times 10^3} \quad \ldots(1)$$

Resonating frequency,

$$f_{ar} = \frac{1}{2\pi LC}\sqrt{1 - \frac{1}{Q^2}}$$

$$2.4 \times 10^6 = \frac{1}{2\pi LC}\sqrt{1 - \frac{1}{16}}$$

$$LC = \frac{15}{4 \times \pi \times 2.4 \times 10^6 \times (2.4 \times 10^6)^2}$$

$$\boxed{LC = 4.1227 \times 10^{-15}} \quad \ldots(2)$$

Using (1) and (2)

$$L\left(\frac{L}{58.82 \times 10^3}\right) = 4.1227 \times 10^{-15}$$

$$L^2 = 2.425 \times 10^{-10}$$

$$\boxed{L = 15.57 \ \mu H}$$

(ii) To calculate value of C:

$$LC = 4.1227 \times 10^{-15}$$

$$C = \frac{4.1227 \times 10^{-15}}{L}$$

$$\boxed{C = 0.264 \ nF}$$

(iii) To calculate the bandwidth:

$$\Delta f = \frac{f_{ar}}{Q}$$

$$= \frac{2.4 \times 10^6}{4}$$

$$\Delta f = 0.6 \times 10^6 \ Hz$$

$$\boxed{BW = 0.6 \ MHz}$$

Ans.:

$$\boxed{\begin{aligned} L &= 15.57 \ \mu H \\ C &= 0.264 \ nF \\ \Delta F &= 0.6 \ MHz \end{aligned}}$$

Ex. 6.54: Find exact resonant frequency in the network shown. Also find Z_{in} at that frequency.

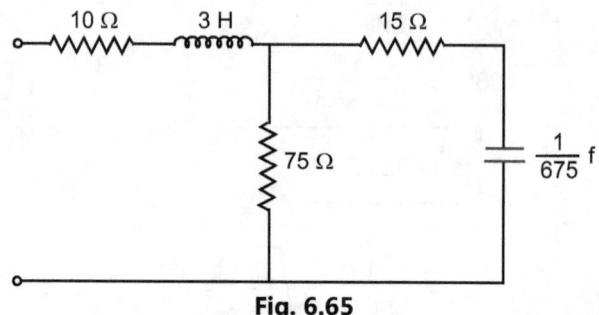

Fig. 6.65

Sol.: Given:
$$Z_1 = 75 \, \Omega$$
$$Z_2 = 15 - \frac{j\omega}{\frac{1}{625}}$$
$$Z_3 = 10 + j3\omega \qquad \because X_L = \omega L = 3\omega$$

Total impedance can be written as:

$$Z = Z_3 + (Z_1 \| Z_2) = Z_3 + \frac{Z_1 Z_2}{Z_1 + Z_2} = (10 + j3\omega) + \frac{75 \times \left(15 - j\frac{625}{\omega}\right)}{75 + \left(15 - j\frac{625}{\omega}\right)}$$

$$= (10 + j3\omega) + \frac{1125\omega - j\,50625}{90\omega - j\,625} = (10 + j3\omega) + \frac{75\omega - 3375\,j}{6\omega - 45\,j}$$

$$= 10 + j3\omega + \left(\frac{75\omega - j3375}{6\omega - j45}\right)\left(\frac{6\omega + j45}{6\omega + j45}\right)$$

$$= 10 + j3\omega + \frac{450\omega - 1425\,j\omega + 15.1875}{\omega^2 6^2 + 45^2}$$

$$Z = \frac{360\omega^2 + 20250 + 108\,j\omega^3 + 450\omega - 14625\,j\omega + 151875}{36\omega^2 + 2025}$$

$$Z = \frac{360\omega^2 + 20250 + 450\omega + 151875}{36\omega^2 + 2025} + j\left(\frac{108\omega^3 - 14625\omega}{36\omega^2 + 2025}\right)$$

At resonating frequency, imaginary part is zero

$$\frac{108\omega^3 - 14625\omega}{36\omega^2 + 2025} = 0$$

$$108\omega^2 = 14625\omega$$
$$108\omega^2 = 14625$$
$$\omega^2 = 135.4$$
$$\omega = 11.6 \text{ Hz}$$
$$\boxed{f_{ar} = 1.8 \text{ Hz}}$$

At antiresonance, imaginary part is zero.

$$Z_{in} = \frac{360\,\omega^2 + 20250 + 450(\omega) + 151875}{36\,\omega^2 + 2025}$$

Substituting
$$\omega = 11.6$$
$$Z_{in} = 32.86\ \Omega$$

Ans.:

> $f_{ar} = 1.8$ Hz
> $Z_{in} = 34.86\ \Omega$

EXERCISE

1. What is a network function? Explain various types of network functions for a one port network and a two port network.
2. Define poles and zeros of a network functions. What are the significance of a pole and zero in a network function?
3. Give the essential properties of driving point function.
4. Give the essential properties of transfer function.
5. Give the essential properties of an driving point function.
6. Explain how time domain behaviour can be obtained from pole-zero plot.
7. Explain how frequency domain behaviour (magnitude plot and phase plot) can be obtained from the pole-zero plot.
8. Explain what is meant by stable and unstable system. Explain how location of pole-zero on S-plane affect the system stability.
9. For the LC ladder network shown obtain the voltage ratio transfer function in the form
$$K\left[\frac{(s^2+a)(s^2+b)}{(s^2+c)(s^2+d)}\right]$$

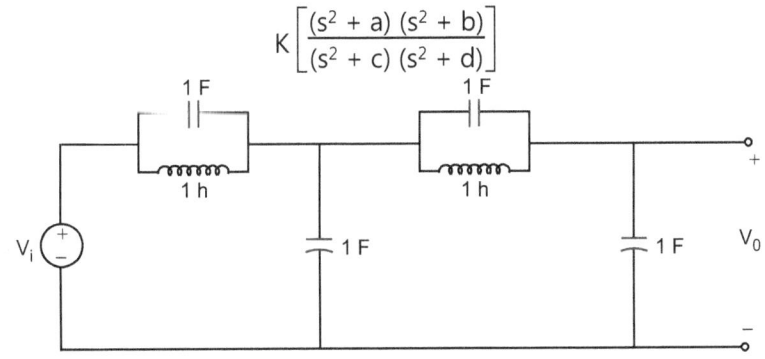

Fig. 6.66: Circuit for Q.9

10. For the Twin T network show that the transfer function is given by
$$\frac{V_o(s)}{V_i(s)} = \frac{s^2 + 1/R^2C^2}{s^2 + \left(\frac{4}{RC}\right)s + \frac{1}{R^2C^2}}$$

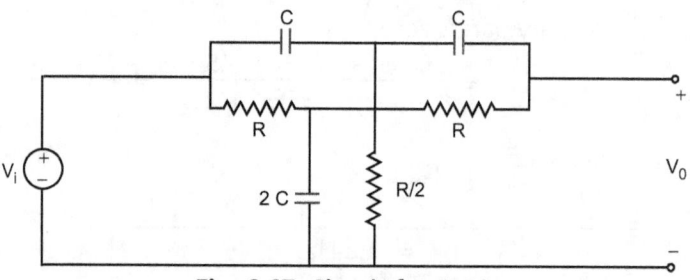

Fig. 6.67: Circuit for Q.10

11. For the symmetrical lattice network show that
$$\frac{V_o(s)}{V_1(s)} = \frac{s^2 - s + 1}{s^2 + s + 1}$$

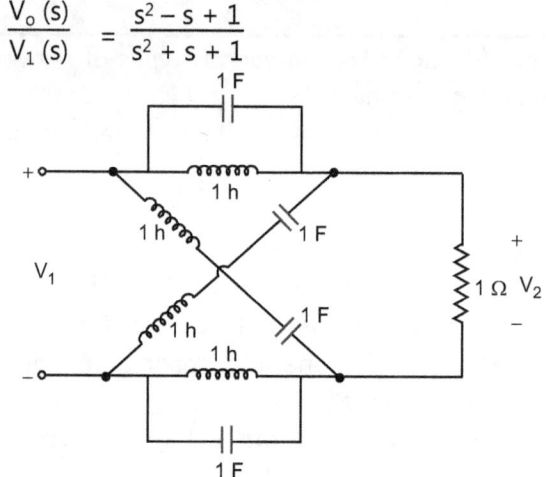

Fig. 6.68: Circuit for Q.11

12. Graphically find residue at poles of the following functions:

    (1) $\dfrac{2s + 5}{(s + 2)(s + 3)}$ (2) $\dfrac{s^2 + 10s + 16}{s^2 + 8s + 7}$

13. Draw the magnitude and phase plot of following functions:

    (1) $\dfrac{s}{(s + 10)^2}$ (2) $\dfrac{s + 10}{(s + 100)}$ (3) $\dfrac{(s + 10)(s + 50)}{(s + 200)}$

14. Explain the effect of quality factor Q on the selectivity and the bandwidth of a parallel resonating circuit.
15. Explain the effect of the generator resistance R_g on the bandwidth and the selectivity of and a parallel resonating circuit.
16. Obtain an expression of the frequency of resonance of a series and a parallel resonating circuit.
17. Parallel resonant circuit is a current amplifier justify.
18. Derive the expression for the bandwidth of an antiresonant circuit.
19. Give important properties and applications of parallel resonant circuits.
20. Two impedances $Z_1 = a + Jb$ and $Z_2 = C - Jd$ are connected in parallel. Determine the condition of resonance in each case.

■■■

www.ingramcontent.com/pod-product-compliance
Lightning Source LLC
Chambersburg PA
CBHW081141290426
44108CB00018B/2407